CompTIA® Network+® (Exam N10-006)

CompTIA® Network+® (Exam N10-006)

Part Number: 093012
Course Edition: 1.1

Acknowledgements

PROJECT TEAM

Author	Media Designer	Content Editor
Peter Lammers	Alex Tong	Catherine M. Albano
Pamela J. Taylor	Devon Watters	Tricia Murphy

Logical Operations wishes to thank the members of the Logical Operations Instructor Community, and in particular Ralph Nyberg and Andrew James Riemer, for contributing their technical and instructional expertise during the creation of this course.

Notices

DISCLAIMER

While Logical Operations, Inc. takes care to ensure the accuracy and quality of these materials, we cannot guarantee their accuracy, and all materials are provided without any warranty whatsoever, including, but not limited to, the implied warranties of merchantability or fitness for a particular purpose. The name used in the data files for this course is that of a fictitious company. Any resemblance to current or future companies is purely coincidental. We do not believe we have used anyone's name in creating this course, but if we have, please notify us and we will change the name in the next revision of the course. Logical Operations is an independent provider of integrated training solutions for individuals, businesses, educational institutions, and government agencies. Use of screenshots, photographs of another entity's products, or another entity's product name or service in this book is for editorial purposes only. No such use should be construed to imply sponsorship or endorsement of the book by, nor any affiliation of such entity with Logical Operations. This courseware may contain links to sites on the Internet that are owned and operated by third parties (the "External Sites"). Logical Operations is not responsible for the availability of, or the content located on or through, any External Site. Please contact Logical Operations if you have any concerns regarding such links or External Sites.

TRADEMARK NOTICES

CompTIA® Network+® (Exam N10-006)

About This Course

The *CompTIA® Network+® (Exam N10-006)* course builds on your existing user-level knowledge and experience with personal computer operating systems and networks to present the fundamental skills and concepts that you will need to use on the job in any type of networking career. If you are pursuing a CompTIA technical certification path, the CompTIA® A+® certification is an excellent first step to take before preparing for the CompTIA Network+ certification.

The *CompTIA® Network+® (Exam N10-006)* course can benefit you in two ways. It can assist you if you are preparing to take the CompTIA Network+ examination (Exam N10-006). Also, if your job duties include network troubleshooting, installation, or maintenance, or if you are preparing for any type of network-related career, it provides the background knowledge and skills you will require to be successful.

Course Description

Target Student

This course is intended for entry-level computer support professionals with a basic knowledge of computer hardware, software, and operating systems who wish to increase their knowledge and understanding of networking concepts and acquire the required skills to prepare for a career in network support or administration, or who wish to prepare for the CompTIA Network+ certification (Exam N10-006). A typical student taking the *CompTIA® Network+® (Exam N10-006)* course should have a minimum of nine months of professional computer support experience as a PC or help desk technician. Networking experience is helpful but not mandatory; A+ certification or equivalent skills and knowledge is helpful but not mandatory.

Course Prerequisites

To ensure your success in this course, you will need basic Windows end-user computer skills. To meet this prerequisite, you can take either of the following LogicalCHOICE courses, or have equivalent experience:

- *Using Microsoft® Windows® 8*
- *Microsoft® Windows® 8 Transition from Windows® 7*

In addition, we highly recommend that you hold the CompTIA A+ certification, or have equivalent skills and knowledge. You may want to take the LogicalCHOICE course *CompTIA® A+®: A Comprehensive Approach (Exams 220-801 and 220-802)* to gain those skills and knowledge.

Course Objectives

In this course, you will describe the major networking technologies and systems of modern networks, and be able to configure, manage, and troubleshoot modern networks.

You will:

- Identify basic network theory concepts and major network communications methods.
- Describe bounded network media.
- Identify unbounded network media.
- Identify the major types of network implementations.
- Identify TCP/IP addressing and data delivery methods.
- Implement routing technologies.
- Identify the major services deployed on TCP/IP networks.
- Identify the infrastructure of a WAN implementation.
- Identify the components used in cloud computing and virtualization.
- Describe basic concepts related to network security.
- Prevent security breaches.
- Respond to security incidents.
- Identify the components of a remote network implementation.
- Identify the tools, methods, and techniques used in managing a network.
- Describe troubleshooting of issues on a network.

The LogicalCHOICE Home Screen

The LogicalCHOICE Home screen is your entry point to the LogicalCHOICE learning experience, of which this course manual is only one part. Visit the LogicalCHOICE Course screen both during and after class to make use of the world of support and instructional resources that make up the LogicalCHOICE experience.

Log-on and access information for your LogicalCHOICE environment will be provided with your class experience. On the LogicalCHOICE Home screen, you can access the LogicalCHOICE Course screens for your specific courses.

Each LogicalCHOICE Course screen will give you access to the following resources:

- eBook: an interactive electronic version of the printed book for your course.
- LearnTOs: brief animated components that enhance and extend the classroom learning experience.

Depending on the nature of your course and the choices of your learning provider, the LogicalCHOICE Course screen may also include access to elements such as:

- The interactive eBook.
- Social media resources that enable you to collaborate with others in the learning community using professional communications sites such as LinkedIn or microblogging tools such as Twitter.
- Checklists with useful post-class reference information.
- Any course files you will download.
- The course assessment.
- Notices from the LogicalCHOICE administrator.
- Virtual labs, for remote access to the technical environment for your course.
- Your personal whiteboard for sketches and notes.
- Newsletters and other communications from your learning provider.
- Mentoring services.
- A link to the website of your training provider.
- The LogicalCHOICE store.

Visit your LogicalCHOICE Home screen often to connect, communicate, and extend your learning experience!

How to Use This Book

As You Learn

This book is divided into lessons and topics, covering a subject or a set of related subjects. In most cases, lessons are arranged in order of increasing proficiency.

The results-oriented topics include relevant and supporting information you need to master the content. Each topic has various types of activities designed to enable you to practice the guidelines and procedures as well as to solidify your understanding of the informational material presented in the course. Procedures and guidelines are presented in a concise fashion along with activities and discussions. Information is provided for reference and reflection in such a way as to facilitate understanding and practice.

Data files for various activities as well as other supporting files for the course are available by download from the LogicalCHOICE Course screen. In addition to sample data for the course exercises, the course files may contain media components to enhance your learning and additional reference materials for use both during and after the course.

At the back of the book, you will find a glossary of the definitions of the terms and concepts used throughout the course. You will also find an index to assist in locating information within the instructional components of the book.

As You Review

Any method of instruction is only as effective as the time and effort you, the student, are willing to invest in it. In addition, some of the information that you learn in class may not be important to you immediately, but it may become important later. For this reason, we encourage you to spend some time reviewing the content of the course after your time in the classroom.

As a Reference

The organization and layout of this book make it an easy-to-use resource for future reference. Taking advantage of the glossary, index, and table of contents, you can use this book as a first source of definitions, background information, and summaries.

Course Icons

Watch throughout the material for these visual cues:

Icon	Description
	A **Note** provides additional information, guidance, or hints about a topic or task.
	A **Caution** helps make you aware of places where you need to be particularly careful with your actions, settings, or decisions so that you can be sure to get the desired results of an activity or task.
	LearnTO notes show you where an associated LearnTO is particularly relevant to the content. Access LearnTOs from your LogicalCHOICE Course screen.
	Checklists provide job aids you can use after class as a reference to performing skills back on the job. Access checklists from your LogicalCHOICE Course screen.
	Social notes remind you to check your LogicalCHOICE Course screen for opportunities to interact with the LogicalCHOICE community using social media.

1 Network Theory

Lesson Time: 2 hours, 30 minutes

Lesson Objectives

In this lesson, you will identify basic network theory concepts and major network communications methods. You will:

- Describe common terminology used in networking.

- Identify the layers and purpose of the OSI model.

- Describe the primary types of networks.

- Describe standard networking configurations.

- Identify the primary data transmission methods on a network.

Lesson Introduction

The CompTIA® Network+® certification covers a wide range of knowledge and skills that apply to different networking job roles. Any networking job role requires a fundamental knowledge of network terminology, components, standards, types, and configurations. In this lesson, you will identify the basic concepts of networking theory.

With a background in CompTIA Network+ information and skills, your networking career can move in many directions. Whether you are a network support technician, installer, or administrator, knowledge of basic networking theory provides the necessary foundation needed for learning more advanced networking concepts. A good grasp of fundamental networking theory will help you succeed in any network-related job role.

TOPIC A

Networking Overview

This lesson introduces the primary elements of network theory. In the information technology industry, there is a set of common terminology used to discuss network theory. In this topic, you will define common terms used in networking.

Networking, like any other technical discipline, has a language of its own. Part of mastering the technology involves familiarity with the language you use to describe that technology. With so many technical terms involved in the field of networking, the information and definitions in this topic will help you get familiar with these terms and the context in which they are used in networking.

Networks

A *network* is a group of devices that are connected together to communicate and share network resources such as files and peripheral devices. No two networks are alike in size or in configuration. Each network, however, includes common components that provide the resources and communications channels necessary for the network to operate.

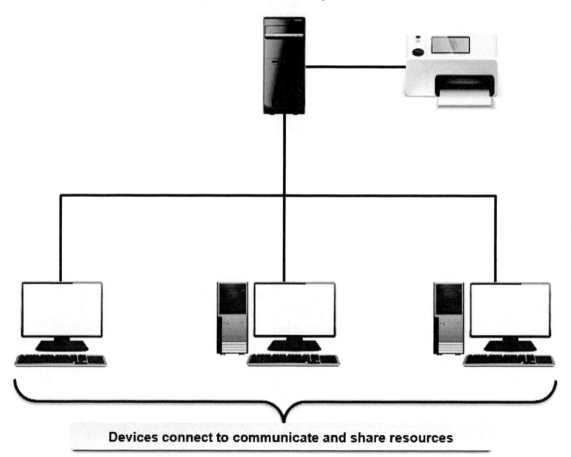

Devices connect to communicate and share resources

Figure 1–1: A simple network.

Network Components

There are several common components that make up a network, each of which performs a specific task.

Network Component	Description
Devices	Hardware such as computers, tablets, cell phones, servers, printers, fax machines, switches, and routers.
Physical media	Media that connects devices to a network and transmits data between the devices.
Network adapters	Hardware that translates data between the network and a device.
Network operating systems	Software that controls network traffic and access to common network resources.

Nodes

A *node* is any device or computer that can connect to a network and generate, process, or transfer data. Every node has addressing information to enable other devices to communicate with it. Network nodes can either be endpoints or redistribution points. *Endpoints* are nodes that function as a source or destination for data transfer. *Redistribution points* are nodes that transfer data, such as a network switch or a router.

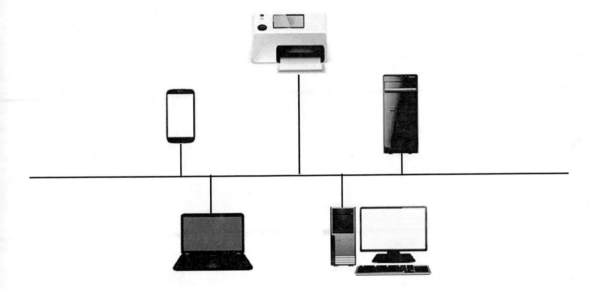

Figure 1–2: Nodes on a network.

 Note: This is a common definition of a node. Some people may refer to a node as a workstation, client, host, etc.

Computers and devices that are connected via network media require a method for communicating with other computers and devices on the network. For communication to occur, there must be a set of rules or *protocols*. Network communication protocols establish the rules and formats that must be followed for effective communication between networks, as well as from one network node to another.

Network Segments

A *segment* is a subdivision of a network that links a number of devices or serves as a connection between two nodes. A segment is bounded by physical internetworking devices such as switches and routers. All nodes attached to a segment have common access to that portion of the network.

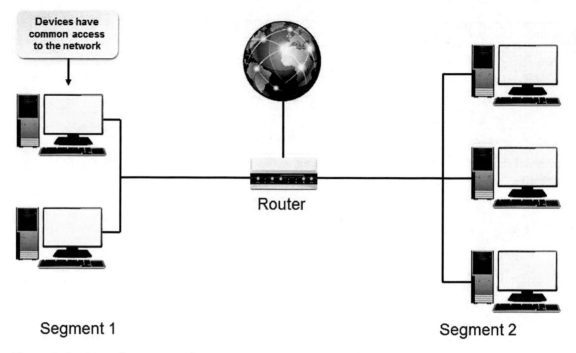

Figure 1-3: Network segments.

The Network Backbone

The *network backbone* is a very-high-speed transmission path that carries the majority of network data. It connects either small networks into a larger structure or server nodes to a network where the majority of client devices are attached. Network backbones can take many different forms, such as a bus, cloud, or mesh. The technology in use on a backbone network can be different from that used on client network sections. Since the backbone cabling connects switches and routers on a network, it can carry more traffic than other types of cabling on the network.

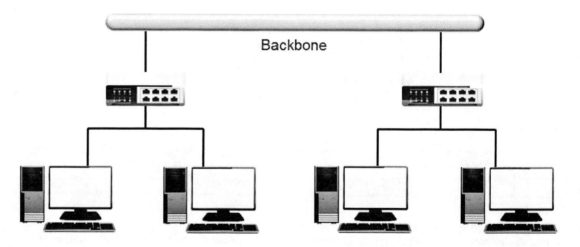

Figure 1-4: Network backbones are high-speed transmission paths that connect networks, network segments, and nodes.

In a local area network (LAN), a typical network backbone is one or more core level switches, or several switches connected together by trunk links. In a wide area network (WAN), a typical backbone is an asynchronous transfer mode (ATM) or frame relay cloud.

Types of Network Backbones

There are several types of network backbones that you may encounter.

Network Backbone Type	Description
Serial	Consists of multiple switches connected by one backbone cable. Typically not scaled for enterprise-wide use.
Distributed/ hierarchical	Consists of multiple switches connected serially to hubs or routers. Due to their hierarchical structure, these networks can be easily expanded without a significant cost impact.
	Serves well as one-site enterprise-wide networks; their switch layers can be configured by geography (such as a floor in a building) or function (such as a workgroup). Distributed backbone networks enable an administrator to segregate workgroups, simplifying their management.
Collapsed	Uses a router or switch as the nexus for several subnetworks. The router or switch must have multiprocessors to bear the frequently high level of network traffic. Router or switch failures in a collapsed backbone can bring down the entire network. Depending on the routers' processing capabilities, data transmission can also be slow.
Parallel	Suits enterprise-wide applications. Like the collapsed backbone network, the parallel backbone network uses a central router or switch but augments the dependent switches with multiple cable connections. These multiple links ensure connectivity to the whole enterprise.

Servers

A *server* is a network computer or process that shares resources with and responds to requests from computers, devices, and other servers on the network. Servers provide centralized access and storage for resources that can include applications, files, printers or other hardware, and services such as email. A server can be optimized and dedicated to one specific function or it can serve general needs. Multiple servers of various types can coexist on the same network.

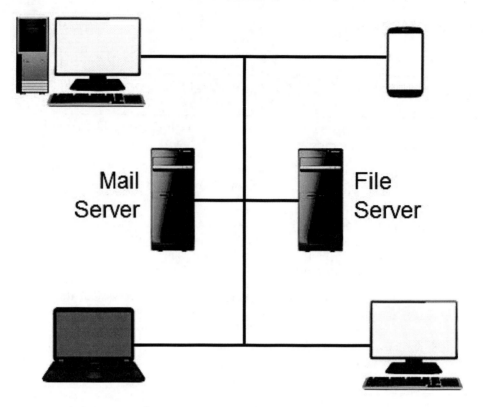

Figure 1-5: Servers performing generic and dedicated tasks.

A server can be a computer or a process running on a device that listens for incoming connection requests from clients. It will accept or reject those incoming connection attempts based on whether or not it provides the service the client is requesting. It can also reject or accept a connection attempt based on security settings configured by the administrator.

Microsoft Windows Server

Microsoft's network operating system is called Microsoft® Windows Server®. The networking features of Windows Server include, but are not limited to:

- The Active Directory service (ADS).
- Integrated network services such as the *Domain Name System (DNS)* and the *Dynamic Host Configuration Protocol (DHCP)*.
- Advanced services such as clustering, public key infrastructure (PKI), routing, and web services.
- User and group security on the file and object levels.
- Advanced security features such as a built-in firewall, file encryption, and Internet Protocol Security (IPSec).

Linux Servers

There are several open-source network operating systems based on the Linux® operating system. Two of the more popular distributions are Red Hat® Enterprise Linux® (RHEL) and SUSE LINUX Enterprise Server® (SLES). Common features of Linux servers include, but are not limited to:

- Lightweight Directory Access Protocol (LDAP)-compliant directory services.
- Network services such as DNS and DHCP.
- Advanced services such as clustering, PKI, routing, and web services.
- User and group security on the file and object levels.
- Advanced security features such as a built-in firewall, file and disk encryption, and IPSec.

Clients

A *client* is a computer or process running on a device that initiates a connection to a server. The client contacts the server attempting to make the connection. The server may or may not accept the connection. The client device has its own processor, memory, and storage, and can maintain its own resources and perform its own tasks and processing. Any type of device on a network can function as a client of another device, when needed.

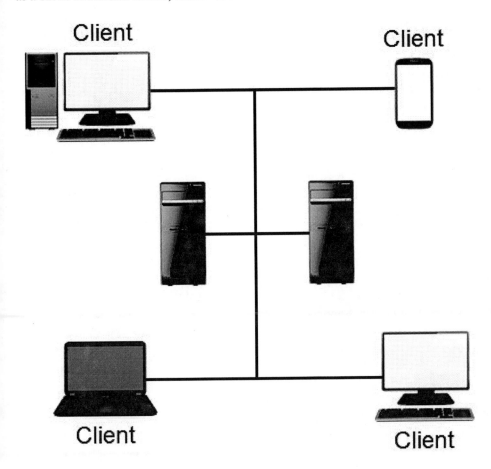

Figure 1-6: Clients connected to a server.

The term "client" most often refers to workstation or desktop computers employed by end users. Any device on the network can function as a client when it uses other computers' resources, such as a Windows Server computer accessing resources on another server.

There are also *thin clients*, which are devices that depend on a server to fulfill their computational needs to some degree. They can range from a *terminal* that has no computing abilities to a normal client device that relies on a server to perform its main functions.

Client Operating Systems

There are many different types of operating systems for client devices, including:

- **Microsoft® Windows®**: Microsoft Windows features an enhanced graphical user interface (GUI), support for a wide range of applications and devices, a minimum of 32-bit processing, native networking support, and a large suite of built-in applications and accessories such as the Internet Explorer® browser. Windows is often factory-installed on new personal computers that are designed for retail sale.
- **Apple® OS X®**: OS X is a GUI-based operating system developed by Apple Inc. for their Macintosh® line of computer systems. It features an enhanced GUI, enhanced support and compatibility with iOS devices, native networking support, and a large suite of built-in

applications and accessories such as the Safari® browser. OS X is factory-installed on new Macintosh computers that are designed for retail sale.

- **Linux operating systems:** Linux OS is a freely distributable open-source, cross-platform operating system based on UNIX® that can be installed on different hardware devices such as PCs, laptops, mobile and tablet devices, video game consoles, servers, etc. No single official Linux desktop exists; rather, desktop environments and Linux distributions select components from a pool of free and open-source software with which they construct a GUI implementing some more or less strict design guide.
- **Android operating systems:** Android™ is a mobile OS based on the Linux kernel and is developed by Google. The Android OS is designed primarily for touchscreen mobile devices such as smartphones and tablet computers.
- **iOS operating systems:** iOS is a mobile OS developed by Apple Inc. and distributed exclusively for Apple® hardware such as their iDevices. The user interface is based on the concept of direct manipulation using multi-touch gestures.

Hosts

A *host* is any device that is connected to a network. It can be a client or a server, or even a device such as a printer, router, or switch. Any device on the network can function as a host when other devices access its resources, such as a server computer having its resources accessed by another server.

TCP/IP Hosts

In the early days of computer networking, all computers were mainframe computers that controlled the activities of network terminal devices. The mainframes were joined together to communicate in the early research networks that laid the foundation for the Internet.

As *Transmission Control Protocol/Internet Protocol (TCP/IP)* was adopted and became ubiquitous and personal computers joined the networks, the term "host" was generalized and is now used to refer to virtually any independent system on a TCP/IP network.

Peer Devices

A *peer* is a self-sufficient computer that acts as both a server and a client to other computers on a network. Peer computing is most often used in smaller networks with no dedicated central server, but both clients and servers in other types of networks can share resources with peer devices.

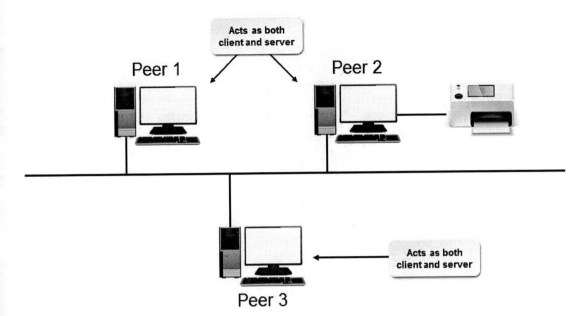

Figure 1-7: Peer devices in a network.

Mainframe Computers

A *mainframe computer* is a powerful, centralized computer system that performs data storage and processing tasks on behalf of clients and other network devices. On a mainframe-based network, the mainframe computer does all computing tasks and returns the resultant data to the end user's device.

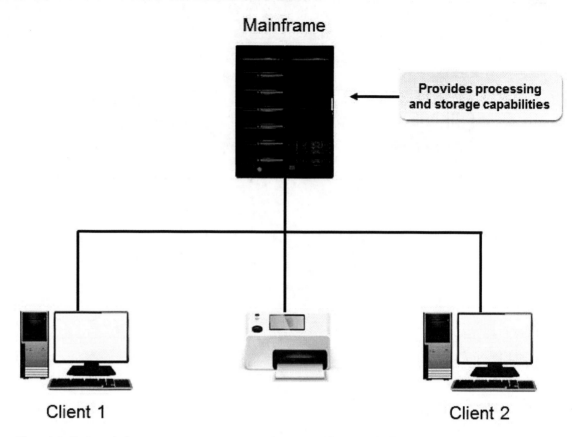

Figure 1-8: A mainframe computer connected to several network devices.

Terminals

A *terminal* is a specialized device on a mainframe-based network that transmits user-entered data to a mainframe for processing and displays the results. Terminals are often called "dumb" because all required processing or memory is located on the mainframe. Terminals usually consist of just a keyboard and a monitor. Standard client devices that need to interact with mainframe computers can run software called a *terminal emulator* so that they appear as dedicated terminals to the mainframe.

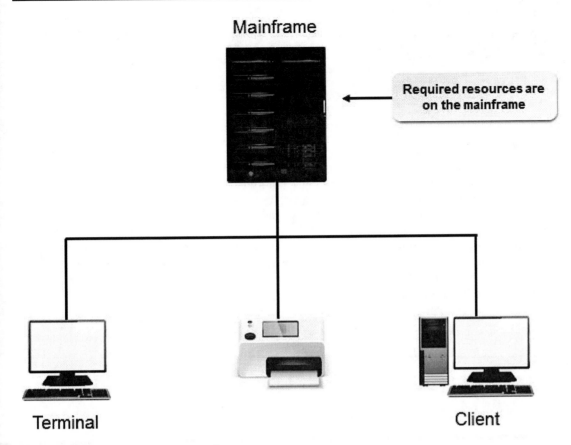

Figure 1-9: A terminal on a network.

Thin clients are often considered to be related to terminals because of their reliance on another device to provide processing power. The main differences between thin clients and terminals are:

- A terminal is typically just a monitor and a keyboard with no processing power. A thin client is typically an actual device with a CPU and RAM, but has no hard drive.
- A terminal connects to a dedicated port on a mainframe. A thin client connects to the network like any other device, and it boots from its network card, downloading the operating system from the network and running it from RAM.

Numbering Systems

Various numbering systems are used in networking. Typically, in day-to-day use, decimal numbering, or base 10, is used. Most are familiar with the place values of ones, tens, hundreds, thousands, and so on. Place values can also be expressed as 10^0, 10^1, 10^2, and so on. Values in each place value can be between 0 and 9. If you get to 9 in a place value, the next number starts with 1 in the next place value and zero in the current place value.

Binary is used whenever an on/off state is needed and when IP addresses are being calculated. Binary is also referred to as base 2 numbering. There are only two numbers used: 0 and 1. The place values are expressed as 2^0, 2^1, 2^2, 2^3, and so on. If you get to 1 in a place value, the next number starts with 1 in the next place value and zero in the current place value.

Hexadecimal numbers are base 16 numbers. The values in each place can be between 0 and F; numbers above 9 are expressed with letters A through F. As with the other numbering systems, place values are used with the first place value being 16^0, followed by 16^1, 16^2, and so on. You are most likely to encounter these types of numbers in MAC addresses.

Octal numbers are base 8 numbers and use the numbers 0 to 7. These are more often used by programmers and are not typically used when viewing networking addresses or routes.

ACTIVITY 1-1
Defining Networking Terminology

Scenario

You have recently been hired to work in the IT department at Greene City Interiors. Your manager informs you that you will be working with a network administrator at Greene City Interiors to assess and configure the network for one of the branch offices that is having problems. They tell you that the branch office previously used a local IT professional to maintain their network, but they have had constant problems. Users have complained about connectivity issues and an absence of some network technologies, preventing them from being able to fully perform their jobs. Your manager says it is your and the network administrator's task to assess the branch office network and devices for any issues, and then implement changes and additions to bring the network up to the Greene City Interiors networking standards.

Before you travel to the branch office, the network administrator wants to gauge your level of knowledge and quizzes you with some basic networking questions.

1. What is a network device that shares resources with and responds to requests from other devices called?
   ○ Client
   ○ Server
   ○ Terminal
   ○ Mainframe

2. What is a network device that transmits data a user enters to a mainframe for processing and displays the results?
   ○ Server
   ○ Mainframe
   ○ Terminal
   ○ Client

3. What is a device that acts as both a server and a client?
   ○ Mainframe
   ○ Client
   ○ Server
   ○ Peer

4. True or False? A mainframe computer transmits data to another device for processing and displays the result to a user.
   ☐ True
   ☐ False

5. In which type of network are multiple switches connected by a single backbone cable?

    ○   Distributed

    ○   Serial

    ○   Collapsed

    ○   Parallel

TOPIC B

Network Standards and the OSI Model

Network implementations are built on common network standards and models of networking that describe how these devices and protocols interconnect. In this topic, you will identify how these devices use an important common standard: the Open Systems Interconnection (OSI) model.

Data communication over a network is a structured process and is described by certain models. The OSI model breaks the data communication process into definite stages, with each stage corresponding to one of its layers. The OSI model has been implemented in many types of networks. Being able to identify the OSI layers and their purpose will enable you to plan the implementation of a network according to the devices, protocols, and transmission methods needed.

The OSI Model

The *Open Systems Interconnection (OSI) model* is a standard means of describing network communication by defining it as a series of layers, each with specific input and output. The model provides a theoretical representation of what happens to information being sent from one device to another on a network. The sending device works from the Application layer down, and the receiving device works on the transmitted data from the Physical layer up. The OSI model was developed by the International Standards Organization (ISO) and has seven layers that are numbered in order from the bottom (Layer 1) to the top (Layer 7).

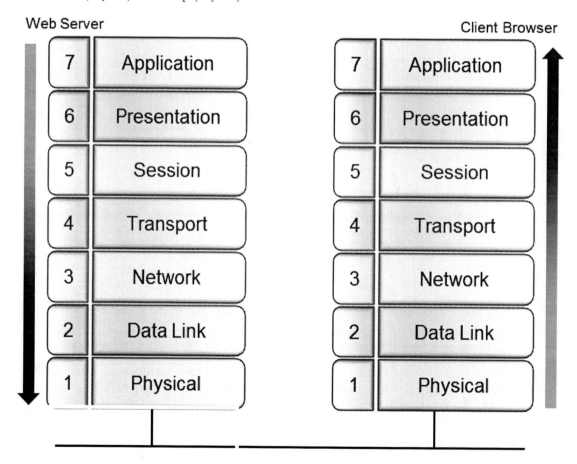

Figure 1-10: Layers in the OSI reference model.

Note: It can be difficult to remember the correct sequence of the OSI layers, it is easy to remember them from the top down, using the mnemonic "All People Seem To Need Data Processing."

OSI Model Layers

The layers of the OSI model, starting from the top, are described in the following table.

Layer Number and Name	Description
Layer 7, Application layer	Enables applications on a network node (device) to request network services such as file transfers, email, and database access. These requests are accomplished through the use of Layer 7 protocols such as Hypertext Transfer Protocol (HTTP), File Transfer Protocol (FTP), Simple Mail Transfer Protocol (SMTP), Internet Message Access Protocol (IMAP), and the like. Proxies and firewalls work at this layer.
Layer 6, Presentation layer	Translates Application layer data into an intermediate form that both client and server can process. Encryption, compression, character sets, multimedia formats, Multi-Purpose Internet Mail Extensions (MIME) types, and codecs exist at this layer. Proxies and firewalls work at this layer.
Layer 5, Session layer	Establishes and controls data communication between applications operating on two different devices, regulating when each device can send data and how much it can send. TCP and User Datagram Protocol (UDP) port numbers exist at this layer. Firewalls also work at this layer.
Layer 4, Transport layer	Performs the actual establishment, maintenance, and teardown of the connection. Optionally divides long communications into smaller segments, including error recognition and correction, and data receipt acknowledgment. TCP and UDP protocols exist at this layer. Packet filtering routers, multilayer switches, and firewalls work at this layer.
Layer 3, Network layer	Adds logical addressing (network addresses) and chooses the best route. IP, Internet Control Message Protocol (ICMP), and Internet Group Management Protocol (IGMP) exist at this layer. Routers, multilayer switches, and firewalls work at this layer.
Layer 2, Data Link layer	Structures the data into a format appropriate for the transmission medium. Adds physical addresses such as media access control (MAC) addresses or frame relay data link connection identifier (DLCI) numbers. Usually includes simple error checking. All WAN and LAN protocols exist at this layer, including Ethernet, token ring, frame relay, Point-to-Point Protocol (PPP), High-Level Data Link Control (HDLC), wireless access protocols, ATM, and X.25. (Some of these protocols extend beyond Layer 2.) Switches and bridges work at this layer.

Layer Number and Name	Description
Layer 1, Physical layer	Transmits bits (binary digits) from one device to another and regulates the transmission stream over a medium (wire, fiber optics, or radio waves). All electrical and mechanical aspects of data transmission exist at this layer, including cabling, connectors, antennas, transceivers, baseband, broadband, signaling types, voltages, waveforms, modulation, frequencies, and clock rates. Network interface cards, hubs, and repeaters work at this layer. **Note:** While it is true that a repeater, hub, or network interface card will also be designed to work with a specific Layer 2 protocol (such as Ethernet or token ring), these devices are generally classified as Layer 1 devices because their primary purpose is connectivity rather than forwarding decisions based on Layer 2 addresses.

The OSI model is an excellent conceptual model to understand networking and to compare the functionality of different devices and protocols. You will often hear experienced engineers and troubleshooters discuss a problem by referring to the relevant OSI layer. Examples include: "I think it's a Layer 2 problem as opposed to a Layer 3 problem," or "Do we really have to use Layer 3 addressing to carry data across a point-to-point cellular call?"

 Note: Some network protocols do not map directly to the OSI model. For example, Multiprotocol Label Switching (MPLS) is often referred to as Layer 2.5 because it exists somewhere between the traditional concept of the Data Link and Network layers.

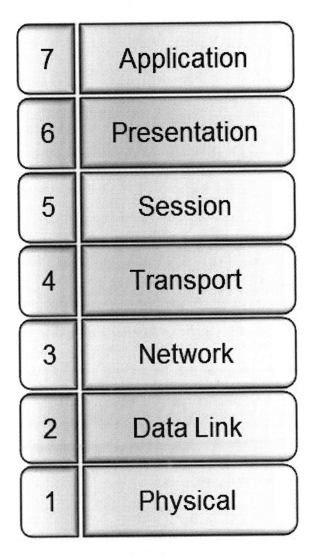

Figure 1–11: The OSI model.

Data Encapsulation

Encapsulation is the process of adding delivery information to the actual data transmitted on each layer. Encapsulation takes place in the transmission end as data is passed down the layers. At the receiving end, the reverse process of removing the added information is done as data passes to the next higher layer. This process is called *de-encapsulation*. The added information is called a header if it is before the data or a trailer if it is added after the data.

Data Packets

A *data packet* is a unit of data transfer between devices that communicate over a network. In general, all packets contain three parts: a header, data, and a trailer. The header part contains the destination and source addresses. The trailer part contains an error checking code. The data part contains the actual information or data that is to be transmitted.

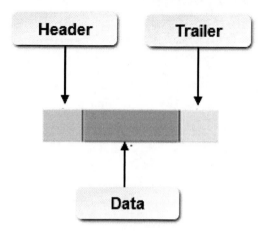

Figure 1-12: Parts of a data packet.

The contents of a packet depend on the network protocol in use.

The terms frame, packet, segment, and datagram are sometimes used interchangeably when referring to data being transmitted over a network. Terms such as these are generally referred to as *protocol data units (PDUs)*. The actual correlation between OSI layers and the appropriate type of PDU is described in the following table.

OSI Layer	PDU Type
Layer 1 (Physical)	Packet
Layer 2 (Data Link)	Frame
Layer 3 (Network)	Packet
Layer 4 (Transport)	Segment or datagram
Layer 5 (Session)	Message
Layer 6 (Presentation)	Message
Layer 7 (Application)	Message

OSI Model and Associated Network Devices

The applications, operating systems, and network technology you choose determine how the OSI model is applied to your network. The applications will vary depending on the user needs. The operating system will vary depending on the needs or preferences of the organization. The network technology will vary depending on the requirements for the network.

The following table summarizes the OSI model layers and the protocols and network devices that are associated with each layer.

OSI Layer	Protocols or Key Characteristics	Network Devices
Layer 7, Application layer	HTTP, FTP, SMTP, IMAP, etc.	Application proxy
Layer 6, Presentation layer	Encryption, compression, character sets, multimedia formats, MIME types, codecs, etc.	Application proxy
Layer 5, Session layer	TCP and UDP port numbers	Firewalls
Layer 4, Transport layer	TCP and UDP protocols	Firewalls

OSI Layer	Protocols or Key Characteristics	Network Devices
Layer 3, Network layer	IP, ICMP, and IGMP protocols	Multi-layer switches, routers, and firewalls
Layer 2, Data Link layer	Ethernet, token ring, frame relay, PPP, HDLC, wireless access protocol, ATM, X.25, etc.	Switches/bridges and access points
Layer 1, Physical layer	Cabling, connectors, antennas, transceivers, baseband, broadband, signaling types, voltages, waveforms, modulation, frequencies, and clock rates. Network interface cards, hubs, repeaters, etc.	Hubs, repeaters, patch panels, cables, and network cards

Networking Standards

A *networking standard* is a set of specifications, guidelines, or characteristics applied to network components to ensure interoperability and consistency between them. Standards determine all aspects of networking such as the size, shape, and types of connectors on network cables as well as the number of devices that can connect to the network. For example, the Institute of Electrical and Electronics Engineers (IEEE) 802.3 standard is used to standardize Ethernet network implementations by providing networking specifications and characteristics.

Standards can be de facto, meaning that they have been widely adopted through use, or de jure, meaning that they are mandated by law or have been approved by a recognized body of experts.

 Note: To help recall which is which, you can think of words like jury and jurisdiction, which are words related to the legal system. These words, and the term de jure, come from the same Latin root.

Standards Organizations

Standards organizations issue standards that are important in the field of networking.

Standards Organization	Description
ISO	The International Organization for Standardization (ISO) is the largest standards-development body in the world comprising the national standards institutes of 162 countries. It is a non-governmental organization issuing voluntary standards in fields from agriculture to textiles.
	Of most significance for networking, in 1984, the ISO developed the OSI model. The OSI model is a seven-layered framework of standards and specifications for communication in networks. The short name ISO is not an abbreviation for the name of the organization in any particular language, but was derived from the Greek word isos, meaning equal.
	Website: **www.iso.org**
IEEE	The Institute of Electrical and Electronics Engineers (IEEE) is an organization dedicated to advancing theory and technology in electrical sciences. The standards wing of IEEE issues standards in areas such as electronic communications, circuitry, computer engineering, electromagnetics, and nuclear science.
	Website: **www.ieee.org**

Standards Organization	Description
ANSI	The American National Standards Institute (ANSI) is the national standards institute of the United States that facilitates the formation of a variety of national standards, as well as promotes those standards internationally. Individually accredited standards bodies perform the standards development under ANSI's guidance. The best-known ANSI standard in the information technology world is a method for representing keyboard characters by standard four-digit numeric codes. Website: **www.ansi.org**
TIA and EIA	The Telecommunications Industry Association (TIA) and the Electronic Industries Alliance (EIA) are two trade associations accredited by ANSI to develop and jointly issue standards for telecommunications and electronics. Websites: **www.tiaonline.org** and **www.eia.org**
ARIN	The Regional Internet Registry (RIR) is an organization that supervises how Internet numbers are allocated and registered in a particular geographical region. There are five RIRs in operation and the American Registry for Internet Numbers (ARIN) is responsible for the United States, Canada, and parts of the Caribbean. The services provided by ARIN include: • IP address allocation. • Registration transaction information with the help of WHOIS, a query/response protocol that is used to query an official database to determine the owner of a domain name or an IP address on the Internet. • Routing information with the help of RIRs that manage, distribute, and register public Internet number resources within their respective regions.
ICANN	The Internet Corporation for Assigned Names and Numbers (ICANN) coordinates the assignments of unique identifications on the Internet, such as domain names, IP addresses, extension names, and Autonomous System (AS) numbers. **Note:** In 1993, an international organization called the *Internet Assigned Number Authority (IANA)* was established to govern the use of Internet IP addresses. Today, that function is performed by ICANN. Website: **www.icann.org**
ISoc	The Internet Society (ISoc) organization coordinates and oversees standards and practices for the Internet. Its mission is to promote the open development, evolution, and use of the Internet for the benefit of all people throughout the world. Website: **www.isoc.org**
IETF	The Internet Engineering Task Force (IETF) is an international open committee that consists of working groups, committees, and commercial organizations that work together to develop and maintain Internet standards and contribute to the evolution and operation of the Internet. All published Internet standards documents, known as Requests For Comments (RFCs), are available through the IETF. Website: **www.ietf.org**

ACTIVITY 1–2
Identifying the Layers in the OSI Model

Scenario
The network administrator at Greene City Interiors now poses questions to you about the OSI model.

1. What layer transmits bits from one device to another and regulates the transmission stream over a medium?
   - ○ Physical
   - ○ Network
   - ○ Transport
   - ○ Data Link

2. In which layer do programs on a network node access network services?
   - ○ Data Link
   - ○ Physical
   - ○ Application
   - ○ Presentation
   - ○ Session

3. Which OSI layer is responsible for establishing connections between two devices?
   - ○ Transport
   - ○ Presentation
   - ○ Application
   - ○ Physical
   - ○ Data Link

4. Which layer packages bits of data from the Physical layer into frames, transfers them from one device to another, and receives acknowledgment from the addressed device?
   - ○ Presentation
   - ○ Session
   - ○ Transport
   - ○ Data Link
   - ○ Application

TOPIC C

Network Types

So far, you have learned about various components that constitute a network. You will now describe how you can replicate these basic network structures on a larger scale. In this topic, you will identify the primary network types.

The area covered by present day networks may be small enough to fit a building or large enough to span continents. Networks of different sizes have different requirements and features, and may use completely different technologies. Companies can deploy a network depending on their size and communications needs. As a network professional, you may work with a network of any possible size or type. A thorough knowledge of the size-based classification of networks and their related technologies will help you choose the network type that is best suited for your needs.

LANs

A *local area network (LAN)* is a self-contained network that spans a small area, such as a single building, floor, or room. In a LAN, all nodes and segments are directly connected with cables or short-range wireless technologies. It does not require a leased telecommunication system to function. Due to their smaller size and fewer number of nodes, LANs provide faster data transfers than other network types. Different technologies can be implemented on a LAN depending on the configuration needs and functionality of the network. Ethernet is the most commonly implemented LAN technology. Other LAN technologies such as token ring, token bus, and Fiber Distributed Data Interface (FDDI) can also be used on LANs.

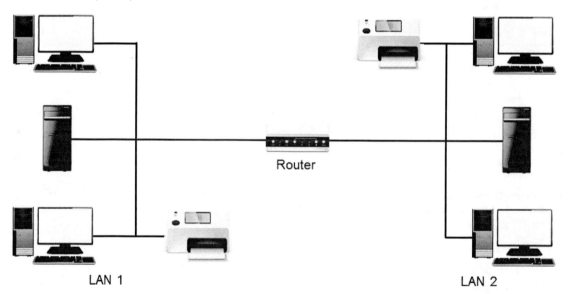

Router

LAN 1   LAN 2

Figure 1-13: Devices connected to form a LAN.

A LAN can be extended or replaced by a *Wireless LAN (WLAN)*, which is a self-contained network of two or more devices connected using a wireless connection. A WLAN spans a small area, such as a small building, floor, or room.

LAN Administration

LAN administration encompasses tasks for managing and maintaining the local network. LAN administration includes the following duties:

• Maintaining devices and cabling.

- Maintaining network software.
- Performing the installation and deployment, upgrades, and troubleshooting for different applications.
- Maintaining a broad range of skills and knowledge about network applications and hardware.

WANs

A *wide area network (WAN)* is a network that spans a large area, often across multiple geographical locations. WANs typically connect multiple LANs and other networks using long-range transmission media. Such a network scheme facilitates communication among users and devices in different locations. WANs can be private, such as those built and maintained by large, multinational corporations, or they can be public, such as the Internet. When a WAN includes sites and networks around the world, it is considered a *global area network (GAN)*.

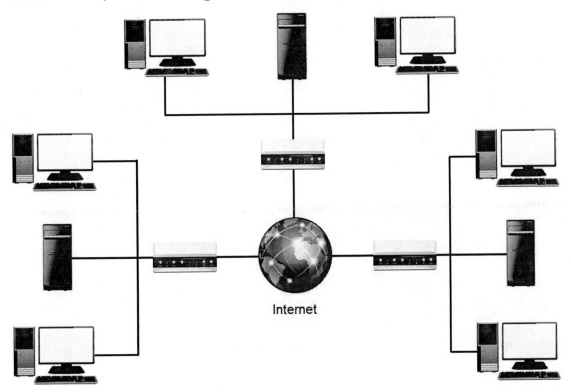

Figure 1–14: A WAN composed of several LANs.

WAN Administration

WAN administration typically includes more complex technical issues than LAN administration, and focuses on resolving network issues rather than user issues. WAN administration includes the following duties:

- Designing and maintaining the connection scheme between remote segments of a network.
- Developing and troubleshooting routing structures.
- Working with both voice and data systems.
- Developing scripts to automate complex network administrative tasks.
- Working on security issues and helping to implement recovery schemes.
- Planning, testing, and implementing hardware and software upgrades.

Network Coverage Areas

There are other network categories based on the geographical areas they cover.

Network Category	Description
MAN	A *metropolitan area network (MAN)* covers an area equivalent to a city or a municipality.
CAN	A *campus area network (CAN)* covers an area equivalent to an academic campus or business park. A CAN is typically owned or used exclusively by an entity.
PAN	A *personal area network (PAN)* connects two to three devices with cables and is most often seen in small or home offices.
	A *wireless personal area network (WPAN)* is a variation of a PAN that connects wireless devices in close proximity but not through a *Wireless Access Point (WAP)* or *access point (AP)*. Infrared and Bluetooth are technologies used for connecting devices in a WPAN.

The Internet

The *Internet* is the single largest global WAN, linking virtually every country in the world. Publicly owned and operated, the Internet is widely used for sending email, transferring files, and carrying out online commercial transactions. All information on the Internet is stored as web pages, which can be accessed through software known as a web browser. Most of the processes related to the Internet are specified by the *Internet Protocol (IP)*, and all the nodes connected to the Internet are identified by a unique address, known as an *IP address*.

Figure 1-15: The Internet consists of devices connected across the world.

Intranets

An *intranet* is a private network that uses Internet protocols and services to share a company's information with its employees. As with the Internet, the employees can access an intranet via a web browser and navigate a company's web pages. However, an intranet is not very useful if it is not connected with the Internet. An intranet contains information that is segregated from the Internet for confidentiality and security reasons.

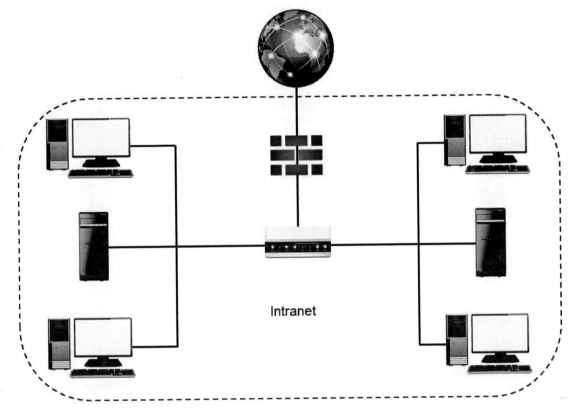

Figure 1-16: An intranet connecting users in a private network.

Extranets

An *extranet* is a private network that grants controlled access to users outside of the network. It is an extension of an organization's intranet. With the help of an extranet, organizations can grant access to users such as vendors, suppliers, and clients to connect to resources on the network.

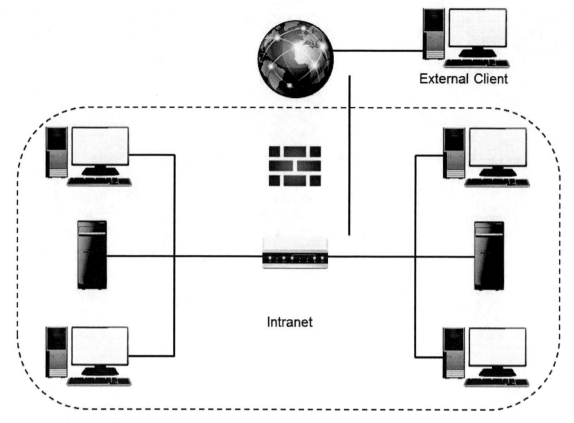

Figure 1-17: An extranet connecting a user outside of the network.

Enterprise Networks

An *enterprise network* is a network that includes elements of both LANs and WANs. It is owned and operated by a single organization to interlink its devices and resources so that users have access whether they are on or off premise. Enterprise networks employ technologies and software designed for fast data access, email exchange, and collaboration. Enterprise networks are scalable and include high-end equipment, strong security systems, and mission-critical applications.

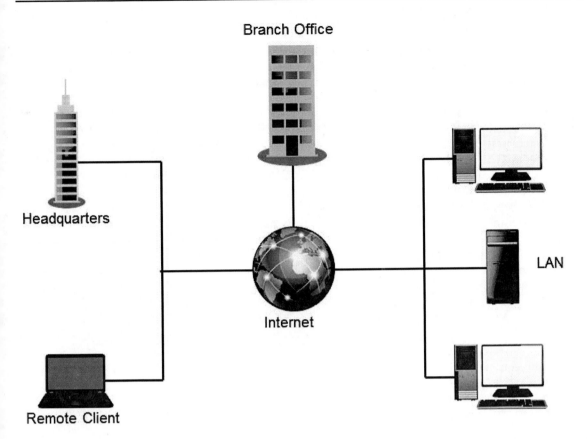

Figure 1-18: An enterprise network.

Specialized Network Types

You might also encounter some specialized networks, such as Industrial Control Systems (ICSs) and medianets.

Industrial Control Systems (ICSs) are networks and systems used to support municipal services and industrial processes such as power generation and distribution, water treatment and distribution, wastewater collection and treatment, oil and natural gas collection and production, chemical synthesis and other production processes, as well as in transportation systems. The two main types of ICSs are Supervisory Control and Data Acquisition (SCADA) systems and Distributed Control Systems (DCSs).

*   *Supervisory Control and Data Acquisition (SCADA) systems* are used in situations where sites are at great geographical distances from one another, and where centralized data collection and management is critical to the industrial operation. Examples of industries where SCADA systems are common include systems like water distribution systems, wastewater collection systems, oil or natural gas pipelines, electrical power grids, and railway transportation systems. A SCADA control center monitors and manages remote sites by collecting and processing data and then sending supervisory commands to the remote station's control devices. Remote control devices, or field devices, are responsible for controlling operations like opening and closing valves, collecting data from sensor systems, and monitoring the environment for alarm conditions.
*   *Distributed Control Systems (DCSs)* are used in process-based industries such as electric power generation; oil refining; water treatment; wastewater treatment; and chemical, food, and automotive production. In most instances, each main process is broken down into a series of sub-processes, each of which is assigned an acceptable tolerance level. Programmable Logic Controllers (PLCs) provide control over these sub-processes by using control loops, and the DCS manages the PLCs. DCSs are used primarily in industries where the parts of the manufacturing system are in close geographic proximity, and where feedback and feed-forward

loops are used to create a closed-loop or closed network system. The ICS server contains the DCS or PLC control software that communicates with subordinate control devices on an ICS network. A remote terminal unit (RTU) connects physical objects to an ICS or SCADA system. The connection established via a microprocessor-controlled device transmits telemetry data to the master system. Data and messages from the master system or server are used to control the objects that are connected.

Note: Do not confuse ICSs with Microsoft's Internet Connection Sharing, which is a way for Microsoft devices to share an Internet connection with other computers.

A *medianet* is a network optimized for rich media, such as voice and video, and is designed to transport a mixture of rich media and other content, such as text. The coordination of multiple types of video, audio, and written documents into a single experience is a critical aspect of a medianet. A medianet does not replace existing network architectures, and is an evolutionary extension in the multimedia space of these existing network architectures. One of the uses for a medianet is to support video teleconferencing (VTC), which is also referred to as video conferencing.

Note: For additional information, check out the LearnTO **Recognize Network Types and Components** presentation in the LearnTOs for this course on your LogicalCHOICE Course screen.

ACTIVITY 1-3
Identifying Network Types

Scenario

The network administrator at Greene City Interiors describes different Greene City Interiors offices and wants you to identify the type of each network.

1. Greene City Interiors has a remote office that accesses its corporate office with relatively high bandwidth. Which network category does it use?

   ○ LAN

   ○ WAN

   ○ CAN

   ○ MAN

2. The Greene City Interiors headquarters occupies four floors in their building. What category does this network fit into?

   ○ LAN

   ○ WAN

   ○ CAN

   ○ MAN

3. This figure represents the Greene City Interiors company with a central office, an attached warehouse, and a remote supplier. Which portions of the network are LANs?

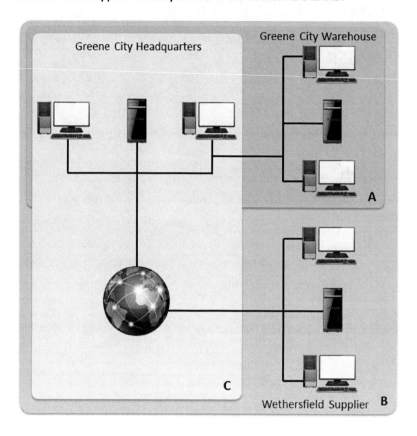

☐ Section A—Greene City Headquarters and Greene City Warehouse

☐ Section B—Greene City Warehouse and Wethersfield Supplier

☐ Section C—Greene City Headquarters

4. This figure represents the Greene City Interiors company with a central office, an attached warehouse, and a remote sales office. Which portion of the network is a WAN?

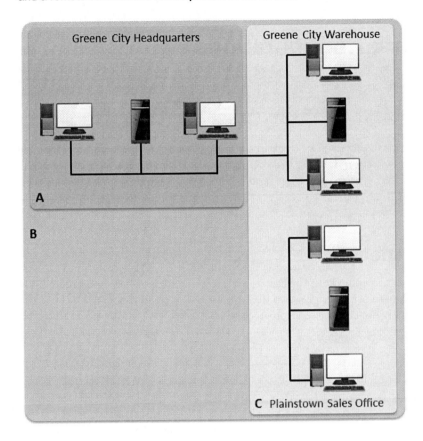

- ○ Section A—Greene City Headquarters
- ○ Section B—Greene City Headquarters and Greene City Warehouse
- ○ Section C—Greene City Warehouse and Plainstown Sales Office

5. Which network type employs elements of both LANs and WANs?
- ○ MAN
- ○ WAN
- ○ CAN
- ○ Enterprise network

TOPIC D

Identify Network Configurations

Up to this point, you have identified the primary components that describe the size and extent of a network. For every network deployed, the actual model of the network will depend on the individual network's requirements that the network is designed for. In this topic, you will identify the standard networking configurations currently in use.

As a networking professional, you will need to work in a variety of network environments that use different technologies, implementation designs, and configurations. The configuration to be used is a result of an analysis of requirements, connectivity methods, and technologies that are being used. Some of these configurations might be more prevalent than others, and you need to understand the different network configurations you might encounter.

Network Configurations

A *network configuration* is a design specification for how the nodes on a network are constructed to interact and communicate. A network configuration determines the degree to which communications and processing are centralized or distributed.

There are three primary network configurations:

- Centralized or hierarchical
- Client/server
- Peer-to-peer

Centralized Networks

A *centralized network* is a network in which a central mainframe computer controls all network communication and performs data processing and storage on behalf of clients. Users connect to the mainframe via dedicated terminals or terminal emulators. Centralized networks provide high performance and centralized management, but they are expensive to implement.

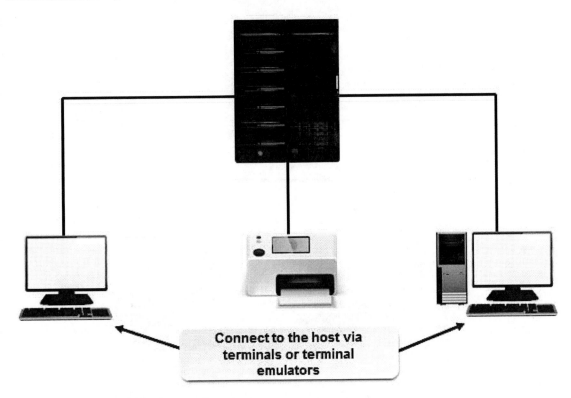

Figure 1-19: A centralized network.

 Note: The term "hierarchical network" can also be used to describe centralized networks.

A pure centralized network is rare in today's environment. Most of the network types you encounter will be decentralized to some extent, with the client/server architecture having some degree of centralization and the peer-to-peer architecture being almost purely decentralized. In a decentralized network, each peer can connect directly with other peers without being managed by a central server. A server provides services to the nodes upon a request from them. A peer-to-peer network is an example of a decentralized network.

Client/Server Networks

A *client/server network* is a network in which servers provide resources to clients. Typically, there is at least one server providing central *authentication* services. Servers also provide access to shared files, printers, hardware storage, and applications. In client/server networks, processing power, management services, and administrative functions can be concentrated where needed, while clients can still perform many basic end-user tasks on their own.

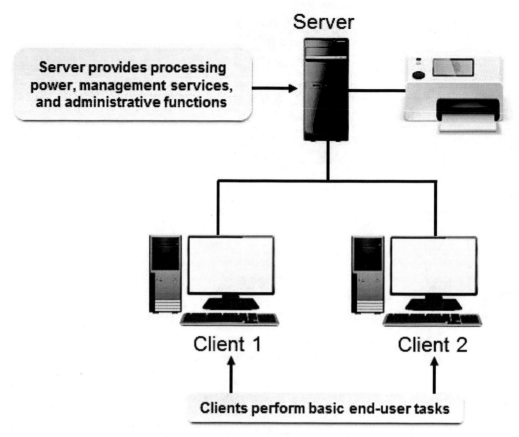

Server provides processing power, management services, and administrative functions

Server

Client 1

Client 2

Clients perform basic end-user tasks

Figure 1-20: Clients and a server in a client/server network.

 Note: You will learn more about authentication services later in the course.

Peer-to-Peer Networks

A *peer-to-peer network* is a network in which resource sharing, processing, and communications control are completely decentralized. All clients on the network are equal in terms of providing and using resources, and each individual device authenticates its users. Peer-to-peer networks are easy and inexpensive to implement. However, they are only practical in very small organizations due to the lack of centralized data storage and administration. A peer-to-peer network is more commonly referred to as a *workgroup*. In a peer-to-peer network, user accounts must be duplicated on every device from which a user accesses resources. Such distribution of user information makes maintaining a peer-to-peer network difficult, especially as the network grows.

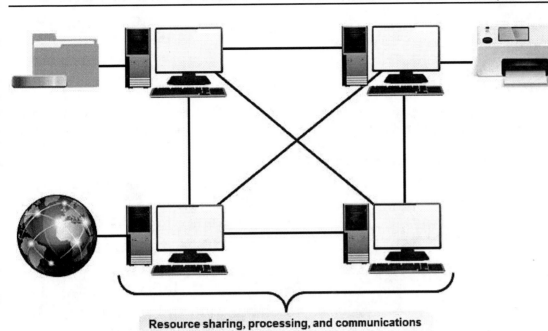

Figure 1-21: Devices in a peer-to-peer network.

Mixed Mode Networks

A *mixed mode network* incorporates elements from more than one of the three standard network configurations. Some mixed mode networks consist of a client/server network combined with a centralized mainframe. An end user's device functions as a client to the network directory server and employs terminal emulation software to authenticate to the mainframe system.

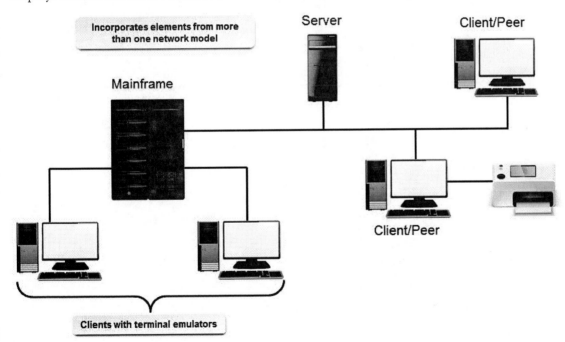

Figure 1-22: A mixed mode network.

A common example of a mixed mode network is a workgroup created to share local resources within a client/server network. For example, you might share one client's local printer with just a few other users. The client sharing the printer on the network does not use the client/server network's directory structure to authenticate and authorize access to the printer.

Network Topologies

A *topology* is a network specification that determines the network's overall layout, signaling, and data-flow patterns. Networks are defined by a combination of their logical and physical topologies. Topologies define the way different nodes are placed and interconnected with each other. They may also describe how the data is transferred between these nodes.

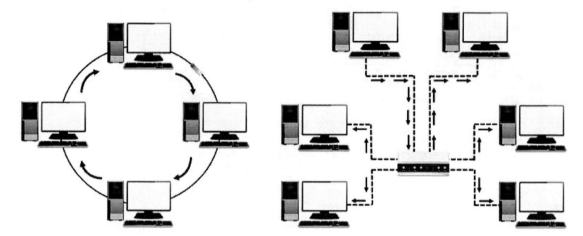

Figure 1–23: Examples of network topologies.

 Note: Physical and logical topologies will be covered in more detail later in the course.

ACTIVITY 1-4
Identifying Network Models

Scenario

The network administrator at Greene City Interiors describes networks used at different offices and wants you to identify the network configuration for each.

---

1. **On a company's network, users access a single computer via a terminal for all of their data processing and storage. Which network model does this network use?**

   ○ Peer-to-peer

   ○ Mixed mode

   ○ Client/server

   ○ Centralized

2. **On a company's network, users directly share files stored on their devices with other users. Additionally, they access shared storage, printing, and fax resources, which are connected to a department-wide server. Which network model does this network use?**

   ○ Peer-to-peer

   ○ Client/server

   ○ Centralized

   ○ Mixed mode

3. **A company has four employees who need to share information and hardware, such as a scanner and printer. They also need Internet access. None of the users have advanced computing skills. Which type of network would best suit their needs?**

   ○ Client/server

   ○ Peer-to-peer

   ○ Centralized

   ○ Mixed mode

TOPIC E

Data Transmission Methods

With the network in place, the next step is to identify methods to transmit data. In this topic, you will identify the primary data transmission methods.

As a network professional, you will probably be expected to monitor network performance and response time. The manner in which data is transmitted between nodes on a network can significantly affect network traffic and performance. You will need to understand the characteristics and potential effects of the network traffic transmission methods, which are implemented on the networks you support, to understand their impact on the network.

Data Transmission

Data transmission is the exchange of data among different computers or other electronic devices through a network. Unlike telephony, which involves only the transmission of voice, data transmission sends non-voice information such as graphics, animations, audio, text, and video over the network. Most of the data transmission takes place through networks and the term "data networks" is synonymous with networks.

Though data is typically stored as files before being transmitted, there are exceptions to this process. In some forms of data communication, such as online chat or video conferencing, data needs to be transmitted as soon as it is generated. In such cases, data is instantaneously converted into a network-compatible format and transmitted without being stored either in main memory or on a disk.

Analog Signals

A *signal* is data transmitted as electromagnetic pulses across a network medium. An *analog signal* carries information as continuous waves of electromagnetic or optical energy. In networking, electrical current commonly generates analog signals, the intensity of which is measured in volts. An analog signal oscillates between maximum and minimum values over time and can take any value between those limits. The size, shape, and other characteristics of the *waveform* describe the analog signal and the information it carries.

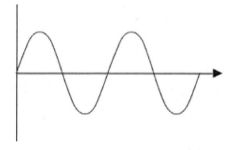

Figure 1–24: Analog signals.

The characteristics of an analog signal can be described or categorized using some specific terms.

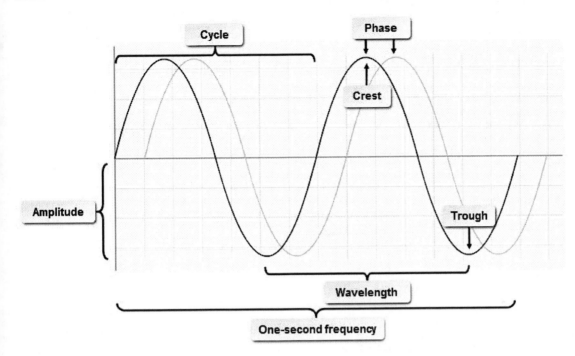

Figure 1-25: Characteristics of an analog signal.

Term	Description
Amplitude	The distance of the crest or trough of a wave from the midpoint of the waveform to its top or bottom. The *amplitude* is one half of the overall distance from the peak to the trough of the wave.
Cycle	One complete oscillation of an analog signal.
Frequency	The number of complete cycles per second in a wave. It is measured in *hertz*, which is one cycle per second. *Frequency* is also called the period of the wave.
Phase	Is where a wave's cycle begins in relation to a fixed point. Thus, two waves of the same frequency that begin at the same time are said to be *in phase*. Two waves that either start at an offset from each other or have different frequencies are *out of phase*.
Wavelength	The distance between two successive crests or troughs in a waveform.

Digital Signals

A *digital signal*, unlike an analog signal that can have many possible values, can have combinations of only two values: one and zero. These values represent the presence and the absence of a signal, respectively. Digital data, which is a sequence of ones and zeros, can be translated into a digital waveform. In computer systems and other digital devices, a waveform can switch between two voltage levels: zero at the ground or a zero voltage state, and one at a positive or negative voltage level.

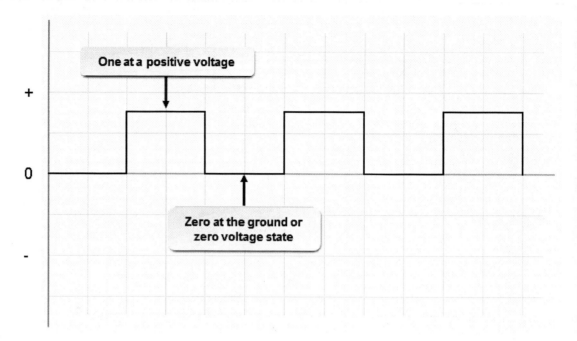

Figure 1-26: Waveform of a digital signal.

Digital Data Transmission

Digital data transmissions use voltage differences to represent the ones and zeros in data. Unlike analog signal transmission, they are not modulated over a carrier. *On-off keying* or *Manchester encoding* converts data into a digital waveform. Each bit takes a predefined time to transmit, and the sender and receiver synchronize their clocks either by transmitting a bit pattern or by monitoring for the reception of the first bit.

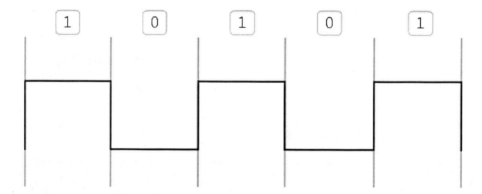

Figure 1-27: Digital data transmission using on-off keying.

Unicast Transmission

Unicast transmission is a method for data transfer from a source address to a destination address. Network nodes not involved in the transfer ignore the transmission. Unicast transmission is the predominant mode of transmission on LANs and the Internet. Unicast communications are also commonly referenced as point-to-point communications. Some familiar unicast applications are *Hypertext Transfer Protocol (HTTP)*, *Simple Mail Transfer Protocol (SMTP)*, and *File Transfer Protocol (FTP)*.

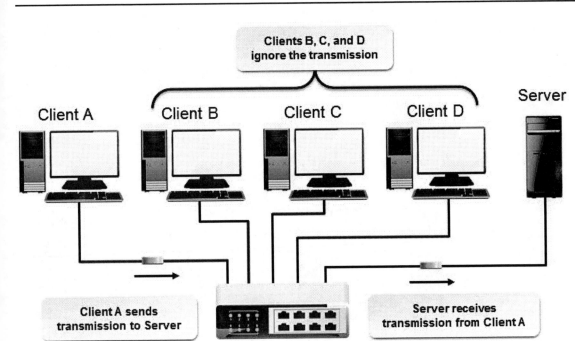

Figure 1-28: Data transfer in a unicast transmission.

Broadcast Transmission

Broadcast transmission is a transmission method in which data is sent from a source node to all other nodes on a network. Network services that rely on broadcast transmissions generate a great deal of traffic. Occasionally, nodes use broadcast transmissions to check for the availability of a particular service on the network. If the service is not available, the nodes broadcast a request for the service. If a server is present, it responds to the request.

Some servers periodically advertise their presence to the network by sending a broadcast message.

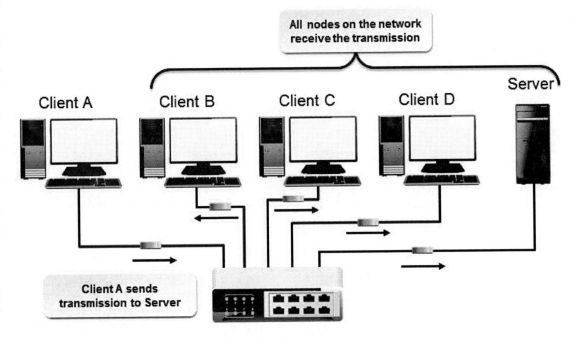

Figure 1-29: Data transfer in a broadcast transmission.

Multicast Transmission

Multicast transmission is a transmission method in which data is sent from a server to specific nodes that are predefined as members of a multicast group. Network nodes not in the group ignore the data. Communication with nodes outside of a multicast group must be done through unicast or broadcast transmissions.

A video server transmitting television signals is an example of multicast transmission.

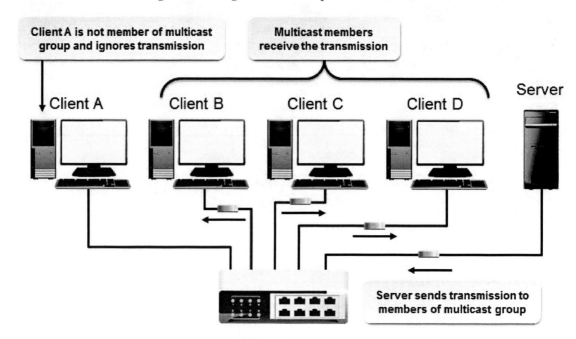

Figure 1–30: Data transfer in a multicast transmission.

Anycast Transmission

Anycast transmission is a transmission method in which data is sent from a server to the nearest node within a group. That node then initiates a second anycast and transmits the data to the next nearest node within the group. The process is repeated until all nodes within the group have received the data. Network nodes not in the group ignore the data.

Anycast is used for updating routing tables in IP version 6 (IPv6) because IPv6 does not use broadcast transmissions. In addition, anycast addresses are often used with IPv6 DNS servers. You can have multiple IPv6 DNS servers scattered around the network using the same anycast address. When a client sends a DNS query to that address, the client's router would route the query to the nearest DNS server.

 Note: IPv6 is covered in greater depth later in the course.

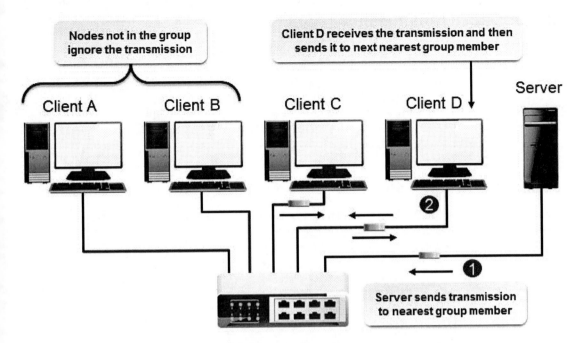

Figure 1-31: Data transfer in an anycast transmission.

 Note: For additional information, check out the LearnTO **Recognize Transmission Types** presentation in the LearnTOs for this course on your LogicalCHOICE Course screen.

Serial Data Transmission

With *serial data transmission,* the transmission of bits occurs as one per clock cycle across a single transmission medium. The transmission of synchronization, start/stop, and error correction bits occurs along with data bits, thus limiting the overall throughput of data. Serial data transmission does not use *direct current (DC)* pulses for transmission. Serial transmission can delineate bytes by using either synchronous or asynchronous techniques. Many common networking systems, such as Ethernet, use serial data transmission. Keyboards, mice, modems, and other devices can connect to your PC over a serial transmission port.

 Note: A clock cycle refers to a signal that synchronizes different parts of a circuit by oscillating between low and high states.

Synchronous and Asynchronous Communications

The receiver of an analog signal must have a way of delineating between bytes in a stream of data. This can be done using either asynchronous or synchronous techniques.

* With *asynchronous communications,* a sender inserts special start and stop bit patterns between each byte of data. By watching for these bit patterns, the receiver can distinguish between the bytes in the data stream.
* With *synchronous communications,* a byte is sent after a standardized time interval. The receiver assumes that one byte is transmitted every interval. However, the two devices must start and stop their reckoning of these intervals at precisely the same time. Synchronous devices include a clock chip. A special bit pattern is inserted at specific intervals in the data stream, enabling the receiving device to synchronize its clock with the sender. After synchronizing the clocks, a receiver can use the predetermined time interval as a means to distinguish between bytes in the data stream.

In asynchronous communications, the two sides negotiate a sustainable speed. In synchronous communications, one side sets the clock rate and the other side slaves to that rate.

Parallel Data Transmission

With *parallel data transmission,* the transmission of multiple bits takes place by using multiple transmission lines. Many bits—even multiple bytes—can be transferred per clock cycle. The transmission of synchronization, start/stop, and error correction bits does not occur along with data bits. They are often sent over additional transmission lines, thus improving the overall throughput of data. Parallel transmission is commonly used on the parallel port on a computer, to which you can connect printers or scanners. Other uses include the system bus inside a PC and the *Small Computer System Interface (SCSI)* data bus.

Baseband Transmission

In *baseband transmissions,* digital signals are sent via DC pulses over a single, unmultiplexed signal channel. As all devices share a common transmission channel, they can send and receive over the same baseband medium, but they cannot send and receive simultaneously.

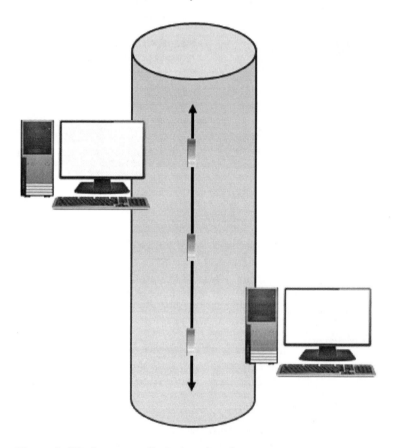

Figure 1–32: Data transfer in baseband transmission.

Broadband Transmission

Broadband transmission uses a single medium to carry multiple channels of data, usually through modulation. Multiple carrier signals, usually at different frequencies, act as different channels, each carrying their own data on the same transmission line. An example of this is broadband Internet access via cable modem. The cable provider assigns each customer two premium TV channels for their Internet data: one for transmit and one for receive. All of the cable TV channels, including those used for data, travel on different carrier frequencies on the same coaxial cable.

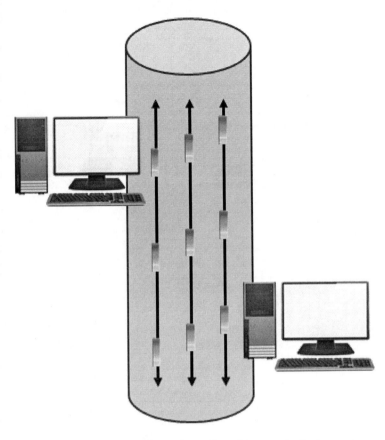

Figure 1–33: Data transfer in broadband transmission.

DOCSIS, the Data Over Cable Service Interface Specification, is the standard used by cable companies to provide high-speed data communication using the existing cable TV system. DOCSIS 3.1 was released in 2013 with specifications to support at least 10 Gigabits per second downstream and 1 Gigabit per second upstream.

Transmission Speeds

Data transmission speed is usually stated in terms of bit rate. However, there is another measure of speed known as baud rate. Though the two aren't the same, they are similar.

* Bit rate: Bits are the zeros and ones that binary data consists of. The bit rate is a measure of the number of bits that are transmitted per unit of time. The bit rate is usually measured in bits per second. This means that, if a wireless network is transmitting 54 megabits bits every second, the bit rate is 54,000,000 bps or 54 Mbps, where bps stands for bits per second and Mbps stands for megabits per second.
* Baud rate: Baud rate measures the number of symbols that are transmitted per unit of time. A symbol consists of a fixed number of bits depending on what the symbol is defined as. The baud rate is measured in symbols per second. If your data encoding uses something other than bits, the baud rate will be lower than the bit rate by the factor of bits per symbol. For example, if there are 3 bits per symbol, the baud rate will be one-third that of the bit rate.

Types of Media Access

Depending upon the traffic on the network media, a node can transmit data on a network. The *media access method* determines whether or not a particular node can transmit data on the network at a given time. Media access methods fall into two categories: contention-based and controlled. With *contention-based* or competitive media access, the nodes themselves negotiate for media access time.

With *controlled* or deterministic media access, a central device or system controls when and for how long each node can transmit.

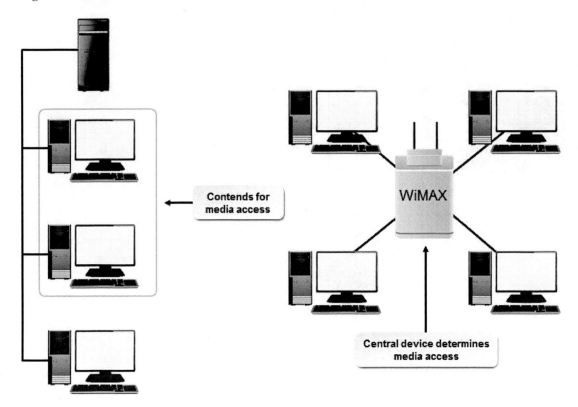

Figure 1-34: Contention-based and controlled media access deployed on networks.

Deterministic access methods are beneficial when network access is time critical. For example, in an industrial setting, key control and safety equipment, such as flow-shutoff sensors in chemical storage facilities, must have a guaranteed transmission time. Deterministic systems ensure that a single node cannot saturate the media; all nodes get a chance to transmit data. However, they require additional hardware and administration to configure and maintain. Contention-based systems are simpler to set up and administer, but timely media access is not guaranteed for any node.

Polling

Polling is a controlled media access method in which a central device contacts each node to check whether it has data to transmit. Each node is guaranteed access to the media, but network time can be wasted if polling nodes have no data to transmit. The polling process is repeated by giving each node access to the media until the media reaches the node that needs to transmit data.

Demand priority is a polling technique in which nodes signal their state—either ready to transmit or idle—to an intelligent (or managed) hub. The hub polls the state of each node and grants permission to transmit. Additionally, a node can signal that its data is high priority. The hub will favor high-priority transmission requests. Safeguards in the protocol prevent nodes from assigning every transmission request as high priority. This is done by ensuring that each node has an equal opportunity to transmit, and a node is not allowed a second normal transmission unless all nodes have completed their first normal transmission.

 Note: The IEEE has not standardized polling in general. However, the IEEE 802.12 standard defines 100VG-AnyLAN, which uses a specific polling technique called demand priority to control media access.

CSMA/CA

Carrier Sense Multiple Access/Collision Avoidance (CSMA/CA) is a contention-based media access method that is primarily used in IEEE 802.11–based wireless LANs. In CSMA/CA, nodes can transmit whenever they have data to send. However, they take steps before they transmit data to ensure that the media is not in use.

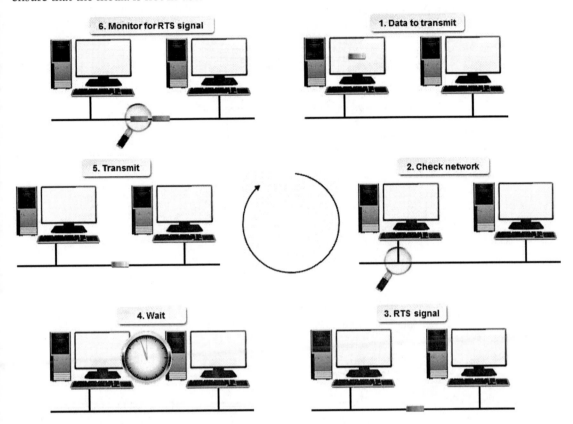

Figure 1-35: The CSMA/CA media access method.

There are six steps in the CSMA/CA process.

Step	Description
Step 1: Data to transmit	A node has data to transmit.
Step 2: Check network	The node determines if the media is available by polling.
Step 3: RTS signal	Optionally, the node may send a Request-To-Send (RTS) signal to the access point.
Step 4: Wait	The node waits until all nodes have had time to receive the jam signal.
Step 5: Transmit	The node transmits data.
Step 6: Monitor for RTS signal	During transmission, the node monitors the media for an RTS signal from any other node that may already be transmitting data. If an RTS signal is received, it stops transmitting and retries after a random delay.

 Note: The 802.11 standard is a family of specifications developed by the IEEE for wireless LAN technology.

CSMA/CD

Carrier Sense Multiple Access/Collision Detection (CSMA/CD) is a contention-based media access method used in Ethernet LANs, where nodes contend for use of the physical medium. Nodes can transmit whenever they have data to send. However, they must take steps to detect and manage the inevitable collisions that occur when multiple nodes transmit simultaneously. The busier a network becomes, the greater the probability of collisions, and the lower the CSMA/CD efficiency.

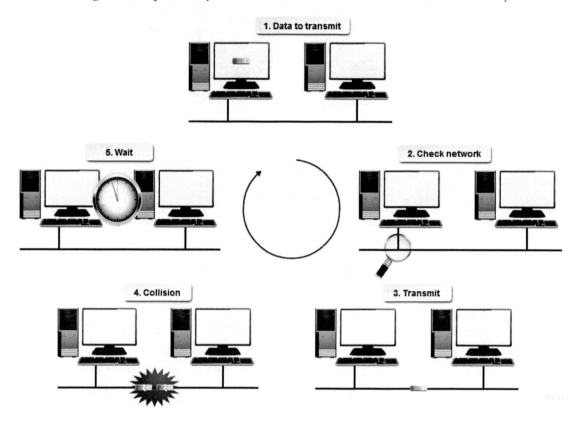

Figure 1–36: The CSMA/CD media access method.

There are six steps in the CSMA/CD process.

Step	Description
Step 1: Data to transmit	A node has data to transmit.
Step 2: Check network	The node determines if the media is available by monitoring for existing transmissions by other nodes (carrier sense).
Step 3: Transmit	The node transmits data if no other node is transmitting. When the media is available, the node transmits, starting with a 7-byte repeating pattern of 1s and 0s. This is called the preamble.
Step 4: Collision	If two nodes transmit at the same time, a collision has occurred. The collision is most likely to occur during the preamble. The transmitting node that detects the collision will continue to send the preamble, along with a 32-bit jam signal. This is a special pattern that warns other nodes to not transmit. In addition, the jam signal will cause the frame to fail its expected CRC check, so that other nodes discard the frame and wait for a retransmission.
Step 5: Wait	The two nodes that collided wait for a random *backoff* period (in milliseconds).

Step	Description
Step 6: Retransmit	After waiting for a suitable backoff interval, the two nodes will retransmit again. Because the backoff interval will not be the same for both nodes, one of the nodes will retransmit first, and the other node will retransmit after.

 Note: CSMA/CD is the access method for Ethernet formalized in the 802.3 standard, a specification issued by IEEE to standardize Ethernet and expand it to include a wide range of cable media.

Multiplexing

The modulation technique *multiplexing* is a controlled media access method in which a central device combines signals from multiple nodes and transmits the combined signal across a medium. To carry multiple signals, the medium or channel is separated logically into multiple, smaller channels. Signals can be multiplexed using *Time-Division Multiplexing (TDM)* or *Frequency-Division Multiplexing (FDM)*. Both multiplexing techniques rely on a central device, called a *multiplexer,* or *mux,* to manage multiplexing from the sending end. At the receiving end, a *demultiplexer,* or *demux,* separates the signals. De-multiplexing is done on the receiving end of a multiplexing transmission. The data is gathered, examined, and passed to the Application layer of the OSI model.

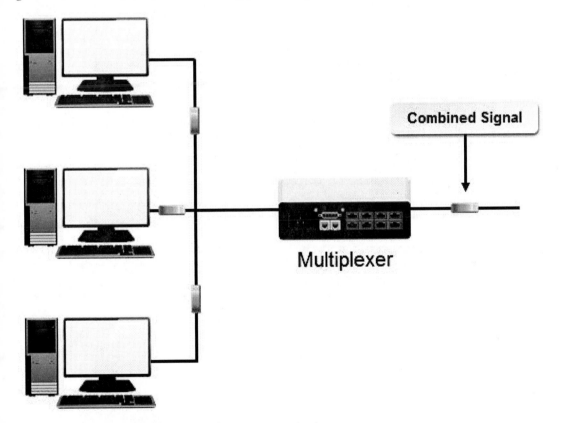

Figure 1–37: The multiplexing media access method.

In TDM, a communication channel is divided into discrete time slots. Each node on a network is assigned a time slot, and each sender is given exclusive access to the medium for a specific period of time. Nodes have exclusive access to the connection between themselves and a mux for that period of time. The mux combines each node's signal, and in turn, sends the resulting combined signal over the primary network medium. Using TDM, multiple baseband signals can be combined and sent over a single medium.

In FDM, data from multiple nodes is sent over multiple frequencies, or channels, using a network medium. Nodes have exclusive access to the connection between themselves and a mux. The mux includes each node's signal onto its own channel, sending the resulting combined signal over the primary network medium. Using FDM, multiple broadband signals can be combined and sent over a single medium.

There are three commonly used connection modes for multiplexing.

Connection Mode	Description
Simplex	The *simplex* mode of communication is the one-way transmission of information. There is no return path. Because the transmission operates in only one direction, simplex mode can use the full bandwidth of the medium for transmission. Radio and television broadcasts are simplex mode transmissions.
Half duplex	The *half duplex* mode of communication permits two-way communications, but in only one direction at a time. When one device sends, the other must receive; then they can switch roles to transfer information in the other direction. Half duplex mode can use the full bandwidth of the medium because the transmission takes place in only one direction at a time.
Full duplex	The *full duplex* mode of communication permits simultaneous two-way communications. A device can both send and receive data simultaneously. Sending and receiving can occur over different channels or on the same channel. Generally, neither the sender nor the receiver can use the full bandwidth for their individual transmission because transmissions are allowed in both directions simultaneously. Full duplex mode also may be called a bidirectional transmission. If someone speaks about "duplex" transmissions, they likely are referring to full duplex mode. Telephone systems are full duplex devices—all persons involved can talk simultaneously. Many modern networking cards support full duplex mode.

 Note: There are full bandwidth transmissions in some network environments, namely full duplexed switched Ethernet.

 Note: For additional information, check out the LearnTO **Identify Connection Modes** presentation in the LearnTOs for this course on your LogicalCHOICE Course screen.

ACTIVITY 1-5
Identifying Data Transmission Methods

Scenario
The network administrator at Greene City Interiors asks you questions to test your knowledge of data transmission methods.

1. Identify the transmission method depicted in the graphic.

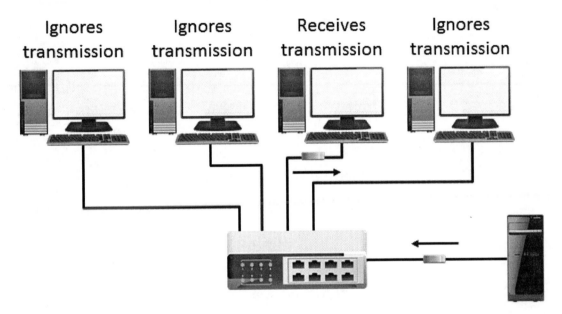

- ○ Unicast
- ○ Broadcast
- ○ Multicast

2. True or False? Multicasting is more efficient in the use of network media than unicast transmission when many clients need to receive the same information from a server.
   - ☐ True
   - ☐ False

3. Which transmission method allows digital signals to be sent as DC pulses over a single, unmultiplexed signal channel?
   - ○ Broadband
   - ○ Parallel
   - ○ Baseband
   - ○ Serial

4. Which of these devices use serial data transmission?

☐ Keyboard

☐ Mouse

☐ USB hard drive

☐ Internal bus

5. True or False? With the deterministic media access method, the nodes themselves negotiate for media access time.

☐ True

☐ False

6. Which transmission method allows data to be sent to a node, and then that node transmits the data to the next nearest node?

○ Broadcast

○ Anycast

○ Baseband

○ Parallel

Summary

In this lesson, you explored basic networking theory and concepts. This information should help you create a solid foundation on which to build your networking skills and knowledge.

In your experience, what network types and configurations have you used?

How will knowing the OSI model help you perform networking tasks?

 Note: Check your LogicalCHOICE Course screen for opportunities to interact with your classmates, peers, and the larger LogicalCHOICE online community about the topics covered in this course or other topics you are interested in. From the Course screen you can also access available resources for a more continuous learning experience.

2 Bounded Network Media

Lesson Time: 3 hours

Lesson Objectives

In this lesson, you will describe bounded network media. You will:

- Identify the common types of bounded copper network media.

- Identify the common types of bounded fiber optic network media.

- Describe the equipment and methods required to install bounded network media.

- Identify noise control methods used in network transmissions.

Lesson Introduction

In the previous lesson, you learned about basic network theory and components. Data moves across a network by using some sort of medium. This medium can be bounded, like cables, or unbounded, like radio waves. In this lesson, you will describe bounded network media.

Bounded network media comes in different types that you can select to best suit the needs of your network. You are likely to work with bounded media daily as part of your duties as a network professional. Understanding the characteristics of bounded media will enable you to properly install and service your networks.

TOPIC A

Copper Media

In this lesson, you will identify various types of bounded network media. To begin, you will describe copper media, including cables and connectors.

Copper media are the most basic networking media type, consisting of various different types. You are likely to work with copper media daily as part of your duties as a network professional. Understanding the characteristics of copper media and the equipment used will enable you to properly install and service your networks.

Network Media

Network media, the conduit through which signals flow, can be either bounded or unbounded. *Bounded media* use a physical conductor. This conductor can be a metal wire through which electricity flows, or a glass or plastic strand through which pulses of light flow. *Unbounded media* do not need a physical connection between devices, and can transmit electromagnetic signals through air using *radio waves, microwaves,* or *infrared radiation.*

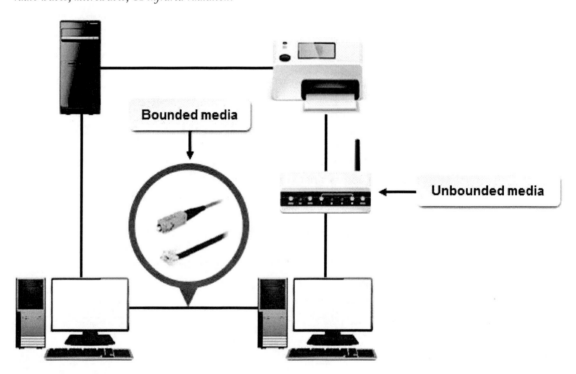

Figure 2-1: Types of network media.

Copper Media

Copper media are a type of bounded media that use one or more copper conductors surrounded by an insulated coating. The conductors can be made from a solid wire or from braided strands of wire. Sometimes *shielding,* in the form of a braided wire or foil, is wrapped around one or more conductors to reduce signal interference from nearby sources of electromagnetic radiation.

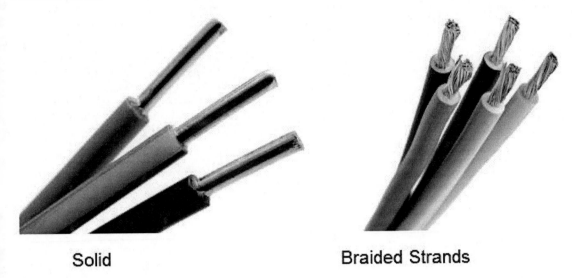

Solid   Braided Strands

Figure 2-2: Solid and braided strands copper wires.

Two of the most prevalent types of copper media used in networks are *twisted pair* and *coaxial cable*.

Twisted Pair Cables

A *twisted pair* cable is a type of cable in which one or more pairs of copper wires are twisted around each other and clad in a color-coded, protective insulating plastic sheath or jacket to form a pair. All pairs are encased in a plastic sheath or jacket. The number of pairs within a cable will vary depending on the type of twisted pair cable. Twisted pair cables typically use shielding around pairs of wires.

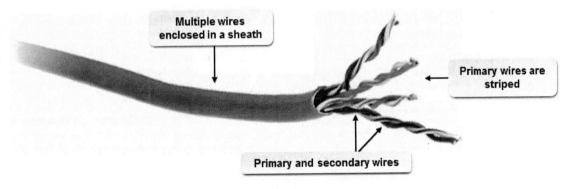

Multiple wires
enclosed in a sheath

Primary wires are
striped

Primary and secondary wires

Figure 2-3: Constituents of a twisted pair cable.

Twisted Pair Cable Types

A twisted pair cable can be of two types: *unshielded twisted pair (UTP)* or *shielded twisted pair (STP)*.

- UTP:
  - Does not include shielding around its conductors.
  - Typically contains four pairs of stranded or solid conductors.
  - Is inexpensive and reliable.
- STP:
  - Includes foil wrapper shielding around its conductors to improve the cable's resistance to interference and noise.
  - Typically contains four pairs of stranded or solid conductors.
  - Is more expensive than UTP.

Note: Twisted pair cables are available in 2-pair, 4-pair, 6-pair, 25-pair, 100-pair, and larger bundles.

Note: A variation of STP, known as screen twisted pair (ScTP) or foil twisted pair (FTP), uses only the overall shield and provides more protection than UTP, but not as much as STP.

Wire colors are standardized. The industry standard for twisted pair is one solid color and the same color with white.

The first four standard color pairs are listed in the following table.

Primary Wire	Secondary Wire
White/blue	Blue
White/orange	Orange
White/green	Green
White/brown	Brown

Twisted Pair Cable Categories

A twisted pair cable comes in different grades, called categories, which support different network speeds and technologies.

Category	Network Type	Maximum Speed	Description	Distance
1	Voice transmission	1 Mbps	CAT1 is not suitable for networking.	Not specified
2	Digital telephone and low-speed networks	4 Mbps	CAT2 is not commonly used on networks.	100 m
3	Ethernet	10 Mbps	CAT3 is currently used for telephone wiring.	100 m
4	IBM token ring	16 Mbps	CAT4 can also be used for 10 Mbps Ethernet.	100 m
5	Fast Ethernet	100 Mbps	CAT5 supports a signaling rate of 100 MHz.	100 m
5e	Gigabit Ethernet	1 Gbps	CAT5e supports a signaling rate of 100 MHz.	100 m
6	Gigabit Ethernet	1 Gbps	CAT6 supports a signaling rate of 250 MHz.	100 m
	10 Gigabit Ethernet	10 Gbps		55 m
6a	10 Gigabit Ethernet	10 Gbps	CAT6a supports a signaling rate of 500 MHz.	100 m
7	10 Gigabit Ethernet	10 Gbps	CAT7 supports a signaling rate of 600 MHz.	100 m

Note: A twisted pair cable's category is typically printed on the cable itself, making identification easier.

Twisted Pair Connectors

Twisted pair has two common types of connectors: the RJ-45 and the RJ-11.

The RJ-45 is an eight-pin connector used by twisted pair cables in networking. All four pairs of wires in the twisted pair cable use this connector.

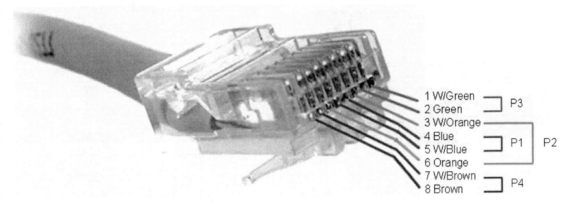

Figure 2-4: Twisted pair connectors—RJ-45 wiring schemes.

Note: The RJ in RJ-11 and RJ-45 is an abbreviation for "registered jack." An RJ-45 connector can also be called an 8P8C connector.

There are two standard wiring schemes for RJ-45: T568A and T568B. It is important that you use the wiring scheme that matches the devices on your network even though all cables are the same.

Pin	T568A (Legacy)	T568B (Current Standard)
1	White/green	White/orange
2	Green	Orange
3	White/orange	White/green
4	Blue	Blue
5	White/blue	White/blue
6	Orange	Green
7	White/brown	White/brown
8	Brown	Brown

You can also connect two UTP cables together by using a *UTP coupler*. This can be handy when you have some shorter cables and you need to run them for a longer distance.

The RJ-11 connector is used with Category 1 cables in telephone system connections and is not suitable for network connectivity. However, because the RJ-11 connector is similar in appearance to the RJ-45 connector, they are sometimes confused. RJ-11 connectors are smaller than RJ-45 connectors, and have either four or six pins.

There is also the RJ-48C connector, which is commonly used for T1 lines and uses pins 1, 2, 4, and 5.

Coaxial Cables

A coaxial cable, or *coax*, is a type of copper cable that features a central conducting copper core surrounded by an insulator and braided or foil shielding. The *dialectric* insulator separates the conductor and shield and the entire package is wrapped in an insulating layer called a sheath or jacket. The data signal is transmitted over the central conductor. A coaxial cable is so named because the conductor and shield share the same axis, or center. They share a common axis or are "co-axial." This arrangement helps prevent electromagnetic interference from reaching the conductor.

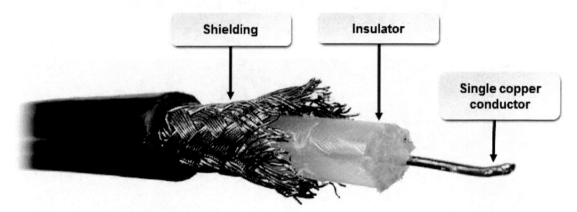

Figure 2–5: Layers of a coaxial cable.

Coaxial Cable Types

Many varieties of coax cables are available, not all of which are used in networking. The wires used in networking can be solid core or stranded core. A solid core wire is made of a single metal or a single strand. A stranded core wire consists of multiple strands or solid cores.

Cable Type	Characteristics
RG59	A 6 mm (0.25 inch) coax cable with 75 ohms impedance.
	RG59 is used for low-power video connections such as digital receivers.
RG6	A coax cable with 75 ohms impedance. RG6 is preferred over RG59.
	This type of cable is often used in routing cable television signals.
RG58/U and RG58A/U	A 5 mm (0.25 inch) coax cable with a stranded core and 50 ohms impedance.
	RG58/U and RG58A/U are used for Ethernet networking.
RG8	A 10 mm (0.5 inch) coax cable with a solid core and 50 ohms impedance.
	RG8 is used for Ethernet networking.
RG9	A 10 mm (0.5 inch) coax cable with a stranded core and 51 ohms impedance.
	RG9 is used for cable television transmission and cable modems.

 Note: The RG specification codes come from their page numbers in the Radio Guide manual, the original military specification (Mil-Spec) for coax cables, which is no longer in use. For example, the RG8 specification appeared on page 8.

Coaxial Connector Types

Connectors are metal devices that are located at the end of a wire. Coaxial connectors are used to connect video equipment and network nodes in a LAN. Signals flow from the wire to network devices through connectors. All connectors are metal plated and some of the metals used are gold, silver, rhodium, nickel, or tin.

Coax network segments must be terminated to prevent signal reflections off the ends of the cable. Cables are terminated by installing a resistor of an appropriate rating, typically 50 ohms, at either end of the cable.

Two broad categories of connectors are typically used in coax cables: F and BNC connectors.

Connector Type	Characteristics
F	A coax connector type used with a 75-ohm cable to connect cable TV and FM antenna cables. It comes in a secure screw-on form or as a non-threaded slip-on connector.
BNC	A cable connector used to terminate a coaxial cable. It is usually used with the RG58/U cable. A Bayonet-Neill-Concelman (BNC) connector has a center pin connected to the center cable conductor and a metal tube connected to the shield of the cable. A rotating ring outside the metal tube locks the cable to the connector. The types of BNC connectors include: • T-connectors • Barrel connectors You can also connect two BNC cables together by using a *BNC coupler*.

Other Copper Cable Types

Although twisted pair, coax, and fiber optic cables are the most prevalent types of cable media used in network installations, you might also encounter several other types of cables.

• A *serial cable* is a type of bounded network media that transfers information between two devices by using serial transmission. Information is sent one bit at a time in a specific sequence. A serial cable most often uses an RS-232 (also referred to as DB-9) connector, but can also use a DB-25 connector. In networking, serial cables are often used to connect routers.

• While not as common as other bounded network media, *IEEE 1394*, commonly known as FireWire®, can be used to connect up to 63 devices to form a small local network. FireWire cables use a shielded cable similar to STP with either four or six conductors. Connections to devices are made with either a six- or four-pin connector.

• A *USB connection* is a personal computer connection that enables you to connect multiple peripherals to a single port with high performance and minimal device configuration. *USB* connections support two-way communications. The USB 3.1 standard increases the signaling rate to 10 Gbit/s, double that of USB 3.0. It is backward compatible with USB 3.0 and USB 2.0.

• The IEEE 1901-2013 standard, also known as *broadband over power lines (BPL)*, is a technology that allows broadband transmission over domestic power lines. This technology aims to use the existing power infrastructure to deliver Internet access to remote areas at a rapid pace. BPL is yet to gain widespread acceptance because of the potential signal interference with other data signals such as wireless transmission and radio waves.

The interference of BPL signals with radio waves affects radio operations, which are the main source of communication during times of natural disaster. In addition, there are concerns about the security of data when it is transmitted as plaintext using BPL, because it is easy to detect and intercept data when the signal travels using a common power source. Accepting and implementing BPL will require enhanced encryption and other security measures.

 Note: Interference and encryption are covered in detail in subsequent lessons.

- The IEEE 1905-2013, more accurately, the IEEE 1905.1-2013 standard, provides a common interface for home networking technologies. The Standard for a Convergent Digital Home Network for Heterogeneous Technologies is designed to reduce network complexity for consumers and helps operators manage various networks throughout homes. There are various wired connections that can be used, but the most common under this standard are Ethernet over HDMI and Ethernet over power line. A device with built-in HDMI 1.4 capabilities allows audio, video, and data communication over an HDMI 1.4 cable. Devices that comply with the nVoy hybrid home networking standard can use Ethernet over power line.

ACTIVITY 2-1
Identifying Bounded Copper Network Media

Scenario

The network administrator at Greene City Interiors now wants to verify that you are familiar with different copper cables and connectors. He shows you different media and asks you to identify them.

1. Identify the type of network cabling shown in the graphic.

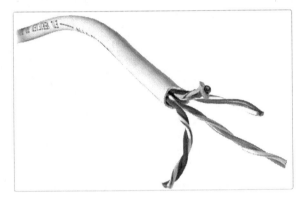

- ○ Twisted pair
- ○ Coax
- ○ Fiber optic
- ○ Video

2. Identify the type of network cabling shown in the graphic.

- ○ Unshielded twisted pair
- ○ Shielded twisted pair
- ○ Coax
- ○ Fiber optic

3. True or False? The connector shown in the graphic is a BNC connector.

☐ True

☐ False

TOPIC B

Fiber Optic Media

In the last topic, you identified common types of copper media. The other main category of bounded media is fiber optics. In this topic, you will identify the different types of bounded fiber optic media.

Fiber optic media is used by many telecommunications companies to transmit telephone signals, Internet communication, and cable television signals. Even if you don't work with it daily, you will still come into contact with fiber optic media as a network professional. Understanding the characteristics of fiber optic media and the equipment used will enable you to properly work with it in your networks.

Fiber Optic Cables

A *fiber optic cable* is a network cable that has a core surrounded by one or more glass or plastic strands. In addition, it contains extra fiber strands or wraps, which are surrounded by a protective outer jacket. The core is the thin glass center through which light travels transmitting data. The core is between 5 and 100 microns thick with cladding made from optical materials such as silica.

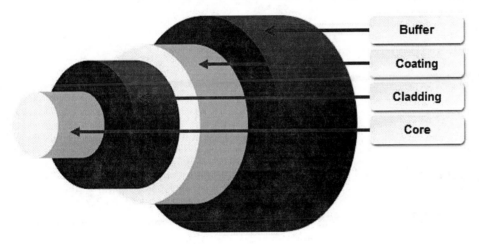

Figure 2-6: Layers in a fiber optic cable.

The cladding reflects light back to the core in patterns determined by the transmission mode. A buffer, often made of plastic, surrounds the cladding and core. To add strength to the cable, strands of synthetic fiber surround the buffer. An outer jacket, sometimes called an armor, wraps and protects the whole assembly. Light pulses from a laser or high intensity LED are passed through the core to carry the signal. The cladding reflects the light back into the core, increasing the distance the signal can travel without a need for regeneration.

 Note: Fiber optic cables are the least sensitive of any cable type to electromagnetic interference.

 Caution: You should not look into the end of an operating fiber optic cable. The intensity of light leaving the end of a singlemode fiber is strong enough to cause temporary or permanent damage to the eye.

Fiber Optic Cable Modes

There are two modes of fiber optic cables available: *multimode* and *singlemode*. Both modes have an outer diameter of 125 microns; that is, 125 millionths of a meter or 5 thousandths of an inch, which is just larger than a single human hair.

- Multimode fiber allows light to travel through its core in multiple rays or modes. Its core of 50 or 62.5 microns works with LED sources for slower networks and with laser for faster networks. Multimode fiber is used mostly for short distances (up to 500 m).
- At only 9 microns, the core of a singlemode fiber is much smaller in diameter than multimode fiber. Within a singlemode fiber, light travels unidirectionally. Singlemode fiber is used with laser to process telephony and cable TV transmissions. Singlemode fiber has a higher transmission rate and up to 50 times more potential distance than multimode fiber.

Singlemode and multimode fibers have different characteristics.

Fiber Optic Cable Mode	Description
Singlemode fiber 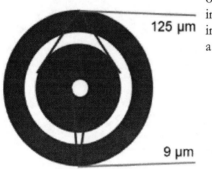	Carries an optical signal through a small core, which allows only a single beam of light to pass. A laser, usually operating in the infrared portion of the spectrum, is modulated in intensity to transmit the signal through the fiber. It provides a bandwidth of up to 30 MHz.
Multimode fiber 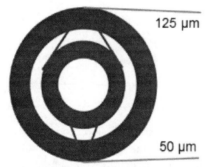	There are two subtypes of multimode fiber: • Step-index multimode fiber contains a core surrounded by cladding, each with its own uniform index of *refraction*. When light from the core enters the cladding, a "step down" occurs due to the difference in the refractive indices. Step-index fiber uses total internal reflection to trap light. • Graded-index multimode fiber possesses variations in the core glass to compensate for differences in the mode path length. Provides up to 2 GHz of bandwidth, which is significantly more than step-index fiber.

Refraction

Refraction occurs when a light ray, passing from one transparent medium to another, bends due to a change in velocity. The change in velocity occurs due to the differences in the density of the two media. The angle of incidence is the same as in reflection. The angle between the normal and the light ray as light enters the second medium is called the angle of refraction.

Color Coding

The color code standard for fiber optic cable is TIA-598C, and it recommends the following colors and labeling be used on fiber optic cables.

Type of Fiber Optic Cable	Application and Color	Suggested Labeling
Multimode (50/125)	• Military application: Orange • Nonmilitary application: Orange	50/125
Multimode (50/125), 850 nm laser-optimized	• Military application: Not defined • Nonmilitary application: Aqua	850 LO 50/125
Multimode (62.5/125)	• Military application: Slate • Nonmilitary application: Orange	62.5/125
Multimode (100/140)	• Military application: Green • Nonmilitary application: Orange	100/140
Singlemode	• Military application: Yellow • Nonmilitary application: Yellow	SM/NZDS or SM
Polarization maintaining singlemode	• Military application: Not defined • Nonmilitary application: Blue	Not defined

Fiber Connectors

Various connectors are used with fiber optic cables.

> **Note:** It often takes a specially trained and certified technician, plus specialized equipment, to install fiber optic connectors. This is because the installation requires in-depth knowledge about fiber optic communication systems and fiber optic cables. Additionally, the installation involves various testing processes, which can be done only by a knowledgeable or certified technician.

Fiber Optic Connector	Description
Straight Tip (ST)	ST connectors are similar in appearance to BNC connectors and are used to connect multimode fibers. They have a straight, ceramic center pin and bayonet lug lockdown. They are often used in network patch panels. ST connectors are among the most popular types of fiber connectors.
Subscriber Connector or *Standard Connector (SC)*	SC connectors are box-shaped connectors that snap into a receptacle. They are often used in a duplex configuration where two fibers are terminated into two SC connectors that are molded together. SC is used with a singlemode fiber.

Fiber Optic Connector	Description
Local Connector (LC) 	LC connectors are used for both singlemode and multimode fiber and a small form factor ceramic ferrule. It is about half the size of an SC or ST connector. LC connectors use an RJ-45–type latching and can be used to transition installations from twisted pair copper cabling to fiber.
Mechanical Transfer Registered Jack (MT-RJ) 	The MT-RJ connector, also called a Fiber Jack connector, is a compact snap-to-lock connector used with multimode fiber. Because the MT-RJ connector is compact, it is easy to use. It is similar in size to the RJ-45 connector. Two strands of fiber are attached with the MT-RJ connector.
Ferrule Connector (FC) 	FC connectors use a heavy duty *ferrule* in the center for more mechanical stability than SMA or ST connectors. A ferrule is a tubular structure made of ceramic or metal that supports the fiber. These connectors are more popular in industrial settings where greater strength and durability are required.
Fiber Distributed Data Interface (FDDI) 	FDDI connectors are used for multimode fiber optic cable and are a push/pull-type, two-channel snap-fit connector. Also called a media interface connector (MIC).
Biconic 	The biconic connector is a screw-on type connector with a tapered sleeve that is fixed against guided rings and screws onto the threaded sleeve to secure the connection. When the connector is inserted into the receptacle, the tapered end of the connector locates the fiber optic cable into the proper position. The biconic connector is one of the earliest connector types.
Sub-multi assembly or sub-miniature type A (SMA) 	SMA connectors are similar to ST connectors, and use a threaded ferrule on the outside to lock the connector in place. It is typically used where water or other environmental factors necessitate a waterproof connection, unlike a bayonet-style connector.

As with copper media, there are also *fiber couplers* available. However, fiber couplers work differently than their copper-media counterparts. Fiber couplers are used when a system has one or more input fibers and one or more output fibers that need to be connected. The connection can be created by thermally fusing the fibers so that the cores get into intimate contact.

Fiber Connector Ferrule Polish

With fiber connectors, there will be some loss in the lightwave transmission. This is caused by the light being reflected directly back down the fiber and disrupting the transmitted signal. To reduce these back reflections, the connector ferrules can be polished to different finishes.

Fiber Connector Ferrule Polish	Description
Physical Contact (PC)	In the PC connector, the end faces are polished to be slightly curved or spherical. This eliminates any air gap and forces the fibers into contact. The back reflection is only about -40 dB. This connector is used in most applications.
Ultra Physical Contact (UPC)	The UPC connector is an improvement to the PC connector. The end faces are given an extended polishing for a better surface finish, which reduces the back reflection to about -55 dB. These connectors are often used in digital, cable television (CATV), and telephony systems.
Angled Physical Contact (APC)	In the APC connector, the end faces are still curved but are angled at an industry-standard 8 degrees. This maintains a tight connection and reduces back reflection to about -70 dB. These connectors are preferred for CATV and analog systems.

Cable Properties Comparison

Twisted pair, coaxial, and fiber optic cables have different properties with regard to transmission speed, distance, duplex, noise immunity, and frequency.

Cable Type	Properties
Twisted pair	**Transmission Speed:** • CAT3: UTP at 10 Mbps. CAT3 cable might still be found in legacy installations that use 10 Mbps hubs or switches. • CAT5: Up to 100 Mbps. CAT5 cable is most commonly found in office installations connecting computers to network drops in wall or floor jacks. It is rapidly being replaced by CAT5e. • CAT5e: Up to 1 Gbps. Category 5e cable is the current de facto standard for Ethernet cabling, and will be found in most new office and home installations. It is less expensive and easier to work with than CAT6, but it has less resistance to EMI and RFI. • CAT6: Up to 1 Gbps. CAT6 cable may be found where higher immunity to EMI/RFI noise is desired than what CAT5e can provide. • CAT6a: Up to 10 Gbps. CAT6a is primarily found in network backbones and data centers. **Distance:** 100 meters per network segment **Duplex:** Supports full-duplex transmission **Noise Immunity (security, EMI):** up to 30 MHz **Frequency:** Up to 600 MHz

Cable Type	Properties
Coaxial	**Transmission Speed:** 10 Mbps **Distance:** 500 meters per network segment **Duplex:** Supports both half-duplex and full-duplex transmission **Noise Immunity (security, EMI):** High **Frequency:** 1 GHz to 10 GHz
Fiber optic	**Transmission Speed:** 40,000 Mbps **Distance:** Multimode fiber is typically used for shorter runs of up to 500 meters, and singlemode for longer runs. The ultra high quality of some fiber cables allows runs of 62 miles or more between repeaters, which are rarely used now. **Duplex:** Supports full-duplex transmission as it consists of two fibers that can be used for simultaneous, bidirectional data transfer. **Noise Immunity (security, EMI):** High **Frequency:** Normally the frequency is very high and its range depends on the bandwidth and the device that you use.

ACTIVITY 2-2
Identifying Bounded Fiber Network Media

Scenario

The network administrator at Greene City Interiors says that you may need to work with fiber network media in the future. They pose different questions to you to assess your knowledge.

1. In an industrial setting, which fiber connector would provide greater strength and durability?
   - ○ Straight tip
   - ○ Biconic
   - ○ Ferrule connector
   - ○ Local connector

2. True or False? Multimode fiber can be used in longer distances than singlemode.
   - ☐ True
   - ☐ False

3. The network administrator says you will need to work with network patch panels. Which fiber connector would you use?
   - ○ Ferrule connector
   - ○ Straight tip
   - ○ Standard connector
   - ○ FDDI

4. The network administrator says that the branch office could be experiencing a high amount of back reflection with their fiber media. Which ferrule polish would you select to reduce the back reflection the most?
   - ○ Ultra physical contact
   - ○ Physical contact
   - ○ Angled physical contact
   - ○ Ferrule connector

TOPIC C

Bounded Network Media Installation

So far in this lesson, you have examined the main types of bounded network media. Now it's time to see how these media can form a network. In this topic, you will describe the equipment and methods required to install bounded network media.

In many cases, the network media will already have been installed into your work environment, but there will be times that you might need to extend or troubleshoot cable installations. Understanding the characteristics of bounded media and the equipment and methods used to install it will enable you to properly install and service your networks.

Network Media Performance Factors

Several factors can affect the performance of network media.

Factor	Description
Noise	*Electromagnetic interference (EMI)* that disrupts the signal. The signal-to-noise ratio decreases as the transmitting distance increases.
Attenuation	The progressive degradation of a signal as it travels across a network medium. Some media types are more susceptible to attenuation than others. Attenuation can also occur when the cable length exceeds the recommended length.
Impedance	The opposition to the flow of electricity in an *alternating current (AC)* circuit. To reduce the risk of signal loss and degradation through reflection, it is important that the transmitting device, the cabling, and any terminators have the same impedance. Impedance is measured in *ohms* (Ω). An ohm is the value of electrical resistance through which one volt will maintain a current of one ampere.

Media Converters

A *media converter* enables networks running on different media to interconnect and exchange signals. Technically, a media converter is considered a transceiver because it transmits and receives signals. Media converters are often built into other devices such as high-end switches.

To install a media converter, simply connect terminated ends of the two media you want to bridge to the converter. You may need to provide electrical power to the converter, but may not need any additional configuration. Many converters are available that allow you to convert from one media type to another.

The following table describes some commonly used media converters.

Converter Type	Description
Multimode fiber to Ethernet	Used to extend an Ethernet network connection over a multimode fiber backbone.
Fiber to coaxial	Used to convert signals on fiber to a coaxial cable.
Singlemode to multimode fiber	Used to transmit multimode fiber signals over singlemode fiber devices and links. It supports conversion between multimode segments on a network that spans a wider coverage area.

Converter Type	Description
Singlemode fiber to Ethernet	Used to extend an Ethernet network connection over a singlemode fiber backbone.

Structured Cabling

The *Telecommunications Industry Association (TIA)* and the *Electronic Industries Association (EIA)* developed the 568 Commercial Building Telecommunication Cabling standard. This standard defines the regulations on designing, building, and managing a cabling system that utilizes structured cabling according to specified performance characteristics to create a system of unified communications.

Structured cabling is based on a hierarchical design that divides cabling into six subsystems.

Subsystem	Description
Demarcation point (demarc)	Contains the telecommunication service entrance to the building, campus-wide backbone connections, and the interconnection to the local exchange carrier's telecommunication facilities. The network demarcation point is usually a foot away from where the carrier's facilities enter the building, but the carrier can designate a different measurement, depending on the needs of the facility. **Note:** A secondary demarc can be installed to provide redundancy. **Note:** The telephone wires coming to your house are an example of a demarcation point. Everything outside your house is the telephone company and everything inside your house is your wiring.
Backbone wiring	Provides connections between equipment rooms and telecommunication closets. Backbone cabling runs through the floors of the building via risers or across a campus. The allowed distance measurements of this cabling depend on the type of cable and the facilities it connects.
Equipment room	Provides the main cross-connection point for an entire facility. Also provides a termination point for backbone wiring connected to telecommunication closets.
Telecommunication closet	Houses the connection equipment for cross-connection to an equipment room along with workstations in the surrounding area. It contains horizontal wiring connections, and entrance facility connections. In an office building with multiple floors, depending on the floor plan, there can be as many telecommunication closets as needed.
Horizontal wiring	Runs from each workstation outlet to the telecommunication closet. The maximum allowed distance from the outlet to the closet is 295 feet. If patch cables are used, an additional 20 feet is allowed both at the workstation and the telecommunication closet, but the combined length cannot be more than 33 feet. Horizontal cabling specifications include: • Four-pair 100 ohms UTP cables • Two-fiber 62.5/125 mm fiber optic cables • Multimode 50/125 mm multimode fiber optic cables
Work area	Consists of wallboxes and faceplates, connectors, and wiring used to connect work area equipment to the telecommunication closet. It is required that a data and voice outlet be available at each wallbox and faceplate.

The TIA/EIA 568 standard also includes recommendations for how network media may best be installed to optimize network performance.

- **568A:** This obsolete standard defined the standards for commercial buildings and cabling systems that support data networks, voice, and video. It further defined cable performance and technical requirements.
- **568B:** This standard, some sections of which are now obsolete, defines the standards for preferred cable types and the minimum acceptable performance levels for:
    - 100 ohm twisted pair
    - STP
    - Optical fiber
- **568C:** The current release is the third in the 568 series. 568C defines the standards for commercial building cabling. It recognizes CAT6a as a media type. It also defines the minimum bend radius for twisted pair cables, both shielded and unshielded. In addition, it specifies the maximum untwist value for CAT6a cable termination.

Premise Wiring

Premise wiring is the collection of cables, connectors, and other devices that connect LAN and phone equipment within a commercial building. In a structured cabling situation, the premise wiring will consist of vertical and horizontal cable runs that radiate out from a central location throughout the building to individual devices.

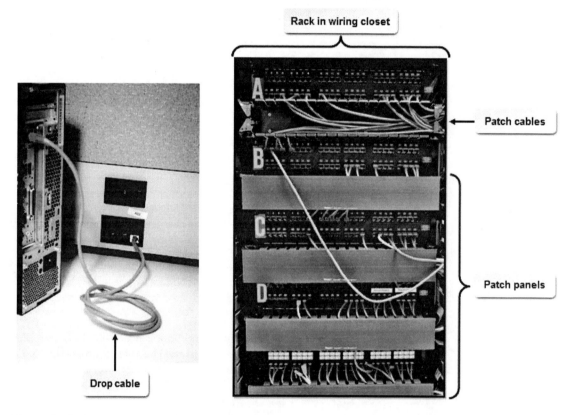

Figure 2–7: Components used in premise wiring.

Many components are used in premise wiring.

Premise Wiring Component	Description
Drop cable	The wire that runs to a PC, printer, or other device connected to a network.
Patch panel	A connection point for drop and patch cables. Typically, a patch panel has one or more rows of RJ-45 or other connectors. Drop cables are connected to the connectors. Cables run between the connectors to connect drop cables as needed.
Patch cable	A cable that is plugged into the patch panel to connect two drop cables. They are most often stranded and not solid core.
Cross-connects	Individual wires that connect two drop cables to a patch panel. Cross-connects are rarely used in modern networks because they are built into the network components. However, they are still frequently used in telephone wiring. • A *main cross-connect (MCC)* is the connecting point between entrance cables, equipment cables, and inter-building backbone cables. It is sometimes referred to as the first-level backbone. • An *intermediate cross-connect (ICC)* is an optional connection point between the MCC and the horizontal cross-connects. • *Horizontal cross-connects (HCC)* provide a point for the consolidation of all horizontal cabling, which extends to individual work areas, such as cubicles and offices. Fiber optic horizontal cabling is limited to 90 meters. Optional consolidation points or transition points are allowable in horizontal cables, although many industry experts discourage their use. • Vertical cabling or *vertical cross-connects* are generally recognized as cables that run vertically between floors in a building, or vertically between equipment in an equipment rack. They are not defined as part of the Structured Cabling standards.
Distribution frames	*Distribution frames* are devices that terminate cables and enable connections with other devices. Many installations will use a combination of a *main distribution frame (MDF)* and several *intermediate distribution frames (IDFs)*. • An MDF contains the devices used to manage the connections between external communication cables coming into the building and the cables of the internal network, via a series of IDFs. An MDF is usually a long steel rack that is accessible from both sides. Termination blocks are arranged horizontally on one side at the front of the rack shelves. The jumpers lie on the shelf and run through vertically arranged termination blocks. • An IDF is a free-standing or wall-mounted rack for managing and interconnecting end user devices, such as workstations and printers, and an MDF. For example, an IDF might be located on each floor of a multi-floor building, routing the cabling down the walls to an MDF on the first floor. The MDF would contain cabling that would connect to external communication cables.
Wiring closet	A *wiring closet*, network closet, or telecommunication closet is a small room in which patch panels are installed. Drop cables radiate out from the wiring closet to the components on the network.

Straight–Through, Crossover, and Rollover Cables

There are generally three main types of networking cables: straight-through, crossover, and rollover cables. Each cable type has a distinct use, and should not be used in place of another. In addition to the differing uses, each cable type has a distinct wiring configuration within the cable itself.

- *Straight-through cables* are used to connect unlike devices, such as computers to hubs or switches. All wire pairs are in the same order at each end of the cable. A straight-through cable is also commonly known as a patch cable.
- *Crossover cables* are used to connect like devices, such as device to device, switch to switch, or router to router. In a crossover cable, the transmit conductor at one end is connected to the receive conductor at the other, allowing both devices to communicate simultaneously.
- A *rollover cable* is used to connect a device to a router's console port. In a rollover cable, one end of the cable is wired exactly the opposite of the other end of the cable, going from one to eight on end A and from eight to one on end B. They do not support data transfer; instead, they provide an interface for programmers to connect to and adjust the router's configuration. Rollover cables are usually flat instead of round, and their outer jacket is often a unique color such as yellow or light blue. Some rollover cables have Ethernet connectors on both ends and will need a DB-9 (RS-232) or RJ-45 adapter to connect to a serial port. They are also referred to as Cisco console cables or Yost cables.

The RJ-45 cable that is commonly used for network connectivity is also referred to as straight-through cable.

In a regular Ethernet UTP patch cable, four wires are used. Pins 1 and 2 transmit and pins 3 and 6 receive. All lines are straight-wired. (Pin 1 is wired to pin 1, pin 2 to pin 2, and so forth.) In a crossover cable, pins 1 and 2 connect to pins 3 and 6, and pins 3 and 6 connect to pins 1 and 2.

Punch Down Blocks

A *punch down block* can be used to connect one group of telephone and network wires with another group in utility or telecommunication closets. They typically support low-bandwidth Ethernet and token ring networks.

There are two primary types of punch down blocks.

Type	Description
66 block	Used in the telephone industry for decades to terminate telecommunications. Supports low-bandwidth telecommunications transmission.
110 block	Punch down block or cable termination block used for structured wiring systems. Using the 110 block system, multipair station cables are terminated, allowing cross-connection to other punch down locations. Supports a higher bandwidth than 66 block and is suitable for use in data applications.

 Note: 110 block (T568A, T568B) supports both T568A and T568B wiring schemes.

Plenum and PVC Cables

A *plenum cable* is a network cable that is jacketed tightly around conductors so that fire cannot travel within the cable. The jacket of the plenum cable does not emanate poisonous gases when it burns. Fire codes require that you install this special grade cabling in the *plenum*, an air handling space, including ducts and other parts of the *heating, ventilating, and air conditioning (HVAC)* system in a building, between the structural and suspended ceilings, and under raised floors, as well as in firebreak walls. Unlike non-plenum cables, plenum cables can run through the plenum and firebreak walls.

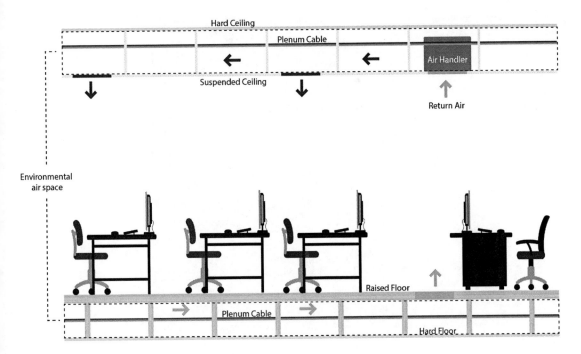

Figure 2-8: Plenum and PVC cables used in an office environment.

Polyvinyl chloride (PVC)-jacketed cabling is inexpensive and flexible. The PVC cable is also referred to as the non-plenum cable. However, when PVC burns, it gives off noxious or poisonous gases. Additionally, PVC jacketing is not formed tightly to the conductors it contains. Tests show that fire can travel within a PVC cable, passing through firebreaks.

 Note: For additional information, check out the LearnTO **Implement Best Practices for Cabling** in the LearnTOs for this course on your LogicalCHOICE Course screen.

Cable Management

If not managed properly, cables can become tangled, making them difficult to work with. *Cable management* is the means of neatly securing electrical, data, and other cables. Cable management is focused on supporting the cables as they are routed through the building from point A to B, and to make any future management of the cables after installation easier.

Figure 2-9: Cable tray.

Cable trays, *cable ladders*, and *cable baskets* can be used to support a cable through cabling routes. Buildings and office furniture are often designed with cable management in mind. Buildings may have dropped ceilings and raised floors to provide easy access and desks may have holes for cables to pass through.

Patch panels are used to connect circuits to the network. Messy patch panels can make finding the correct cable difficult when you need to add, remove, or replace a cable. Remove unused cables from the patch panel not only to make it neater, but also to prevent unauthorized network access. Consider purchasing patch panels with locking covers to prevent unauthorized access to add or remove cables. Make cables the right length: too short cables can pull on connectors and too long cables can make cable management difficult.

Labeling cables is another important aspect of cable management. Labels should help you accelerate tracing a cable to see where it runs to. This can be achieved by numbering the cables and labeling each end of the cable with the same number. Labeling can also be used to identify the properties of the cable, such as the length, type, and so on. Labeling of equipment, ports, and cables is so important, that TIA created a standard for labeling items. TIA-606B specifies standards for labeling and record keeping. All changes should be managed through Move/Add/Change (MAC) documents. Labels need to be printed (not handwritten) and securely attached to the port, cable, system, circuit, or patch panel. The standard specifies how port labeling, system labeling, circuit labeling, and patch panel labeling should be structured. Cables should be labeled within 12 inches of each end of the cable. Patch panel ports should be labeled above the port. Circuits should be individually labeled with the FS-AN. The identifier on the label should confirm to the FS-AN naming convention:

FS-AN character(s)	Description
F	The floor number and telecommunications space.
S	A letter that identifies the telecommunications space within the "F" area.
A	One or two characters (letters or numbers) corresponding to a patch panel that makes up the horizontal cross-connect.

FS–AN character(s)	Description
N	Two to four numbers corresponding to the patch panel port where the cable connects to the patch panel.

Power Management

Power management is an important consideration when installing devices in a wiring closet. You need to ensure that there are sufficient power outlets available and that they can accommodate the number of devices that will require power. In addition, those devices need to be protected from power quality problems that can damage equipment and from power outages. Uninterruptible power supply (UPS) systems provide three functions that affect the availability of network equipment.

• They serve as a source of backup power in the event of an outage.
• They provide power conditioning by removing sags, noise, and other power quality problems.
• They provide real-time monitoring and controlled shutdown of protected equipment.

Figure 2–10: A UPS system.

In addition to the benefits and efficiencies provided by UPSs, other power management features need to be considered in maintaining a healthy network environment.

Power Management Feature	Description
Power converters	In networking, you are most likely to encounter power converters as transformers for devices. You might also see them in voltage regulators and the mains power supply.
Circuits	Be sure there are enough circuits to supply power to all of your devices without overloading any one circuit. Circuit breakers will shut the circuit down if it is overloaded.
Inverters	An inverter or power inverter is a device that converts DC current to AC current. For networking you need an inverter that supplies a stable DC power source so that there are few, close to no, power fluctuations as these could harm the networking equipment.
Power redundancy	Power redundancy is built into many servers in the form of duplicate power supplies. For any device that you rely on to conduct business, you should consider whether power redundancy is available and affordable. Which is more expensive: redundant power or down time?

Device Placement

When installing devices in a wiring closet, you need to consider the placement of those devices so that your setup and maintenance activities are not hampered. Make sure that the devices are placed within reach of a power source and that power cords are not in high foot-traffic areas. Devices that need to connect to other devices should be within a reasonable distance of each other. Devices should also be physically accessible by the people who need to perform administration tasks on them. Proper airflow for cooling must be taken into account so that devices do not overheat.

Rack Systems

A *rack system* is a standardized frame or enclosure for mounting electronic equipment and devices. They allow for dense hardware configurations without occupying excessive floorspace or requiring shelving. The 19-inch rack format is an industry standard. Each piece of equipment or device is fastened to the rack frame with screws. Equipment that is designed to be placed in a rack system is usually identified as a rack mount, rack-mounted system, rack-mount instrument, rack-mount chassis, subrack, or rack-mountable. All types of electronics and computing devices come in rack-mounted packages, including servers, switches, routers, telecommunications components, tape drives, and audio and video equipment.

Figure 2-11: Example of a rack system.

Rack systems can be two-post racks or four-post racks. Two-post racks are designed for lightweight equipment such as switches. Four-post racks are designed for heavier equipment such as servers. These racks are typically bolted to the floor for stability and security. Server rail racks use rails to mount the systems to the racks. Rack mount systems might include the rails, or you might need to purchase them separately. Some server rail racks are fixed mounts. Others are sliding rails, making it easier to access the rear of the device. Free-standing racks are usually heavier duty racks that don't need to be bolted to the floor for stability.

Guidelines for Installing Bounded Network Media

 Note: All of the Guidelines for this lesson are available as checklists from the **Checklist** tile on the LogicalCHOICE Home screen.

Consider these best practices and guidelines when you are installing bounded network media:

- Create a list of requirements for your network so that you can work toward meeting them. These requirements may include how many users will need to connect, the physical area it will need to cover, external connections, etc.
- Consider the factors can affect the performance of network media, such as electromagnetic interference, attenuation, and impedance.

- Consider the environment's limitations, such as the amount of ventilation for the network closet, access to power, or space to run cables that can affect your network.
- Employ converters that enable different media to interconnect and exchange signals.
- Follow the 568 Commercial Building Telecommunication Cabling standard when dealing with structured cabling.
- Make proper use of premise wiring components.
- Use plenum cables in designated plenum spaces of a building to comply with fire codes, and use PVC in nonplenum spaces.
- Employ good cable management techniques to properly support cables and to keep them organized.
- Ensure that your wiring closet has adequate power for networking equipment, and that you protect the equipment from power quality problems that can damage equipment and from power outages.
- Use rack systems to maximize the use of space for equipment in a wiring closet.
- Consider the limitations of the equipment and how they might affect your network.
- Consider the compatibility requirements of all of your equipment to ensure that it will all work together the way you need it to.

ACTIVITY 2-3
Identifying Bounded Network Installation Media

Scenario

The network administrator at Greene City Interiors says that you may need to install or repair some bounded network media. They ask you some questions and to identify network media used in the network.

1. Which of the following are reasons why a plenum cable is commonly used in air handling spaces and run through firebreaks?

   ☐   It does not give off poisonous gases when burning.

   ☐   Fire cannot travel through the cable because of the insulated metal shield that surrounds the conductors.

   ☐   Fire cannot travel through the cable because the jacket is closely bound to the conductors.

   ☐   It is more durable than using a PVC cable.

2. Which is not a factor that can affect the performance of network media?

   ○   Refraction

   ○   Attenuation

   ○   Impedance

   ○   Noise

3. Which structured cabling subsystem provides connections between equipment rooms and telecommunication closets?

   ○   Horizontal wiring

   ○   Attenuation

   ○   Cross-connects

   ○   Backbone wiring

4. Identify the cable types that connect the devices in the classroom.

5. Identify the types of connectors used in the classroom network.

6. Your instructor will provide samples of a variety of media and connector types. Identify each of the media and connectors.

TOPIC D

Noise Control

You have identified many types of bounded transmission media—the conduits over which network communications flow. This flow of communications can be impaired by interference such as noise. In this topic, you will describe noise and noise control techniques used on your network media.

Any number of things can cause interference with the transmission on your network—radio, TV, cell phones, and radar to name a few. The one constant is that noise always slows a network's performance and reduces its reliability. When the receiving node has to try to make sense of a mix of different signals, it ends up asking the sending node to resend data multiple times. In order to reduce noise on your network, you need to understand the sources of noise and how to protect your network against them.

Electrical Noise

Electrical noise, also known as interference in wireless networks, refers to unwanted signals that are present in the network media. Noise interferes with the proper reception of transmitted signals. Noise can come from natural sources, such as solar radiation or electrical storms, or from man-made sources, such as electromagnetic interference from nearby motors or transformers.

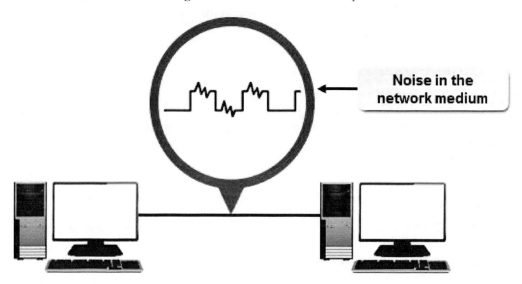

Figure 2-12: Electrical noise on a signal transmission.

Sources of Electrical Noise

A variety of sources contribute to electrical noise.

Noise Source	Description
Ambient noise	Ambient noise can come from many sources, including solar disturbances that affect the Earth's magnetosphere, or nearby radio broadcasting towers. These forms of noise affect both bounded and unbounded media, with longer network segments being affected more than shorter ones.

Noise Source	Description
Power wires	High-tension power lines or a building's own electrical wiring can create electrical noise. Network cables that run parallel to electric wires are more susceptible to electrical noise than those that run perpendicular.
Metal-based network transmission media	Network wiring, particularly unshielded twisted pair, will also generate its own electrical noise. Any time a current flows through a metal conductor, a magnetic field is generated around that conductor. If the magnetic field is close enough to cut across neighboring wires, it will induce a voltage in those wires, thus creating an unwanted signal. This is known as crosstalk.
Electric motors	Electric motors, such as those used in elevators, refrigerators, water fountains, and HVAC equipment, create noise while running, but this is more when they start up. Motors require a huge amount of electricity to start up, causing a burst of noise. These bursts can create temporary outages that resolve themselves when the motor reaches full speed or stops.
Electrical heat-generating devices	Like electric motors, electric heating elements use a lot of electricity and cause a significant amount of electrical noise while running.
Fluorescent, neon, and HID lights	Fluorescent, neon, and high-intensity discharge (HID) lighting devices produce a large amount of electrical noise, generally due to the transformers and ballasts required to make these lights work. Interior overhead lights, building security lights, and decorative lighting can create enough noise during operation to interfere with networking signals traveling over either bounded or unbounded media.

Other Effects of Noise

In addition to the noise that affects data networking media, noise can affect the electricity that powers computing devices. Surges or dips can result in the electric current, which can damage equipment, and cause application or operating system software crashes, or even system restarts.

Electric motors, heating elements, solar disturbances, or natural disasters can cause transient power problems. Most devices include power conditioning components that handle at least some of these power fluctuations. However, sensitive equipment should be protected through the use of specialized power conditioning devices, such as an uninterruptible power supply (UPS) or a surge protector.

 Note: Power conditioning will be covered in greater depth later in the course.

Grounding

Electrical devices often must be connected to a ground point for safety. In these situations, the ground connection serves as a way to direct high voltages safely away from humans and other devices, sending them instead into the ground.

Grounding is the connection of a shield or conductor to an electrical ground point, such as a pipe or wire that is in contact with the ground. Grounding at one point in a segment helps prevent noise on the data conductor by shunting noise signals to the ground. Connecting to the ground at multiple points can introduce noise onto the line, degrading network performance.

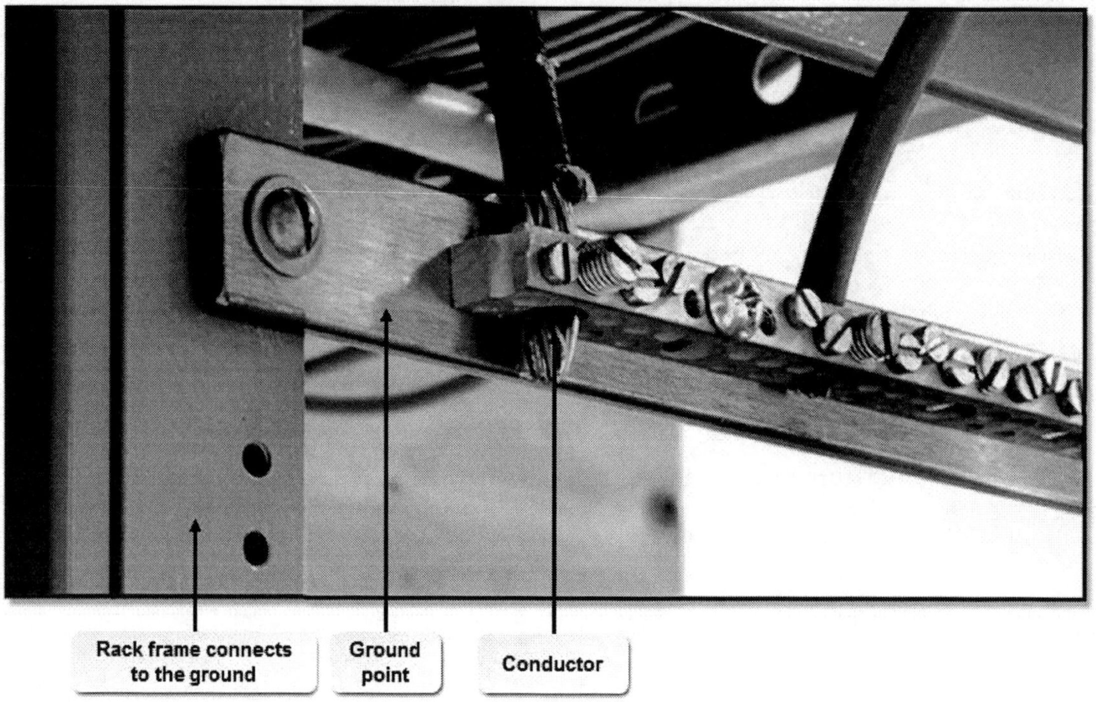

Figure 2-13: Grounding using a rack frame.

You should ground networking and other sensitive electronic equipment to dedicated ground points rather than to pipes and conduits. Electricians refer to this sort of ground connection as an isolated ground and will use an orange socket for such circuits.

Shielding

Shielding is the method of placing the grounded conductive material around the media. This prevents the introduction of noise into the media by deflecting the noise to the ground. Because of this, the connection between the ground and the shield is called a *drain*. Shields are drained in only one location to prevent a ground loop, a phenomenon in which the shield introduces noise in the data signal.

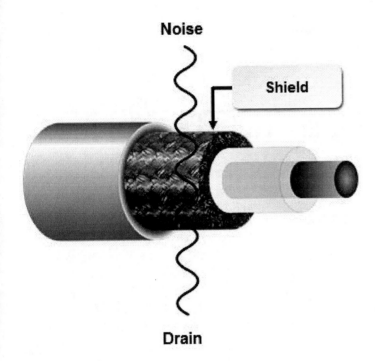

Noise

Shield

Drain

Figure 2-14: Shielding used in coaxial cable.

All other jacks and termination points must also be grounded.

Common forms of shielding include the copper braid in coaxial cable, or foil wrapped around wire pairs in shielded twisted pair (STP).

Noise Control with Twisted Pair

The twists in the twisted pair cable determine how resistant the cable will be to noise, and in particular, to crosstalk. When data wires lie next to each other, they generate crosstalk in each other. This effect accumulates over distance. Twists effectively move adjacent wires away from each other on a regular interval, providing less opportunity for crosstalk to occur. The more twists, the more the crosstalk is disrupted.

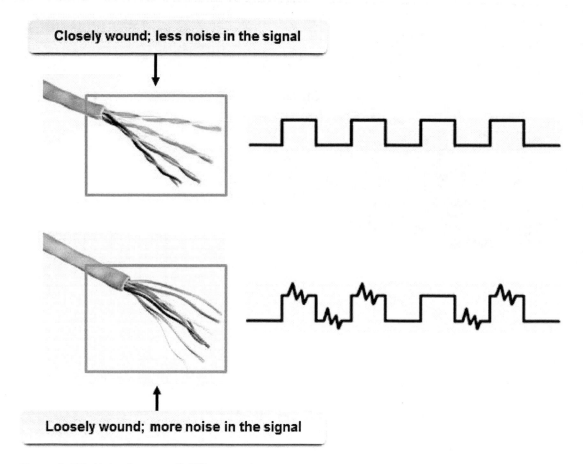

Closely wound; less noise in the signal

Loosely wound; more noise in the signal

Figure 2-15: Noise impact of different twists.

 Note: The tightness of the twists in twisted pair is called the "twist ratio."

The primary difference between twisted pair cable categories is the number of twists per inch. However, to fully support the network speeds for which they are rated, you must take care when adding connectors to these cables. You should not unwind the pairs too much or you will eliminate the noise-canceling benefits of the twists. The more twists per foot and the more consistently the twists are arranged, the more resistant to noise a cable will be.

As a rule, you should not unwind to more than 3/8 of an inch (about 10 mm) for a Category 5 cable. A Category 3 cable is more tolerant to unwinding of twists. A Category 6 cable requires special connectors that maintain the twists inside the connector.

 Note: Twisted pair is effective in office environments in which the amount of electromagnetic interference (EMI) and radio frequency interference (RFI) are relatively low. In high-noise environments such as machine shops and hospital radiology departments, consider using fiber optic cabling, which is immune to EMI/RFI.

Noise Reduction Considerations

The installation techniques you follow can affect the amount of noise introduced into a network cable. There are several considerations that you can use to limit the impact of noise on your network.

Consideration	Description
Separate data and electric cables	Do not run data and electricity cables in the same trays, raceways, and conduits. Avoid running network cables parallel to each other when you can, because crosstalk is worst when cables run in parallel. Make sure to comply with any building codes.
Fluorescent lights	Keep network cables at least 20 inches from fluorescent lights as they can cause electromagnetic interference. If you must run data cables across or near these lights, do so in such a way that exposes the smallest length of cable to the light.
Power ground	Ground all equipment and electrical circuits according to the manufacturer's instructions and local building codes.
Connector installation	Follow standards, specifications, and manufacturer's directions when installing network cables. Do not unwind conductor pairs any more than required or allowed. Make sure connectors are firmly attached and connected to the appropriate jacks.
Use of other media	Consider using fiber optic cabling in environments where the noise is unmanageable.

As a general rule, consult local building codes any time you are working with power and ground issues.

ACTIVITY 2-4
Identifying Electrical Noise Control Measures

Scenario

The network administrator at Greene City Interiors asks you questions about electrical noise and its effects.

1. **What is electrical noise?**

   ○ Solar radiation or man-made sources of data signals

   ○ Extraneous signals introduced onto network media

   ○ The reception of transmitted signals from a source

   ○ Extraneous signals that enhance the quality of received transmission

2. **The network administrator says that the branch office is experiencing electrical noise. What are some of the possible sources?**

   ☐ Fluorescent lights

   ☐ Solar storms

   ☐ Wind storms

   ☐ HVAC equipment

3. **True or False? Differential signaling reduces electrical noise by distinguishing between the signals on two different inputs.**

   ☐ True

   ☐ False

4. **What is the process of installing a resistor on the end of a cable to prevent signal reflections?**

   ○ Draining

   ○ Grounding

   ○ Terminating

   ○ Shielding

5. **True or False? The unwinding of a twisted pair cable's conductors does not affect its performance characteristics.**

   ☐ True

   ☐ False

Summary

In this lesson, you identified bounded network media. By recognizing the common types of copper and fiber media and connectors used in today's networks, you will be better prepared to use bounded media to connect devices to a network.

What types of cables do you have experience working with?

What challenges have you experienced when trying to install bounded media?

 Note: Check your LogicalCHOICE Course screen for opportunities to interact with your classmates, peers, and the larger LogicalCHOICE online community about the topics covered in this course or other topics you are interested in. From the Course screen you can also access available resources for a more continuous learning experience.

3 | Unbounded Network Media

Lesson Time: 2 hours

Lesson Objectives

In this lesson, you will identify unbounded media. You will:

- Describe the basics of wireless networking.

- Identify the components of a wireless network implementation.

- Install a wireless network.

Lesson Introduction

In the previous lesson, you identified bounded network media. With more and more wireless network implementations, you will need different types of media to meet the needs of your wireless network. In this lesson, you will identify unbounded network media.

Unbounded media technologies have two distinct advantages for businesses over bounded media: first, they are generally easier to install and configure; and second, they afford clients a lot of mobility. They are usually not as secure as bounded media, as the signals are subject to interception. Wireless technologies implementations offer various advantages, and you need to understand their limitations to compensate for their disadvantages in your network environments.

TOPIC A

Wireless Networking

In this lesson, you will describe unbounded network media. Several types of wireless communications are supported by unbounded media, so it's important to have a basic understanding of those communication types. In this topic, you will describe the basics of wireless networking,

Wireless Communication

Wireless communication is a type of communication in which signals are transmitted over a distance without the use of a physical medium. Information, data or voice, is transmitted as electromagnetic waves, such as radio and microwaves, or as light pulses. Wireless communication enables users to move around while remaining connected to the network.

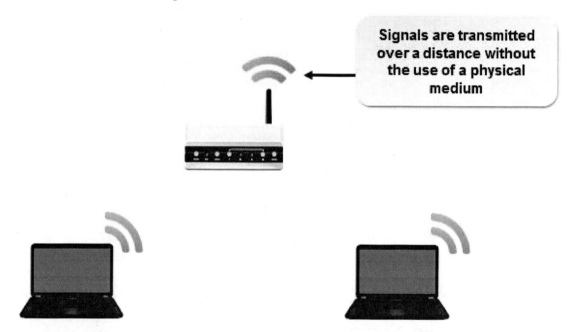

Signals are transmitted over a distance without the use of a physical medium

Figure 3–1: Communication on a wireless network.

Wireless media are also referred to as unbounded network media, where data signals are transmitted through the air instead of cables. Wireless communication permits connections between areas where it would be difficult or impossible to connect using wires, such as in hazardous areas, across long distances, or inside historic buildings.

Wireless connections can be point-to-point, multipoint, or broadcast.

- Point-to-point communication is a direct connection between two nodes. Data transmitted by one node goes directly to the other. Cellular communications are point-to-point communications. Typically, point-to-point wireless connections are used to link distant buildings or networks as part of a campus area network (CAN), a metropolitan area network (MAN), or a wide area network (WAN).
- Multipoint communication involves connections between many nodes. Each multipoint connection has more than two endpoints. A signal transmitted by any device through a medium is not private. All devices that share the medium can detect the signal but cannot receive it. Wireless networks are an example of multipoint communication.

- Broadcast communication is a communication method in which data goes from a source node to all other nodes on a network. Each node receives and acts on the data. Radio communication is an example of broadcast communication.

The IEEE 802.11 Standard

The *802.11* standard is a family of specifications developed by the Institute of Electrical and Electronics Engineers (IEEE) for the wireless LAN technology. 802.11 specifies an over-the-air interface between a wireless client and a base station or between two wireless clients. 802.11 defines the access method as Carrier Sense Multiple Access/Collision Avoidance (CSMA/CA). It specifies spread spectrum radio devices in the 2.4 GHz band for reliability. The 802.11b standard also defines a multichannel roaming mode and automatic data rate selection. The 802.11ac standard provides faster wireless connections, better range, improved reliability, and improved power consumption than previous wireless standards. 802.11ac routers can also have up to eight antennas.

Latency is the time taken by a data packet sent through a wireless connection from a requesting device to the receiving device and back. Latency includes the time taken for checking the data packets, correcting errors, and resending data lost in transit. Some of the wireless technologies based on the 802.11 specifications are more prone to latency and interference than Gigabit Ethernet.

Multiple input, multiple output (MIMO) uses multiplexing to increase wireless network range and bandwidth. MIMO uses algorithms to send and receive data using multiple antennas, using multiple antenna pathways to send additional data. It can also recombine signals it receives to increase capacity and provide more reliable connections. Multi-user MIMO (MUMIMO) allows multiple independent radio antennas to access a system. Using MUMIMO, multiple users can access the same channel. It uses spatial degrees of freedom to allow multiple user access to receive data from the access point to the wireless devices.

The 802.11 standards provide specifications for different wireless technologies.

Standard	Transmission Speed (Mbps)	Frequency (GHz)	Geographic Range (meters)	MIMO Streams
802.11a	54	5	20	1
802.11ac	433 per channel	5	35	8
802.11b	11	2.4	100	1
802.11g	54	2.4	100	1
802.11n	150	2.4 or 5	70	4

 Note: The 802.11a standard is not cross-compatible with 802.11b and g.

There are also the 802.11a-ht and 802.11g-ht standards. These are the same as the base standard but they have high throughput (ht), making the transmission speed the same as 802.11n.

Frequencies and Overlap of Wireless Channels

The 802.11b and g specifications define 14 channels within the Industrial, Scientific, and Medical (ISM) 2.4 GHz band. Each channel is composed of a range of frequencies transmitting at low power, rather than a single frequency transmitting at high power. The data from a single transmitting node is spread across all frequencies in the channel. Because the overall frequency range of the ISM band is limited, the channels have been implemented with substantial overlap. Special codes embedded in the signal give each transmitting node a distinguishing pattern, so that several nodes can share the same channel at once. At some point, however, the channel becomes saturated with too many nodes sharing not only the frequencies from their own channel, but also portions of adjacent channels.

1	2	3	4	5	6	7	8	9	10	11	12	13	14	Channel
2.412	2.417	2.422	2.427	2.432	2.437	2.442	2.447	2.452	2.457	2.462	2.467	2.472	2.484	Center Frequency (GHz)

Figure 3–2: Frequencies and overlap of wireless channels.

The only three channels that have no overlap with each other are 1, 6, and 11. Nonetheless, they still have overlap with the other channels. In addition, most wireless access points come configured out of the box with one of these channels. Because of their popularity, these channels may in practice be busier than some of the others. You should use a wireless spectrum analyzer such as InSSIDer to find which channels in your area are actually the least busy. Newer access points will auto-negotiate their channel.

Radio Networking

Radio networking is a form of wireless communications in which signals are sent via *radio frequency (RF)* waves in the 10 KHz to 1 GHz range. Radio networking is subject to electrical interference from power lines, a building's metal structural components, and atmospheric conditions.

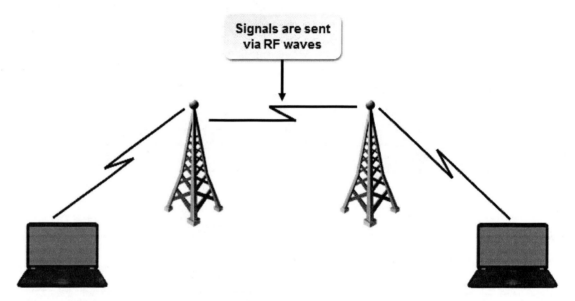

Figure 3–3: Communications on a radio network.

 Note: U.S. regulatory agencies define the limits on which frequencies and how much power can be used to transmit radio signals. In the United States, the Federal Communications Commission (FCC) regulates radio transmission.

Broadcast Radio

Broadcast radio is a form of RF networking that is non-directional, uses a single frequency for transmission, and comes in low- and high-power versions. Low-power RF transmissions travel a short distance, often no more than 70 meters, but are inexpensive and relatively easy to install. High-power RF transmissions travel longer distances; however, specially trained technicians are often required to install this more expensive type of system.

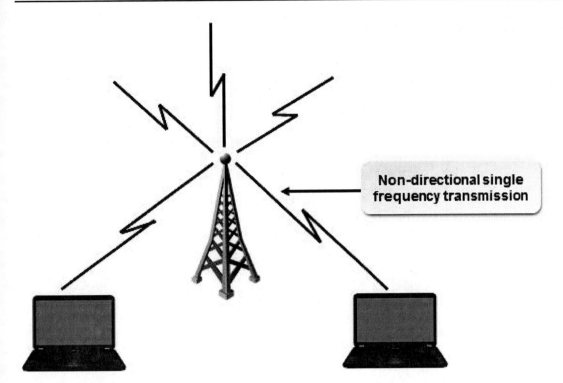

Figure 3-4: Communications using broadcast radio.

Spread Spectrum

Spread spectrum is a form of radio transmission in which the signal is sent over more than one frequency. Because signals are transmitted over different frequencies, it is more difficult to eavesdrop and capture the signals. Additionally, distinguishing between the signal and background noise is more difficult.

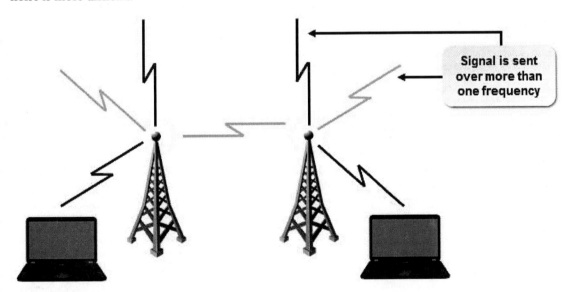

Figure 3-5: Spread spectrum radio.

Signal Distribution Methods

Spread spectrum uses either frequency hopping or direct sequencing techniques to distribute the signal across the radio spectrum.

Spread Spectrum Type	Description
Orthogonal Frequency Division Multiplex (OFDM)	*OFDM* uses multiple frequencies simultaneously to send data. A high-speed data stream is converted into multiple low-speed data streams via Serial-to-Parallel (S/P) conversion. Each data stream is modulated by a subcarrier. This produces multiple flat-fading subchannels. It is used in applications such as digital television and audio broadcasting, digital subscriber line (DSL) Internet access, wireless networks, powerline networks, and 4G mobile communications.
Direct Sequence Spread Spectrum (DSSS)	*DSSS* uses multiple frequencies simultaneously to send data. Additionally, Error Detection and Correction (EDAC) techniques are used to reduce data transmission errors. In DSSS, a data signal is converted into multiple data signals called *chips*. The set of chips is sent across a wide band of adjacent frequencies. Upon receiving the data, the receiver combines and converts the signals back into the original. Because of the included EDAC information, the signal can often be reconstructed only if some of the frequencies are received clearly. It is used in satellite navigation systems such as GPS; cordless phones operating in the 900 MHz, 2.4 GHz, and 5.8 GHz bands; IEEE 802.11b 2.4 GHz Wi-Fi; and radio-controlled model automotive vehicles.

Infrared Transmission

Infrared transmission is a form of wireless transmission in which signals are sent as pulses of infrared light. Infrared signals transmit at frequencies between 300 GHz and 300,000 GHz and in the range just below visible light in the electromagnetic spectrum. Receivers need an unobstructed view of the sender to successfully receive the signal, though the signal can reflect off hard surfaces to reach the recipient. Many infrared-compatible devices follow the standards set forth by the Infrared Data Association (IrDA). Infrared transmissions are still used in legacy remote control systems, security sensors that can be wired to the network, and manufacturing plants in which sensors are wired to the network.

Bluetooth

Bluetooth 4.1 is a wireless technology that facilitates short-range wireless communication between devices such as personal computers, laptops, cellular phones, tablets, and gaming consoles, thus creating a wireless personal area network (WPAN). Up to eight Bluetooth devices, usually less than 30 meters apart, can be connected to each other at a point in time. Bluetooth establishes a link using an RF-based media and does not need line-of-sight to make connections.

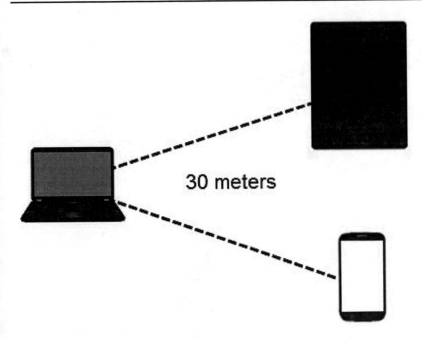

Figure 3-6: Bluetooth communications.

 Note: The "Bluetooth" technology is named in memory of a Danish king named Harald Bluetooth.

Bluetooth uses the 2.4 GHz spectrum to communicate a 24 Mbps connection between two devices as far as 100 meters apart, but in most cases only 30 meters. Examples include Bluetooth wireless keyboards, mice, headsets, and recent-model cars. Bluetooth is also used (in conjunction with near field communications, or *NFC*) as the back-end transport mechanism for when you tap your smartphone to a point of sale machine such as an ATM card reader in a market.

Microwave Transmission

Microwave transmission is a form of point-to-point wireless transmission in which signals are sent via pulses of electromagnetic energy in the microwave region of the electromagnetic spectrum. It transmits signals at a frequency range of 1 GHz to 300 GHz. Receivers need an unobstructed view of the sender to successfully receive the signal, and depending on the frequency in use, transmission can be affected by environmental conditions such as fog, birds, and so on. Signals can be reflected off satellites to increase the transmission distance. Microwave transmission technologies are often used in WANs and MANs.

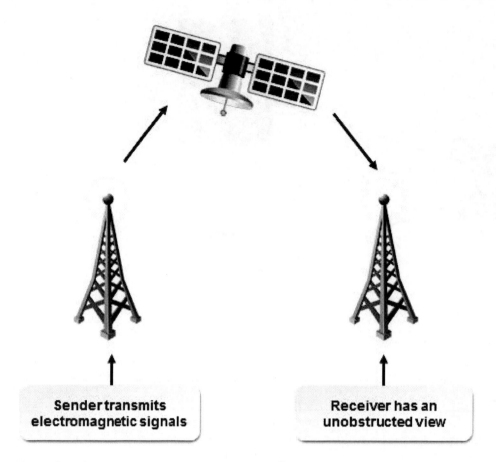

Figure 3–7: Microwave transmission using satellites.

Mobile carriers often use point-to-point microwave connections as part of their backhaul network. A *backhaul* is the connection between the provider's core network and its smaller distribution-level (regional) subnetworks.

Microwave is also used by wireless Internet service providers (WISPs) to provide broadband Internet access to customers in areas where wired connections are not practical. Examples include rural areas, or developing nations that lack the infrastructure for copper or fiber connections. Microwave transmissions are used in the great plains areas to connect locations that are miles away. Transmitting towers or satellites are used to beam two-way microwave signals to the customer's dish antenna.

ACTIVITY 3-1
Identifying Wireless Transmission Technologies

Scenario

The network administrator at Greene City Interiors informs you that you will need to assess the wireless network at the branch office. You need to identify and distinguish between the various types of unbounded media used to create wireless links between network nodes.

1. Select the characteristics of unbounded media.

   ☐ Use a physical medium.

   ☐ Transmit both voice and data signals.

   ☐ Use electromagnetic energy.

   ☐ Operate only within a 10-mile radius.

2. At what radio frequency does Bluetooth operate?

   ○ 5 GHz

   ○ 2.4 GHz

   ○ 300 GHz

   ○ 100 GHz

3. Which form of wireless transmission transmits signals in the 10 KHz to 1 GHz frequency range?

   ○ Radio

   ○ Infrared

   ○ Spread spectrum

   ○ Microwave

4. Which forms of wireless media operate only when there are no obstacles in the transmission path?

   ☐ Infrared

   ☐ Radio

   ☐ Microwave

   ☐ Broadcast

5. Which unbounded media transmission method uses multiple frequencies to reduce interference and the likelihood of eavesdropping?

   ○ Infrared

   ○ Microwave

   ○ Spread spectrum

   ○ Broadcast radio

TOPIC B

Wireless Network Devices and Components

In the last topic, you described basic concepts related to wireless networking. In order for your wireless network to function properly, you need to understand the different wireless devices and how they are used. In this topic, you will identify wireless network devices and components.

Wireless Access Points

A *wireless access point (WAP)*, or access point (AP), is a device that provides a connection between wireless devices and can connect to wired networks. It has a network interface to connect to the wired network and an antenna or infrared receiver necessary to receive wireless signals. The WAP can be a wireless router in a large environment or in a small office/home office. The *Service Set Identifier (SSID)* is a 32-bit alphanumeric string that identifies a WAP and all devices attached to it. Wireless connectivity devices such as the WAP or wireless routers come with a default SSID. Many access points include security features that enable you to specify which wireless devices can make connections to the wired network.

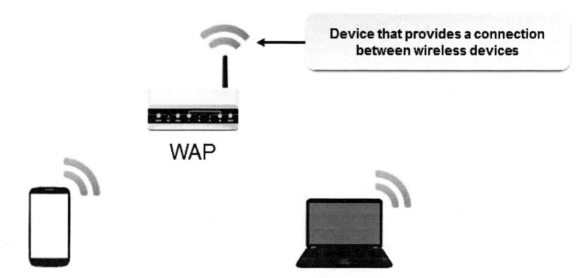

Device that provides a connection between wireless devices

WAP

Figure 3–8: A WAP connecting to a wired network.

 Note: IEEE 802.11 does not specify how two WAPs should communicate. To ensure compatibility, it is best to use WAPs from the same manufacturer.

A client device uses its SSID to identify itself to the wireless network. An SSID mismatch can occur when a device receives a packet that contains a different SSID than its own. Devices need to be configured with the same SSID as the WAP in order to communicate with it. A mismatch of SSIDs can block communication between the device and the WAP. Currently, there are fewer episodes of SSID mismatch, because the configuration is done automatically.

When determining device density, you need to consider the number of users who will be accessing the WAPs, the number of access points available, and the square footage covered by the access points. Typically, consumer-based WAPs are hardware based to allow about 10 devices to connect. Enterprise WAPs use hardware and software to increase the number of concurrent wireless devices that can connect to the access point.

Wireless Controllers

Wireless controllers provide wireless LAN management for multiple access points. The network administrator uses a wireless controller in combination with the Lightweight Access Point Protocol (LWAPP) to manage lightweight access points. The wireless controller automatically handles the configuration of wireless access points. A wireless controller can be a physical device or a software application.

LWAPP is a protocol that controls multiple Wi-Fi wireless access points. This can reduce the amount of time spent on configuring, monitoring, or troubleshooting a large network.

Wireless Bridges

A wireless bridge can be used to connect two wired networks by using a wireless connection. A wireless bridge receives the signal from a wireless router and sends it out to other wired devices. The wireless bridge needs to be within range of the wireless router's signal and also within cable length of the other wired devices.

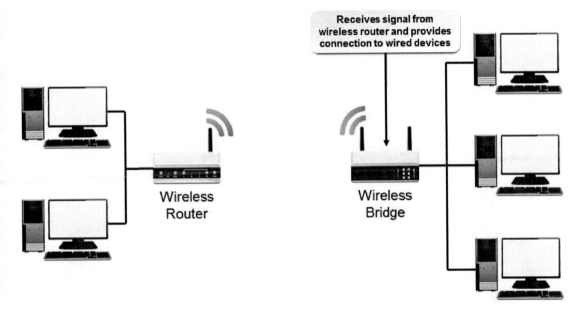

Figure 3-9: A wireless bridge connecting two wired networks.

Wireless Antennas

A *wireless antenna* is a device that converts high frequency signals on a cable into electromagnetic waves and vice versa. In wireless communication, an antenna is used to receive or transmit radio waves. The frequency at which an antenna can send or receive radio waves depends on the physical dimensions of the antenna. The higher the frequency, the shorter the wavelength of the signal, and the shorter the antenna will be. You can choose different antenna types to use in different wireless networking situations. Different styles of antennas vary in their *gain* or signal strength, and the shape or the radiation pattern of the transmission beam.

Wireless Tower   **Dish Antenna**

Figure 3-10: A wireless antenna converts high frequency signals on a cable into electromagnetic waves.

Gain is an increase in the amplitude of a radio wave. Gain can occur due to the use of external sources such as amplifiers that amplify a radio signal. It has both positive and negative effects. Typically, high gain is advantageous, but there may be situations in which the amplitude of a radio wave is already very close to the legal value and added power could be a serious problem. You also need to be aware of the FCC's rules for unlisted wireless equipment and make sure wireless signals stay within the established limits.

Wireless signals are not bound by the same physical limitations of wired media. Wireless signals that travel where they are not intended is known as *bleed*. For example, the wireless signal in an office is not restricted to that office, and someone outside might also use the signal. Some antennas and access points allow administrators to restrict the range of a wireless signal by reducing the strength of the wireless signal output.

Antenna polarization is a very important consideration when selecting an antenna. Most communications systems use vertical, horizontal, or circular polarization. Knowing the difference between polarizations and how to maximize their benefit is very important to the antenna user. Most antennas radiate either linear or circular polarization. A linear polarized antenna radiates wholly in one plane containing the direction of propagation. In a circular polarized antenna, the plane of polarization rotates in a circle making one complete revolution during one period of the wave. A vertically polarized (linear) antenna has its electric field perpendicular to the Earth's surface. Horizontally polarized (linear) antennas have their electric field parallel to the Earth's surface. A circular polarized wave radiates energy in both the horizontal and vertical planes and all planes in between.

The default antennas on APs are typically omnidirectional, covering an area that is mostly circular except for areas where the signal is impacted by things like walls, motors, and other RF obstacles. Placing the antenna in a central location and then allowing AP coverage areas to overlap is one way to ensure coverage, but not likely the best choice. APs that use MIMO antennas do not provide circular coverage. These MIMO antennas take advantage of multiple path signal reflections to extend coverage areas; however, you still might have gaps in coverage. Purchasing additional APs is often the way administrators cover the gaps, but you should consider using directional antennas instead.

Wireless Antenna Types

Antennas can be grouped into one of two broad categories.

Antenna Category	Description

Directional antenna

A type of antenna that concentrates the signal beam in a single direction, sometimes referred to as a *unidirectional antenna.*. They have a relatively narrow, focused transmission beam and a relatively high gain. Because they transmit primarily in a single direction, the sending and receiving stations must be precisely aligned. The high gain provides for good signal quality and the narrow beam ensures that only a narrow transmission area needs to be clear of interference.

Directional antennas are used in a point-to-point network to connect one station to another. Directional antennas include the parabolic dish antenna, backfire antenna, yagi antenna, and panel antenna. Some of these antennas can be semi-directional, which are designed to provide specific, directed signal coverage over large areas. Others can be bidirectional, which have two high-gain directions, usually oriented opposite to each other in space. Other antennas can provide 180-degree coverage in a single direction.

Omni-directional antenna

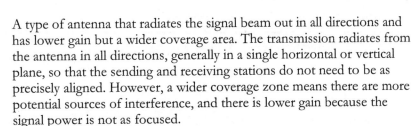

A type of antenna that radiates the signal beam out in all directions and has lower gain but a wider coverage area. The transmission radiates from the antenna in all directions, generally in a single horizontal or vertical plane, so that the sending and receiving stations do not need to be as precisely aligned. However, a wider coverage zone means there are more potential sources of interference, and there is lower gain because the signal power is not as focused.

Omni-directional antennas are used in multipoint and distributed networks. Omni-directional antennas include the ceiling dome or "blister" antenna, blade antenna, and various rod-shaped antennas.

 Note: The wireless antenna in a laptop typically runs along the lid of the display.

ACTIVITY 3-2
Identifying Wireless Devices and Components

Scenario

The network administrator at Greene City Interiors says that you will also need to ensure that the wireless network at the branch office is using the correct devices to provide the coverage they need. They ask you questions related to the wireless devices you will encounter.

1. Select the characteristics of directional antennas.

   ☐ Used in point-to-point networks

   ☐ Have low gain

   ☐ Transmit narrow and focused beams

   ☐ Are prone to interference

2. Which device can be used to connect two wired networks using a wireless connection?

   ○ Wireless bridge

   ○ Wireless controller

   ○ Wireless access point

   ○ Wireless antenna

3. What is the purpose of an SSID?

   ○ Control multiple Wi-Fi wireless access points.

   ○ Identify each device on a wireless network.

   ○ Identify a WAP and all devices attached to it.

   ○ Identify the protocol of a wireless network.

TOPIC C

Install a Wireless Network

So far in this lesson, you explored wireless networking concepts and identified the components of a wireless LAN implementation. It's time to put that information to use. In this topic, you will install a wireless network.

Wireless networks are the network of choice in most environments today because they are relatively easy to install and are flexible. Even more important, with users increasingly needing to connect on the move by using different devices, roaming users in both business and leisure environments want the freedom to use their computing devices for work or recreation wherever they are, without a physical connection to the network. With its increasing popularity and widespread appeal, you will undoubtedly be faced with installing, managing, or troubleshooting a wireless network.

Wireless Antenna Performance Factors

It is important to consider various performance factors before installing antennas for infrared, radio, or microwave wireless technologies.

Wireless Technology Type	Performance Factors
Infrared	The maximum transmitting distance of an infrared wireless installation is affected by these factors: • Sunlight. • Obstacles. • Smoke, dust, or fog.
Radio	The maximum transmitting distance of a radio wireless installation is affected by all of these factors: • Signal characteristics of the antenna. • Environment conditions such as wire mesh in wall construction, thick walls, and so on. • Ambient electrical noise. • Conductive obstacles in the path. • Presence of other electrical equipment. • Data transmission rate.
Microwave	The maximum transmitting distance of a microwave wireless installation is affected by all of these factors: • Weather. • Signal characteristics of the antenna. • Line of sight. • Distance between transmitting stations.

 Note: Although there are a few exceptions, most notably in developing nations, most radio-based wireless is in the microwave frequency range.

WLAN Overview

A *wireless LAN (WLAN)* is a self-contained network of two or more devices connected by using a wireless connection. A WLAN spans a small area, such as a small building, floor, or room. A typical WLAN consists of client systems such as desktops, laptops, smartphones, or tablets, and wireless connectivity devices such as access points. The access points interconnect these client systems in a wireless mode, or they can connect them to a wired network. WLANs enable users to connect to the local network or the Internet, even on the move. A physical location that enables users to access the Internet over a WLAN is referred to as a hotspot. This can be created from a hardware device designed specifically to be a hotspot, or you can enable a hotspot on a computer or mobile phone to allow Internet access.

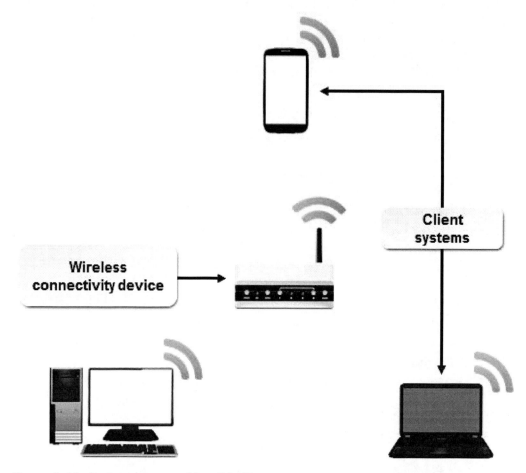

Figure 3-11: Devices connected in a WLAN.

Devices can have simultaneous wired and wireless connections to a network. In these cases, one will be used over the other. If that connection is lost then it will switch over to the other connection after a brief interruption in connection.

When you are examining the throughput of your wireless network, you should also consider the goodput. Goodput is the data exchanged at the application level, without considering the additional packet information needed to transfer data over the network.

WLAN Architecture

Several components comprise a WLAN architecture.

WLAN Architecture Component	Description
Station (STA)	A device that can use the IEEE 802.11 protocol. A wireless STA contains an adapter card, a PC card, or an embedded device to provide wireless connectivity.
Access point (AP)	A device or software that facilitates communication and provides enhanced security to wireless devices. It also extends the physical range of a WLAN. The AP functions as a bridge between wireless STAs and the existing network backbone for network access.
Service sets	The service set defines the way a WLAN is configured. There are three ways to configure a WLAN—BSS, IBSS, and ESS.
Basic Service Set (BSS) and Basic Service Set Identifier (BSSID)	A set of devices with an AP connected to a wired network and one or more wireless stations or clients. A BSS can effectively extend the distance between wireless endpoints by forwarding signals through the WAP. The BSSID is a unique address that identifies the BSS.
Extended Service Set (ESS) and Extended Service Set Identifier (ESSID)	A configuration of multiple BSSs used to handle mobility on a wireless network. BSSs are connected to a common distribution system such as a wired network. ESS enables users to move their mobile devices, such as laptop computers, outside of their home BSS while keeping their connection. It also enables data to be forwarded from one BSS to another through the network backbone. The ESSID identifies the extended service set. In most cases, the term service set identifier (SSID) is used.
Independent Basic Service Set (IBSS)	A peer-to-peer network where each wireless station acts as both a client and a wireless AP. Each wireless station can both transmit and receive data.
Distribution System (DS)	A wired connection between a BSS and a premise-wide network that enables mobility to devices and provides access to available network resources.

DCF

802.11 defines *Distributed Coordination Function (DCF)* as a collision avoidance method that controls access to the physical medium. Each station checks the status of the wireless medium before beginning transmission. If a station determines that the network is busy, the station must wait for a random backoff period before it can try to access the network again. In a network where many stations contend for the wireless medium, if multiple stations sense the channel busy and defer access, they will also virtually simultaneously discover that the channel is open and then try to transmit, possibly causing collisions. That is why a random backoff interval is used.

802.11 Modes

The 802.11 standard supports two modes: the infrastructure mode and the ad-hoc mode.

Mode	Description
Infrastructure mode	The *infrastructure mode* utilizes one or more WAPs to connect workstations to the cable backbone. Infrastructure mode wireless networks use either BSS or ESS. Infrastructure mode uses the hub-and-spoke topology.

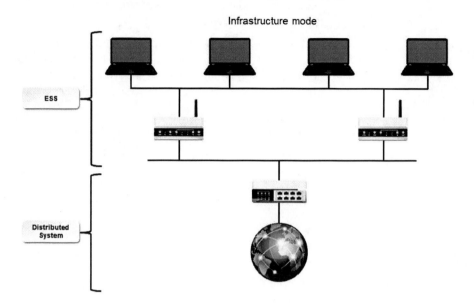

Ad-hoc mode	The *ad-hoc mode*, also referred to as IBSS, utilizes a peer-to-peer configuration in which each wireless workstation talks directly to other workstations. Ad-hoc mode uses the mesh topology.

Ad-hoc mode

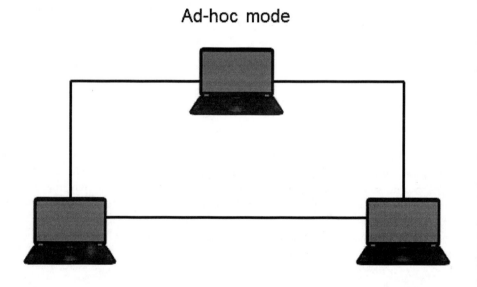

SSID Broadcasts

SSID broadcasts are a continuous announcement by a wireless access point that transmits its name, or SSID, so that it is discoverable by wireless devices searching for a network connection. An SSID broadcast is sometimes referred to as a beacon. When a WAP is secured with a password, devices might see the SSID but be unable to connect to it.

Mobile Devices

More and more mobile devices, such as cell phones, tablets, and laptops, are connecting to wireless networks. Connecting these devices is similar to connecting a desktop computer that has a wireless network interface card (NIC).

Mobile Device	Description
Mobile phone	Mobile phones range from simple mobile phones to smartphones. Connecting a mobile phone requires locating where in the interface to select the wireless network and input the security key.
Laptop	Laptops are connected in the same manner as desktop computers.
Tablet	Tablets are computing devices that contain a touchscreen display for input. Connecting a tablet requires locating where in the interface to select the wireless network and input the security key.
Gaming device	Gaming devices come in many different forms and are primarily used for playing games. Depending on the environment, these may not be appropriate to connect to the network. Connecting a gaming device requires locating where in the interface to select the wireless network and input the security key.
Media device	Media devices allow access to a particular form of media such as music, movies, and more. Examples of media players are MP3 players and Internet TV devices. Connecting a media device requires locating where in the interface to select the wireless network and input the security key.

Guidelines for Implementing a Basic Wireless Network

 Note: All of the Guidelines for this lesson are available as checklists from the **Checklist** tile on the LogicalCHOICE Home screen.

By considering several key factors of wireless network installation along with the cost of implementing and maintaining a secure wireless network, a network professional both demonstrates the proper installation methods and ensures maximum network functionality.

Implement a Wireless Network

To implement a basic wireless network, follow these guidelines:

- Create a list of requirements for your network so that you can work toward meeting them. These requirements may include how many users will need to connect, the physical area it will need to cover, external connections, and more.
- Consider the devices you will need and any requirements they have.
- Consider the environmental limitations such as the amount of ventilation for a network closet or access to power that can affect your network.
- Consider the limitations of the equipment and how they might affect your network.
- Consider the compatibility requirements of all of your equipment to ensure that it will all work together the way you need it to.
- Choose the appropriate 802.11 technology for your needs, such as 802.11a, ac, b, g, or n.
- Choose the appropriate AP placement locations for your network.
  - Obtain a scale drawing of the building. This will assist you in all areas of AP placement.
  - Determine the range of the AP for the wireless technology you have chosen. This will help you to better determine how many APs you will need to ensure adequate coverage for the space.

- Balance the number of users who will have access to the AP, and ensure that the AP can cover all employees in the range of the AP. More employees in a given area means more APs.
- Tour the area in the range of the AP and check to see if there are any devices that will interfere with the wireless network. This can include devices such as microwave ovens, Bluetooth-enabled devices, or an existing wireless network—whether from a community network, a neighboring building, or another floor of your company's building. These devices or networks can possibly interfere with your new implementation.
- Consider whether the AP will be exposed or concealed in the ceiling or placed in a secure room.
- Ensure that there are no obstacles in the path of the AP, such as doors, closed windows, walls, and furniture, that the wireless signal will need to pass through on its way to a client. If there are too many obstacles in the path, adjust the placement of your AP accordingly.
- Consider bringing in a consultant to help with the site survey, especially if you do not have access to someone who has good knowledge of wireless networks. The survey may include a heat map.
- Install the APs. The specific steps for installing the AP will vary by vendor, but the common steps may include:
    - Connecting the AP to a router.
    - Configuring the DHCP service as appropriate.
    - Configuring the appropriate encryption schemes.
    - Configuring channels and frequencies.
    - Setting the SSID/ESSID and an 802.11 beacon.
    - If necessary, creating an access control list (ACL). The ACL contains a list of users who have access to the wireless network.
    - Configuring the network adapters of the devices that will connect to the AP.
- Test to ensure that the installation is appropriately sized, secure, and operational. Make sure these tests are done under real world conditions so that you have an accurate test.
- Document the steps and establish a baseline for future installations.

Wireless Access Point Placement

While deciding on placement of WAPs, you need to consider several important factors.

- **Building layout:** The building layout is a very important factor when deciding on the positions at which to place WAPs. A scaled building layout of the coverage area will help in deciding on the areas where you require wireless access. Use the layout to identify locations of possible interference and obstacles. Also, the layout helps in locating strategic spots where you can place the WAPs.
- **Coverage area:** The area covered by an access point is called a *cell*. If the cell area is large, then you need to consider increasing the number of WAPs. Overlapping cells with multiple access points provide continuous access for devices.
- **Clients:** The number of clients accessing the WAP plays a major role in deciding on the placement of the WAP. Depending on the number of clients, you need to decide on the number of WAPs to install.
- **Obstacles:** Obstacles in the path of transmission of RF waves sometimes absorb the signals when they pass through, whereas others might reflect the signals, resulting in signal loss. Avoiding obstacles such as doors, walls, and windows between access points and devices can considerably reduce signal loss.
- **Interference:** Radio frequency interference from other devices such as mobile phones and microwave ovens can affect signals from WAPs. Removing other devices that can cause radio frequency interference will significantly reduce signal interference.

 Access the Checklist tile on your LogicalCHOICE course screen for reference information and job aids on How to Install a Wireless Access Point.

ACTIVITY 3-3
Installing a Wireless Router

Before You Begin
You are logged in as the administrator for the domain Child##.GCInteriors. Your password is P@ssw0rd12.

You will need an Internet connection to access the emulator.

Scenario
The network administrator at Greene City Interiors informs you that the wireless network is not as secure as it should be. Many of the employees in the branch office are mobile users, and they need to connect to the company network and the Internet through devices such as laptops and smartphones. The network administrator is concerned that attackers may try to steal client information. He says that employees often run applications and transfer customer data and sales information across the network. It is your responsibility to make sure that the routers employees must connect to are configured to prevent unauthorized access.

 Note: Activities may vary slightly if the software vendor has issued digital updates. Your instructor will notify you of any changes.

1. Connect to the wireless router's configuration interface.
   a) Open **Internet Explorer**.
   b) In the **Address** bar, enter *http://ui.linksys.com*
   c) From the list of routers, select the **E1200** link.
   d) Select the **2.0.04/** link.
   e) In the **Warning** message box, check the **Do not show me this again** check box and select **OK**.

    Note: This website emulates a common router configuration interface. When working with a real device, you will typically connect to http://192.168.1.1 and be prompted to enter a user name and password. For a list of default user names and passwords by router, navigate to http://www.routerpasswords.com.

2. Set an SSID for your wireless network.
   a) On the menu bar at the top of the page, select the **Wireless** tab.
   b) If necessary, select **Manual**.
   c) In the **Network Name (SSID)** text box, double-click and type *child##.gcinteriors*

    Note: Because you are using an emulator, you can use all lowercase letters in the **Network Name (SSID)** text box.

   d) Select **Save Settings** and, in the **Message from webpage** message box, select **OK**.
   e) Select **Save Settings** again, and then select **Continue**.

3. Set WPA2 encryption with a passphrase.
   a) Under the **Wireless** tab on the menu bar, select the **Wireless Security** link.
   b) From the **Security Mode** drop-down list, select **WPA2 Personal**.
   c) In the **Passphrase** text box, type *!Pass1234*
   d) Select **Save Settings**, and then select **Continue**.

4. Configure the router's administration settings.

   a) On the menu bar, select the **Administration** tab.

   b) In the **Router Password** text box, double-click the existing password (represented by asterisks) and type *P@ssw0rd*

   c) In the **Re-Enter to Confirm** text box, type the same password.

   d) In the **Local Management Access** section, uncheck the **HTTP** check box and check the **HTTPS** check box.

   e) In the **Local Management Access** section, for the **Access via Wireless** option, select **Disabled.**

   f) In the **Remote Management Access** section, verify that **Remote Management** is disabled.

   g) At the bottom of the web page, select **Save Settings**.

   h) On the **Your settings have been successfully saved** page, select **Continue**.

   i) Close **Internet Explorer**.

5. Greene City Interiors has installed a wireless network. There are ceiling dome transmitters at various locations in your building, and you have upgraded the users' laptops with wireless NICs. There is one wireless antenna to serve the warehouse area. The coverage area is adequate; however, users in the warehouse report intermittent connectivity problems as they move in and out of the tall metal storage shelving. What problem do you suspect?

6. A user on your network uses a tablet computer to keep track of her calendar and contact list. She synchronizes the tablet data frequently with her laptop computer via the systems' infrared ports. She complains that she intermittently loses the infrared connection between the two devices. You visit her workstation and find that she is seated in close proximity to a large window. What problem do you suspect?

Summary

In this lesson, you identified unbounded network media. By understanding the various advantages and limitations of wireless networks, you will be better able to implement them in your network environments.

In your opinion, what are the primary considerations for implementing a wireless network?

What problems have you encountered when setting up a wireless network?

 Note: Check your LogicalCHOICE Course screen for opportunities to interact with your classmates, peers, and the larger LogicalCHOICE online community about the topics covered in this course or other topics you are interested in. From the Course screen you can also access available resources for a more continuous learning experience.

4 Network Implementations

Lesson Time: 3 hours

Lesson Objectives

In this lesson, you will identify the major types of network implementations. You will:

- Describe the primary physical network topologies.

- Describe the primary logical network topologies.

- Identify the components of an Ethernet network implementation.

- Describe the characteristics and functions of network devices.

- Identify characteristics and functions of VLANs.

Lesson Introduction

In the previous lessons, you identified bounded and unbounded network media. All of these media are used in different types of network implementations. In this lesson, you will identify the major types of network implementations.

Networking is a fundamental aspect of all computer infrastructure. The ability to link and communicate between clients, servers, and mainframes is vital for the dissemination of voice and data traffic. As a network engineer, you will need to handle different types of networks. You need to be aware of the characteristics of the different types of networks to implement the most suitable network so that its performance is fully optimized.

TOPIC A

Physical Network Topologies

Now you are ready to see how network components can combine to create large structural units called network topologies. In this topic, you will identify the primary physical network topologies.

Network topologies influence the flow of data through a network and the design of communication protocols to a large extent. Getting to know the different topologies is essential to designing or troubleshooting a network. Knowledge of the physical topology of a network is critical for you to be able to successfully execute many network management tasks, including fault monitoring and problem isolation. No matter what your role, you will need to understand the characteristics of the network topology you are working with, and identify how the topology affects network performance and troubleshooting.

Physical vs. Logical Topologies

A *physical topology* describes a network's physical wiring layout or shape, whereas a *logical topology* describes the paths through which data moves. The physical and logical topologies can be different for a network. Common physical topologies include a bus, ring, star, and mesh.

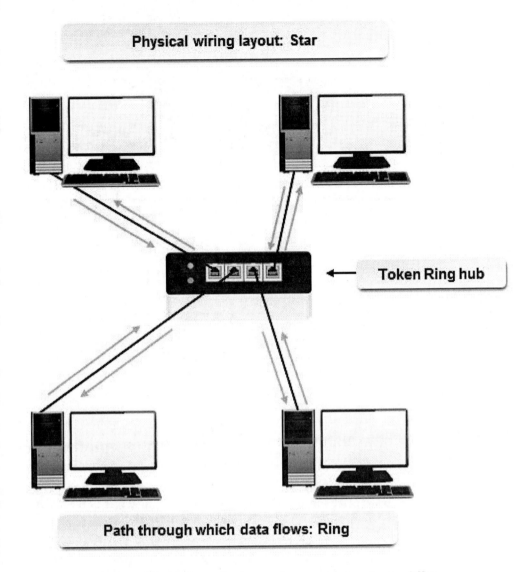

Physical wiring layout: Star

Token Ring hub

Path through which data flows: Ring

Figure 4–1: Physical and logical topologies on the same network can differ.

Physical Bus Topology

A *physical bus topology* is a network topology in which the nodes are arranged in a linear format, and a T-connector connects each node directly to the network cable. The cable is called the bus and serves as a single communication channel. Signals can reflect off the ends of the cable, so you must install 50 ohm *terminators* to prevent this reflection. Attaching a terminator at both ends of the network cable prevents a condition called *signal bounce*, in which signals endlessly move from one end of the wire to the other. Terminators impede or absorb signals so they cannot reflect onto the wire.

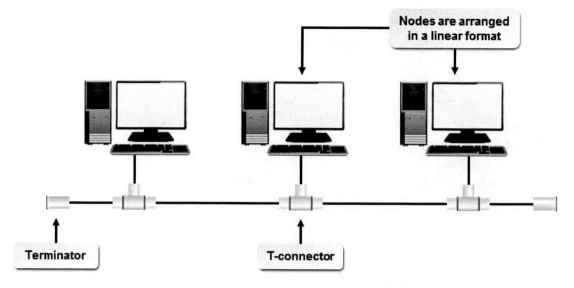

Figure 4–2: A physical bus topology.

 Note: You must ground a bus network on one end to reduce static electricity.

Using 10BASE-2 coaxial cable (ThinNet) to connect computers is a classic example of a physical bus topology.

The bus topology has a few disadvantages. A bus network:

- Is easy to implement but can be unreliable, because the entire bus fails if there is a break in the network cable.
- Transmits data more slowly than the other topologies, as only two nodes can communicate at any time.

On a bus, as all communication takes place through the same path, only a single pair of terminals can communicate at a time. Data is transmitted on a bus in a sequence of steps:

1. Each node on a bus listens passively to the channel until it receives a signal. The data signal passes by every node, but not through the node.
2. The node transmits data when the bus is free, and the allocation of the channel to nodes is done on a first-come, first-served basis.
3. If two nodes try to transmit data at exactly the same time, a collision occurs on the wire. A 32-bit jam signal is sent to indicate that a collision has occurred. Each node then waits a random period of time before retransmission in order to avoid further collisions.
4. The transmission fills the entire media of the bus, moving nearly instantaneously along the entire pathway. It passes the network interface card of all nodes. Each node examines the destination MAC address to determine whether or not the transmission is intended for it, and whether or not it should process the transmission.
5. The destination node picks up the transmission.
6. If none of the nodes accept the transmitted data, such as in the case of the destination node being switched off, the data packet is absorbed by the terminator.

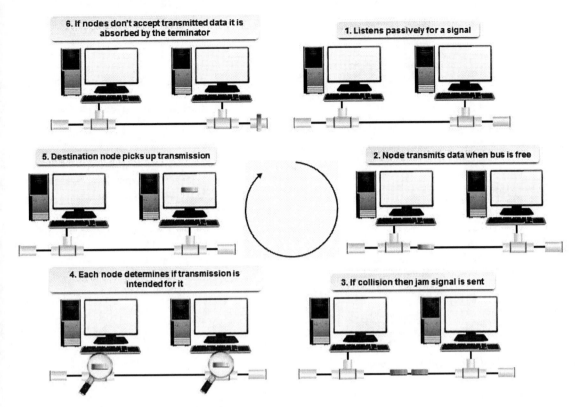

Figure 4-3: Data transmission on a bus.

Termination

Termination is the application of a resistor or other device to the end of a cable. Adding a terminator ensures that the ends of the cable do not represent an abrupt change in impedance, causing signal reflections and noise. The electrical characteristics of a terminator must match those of the cable and other components.

 Note: In legacy networking equipment, you had to install terminators yourself. They are now typically built into the networking devices you use.

Generally, you must match the impedance of all devices and cables to achieve proper signal flow. Signals can reflect off the points where impedance changes, such as at a connector between devices or cable segments of mismatched impedance. Signals flow smoothly across connections when impedances match.

 Note: A cable's impedance is typically marked on its outer jacket.

Physical Ring Topology

A *physical ring topology* is a network topology in which each node is connected to the two nearest nodes: the upstream and downstream neighbors. The flow of data in a ring network is unidirectional to avoid collisions. All nodes in the network are connected to form a circle. There is no central connecting device to control network traffic, and each node handles all data packets that pass through it. Data moves in one direction through each node that scans data packets, accepts packets destined for it, and forwards packets destined for another node.

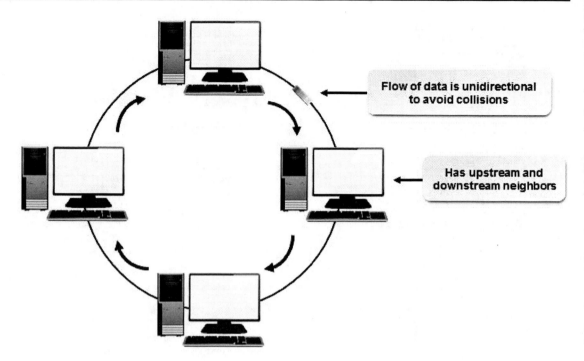

Figure 4-4: A physical ring topology.

Each node in the ring topology acts as a repeater and boosts the signal when it retransmits the data packet. This boost in the signal ensures that the signal quality is high. Ring topologies are potentially unreliable, as the failure of a single node can bring down the entire network.

A variant of the ring topology is the *dual ring topology,* which allows the use of two counter-rotating rings, in which each ring carries data in the opposite direction. Dual ring configurations are faster, as data can be sent through the shortest path between a sender and the receiver. It is a more reliable topology because in case of a breakage in the inner or outer ring, the two nodes on either side of the break connect the two rings together, essentially closing the loop into a single ring. The topology is thus automatically reconfigured to a single-ring data flow, reducing downtime on the network.

Physical Star Topology

A *physical star topology* is a network topology that uses a central connectivity device, such as a switch, with individual physical connections to each node. The individual nodes send data to the connectivity device, and the device then forwards data to the appropriate destination node. In legacy implementations, hubs were also used in physical star topologies, where nodes sent data to the hub, which simply passed it through to all attached nodes. Star topologies are reliable and easy to maintain, as a single failed node does not bring down the whole network. However, if the central connectivity device fails, the entire network fails.

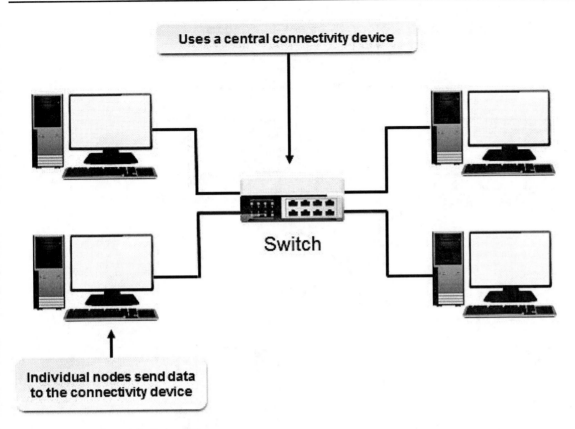

Figure 4-5: A physical star topology.

Although star topologies are extremely common in client/server networks, a mainframe-based computing system is also a classic example of a physical star topology. Each node has a connection to the mainframe computer and is not aware of other nodes on the network.

Physical Mesh Topology

A *physical mesh topology* is a network topology in which each node is directly connected to every other node, similar to the physical point-to-point topology. This configuration allows each node to communicate with multiple nodes at the same time. All nodes have dedicated links with other nodes, so there is no congestion on the network and data travels very fast. Because no node can be isolated from the network, this topology is extremely reliable. It is also difficult to implement and maintain because the number of connections increases exponentially with the number of nodes. Mesh topologies typically provide reliable communications between independent networks.

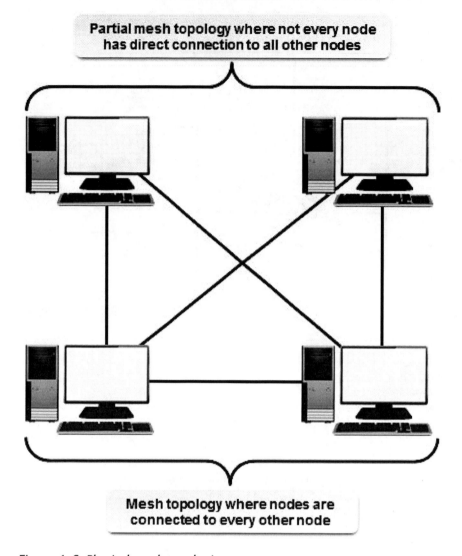

Partial mesh topology where not every node has direct connection to all other nodes

Mesh topology where nodes are connected to every other node

Figure 4-6: Physical mesh topologies.

When all nodes are connected to all nodes, this is referred to as full mesh.

The *partial mesh* topology is a variation of the mesh topology in which only a few nodes have direct links with all the other nodes. This differentiates it from the full mesh topology where all nodes have direct links with others. It is less complex, less expensive, and contains fewer redundancies than a full mesh topology. A partial mesh topology is also sometimes referred to as a redundant star.

The connections between major divisions of the Internet use a mesh topology, making the Internet the largest partial mesh network in the world. A wireless ad-hoc network between multiple laptops is also an example of a physical mesh. In addition, a frame relay or asynchronous transfer mode (ATM) cloud may also have a physical full mesh or partial mesh topology.

Hybrid Topologies

A *hybrid topology* is any topology that exhibits the characteristics of more than one standard topology. Each section of the network follows the rules of its own topology. Hybrid topologies can be complex to maintain because they typically incorporate a wide range of technologies. Most large networks consist of several smaller subnetworks, and each subnetwork may have a different topology.

Figure 4–7: The star bus topology connects star networks to a bus.

 Note: Hybrid topologies are typically not designed as such. They usually arise when administrators connect existing network implementations independently by using different topologies.

Common types of hybrid topologies are described in the following table.

Hybrid Topology	Formed By
Star-bus	Linking the central nodes of several star networks by using a common bus, or network backbone. Inside each subnetwork, data flows as it would on a star network, and each of these star networks is treated as a node on the larger bus network. To move data from one subnetwork to another, it must be placed on the common bus. Star-bus topologies are commonly found in local area networks (LANs).
Extended-star (or star-of-stars)	Connecting the central nodes of two or more star networks with a new common node. To move data from one subnetwork to another, it must be forwarded through the new common node. Extended star topologies are commonly found in LANs.
Star-ring	Connecting the central nodes of multiple star networks in a ring. The data flow between different subnetworks is through this ring. Data is sent in a circular pattern around the star configuration. Star-ring topologies are commonly found in metropolitan area networks (MANs).

ACTIVITY 4–1
Identifying Physical Network Topologies

Scenario

The network administrator at Greene City Interiors wants you to identify different physical network topologies by observing how the networks are connected.

1. Identify the physical network topology depicted in the graphic.

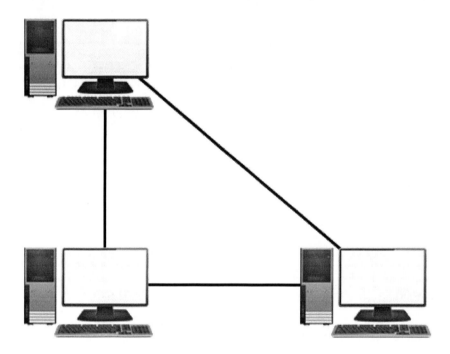

- ○ Star
- ○ Bus
- ○ Mesh
- ○ Ring

2. Identify the physical network topology depicted in the graphic.

- ○ Mesh
- ○ Bus
- ○ Star
- ○ Hybrid

3. Identify the physical network topology depicted in the graphic.

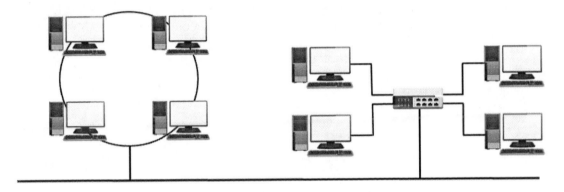

- ○ Mesh
- ○ Bus
- ○ Star
- ○ Hybrid

TOPIC B

Logical Network Topologies

In the last topic, you identified physical network topologies. The path of data flow does not always correspond to the physical wiring layout of the network, so you also need to consider how logical data paths work. In this topic, you will identify logical network topologies.

You may be faced with a situation in which you need to troubleshoot a logical segment of your network and ensure the flow of data between two links when the physical topology seems just fine. Logical network topologies provide information that physical topologies do not provide, such as the data transmission path between a sender and a receiver and the different places where this path converges or diverges. This information will also help you plan transmission links and resource sharing capabilities and identify network routes while troubleshooting.

Logical Bus Topology

A *logical bus topology* is a network topology in which nodes receive the data transmitted all at the same time, regardless of the physical wiring layout of the network. A common implementation is physical star-logical bus. In this topology, even though nodes connect to a central switch and resemble a star, data appears to flow in a single, continuous stream from the sending node to all other nodes through the switch. Because the transmission medium is shared, only one node can transmit at a time.

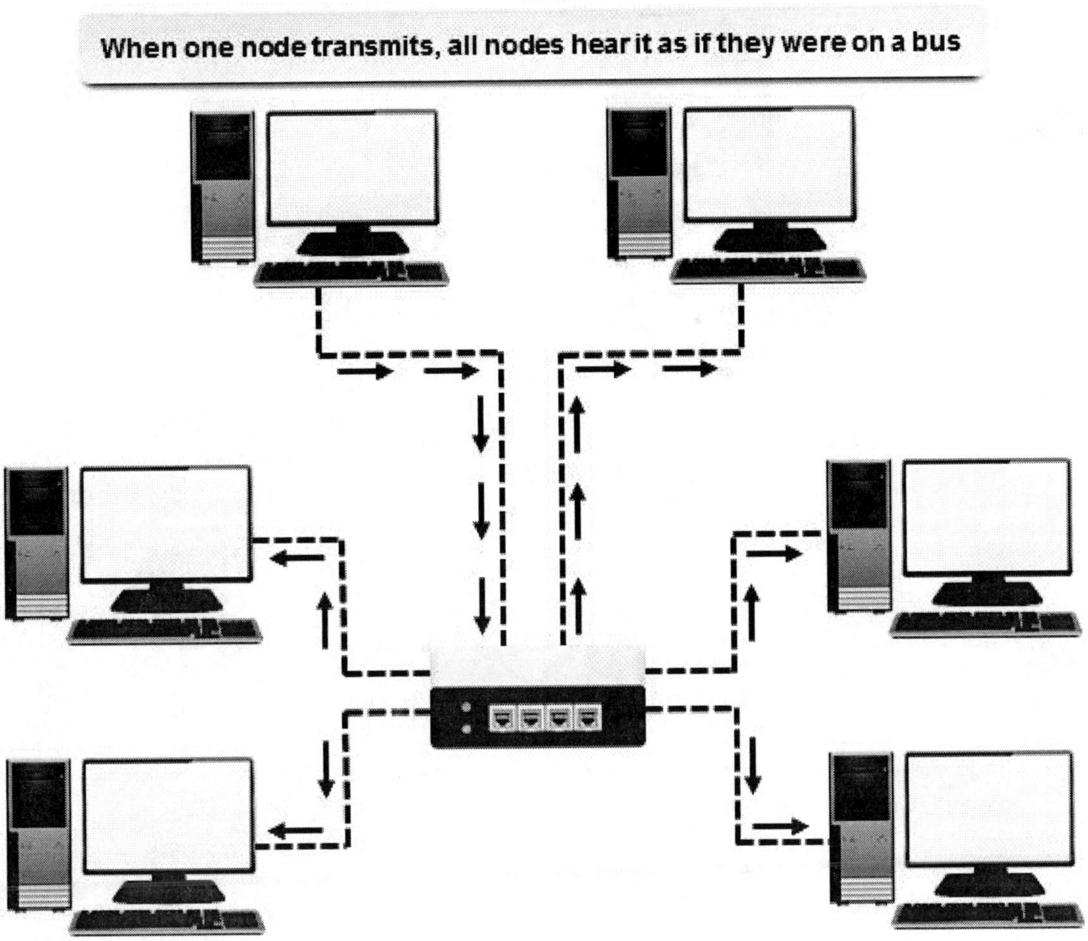

When one node transmits, all nodes hear it as if they were on a bus

Figure 4–8: A logical bus topology.

A typical example of the logical bus topology is when several workstations are connected to a hub.

Logical Ring Topology

A *logical ring topology* is a network topology in which each node receives data only from its upstream neighbor and retransmits data only to its downstream neighbor, regardless of the physical layout of the network. In a LAN, the logical ring topology has generally been implemented as a physical star (physical star-logical ring). In the days of token ring, a central hub (multistation access unit or MSAU) would connect the devices in a star shape, but the wiring was such that the electrical path was actually a never-ending loop, passing from the hub to a node, back to the hub, to another node, back to the hub, and so forth.

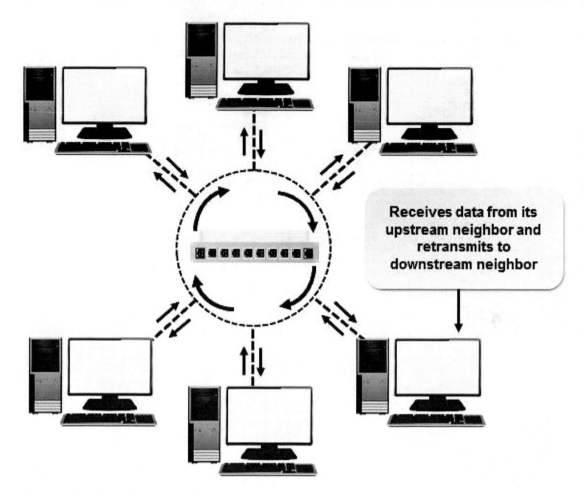

Receives data from its upstream neighbor and retransmits to downstream neighbor

Figure 4–9: A logical ring topology.

In today's networks, a logical ring is typically not implemented in LANs.

Logical Star Topology

The implementation of a *logical star topology* on a different physical topology is less common than a logical ring or a logical bus, but the logical star topology running on a physical star topology is the single most common implementation in modern LANs. After that, logical star topologies are often implemented on a physical bus topology (physical bus-logical star).

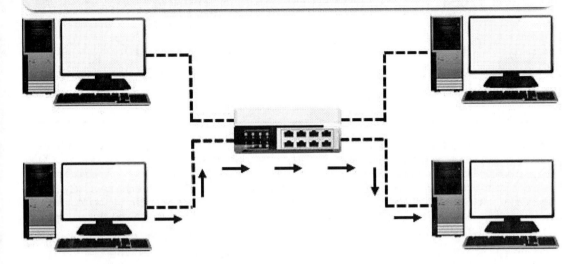

Figure 4-10: A switch managing signaling between nodes in a logical star topology.

In a physical bus-logical star topology, although all nodes are wired onto the same bus cable, a central device polls each node to see if it needs to transmit data. The central device also controls how long a node has access to the cable. A multiplexer (mux) manages individual signals and enables them to share the media.

ACTIVITY 4-2
Identifying Logical Network Topologies

Scenario

The network administrator at Greene City Interiors describes different logical topology scenarios to you and asks you configuration questions based on them.

---

1. One of your servers is suffering from intermittent poor performance. As the CPU, RAM, and disk utilization are normal, you suspect it is the target of a network-based hacking attack. You would like to place a sniffer with a protocol analyzer next to the server's network interface to monitor traffic. The server is connected to an Ethernet switch, but the switch does not have port mirroring capability. You also do not want to add to the server's load by running the sniffer on the server itself. What logical network topology do you need to place a sniffer next to the server, and how would you implement it?

   ○ You need to configure the server and the sniffer in a logical bus. Unplug the server from its switch port, plug a hub in its place, and then plug both the switch and the sniffer into the hub.

   ○ You need to configure the server and the sniffer in a logical star. Plug the sniffer into the switch port that is next to the server's switch port.

   ○ You need to configure the server and the sniffer in a logical ring. Unplug the server from the switch port, plug a hub into the switch, and then plug the server and the sniffer into the token ring hub.

2. Briefly explain the thought process you used to arrive at the answer in the preceding question.

3. You are part of a team helping to troubleshoot and upgrade the network at an older facility. Until the new equipment arrives, you need to restore connectivity to some old mini mainframe computers and other workstations. None of the computers can communicate with any other computer. All of the computers connect to a central hub device. You inspected the hub and noticed that the chassis has no place for status lights, no power switch, and does not appear to have any way to plug into power. All of the connectors, which are unusually large, seem to be firmly plugged into the hub. Meanwhile, your colleague discovered a frayed-looking connector at the back of one of the computers. You are able to bring the network back up by holding the connector in place, though as soon as you let go the network goes down again. You are wondering how the failure of a single node could impact the entire network. What do you think is the problem?

   ○ Although the network is hub and spoke (physical star), it is a logical bus. The break at the end of one of the spokes is causing reflections in the signal, thus bringing the network down.

   ○ Although the network is a hub and spoke (physical star), it is also a logical star. The break at the end of one of the spokes is disrupting network continuity for all nodes.

   ○ Although the network is a hub and spoke (physical star), it is a logical ring. The broken connector at one computer is breaking the ring, thus taking the network down. When you manually hold the connector in place, the wiring reconnects and the ring resumes conducting traffic.

4. Briefly explain the thought process you used to arrive at the answer in the preceding question.

5. You are troubleshooting intermittent connectivity in a departmental network. In the entire department, two devices continue to have connectivity problems. All of the other devices seem to be fine. Each device is plugged into a wall jack by using a CAT5 cable with RJ-45 connectors. Because the wiring is in the wall, you are unable to determine where the wiring leads to. You suspect that a locked door in the hallway leads to a wiring closet. While you are waiting for maintenance to arrive and unlock the door, your assistant theorizes that the problem is that the network is in a ring topology, that there is a break somewhere in the cable, and the reason why the two nodes cannot connect is that they exist on either side of the break. Do you agree with this theory?

   ○   No, you disagree. Because only two nodes are affected, your idea is that this is a logical star, keeping the problem limited to those nodes only.

   ○   Yes, you agree. Since only two nodes are affected, you agree that this must be a logical ring, and that the two affected nodes must be on either side of the break.

   ○   No, you disagree. Because only two nodes are affected, you think that they must be at the far end of a logical bus, and that the break in the cabling is between them and the rest of the network.

6. Briefly explain the thought process you used to arrive at the answer in the preceding question.

TOPIC C

Ethernet Networks

In the previous topics, you identified physical and logical network topologies. Next, you will examine the most common implementation of network topologies. In this topic, you will identify the components used in an Ethernet network implementation.

Ethernet continues to dominate the wired LAN scenario, and is known for its simplicity and wide applicability. Its popularity is largely based on its ease of installation and upgradability. Large and small networks use Ethernet technology to provide both backbone and end-user services. Due to the wide deployment of Ethernet today, you will undoubtedly be required to manage and troubleshoot Ethernet networks.

NICs

A *network interface card (NIC),* also called a network adapter or network card, is a device that serves as an interface between a network node and the network. To connect to a network, whether wired or wireless, a node must have a NIC installed. NICs can be:

- Built into the motherboard of a computer or other network device.
- Internally connected to a computer by using one of the expansion slots on the computer's motherboard.
- Externally connected to a computer or other network device by using a USB, CompactFlash®, or FireWire® port.

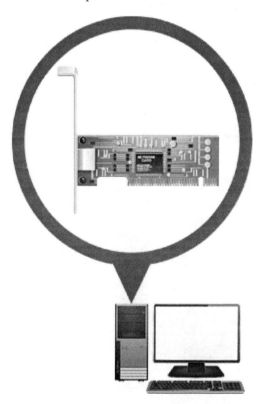

Figure 4-11: A NIC on a computer.

Most NICs can operate in full duplex or half duplex mode. There is also an auto negotiation feature, where devices perform self-configuration to achieve the best possible mode of operation across a link.

- A full duplex NIC enables a device to send and receive data simultaneously using separate channels or wire pairs for transmitting and receiving. If the NIC is connected to a switch that is also in full duplex mode, it can transmit and receive at maximum speed. This means that a 100-MB full duplex connection can carry 200 MB of data at any time. In addition, because a switch forms a miniature network between a node and itself (with no other nodes involved), there is no chance of data collision.

 Note: While an eight-port 100-MB switch in full duplex mode can theoretically carry 1,600 MB of data, in reality only high-end switches can deliver full throughput.

- A half duplex NIC can send or receive data, but not both, at any one time.

In many cases, the NIC is configured to use auto negotiation by default, but there are times when this is not the optimal configuration. If a NIC is set to auto negotiate duplex, and it is connected to a full duplex–only switch or router, the auto-negotiate port will negotiate to half duplex because the full duplex port does not send any negotiation signals. This will cause a duplex mismatch, which can severely affect performance.

 Access the Checklist tile on your LogicalCHOICE course screen for reference information and job aids on How to Install a NIC into an Expansion Slot.

Transceivers

A *transceiver* is a device that has both a transmitter and a receiver integrated into it and, as a result, can both send and receive data. Most modern transceivers are built into the network card. In networking, the transceiver supports the NIC in allowing data transmission through the medium.

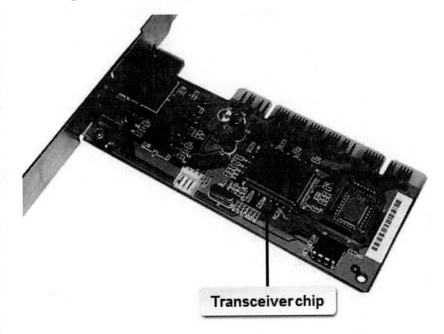

Figure 4-12: A transceiver on a network card.

A *gigabit interface converter (GBIC)* is a transceiver used to convert electrical signals into optical signals and vice versa. It is used as an interface for high-speed networking and to upgrade the network, without needing to replace all components in the motherboards. For instance, if different optical technologies are used, GBICs can be used to specifically configure that link on the network. Based on the wavelength of laser light generated within the GBIC generator, GBICs can be categorized into short-wave GBICs and long-wave GBICs. The short-wave GBIC is used for connecting devices that are between 0.5 meters and 500 meters apart. Meanwhile, the long-wave GBIC is used for connecting devices that are between 2 meters and 6 miles apart.

A *small form factor pluggable (SFP)* transceiver is most commonly used in 2 Gbps and 4 Gbps Fibre Channel components to interconvert electrical signals and optical signals. SFPs are similar to GBICs in their architecture, but they allow higher port density than GBICs.

A *MAC transceiver*, also known as an Ethernet transceiver or AUI-to-Ethernet transceiver, is a passive device that connects a 15-pin AUI Ethernet connector to an RJ-45 Ethernet connector. It was used as an adapter to connect twisted pair to the old *attachment unit interface (AUI)* Ethernet ports. This transceiver helped extend the life of the popular Cisco 2500 series router that had only an AUI Ethernet port.

IEEE 802.x Standards

The *802.x standards* are a family of networking standards developed by the IEEE in 1980 to address the rapid developments in networking technology. The 802.x standards are divided into subcategories to address different networking requirements.

The more popular groups of standards are described in the following table.

IEEE Standard	Description
802.2	The *802.2 standard* was developed to address the need for MAC-sub-layer addressing in switches. The 802.2 standard specifies the frame size and transmission rate. Frames can be sent over Ethernet and *Token ring* networks by using either copper or fiber media.
802.3	The original Ethernet network implementation was developed by Xerox® in the 1970s. The IEEE issued the *802.3 standard* to standardize Ethernet and expand it to include a wide range of cable media. In addition to the media type, 802.3 also specifies transmission speeds and the signaling method. This type of network is most efficient in a physical star-logical bus topology.
802.3af	The *802.3af standard* describes Power over Ethernet (PoE) technology, which enables networks to deliver electrical power and standard data over Ethernet cabling. Up to 15.4 W of DC power can be supplied to each powered device, with 12.95 W being ensured to the powered device due to power dissipation during delivery.
802.3at	The *802.3at standard* is an update to 802.3af and describes Power over Ethernet Plus (PoE+) technology, which enables networks to deliver electrical power and standard data over Ethernet cabling. With PoE+, up to 30 W of power can be supplied to each powered device, with 25.5 W being assured to the powered device.
802.11	The *802.11 standard* describes Layer 1 and Layer 2 specifications for wireless LANs in the 2.4-, 3.6-, 5-, and 60-GHz frequency bands. Numerous amendments to the standards have been adopted as Wi-Fi technology has evolved.

Ethernet (IEEE 802.3)

Ethernet is a set of networking technologies and media access methods specified for LANs. IEEE has defined the 802.3 specifications and standards for Ethernet implementations. Ethernet enables computers to communicate over small distances using a wired medium. Ethernet has evolved as the most widespread technology for wired LANs. Most Ethernet networks use twisted pair cables at the access layer (where computers plug in) and either high-speed twisted pair or fiber optic cable for the network backbone.

The original 802.3 specification for Ethernet included both OSI Layer 1 and Layer 2 protocols. In today's networks, however, we tend to associate Ethernet only with Layer 2, because Ethernet can now be carried on a variety of physical media and is not restricted to only thick or thin coaxial cable.

Traditional Ethernet networks used a shared medium, as they were all connected to the same bus and competed for bandwidth by using the CSMA/CD media access control (MAC) method. Modern Ethernet implementations are considered to be *switched Ethernet*, where there are one or more direct point-to-point connections between hosts or network segments. The switch enables each device to use the full bandwidth of the medium. In switched Ethernet, switches read the destination Layer 2 (MAC) address and forward the frame only to the destination node. A 24-port switch can, in theory, handle 12 pairs of conversations simultaneously.

ThinNet and ThickNet

Although today's networks commonly use twisted pair cabling in their Ethernet implementations, you might still encounter some coaxial cables. The following table describes the most common coaxial cables used in Ethernet networking.

Name	Description
ThinNet	*ThinNet* is the name given to Ethernet networking that uses RG58/U or RG58A/U cabling. ThinNet is wired in a bus configuration where segments can be up to 185 meters (607 feet) long. ThinNet connections are made with a BNC connector. Devices connect to the network with T-connectors, and each end of the cable must be terminated with a 50-ohm resistor.
ThickNet	*ThickNet* is the name given to Ethernet networking that uses RG8 cabling. ThickNet is not commonly used today, but was popular as a network backbone because ThickNet segments can be up to 500 meters (or 1,640 feet) long.
	Networking devices are not directly connected to the ThickNet cable. Instead, transceivers are connected to the cable with a *vampire tap*, which is a clamshell-like device that pierces an RG8 cable, to make contact with its conductors. This permits a networking device to connect to the ThickNet segment.
	Transceivers can be installed as needed at intervals of 2.5 meters along the length of the cable. The networking device connects to the transceiver via a 15-pin AUI connector and a short section of cable called a drop cable. An AUI connector is also known as a DIX connector, which gets its name from the three companies that invented it: Digital Equipment Corporation (DEC), Intel, and Xerox.
	Connections between ThickNet segments are made with a screw-type connector called an N-connector. ThickNet segments must be terminated with a 50-ohm resistor.

Ethernet Frames

An *Ethernet frame* is a data packet that has been encoded at the Data Link layer (Layer 2) for transmission from one node to another on an Ethernet network. The basic Ethernet frame contains seven fields.

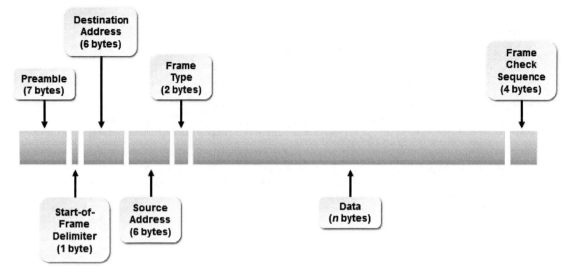

Figure 4-13: Fields in an Ethernet frame.

Ethernet Frame Field	Description
Preamble (PRE)	(7 bytes) A pattern of ones and zeros used to signal the start of the frame and provide synchronization and timing information. The preamble notifies all nodes that there is data to follow.
Start-of-Frame Delimiter (SFD)	(1 byte) The SFD identifies the beginning of the data field.
Destination Address (DA)	(6 bytes) This is the MAC address of the computer to which the frame is being transmitted; it can be a unicast, multicast, or broadcast address.
Source Address (SA)	(6 bytes) This is the MAC address of the computer transmitting data—the SA is always a unicast address.
Frame type	(2 bytes) This is the length of the entire Ethernet frame in bytes, or the frame type ID of the frame. This field can hold a value between 0 and 65,534, but the maximum value is usually less than 1,500.
Data	(*n* bytes) The payload of the frame (or the information being sent). It must be a minimum of 46 bytes long and can be a maximum of 1,500 bytes. If the length of data is less than 46 bytes, the data field must be extended by adding a filler to increase the length to a minimum of 46 bytes.
Frame Check Sequence (FCS)	(4 bytes) The FCS checks the frame by using a 32-bit cyclic redundancy check (CRC) value. The FCS allows the receiving device to detect errors in the Ethernet frame and reject it if it appears damaged.

MAC Addresses

A *MAC address*, also called a physical address, is a unique, hardware-level address assigned to every networking device by its manufacturer. MAC addresses are 6 bytes long. The first 3 bytes uniquely identify the manufacturer and are referred to as the *organizationally unique identifier (OUI)*. The remaining 3 bytes identify the device itself and are known as the Universal LAN MAC address. MAC addresses can be assigned manually.

 Note: The OUI may also be called the block ID and the universal LAN MAC address may also be called the device ID.

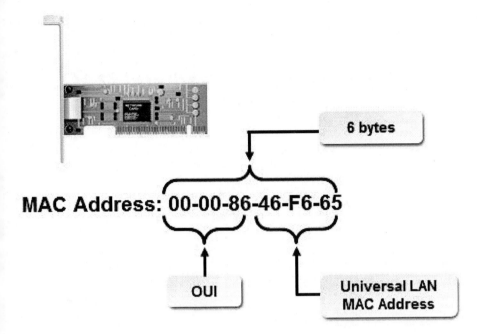

Figure 4-14: A MAC address.

MAC addresses use hexadecimal numeral system, a positional numeral system with a base of 16. It uses 16 distinct symbols, 0 through 9 to represent values 0 to 9, and A, B, C, D, E, F to represent values 10 to 15.

On a local network it is often necessary for one host to send messages to all the other hosts at the same time. This can be done by using broadcast messaging. A message can contain only one destination MAC address, but there is a unique MAC address that is recognized by all hosts. The broadcast MAC address is a 48-bit address made up of all ones. Because MAC addresses are in hexadecimal form, the broadcast MAC address notation is FF:FF:FF:FF:FF:FF. Each F in the hexadecimal notation represents four ones (1s) in the binary address.

ACTIVITY 4-3
Identifying the Local Network Card and MAC Address

Before You Begin
You are logged in as the administrator for the domain Child##.GCInteriors. Your password is P@ssw0rd12.

Scenario
At the Greene City Interiors branch office, you have been tasked by the network administrator to verify that each computer has a functioning network card and that each NIC has a unique MAC address.

---

1. Identify your physical NIC.
   a) Examine the back of your physical computer and locate the NIC.

    Note: If you are using a virtual machine, then examine the back of the host computer.

    Note: The NIC will have a network cable plugged into it, unless the computer is using a wireless connection.

   b) Observe the link light.

2. Verify your logon identity.
   a) Select **Start**.
   b) Select **Control Panel**.
   c) In the Control Panel window, select **User Accounts**.
   d) In the User Accounts window, in the right pane, select the **User Accounts** link.
   e) Select the **Manage User Accounts** link.
   f) Verify that your user name is selected and select **Properties**.
   g) Observe your domain user name in the title of the dialog box. Close the **CHILD##\Administrator Properties** and **User Accounts** dialog boxes.

3. Identify the network card type.
   a) In the User Accounts window, select the **Control Panel Home** link.
   b) In the Control Panel window, select the **Hardware** link.
   c) In the **Devices and Printers** section, select the **Device Manager** link.
   d) In the Device Manager window, in the objects list, double-click **Network adapters** to expand it.

    Note: Your card type might be different from the one displayed in the graphic of step 3e.

e) Identify the network card type and then close all open windows.

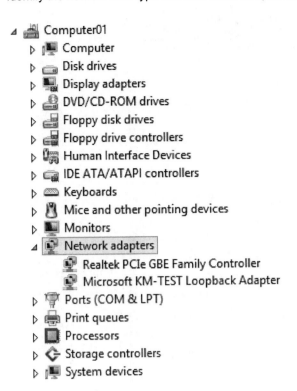

4. Open the **Ethernet Status** dialog box.
   a) Select **Start→Control Panel**.
   b) In the Control Panel window, select the **Network and Internet** link.
   c) In the Network and Internet window, select the **Network and Sharing Center** link.
   d) In the Network and Sharing Center window, in the left pane, select **Change adapter settings**.
   e) In the Network Connections window, right-click **Ethernet** and select **Status**.

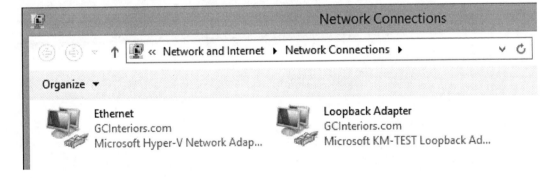

5. Identify your computer's MAC address.

a) In the **Ethernet Status** dialog box, select **Details.**

b) In the **Network Connection Details** dialog box, identify the **Physical Address** value to determine your computer's MAC address.

c) Close all open dialog boxes and windows.

The 10Base Standards

The *10Base standards* describe the media type and the speeds at which each type of media operates. The cable standard specification contains three components:

- A number indicating media speed
- The signal type (baseband or broadband)
- A code for either copper or fiber media

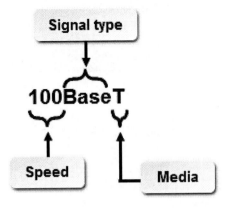

Figure 4-15: Name breakdown of the 10Base standard.

There are several standards and specifications for 10 Mbps Ethernet, the most common of which are described in the following table.

Standard	IEEE Specification	Medium	Distance (meters)
10Base-2	802.3a	ThinNet coax	185
10Base-5	802.3	ThickNet coax	500
10Base-T	802.3i	CAT5 UTP	100
10Base-F	802.3j	Fiber	2,000
10Base-FB	802.3j	Fiber	2,000
10Base-FL	802.3j	Fiber	2,000
10Base-FP	802.3j	Fiber	500

Fast Ethernet

Fast Ethernet is an Ethernet technology that can transmit data at speeds of 100 Mbps. It can use either coaxial cables or optical fibers. It is used as a backbone network to interconnect several LANs.

There are several standards and specifications for 100 Mbps or Fast Ethernet, the most common of which are described in the following table.

Standard	IEEE Specification	Medium	Distance (m)
100Base-T	802.3u	CAT5 UTP	100
100Base-T4	802.3u	CAT3, 4, or 5 UTP	100
100Base-TX	802.3u	CAT5 UTP or STP	100
100Base-FX	802.3u	Multimode or single mode fiber	412 (half duplex), 2,000 (full duplex), 15,000–20,000 (full duplex)

Gigabit Ethernet

Gigabit Ethernet is an Ethernet technology that can transmit data at speeds of 1,000 Mbps and primarily uses optical fibers for transmission. It can be used for distances ranging from 500 to 5,000 meters depending on the type of optical fiber used. The hardware required for Gigabit Ethernet is very expensive when compared with other types of Ethernet.

There are several standards and specifications for 1,000 Mbps or Gigabit Ethernet, the most common of which are described in the following table.

Standard	IEEE Specification	Medium	Distance (m)
1000Base-T	802.3ab	CAT5 CAT6 UTP	100
1000Base-TX	802.3ab	CAT6 UTP CAT7 UTP	100
1000Base-X	802.3z	Shielded Balanced coax	25 to 5,000
1000Base-CX	802.3z	Shielded Balanced coax	25
1000Base-SX	802.3z	Multimode fiber Wavelength: 850 nm	550 in practice (220 per specification)
1000Base-LX	802.3z	Single-mode fiber Wavelength: 1,300 nm	5,000
1000Base-LX	802.3z	Multimode fiber Wavelength: 1,300 nm	550
1000Base-LH	802.3z	Single-mode fiber Wavelength: 1,300 nm	10,000
1000Base-LH	802.3z	Multimode fiber Wavelength: 1,300 nm	550

10 Gigabit Ethernet

10 Gigabit Ethernet is currently the highest speed at which Ethernet operates. It can achieve speeds of 10 Gbps, which is 10 times faster than Gigabit Ethernet.

There are several standards and specifications for 10 Gbps or 10 Gigabit Ethernet, the most common of which are described in the following table.

Standard	IEEE Specification	Medium and Characteristics	Speed (in Gbps)	Distance (m)
10GBase-X	802.3ae	Multimode fiber Wavelength: 850 nm	9.9	65
10GBase-SR	802.3ae	Multimode fiber Wavelength: 850 nm	10.3	300
10GBase-SW	802.3ae	Multimode fiber Wavelength: 850 nm	9.9	300

Standard	IEEE Specification	Medium and Characteristics	Speed (in Gbps)	Distance (m)
10GBase-LR	802.3ae	Single mode fiber Wavelength: 1,310 nm Dark fiber	10.3	10,000
10GBase-LW	802.3ae	Single mode fiber Wavelength: 1,310 nm Synchronous Optical Network (SONET)	9.9	10,000
10GBase-ER	802.3ae	Single mode fiber Wavelength: 1,550 nm Dark fiber	10.3	40,000
10GBase-EW	802.3a	Single mode fiber Wavelength: 1,550 nm SONET	9.9	40,000
10GBase-T	802.3an	CAT5e, 6, or 7 UTP	10	100
10GBase-CX4	802.3ak	Four thin twin-axial cables	4×2.5	25

Note: SONET is described in detail later in the course.

Note: A nanometer (nm) is one trillionth of a meter (10^{-9}).

PoE

Power over Ethernet (PoE) uses the IEEE 802.3af standard for transferring both electrical power and data to remote devices over twisted-pair cable in an Ethernet network. This technology allows you to place devices such as network switches, Voice over IP (VoIP) phones, wireless access points, and cameras in locations where it would be inconvenient or impossible to run electrical power for the device. PoE provides up to 15.4 W of power and requires CAT5 or higher copper cable.

The updated IEEE 802.3at standard, also known as *Power over Ethernet+ (PoE+)*, provides up to 25.5 W of power per port and is backward compatible with all existing IEEE 802.3af devices. PoE+ allows for a broader range of devices to be powered such as:

- Cameras with pan/tilt/zoom capabilities
- Door controllers
- Point-of-sale terminals

Many switches provide PoE directly from their switch ports. This is used to power VoIP phones that are plugged into the switch. Another common implementation is a small device that plugs into AC power at the wall. This device is a special power supply that is inserted between the switch and the device that needs power (such as a camera, access point, or radio transmitter). It applies the needed DC power onto the Ethernet cable that leads to the connected device. This allows the camera or access point to be mounted on a pole or under the eave of a roof, where power is not normally available.

ACTIVITY 4-4
Describing Ethernet Networks

Scenario

Now that you have done an initial assessment of the Greene City Interiors branch office network, the network administrator wants to quiz you on Ethernet networks in general.

1. **Which of the following is an example of a proper MAC address?**

   ○ 192.168.1.1

   ○ FG:12:1A:N0:22:42

   ○ 00:25:1D:12:3E:48

   ○ 01:15:2E:10:2B:48:5A

2. **True or False? The 802.2 standard specifies the frame size and transmission rate of the Ethernet technology.**

   ☐ True

   ☐ False

3. **Which field of the Ethernet frame provides error detection information?**

   ○ PRE

   ○ FCS

   ○ SFD

   ○ SA

4. **Which is a Gigabit Ethernet standard?**

   ○ 100Base-T

   ○ 1000Base-LX

   ○ 10Base-F

   ○ 10000Base-P

TOPIC D

Network Devices

Before you start setting up a network, you need to be aware of the devices that you need on a network. In this topic, you will identify several types of network devices.

Switches and routers are fundamental network connectivity devices, so you are likely to encounter them in the network environments that you support. In addition, there are other types of networking devices that you might be asked to support. Understanding the capabilities of these devices will prepare you to support a wide variety of network environments.

Switches

A *switch* is a network device that acts as a common connecting point for various nodes or segments. Working at Layer 2 of the OSI model, switches make forwarding decisions based on Layer 2 (MAC) addresses. A switch listens for the MAC addresses of all the nodes plugged into it, and builds a table in memory that maps each MAC address with its associated port. When an Ethernet frame comes into the switch, the switch reads the destination MAC address from the header and consults its table to determine which port to repeat the frame out of. In this way, switches can keep conversations limited to only the nodes that are involved. Thus, a 24-port switch can have 12 pairs of conversations going on at the same time.

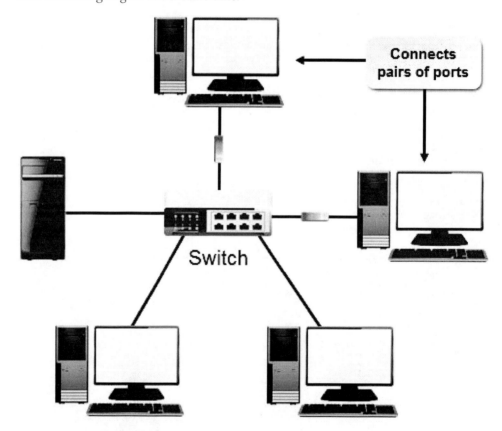

Figure 4-16: Switches in a network.

In order to perform switch management, you will need to supply the appropriate user name and password. This can be configured through the AAA configuration services. This sets up the authentication (identify user through login and password), authorization (access control), and accounting (logging information and forwarding it to a AAA server for auditing and reporting).

Configuration of the switch can be performed using a management console or a virtual terminal. Multiple administrators can be connected and configure the switch management features.

In-band management requires that software be loaded and in-band connectivity between the managed system and the device. It is less expensive to implement than out-of-band management, but is not as robust as it does not allow you to access the firmware or deal with boot problems. Out-of-band management uses a dedicated channel or port to manage the device. Out-of-band management enables you to access firmware and diagnose and correct boot issues.

You can assign the switch IP address through the switch setup program, or DHCP. Switches can be configured with the IP address of the next-hop router interface that is directly connected to the switch where a default gateway is being configured. The default gateway receives IP packets with unresolved destination IP addresses from the switch.

Unmanaged vs. Managed Switches

Unmanaged switches are devices that perform switching without user intervention. In other words, the functions of an unmanaged switch cannot be controlled. On the other hand, a managed switch provides complete control over how the device functions. It is typically assigned its own IP address and can be managed either directly through the use of a console cable, a Telnet or as a stage connection, or a web browser. Managed switches allow administrators to create virtual local area networks (VLANs) within the network.

Routers

A *router* is a networking device that connects multiple networks. Operating at Layer 3 of the OSI model, it makes forwarding decisions based on Layer 3 addresses, such as Internet Protocol (IP) addresses. When a packet comes in one of the router's interfaces, the router reads the destination IP address and forwards the packet out the appropriate interface. If necessary, it will strip off the packet's Layer 2 encapsulation and replace it with encapsulation that is appropriate for the outgoing transmission medium; for example, replacing Ethernet with Point-to-Point Protocol (PPP).

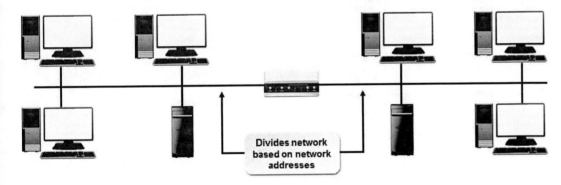

Figure 4-17: Router on a network.

Routers can work only with *routable protocols,* which are network protocols that provide separate network and node addresses. Examples of routable protocols include IP, Internetwork Packet eXchange (IPX), and AppleTalk.

 Note: Routers are often referred to as default gateways or hops.

 Note: For additional information, check out the LearnTO **Follow a Routing Path** presentation in the LearnTOs for this course on your LogicalCHOICE Course screen.

A rollover cable is often used to initially configure a network device such as a router or switch. Used most notably by Cisco Systems, the rollover cable connects the device's console port to a PC's serial port, enabling the administrator to use a PC to access the device's configuration console. Using a PC is necessary because routers and switches do not have any ports to plug in a monitor or keyboard.

Types of Routers

Routers can be classified into three main categories: access, distribution, and core.

Router Type	Description
Access routers	Routers used in *small office/home office (SOHO)* networks. They are located at customer sites and are inexpensive.
Distribution routers	Routers that collect data from multiple access routers and redistribute them to an enterprise location such as a company's headquarters. The routing capabilities of a distribution router are greater than those of access routers.
Core routers	Core routers are located at the center of network backbones. They are used to connect multiple distribution routers located in different buildings to the backbone.

Gateways

The word *gateway* is a generic term for any device or software that translates one network protocol to another. Working at OSI Layer 3 or above, gateways connect incompatible systems by taking an incoming packet, stripping off the lower-level encapsulation of the original protocol, and re-encapsulating the packet with a new protocol.

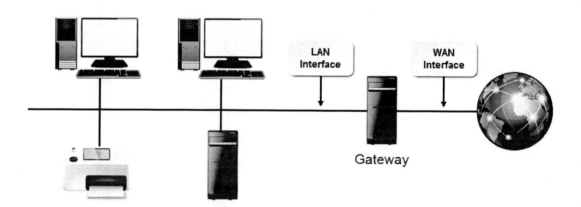

Figure 4-18: A gateway connecting a LAN to a WAN.

For example, a router can translate between Ethernet and token ring by stripping off the Layer 2 Ethernet encapsulation and replacing it with token ring encapsulation (also at Layer 2). Some gateways can strip off entire protocol stacks, leaving only the data payload, re-inserting the data into an entirely new packet. For example, a gateway could connect an IP network to an IPX network, stripping off the entire Transmission Control Protocol/Internet Protocol (TCP/IP) stack and replacing it with Internetwork Packet eXchange/Sequenced Packet eXchange (IPX/SPX).

 Note: It is important not to confuse a gateway with the default gateway in TCP/IP, which just forwards IP data packets.

Firewalls

A *firewall* is a software program or a hardware device or a combination of both that protects a device or network from unauthorized data by blocking unsolicited traffic. Firewalls generally are configured to block suspicious or unsolicited incoming traffic, but allow incoming traffic sent as a response to requests from internal hosts.

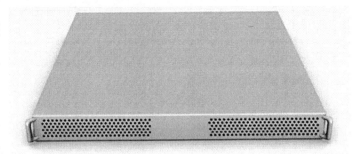

Figure 4-19: A hardware firewall.

Analog Modems

An *analog modem* is a device that modulates signals to encode digital information and demodulates signals to decode the transmitted information. A common type of modem is one that takes the digital data of a device and turns it into modulated electrical signal for transmission over telephone lines, which is then demodulated by another modem at the receiver side to recover the digital data. Though modems are not used much anymore, they can be used in locations where you have no other options for connections.

Figure 4-20: A USB analog modem.

Modems are generally classified by the amount of data they can send in a given unit of time, usually expressed in bits per second (bps). Modems can also be classified by their symbol rate, measured in baud. The baud unit denotes symbols per second, or the number of times per second the modem sends a new signal.

Carrier detect is used by a modem to let the computer know that a carrier is available to send and receive data. It is a control signal on an RS-232 serial cable between the computer and the modem. Carrier sense uses a handshake signal to let the computer know a carrier is available. It can be used to alert a UNIX host that a terminal is on before the host sends the logon screen to the terminal.

Network Controllers

Network controllers support large-scale interactive networks and communication between set-tops and application servers. A set-top is an information appliance device that contains a television-tuner input and displays output to a television set. They are used in cable television, satellite television, and over-the-air television systems. Network controllers are used in digital cable networks and enable such services as video-on-demand (VOD), catalog shopping, web browsing, and email. Network controllers act as a gateway between the IP network, which connects application servers, and the digital cable network, which connects set-tops.

Legacy Network Connectivity Devices

Due to technological advancements in the field of networking, some of the network connectivity devices have become outdated. Although some of them are no longer available as separate devices, their functionality is built into devices such as routers and switches.

Network Device	Description
Repeater	A *repeater* is a device that regenerates a signal to improve signal strength over transmission distances. By using repeaters, you can exceed the normal limitations on segment lengths imposed by various networking technologies.
	Repeaters are used frequently with coax media, such as cable TV, and were also deployed in networks that used coax cabling. On today's networks, repeaters are not commonly needed because other devices perform that function, but they are sometimes used in fiber networks. Wireless network repeaters and bridges are frequently used to extend the range of a wireless access point (WAP). Repeaters are not needed when you are using twisted pair because other devices act as repeaters.
Hub	A *hub*, or *multiport repeater*, is a networking device used to connect the nodes in a physical star topology network into a logical bus topology. A hub contains multiple ports to which the devices can be connected. When a data packet from the transmitting device arrives at a port, it is copied and transmitted to all other ports so that all other nodes receive the packets. However, only the node to which it is addressed reads and processes the data while all other nodes ignore it.
	Two common types of hubs used were passive and active.
	• A *passive hub* simply has its ports wired together physically. It connects devices plugged into it without the use of power. Acting like a patch panel, it merely makes the electrical connection without repeating or transmitting any frames. A token ring MSAU is an example of a passive hub.
	• An *active hub* is a true multiport repeater. It receives incoming frames and retransmits those frames out all ports. An Ethernet hub is an example of an active hub.
	In today's networks, hubs have been replaced by switches.
Bridge	A *bridge* is an older version of a switch. It has the same basic functionality of a switch, but it has fewer ports and is software based, rather than hardware based (like a modern switch).

Collision and Broadcast Domains

A *collision domain* is a network segment in which a collision can happen. In a collision domain, nodes contend for access to the same physical medium. This occurs on a logical bus, where the transmission of a single node is heard by all nodes. A single hub creates a single collision domain, because all nodes hear all transmissions from all other nodes. Likewise, a coax bus (which is both a physical and logical bus) is a single collision domain because the transmission of one node fills the entire medium, potentially colliding with other nodes that try to transmit.

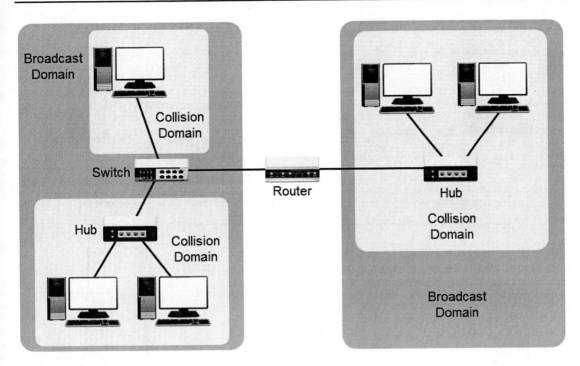

Figure 4-21: Collision domains on a network.

A switch, because of its microsegmentation, effectively eliminates collisions. Each port on the switch becomes its own collision domain because it will forward traffic to only the one recipient that is connected to it. A 24-port switch will effectively have 24 collision domains. And, if the switch ports are placed in full duplex mode, there will be no collisions of any sort because one pair of wires will be used for transmitting and another pair for receiving. Should a user plug a hub into a switch port, that port becomes a collision domain for all of the nodes plugged into the hub.

A *broadcast domain* is a network segment on which broadcasts occur. Microsegmentation will not stop broadcasts. Because switches flood broadcasts out all ports by default, a single switch, or any number of switches connected together, comprise a single broadcast domain. Routers block broadcasts by default, so they become the point at which the broadcast domain ends. If a router has two Ethernet interfaces, the network has two broadcast domains, one on either side of the router.

Switches and Network Performance

Switches make forwarding decisions based on Layer 2 (MAC) addresses. They do this through a process called *microsegmentation*, in which all nodes are logically separated from each other until there is a need to connect them. A switch listens to the transmissions of all of the nodes plugged into its ports. It learns the MAC addresses of each of the nodes and puts those MAC addresses into a table in memory. The table associates each MAC address with the port that it is plugged into. This table is called a MAC table or content addressable memory (CAM) table. When a node sends a frame to another node, the switch examines the Ethernet header for the destination MAC address. It refers to its MAC table to see which port it must forward the frame out of. It does not repeat the frame out any other port except the one that is required. In this way, conversations are limited to the nodes involved. If the switch receives a frame that has an unknown unicast (the address is not in the MAC table), multicast, or a broadcast destination MAC address, the switch will flood the frame out all ports except for the port that it received the frame from.

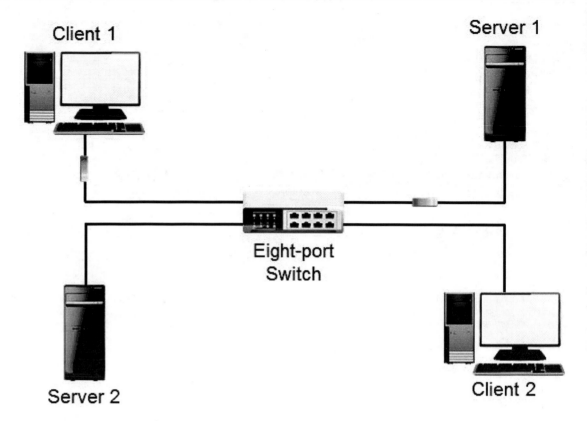

Figure 4-22: An eight-port switch connecting several devices.

Switching offers a dramatic performance improvement over hubs, which simply flood all frames out all ports regardless of which port the intended recipient is plugged into. Most switches allow you to configure the port speed and duplex settings to allow for greater control of the switch performance. The speed and duplex options are similar to those used for NICs, as seen in the previous topic.

A *managed switch,* also called an *intelligent switch,* is one that includes functions that enable you to monitor and configure its operation. Typically, you connect to the switch by using a web browser or via a dedicated management port.

Switch Types and Operating Modes

There are several types of switches available for your network.

Switch Type	Description
Multilayer	A multilayer switch performs both routing and switching. Also referred to as a Layer 3 switch or a Layer 2–3 switch, it can perform only limited routing functions and supports only Ethernet connections. Multilayer switches support the configuration of virtual local area networks (VLANs), which are discussed later in this topic.

Switch Type	Description
Content	A content switch supports load balancing among server groups and firewalls, and web cache and application redirection, in addition to other server management functions. Content switches are often referred to as 4–7 switches as they primarily work on Layers 4 and 7 of the OSI model. They make intelligent decisions about data by analyzing data packets in real time, and understanding the criticality and type of the request. Content switching supports load balancing for servers by directing traffic to assigned server groups that perform the function. This increases the response time for requests on the network. Although complex to implement, a content switch can perform many critical functions on a network and increase throughput.

Note: Basic or traditional switches operate at the Data Link layer of the OSI model (Layer 2). However, modern switches include more complex capabilities and can operate at the Network (Layer 3) and Transport layers (Layer 4). Higher layer switches are often called application or routing switches.

There are also several different operating modes for switches.

Switching Mode	Description
Cut-through	In cut-through switching, the switch forwards a data packet as soon as it receives it; no error checking or processing of the packet is performed. The switch performs the address table lookup immediately upon receiving the **Destination Address** field in the packet header. The first bits in a packet are sent out of the outbound port on a switch immediately after it receives the bits. The switch does not discard packets that are corrupt and fail error checking.
Fragment-free	In fragment-free switching, the switch scans the first 64 bytes of each packet for evidence of damage by a collision. If no damage is found, it forwards the packet; otherwise, it discards it. Fragment-free switching reduces network congestion by discarding fragments. It is similar to the cut-through switching method, but the switch waits to receive 64 bytes before it forwards the first bytes of the outgoing packet.
Store-and-forward	In store-and-forward switching, the switch calculates the cyclic redundancy check (CRC) value for the packet's data and compares it to the value included in the packet. If they match, the packet is forwarded. Otherwise, it is discarded. This is the slowest type of switching mode. The switch receives the entire frame before the first bit of the frame is forwarded. This allows the switch to inspect the *frame check sequence (FCS)* before forwarding the frame. FCS performs error checking on the trailer of an Ethernet frame.

STP (IEEE 802.1d)

The *Spanning Tree Protocol (STP)* is a Layer 2 protocol used to prevent switching loops. Whenever there are redundant paths between switches, where either two switches are connected using two different links or a ring of switches is connected to each other, a switching loop will occur. Because switches, by their nature, flood broadcasts and multicasts out all ports, the first Address Resolution Protocol (ARP) frame sent by a client trying to find a neighbor or a router will cause a Layer 2 broadcast storm. The ARP broadcast will go down one link to the next switch, which will send the broadcast back up the redundant link. This feedback loop will continue indefinitely until there is manual intervention by an administrator. It will cause network utilization to go to near maximum capacity, and the CPU utilization of the switches to jump to 80 percent. This makes the switched segment effectively unusable until the broadcast storm stops.

STP prevents switching loops and broadcast storms because switches use it to determine if there are any redundant links that may cause a loop. During the STP process, all switches in the same broadcast domain elect among them a root bridge (switch), which acts as a reference point for all of the other switches. A switch will then listen for special frames coming from the root to determine if those frames are coming into different ports. If the frames are coming into different ports, then there is a redundant link. The switch will then temporarily block its redundant link, thus eliminating the possibility of a loop. Should the first link fail for some reason, the switch will then unblock the redundant link so that there is connectivity on the network.

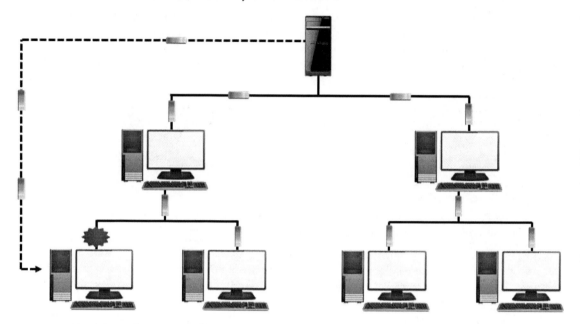

Figure 4-23: A loop-free path created by STP.

STP is an old protocol. Its full process to determine redundancy actually takes 50 seconds, which is considered too long by modern standards. It has since been replaced by the Rapid Spanning Tree Protocol (RSTP), IEEE 802.1w, which takes only 20 seconds to identify and rectify loops. There is also *Shortest Path Bridging (SPB)*, which is another replacement for STP. It is intended to simplify the creation and configuration of networks, while enabling multipath routing.

Switches on which the STP is enabled can be in one of five port states. The switches use Bridge Protocol Data Units (BPDUs) to exchange data between bridges and calculate route costs.

State	What Happens in This State
Blocking	User data is not sent or received. BPDU data is received, but the port only goes into another state if other links are unavailable and the spanning tree algorithm determines that the port should change to the forwarding state.
Listening	BPDUs are processed by the switch. It does not forward frames. It waits for information to determine if it should return to the blocked state. It does not update the MAC tables.
Learning	Learns source addresses from received frames. Addresses are added to the switching database. MAC address table is updated. No frames are forwarded.
Forwarding	Data is sent and received on a port in this state. BPDUs are monitored to determine if the port should return to the blocked state.

State	What Happens in This State
Disabled	A port that has been manually disabled.

 Access the Checklist tile on your LogicalCHOICE course screen for reference information and job aids on How to Install and Configure Network Devices.

ACTIVITY 4-5
Identifying Network Connectivity Devices

Scenario

The network administrator at Greene City Interiors wants to question you on the types of network devices you may have to work with at the branch office.

1. True or False? The main purpose of a switch is to optimize performance by providing users with higher bandwidth for transmission.

   ☐ True

   ☐ False

2. You need to connect multiple networks that use the same protocol. Which networking device would best meet your needs?

   ○ Router

   ○ Firewall

   ○ Gateway

   ○ Switch

3. Which of these network devices is a common connecting point for various nodes or segments?

   ○ Hub

   ○ Router

   ○ Gateway

   ○ Switch

4. True or False? A gateway subdivides a LAN into segments.

   ☐ True

   ☐ False

5. Which statements are valid for a gateway?

   ☐ It can connect networks with dissimilar protocols.

   ☐ It can be implemented in a router.

   ☐ It can be implemented only as a computer program.

   ☐ It can be implemented as hardware or software.

6. You have a logical bus network formed by connecting devices with twisted-pair cables. As you expect considerable traffic on the network, you need maximum transmission speeds between the nodes on the network. Which network device would you use to handle this requirement?

   ○ Router

   ○ Modem

   ○ Switch

   ○ Gateway

7. True or False? A collision domain associates itself only with a single broadcast domain.

☐ True

☐ False

8. What is used to prevent switching loops?

○ Gateway

○ Spanning Tree Protocol

○ Collision Domain

○ Switch

TOPIC E

VLANs

In the last topic, you identified several types of network connectivity devices, including switches. One of the primary benefits of using switches is to implement the concept of VLANs to segment a network. You will need to understand what VLANs are before you can properly implement them. In this topic, you will identify characteristics and functions of VLANs.

VLANs

A *virtual LAN (VLAN)* is a logical grouping of ports on the switch. An administrator determines which ports are grouped together. Nodes that plug into those ports can communicate only with nodes that belong to the same VLAN. They cannot communicate with nodes that belong to other VLANs. This effectively divides a physical switch into multiple, smaller logical switches.

When a VLAN port group is extended to another device, then tagging is used. Since communications between ports on two different switches travel via the uplink ports of each switch involved, every VLAN containing such ports must also contain the uplink port of each switch involved, and these ports must be tagged. This also applies to the default VLAN. The default VLAN is the default VLAN on a switch that is used unless another VLAN is created and specified. On a Cisco switch, that default VLAN is VLAN1, which cannot be removed or renamed. If the VLAN port group exists on only a single device, then those ports would be untagged. A Native VLAN is a VLAN that handles traffic that is not tagged.

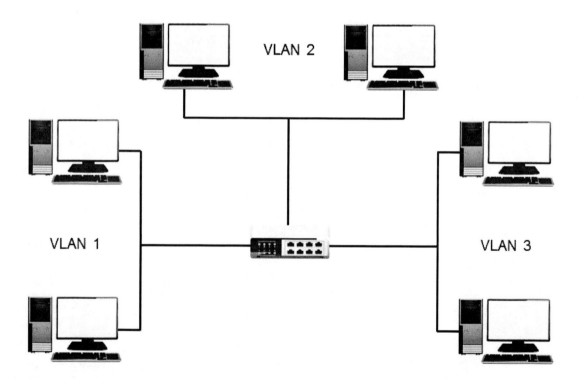

Figure 4–24: Example of three VLANs.

There are several common uses for VLANs, including:

- Traffic management, especially to reduce the impact of broadcasting, which is a natural and unavoidable part of Ethernet networking. If a node transmits a Layer 2 broadcast, such as an

ARP broadcast to discover some other node's MAC address, the switch will forward the frame only out the ports that belong to the same VLAN, rather than flood the broadcast out all ports.

- Security. Instead of buying a separate switch to isolate a group of computers, the administrator can put them in their own VLAN. In this way, each department can have its own VLAN, and not interfere with the traffic of other departments. For example, it is very common to have a separate VLAN just for guests who connect to a guest wireless access point (WAP) in the office lobby.

- To separate nodes based on traffic type and the need for Quality of Service. For example, it is commonplace to put all VoIP phones on their own VLAN, so there is no interference coming from nodes that are sending email or downloading large files on the same network. The switches and routers can then be configured to give the VoIP VLAN priority over other VLANs.

A great convenience of VLANs is that they can be extended beyond a single switch. Switches can connect to each other using trunk links that will carry all VLAN traffic from one switch to the next. In this way, a single VLAN can extend across an entire campus and not be limited to one switch or one building.

Ethernet-based MANs also use VLAN tagging to keep different customers' traffic separate.

VLAN Assignment

The use of VLANs must be carefully planned. Because the switch will not forward frames between VLANs, the administrator must determine which nodes should be grouped together into the same VLAN. If a node in one VLAN needs to communicate with a node in another VLAN, some other mechanism must be used to allow that communication. The common practice is to assign each VLAN its own set of IP addresses (IP subnet) and to have a router route packets between the VLANs.

Assigning ports to VLANs can be done in one of two ways: manually configuring each port on a switch to belong to a particular VLAN, or associating a VLAN with a node's MAC address. If the latter is done, a database must be configured ahead of time that maps the VLANs to the MAC addresses. The convenience of using this technique is that if a user moves freely between locations, plugging a device into different ports, the node always stays in the same VLAN.

Generally, a single port on the switch can belong to only one VLAN at a time. The exceptions are ports that have been configured to be trunk ports to connect to other switches, or ports that are configured for port mirroring.

Port Mirroring

Port mirroring is the practice of duplicating all traffic on one port in a switch to a second port, effectively sending a copy of all the data to the node connected to the second port. This is known as local port mirroring. Remote port mirroring implements port mirroring between multiple devices. In this case, the source port is on one device and the destination port is located on a different device. Port mirroring is useful as a diagnostic tool when you need to monitor all traffic going to a particular port or node with minimal impact on the network performance.

Trunking

Trunk links can be combined to increase bandwidth and reliability in a process called *trunking.*. This is also known as link aggregation, port bonding, port teaming, EtherChannel, and NIC bonding, among other names. Although a variety of manufacturer-implemented techniques exist, IEEE 802.1AX-2008 defines a standard for link aggregation. Within the IEEE specification, the Link Aggregation Control Protocol (LACP) provides a method to control the bundling of several physical ports together to form a single logical channel. LACP allows a network device to negotiate an automatic bundling of links by sending LACP packets to the peer. The primary purpose of link aggregation is to allow redundant links to combine their bandwidth together without causing spanning tree loops. Link aggregation is typically implemented between switches, although it can be implemented between a node and a switch.

Linking two 1-Gbps ports on a server to two 1-Gbps ports on a switch can result in 2 Gbps aggregate throughput. Depending on the implementation, this can result in a redundant connection in case one of the cables or ports fails. However, this still leaves the possibility of the entire switch failing, so some hardware vendors provide proprietary methods for trunking ports across two physically separate switches. Trunking can be used to connect a variety of network hardware, including switch-to-switch, server-to-switch, server-to-server, or switch-to-router.

IEEE 802.1q

Because trunk links carry all VLAN traffic, there must be some mechanism for identifying which frame belongs to which VLAN as it moves from switch to switch. IEEE 802.1q is the most commonly used trunk link protocol to address this issue. 802.1q inserts a special tag in the Ethernet header identifying the VLAN for that frame. The switch at the other end of the trunk link will read that tag and forward the frame to the appropriate VLAN.

A competitor to 802.1q is Cisco's inter-switch link (ISL). This protocol encapsulates an Ethernet frame into a proprietary format that identifies the VLAN. ISL is an older protocol. Most Cisco switches now use 802.1q.

VLAN Pooling

VLAN pooling is a mechanism whereby WAPs can choose among several different available VLANs to assign to incoming client connections. This strategy distributes and load-balances wireless client traffic among multiple VLANs so that no single network segment is overwhelmed by too many wireless client connections.

VTP

The *VLAN Trunking Protocol (VTP)* is the messaging protocol that switches use to update each other's VLAN databases. Developed by Cisco, it allows switches to quickly advertise to each other when a VLAN is created or deleted. This saves an administrator some manual labor. If the administrator wishes to extend a VLAN across several switches, he or she would have to manually configure each switch with the same VLANs. With VTP, this is done automatically.

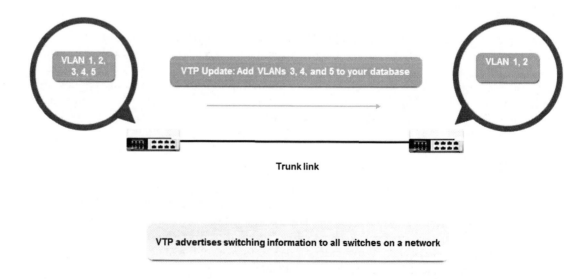

Figure 4-25: VTP advertises switching information to all switches on a network.

There are three VTP modes that a switch can use: server, client, and transparent.

- **Server mode:** This is the default mode for VTP on a switch. In the server mode, a switch can modify VLANs. This information is then transmitted to all the other switches that are configured to the same group using VTP.
- **Client mode:** In the client mode, a switch cannot modify VLANs but will receive configuration information from other switches.
- **Transparent mode:** In the transparent mode, a switch receives configuration messages from other switches but does not process them. Configuration changes to the VLAN are not transmitted to other switches in the group.

ACTIVITY 4–6
Describing VLANs

Scenario

The network administrator at Greene City Interiors informs you that the branch office has VLANs configured. They ask you questions to discover how much you know about VLANs.

---

1. **What are some of the common uses for employing VLANs?**

   ☐ Security

   ☐ Separate traffic types for Quality of Service

   ☐ Increase bandwidth and reliability

   ☐ Traffic management

2. **Why should VLANs be carefully planned before implementing them?**

3. **True or False? VLANs can be extended beyond a single switch.**

   ☐ True

   ☐ False

4. **When would you use port mirroring?**

Summary

In this lesson, you identified devices and standards related to network implementations. By being aware of the characteristics of the different types of networks and devices, you will be able to implement a suitable network for your environment.

Describe your network topology, being sure to describe both the physical and logical aspects.

If you have experience in using VLANs, share it. If not, brainstorm ideas for using them.

 Note: Check your LogicalCHOICE Course screen for opportunities to interact with your classmates, peers, and the larger LogicalCHOICE online community about the topics covered in this course or other topics you are interested in. From the Course screen you can also access available resources for a more continuous learning experience.

5 | TCP/IP Addressing and Data Delivery

Lesson Time: 3 hours, 30 minutes

Lesson Objectives

In this lesson, you will identify TCP/IP addressing and data delivery methods. You will:

- Identify the key protocols in the TCP/IP protocol suite.

- Describe data addressing on TCP/IP networks.

- Identify default IP addressing schemes.

- Create custom IP addressing schemes.

- Describe IPv6 address implementation.

- Identify techniques to ensure reliable network data delivery.

Lesson Introduction

You need to be aware of TCP/IP addressing and data delivery methods to implement TCP/IP on your network. In this lesson, you will identify the addressing and data delivery methods of TCP/IP.

You must be able to identify each individual system that is connected, and the addressing scheme and data flow on the network. This knowledge will become necessary to perform fault management and zero-in on the faulty node. It will also allow you to isolate the system from the network, and recognize and troubleshoot the problem while ensuring that the network is fully functional.

TOPIC A

The TCP/IP Protocol Suite

In this topic, you will describe TCP/IP addressing and data delivery, which is performed by the TCP/IP protocol suite. TCP/IP consists of a suite of complementary protocols and standards that work together to provide the functionality on TCP/IP networks. In this topic, you will identify the protocols that are in use on a TCP/IP network.

The TCP/IP protocol suite includes many services that made TCP/IP the universal de facto, standard networking protocol. The TCP/IP protocol suite defines how applications on separate nodes establish a connection and track communications. To ensure that your network is receiving the benefits that the TCP/IP suite of protocols and standards provide, you need to know what those protocols are, and how they can benefit your network.

The TCP/IP Model

The *TCP/IP model* is a four-layer model developed by the United States Department of Defense. To some extent, it is similar to the OSI model. The TCP/IP model was developed to allow the addition of new technologies and create a more flexible architecture, which can easily allow the modification of existing protocols. This architecture later became known as the TCP/IP model after two of its most important protocols: TCP and IP.

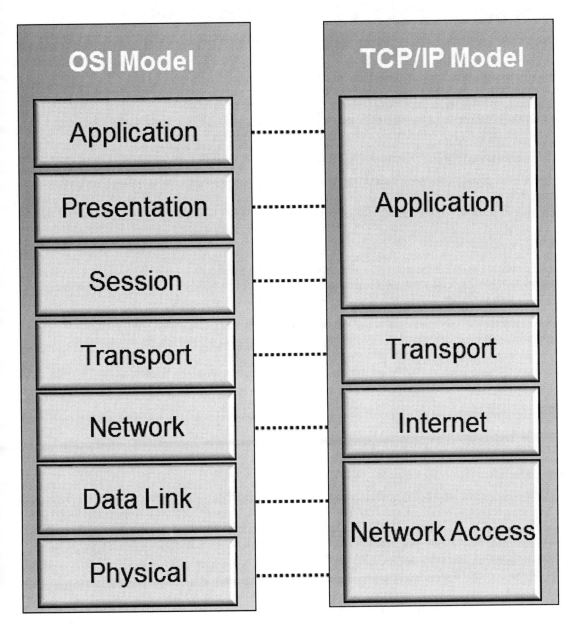

Figure 5-1: The layers in the TCP/IP network model.

Some vendors use different names for the layers, but you will always have four layers describing the TCP/IP model.

Encapsulation on TCP/IP Networks

If an application is initiated on the TCP/IP network, data is sent from the Application layer to the Transport layer. The Transport layer adds a header to the datagram and moves the datagram to the Internet layer. In the Internet layer, another header is added to the datagram and passed to the Network Interface layer, which adds a header and a trailer. The entire packet with the header and trailer information is sent to ensure its proper delivery. Upon receiving the data, the device removes the corresponding headers and trailers from the data and moves it up through the stack to the Application layer.

Connection–Oriented and Connectionless Protocols

Protocols can be divided into two categories depending upon the types of connections they establish. They are connection-oriented and connectionless protocols. *Connection-oriented protocols* are a data transmission method in which a connection is established before any data can be sent, and where a stream of data is delivered in the same order as it was sent. *Connectionless protocols* are a data transmission method that does not establish a connection between devices and where data may be delivered out of order and may be delivered over different paths. TCP is an example of a connection-oriented transport protocol, and UDP is an example of connectionless.

Connection-oriented protocols operate in three phases.

1. In the first phase, a connection is established and the devices negotiate the parameters for the connection.
2. During the second phase, the devices transfer data.
3. And in the third phase, the connection held by the devices is released and is torn down as it is no longer required.

Connectionless protocols do not have any explicit setup or release phases, and are always in the data transfer phase. If a device has data to be sent to the other, it just sends it. Connection-oriented systems can function only in bidirectional communication environments.

Connectionless communication is achieved when information is transmitted from a source to a destination without checking to see if the destination is prepared to receive the information. In environments where it is difficult to transmit data to a destination, the sender may have to retransmit the information multiple times before the destination receives the complete message.

TCP

The TCP/IP protocol suite includes two Transport-layer protocols: *Transmission Control Protocol (TCP)* and *User Datagram Protocol (UDP)*. These protocols correspond to Layer 4 of the OSI model. TCP carries the majority of traffic in today's networks.

TCP is a connection-oriented, guaranteed-delivery protocol used to send data packets between devices over a network such as the Internet. It is part of the Internet protocol suite along with the *Internet Protocol (IP)*. TCP is responsible for breaking up data into segments, reassembling them at the other end, resending data lost in transit, and resequencing data. It sends data, waits for an acknowledgement, and retransmits if necessary.

The Three–Way Handshake

TCP uses a three-way handshake to establish a connection. Before a client attempts to connect with a server, the server must perform a passive open. To do this, the server binds to and listens at a port to open it up for connections. Once the passive open is established, a client may initiate an active open. To establish a connection, the three-way handshake occurs:

1. SYN: The active open is performed by the client sending a SYN packet to the server. The client sets the packet's sequence number to a random value A.
2. SYN-ACK: In response, the server replies with a SYN-ACK packet. The acknowledgment number is set to one more than the received sequence number (i.e., A+1), and the sequence number that the server chooses for the packet is another random number, B.
3. ACK: Finally, the client sends an ACK packet back to the server. The sequence number is set to the received acknowledgement value (i.e., A+1), and the acknowledgement number is set to one more than the received sequence number (i.e., B+1).

Now both the client and server have received an acknowledgment of the connection. The first two steps establish the connection parameter for one direction and it is acknowledged. The last two steps establish the connection parameter for the other direction and it is acknowledged. With these, a full-duplex communication is established.

UDP

The User Datagram Protocol (UDP), also known as the Universal Datagram Protocol, is a connectionless Transport-layer protocol in the IP suite. UDP is a best-effort delivery protocol and is used with IP in the same way TCP is. It uses a smaller, simpler header than TCP does, which provides for faster service. And because it is a connectionless protocol, it provides faster service because it does not wait for acknowledgement.

UDP is commonly used in streaming media such as Voice over IP (VoIP), real-time video (as opposed to video-on-demand), and network management applications in which a device is polled regularly for its health. It is used when performance is more important than the ability to receive all of the data.

IP

Internet Protocol (IP) is a Network-layer (OSI Layer 3) protocol that is responsible for routing individual datagrams and addressing. Responsible for packet formatting and the logical addressing scheme, IP is a connectionless protocol and acts as an intermediary between higher protocol layers and the network. It makes no guarantees about packet delivery, corruption of data, or lost packets. IP can carry either TCP or UDP as its payload. When IP is used with TCP, then IP provides the connection and TCP provides reliability because it is a guaranteed-delivery protocol.

ICMP

The *Internet Control Message Protocol (ICMP)* is used with IP that attempts to report on the condition of a connection between two nodes. ICMP messages notify a sender of network conditions by reporting on errors. ICMP is connectionless and works at OSI Layer 3. If a node is sending data so quickly that the receiving node's buffers flood, the receiving node sends an ICMP source quench message to slow down data transmission from the sending node.

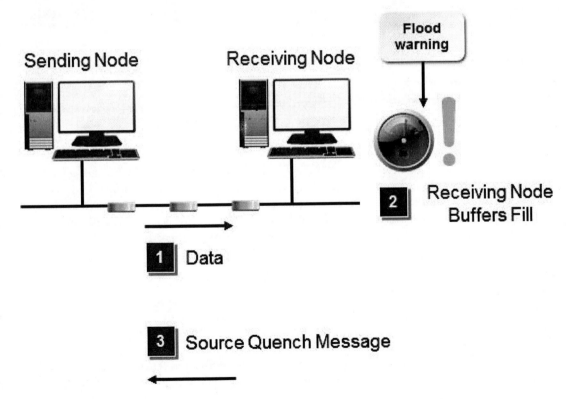

Figure 5-2: ICMP reports on the condition of a connection between two nodes.

A router could also send an ICMP **Destination unreachable** or **Expired in transit** message to a sender. When you ping from one device to another, you are using ICMP **echo** and **echo reply** messages. ICMP exists at Layer 3 of the OSI model (the Internet layer of the TCP/IP model).

Often, ICMP traffic is blocked on networks for security reasons.

A common example of ICMP traffic is using the *ping* utility to check connectivity.

IGMP

The *Internet Group Management Protocol (IGMP)* is a protocol in the TCP/IP suite that supports multicasting in a routed environment. Operating at Layer 3 of the OSI model (the Internet layer of the TCP/IP model), it provides one-to-many communications and is used to inform all systems on a network as to what host currently belongs to which multicast group. The routers need to support IGMP and multicast packet routing. Routers use IGMP to periodically send out queries to hosts inquiring about group membership. IGMP on the node responsible for multicast traffic sends a message to the router informing it of the multicast session in progress. The router uses IGMP to poll its interfaces for members of the multicast group, and then forwards the multicast transmission to group members. Hosts send out notifications, called host membership reports, as response to the query. Upon receiving the response from hosts, routers forward the multicast transmission to group members. IGMP can be used for one-to-many networking applications such as streaming videos or deploying images to multiple machines, and allows for more efficient use of resources.

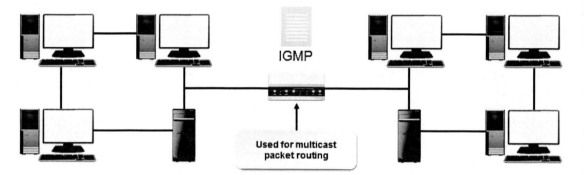

Figure 5–3: IGMP directs multicast traffic to members of the multicast group.

> **Note:** Routing is covered in greater detail later in the course.

ARP

The *Address Resolution Protocol (ARP)* maps an IP address to a physical or media access control (MAC) address recognized within a local network. ARP resides on Layer 2, or the Data Link layer of the OSI model (Network Interface layer of the TCP/IP model), encapsulated by an Ethernet header. ARP enables you to dynamically discover the mapping of a Layer 3 IP address to a Layer 2 MAC address.

ARP supports IP by resolving IP addresses to MAC addresses. Address resolution in ARP is performed in the following three steps:

1. ARP receives an IP address from IP.
2. If ARP has the MAC address in its cache, it returns it to IP. If not, it issues a Layer 2 broadcast to resolve the IP address.
3. A target node with the corresponding IP address responds with a Layer 2 unicast that includes its MAC address. ARP adds the MAC address into its cache and then sends it to IP as requested.

ARP plays a critical role in address resolution. If IP needs to deliver a packet to an IP address on the local network, it needs to obtain the MAC address of the destination node directly from ARP.

However, if IP needs to deliver a packet to an IP address on a remote network, it needs only the MAC address of the default gateway, and not of the destination node.

Protocol Analyzers

A *protocol analyzer*, or a *network analyzer* or packet analyzer, is diagnostic software that can examine and display data packets that are being transmitted over a network. It can examine packets from protocols that operate in the Physical, Data Link, Network, and Transport layers of the OSI model. Protocol analyzers can gather all information passed through a network, or selectively record certain types of transactions based on various filtering mechanisms. On a wired network, it is possible to gather information on all or just part of a network. On a wireless network, traffic can be captured one wireless channel at a time.

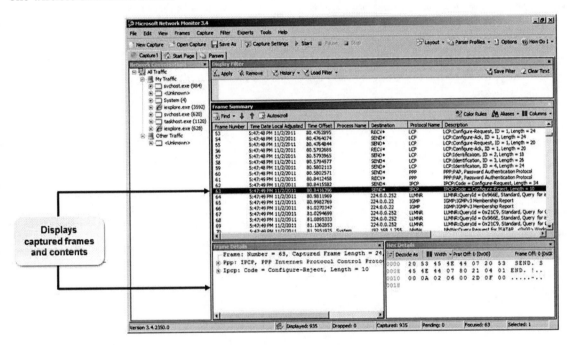

Figure 5-4: A protocol analyzer with captured data.

There are numerous uses for a protocol analyzer, including:

- Analyzing current network traffic patterns and potential problems
- Detecting possible network intrusions
- Monitoring network usage for performance analysis
- Filtering undesirable network traffic
- Launching an eavesdropping attack

Different protocol analyzers have different levels of functionality. Some have only software components; others use a combination of hardware and software to gather and analyze network information. High-end solutions usually provide support for more protocols, higher speeds, more analytical information, and the ability to send test traffic. The product you will use depends on your environment and the needs of your network.

- Most Windows devices include a basic protocol analyzer tool called Network Monitor that enables you to save each network capture to a log. There are two versions of Network Monitor. The first is one that ships with Windows but is not installed by default. You must add it by using **Add/Remove Windows Components**. This version of Network Monitor can capture only packets that travel to or from the device on which it is installed. There is also a full version of Network Monitor that is included with Systems Management Server, and can be installed separately from the full Systems Management Server product. This version can capture packets sent to or from any device on the network.

Note: Network Monitor can be downloaded from **http://www.microsoft.com/download/en/details.aspx?id=4865**.

- Most Linux distributions include tcpdump, a popular command-line utility for capturing packets. tcpdump can capture IP addresses, MAC addresses, session state and header information as well as data. The capture can be watched in real time, or saved to a file that can be imported and opened by other protocol analyzers. In addition to tcpdump, many Linux system administrators use Wireshark® to capture and analyze traffic on the network.

- The netstat utility is included with most UNIX and Linux distributions. netstat can provide a wide range of information, including open ports and sockets, packets transmitted on those ports, routing tables, and multicast memberships.

To capture all packets sent on a network, protocol analyzers require a network adapter and driver that support *promiscuous mode* operation. Promiscuous mode enables the device running the analyzer to recognize all packets being sent over the network, irrespective of the source or destination.

In promiscuous mode, a network card passes all network events to the operating system. In normal modes of operation, network traffic that is not intended for the adapter that received it is filtered out and not passed to the operating system, including the error conditions that the protocol analyzer is designed to detect.

ACTIVITY 5-1
Identifying Protocols on a TCP/IP Network

Before You Begin

You are logged in as the administrator for the domain Child##.GCInteriors. Your password is P@ssw0rd12.

Scenario

At the Greene City Interiors branch office, the network administrator has asked you to identify the protocols that are in use on the network.

---

1. Use Network Monitor to capture data.
   a) On the desktop, double-click **Microsoft Network Monitor 3.4**.
   b) In the **Microsoft Update Opt-In** message box, select **No**.
   c) Maximize the Microsoft Network Monitor 3.4 window.
   d) In the **Select Networks** pane, in the **Friendly Name** list, check the **NDISWANBH** check box.

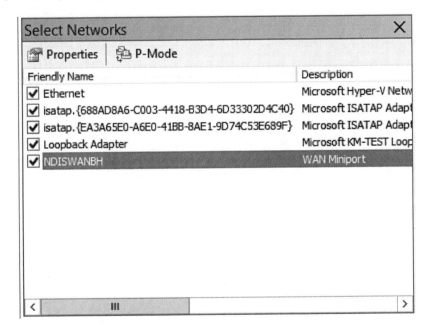

   Your adapter list may look somewhat different.
   e) On the toolbar, select **New Capture**.
   f) Select **Start**.

2. Generate network traffic.
   a) Open **Windows PowerShell,** and in the Windows PowerShell window, type `ping 192.168.2.200` and press **Enter**.
   b) Type `ping 192.168.2.XX` and press **Enter**, where XX corresponds to another students' IP address in the classroom. Repeat the ping a few times to generate traffic.
   c) Close the Windows PowerShell window.

3. Stop the Network Monitor capture of traffic and review the capture log.

a) In the Network Monitor window, on the toolbar, select **Stop**.
b) Select some frames and view the contents in the details pane.
c) In the **Display Filter** pane, in the text field, type *arp* and then select **Apply**.

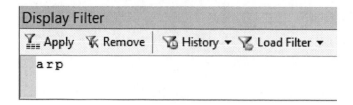

d) View the plaintext content of the ARP frames.
e) In the **Display Filter** pane, in the text field, type *icmp* and then select **Apply**.
f) View the plaintext content of the ICMP frames.
g) When you have finished, close the Microsoft Network Monitor 3.4 window without saving.

TOPIC B

IPv4 Addressing

You are familiar with different protocols and their functions on a TCP/IP network. To ensure that a network request arrives at its intended destination, you need to ensure that it follows the correct data addressing scheme. In this topic, you will identify data addressing methods on TCP/IP networks.

Data, while being sent or received on a TCP/IP network, is packaged with the addresses of the sending and receiving nodes. Packaging data for delivery so that it can be routed to the correct destination is the cornerstone of networking. Incorrectly packaging or addressing data will result in users experiencing symptoms of network communication problems. If you understand how a client packages data and then addresses it to travel to its destination on your network, you can use this information to detect causes of network communication problems.

Data Transmission on IP Networks

On a TCP/IP network, a sender transmits a protocol data unit (PDU) and waits for an acknowledgement of its receipt from a recipient—a TCP "ACK" signal. If the recipient is busy, the sender waits until it receives an ACK, after which it transmits the next PDU. Throughput can increase if data is sent as larger PDUs, with the recipient needing to send fewer acknowledgements.

PDUs that exist at Layer 4 are segments (for TCP) and datagrams (for UDP).

Introduction to IP Addressing

To implement TCP/IP on a network, administrators need to configure three settings on each network node:

- IP address
- Subnet mask
- Default gateway

The three main benefits of using IP on a network are:

- IP addresses and subnet masks enable each individual network to have a unique network address.
- Every network node can determine if a PDU is destined for a node on the local network or on a remote network.
- Routers can use network addresses and default gateways to send PDUs to the correct networks.

Binary and Decimal Conversion

Humans normally perform calculations by using the decimal (base 10) numbering system. Electronic machines, however, perform calculations by using the *binary (base 2) numbering system*. In the decimal numbering system, each position, starting from the rightmost, signifies a higher power of 10. Similarly, in the binary numbering system, each position, starting from the rightmost, signifies a higher power of 2.

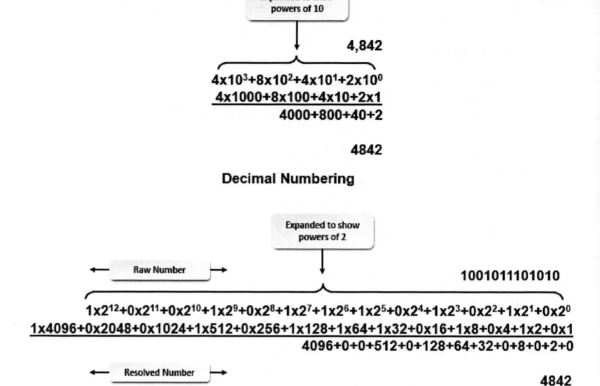

Decimal Numbering

Binary Numbering

Figure 5–5: Decimal and binary numbers.

For a given value of *n*, the decimal values of 2^n vary accordingly.

Exponent Value	Decimal Value
2^0	1
2^1	2
2^2	4
2^3	8
2^4	16
2^5	32
2^6	64
2^7	128

The following table shows 8-bit binary numbers and their decimal equivalents, along with the numeric conversion used to go from binary to decimal.

Binary Number	Conversion	Decimal Value
00000001	$0+0+0+0+0+0+0+2^0$	1
00000011	$0+0+0+0+0+0+2^1+2^0$	3
00000111	$0+0+0+0+0+2^2+2^1+2^0$	7
00001111	$0+0+0+0+2^3+2^2+2^1+2^0$	15

Binary Number	Conversion	Decimal Value
00011111	$0+0+0+2^4+2^3+2^2+2^1+2^0$	31
00111111	$0+0+2^5+2^4+2^3+2^2+2^1+2^0$	63
01111111	$0+2^6+2^5+2^4+2^3+2^2+2^1+2^0$	127
11111111	$2^7+2^6+2^5+2^4+2^3+2^2+2^1+2^0$	255

Windows Calculator

You can use the **Calculator** accessory that is built into the Windows operating systems to convert decimal and binary numbers. Switch the calculator to the **Programmer** view, type a number, and use the **Dec** and **Bin** radio buttons to convert the number from one format to another.

Other Numbering Systems

As you work with computing devices and networks, you are likely to encounter other number systems, such as:

- The *octal (base 8) numbering system*, where each digit is the equivalent of three binary digits. Each position, starting from the rightmost, signifies a higher power of eight.
- The *hexadecimal (base 16) numbering system*, where each digit is the equivalent of four binary digits. Each position, starting from the rightmost, signifies a higher power of 16. This numbering system is sometimes referred to as hex, and the symbols used are 0 through 9 and A through F.

IP Addresses

An *IP address* is a unique binary address assigned to a device so that it can communicate with other devices on a TCP/IP network. IPv4 addresses are 32 bits in length, whereas IPv6 addresses are 128 bits long. An IP address consists of two portions: the network address portion that is common to all hosts and devices on a physical network, and the host address portion, which is unique to the individual host. However, you probably won't be able to determine which part of the IP address is the network address and which is the node address unless you apply a subnet mask.

All devices on a TCP/IP network, such as computers, tablets, routers, and printers, each have a unique IP address.

 Note: Throughout the rest of this course, the terms "IP address" and "IPv4 address" both refer to an IPv4 address; all references to "IPv6" addresses are cited as IPv6 addresses. IPv6 is discussed in detail later in this lesson.

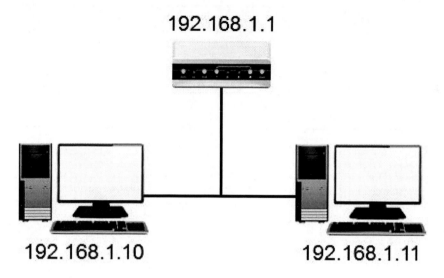

Figure 5-6: An IP address enables devices to connect with each other.

Dotted Decimal Notation

IP addresses are usually displayed in dotted decimal notation, rather than in binary. The dotted decimal notation consists of four decimal numbers separated by three dots. Each decimal number is called an octet and represents eight binary bits. Each decimal number can range from 0 to 255. When pronouncing a dotted decimal number, include the separator dots.

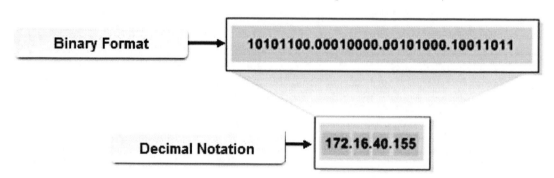

Figure 5-7: Decimal notation of an IP address.

Subnet Masks

A *subnet mask* is a number assigned to each host for dividing the IP address into network and node portions. This segregation makes TCP/IP routable. A subnet mask removes the node ID from the IP address, leaving just the network portion. A subnet mask is a series of continuous binary 1s that end abruptly at some point, followed by all 0s. Where the 1s end and the 0s begin marks the dividing line between network ID and host ID.

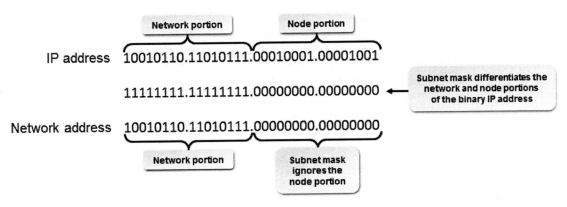

Figure 5-8: The subnet mask of an IP address.

Default subnet masks use the value of eight 1s in binary, or 255 in decimal, to mask an entire octet of the IP address. Groups of IP addresses have specific default subnet masks.

Default Subnet Mask	Value of the First Octet of IP Address
255.0.0.0	1–127, with some being reserved
255.255.0.0	128–191
255.255.255.0	192–223

The following are examples of permitted subnet masks:

- 255.0.0.0
- 255.255.0.0
- 255.255.255.0
- 255.255.128.0
- 255.255.255.244

Examples of illegal subnet masks are:

- 255.0.255.0
- 255.255.292.255
- 255.240.254.0
- 255.255.0.192

Applying a Subnet Mask

To apply a subnet mask, you can convert both the IP address and subnet mask to binary. Then, you can use a technique called binary ANDing to combine the two binary numbers. The result of ANDing these two numbers together is to yield the network number of that address. The binary AND operation involves two rules:

- 0 AND any other value equals 0.
- 1 AND 1 equals 1.

 Note: There are other ways to accomplish this, which you will see later in this lesson.

Subnets

Subnetting is the process of logically dividing a network into smaller subnetworks or *subnets*, with each subnet having a unique address. The conventional addressing technique has IP addresses with two hierarchical levels, namely the network ID and host ID. However, in subnet addressing, the host portion is further subdivided into the subnet ID and host ID, so subnet addressing is designed with three hierarchical levels: a network ID, subnet ID, and host ID. You should understand, however, that there is only one subnet mask applied to the IP address. For example, you can think of a subnet as part of your postal address. Each set of numbers represents a geographic area, and as it moves from the left to the right the geographic area becomes more specific. With the IP address of 192.168.12.10, 192 is your country or state, 168 is your city, 12 is your street, and 10 is your house number.

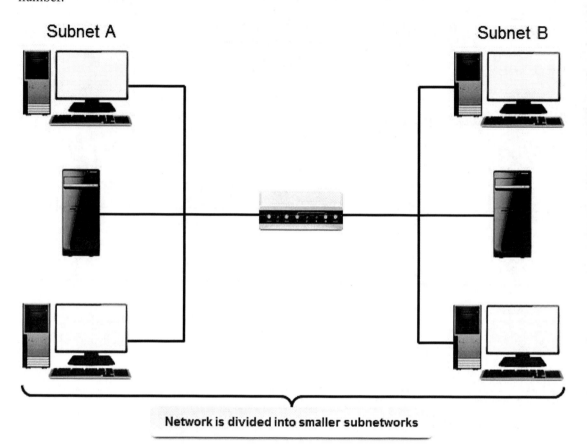

Figure 5-9: A network divided into two subnets.

The primary purpose for subnetting is to conserve IP addresses. If there are more IP addresses than nodes on a network, those extra IP addresses go to waste. Subnetting reduces the number of available IP addresses for a specific subnetwork, making the unused addresses available for other subnetworks. Two additional benefits of creating subnets are to improve network performance and to provide a more secure network environment. For performance enhancement, an administrator would most likely divide the network into groups of devices that frequently interact with each other, and for security enhancement, the administrator might divide the network based on servers that have restricted applications or sensitive data.

ACTIVITY 5-2
Identifying TCP/IP Information

Before You Begin
You are logged in as the administrator for the domain Child##.GCInteriors. Your password is P@ssw0rd12.

Scenario
At the Greene City Interiors branch office, you need to identify the IPv4 and MAC addresses of some devices to create a subnet. You also need to identify the names of a few devices so that you can join them to the domain on your network. You need to reassign the devices to a different subnet on your organization's network and you want to gather information such as the subnet mask and default gateway. You need to check this TCP/IP information on each computer.

---

1. Display system properties.
   a) From the **Start** page, open **Control Panel**.
   b) In the Control Panel window, verify that the **View by** drop-down box is set to **Category**, and then select the **System and Security** link.
   c) In the System and Security window, select the **System** link to display the system properties.

    Note: Your computer's full name might differ from the name displayed in the graphic.

   d) In the System window, in the **Computer name, domain, and workgroup settings** section, in the **Full computer name** field, identify your computer's full name.

   Computer name, domain, and workgroup settings

Computer name:	Computer01	🛡️Change settings
Full computer name:	Computer01.Child01.GCInteriors.com	
Computer description:		
Domain:	Child01.GCInteriors.com	

   e) Close the System window.

2. View the TCP/IP information assigned to your NIC.
   a) Open **Control Panel.**
   b) In the Control Panel window, select the **Network and Internet** link.
   c) In the Network and Internet window, select the **Network and Sharing Center** link.
   d) In the Network and Sharing Center window, select the **Change adapter settings** link.
   e) Right-click **Ethernet** and select **Status**.
   f) In the **Ethernet Status** dialog box, select **Details**.

g) In the **Network Connection Details** dialog box, in the properties list, identify the physical address, IPv4 address, and subnet mask. You will work with the DHCP server and DNS server information later in the course.

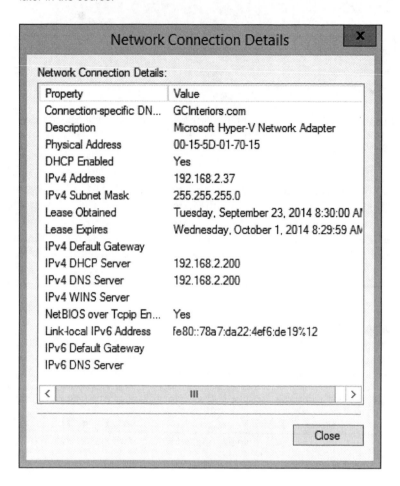

h) Close all open dialog boxes and windows.

IP Address Assignment Rules

While assigning IP addresses to nodes in a network, you need to follow certain rules:

- Every node (host) that connects to a network must have a unique IP address.
- Every subnet must have a unique network ID.
- All hosts on the same network/subnet must have the same network ID and same subnet mask.
- The host part of an IP address cannot be all 1s or all 0s.
- The IP address 127.0.0.1 is reserved for testing and cannot be used as a host ID.

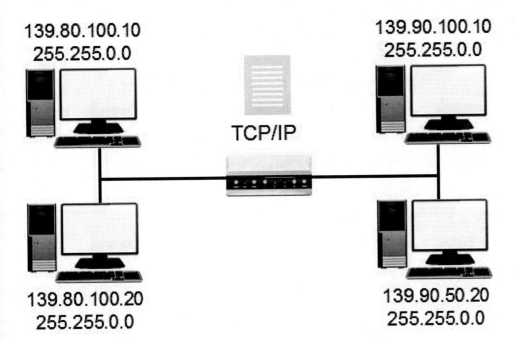

Figure 5-10: IP addressing on subnets.

ACTIVITY 5-3
Converting Binary and Decimal Numbers

Scenario

At the Greene City Interiors branch office, the network administrator wants you to make sure you understand how to convert binary numbers into decimal numbers. The administrator reminds you that binary is a base 2 numbering systems and gives you some numbers to convert.

Use the following figure to help you with your conversion.

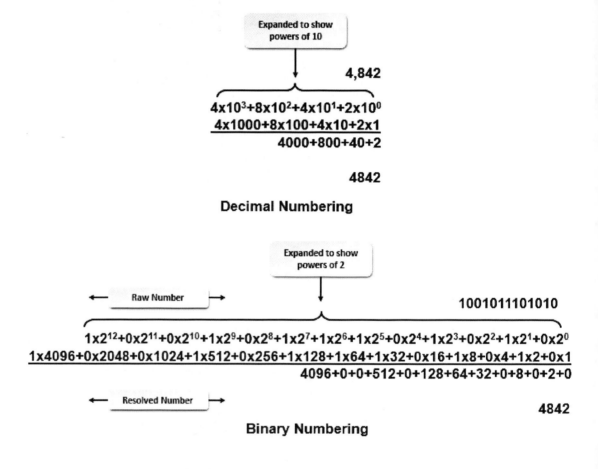

1. Convert the binary number of 10110010 to its decimal equivalent.

2. Convert the binary number of 10111011 to its decimal equivalent.

3. Convert the binary number of 1010001 to its decimal equivalent.

4. Use the calculator app on your computer and select the Programmer view (or an equivalent display mode that includes binary and decimal number options) and verify each of your conversions from steps 1, 2, and 3.

TOPIC C

Default IP Addressing Schemes

In the previous topic, you described data addressing on a TCP/IP network. Now that you are aware of the basic concepts of IP addressing, you can start identifying ways to assign IP addresses. In this topic, you will identify the default addressing schemes used in TCP/IP networks.

On the Internet, TCP/IP addresses must be regulated with a common scheme to ensure that there are no duplicate addresses worldwide. Companies and Internet Service Providers (ISPs) often lease addresses for their networks and customers to gain Internet access, but it can be expensive for a company to lease IP addresses for every client that needs Internet access.

IP Address Classes

The IPv4 address space consists of five blocks of addresses, called address classes, for use on specific networks based on their size.

- *Class A* addresses provide a small number of network addresses for networks with a large number of nodes per network. Used only by extremely large networks, Class A addresses are too expensive for use by most organizations. The technical definition of a Class A address is any address where the first octet (on the left) begins with 0.
- *Class B* addresses provide a balance between the number of network addresses and the number of nodes per network. Most organizations lease Class B addresses for use on networks that connect to the Internet. The technical definition of a Class B address is any address where the first octet (on the left) begins with 10.
- *Class C* addresses provide a large number of network addresses for networks with a small number of nodes per network. The technical definition of a Class C address is any address where the first octet (on the left) begins with 110.
- *Class D* addresses are set aside to support multicast transmissions. Any network can use them, regardless of the base network ID. A multicast server assigns a single Class D address to all members of a multicast session. There is no subnet mask. Class D addresses are routable only with special support from routers. The technical definition of a Class D address is any address where the first octet (on the left) begins with 1110.
- *Class E* addresses are set aside for research and experimentation. The technical definition of a Class E address is any address where the first octet (on the left) begins with 1111.

Characteristics of each address class are listed in the following table.

Address Class	Address Range	Example	Additional Comments
Class A	1.0.0.0 to 126.255.255.255	10.28.220.19	Class A addresses can have up to 126 networks, each with up to 16,777,214 nodes.
			The practical range for a class A address is from 1.0.0.0 to 126.255.255.255. The *actual* class A range is from 0.0.0.0 to 127.255.255.255. However, both 0 and 127 in the first octet are reserved for special purposes, and are not assigned to nodes. Nodes use 0.0.0.0 to indicate that they currently have no IP address. 127 is reserved for diagnostics such as the loopback address (127.0.0.1).
			The default subnet mask for Class A networks is 255.0.0.0.
Class B	128.0.0.0 to 191.255.255.255	155.128.20.106	Class B addresses can have up to 16,382 networks, each with up to 65,534 nodes.
			The default subnet mask for Class B networks is 255.255.0.0.
Class C	192.0.0.0 to 223.255.255.255	201.208.120.86	Class C addresses can have up to 2,097,150 networks, each with up to 254 nodes.
			The default subnet mask for Class C networks is 255.255.255.0.
Class D	224.0.0.0 to 239.255.255.255	230.43.160.48	Addresses are set aside to support multicast transmissions.
Class E	240.0.0.0 to 255.255.255.255	250.217.39.190	Addresses are set aside for research and experimentation.

Note: To test a network node, enter `ping 127.0.0.1`, `ping loopback`, or `ping localhost` to verify that TCP/IP is functioning on a node.

Available Host and Network Addresses

Because neither the node portion nor the network portion of an IP address can be all 1s or all 0s, certain host addresses in each address class are invalid for individual hosts. For example, on a Class A network that uses the default subnet mask, the host address 10.0.0.0 is not valid because the host portion is all 0s—the address is identical to the network address. Similarly, the Class A address 120.255.255.255 is not valid because the host portion is all 1s. A host address with all 1s has a special purpose; it is used as a broadcast address. The address 127.255.255.255 would be used for broadcasts to the local subnet.

The number of host addresses or network addresses available on networks in each class depends upon how many bits are in the network portion or host portion of the address.

- The formula to calculate available host addresses is 2^n-2, where n is the number of host bits. Two addresses in each block are unavailable because host addresses cannot be all ones or all zeros.
- Similarly, the formula to calculate available network addresses is 2^a, where a is the number of network bits. For network addresses, you do not need to reserve two addresses as you do with host addresses.

Private IP Addresses

Private IP addresses are addresses that organizations use for nodes within enterprise networks requiring IP connectivity and not external connections to the Internet. There are IP addresses in three of the address classes (A, B, and C) that are reserved as private IP addresses. When an Internet router receives a data packet bound for one of these reserved IP addresses, it recognizes the address as nonroutable and does not forward it outside the network. Private IP addresses can be used freely on internal networks. Any IP addresses outside of the private IP address ranges are considered public addresses. These are globally routable unicast IP addresses.

An organization can use private IP addresses without contacting an Internet registry or the ICANN. These addresses are not injected into the global Internet routing system. Therefore, different organizations can use the address space simultaneously. Problems arising due to the shortage of IP addresses are partly resolved by private IP addresses.

 Note: In order for a device with an assigned private IP address to access Internet resources or other external networks, the private IP address needs to be converted to a routable address. This is usually accomplished through a gateway or by a router.

There are also link-local addresses, which are network addresses that are valid only for communications within the network segment or the broadcast domain that the host is connected to. Link-local addresses are usually not guaranteed to be unique beyond a single network segment and routers therefore do not forward packets with link-local addresses.

The private IP address ranges are:

- 10.0.0.0 to 10.255.255.255
- 172.16.0.0 to 172.31.255.255
- 192.168.0.0 to 192.168.255.255

Private IP Address Conflicts

Because they do not get forwarded across external routers, private IP addresses do not cause duplicate IP address conflicts on the Internet. They can, however, cause duplicate IP address problems on an internal network. Private addresses are actual IP addresses that are used by most organizations internally. They are even used across routers inside the company's intranet.

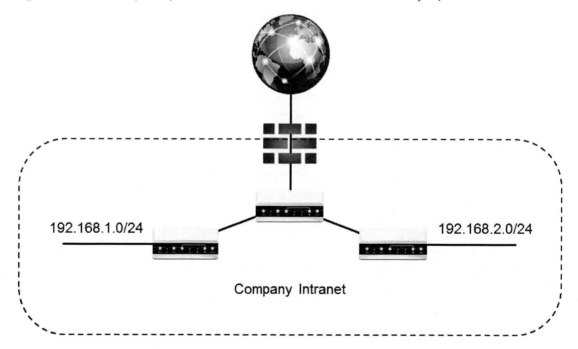

Figure 5-11: Private IP addresses used across routers on an intranet.

If the company's network is not designed well, there is a chance that the same private IP address block will be used in different parts of the internal network, causing problems.

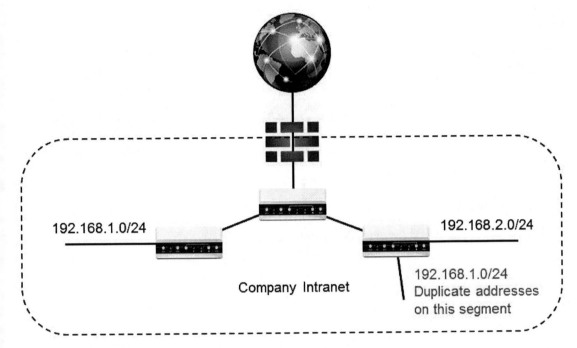

Figure 5–12: Duplicate private IP addresses.

Another common cause of duplicate address problems occurs when two small locations use the same internal IP addressing scheme and then connect across the Internet via a VPN. Because the VPN acts as a direct connection between these networks, routers cannot make forwarding decisions if both sides use the same IP addresses.

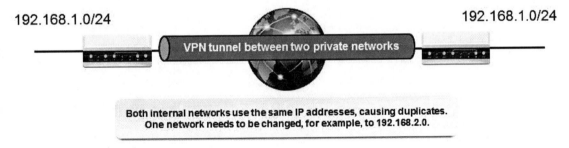

Figure 5–13: Duplicate IP addresses across a VPN tunnel.

Default Gateways

A *default gateway* is the IP address of a router that routes remote traffic from the device's local subnet to remote subnets. Typically, it is the address of the router connected to the Internet. A TCP/IP host does not need a default gateway address if the device does not need to communicate with devices outside its local subnet. In this case, it needs only the MAC address. You need to configure a node with an IP address, a subnet mask, and a default gateway to communicate on the Internet or any other external network. You will need only an IP address and a subnet mask to communicate with other nodes on your network.

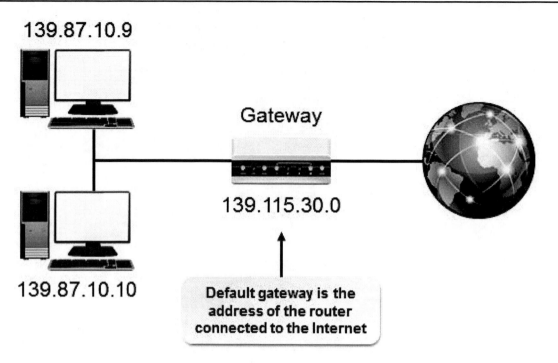

Figure 5-14: The default gateway routes traffic to remote subnets.

 Note: You can enter `ipconfig` at the command prompt to view the TCP/IP parameters on your Windows device. In Linux, this command is `ifconfig`.

ACTIVITY 5-4
Identifying Default IP Addressing Schemes

Scenario

At the Greene City Interiors branch office, you now need to verify the subnet mask and gateway of a few devices and verify that they are on the correct subnet and are configured properly. You need to check this TCP/IP information on each device.

1. Identify IP address information.
   a) Open **Windows PowerShell**.
   b) In the Windows PowerShell window, type *ipconfig* and press **Enter**.

```
Ethernet adapter Ethernet:

        Connection-specific DNS Suffix  . : GCInteriors.com
        Link-local IPv6 Address . . . . . : fe80::78a7:da22:4ef6:de19%12
        IPv4 Address. . . . . . . . . . . : 192.168.2.37
        Subnet Mask . . . . . . . . . . . : 255.255.255.0
        Default Gateway . . . . . . . . . : 192.168.2.200
```

   Your results will be slightly different.

2. For the Ethernet adapter named Ethernet, what are the IPv4 Address, Subnet Mask, and Default Gateway?

3. How will you determine the class of this IPv4 address?

4. How many valid IP addresses are available for internal hosts?

TOPIC D

Create Custom IP Addressing Schemes

In the previous topic, you identified default IP addressing schemes. Administrators can also create customized IP addressing schemes. In this topic, you will create custom IP addressing schemes.

Because of the fixed number of default networks and hosts on Class B and Class C networks, many companies have been forced to either lease Class B networks and then divide them up into multiple subnetworks within their company, or combine multiple smaller subnets into one highly subnetted network using Class C networks to facilitate the total number of nodes. As a network administrator, you will need to create subnets that meet the requirements of the current IP addressing scheme and are fully functional on any IP network.

Custom Subnets

A *custom subnet* is a collection of leased IP addresses that are divided into smaller groups to serve a network's needs. A custom subnet has a custom subnet mask applied to the IP address, so that what the node sees as its local network is a subset of the whole default network address block. A default gateway is configured for each subnet to route traffic between subnets.

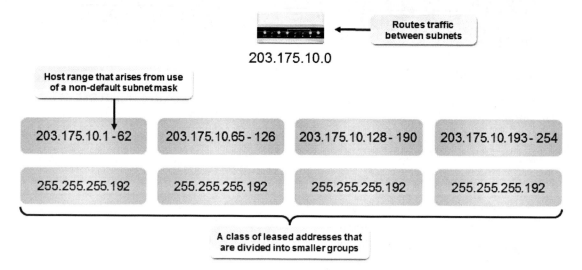

Figure 5–15: A custom subnet mask applied to the IP address.

Custom Subnet Masks

You can use a *custom subnet mask* to divide a single IP address block into multiple subnets. A custom subnet mask borrows node bits in a contiguous block from the left side of the node portion of the address, and uses them as network bits. This divides a single network address into multiple networks, each containing fewer nodes. Custom subnet masks are sometimes referred to as variable length subnet masks (VLSMs).

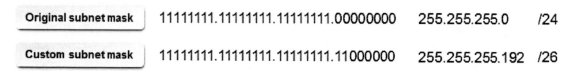

Figure 5–16: A custom subnet mask borrows node bits in a contiguous block.

There are different possible combinations of custom subnet masks on a Class C network.

Last Octet of New Mask (Binary)	New Mask (Decimal)	Number of Added Networks	Nodes per Network
10000000	255.255.255.128	2	126
11000000	255.255.255.192	4	62
11100000	255.255.255.224	8	30
11110000	255.255.255.240	16	14
11111000	255.255.255.248	32	6
11111100	255.255.255.252	64	2
11111110	255.255.255.254	Not allowed in Class C	
11111111	255.255.255.255	Not allowed in Class C	

CIDR

Classless inter-domain routing (CIDR) is a classless addressing method that considers a custom subnet mask as a 32-bit binary word. Mask bits can move in one-bit increments to provide the exact number of nodes and networks required. The CIDR notation combines a network address with a number to represent the number of 1 bits in the mask. With CIDR, multiple class-based networks can be represented as a single block.

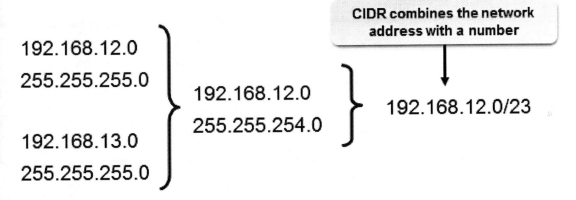

Figure 5–17: CIDR.

 Note: CIDR can also be referred to as classless routing or supernetting. Because of its efficiencies, CIDR has been rapidly adopted, and the Internet today is largely a classless address space.

CIDR and VLSM

VLSM and CIDR are essentially the same thing. They both use slash notation to represent a custom subnet mask. The difference is that VLSM refers to lengthening the mask to create multiple subnets out of a single network, whereas CIDR refers to shortening the mask to aggregate smaller networks into a larger network for routing purposes on the Internet.

CIDR Subnet Mask Values

There are different values possible for each CIDR subnet mask. The /24, /16, and /8 CIDR masks correspond with the classful ranges of Class C, Class B, and Class A, respectively.

CIDR Mask (Number of Network Bits)	Number of Possible Nodes	Standard Subnet Mask in Dotted Decimal
/32	N/A	255.255.255.255
/31	N/A	255.255.255.254
/30	2	255.255.255.252
/29	6	255.255.255.248
/28	14	255.255.255.240
/27	30	255.255.255.224
/26	62	255.255.255.192
/25	126	255.255.255.128
/24	254	255.255.255.0
/23	510	255.255.254.0
/22	1,022	255.255.252.0
/21	2,046	255.255.248.0
/20	4,094	255.255.240.0
/19	8,190	255.255.224.0
/18	16,382	255.255.192.0
/17	32,766	255.255.128.0
/16	65,534	255.255.0.0
/15	131,070	255.254.0.0
/14	262,142	255.252.0.0
/13	524,286	255.248.0.0
/12	1,048,574	255.240.0.0
/11	2,097,150	255.224.0.0
/10	4,194,304	255.192.0.0
/9	8,386,606	255.128.0.0
/8	16,777,214	255.0.0.0
/7	33,554,430	254.0.0.0
/6	67,108,862	252.0.0.0
/5	134,217,726	248.0.0.0
/4	268,435,544	240.0.0.0
/3	536,870,910	224.0.0.0
/2	1,073,741,824	192.0.0.0
/1	N/A	N/A

The Custom Subnetting Process

Because IP addressing uses the binary numbering system, every time you move the subnet mask to the right one bit, you are dividing by two.

- If you move the subnet mask one bit to the right, you are dividing one network in half, giving you two subnets.
- If you move the subnet mask one more bit to the right (two bits total) you are dividing the two parts again, giving you four subnets.
- If you move the mask yet again (three bits total), you are dividing again, giving you a total of eight subnets.

This is rather like watching cells divide under a microscope. For example, suppose you have the network 192.168.1.0 /24. This is a typical Class C network block. The total range of addresses on the host side is 256 (0 to 255). The two outside addresses, 0 and 255, have special meaning and cannot be assigned to hosts.

- 0 (192.168.1.0) is the subnet ID.
- 1 (192.168.1.1) is the first legitimate host ID, and 254 (192.168.1.254) is the last legitimate host ID.
- 255 (192.168.1.255) is the broadcast ID.

In binary, the subnet mask looks like this:

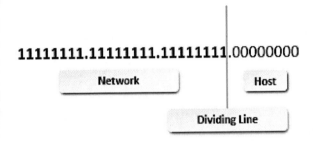

Now, imagine that you need to divide this network into two parts. To do this, you need to move the mask to the right one bit. When you move the mask to the right one bit, borrowing a bit from the host side, the new mask is now no longer /24, it is /25. In binary, it now looks like this:

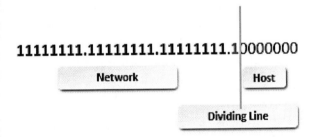

You have divided the network into two halves, each receiving half of the original block of host addresses. That's 128 addresses per subnet.

Address Range	Subnet ID	First Host ID	Last Host ID	Broadcast ID
0 to 127	0	1	126	127
128 to 255	128 (192.168.1.128)	129 (192.168.1.129)	254 (192.168.1.254)	255 (192.168.1.255)

The new subnet mask for both of these subnets is no longer /24, it is now /25. In dotted decimal, that is 255.255.255.128.

Here's another example. Suppose you need to take the same original network of 192.168.1.0/24 and divide it into four subnets. You will need to move the mask **2** bits to the right.

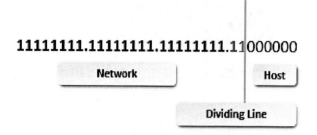

11111111.11111111.11111111.11000000

Network   Host

Dividing Line

The new mask for the four subnets is now /26, or 255.255.255.192.

When you divide the original network into four parts, each receives one-fourth of the original block of host addresses.

Address Range	Subnet ID	First Host ID	Last Host ID	Broadcast ID
0 to 63	0	1	62	63
64 to 127	64	65	126	127
128 to 191	128	129	190	191
192 to 255	192	193	254	255

The Delta Method

There is a simpler way to identify the range of addresses for new subnets. It's called the delta method. It uses bit positions to determine the subnet ID increment. In the delta technique, you follow these steps:

1. Identify the bit position of the original subnet mask.
2. Determine how many subnets you need.
3. Based on the number of subnets needed, determine how many bits to move the mask. You can use this image to determine how many bits to move the mask from its original position.

$$\frac{128}{7} \qquad \frac{64}{6} \qquad \frac{32}{5} \qquad \frac{16}{4} \qquad \frac{8}{3} \qquad \frac{4}{2} \qquad \frac{2}{1} \qquad \frac{1}{0}$$

4. Identify the delta.

   a. Expand the last octet and use the top row of the previous image to insert the decimal equivalents of each bit position.

   _ _ _ _ _ _ _ _ . _ _ _ _ _ _ _ _ . _ _ _ _ _ _ _ _ .128 64 32 16 8 4 2 1

   b. Move the mask from the old position to the new position. The number to the left of where the mask ends is the delta.

5. Assign subnet IDs and host address ranges based on the delta.

Remember that the more you move the subnet mask, the more subnets you have. Fewer bits remain for the hosts, so there are fewer hosts per subnet.

For example, you have the network 192.168.1.0/24 and you need two subnets.

1. The bit position of the original subnet mask is:

11111111.11111111.11111111.00000000

2. You know you need two subnets.
3. Based on the need for two subnets, you need to move the mask one bit. This changes the mask from 24 to 25. The dotted decimal equivalent of /25 is 255.255.255.128.
4. Identify the delta.

   a. Expand the last octet and use the top row of the previous image to insert the decimal equivalents of each bit position.

   _ _ _ _ _ _ _ _ . _ _ _ _ _ _ _ _ . _ _ _ _ _ _ _ .128 64 32 16 8 4 2 1

   b. Move the mask from the old position, 24, to the new position, 25. The number to the left of where the mask ends is the delta; in this example, it is 128.

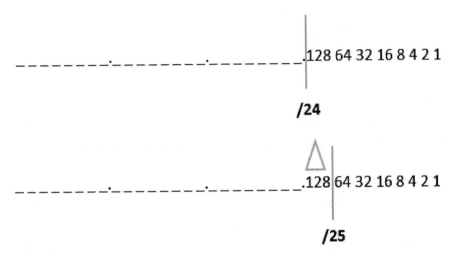

5. Assign subnet IDs and host address ranges based on the delta, 128. This means that you need to increment the subnets by 128.

Subnet Name	Subnet ID	First Host ID	Last Host ID	Broadcast ID
Subnet 0	192.168.1.0/25	192.168.1.1	192.168.1.126	192.168.1.127
Subnet 128	192.168.1.128/25	192.168.1.129	192.168.1.254	192.168.1.255

You can subnet this way in any octet, although it is not likely that you will do it in the first octet. Also, the farthest you can go in the fourth octet is to take the mask to /30. In a /30 mask, the delta is 4, so you would only have two IP addresses available for hosts. This is commonly used for point-to-point WAN links where there would be only two nodes that need addresses, a router on either side of the WAN link.

Network ID Calculation

Sometimes, you will need to determine the base network ID of an IP address on a network that has already been subnetted. For instance, say you have the IP address 206.234.120.87/20, and you need to know the base network ID.

1. Start by identifying the octet that contains both network and node bits, by examining the subnet mask for /20.

11111111.11111111.11110000.00000000

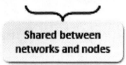

Shared between
networks and nodes

2. Convert the shared octet for the IP address to binary; add leading zeros as needed to create an 8-bit number. In this example, the third octet is 120, which has the binary equivalent of 1111000, so you need to add a 0 to the left to create an 8-bit number.

206.234.01111000.87

3. Remove the node bits from the shared octet by applying the subnet mask.

206.234.01111000.87

255.255.11110000.0

206.234.01110000.0

4. Convert the shared portion of the IP address back to decimal to determine the base network ID. In this case, 0111000 is 112, so the base network ID is 206.234.112.0.

 Note: For additional information, check out the LearnTO **Create Multiple Networks by Using Custom Subnet Masks** presentation in the LearnTOs for this course on your LogicalCHOICE Course screen.

Guidelines for Creating Custom IP Addressing Schemes

 Note: All of the Guidelines for this lesson are available as checklists from the **Checklist** tile on the LogicalCHOICE Home screen.

You can use the following guidelines to help you create custom subnets:

- For simplicity's sake, assign an entire Class C octet to a subnet when possible.
- If your subnet has over 100 workstations as well as many transient DHCP clients (such as laptops or mobile devices), consider using a shorter mask to create a larger address pool (/23 or /22).
- Make sure none of your subnets have overlapping IP addresses.

You can use the following guidelines to help you create custom subnet masks:

- Use the table to quickly map the number of needed subnets to the number of borrowed mask bits.
- For simplicity's sake, do not use custom subnet masks (VLSM) unless necessary.
- Exception to the above: When assigning subnets to point-to-point WAN links, use a /30 mask to conserve IP addresses.

You can use the following guidelines to help when you use CIDR:

- Use CIDR notation (as opposed to dotted decimal) for VLSM.
- When subnetting, physically organize the topology of your network so that the subnets can be aggregated together into a supernet by a single border router.

You can use the following guidelines to help you with the subnetting process:

- Determine the number of subnets you need based on the number of geographical locations you have, the number of VLANs you have, or the need to isolate segments into their own subnet for security reasons.
- Use the delta method to determine the subnet ID increments, as well as the IP address ranges for each subnet.

- Use the number of subnets and number of mask bits table to help you with the subnetting process.

You can use the following guidelines to help you with the delta method:

- Draw the number of mask bits in a diagram to help you visually identify the old and new mask positions.
- Use the number of subnets and number of mask bits table to help you identify the delta.

You can use the following guidelines to help you with network ID calculation:

- Keep in mind that the network (subnet) ID must always be an increment of a binary number (1, 2, 4, 8, 16, 32, 64, or 128).
- Use a diagram of bits to help you identify the delta and thus the network ID increments.

 Access the Checklist tile on your LogicalCHOICE course screen for reference information and job aids on How to Create Custom IP Addressing Schemes.

ACTIVITY 5-5
Creating Custom IP Addressing Schemes

Scenario
At the Greene City Interiors branch office, you have been asked to implement TCP/IP on a divided network. Your network ID is currently 192.168.1.0/24. You need to divide this in half (two subnets).

1. How many bits do you need to move the mask?

2. What is the new mask?

3. What is the delta?

4. What are the subnet IDs for each network?

5. What are the first and last assignable IP addresses for each subnet?

6. What is the broadcast for each subnet?

7. What are the recommended IP addresses for each router interface?

TOPIC E

IPv6 Address Implementation

In the previous topics, you learned about IPv4, which is the original version of the TCP/IP protocol and is in use on thousands of networks. In contrast, IP version 6 (IPv6) is a newer standard that is currently being implemented on networks and is expected to eventually replace IPv4. In this topic, you will describe IPv6 address implementation.

As a network professional who supports TCP/IP networking, you should be aware of the limitations of the IPv4 addressing scheme. IPv6 is an addressing scheme available to network administrators who need to overcome these limitations. If you support or configure networks that include the IPv6 addressing scheme, you need to understand its characteristics as well as how it can interoperate with existing IPv4 implementations.

IPv4 Address Space Limitations

Limitations of the IPv4 address space include:

- The 32-bit IP address space itself, which provides only a theoretical maximum of 2^{32}, or approximately 4,295 billion, separate addresses.
- The division of the address space into fixed classes, with the result that node addresses falling either between classes or between subnets are unavailable for assignment.
- The fact that IP address classes provide a small number of node addresses, leading to difficulty matching IP address leases to a company's needs and IP addresses being wasted.
- The depletion of Class A and Class B IP address assignments.
- Unassigned and unused address ranges within existing Class A and Class B blocks.

IPv6

IP version 6, or *IPv6,* the successor to IPv4, is an addressing scheme that increases the available pool of IP addresses by implementing a 128-bit binary address space. This equates to 340 trillion trillion trillion addresses. IPv6 also includes new features, such as simplified address headers, hierarchical addressing, support for time-sensitive network traffic, required security, and a new structure for unicast addressing.

IPv6 is not compatible with IPv4, so at present it is narrowly deployed on a limited number of test and production networks. Full adoption of the IPv6 standard will require a general conversion of IP routers to support interoperability.

 Note: For more information on IPv6, see the IP Version 6 Working Group charter at **www.ietf.org/html.charters/ipv6-charter.html** by the Internet Engineering Task Force (IETF).

Some of the other benefits of IPv6 include:

- One of the goals of IPv6 is to keep the IP headers as small as possible, to make access to the address more efficient and quicker. Non-essential information in IPv6 headers is moved to optional extension headers.
- Stateless auto-reconfiguration of hosts allows an IPv6 host to configure automatically when connected to a routed IPv6 network.
- A new field in the IP header of IPv6 packets enables IP to guarantee the allocation of network resources when requested by time-dependent services such as voice and video transmission.
- IPv6 implements network-layer encryption and authentication with IPSec.

Note: IPSec is covered later in the course.

Transmission Types

IPv6 uses three different transmission types: unicast, multicast, and anycast. Broadcast addresses are not used for IPv6, and have been replaced with multicast addressing. IPv6 unicast is similar to the unicast address in IPv4, which has a single address identifying a single interface.

Multicast in IPv6 is similar to IPv4 broadcast addressing in which a packet sent to a multicast address is delivered to every interface in a group. The difference in IPv6 is that it is targeted and only hosts that are members of the multicast group receive the multicast packets.

Anycast is a transmission method in which data is sent from a server to the nearest node within a group. That node then initiates a second anycast and transmits the data to the next nearest node with the group. The process is repeated until all nodes within the group have received the data. Network nodes not in the group ignore the data.

 Note: Anycast was covered at the beginning of the course.

IPv6 Addresses

An *IPv6 address* is a 128-bit binary number assigned to a computer on a TCP/IP network. Some of the bits in the address represent the network segment; the other bits represent the host itself. IPv6 addresses are not case-sensitive.

For readability, the 128-bit binary IPv6 address is usually separated by colons into eight groups of four hexadecimal digits. Each quartet of four hexadecimal digits equals 16 bits:

2001:0db8:85a3:0000:0000:8a2e:0370:7334

While all eight groups must have four digits, leading zeros can be omitted:

2001:db8:85a3:0:0:8a2e:370:7334

and groups of consecutive zeros are replaced with two colons:

2001:db8:85a3::8a2e:370:7334

Some types of IPv6 addresses contain long sequences of zeros. A contiguous sequence of 16-bit blocks set to 0 in the colon-hexadecimal format can be compressed to :: (known as double-colon). To avoid ambiguity, you can perform the double-colon substitution only once per address.

A 128-bit address provides 2^{128} potential address combinations, which equals 340 billion trillion trillion (340 undecillion) possible addresses. Not all of those addresses will be publicly routable.

In IPv6, everything to the left of the mask is referred to as the "prefix." That is the terminology in IPv6 rather than "network ID." Instead of "octets" it has "quartets" between the colons. Different levels in the IP addressing hierarchy have different prefix lengths, and hence different subnet mask assignments:

- Regional Internet Registries (RIRs like the American Registry for Internet Numbers, or ARIN, and the Asia-Pacific Network Information Centre, or APNIC): The first 12 bits of an address refer to the Internet registry responsible for that region. Example: 2000::/12. In this case, the RIR is responsible for the address range of 2000::/12 to 200F:FFFF:FFFF:FFFF::/64.
- ISPs are assigned /32: The first 32 bits (including the first 23 bits) refers to the ISP. Example: 2001:db8::/32.
- Organizations at a specific location are assigned /48: The first 48 bits (including the two mentioned above) refer to the organization (called the "end site" or "site"). Example: 2001:db8:A00::/48—the A00 part refers to the organization/company (note the /48 mask). This designation is why companies and organizations might be referred to as "the 48s."

- Subnets within an organization are assigned /64: If there are no subnets, then the organization's main network ID with a trailing zero is used for the prefix. Example: Here is the prefix for subnet zero: 2001:db8:A00:0/64. It is more commonly written as 2001:db8:A00::/. This next example is the prefix for subnet 2: 2001:db8:A00:2::/64.
- Hosts are usually assigned a /64 mask. This example is assigned to the first host (probably the router) in the 2001:db8:A00::/64 network: 2001:db8:A00:1::1/64.

Figure 5-18: IPv6 subnet mask assignments.

IPv4 addresses differ from IPv6 addresses in several ways.

- IPv4 addresses use 32 bits as opposed to the 128 bits used in IPv6 addressing.
- The header information structure is different between IPv4 and IPv6 addresses. IPv6 headers are simpler, but expandable if you need to include options.

The loopback address for an IPv6 host is ::1. The default route address (meaning anything unknown is sent to the default gateway) is ::/0. This corresponds with the IPv4 default route of 0.0.0.0/0.

A host computer running IPv6 can use an IEEE standard called the extended unique identifier (EUI) to self-assign its node address. With EUI, the MAC address is padded in the center with FFFE, extending it to 64 bits in length. For instance, a MAC address of 01-00-11-22-33-44 would be changed to 0100:11FF:FE22:3344 to become the last 64 bits of the node's IPv6 address. While not a requirement, most vendors are adopting this format, as it's the easiest to implement.

IPv6 replaces classful addresses with a more flexible and logical unicast addressing structure. There are different categories of unicast addresses that serve different functions.

Unicast Address Type	Description
Global addresses	Globally routable public addresses. Also known as aggregatable global unicast addresses, they are designed such that they can be summarized for efficient routing. Global addresses are the equivalent of the entire IPv4 public address space.
Site-local addresses	Addresses used for internal networks that are not routable on the Internet. The equivalent of the IPv4 private, nonroutable address blocks. Site-local addresses begin with FEC0::/10. In Sept 2004, the Internet Assigned Numbers Authority (IANA) requested the IETF deprecate this address type because it was ambiguous and could lead to misconfigurations resulting in network security leaks. Site-local addresses have been replaced with "unique local addresses" in the block fc00::/7. Of that block, fd00::/8 has been set aside for the 48s to use in their internal networks.
Link-local addresses	Addresses that are used to communicate and automatically assigned on private network segments with no router. Link-local addresses always begin with FE80. They are the equivalent of self-assigned IPv4 automatic private IP addressing (APIPA) addresses.

Unicast Address Type	Description
IPv6 transitional addresses	Addresses used on mixed networks to support routing of IPv6 data across IPv4 networks. This class will be phased out when all routers convert to IPv6. An example of transitional addresses is Microsoft's IPv4-compatible version that Windows sometimes uses during 6-4 transition. In this version, the host ID is not the EUI, but instead the 4 octets of the IPv4 address. So, for example, if the IPv4 address is 192.168.1.26, the IPv6 address is 2001:0db8:85A3:0:192:168:1:26/64.
	2002::/16 is a 6-to-4 routing prefix, meaning that networks that are in transition using 6-to-4 will use this prefix.

IPv6 Tunneling

One of the ways that IPv6 can be implemented is through the *tunneling* process. Like encapsulation, tunneling envelops a data packet in a form that is acceptable to the carrier. In this instance, you are encapsulating IPv6 packets to traverse IPv4 networks such as the Internet. An example of this is Microsoft DirectAccess, which creates an "Always On" VPN between a client and the corporate network. To make sure the packets can travel across all ISPs, the client encapsulates the IPv6 packets into IPv4 (Teredo tunneling on Windows OS and Miredo tunneling on Linux and Mac OS). The IPv4 encapsulation is removed at the corporate network end.

There is also 6to4, which is an Internet transition mechanism that allows IPv6 packets to be transmitted over an IPv4 network without the need to configure explicit tunnels. Special relay servers are also in place that allow 6to4 networks to communicate with native IPv6 networks. The 4to6 Internet transition mechanism is the same but in reverse, allowing IPv4 packets to be transmitted over an IPv6 network.

Router Solicitation and Advertising

IPv6 routers regularly advertise information on the links to which they are connected. These advertisements are Internet Control Message Protocol Version 6 (ICMPv6) router advertisement (RA) messages, sent to the multicast group ff02::1. All the nodes on a link that belong to this group, and nodes configured for autoconfiguration, analyze those messages. Upon reception of an RA message, an autoconfiguring node not already configured with the corresponding global address will prepend the advertised prefix to the unique identifier.

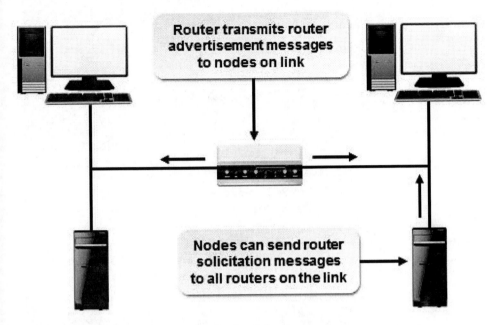

Figure 5-19: Router advertisement and solicitation messages.

Nodes can send router solicitation (RS) messages to all the routers on the link. Nodes that have not configured an address yet use the unspecified address "::". The routers then answer immediately with an RA message containing a global prefix. The node is then able to extract a prefix and build its global address.

Protocol Binding

Assigning a protocol to a network interface card (NIC) is referred to as *protocol binding*. As protocols govern data transmission, it is critical to bind the protocol to the network interface as it creates a path for the flow of data. Multiple protocols can be bound to a NIC, and the NIC can use any of the protocols that are bound to it to communicate with other nodes on the network.

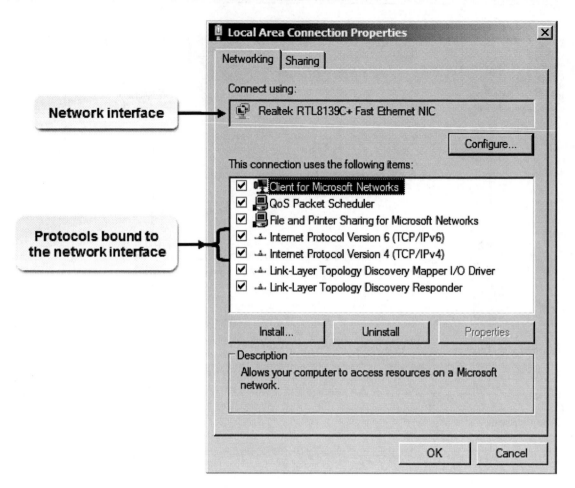

Figure 5-20: Protocols bound to a NIC.

Dual-stack is the side-by-side implementation of IPv4 and IPv6. This is where both protocols run on the same network infrastructure, and there's no need to tunnel IPv6 inside IPv4 or vice versa. Windows has provided dual-stack support since Windows Vista®.

In a scenario where a network interface is bound with multiple protocols, it attempts to connect to a receiving node by sequentially testing the available protocols until it gets a response from the receiving node using a protocol. This carries an inherent risk that the protocol that the node responds to might not be the most efficient one—it is simply the first compatible protocol in the sender's protocol list that the two nodes have in common.

In Windows, you can specify the binding order in which to bind protocols to a network interface. When you set the binding order to prefer the protocol you most frequently use on your network, your system does not attempt to use other protocols to access the network, thus increasing the efficiency of the connection.

In Linux, the `ifconfig` command will display whether or not you are using IPv6. You can disable IPv6 by editing /etc/sysctl.conf. You would add the following lines to the file and restart the sysctl service:

```
net.ipv6.conf.all.disable_ipv6 = 1
net.ipv6.conf.default.disable_ipv6 = 1
net.ipv6.conf.lo.disable_ipv6 = 1
```

Guidelines for Implementing IPv6 Addressing

IPv6 has many advanced features that are not available in IPv4. Although IPv6 is being implemented in test and production networks, IPv4 is implemented on a larger scale. As there are many IPv4 networks, when implementing IPv6 on a network, you need to follow these guidelines to ensure backward compatibility with IPv4.

To implement IPv6 on an IPv4 network, follow these guidelines:

- Implement IPv6 in phases throughout the organization.
- Ensure interoperability between IPv4 and IPv6 during the initial phase of the transition from IPv4 to IPv6, rather than trying to replace IPv4 completely with IPv6.
- Remember that the network classes used in IPv4 will not apply to IPv6.
- Configure AAAA domain name service (DNS) records for IPv6 although IPv4 DNS services make use of A records.
- Upgrade the necessary hardware to support IPv6. This includes all nodes, hosts, and routers on the network.
- Ensure that the IPv6 environment, once implemented, is scalable to support the future requirements of your network.
- Ensure that IPv6 packets that are sent on an IPv4 network are encapsulated. This can be done by tunneling.

ACTIVITY 5-6
Implementing IPv6 Addressing

Scenario

At the Greene City Interiors branch office, you have been tasked with discovering if IPv6 is enabled on network devices. You need to check this IPv6 information on each device.

1. Identify IP address information.

   a) Open **Windows PowerShell**.

   b) In the Windows PowerShell window, type *ipconfig* and press **Enter**.

```
Ethernet adapter Ethernet:

     Connection-specific DNS Suffix  . : GCInteriors.com
     Link-local IPv6 Address . . . . . : fe80::78a7:da22:4ef6:de19%12
     IPv4 Address. . . . . . . . . . . : 192.168.2.37
     Subnet Mask . . . . . . . . . . . : 255.255.255.0
     Default Gateway . . . . . . . . . : 192.168.2.200
```

   Your results will be slightly different.

2. For the Ethernet adapter named Ethernet, what is the IPv6 address?

3. What type of IPv6 address do you have?

TOPIC F

Delivery Techniques

In terms of network data delivery, you have identified two pieces of the puzzle—data addressing and network connection mechanisms. Once you have the data properly packaged and addressed, and a functional network connection established between the source and destination computers, you are ready to transmit data across the network. In this topic, you will identify the techniques that ensure that data is transmitted completely and accurately across a network.

Data that is sent through a network can encounter several variables that can delay or even alter the data before it is received. The challenge for network administrators is to implement delivery techniques within the network to ensure the integrity of data transmission across the network. When implemented, these delivery techniques can detect errors in data transmissions and recover from the errors by using recovery mechanisms.

Connections

A *connection* is a virtual link between two nodes established for the duration of a communication session. Connections provide flow control, packet sequencing, and error recovery functions to ensure reliable communications between nodes.

Connection services ensure reliable delivery by detecting and attempting to correct transmission problems.

Connection Service	Description
Unacknowledged connectionless	This service provides no acknowledgement of successfully transmitted data. The application must provide its own reliability checks. Simplex communications use this type of service.
Acknowledged connectionless	Nodes do not establish a virtual connection. However, they do acknowledge the successful receipt of packets. Web (HTTP) communications use this type of connection service.
Connection-oriented	Nodes establish a virtual connection for the duration of the session. Nodes negotiate communication parameters and typically share security information to establish a connection.
	This connection service provides the means for flow control, packet sequencing, and error recovery functions. Traditional, non-web-based networking applications often use connection-oriented services.

Flow Control

Flow control is a technique for optimizing data exchange between systems. If too much data is sent at once, the receiving node can become overwhelmed, dropping packets that arrive too quickly to process. If too little data is sent, the receiver sits idle waiting for more data to arrive. Buffering and data windows are two flow control techniques commonly used in networking.

TCP, being a connection-oriented protocol, uses flow control to help regulate the flow of data between hosts and manage the session. UDP, being connectionless, makes no attempt at flow control.

Buffering

Buffering is a flow control technique in which data received is stored on a temporary high-speed memory location, called a buffer, until the main system components are ready to work with the data. In a networking situation, the network card itself handles buffering so that the processor does not have to become involved. Buffering is also used when reading information from the disk or RAM, in which case the buffer is more often called a *cache*.

A cache controller, a specialized processor chip, manages caching so that the processor does not have to.

Even with a high-speed buffer, data can sometimes arrive too quickly to be handled. This situation is called *flooding*. To avoid flooding, receiving devices typically send a squelch signal to the sender when the buffer is approximately 75 percent full. Upon receiving a squelch signal, the sender will slow or halt further data transmissions until the receiver catches up.

Both TCP and UDP use buffering to protect the receiver from being overwhelmed by incoming data.

- TCP has a built-in mechanism to continuously communicate the receiver's buffer size to the sender, so that the sender knows how much data it can send at any one time without waiting for an acknowledgement from the receiver.
- UDP has no such mechanism. Instead, it discards any packets it cannot accommodate, expecting the application to manage any errors. Because most UDP applications incorporate a continuous stream of content (voice, live video) or repeated requests (Simple Network Management Protocol [SNMP] management, DNS queries), buffer-related errors are tolerated and compensated for by the application.

Data Windows

Data windows constitute a flow control technique in which multiple packets are sent as a unit called a block or a window. The recipient acknowledges each window rather than each packet, resulting in higher throughput. Two types of data windows are available: fixed length and sliding. Data windows define how much data can be sent without waiting for an acknowledgment. The flow control window, whose size is set by the receiver, ensures that packets are sent at the same speed as the receiver's processing. The size of a data window is set by a sender.

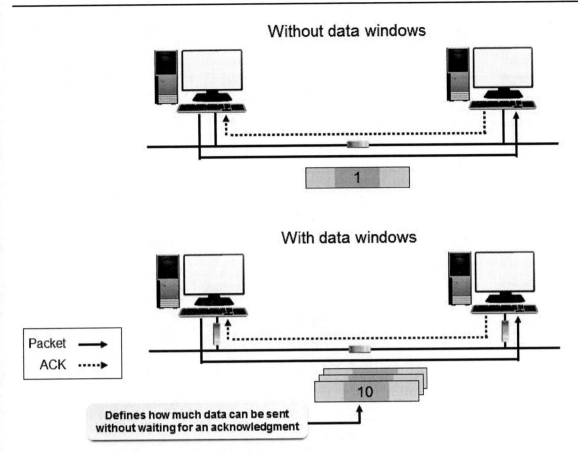

Figure 5-21: Multiple packets sent as a block.

In the simplest case, a sender transmits one packet and then waits for an acknowledgement from the recipient, an ACK signal. If the recipient is busy, the sender sits idle until it receives the ACK, after which it sends the next packet. Throughput can be increased if data is sent in larger packages, with the recipient sending fewer acknowledgements.

The data window size can be fixed or variable. With *fixed-length windows*, every block contains the same number of packets. To avoid flooding the buffers of some devices, fixed-length windows are typically small. So, while fixed-length windows are more efficient than sending individual packets, they are less efficient than sliding windows.

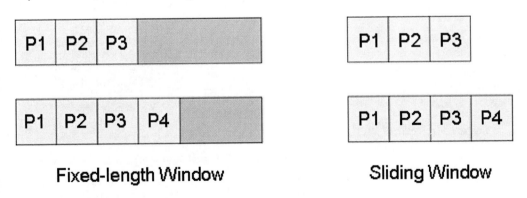

Figure 5-22: Data window sizes can be fixed or variable.

Sliding windows use variable block sizes. The first block sent contains a small number of packets. Each subsequent block is a bit larger, until the sender floods the buffers of the recipient. Upon receiving the squelch signal, the sender reduces the window size and resumes transmission. The window size is continually reevaluated during transmission, with the sender always attempting to send the largest window it can to speed throughput.

TCP uses sliding windows to communicate the receiver's buffer size to the sender. A receive buffer is merely an amount of RAM allocated to a process for it to hold incoming or outgoing data until it is finished processing it. A host's TCP receive buffer will expand or contract in size, depending on how much RAM the operating system can spare at the moment. In the header of every TCP segment is a 16-bit Window Size field that tells the sender how much the receiver can handle at that moment. The sender will then accordingly increase or decrease the number of segments it sends before pausing and waiting for an acknowledgement.

Error Detection

Error detection is the process of determining if transmitted data has been received correctly and completely. Typically, the sender attaches extra bits in the form of an *error detection code (EDC)* to the footer of the transmitted data to indicate its original contents. The receiver generates an EDC and compares it with the transmitted EDC to determine if the data has been altered en route.

- If the EDCs match, the receiver processes the data.
- If the receiver finds an error, it requests retransmission of the data.

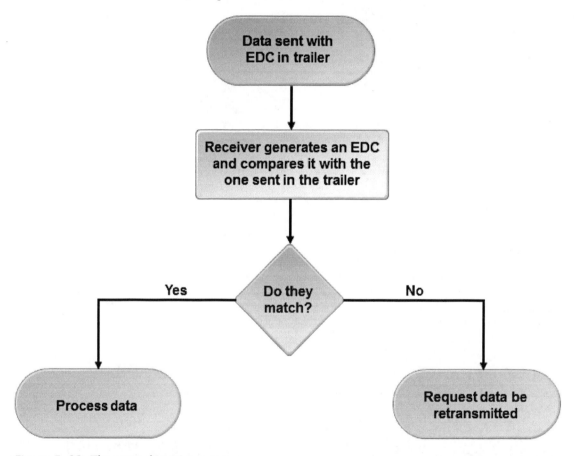

Figure 5–23: The error detection process.

Error detection can also include a correction component, *error detection and correction (EDAC)*, wherein if data has an error, the receiver can rebuild the data.

Parity Checking

Parity check is a process used to detect errors in memory or data communication. In this process:

1. A device checks the data sent and received on a word-by-word basis.

2. The sender adds one bit to each word of the data and then transmits to the receiver. If the number of 1s is odd, the bit will be another one, if the number of 1s is even, then the bit is zero.

3. The receiver compares the number of 1s within a transmitted byte to those received.

4. If the count matches, the data is assumed to be valid. If a word is determined to be corrupt, the receiver requests retransmission of the data.

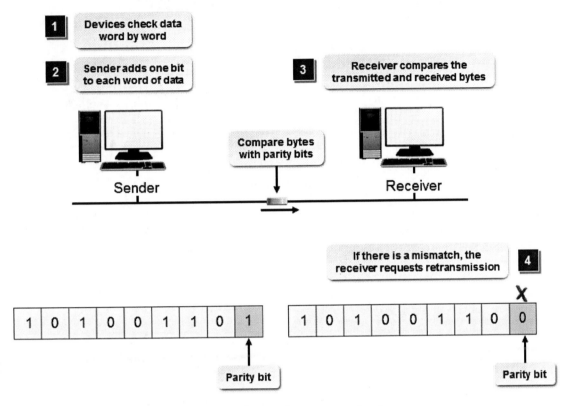

Figure 5-24: Parity check detects errors during data communication.

Cyclic Redundancy Checking

Cyclic redundancy check (CRC) is an error detection method in which a predefined mathematical operation is used to calculate a CRC code. In this error detection process:

1. The sender attaches the CRC to a block of data and transmits it to a receiver.

2. The receiver calculates its own CRC value for the data block and compares it to the transmitted CRC.

3. If the values match, the receiver assumes the data was unaltered during transmission.

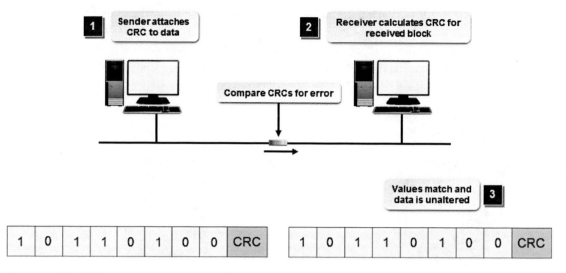

Figure 5-25: CRC used to detect errors in transmitted data.

Typically, CRC checks are applied to large blocks of data, such as all the data sent in a packet. Thus, fewer error detection bits must be transmitted with the data in a packet. However, if a CRC check fails, the entire block must be retransmitted. In general, though, CRC checking uses less network bandwidth than parity checking.

ACTIVITY 5-7
Identifying Data Delivery Techniques

Scenario

At the Greene City Interiors branch office, the network administrator asks you to identify the characteristics of reliable data delivery techniques.

1. Which techniques would you use for error detection?
   - ☐ Sliding windows
   - ☐ Parity checking
   - ☐ CRC
   - ☐ EDAC

2. True or False? Parity checking adds overhead to network transmissions.
   - ☐ True
   - ☐ False

3. Which statement is true of sliding and fixed-length windows?
   - ○ Sliding windows are groups of packets selected at random from transmitted data, whereas fixed-length windows always include the same sequence of packets.
   - ○ Fixed-length windows always contain the same number of packets, while sliding windows contain 8, 16, or 32 packets.
   - ○ Sliding windows contain a variable number of packets in a block, whereas fixed-length windows always contain the same number.
   - ○ Fixed-length windows contain a variable number of packets in a block; sliding windows always contain the same number.

4. Buffer flooding is the process of:
   - ○ Sending data at a speed the receiver can handle.
   - ○ Corrupting the buffers in the receiver.
   - ○ Filling the buffer of the receiver with padding (empty) packets.
   - ○ Overfilling the buffers in the receiver.

Summary

In this lesson, you described TCP/IP addressing. Being able to identify each individual system that is connected, and the TCP/IP addressing scheme, is critical to properly work with networks.

Where would you expect to use custom subnet masks?

What measures have you taken to prepare for implementing IPv6?

 Note: Check your LogicalCHOICE Course screen for opportunities to interact with your classmates, peers, and the larger LogicalCHOICE online community about the topics covered in this course or other topics you are interested in. From the Course screen you can also access available resources for a more continuous learning experience.

6 Routing

Lesson Time: 2 hours, 30 minutes

Lesson Objectives

In this lesson, you will implement routing technologies. You will:

- Enable static routing.

- Implement dynamic IP routing.

Lesson Introduction

In the previous lesson, you learned how the TCP/IP protocol suite uses IP addressing on networks to enable communication. To facilitate communication across different networks, including the Internet, you will need to use routers and routing techniques. In this lesson, you will implement routing technologies.

It is not enough to just know how millions of networks across the globe connect to form a single network. You should also know how these interconnected networks talk to each other and share data, and how information is transferred from a source to a destination almost instantaneously. Because routers are the workhorses of all internetworks, including the Internet, you will need to understand routing basics no matter what kind of network you support.

TOPIC A

Enable Static Routing

In this lesson, you will implement various routing technologies. To begin, you will implement a static IP routing implementation.

It is common for routers to use manually configured routing entries. Even if dynamic routing is used in a network, static routing may also be used to maximize routing efficiency in some cases. A solid understanding of static routing will therefore be important for you to administer networks.

Routing

Routing is the process of selecting the best route for transferring a packet from a source to its destination on a network. A router applies appropriate algorithms to generate and maintain an information base about network paths. It considers various routing metrics such as the bandwidth and reliability of the path, and communication costs while evaluating available network paths to determine the optimal route for forwarding a packet. Once the optimal route for a packet is assigned, packet switching is done to transport the packet from the source host to a destination host. The action of forwarding a packet from one router to the next is called a *hop*.

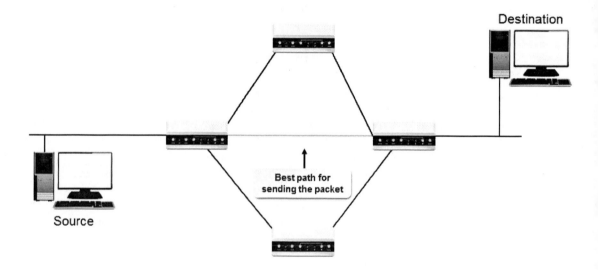

Figure 6-1: A router selects the best path for transferring packets.

Software-Based Routing in Windows Server

Although not as common as hardware-based routers, Windows Server computers with two or more network interface cards (NICs) installed can use the Routing and Remote Access software to function as routers. For testing purposes, instead of installing two NICs, you can install a software-based interface called the Microsoft® Loopback Adapter on your Windows® system, which can simulate the presence of an additional NIC.

Routes

A *route* is the path used by data packets to reach the specified destination, using the gateway as the next hop. Routes are added to the routing table, which stores information about connected and remote networks. Connected networks are directly attached to one of the router's interfaces, which are the gateways for the hosts on different local networks. Because remote networks are not directly connected to the router, routes to these networks must be manually configured on the router by the network administrator or set automatically by using dynamic routing protocols.

Comparing Routing and Switching

When devices communicate with different networks through switches, they are limited to adjacent networks because switches use the media access control (MAC) address of a device to locate it. Routers, on the other hand, are designed to interconnect multiple networks and support connectivity to distant networks. They use a map of the network to make decisions on where to forward data packets. Routers primarily determine the next hop for data. Another advantage that a router has over a switch is that it can read the port number and determine not only the data's destination by using the IP address, but also what kind of data it is transmitting. Broadcasts can either be forwarded or dumped based on the settings of the router.

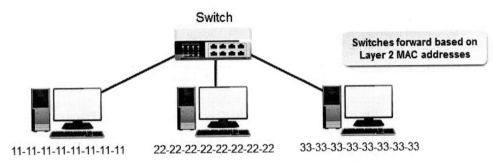

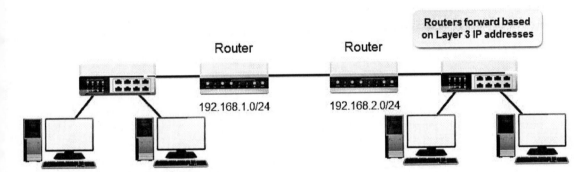

Figure 6-2: Comparing routing and switching.

Switches make forwarding decisions based on Layer 2 MAC addresses. Routers make forwarding decisions based on Layer 3 network addresses. These are typically IP addresses, although they can also include Internet Packet Exchange (IPX), AppleTalk, Open Systems Interconnection (OSI) Connectionless Network Protocol (CLNP), and other types of Layer 3 protocol addresses.

Routers also connect dissimilar Layer 2 network segments. A router will strip off the Layer 2 header of the incoming packet and replace it with the appropriate Layer 2 header before forwarding the packet out the destination interface. For example, a router can connect Ethernet to token ring, Ethernet to frame relay, High-Level Data Link Control (HDLC) to Point-to-Point Protocol (PPP), 802.11 to Ethernet, and so forth.

The IP Data Packet Delivery Process

IP assigns the correct source and destination IP address to a data packet. The process of delivering a data packet by IP consists of four steps:

1. The data payload has been prepared by either the Transmission Control Protocol (TCP) or the User Datagram Protocol (UDP). If necessary, name resolution has already taken place.

2. The Transport-layer protocol passes the segment/datagram down to IP.
3. IP encapsulates the segment/datagram into an IP packet that includes the source and destination IP addresses.
4. IP passes the packet to the Network Interface layer for Layer 2 addressing and transmissions.

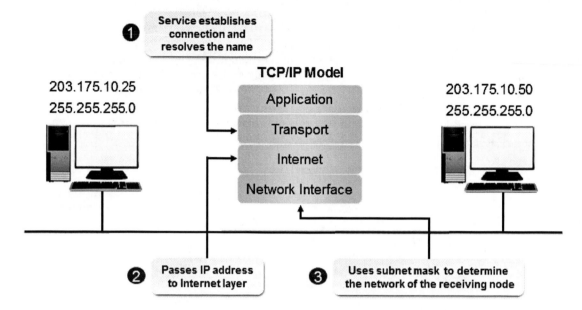

Figure 6-3: The process of IP data packet delivery.

The Local and Remote Delivery Process

In the local and remote delivery process:

1. A network node uses a subnet mask to determine whether a data packet is bound for the local subnet or must be routed to a remote subnet.
2. The node applies the subnet mask to its own IP address to determine its own network ID.
3. It then applies the subnet mask to the packet's destination address to determine the destination network ID.
4. Once the node has applied the subnet mask, it compares the two network IDs.
5. If they are the same, then the two nodes are on the same subnet and the node can deliver the packet.
6. If the two networks are different, then the two nodes are remote to each other and the data is routed to the remote network.

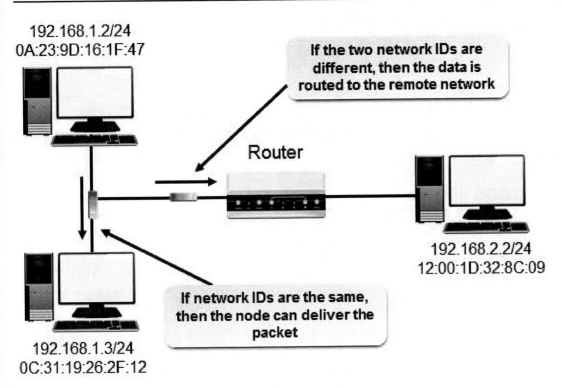

Figure 6-4: Steps involved in the local and remote delivery process.

 Note: The process of determining local and remote addresses based on IP addresses falls under the Network layer's routing protocol function.

Static Routing

Static routing uses table mappings that the network administrator establishes manually in the router prior to routing. Static route mappings do not change unless the network administrator alters them. Static routes remain in a routing table, and traffic is forwarded regardless of whether the destination is active or inactive.

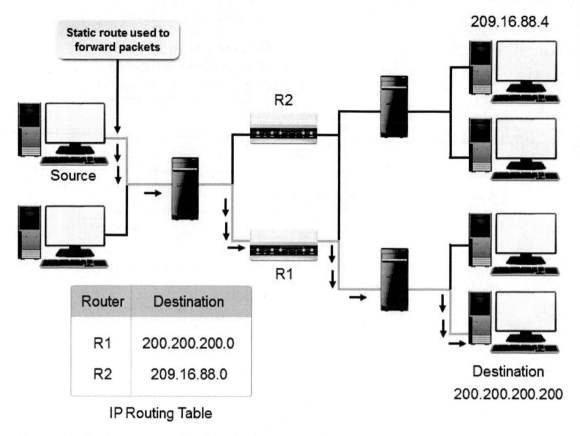

Static route used to forward packets

R2

R1

Source

209.16.88.4

Router	Destination
R1	200.200.200.0
R2	209.16.88.0

IP Routing Table

Destination
200.200.200.200

Figure 6–5: Static routes can be altered only by a network administrator.

Static routing is useful in small networks in which there are no redundant routes and the topology will not change. It is also commonly used when it is not desirable for routers to use bandwidth to update each other with dynamic routes. This is particularly true where there is very little available bandwidth, or routers must dial each other on demand to pass the traffic across a phone line (demand dial routing). In addition, a router will always trust an administrator-configured static route over any route it learned dynamically from other routers.

A device configured with a static default gateway cannot switch to an alternate gateway even if one exists. There exists a class of redundancy protocols known as FHRPs (First Hop Redundancy Protocols) that include VRRP (Virtual Router Redundancy Protocol) and HSRP (Hot Standby Router Protocol). These protocols protect against a single point of failure for the default gateway and may also provide load balancing if multiple uplinks are available at first-hop routers.

VRRP and HSRP enable multiple routers on a LAN to work together sharing a single virtual IP address. The virtual IP address is configured as the default gateway in each device. In a group, one router is elected to handle all requests sent to the group IP address. It is called the active router with HSRP and the master router with VRRP. There is at least one standby router with HSRP and at least one backup router with VRRP.

Routing Tables

A *routing table* is a database created manually or by a route-discovery protocol that contains network addresses as perceived by a specific router. Routers refer to this table to determine where to forward packets. If a router attached to four networks receives a packet from one of them, it would have to determine which of the three other networks is the best route to transfer the packet to its destination. Each router uses its routing table to forward a packet to another network or router until the packet reaches its destination. You can specify the maximum number of hops packets can take from a sender to a receiver.

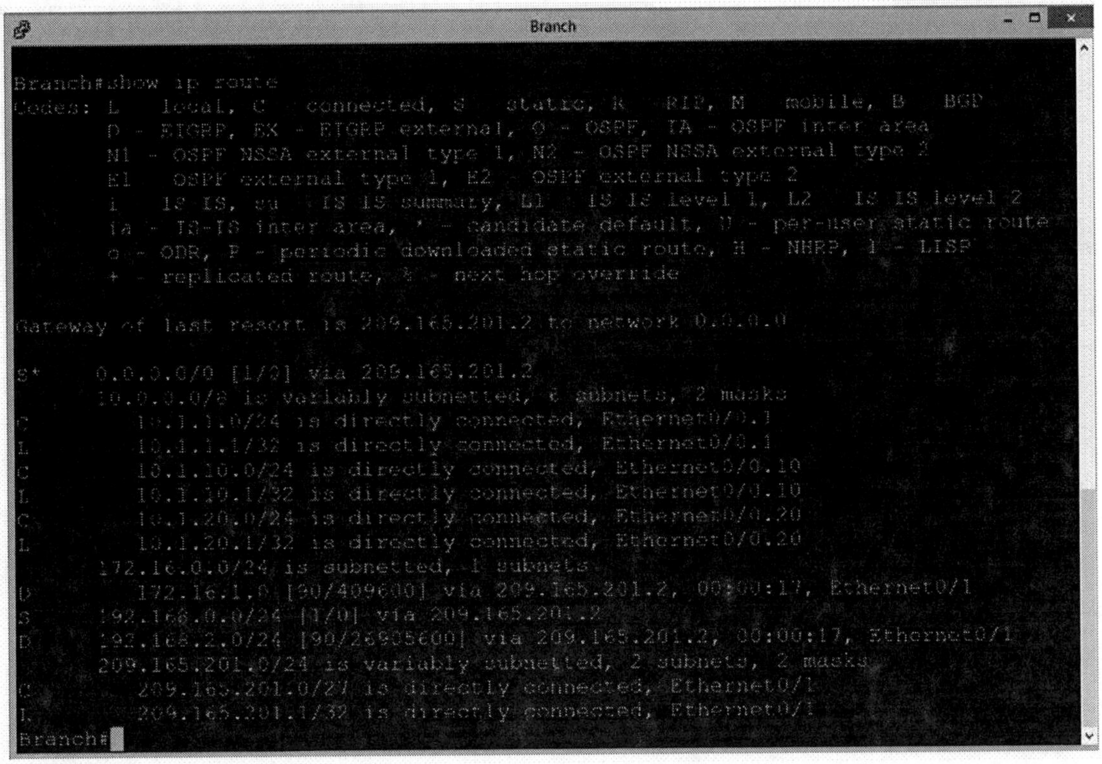

Figure 6-6: A routing table.

The number of hops along a route between two networks constitutes that route's *cost*. However, a cost can also consist of other specifications, such as the transmission speed. Typically, a router maintains the most cost-effective route in its table.

Routing metrics are metrics used by a router to make routing decisions. The metrics are typically one of the fields in a routing table. Metrics are used to determine whether one particular route should be chosen over another. Router metrics can contain any number of values and are typically based on information such as path length, bandwidth, load, hop counts, costs, latency, maximum transmission unit (MTU), administrative distance, and Shortest Path Bridging (SPB).

Static Routing Tables

Static routing tables are manually configured on a router. They are easy to set up and are sometimes used on a small network. Also, as long as a network is relatively unchanging, static routing tables are ideal for an extranet in which the border router of an autonomous system (AS) is pointed toward the border router of an external network.

The advantage of static routing is that it does not cause additional network traffic by sending routing table updates to other routers. It provides extra security from other systems' rogue routers sending information to the AS routers. Also, the routing table can be configured to cover only the necessary portion of the network. That way, the router does not expend resources for maintaining its routing table.

The biggest disadvantage of static routing tables is that they require manual maintenance. Network changes need to be updated manually on all routers affected by the change. Because of this, static routing is prone to configuration errors, and is less efficient than dynamic routing.

Routing Table Entries

Routing table entries fall into four general categories:
* Direct network routes, for subnets to which the router is directly attached.

- Remote network routes, for subnets that are not directly attached.
- Host routes, for routes to a specific IP address.
- Default routes, which are used when a better network or host route is not found.

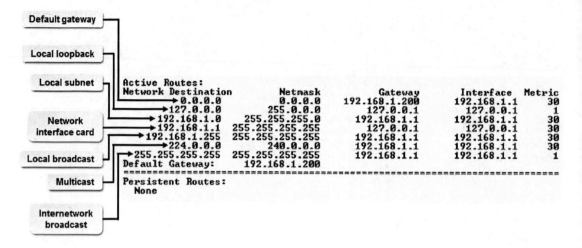

Figure 6-7: Routing table entries.

All IP host computers have a routing table with default entries so that the host can deliver packets to common destinations.

Entry	Description
Default gateway (destination: 0.0.0.0)	The default gateway entry appears if the local host has been configured with a default gateway address.
Local loopback (destination: 127.0.0.1)	The local loopback entry provides a delivery route for packets addressed to the local loopback address (127.0.0.1).
Local subnet (destination: network portion of local IP address plus host address of all 0)	The local subnet entry identifies the route to the local network. An example of a destination address can be 140.125.0.0.
Network interface (destination: local IP address)	The network interface entry identifies the route to the host's local network card. An example of a destination address can be 140.125.10.25.
Subnet broadcast address (destination: network portion of local IP address plus host address of all .255)	The subnet broadcast entry identifies the route for broadcasts on the local subnet. An example of a destination address can be 140.125.255.255.
Multicast broadcast address (destination: 224.0.0.0)	The multicast broadcast entry identifies the address for sending multicast transmissions.
Internetwork broadcast address (destination: 255.255.255.255)	The internetwork broadcast entry identifies the route for broadcasts to the entire network. However, most routers will not pass these broadcasts.

 Note: When reading routing tables, it can be helpful to think of each row as a single routing table entry, and each column as a characteristic of that route.

In Linux, there are three commands you can use to display a routing table. Any will work, but you have to run the commands as root (administrator):

```
route
netstat -rn
ip route list
```

Routes can be added to the routing table based on their *administrative distance*. Administrative distance is a numerical value assigned to a routing protocol, static route, or a directly connected route to signify more desirable routes. A routing protocol with a lower administrative distance is considered "better" and is given priority over routing protocols that have higher administrative distances when multiple paths to the same destination exist. The "better" route is selected by the router and is inserted into the router's routing table to be used to route traffic.

SPB allows all paths to be active with multiple equal cost paths. SPB combines an Ethernet data path with an Intermediate System to Intermediate System (IS-IS) link state control protocol running between shortest path bridges. The link state protocol is used to discover and advertise the network topology and compute shortest path trees from all bridges.

Routing Entry Components

Routing entries are entries in routing tables that provide routing information to a router. There are several components to each entry in a routing table.

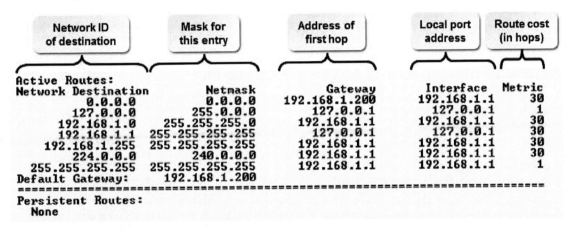

Figure 6-8: Components of a routing table entry.

Routing Entry Component	Description
Network destination or network address	The destination field contains the network ID of a destination address and is the search point when processing the routing table. It can be listed as a complete address, but the router will be more efficient if destination entries are listed as network IDs. This way, only one entry is added to the routing table for an entire subnet, no matter how many nodes are on it.
Network mask	A network mask is specific to a routing entry. It determines the extent to which a packet's destination address needs to match the network destination field of a routing entry before that route is used to deliver the packet.
Gateway	The gateway field indicates the address to which the packet is delivered on its first hop. It can be the local loopback address, a local IP address, the host's own default gateway address, or the address of an adjacent router.
Interface	The interface is the IP address of the local port that a host uses to send data. Once a destination entry is found, data is sent to the interface entry listed in the same line as the destination.

Routing Entry Component	Description
Metric	A metric is the cost of the route, and it is determined by the number of hops. The metric is used to determine which route to use when there are multiple routes to a destination.

The route Command

Routes to destinations that are not in the default routing table must be added manually. On Windows Server® 2012 R2, you can use the route command to manage the static routing table.

Command	Used To
route print	Display the routing table entries.
route add	Add static entries.
route delete	Remove static entries.
route change	Modify an existing route.
route -p	Make the specified route persistent across reboots, when used in conjunction with the add command.
route -f	Clear a routing table of all entries.

The Routing Process

There are three steps in the routing process:

1. A router receives data and reads its destination IP address.
2. The router reads its routing table, which lists the locations of other routers on the network.
3. Once it decides on a route, it removes the old destination MAC address and attaches the MAC address of the next hop in the data's path. The packet's ultimate destination IP address never changes. By enabling the router to change the destination MAC address, the data moves through multiple local networks.

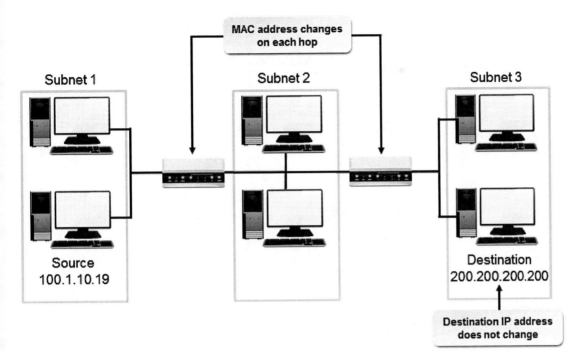

Figure 6-9: The routing process.

The number of routing tables will increase as your network grows. *Route aggregation* can save space in the routing table and simplify routing decisions by aggregating routes to multiple smaller networks. Routing advertisements to neighboring gateways are reduced.

Autonomous Systems

An *autonomous system (AS)* or a *routing domain* is a self-contained network or group of networks governed by a single administration. An AS can connect to other networks or other autonomous systems, but does not share routing information outside of the AS. Each AS has a unique identification number assigned by the Internet Assigned Numbers Authority (IANA). Depending on whether routing takes place within an autonomous system or among different autonomous systems, it is referred to as *intra-domain routing* or *inter-domain routing*. Each autonomous system may choose different routing algorithms for intra-domain routing, but only one algorithm can be used for inter-domain routing. IS-IS and Open Shortest Path First (OSPF) are interior (intra-domain) routing protocols designed to work within an autonomous system. IS-IS is an OSI link-state routing protocol that dynamically routes packets between routers or intermediate systems. OSPF is an Internet link-state protocol based on IS-IS.

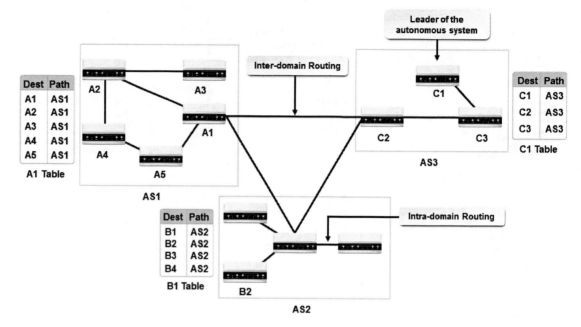

Figure 6–10: Routing in an autonomous system.

An autonomous system number (ASN) is a 16-bit number assigned by the American Registry for Internet Numbers (ARIN). Nearly all ISPs, as well as many large organizations, have their own ASNs, which uniquely identify each network on the Internet.

Classification of Autonomous Systems

Autonomous systems can be classified as *transit* and *stub autonomous systems*.

Autonomous System	Description
Transit	The source or destination node does not reside within an autonomous system. The autonomous system allows the traffic to reach another network. ISPs are examples of transit autonomous systems.
Stub	Either the source node or destination node must exist within an autonomous system. The stub autonomous system does not allow transit traffic.

Router Roles in Autonomous Systems

Routers can play three different roles in autonomous systems.

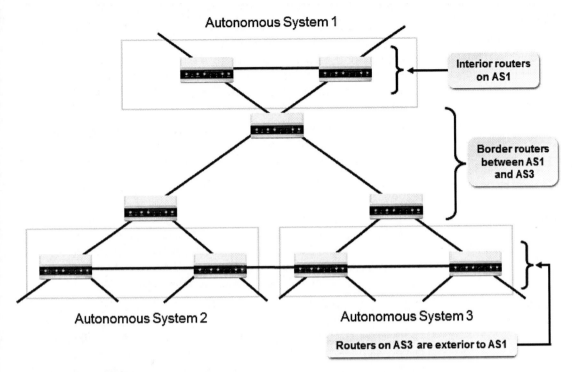

Figure 6-11: Router roles in an autonomous system.

Router Role	Description
Interior router	*Interior routers* are arranged inside an AS, and the AS administrator controls them. All interfaces on an interior router connect to subnets inside the AS. Interior routers use IGPs. Interior routers do not provide connections to external networks.
Exterior router	*Exterior routers* are entirely outside of an AS. These routers matter to the AS only if they handle data from the AS. Exterior routers use EGPs. Routers that operate on the Internet backbone are exterior routers.
Border or edge router	*Border routers* or *edge routers* are situated on the edge of an AS. They have one or more interfaces inside the AS and one or more interfaces that provide a connection to remote networks. Border routers are usually managed by the administrator of an AS and can be placed between two private networks or between a private network and its ISP to direct requests to the Internet.

An *interior gateway protocol (IGP)*, as the name suggests, is a protocol responsible for exchanging routing information between gateways within an AS. In contrast, an *exterior gateway protocol (EGP)* exchanges routing information between two neighboring gateways. EGPs can also use IGPs to resolve a route within the AS. Examples of IGPs include Routing Information Protocol (RIP), OSPF, Enhanced Interior Gateway Routing Protocol (EIGRP), IS-IS, and Interior Gateway Routing Protocol (IGRP). Examples of EGPs include Exterior Gateway Protocol (EGP) (a legacy Internet routing protocol) and Border Gateway Protocol (BGP).

Routing Methods in Autonomous Systems

There are different methods for routing inside an autonomous system: between adjacent networks and between distant networks.

Routing Method	Description
Inside an autonomous system	When routing inside an autonomous network, data transmission begins at a device and does not leave the AS. That means that when any node sends data, it can send it only to a node on the same local network. Nodes use the Address Resolution Protocol (ARP) to obtain the local destination's MAC address.
	When a node needs to send data to a remote network, it sends it to the IP address configured as the node's default gateway. When a node sends data to an address on its own subnet, it sends it directly to the address. When a node needs to send data to a node anywhere inside the AS, all routers in the AS should be aware of the path to the destination node.
Between adjacent networks	Adjacent networks share border routers, and because any router inside an AS knows a direct path to the adjacent network, it knows how to deliver data to the correct border router. That border router then passes the data on to the appropriate network. This configuration gives an AS a single point of contact between adjacent networks.
Between distant networks	Distant networks are not directly aware of the location of a destination network. You have accessed a distant network if you have sent a request to the Internet for a web page. An AS router cannot know all of the details in the path to a website. In this situation, the routers send the data to a default gateway. If the router serving as the default gateway does not know the destination, it transmits the packet to its own default gateway. Data moves from default gateway to default gateway until it either reaches a router that knows a route to the destination, or the time-to-live (TTL) hop limit expires and the packet expires on the network.

 Access the Checklist tile on your LogicalCHOICE course screen for reference information and job aids on How to Configure Routing and Remote Access.

ACTIVITY 6-1
Enabling Static Routing

Scenario

At the Greene City Interiors branch office, you want to implement software-based routing by using Windows Server 2012 R2 routing features. You are going to test a router in a lab environment to simulate the production router. You need to enable routing on the server that you will be testing.

---

1. Enable routing and remote access.

   a) If Server Manager is not running, select **Start→Server Manager**.

   b) In the Server Manager window, select the **Add roles and features** link.

   c) In the **Add Roles and Features Wizard**, on the **Before You Begin** page, select **Next**.

   d) On the **Select installation type** page, verify that **Role-based or feature-based installation** is selected, and select **Next**.

   e) On the **Select destination server** page, verify that **Computer##.Child##.GCInteriors.com** is selected, and select **Next**.

   f) In the **Select server roles** list, check the **Remote Access** check box and select **Next**.

   g) On the **Select features** page, select **Next**.

   h) On the **Remote Access** page, select **Next**.

   i) On the **Select role services** page, in the **Role services** list, check the **Routing** check box.

   j) In the **Add Roles and Features Wizard** dialog box, select **Add Features** to add all the suggested features.

   k) Select **Next**.

   l) On the **Web Server Role (IIS)** page, select **Next**.

   m) On the **Select role services** page, select **Next**.

   n) On the **Confirm Installation Selections** page, select **Restart the destination server automatically if required**.

   o) In the **Add Roles and Features Wizard** dialog box, select **Yes**.

   p) Select **Install,** and when the installation is complete select **Close**.

2. Verify that routing and remote access is enabled.

   a) In the Server Manager window, select **Tools→Routing and Remote Access**.

   b) In the console tree, select **Computer## (local),** and then select **Action→Configure and Enable Routing and Remote Access**.

   c) In the **Routing and Remote Access Server Setup Wizard**, click **Next**.

   d) Verify that the **Remote access (dial-up or VPN)** option is selected and select **Next**.

   e) Check the **VPN** check box and select **Next**.

   f) From the **Network interfaces** list, select **Loopback Adapter** and select **Next**.

   g) Verify that the **Automatically** option is selected and select **Next** to assign IP addresses automatically to remote clients.

   h) Verify that the **No, use Routing and Remote Access to authenticate connection requests** option is selected, and select **Next**.

   i) Select **Finish** and, if necessary, select **OK**.

j) Observe that the Routing and Remote Access service has been enabled, indicated by the green upward pointing arrow next to the Computer## object in the left pane.

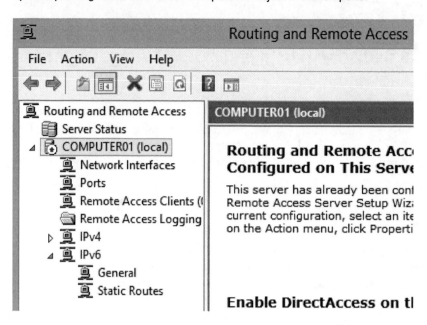

k) Close all open windows except for the Server Manager window.

ACTIVITY 6-2
Identifying Routing Entries

Scenario

At the Greene City Interiors branch office, you want to identify the default routing entries on the Windows Server 2012 R2 computer that you have enabled as a router. Refer to the following IPv4 route table to complete this activity.

```
IPv4 Route Table
===========================================================================
Active Routes:
Network Destination        Netmask          Gateway       Interface  Metric
          0.0.0.0          0.0.0.0    192.168.1.200    192.168.1.11    276
        127.0.0.0        255.0.0.0         On-link        127.0.0.1    306
        127.0.0.1  255.255.255.255         On-link        127.0.0.1    306
  127.255.255.255  255.255.255.255         On-link        127.0.0.1    306
       172.16.0.0      255.255.0.0         On-link       172.16.0.1    286
       172.16.0.1  255.255.255.255         On-link       172.16.0.1    286
   172.16.255.255  255.255.255.255         On-link       172.16.0.1    286
      192.168.1.0    255.255.255.0         On-link     192.168.1.11    276
     192.168.1.11  255.255.255.255         On-link     192.168.1.11    276
    192.168.1.255  255.255.255.255         On-link     192.168.1.11    276
        224.0.0.0        240.0.0.0         On-link        127.0.0.1    306
        224.0.0.0        240.0.0.0         On-link       172.16.0.1    286
        224.0.0.0        240.0.0.0         On-link     192.168.1.11    276
  255.255.255.255  255.255.255.255         On-link        127.0.0.1    306
  255.255.255.255  255.255.255.255         On-link       172.16.0.1    286
  255.255.255.255  255.255.255.255         On-link     192.168.1.11    276
===========================================================================
```

1. Which route determines the destination for packets to the 172.16.0.0 network? What adapter will they be delivered to?

2. Which interfaces will receive internetwork broadcasts?

3. You connect a second router in parallel to the default gateway for testing purposes. Its IP address is 192.168.1.254. Both routers lead to the 10.10.10.0/24 network. You want to ping 10.10.10.22. How can you configure your host to use the second router to reach the 10.10.10.0 network without changing the default gateway on your host?

TOPIC B

Implement Dynamic IP Routing

In the previous topic, you identified the components of a static routing implementation. Routing can also be implemented dynamically. In this topic, you will implement dynamic routing.

Dynamic routing, like dynamic IP addressing, is the technology of choice in larger network environments. As a network professional, you should understand dynamic routing technologies and how you can implement them so that you can support routed environments of all sizes and types. This will ensure that each device is properly identified on the network.

Dynamic Routing

Routers that support *dynamic routing* perform route discovery operations to build and update routing tables themselves by using specially designed software. Routers transmit data to adjacent routers providing information about the networks they are currently connected to and networks they can reach. In the dynamic routing process, routing entries are created automatically. Dynamically built routing tables can show a more accurate picture of a network because they are updated more often than static tables. This is because the routers, not the administrator, update the tables. If the network suffers traffic congestion or device failures, a router running dynamic routing protocols can automatically detect the problem and calculate a different routing path. This feature is a huge advantage on large networks that have many routers or multiple paths to each endpoint.

Route redistribution is when a route from one routing protocol is distributed into another protocol. This allows two different protocols to share and advertise routes to each other. By default, routers advertise and share routes only with other routers running the same protocol.

Comparing Static and Dynamic Routing

In static routing, routing entries are created manually in configuration files. This file is loaded when the router starts. Static routing is used when there are fewer devices on the network. Dynamic routing uses special software designed for routing devices. This software automatically creates routing entries for the router to connect all devices on the network.

On systems that support both static and dynamic routing, the static routing will take precedence.

Distance-Vector Routing

Distance-vector routing is used on packet-switched networks to automatically calculate route costs and routing table entries. Routers calculate the direction and distance between any two points and route packets based on their calculation of the fewest number of hops. Basically, distance vector means "how far" and "in what direction."

This is the general process for distance-vector routing:

1. Each router passes a copy of its routing table to its neighbors and maintains a table of minimum distances to every node.
2. The neighbors add the route to their own tables, incrementing the metric to reflect the extra distance to the end network. The distance is given as a hop count; the vector component specifies the address of the next hop.
3. When a router has two routes to the same network, it selects the one with the lowest metric, assuming that it is faster to route through fewer hops.

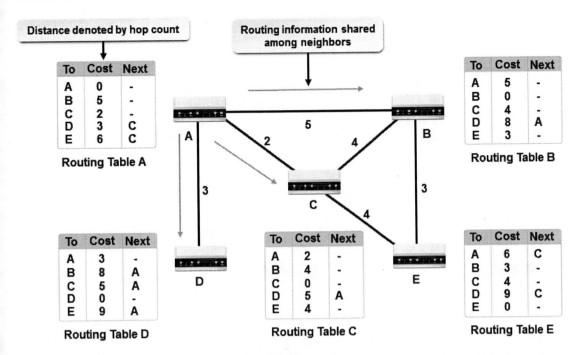

Figure 6-12: Routers maintain a table of minimum costs.

Routing Information Protocol (RIP) and RIPv2 implement distance-vector routing.

 Note: Distance-vector protocols use the Bellman-Ford algorithm to calculate route paths.

Link-State Routing

Link-state routing floods routing information to all routers within a network. It attempts to build and maintain a more complex route database with more information about the network. Routers can exchange information about a route, such as its quality, bandwidth, and availability. This way, the routers can make a decision about sending data through the network based on more information than just the hop count.

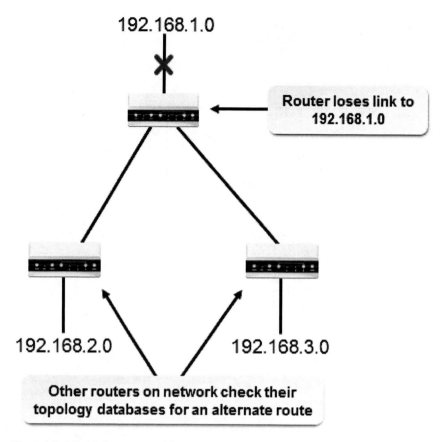

192.168.1.0

Router loses link to 192.168.1.0

192.168.2.0   192.168.3.0

Other routers on network check their topology databases for an alternate route

Figure 6-13: Link-state routing.

Link-state algorithms broadcast small updates and converge quickly, a feature that makes them less prone to routing loops. However, link-state algorithms are more expensive to implement because they require more power and memory. The *Open Shortest Path First (OSPF)* protocol implements link-state routing.

In link-state routing, routers update each other only when one of their links changes state. Otherwise, they do not communicate except for sending a periodic "hello" packet to assure their neighbor routers that they are still functioning on the network.

Comparing Distance-Vector and Link-State Routing

The primary advantages of distance-vector routing are that it is very easy to configure and is suitable for small networks. The primary disadvantages of distance-vector routing include the fact that routers send updates to their neighbors on a periodic basis whether the network is changed or not. This consumes extra bandwidth unnecessarily. In addition, distance-vector routers are aware only of their directly connected neighbors, and do not have a complete topology map of the network. They must trust that routing updates that their neighbors provide them are accurate. This provides opportunities for hacking, network "black holes," and infinite routing loops (a condition in which two routers each assume the other has a path to the destination when in truth neither does, so the routers pass a packet back and forth to each other indefinitely).

The primary advantage of link-state routing is that all routers build and maintain a complete topology database of the entire network (or at least their area of the network). This means should one link fail, these routers can very quickly adapt by consulting their own databases for alternate routes, rather than relying upon neighboring routers to inform them of possible alternate routes.

The primary disadvantage of link-state routing is that it requires a well-designed, hierarchical network with a central backbone area that all traffic and route updates pass through. Link-state routing protocols do not perform well when the network is designed poorly, when the network is discontiguous, or when the IP addresses cannot be summarized by the border routers.

Hybrid Routing

A *hybrid routing protocol* is one that uses the best of both distance-vector and link-state routing methods. Cisco's Enhanced Interior Gateway Protocol (EIGRP) is an example of a hybrid routing protocol. As with the distance-vector protocol RIP, EIGRP depends on neighboring routers to advertise the cost of each route. And as with the link-state protocol OSPF, EIGRP maintains a topology table of the entire network, indicating possible alternate routes should the best route fail.

Path-Vector Routing

Path-vector routing is used in inter-domain routing, and a router keeps track of the route from itself to the destination. However, rather than recording every individual node, path-vector routing can treat entire autonomous systems as nodes. As the AS border or exterior routers pass routing information from one to the next, each adds its presence to the path and forwards the route to the next autonomous system in the chain. If the destination address is within an AS, the border router passes the packet on to interior routers.

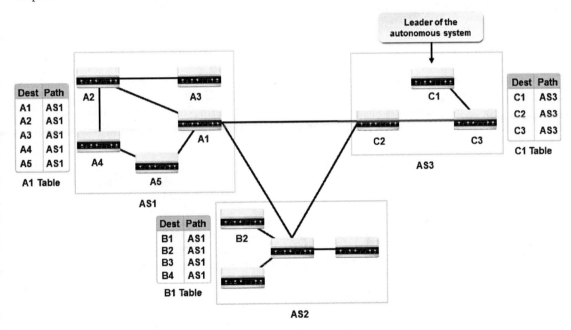

Figure 6-14: The path-vector routing table of different autonomous systems.

Border Gateway Protocol (BGP) is an example of a path vector routing protocol.

Path-vector routing is enhanced by its inclusion of routing policies, which are implemented by administrators to enable routers to react to situations such as network congestion, offline nodes, and potentially duplicate routes. Path-vector routing has roots in distance-vector routing, but was designed to scale up to much larger networks.

Route Convergence

In dynamic routing, when the network topology or conditions change, each router must first learn of the change and then calculate the effect and update its routing tables. *Route convergence* is the period of time between a network change and the router updates to reach a steady state once again. During route convergence, data delivery can be unreliable, as the routing table may not be updated with the route information.

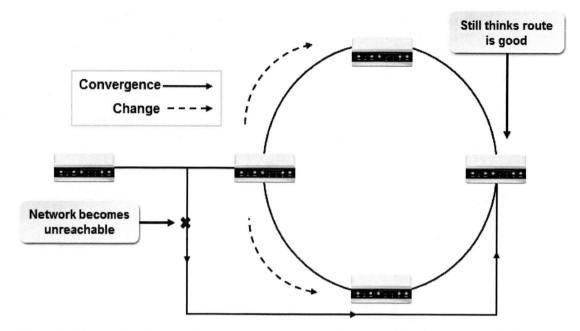

Figure 6–15: A router changes the route when a part of the network becomes unreachable.

Routing Loops

A *routing loop* is a routing process in which two routers discover different routes to the same location that include each other, but have incorrect information and thereby never reach the endpoint. Data caught in a routing loop circles around until its TTL expires. Routing loops can be difficult to detect and to troubleshoot; the best prevention is proper router configuration.

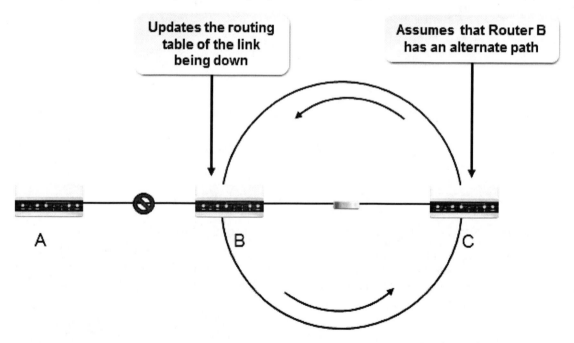

Figure 6–16: A routing loop created between routers B and C.

For example, Routers A, B, and C are connected in a line. When the link between A and B goes down, it prompts B to update its routing table. But, this update does not reach C on time, and it sends its regular update to B. This leads B to assume that C has found an alternate path to reach A.

An endless loop is created because B tries to send packets addressed to A via C, which redirects the packets to B. This routing loop continues until the TTL of the data expires.

Count-to-Infinity Loops

A *count-to-infinity loop* can occur when a router or network goes down and one of the other routers does not realize that it can no longer reach the route. This loop results in the remaining routers broadcasting incorrect information and updating each other's routing tables to create an endless cycle of hop count recalculation. This cycle continues to infinity, which is configured as 16 hops in most routing implementations.

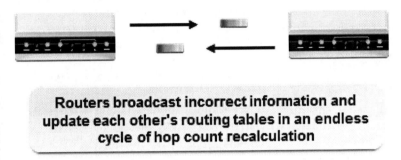

Routers broadcast incorrect information and update each other's routing tables in an endless cycle of hop count recalculation

Figure 6-17: A count-to-infinity loop.

Consider a network containing four routers that connect five networks. In calculating the cost to network E, router 3 figures its cost to be one hop, router 2 figures two hops, and router 1 figures three hops. If router 4 fails, router 3 must recalculate its routing table by using information from other routers. However, router 3 still thinks that it can reach network E, and uses information advertised from router 2 to calculate its table.

According to router 2, network E is still two hops away, so router 3 broadcasts that its cost to network E is three hops. Router 1 receives the new information from router 3, updates its table, and then broadcasts this information. Router B also recalculates accordingly and the infinite loop continues.

Split Horizon and Poison Reverse

One workaround to the count-to-infinity problem is the *split horizon* method, where a router does not include any routes to the router from which it discovered its own location in its broadcasts.

Another workaround to the count-to-infinity problem is called a *poison reverse*. Unlike in split horizon, routers using poison reverse broadcast routes back to the router from which they calculated their location, but instead of giving a true hop count, to discourage use of the route, the router broadcasts a hop count of 16, as a warning not to use the value specified and as an intimation that the route was learned from router 1.

Router Discovery Protocols

Router discovery protocols are used to identify routers on the network.

Protocol	Description
RIP	*RIP* is a distance-vector routing protocol that is easy to configure, works well inside simple autonomous systems, and is best deployed in small networks with fewer numbers of routers and in a non-dynamic environment. Most equipment that supports RIP is lower in cost than that which supports more complicated router discovery protocols. RIP broadcasts the entire routing table, including known routes and costs, every 30 seconds. This places a lot of router discovery traffic on the network. When RIP builds its routing table, it does not take into account network congestion or link speed. A router records the route with the lowest metric to a location and removes the others. RIP is very stable, but convergence is slow. RIP is prone to count-to-infinity loops and does not support many of the new features expected on modern networks such as multicast addressing. RIP has been replaced with RIP version 2 (RIP v2).
RIP v2	RIP v2 enhances RIP by supporting the following features: • **Next Hop Addressing:** Includes IP address information in routing tables for every router in a given path to avoid sending packets using additional routers. • **Authentication:** Enables password authentication and the use of a key to authenticate routing information to a router. • **Subnet mask:** Supports additional subnets and hosts on an internetwork by supporting VLSMs and including length information along with the routing information. • **Multicast addressing:** Decreases the workload of non–RIP v2 hosts by communicating only with RIP v2 routers. RIP v2 packets use 224.0.0.9 as their IP multicast address. • **IPv6 support:** Supports IPv6 networking. Most hosts and routers support RIP, so ensure that the RIP v2 mode you configure works with your current RIP configuration. **Note:** For more information on RIP v2, see RFC 1387 "RIP Version 2 Protocol Analysis." You might also be interested in RFCs 1388 and 1389 for RIP II information.
OSPF	On IP internetworks, link-state routing is usually accomplished by the *OSPF* protocol. Each OSPF router uses the information in its database to build the shortest possible path to destinations on the internetwork. Although OSPF uses less bandwidth than distance-vector protocols, it requires more memory and CPU resources. OSPF uses Dijkstra's algorithm for computing the best path through a network. OSPF supports IPv4 and IPv6.
BGP	*BGP* is a hybrid routing protocol used to establish routing between ISPs. BGP is the routing protocol used to connect Internet backbones. BGP maintains a table of IP networks among autonomous systems. BGP was created as a fully decentralized routing protocol to replace EGP in order to decentralize the Internet. The current version is BGP v4, which supports IPv4 and IPv6. Although BGP was created to replace EGP, BGP is considered an interautonomous routing protocol. When it is used to route information between ASs, it is called External BGP (EBGP), but when EGP is used to route information within an AS, it is referred to as Internal BGP (IBGP).

Protocol	Description
IGRP	*Interior Gateway Routing Protocol (IGRP)* is a distance-vector routing protocol developed by Cisco® as an improvement over RIP and RIP v2. It was designed to be deployed on interior routers within an AS. IGRP introduced a composite metric, enabling an administrator to manually configure and add to the hop count up to four metric values to give extra value to the metric. Because of this, IGRP can support multiple routes to the same network and can even support load balancing across routes with identical metrics.
EIGRP	*Enhanced Interior Gateway Routing Protocol (EIGRP)* is a proprietary routing protocol by Cisco and considered a hybrid protocol. It includes features that support classful and classless subnet masks, and it can be used on multilayer switches. Additional updates reduce convergence times and improve network stability during changes. To ensure that EIGRP is a viable solution for interior routing, EIGRP removed routing protocol dependence on the network protocol. This means that routing tables can be built for several different protocols, such as IPv6. In March 2013, Cisco made EIGRP an open standard.
IS-IS	*Intermediate System to Intermediate System (IS-IS)* is a link-state routing protocol that is natively an OSI Network-layer protocol. IS-IS is similar to OSPF (they both use Dijkstra's algorithm) but IS-IS is able to support more routers than OSPF and does not support only a specific type of network address. This made IS-IS easily adaptable to support IPv6.

RIP v2 vs. OSPF

There are differences in characteristics of RIPv2 and OSPF.

Characteristic	RIP v2	OSPF
Size of metric	16—This means that a RIP v2 network cannot be larger than 16 hops. This maximum is further reduced when costs other than 1 are used for certain routes.	Limited only by the number of bits in the metric field (65,535). Because OSPF does not suffer from the count-to-infinity problem, it can be the basis for much larger internetworks, and administrators can assign costs to optimize routing without limiting the size of the network.
Maximum number of routers	15—This value is related to the allowable metric size.	65,535. This value is related to the allowable metric size.
Variable-length subnets	Only with RIP v2; RIP treats subnets as part of the internal structure of the network and assumes that all subnets are of equal length. With RIP, all subnets must be contiguous, connected, and hidden from remote networks.	Supported by default; because OSPF treats the subnet mask as part of the protocol information, the restrictions that affect RIP do not apply.
Convergence	Poison reverse or split horizon must be used to counteract the count-to-infinity problem. RIP must calculate all routes before broadcasting the information.	Link State Acknowledgements (LSAs) provide rapid convergence among tables; no count-to-infinity problem arises. OSPF passes along LSAs as soon as they are received, meaning that nodes can adjust their routing tables at practically the same time.

Characteristic	RIP v2	OSPF
Broadcast traffic	The entire routing table is broadcast every 30 seconds.	A Hello packet is broadcast to establish and maintain neighbor relationships, and is typically sent every 10 seconds by default.

 Access the Checklist tile on your LogicalCHOICE course screen for reference information and job aids on How to Implement Dynamic IP Routing.

ACTIVITY 6-3
Implementing Dynamic IP Routing

Before You Begin
You will need to work with a partner if you want to view the results of step 3 of this activity.

Scenario
At the Greene City Interiors branch office, you have decided that static routing will not meet the needs of the network because it is too large. You plan to implement dynamic routing and need to install a routing protocol on your Windows Server 2012 R2 router.

1. Add RIP v2 as the routing protocol.
   a) In Server Manager, select **Tools→Routing and Remote Access**.
   b) In the Routing and Remote Access window, expand **COMPUTER## (local)**, expand **IPv4**, and select **General**.
   c) Select **Action→New Routing Protocol**.
   d) In the **New Routing Protocol** dialog box, select **RIP Version 2 for Internet Protocol** and select **OK** to add RIP v2 as the routing protocol.

2. Add the RIP interfaces.
   a) In the console tree, under **IPv4**, select **RIP**.
   b) Select **Action→New Interface**.
   c) In the **New Interface for RIP Version 2 for Internet Protocol** dialog box, verify that **Ethernet** is selected and select **OK**.
   d) In the **RIP Properties - Ethernet Properties** dialog box, select **OK** to accept the default settings.
   e) Select **Action→New Interface**.
   f) Verify that the **Loopback Adapter** is selected and select **OK**.
   g) Select **OK** to accept the default settings.

3. Examine the dynamic routes.
   a) With RIP selected, select **Action→Show Neighbors**.
      It might take a few minutes for the neighbors to be listed.

b) Observe that you have neighbor routers running RIP. Close the RIP Neighbors window.

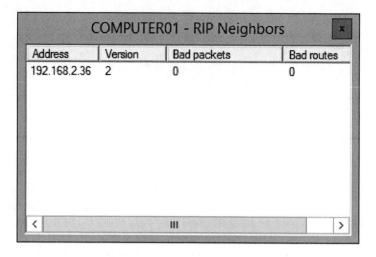

c) Close the Routing and Remote Access window.

Summary

In this lesson, you implemented routing. Knowing how routers interconnect networks so they can talk to each other and share data is important no matter what kind of network you support.

At your workplace, what sorts of situations might you use static routing for?

What dynamic routing protocol do you think you would recommend for implementation? Why?

 Note: Check your LogicalCHOICE Course screen for opportunities to interact with your classmates, peers, and the larger LogicalCHOICE online community about the topics covered in this course or other topics you are interested in. From the Course screen you can also access available resources for a more continuous learning experience.

7 | TCP/IP Services

Lesson Time: 2 hours, 30 minutes

Lesson Objectives

In this lesson, you will identify the major services deployed on TCP/IP networks. You will:

- Assign IP addresses statically and dynamically.

- Identify host name resolution methods on a TCP/IP network.

- Identify common TCP/IP commands and their functions.

- Identify common protocols and services in use on a TCP/IP network.

Lesson Introduction

In addition to providing addressing and routing services, the TCP/IP protocol suite also includes services that aid in managing your TCP/IP network. In this lesson, you will identify the services that are part of the TCP/IP protocol suite that can be used on your network.

To manage a TCP/IP network, you need to understand IP addressing methods. But you also have to be able to implement an addressing scheme and provide ongoing support. To do that, you will need to understand and use TCP/IP services and tools that enable you to configure, monitor, and troubleshoot your TCP/IP network.

TOPIC A

Assign IP Addresses

Each node needs an IP address to communicate on a TCP/IP network. An administrator can manually assign these IP addresses, or the assignment can be done automatically without manual intervention. In this topic, you will assign IP addresses statically and dynamically.

Depending on the scope and size of your network, it may be just as easy to manually assign IP addresses to all your nodes as it is to install and maintain a service to do it for you dynamically. By understanding the different methods available to you for assigning IP addresses, you can choose the method that best suits your network.

Static and Dynamic IP Addressing

On a Transmission Control Protocol/Internet Protocol (TCP/IP) network, you can assign IP address information statically to nodes by manually entering IP addressing information on each individual network node. Or, you can assign IP addresses dynamically, by using the *Dynamic Host Configuration Protocol (DHCP)* service.

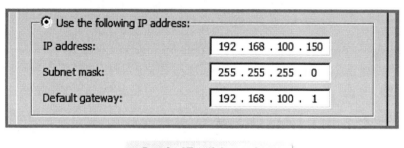

Static IP addressing

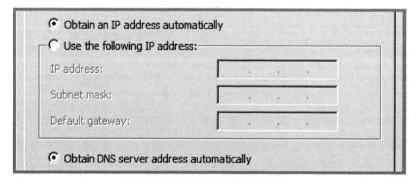

Dynamic IP addressing

Figure 7-1: Static and dynamic IP addresses assignment.

Static IP Address Assignment

Configuring TCP/IP statically on a network requires that an administrator visit each node to manually enter IP address information for that node. If the node moves to a different subnet, the administrator must manually reconfigure the node's TCP/IP information for its new network location. In a large network, configuring TCP/IP statically on each node can be very time consuming, and prone to errors that can potentially disrupt communication on the network. Static addresses are typically assigned only to systems with a dedicated functionality, such as router interfaces, network-attached printers, or servers that host applications on a network.

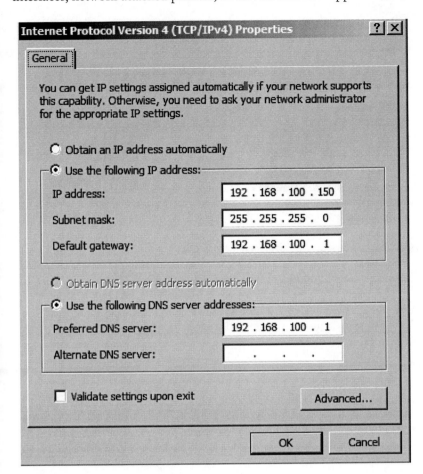

Figure 7-2: Static IP address assignment.

DHCP

DHCP is a network service that automatically assigns IP addresses and other TCP/IP configuration information on network nodes configured as DHCP clients. A DHCP server allocates IP addresses to DHCP clients dynamically, and should be configured with at least one DHCP *scope*. The scope defines the group of IP addresses that a DHCP server can use.

When a DHCP server enables the scope, it automatically leases TCP/IP information to DHCP clients for a defined lease period (normally eight days). The scope contains a range of IP addresses and a subnet mask, and can contain other options, such as a default gateway and Domain Name System (DNS) addresses. A scope also needs to specify the duration of the lease, and usage of an IP address after which the node needs to renew the lease with the DHCP server. The DHCP server determines this duration, which can be set for a defined time period or for an unlimited length of time.

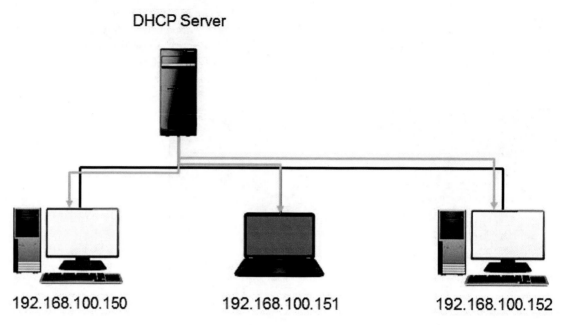

Figure 7-3: A DHCP server dynamically assigns IP addresses to clients.

The Dynamic Host Configuration Protocol version 6 (DHCPv6) is a network protocol for configuring IPv6 hosts with IP addresses, IP prefixes, and other configuration data required to operate in an IPv6 network. It is the IPv6 equivalent of DHCP for IPv4 networks. IPv6 hosts may automatically generate IP addresses internally using stateless address autoconfiguration, or they may be assigned configuration data with DHCPv6.

DHCP Options

DHCP options enable you to configure specific values such as the address of the default gateway, the DNS server, the domain name suffix of the interface, and other IP-related information, relieving the administrator from having to manually configure these parameters. You can modify scope options at the scope, server, class, or client-specific levels. You can modify DHCP options on a DHCP server by using the **DHCP Options Properties** dialog box.

There are different categories of options for DHCP. These options will always apply to all clients unless they are overridden by other settings at the client's end.

Category	Includes Options That Are Applicable
Global options	Globally for all DHCP servers and their clients
Scope options	To clients that obtain leases within a particular scope
Class options	To clients that specify a class when obtaining a scope lease
Reserved client options	To any client with a scope reservation for its IP address

DHCP Reservations

Reservations are lease assignments in DHCP that enable you to configure a permanent IP address for a particular client on the subnet. DHCP reservations are based on the client's media access control (MAC) address. Reserved IP addresses differ from statically configured IP addresses; when there are any changes in network parameters on the DHCP server, IP addresses receive the changes when they renew their leases.

The DHCP Lease Process

The DHCP lease process contains four main phases.

1. **Discover:** Once a node comes online and loads a simple version of TCP/IP and it's ready to communicate with a DHCP server, it transmits a broadcast called a *DHCP discover* to the network's broadcast address of 255.255.255.255 to see if any DHCP servers are online and then request an IP address.
2. **Offer:** DHCP servers that are online respond with a directed lease offer packet that contains an IP address that the node can lease.
3. **Request:** The node accepts the first offer it receives and returns a request to lease the IP address from the DHCP server, called a *DHCP request.*
4. **Acknowledge:** The DHCP server acknowledges the request from the node with a DHCP ACK, which has the IP address and settings required for the leasing time and starts the lease. The DHCP server also updates the IP address in its database as being in use, to avoid reassigning the address.

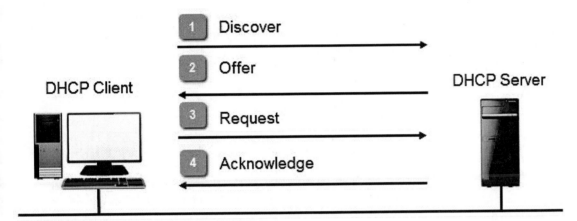

Figure 7–4: Steps in the DHCP lease process.

 Note: For additional information, check out the LearnTO **Follow the DHCP Lease Process** presentation in the LearnTOs for this course on your LogicalCHOICE Course screen.

BOOTP

BOOTP (the Bootstrap Protocol) is the predecessor of DHCP. It was developed to assign IP addresses to diskless workstations that had no way of storing their operating system. After providing the IP address from a configuration server, the workstation would then seek to download its operating system from the network. With BOOTP, clients do not lease their addresses. Instead, they are assigned an IP address from a list on the configuration server. Although BOOTP has largely been superseded by DHCP, it is still used by enterprise organizations to roll out large numbers of "bare metal" boxes that have no OS initially. The devices boot from their network cards, sending out a BOOTP request for an IP address. After obtaining their address, they then seek to discover a Trivial File Transfer Protocol (TFTP) server that they can download their operating system from. BOOTP uses the same port, UDP 67, as DHCP. Most DHCP servers can be configured to respond to both BOOTP and DHCP client requests.

DHCP Relay Agent

A DHCP relay agent is a service that captures a BOOTP or DHCP broadcast and forwards it through the router as a unicast transmission to the DHCP server on another subnet. BOOTP uses a local broadcast that cannot be sent through routers on the network. As an administrator of a TCP/IP network using DHCP, you must either have a DHCP server on each subnet and configure the router to forward the broadcasts, or configure a *DHCP relay agent.* Having multiple DHCP servers also ensures a higher degree of fault tolerance as the unavailability of a DHCP server on a subnet does not prevent nodes from requesting or renewing their leases. The Internet Protocol Helper (IP Helper) is an API used by C and C++ programmers to retrieve and modify network configuration settings on the local computer. An IP Helper address can be used to forward DHCP broadcasts to their destination. One DHCP server can be used to examine address leases for all network devices and manage network IP subnetworks.

The DHCP server returns an offer to the relay agent, which in turn presents the offer to the client. Once the client has its lease, it also has the DHCP server's IP address, so it does not need to use the relay agent to renew the lease. An important factor you need to consider on a network with multiple subnets is that the routers on the network must be RFC 1542–compliant to allow a DHCP server to receive the broadcast message from a node.

IP Addresses Recovery

The DHCP lease process is important to the overall performance of a DHCP system. By leasing addresses to clients instead of permanently assigning them, a DHCP server can recover addresses leased to offline clients that no longer need the addresses.

A typical DHCP lease lasts for eight days, but the lease can be as short as one day, one hour, or even less depending on organizational requirements. For example, many organizations limit wireless DHCP leases to one day for security purposes.

APIPA

Automatic Private IP Addressing (APIPA) is a service that enables a DHCP client device to configure itself automatically with an IP address in the range of 169.254.0.1 to 169.254.255.254, in case no DHCP servers respond to the client's DHCP discover broadcast. In case of a DHCP server failure, when the clients on the network cannot obtain IP addresses, the clients can use APIPA to assign themselves an IP address in the 169.254.x.x address range to enable communication with other clients. Thus, APIPA enables DHCP clients to initialize TCP/IP and communicate on the local subnet even in the absence of an active DHCP scope. APIPA addresses are not routable, so devices with APIPA addresses cannot communicate outside of the local subnet.

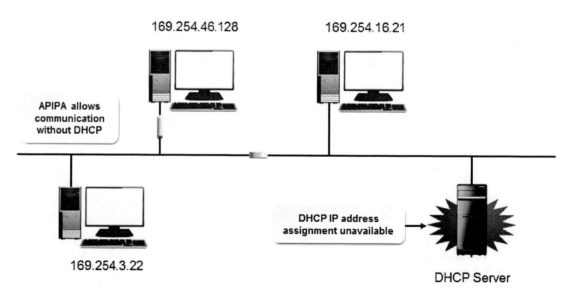

Figure 7–5: Automatically assigned private IP addresses.

 Note: If a client cannot reach destinations outside of the local subnet, check the device's IP address. If the client shows an APIPA address, it signals that the client is configured to use DHCP and that a DHCP server is unavailable.

APIPA is not a practical replacement for receiving a DHCP lease. Instead, its most common usage is as a diagnostic tool. The presence of an APIPA address informs IT support personnel that a client attempted to receive a DHCP lease but failed, and therefore self-assigned its own IP address.

APIPA Support

APIPA is available on client systems including: Windows® 7 and Windows 8, and server operating systems including: Windows 2008, Windows 2008 R2, Windows 2012, and Windows 2012 R2, as well as Macintosh®. Because APIPA requires no administrative configuration, it was once thought that APIPA addressing could be used for small offices where local subnet communication is all that is required. In reality, however, nearly all offices in today's modern networks implement Internet access. APIPA cannot assign the address of the default gateway or DNS server. To assign these values, the administrator would have to manually configure these settings in every client. Additionally, you cannot have a self-assigned IP address with a manually configured default gateway. This makes APIPA an untenable addressing alternative.

IP Configuration Utilities

You can use the IP configuration utility for your operating system to view and change TCP/IP configuration information.

Utility	Description
ipconfig	Displays connection-specific DNS suffix, IP address, subnet mask, and default gateway information. Must be run from a command line. To display additional information about a computer's IP configuration, use the command ipconfig /all. Supported on all Windows server systems and client systems.
ifconfig	Displays the status of currently active network interface devices. Using options, you can dynamically change the status of the interfaces and their IP address. Supported on Linux and UNIX.
dhclient	Enables you to configure and manage DHCP settings on the network interfaces of a computer. Supported on Linux and UNIX.

 Note: You can manually release and renew a DHCP lease in Linux by issuing the following command at a command prompt: sudo dhclient -v -r

ipconfig Options for DHCP

The Windows ipconfig utility provides options for managing dynamic address leases:

- ipconfig /release forces the release of an IP address used by a client.
- ipconfig /renew requests the renewal of an IP address for a client.

The system first attempts to obtain a DHCP address, and if a DHCP server fails to respond, it will switch to APIPA addressing.

The ping Command

The ping command is used to verify the network connectivity of a device, and also to check to see if the target device is active. It verifies the IP address, host name, and reachability of the remote device by using and listening for echo replies. ping uses ICMP to check the connections with remote hosts by sending out echo requests as ICMP ECHO_REQUEST packets to the host whose name or IP address you specify on the command line. ping listens for reply packets. The ping command can be used in both Windows and Linux, as well as FreeBSD (which is what Mac OS X is built on), but the syntax options are not the same. For a list of options in Windows, enter ping /?. For Linux and FreeBSD, enter man ping.

```
C:\>ping 192.168.1.200
Pinging 192.168.1.200 with 32 bytes of data:
Reply from 192.168.1.200: bytes=32 time<1ms TTL=128
Reply from 192.168.1.200: bytes=32 time<1ms TTL=128
Reply from 192.168.1.200: bytes=32 time<1ms TTL=128
Reply from 192.168.1.200: bytes=32 time<1ms TTL=128

Ping statistics for 192.168.1.200:
    Packets: Sent = 4, Received = 4, Lost = 0 (0% loss),
Approximate round trip times in milli-seconds:
    Minimum = 0ms, Maximum = 0ms, Average = 0ms
```

Figure 7–6: Using ping tests the connectivity between two hosts.

Syntax

The syntax of the ping command is:

```
ping target
```

The *target* variable specifies the IP address or DNS name of a device on the network. ping uses the DNS setting to resolve the DNS name into an IP address.

Options

You can ping a device or an IP address. You can also ping the loopback address (127.0.0.1) to test whether TCP/IP has initialized on an individual device. If the computer has a default gateway, you can ping remote systems.

To list other options for the ping command, enter ping /? at the command prompt. Some of the options include setting the packet size, changing the *time-to-live (TTL)* value, and specifying how many times to ping the host.

Option	Description	Example
Packet size	By default, data packets are sent as 32 bytes. You can specify a larger size to test response time, the maximum size being 65,500 bytes. To change the packet size, use the -l option followed by the packet length.	ping *target* [-l *size*]
TTL	A value that determines how many hops an IP packet can traverse before being discarded. Each hop is a router that was crossed.	ping *target* [-i *TTL*]
Packet count	Specifies the number of packets with which a remote host is pinged. The default is four packets. You can specify a higher number of packets with the -n option.	ping *target* [-n *packet count*]
Continuous ping	Pings the specified host until the command is interrupted by pressing Ctrl+C.	ping *target* -t

Option	Description	Example
IPv6	Ping using IPv6.	`ping target -6` **Note:** To ping IPv6 on Linux, use the `ping6` command.

ICMP Blocking

As a security measure, some public Internet hosts and routers might be configured to block incoming packets that are generated by the `ping` command. (They might also block packets from other TCP/IP diagnostic utilities such as the `tracert` command.) It is not the `ping` command that is blocked but the ICMP traffic that is blocked. Pinging these hosts will fail even if the host is online. Keep this in mind when you try to ping large public Internet sites; if you are trying to determine if one of these sites is up and running, a better method is simply to use a web browser to connect to the site directly.

Ports

A *port* is a number that represents a process running on a network. Ports are associated with OSI Layer 5, but in every packet, there will be both a source and destination port embedded in the Transmission Control Protocol (TCP) or User Datagram Protocol (UDP) header. Both clients and servers use port numbers to identify themselves. Because a single device can be running many client and server processes at the same time, each process has its own port number to keep it unique. Ports are used to keep separate network conversations separate. For example, if you open several browsers at once, even to the same website, each browser has its own port number. This prevents the content in one browser from suddenly appearing in another browser.

If your device offers any type of service on the network, that service will listen on its designated port for incoming connections. You can examine all of the ports that are being listened on or are currently in use on your device by entering the `netstat -na` command at a command prompt.

All ports are assigned a number in a range from 0 to 65,535. The Internet Assigned Numbers Authority (IANA) separates port numbers into three blocks: well-known ports, which are preassigned to system processes by IANA; registered ports, which are available to user processes and are listed as a convenience by IANA; and dynamic ports, which are assigned by a client operating system as needed when there is a request for service.

There are three blocks of port numbers that are commonly used.

Block	Description
Well-known ports	**Port range:** 0 to 1,023 These ports are preassigned for use by common, or well-known, services. Often, the services that run on these ports must be started by a privileged user. Services in this range include Hypertext Transfer Protocol (HTTP) on TCP port 80, Internet Message Access Protocol (IMAP) on TCP port 143, and DNS on UDP port 53. In addition, port 0 is not used.
Registered ports	**Port range:** 1,024 to 49,151 These ports are registered by software makers for use by specific applications and services that are not as well-known as the services in the well-known range. Services in the registered port range include Socket Secure (SOCKS) proxy on TCP port 1080, and Xbox Live on TCP and UDP port 3074.

Block	Description
Dynamic or private ports	**Port range:** 49,152 to 65,535 These ports are set aside for use by unregistered services and services (typically, client applications) needing a temporary connection.

Well-Known TCP and UDP Port Numbers

Commonly used port numbers are listed in the following table, along with the protocols and services that use those ports.

Port Number	Protocol	Service Name	Service
7	TCP, UDP	echo	Echo
20	TCP	ftp-data	File Transfer [Default Data]
21	TCP	ftp	File Transfer [Control]
22	TCP, UDP	ssh	Secure Shell (SSH)
23	TCP, UDP	telnet	Telnet
25	TCP	smtp	SMTP
53	TCP, UDP	dns	DNS
67	TCP, UDP	bootps	DHCP (BOOTP) server
68	TCP, UDP	bootpc	DHCP (BOOTP) client
69	UDP	tftp	TFTP
80	TCP	http	HTTP
110	TCP	pop3	Post Office Protocol, version 3 (POP3)
123	UDP	ntp	Network Time Protocol (NTP)
137	UDP	netbios	Network Basic Input/Output System (NetBIOS) naming service
138	UDP	netbios	NetBIOS datagram distribution service
139	TCP	netbios	NetBIOS session service
143	TCP, UDP	imap	IMAP
161	UDP	snmp	Simple Network Management Protocol (SNMP)
194	TCP	irc	Internet Relay Chat (IRC)
389	TCP, UDP	ldap	Lightweight Directory Access Protocol (LDAP)
443	TCP	https	HTTP-secure
445	TCP	smb	Server Message Block (SMB)
546	TCP, UDP	dhcpv6-client	DHCPv6 client
547	TCP, UDP	dhcpv6-server	DHCPv6 server
1720	TCP	h.323	H.323 Call Setup

Port Number	Protocol	Service Name	Service
2427	UDP	mgcp	Media Gateway Control Protocol (MGCP) gateway traffic
2727	TCP	mgcp	MGCP callagent traffic
3389	TCP, UDP	rdp	Remote Desktop Protocol (RDP)
5004	TCP, UDP	rtp	Real-time Transport Protocol (RTP) media data
5005	TCP, UDP	rtp	RTP control protocol
5060	TCP, UDP	sip	Session Initiation Protocol (SIP) unencrypted signaling traffic
5061	TCP, UDP	sip	SIP encrypted traffic

 Note: Although port 3389 does not fall within the specified range of well-known ports, this is one of the port numbers that you will need to remember.

 Note: The complete list of well-known ports and other port number assignments is available online at **www.iana.org/assignments/port-numbers**

Sockets

A *socket* is an identifier for an application process on a TCP/IP network. It is the combination of the IP address (or host name) and port number.

For example, if your web server is installed on 193.44.234.3, the socket for the HTTP process is 193.44.234.3:80.

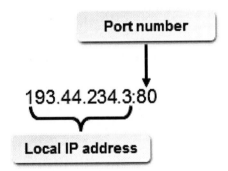

Figure 7–7: Format of an IP address socket.

A socket can be open for any protocol, or it can be limited to a specific protocol (as defined in firewall rules).

Winsock is the technical specification that defines how Windows network software accesses network services such as TCP/IP. It defines a standard interface between a Windows TCP/IP client application and the underlying TCP/IP protocol stack. The Berkeley sockets interface is the interface between the TCP/IP based network and the network applications that use it. It is the socket interface used by UNIX and Linux.

 Access the Checklist tile on your LogicalCHOICE course screen for reference information and job aids on How to Assign IP Addresses.

ACTIVITY 7-1
Assigning IP Addresses

Before You Begin
Your computer is currently configured to lease an IP address from the classroom DHCP server.

Instructor-Only Steps (to be performed only on the DC)

To deactivate the DHCP scope:

1. Log in as **Administrator** with *P@ssw0rd12* as the password.
2. In **Server Manager**, select **Tools→DHCP**.
3. In the console tree, expand **dc.gcinteriors.com, IPv4**.
4. Right-click the **Scope** object.
5. Select **Deactivate**.
6. In the **DHCP** dialog box, select **Yes**.
7. Minimize the DHCP window. You will need to activate the DHCP scope later in step 7 of the actual activity.

Scenario

At the Greene City Interiors branch office, you believe there might be a problem with the DHCP server and it will require that it be offline for several hours. Before you take it offline you want to configure the IP addresses of workstations manually so that they will continue to have access to the network. Once the DHCP server is back online you will switch the workstations back to DHCP.

The IP address range that you have identified for the workstations is 192.168.2.25 to 192.168.2.95. The subnet mask is 255.255.255.0, and the IP address of the DNS server is 192.168.2.200. The DNS server is also the default gateway on the network.

 Note: You will examine DNS servers in depth in the next topic.

---

1. Configure your computer with the static IP address 192.168.2.##, where .## is your student number plus 24, the subnet mask 255.255.255.0, the default gateway 192.168.2.200, and the DNS server 192.168.2.200.

   a) From the **Start** screen, select **Control Panel**.
   b) In the Control Panel window, select the **Network and Internet** link.
   c) In the Network and Internet window, select the **Network and Sharing Center** link.
   d) In the Network and Sharing Center window, in the left pane, select the **Change adapter settings** link.
   e) Right-click **Ethernet** and select **Properties**.

    Note: Your adapter name may be slightly different.

   f) In the **Ethernet Properties** dialog box, in the **This connection uses the following items** section, select **Internet Protocol Version 4 (TCP/IPv4)** and select **Properties**.
   g) In the **Internet Protocol Version 4 (TCP/IPv4) Properties** dialog box, on the **General** tab, select the **Use the following IP address** option.
   h) In the **IP address** text box, type *192.168.2.##*, where *##* is your student number plus 24.
   i) Select the **Subnet mask** text box.

j) Observe that the default subnet mask for the IP address is auto-populated.

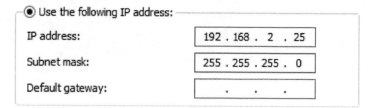

k) In the **Default gateway** text box, type *192.168.2.200*
l) Verify that the **Use the following DNS server addresses** option is selected and that, in the **Alternate DNS server** text box, *192.168.2.200* is entered.

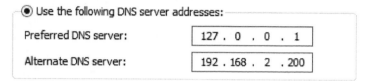

m) Select **OK** to close the **Internet Protocol Version 4 (TCP/IPv4) Properties** dialog box.
n) Select **Close** to close the **Ethernet Properties** dialog box. Minimize the Network Connections window.

2. Test your ability to communicate over TCP/IP with the DNS server.
    a) Open **Windows PowerShell**.
    b) In the Windows PowerShell window, type *ping 192.168.2.200* and press **Enter**.

```
PS C:\Users\Administrator> ping 192.168.2.200

Pinging 192.168.2.200 with 32 bytes of data:
Reply from 192.168.2.200: bytes=32 time<1ms TTL=128
Reply from 192.168.2.200: bytes=32 time<1ms TTL=128
Reply from 192.168.2.200: bytes=32 time<1ms TTL=128
Reply from 192.168.2.200: bytes=32 time<1ms TTL=128

Ping statistics for 192.168.2.200:
    Packets: Sent = 4, Received = 4, Lost = 0 (0% loss),
Approximate round trip times in milli-seconds:
    Minimum = 0ms, Maximum = 0ms, Average = 0ms
```

c) Observe that the `ping` command returns four replies, indicating that the connection to the server was successfully established.

d) At the prompt, type *netstat* and press **Enter**.

```
PS C:\Users\Administrator> netstat

Active Connections

  Proto  Local Address          Foreign Address        State
  TCP    192.168.2.25:53143     Computer01:domain      TIME_WAIT
  TCP    192.168.2.25:54468     Computer01:domain      TIME_WAIT
  TCP    192.168.2.25:57075     Computer01:domain      TIME_WAIT
  TCP    192.168.2.25:59396     Computer01:domain      TIME_WAIT
  TCP    [::1]:389              Computer01:49161       ESTABLISHED
  TCP    [::1]:389              Computer01:49162       ESTABLISHED
  TCP    [::1]:389              Computer01:49186       ESTABLISHED
  TCP    [::1]:49161            Computer01:ldap        ESTABLISHED
  TCP    [::1]:49162            Computer01:ldap        ESTABLISHED
  TCP    [::1]:49186            Computer01:ldap        ESTABLISHED
  TCP    [fe80::78a7:da22:4ef6:de19%12]:135   Computer01:57027    ESTABLISHED
  TCP    [fe80::78a7:da22:4ef6:de19%12]:389   Computer01:49222    ESTABLISHED
  TCP    [fe80::78a7:da22:4ef6:de19%12]:389   Computer01:49225    ESTABLISHED
  TCP    [fe80::78a7:da22:4ef6:de19%12]:49156 Computer01:49224    ESTABLISHED
  TCP    [fe80::78a7:da22:4ef6:de19%12]:49156 Computer01:52976    ESTABLISHED
  TCP    [fe80::78a7:da22:4ef6:de19%12]:49156 Computer01:57028    ESTABLISHED
  TCP    [fe80::78a7:da22:4ef6:de19%12]:49222 Computer01:ldap     ESTABLISHED
  TCP    [fe80::78a7:da22:4ef6:de19%12]:49224 Computer01:49156    ESTABLISHED
  TCP    [fe80::78a7:da22:4ef6:de19%12]:49225 Computer01:ldap     ESTABLISHED
  TCP    [fe80::78a7:da22:4ef6:de19%12]:52976 Computer01:49156    ESTABLISHED
  TCP    [fe80::78a7:da22:4ef6:de19%12]:57027 Computer01:epmap    ESTABLISHED
  TCP    [fe80::78a7:da22:4ef6:de19%12]:57028 Computer01:49156    ESTABLISHED
```

e) Observe the current active open ports on your computer.

f) Minimize the Windows PowerShell window.

3. Configure your computer to use DHCP.

Note: The DHCP server is now back online, so you need to configure the workstations to use DHCP again.

a) In the Network Connections window, right-click **Ethernet** and select **Properties**.

b) In the **Ethernet Properties** dialog box, in the **This connection uses the following items** section, select **Internet Protocol Version 4 (TCP/IPv4)** and select **Properties**.

c) In the **Internet Protocol Version 4 (TCP/IPv4) Properties** dialog box, select the **Obtain an IP address automatically** option and select **OK**.

d) Select **Close**.

e) Close the Network Connections and Network and Sharing Center windows.

4. Verify your IP information.

a) In the Windows PowerShell window, type *ipconfig /renew* and press **Enter**.

b) At the prompt, type *ipconfig* and press **Enter**.

Note: APIPA configuration can take a moment because the system first attempts to contact a DHCP server before self-assigning the APIPA address. If `ipconfig /renew` shows your IP address and subnet mask as null (all zeros), wait a minute and run `ipconfig /renew` again or type `ipconfig / all`.

c) Verify that the **Ethernet adapter Ethernet** section displays the IP address and subnet mask from the 169.254.0.0 APIPA network.

```
Ethernet adapter Ethernet:

   Connection-specific DNS Suffix  . :
   Link-local IPv6 Address . . . . . : fe80::78a7:da22:4ef6:de19%12
   Autoconfiguration IPv4 Address. . : 169.254.222.25
   Subnet Mask . . . . . . . . . . . : 255.255.0.0
   Default Gateway . . . . . . . . . :
```

5. Test your ability to communicate over TCP/IP with the DNS server.

   a) At the prompt, type *ping 192.168.2.200* and press **Enter**.

   b) Verify that the destination is unreachable and the error message "PING: transmit failed. General failure" is displayed. Because you are using a nonroutable APIPA address, you cannot communicate with the DNS server.

```
PS C:\Users\Administrator> ping 192.168.2.200

Pinging 192.168.2.200 with 32 bytes of data:
PING: transmit failed. General failure.
PING: transmit failed. General failure.
PING: transmit failed. General failure.
PING: transmit failed. General failure.

Ping statistics for 192.168.2.200:
    Packets: Sent = 4, Received = 0, Lost = 4 (100% loss),
```

6. Test your ability to communicate with another computer on the APIPA network.

   a) At the prompt, type *ping 169.254.#.#* and press **Enter**, where **#.#** is a part of the address of another computer in the classroom.

```
PS C:\Users\Administrator> ping 169.254.250.100

Pinging 169.254.250.100 with 32 bytes of data:
Reply from 169.254.250.100: bytes=32 time<1ms TTL=128
Reply from 169.254.250.100: bytes=32 time<1ms TTL=128
Reply from 169.254.250.100: bytes=32 time=6ms TTL=128
Reply from 169.254.250.100: bytes=32 time<1ms TTL=128

Ping statistics for 169.254.250.100:
    Packets: Sent = 4, Received = 4, Lost = 0 (0% loss),
Approximate round trip times in milli-seconds:
    Minimum = 0ms, Maximum = 6ms, Average = 1ms
```

   b) Observe from the results that you are able to communicate with the other system on the APIPA network.

7. Instructor-Only Steps (to be performed only on the DC)

   a) Maximize the DHCP window.

   b) Right-click the **Scope** object.

   c) Select **Activate**.

   d) Close the DHCP window.

8. Force your computer to lease an IP address from the DHCP server.

 Note: Do not proceed with this step until after the instructor has performed step 7.

   a) At the prompt window, type *ipconfig /renew* and press **Enter**.

Note: You may receive a message that an error occurred while renewing the loopback adapter. This can be ignored because you are trying to renew only the Ethernet adapter.

b) Observe that the IPv4 address 192.168.2.## is obtained from the DHCP server.

9. Test your ability to communicate over TCP/IP with the DNS server.

a) At the prompt, type *ping 192.168.2.200* and press **Enter** to ping the DNS server.

b) Observe that you are able to communicate with the DNS server.

c) At the prompt, type *netstat* and press **Enter**.

```
PS C:\Users\Administrator> netstat

Active Connections

  Proto  Local Address            Foreign Address        State
  TCP    192.168.2.37:135         COMPUTER02:62885       ESTABLISHED
  TCP    192.168.2.37:51044       Computer01:domain      TIME_WAIT
  TCP    192.168.2.37:59573       Computer01:domain      TIME_WAIT
  TCP    192.168.2.37:59763       Computer01:domain      TIME_WAIT
  TCP    192.168.2.37:63148       Computer01:domain      TIME_WAIT
  TCP    [::1]:389                Computer01:49160       ESTABLISHED
  TCP    [::1]:389                Computer01:49161       ESTABLISHED
  TCP    [::1]:389                Computer01:49170       ESTABLISHED
  TCP    [::1]:389                Computer01:49199       ESTABLISHED
  TCP    [::1]:3268               Computer01:49201       ESTABLISHED
  TCP    [::1]:49160              Computer01:ldap        ESTABLISHED
  TCP    [::1]:49161              Computer01:ldap        ESTABLISHED
  TCP    [::1]:49170              Computer01:ldap        ESTABLISHED
  TCP    [::1]:49199              Computer01:msft-gc     ESTABLISHED
  TCP    [fe80::78a7:da22:4ef6:de19%12]:389  Computer01:49195   ESTABLISHED
  TCP    [fe80::78a7:da22:4ef6:de19%12]:389  Computer01:49198   ESTABLISHED
  TCP    [fe80::78a7:da22:4ef6:de19%12]:49156  Computer01:49197   ESTABLISHED
  TCP    [fe80::78a7:da22:4ef6:de19%12]:49156  Computer01:49243   ESTABLISHED
  TCP    [fe80::78a7:da22:4ef6:de19%12]:49195  Computer01:ldap    ESTABLISHED
  TCP    [fe80::78a7:da22:4ef6:de19%12]:49197  Computer01:49156   ESTABLISHED
  TCP    [fe80::78a7:da22:4ef6:de19%12]:49198  Computer01:ldap    ESTABLISHED
  TCP    [fe80::78a7:da22:4ef6:de19%12]:49242  Computer01:epmap   TIME_WAIT
  TCP    [fe80::78a7:da22:4ef6:de19%12]:49243  Computer01:49156   ESTABLISHED
```

d) Observe the current active open ports on your computer.

e) Close the Windows PowerShell window.

TOPIC B

Domain Naming Services

Each node that has an IP address assigned to it can also have a descriptive name that is more commonly used to identify it on the network. These descriptive names are easier for users to remember and use than their 32-bit IP addresses. In this topic, you will identify methods for host name resolution for TCP/IP networks.

Without host name resolution services, you have to connect to other computers and websites using their numeric IP addresses. However, for a user, it is easier to remember a descriptive name such as **www.greenecityinteriors.example** than its assigned 32-bit IP address. When you configure host name resolution services on your network, you can connect to other devices and websites by using their names instead of a string of numbers.

Host Names

A *host name* is a unique name given to a node on a TCP/IP network. It enables users and technicians to recognize the node more easily. A naming service, which is software that runs on one or more nodes, maps the node address to an IP address or a MAC address.

Domain Names

A *domain* is a grouping of devices on the Internet or on another network based on the nature of their operations. A domain enables communication between its systems as a unit and other networks on the Internet, instead of maintaining individual connections for each of its systems. Although there are several types of domains, some of the common ones are commercial, governmental, and educational domains. Domains are identified by their unique names; for example, com, gov, and edu.

A *domain name* is a unique name that identifies an entity on the Internet. Also known as site names, domain names appear as part of the complete address of a web resource. They are usually registered by organizations as their website address. A period is used to separate domain name labels, which can have no more than 63 characters.

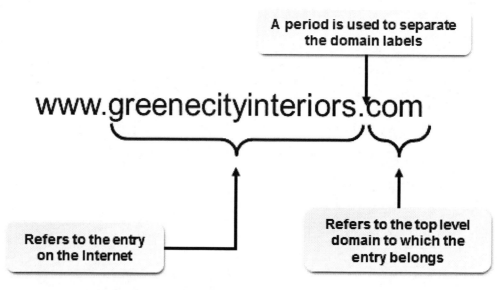

Figure 7–8: Components of a domain name.

A domain name identifies a collection of devices on the network of a particular domain. A host name is a unique name that identifies a specified device in a network. Therefore, host names are subsets of domain names.

FQDN

A host name combined with the host's domain name forms the node's *Fully Qualified Domain Name (FQDN)*. A name resolution service maps the FQDN of the node to its IP address so that users can use names instead of IP addresses to communicate with other network nodes and the Internet.

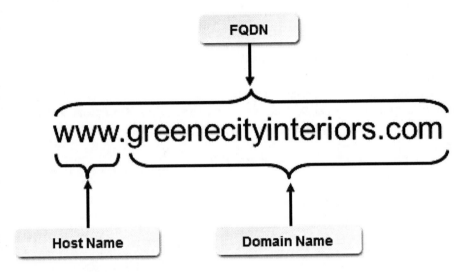

Figure 7-9: The FQDN contains a host name and a domain name.

FQDNs are written using standard dot-delimited notation, and a dot separates each section of the name. The maximum length of an FQDN is 255 characters; each dot-delimited section can be up to 63 characters long. A network node can have more than one host name assigned to it. Its primary name is its host name; the other names are called canonical names (CNAMEs), or aliases.

You can use the hostname command in either Windows or Linux to discover the host part of your computer's DNS name. In Windows, you can use the command ipconfig /all to discover your FQDN. In Linux, you can use the command hostname --fqdn.

ACTIVITY 7-2
Identifying the Local Host Name

Scenario

At the Greene City Interiors branch office, you need to document the host name of each device to ensure that there will be no duplicate names on the network.

---

1. Identify the host name and FQDN by using System Properties.

   a) Select **Start→Control Panel**.

   b) In the Control Panel window, select the **System and Security** link.

   c) In the System and Security window, under **System**, select the **See the name of this computer** link.

   d) In the System window, in the **Computer name, domain, and workgroup settings** section, identify the computer's name.

   e) In the **Full computer name** section, identify the computer's FQDN.

   > Computer name, domain, and workgroup settings
   >
   > Computer name: Computer01
   >
   > Full computer name: Computer01.Child01.GCInteriors.com
   >
   > Computer description:
   >
   > Domain: Child01.GCInteriors.com

   f) Identify the host name from the first portion of the FQDN.

2. Identify the host name by using the `hostname` command.

   a) Open **Windows PowerShell**.

   b) In the Windows PowerShell window, type ***hostname*** and press **Enter** to display the host name of the system.

   c) Observe the host name that is displayed.

3. Identify the FQDN by using the `ipconfig` command.

   a) Type **ipconfig /all | more** and press **Enter** to view the first page of the network details.

   b) Identify the host name and then press the **Spacebar** to view the next page of the network details.

   ```
   Windows IP Configuration

       Host Name . . . . . . . . . . . . : Computer01
       Primary Dns Suffix  . . . . . . . : Child01.GCInteriors.com
   ```

   c) In the **Ethernet adapter Ethernet** section, in the **Connection-specific DNS Suffix** section, identify the DNS suffix.

   d) Close the Windows PowerShell and System windows.

Name Resolution

Name resolution is the process of identifying a network node by translating its host or domain name into the corresponding IP address. Several popular name resolution systems are available, but the most prevalent is DNS, which is used on the Internet and practically all TCP/IP based networks.

DNS services on an IP network are comparable in functionality to directory assistance in the telephone system. When a client needs the number, it contacts the DNS server, provides the name, and requests the DNS server to look up the number for it.

DNS

The *Domain Name System (DNS)* is a TCP/IP name resolution service that translates FQDNs into IP addresses. It consists of a system of hierarchical databases that are stored on separate DNS servers on all networks that connect to the Internet. These servers list IP addresses and related device names. Because DNS servers store, maintain, and update databases, they respond to DNS client name resolution requests to translate host names into IP addresses. All these servers work together to resolve FQDNs. On internal networks, a local DNS service can resolve host names without using external DNS servers.

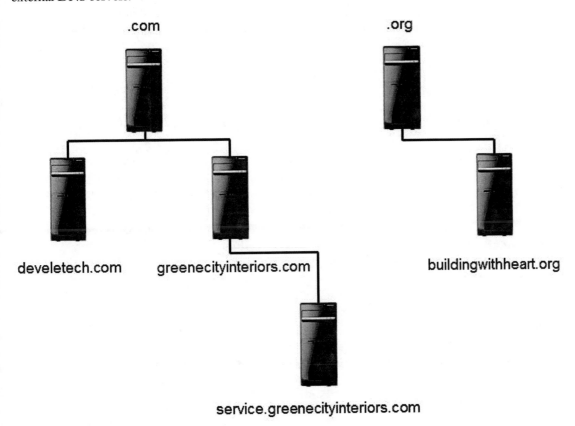

Figure 7-10: DNS server domains.

DNS Components

The DNS database is divided logically into a hierarchical grouping of domains. It is divided physically into files called *zones*. The zone files contain the actual IP-to-host name mappings for one or more domains. The zone file is stored on the DNS server that is responsible for resolving host names for the domains contained in the zone. For example, a zone might be responsible for mapping host names to IP addresses within the gcinteriors domain within the .com namespace. Each network node in that domain will have a host record within the domain's zone file. The record includes the node's host name, FQDN, and assigned IP address.

For example, a host named 2012srv in the gcinteriors.com domain might have an IP address of 74.43.216.152. That host would have a host record that maps the 2012srv.gcinteriors.com name to the IP address of 74.43.216.152. That host record will appear in the gcinteriors.com zone file on the DNS server that is responsible for the gcinteriors.com domain.

Records can be entered into a DNS database either statically or dynamically. A static record is entered manually by an administrator and does not change unless the administrator manually updates it. A network node can request to add a dynamic DNS record that can change dynamically. Dynamic DNS is a method of automatically updating a name server in DNS, often in real time, with the active DNS configuration of its configured host names, addresses, or other information. For example, if a client is using DHCP to get its IP address, each time it leases a new address, it can request an update of its DNS host record.

Types of DNS Servers

There are different types of DNS servers, including default DNS servers and authoritative name servers.

As with the default gateway, you can configure default DNS servers that match host names to IP addresses. These specialized servers maintain databases of IP addresses and their corresponding domain names. For example, when you type **www.yahoo.com** into your browser address bar, the name is resolved by DNS to the IP addresses of the Yahoo server farm.

You can configure default DNS servers statically or automatically.

- If you are configuring static IP addresses, include the IP addresses of the default DNS servers as you configure each client.
- If you are using DHCP, use the DHCP scope options to specify the IP addresses of the default DNS servers.

An *authoritative name server (ANS)* is a DNS server that possesses an actual copy of the records for a zone, as opposed to just caching a lookup from another DNS server. It responds to name-related queries in one or more zones. The most important function of the ANS is delegation, which means that part of a domain is delegated to other DNS servers.

The start of authority (SOA) is the first DNS server to create the zone. It is typically the primary DNS server, meaning that it holds the only writable copy of the zone. Additional authoritative servers can be secondary DNS servers, meaning that they hold read-only copies that they obtain from the primary (their master).

Primary and Secondary DNS Servers

When configuring a client's DNS settings, it is common to specify both a primary and a secondary DNS server to provide a more reliable name resolution process. When two DNS servers are listed in a client's TCP/IP settings, the client queries the primary server first. If the primary server does not answer, the client queries the secondary server. If the primary server returns a "Name Not Found" message, the query is over and the client does not query the secondary server. This is because both DNS servers can do recursive and iterative queries, and both primary and secondary servers should be able to contact the same resources. If one cannot access the resource, the other will not be able to either.

Types of DNS Records

Different types of DNS records are available that serve specific purposes.

Record Type	Purpose
Address (A)	Maps a host name to its IP address by using a 32-bit IPv4 address.
IPv6 address (AAAA)	Maps a host name to its IP address by using a 128-bit IPv6 address.
Canonical name (CNAME)	Maps multiple canonical names (aliases) to an A record.
Mail Exchanger (MX)	Maps a domain name to a email server list.
Name Server (NS)	Assigns a DNS zone to access the given authoritative name servers.

Record Type	Purpose
Pointer (PTR)	Maps an IP address to the host name for the purpose of reverse lookup.
Start of Authority (SOA)	Specifies authoritative information about a DNS zone.
Service Locator (SRV)	Specifies a generic service location record for newer protocols.

The DNS Hierarchy

DNS names are built in a hierarchical structure. This allows DNS servers on the Internet to use a minimum number of queries to locate the source of a domain name. The top of the structure—represented by a period—contains root name servers. Below that is the top-level domain name, then the first-level domain name, and so on, until the FQDN for an individual host is complete.

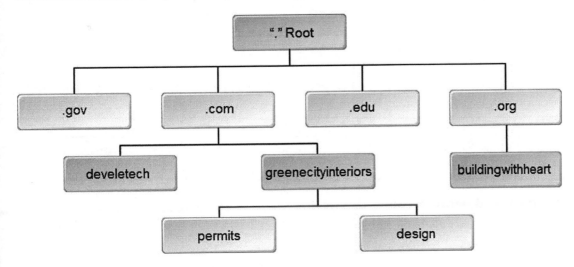

FQDN = design.greenecityinteriors.com

Figure 7–11: Hierarchical structure of a DNS.

The DNS Name Resolution Process

In the DNS process, DNS servers work together as needed to resolve names on behalf of DNS clients.

Step	Description
Step 1: Client request	The DNS request is passed to a DNS Client service for resolution by using locally cached information on the client. If the DNS request cannot be resolved locally, it sends a DNS query to the DNS resolver. A DNS name resolution request message is generated by the resolver, which is transmitted to the DNS server address specified during configuration.
Step 2: Preferred DNS server	The DNS server, upon receiving the request, first checks if the requested name is in its DNS cache entries or its local DNS database, and returns the IP address to the client. If there is no match for the requested name, the DNS server sends the request to a root name server asking which DNS server has the entries for the appropriate top-level domain.

Step	Description
Step 3: Root name server	Upon receiving the request, the root name server reads the top-level domain of that name and sends a message that contains the IP address of the server for that top-level domain. The root name server then sends a reply to the client's DNS server.
Step 4: Top-level domain server	The client's DNS server contains the IP address of the top-level domain of the requested name. The DNS server then contacts the top-level domain's DNS server to resolve the name. The top-level domain server reads the second-level domain of the requested name, and if it can resolve the name, it sends the desired IP address back to the client's DNS server.
Step 5: Other domain servers	If the top-level domain cannot resolve the name because of additional levels in the FQDN, it sends the IP address to the second-level DNS server.
Step 6: Host name resolution	This communication between DNS servers continues until it reaches the level in the DNS hierarchy where a DNS server can resolve the host name.
Step 7: Host address	The preferred DNS server provides the client with the IP address of the target host.

 Note: For additional information, check out the LearnTO **Follow the DNS Name Resolution Process** presentation in the LearnTOs for this course on your LogicalCHOICE Course screen.

Recursive and Iterative Name Queries

There are two kinds of DNS queries: recursive and iterative.

- A *recursive query* is when the client requests that its preferred DNS server find data on other DNS servers. A recursive request starts with the client requesting a name to be resolved to an IP address of its preferred DNS server. If the preferred server cannot resolve the name, it sends a request, on behalf of the client, to another DNS server.
- An *iterative query* occurs when the client requests only the information a server already has in its cache for a particular domain name. If the receiving server cannot resolve the request, it notifies the client, but does not forward the request on to any other server.

Recursive queries usually take place between end-user client systems and their preferred DNS servers. Once the recursive query is in process, queries between DNS servers are usually iterative.

In most cases, a DNS client will perform a recursive query, and wait upon its DNS server to locate the address for it. The DNS server in turn will either perform an iterative search on the Internet, or will also do a recursive query, asking another DNS server to perform the search for it.

Legacy Name Resolution Methods

The most common name resolution methods that have been used in the past are the HOSTS file, NetBIOS, and Windows Internet Name Server (WINS).

A *HOSTS file* is a plaintext file configured on a client device containing a list of IP addresses and their associated host names, separated by at least one space. Comments may be included after the host name if preceded by the # symbol and separated from the host name by at least one space. The hosts file exists in both Linux and Windows. It can be edited in both operating systems to manually map host names to IP addresses.

The HOSTS file provides an alternative method of host name resolution. An external client can use a HOSTS file to resolve names on your internal network without accessing your internal DNS server. You have to manually configure each host name entry in a HOSTS file.

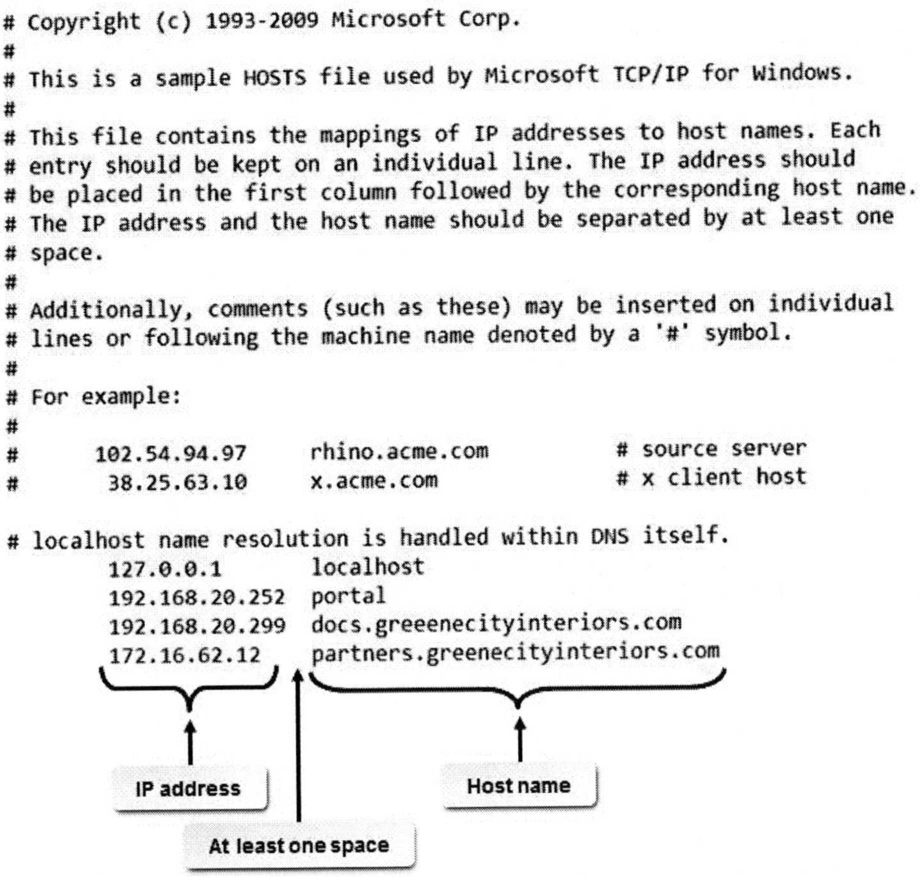

```
# Copyright (c) 1993-2009 Microsoft Corp.
#
# This is a sample HOSTS file used by Microsoft TCP/IP for Windows.
#
# This file contains the mappings of IP addresses to host names. Each
# entry should be kept on an individual line. The IP address should
# be placed in the first column followed by the corresponding host name.
# The IP address and the host name should be separated by at least one
# space.
#
# Additionally, comments (such as these) may be inserted on individual
# lines or following the machine name denoted by a '#' symbol.
#
# For example:
#
#       102.54.94.97       rhino.acme.com            # source server
#       38.25.63.10        x.acme.com                # x client host

# localhost name resolution is handled within DNS itself.
        127.0.0.1          localhost
        192.168.20.252     portal
        192.168.20.299     docs.greeenecityinteriors.com
        172.16.62.12       partners.greenecityinteriors.com
```

IP address   **At least one space**   **Host name**

Figure 7-12: Entries in a HOSTS file.

A device will always consult its HOSTS file first to see if the desired IP address is there before querying a DNS server. The HOSTS file requires a lot of maintenance, so it is recommended that you use it only when other methods of host name resolution are not supported, or temporarily unavailable for troubleshooting purposes.

NetBIOS is a simple, broadcast-based naming service. A NetBIOS name can be any combination of alphanumeric characters excluding spaces and the following characters: / : * ? " ; \ |. The length of the name cannot exceed 15 characters. The 16th character is reserved.

WINS is an implementation of the NetBIOS Name Service (NBNS), a name server and service for NetBIOS computer names. It is an older type of naming service used on Windows-based networks.

ACTIVITY 7–3
Creating a DNS Record

Scenario

At the Greene City Interiors branch office, you have a server that acts as both a web server and an FTP server. Some users get confused when they are told to access the web server when they want to use FTP. You decide to create an alias in DNS that will allow users to use a different name when they want to access FTP.

---

1. Display the **New Resource Record** dialog box.
   a) In **Server Manager**, select **Tools→DNS**.
   b) In the DNS Manager window, in the console tree, expand **Computer##, Forward Lookup Zones**, and select **Child##.GCInteriors.com**, where ## is the student number.

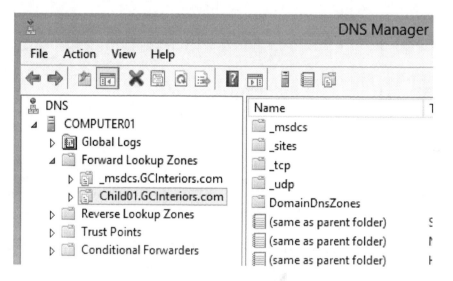

   c) Select **Action→New Alias (CNAME)** to display the **New Resource Record** dialog box.

2. Add a new host entry for your server with an associated pointer record.
   a) In the **New Resource Record** dialog box, in the **Alias name (use parent domain if left blank)** text box, type *FTP##*
   b) In the **Fully qualified domain name (FQDN) for target host** text box, type *computer##.child##.GCInteriors.com* and select **OK**.

3. Check the connectivity with your server.
   a) Open **Windows PowerShell**.
   b) At the prompt, type *ping FTP##* and press **Enter**.

c) Observe that you are able to communicate with the server and get four successful responses. Type *exit* and press **Enter** to close the window.

```
PS C:\Users\Administrator> ping FTP01

Pinging computer01.Child01.GCInteriors.com [192.168.2.37] with 32 bytes of data:
Reply from 192.168.2.37: bytes=32 time<1ms TTL=128
Reply from 192.168.2.37: bytes=32 time<1ms TTL=128
Reply from 192.168.2.37: bytes=32 time<1ms TTL=128
Reply from 192.168.2.37: bytes=32 time<1ms TTL=128

Ping statistics for 192.168.2.37:
    Packets: Sent = 4, Received = 4, Lost = 0 (0% loss),
Approximate round trip times in milli-seconds:
    Minimum = 0ms, Maximum = 0ms, Average = 0ms
```

d) Close the DNS Manager window.

TOPIC C

TCP/IP Commands

In the previous topic, you identified host name resolution services. Another set of services that are available on IP networks is a robust administrative tool set. In this topic, you will identify the commands in the TCP/IP protocol suite that can help you ensure smooth connectivity in your TCP/IP network.

TCP/IP commands enable you to gather information about how your systems are communicating over a TCP/IP network. When used for troubleshooting, these commands can provide critical information about communication lapses and their causes.

Commands and Utilities for IP Networks

There are several commands and utilities available for you to configure, manage, and troubleshoot IP networks. Some you've already seen, such as using `ipconfig` to see if the default gateway is configured, and using `ping` to check for basic network connectivity. Other commands and utilities that you will probably find useful include:

- `route`
- `tracert` in Windows, and `traceroute` in UNIX and Linux
- `pathping`
- `mtr` utility in UNIX and Linux

The tracert Command

The *tracert* command determines the route data takes to get to a particular destination. The node sends out messages with incrementally increasing TTL values, which cause the packets to expire at each successive router in the path. Internet Control Message Protocol (ICMP) "Time Exceeded" messages are then sent back from the routers to the node running `tracert`. Each time a packet is sent, the TTL value is reduced before the packet is forwarded, thus allowing TTL to count how many hops it is away from the destination.

`traceroute` is the Linux equivalent of the `tracert` command, which is Windows-based.

Note: If you run the `tracert` command repeatedly for the same destination, you will normally see different results after a relatively short period of time. This is because TCP/IP is auto-correcting and takes the fastest route possible across the global network of Internet routers.

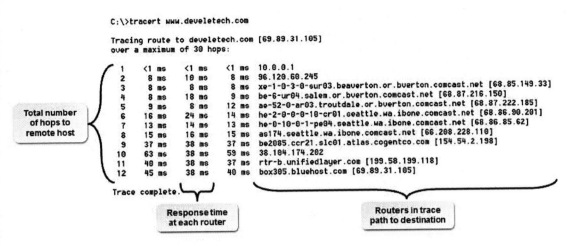

```
C:\>tracert www.develetech.com

Tracing route to develetech.com [69.89.31.105]
over a maximum of 30 hops:

  1    <1 ms    <1 ms    <1 ms  10.0.0.1
  2     8 ms    10 ms     8 ms  96.120.60.245
  3     8 ms     8 ms     8 ms  xe-1-0-3-0-sur03.beaverton.or.bverton.comcast.net [68.85.149.33]
  4     8 ms    18 ms     9 ms  be-6-ur04.salem.or.bverton.comcast.net [68.87.216.150]
  5     9 ms     8 ms    12 ms  ae-52-0-ar03.troutdale.or.bverton.comcast.net [68.87.222.185]
  6    16 ms    24 ms    14 ms  he-2-0-0-0-10-cr01.seattle.wa.ibone.comcast.net [68.86.90.201]
  7    13 ms    14 ms    13 ms  he-0-10-0-1-pe04.seattle.wa.ibone.comcast.net [68.86.85.62]
  8    15 ms    16 ms    15 ms  as174.seattle.wa.ibone.comcast.net [66.208.228.110]
  9    37 ms    38 ms    37 ms  be2085.ccr21.slc01.atlas.cogentco.com [154.54.2.198]
 10    63 ms    38 ms    59 ms  38.104.174.202
 11    40 ms    38 ms    37 ms  rtr-b.unifiedlayer.com [199.58.199.118]
 12    45 ms    38 ms    40 ms  box305.bluehost.com [69.89.31.105]

Trace complete.
```

Total number of hops to remote host

Response time at each router

Routers in trace path to destination

Figure 7-13: tracert output for www.develetech.com.

Network Firewalls

If a network firewall is configured to not allow a `tracert` or `ping` through, you might not be able to trace the route all the way to the end; it might appear to end at the firewall. If you get the message "Destination Unreachable," a router is not able to figure out how to get to the next destination. Even though it does not tell you what is wrong, it alerts you to the router where the problem is occurring.

You can use various options with the `tracert` command.

tracert Options

Option	Description
`-d`	If you are having trouble resolving host names when using `tracert`, use the `-d` option to prevent `tracert` from trying to resolve host names. It also speeds up response time because it is not spending time resolving host names.
`-h max_hops`	The default number of hops `tracert` will attempt to reach is 30. Using the `-h` option, you can specify more or fewer hops for it to check.
`-j host-list`	You can use the `-j` option to force the outgoing datagram to pass through a specific router.
`-w timeout`	If many of your responses on the `tracert` are timing out, by using the `-w` option, you can increase the number of milliseconds to wait before continuing. If, after increasing the value, destinations are then reachable, you probably have a bandwidth issue to resolve.

The pathping Command

The *pathping* command provides information about latency and packet loss on a network. `pathping` combines the functionality of the `ping` and `tracert` commands. Similar to `ping`, `pathping` sends multiple ICMP echo request messages to each router between two hosts over a period of time, and then displays results based on the number of packets returned by each router.

It is similar to `tracert` as it identifies the routers that are on the path. In the output, it also displays the path to the remote host over a maximum of 30 hops. In addition, it displays details of packet transfer between the hosts in a time span of over 25 seconds, and the system names and their IP addresses. `pathping` can be used to isolate a router or subnet with issues as it can display the degree of packet loss at any given router or link.

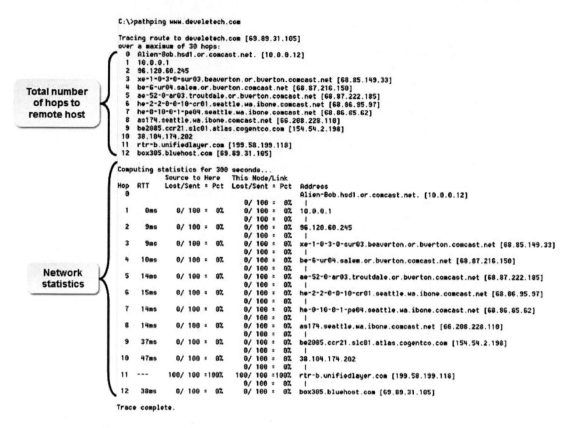

Figure 7-14: pathping output for www.develetech.com.

pathping Options

The `pathping` command can be used with different options that allow you to customize the results of the command to your network requirements.

Option	Description
-h *maximum hops*	Specify the maximum number of hops to locate a destination.
-i *address*	Specify a source IP address.
-n	Specify that host name resolution can be skipped.
-4 *address*	Specify the IPv4 addresses that are to be used.
-6 *address*	Specify the IPv6 addresses that are to be used.

The MTR Utility

The My traceroute (*MTR*) utility combines `ping` and `traceroute` into a single function. MTR displays the routers traversed, the average time taken for round trip, and packet loss of each router. This utility helps network administrators identify latency or packet loss between two routers. MTR is used on UNIX-based systems.

 Note: The General Public License (GNU) is responsible for licensing and distributing MTR.

ACTIVITY 7–4
Using TCP/IP Commands

Scenario

At the Greene City Interiors branch office, a node on the network has problems communicating with the DNS server. As the network administrator, you have reconfigured the network setting on the node. You want to ensure that the connectivity is successful before you reassign the device to a user.

1. Use the `ping` command to verify that the DNS server is available.
   a) Open **Windows PowerShell**.
   b) In the Windows PowerShell window, type *ping DC* and press **Enter**.
   c) Observe that the results display the DNS server's IP address as 192.168.2.200.

```
PS C:\Users\Administrator> ping DC

Pinging DC.GCInteriors.com [192.168.2.200] with 32 bytes of data:
Reply from 192.168.2.200: bytes=32 time<1ms TTL=128
Reply from 192.168.2.200: bytes=32 time<1ms TTL=128
Reply from 192.168.2.200: bytes=32 time<1ms TTL=128
Reply from 192.168.2.200: bytes=32 time<1ms TTL=128

Ping statistics for 192.168.2.200:
    Packets: Sent = 4, Received = 4, Lost = 0 (0% loss),
Approximate round trip times in milli-seconds:
    Minimum = 0ms, Maximum = 0ms, Average = 0ms
```

2. Use the `tracert` command to trace the route from your system to the DNS server.
   a) In the Windows PowerShell window, type *tracert /?* and press **Enter** to view the syntax of the `tracert` command.
   b) Observe the syntax of the command displayed in the **Usage** section and the various options of the command along with their description.

```
PS C:\Users\Administrator> tracert /?

Usage: tracert [-d] [-h maximum_hops] [-j host-list] [-w timeout]
               [-R] [-S srcaddr] [-4] [-6] target_name

Options:
    -d                 Do not resolve addresses to hostnames.
    -h maximum_hops    Maximum number of hops to search for target.
    -j host-list       Loose source route along host-list (IPv4-only).
    -w timeout         Wait timeout milliseconds for each reply.
    -R                 Trace round-trip path (IPv6-only).
    -S srcaddr         Source address to use (IPv6-only).
    -4                 Force using IPv4.
    -6                 Force using IPv6.
```

   c) In the Windows PowerShell window, type *tracert -d 192.168.2.200* and press **Enter**.

    d) Verify that there was only one hop because it is on the same local network as your system.

```
PS C:\Users\Administrator> tracert -d 192.168.2.200

Tracing route to 192.168.2.200 over a maximum of 30 hops

  1    <1 ms    <1 ms    <1 ms  192.168.2.200

Trace complete.
```

    e) Type *cls* and press **Enter** to clear the screen.

3. Use the `pathping` command to display statistics related to network traffic.
    a) At the prompt, type *pathping DC* and press **Enter**.
    b) Observe that the results display the IP address and the system name. Verify that there are no packet errors.

```
PS C:\Users\Administrator> pathping DC

Tracing route to dc.gcinteriors.com [192.168.2.200]
over a maximum of 30 hops:
  0  Computer01.Child01.GCInteriors.com [192.168.2.37]
  1  DC [192.168.2.200]

Computing statistics for 25 seconds...
            Source to Here   This Node/Link
Hop  RTT    Lost/Sent = Pct  Lost/Sent = Pct  Address
  0                                            Computer01.Child01.GCInteriors.com [192.168.2.37]
                                0/ 100 =  0%   |
  1    0ms    0/ 100 =  0%     0/ 100 =  0%   DC [192.168.2.200]

Trace complete.
```

    c) Close the Windows PowerShell window.

TOPIC D

Common TCP/IP Protocols

You have identified common TCP/IP commands and their functions. The TCP/IP protocol suite also includes protocols that work at different layers of the protocol stack. In this topic, you will identify common TCP/IP protocols and services and the functions they provide on your network.

Once network communication has been established at the lower layers of the protocol stack, users will deploy applications to complete tasks using that communication link. These tasks can include transferring and sharing files, reading and sending email, reading and posting messages on a newsgroup, and browsing the web. The TCP/IP upper-layer protocols and services make accomplishing these tasks possible. By understanding the function of each of the TCP/IP protocols, you can choose the appropriate protocol for the desired user task.

The TCP/IP Protocol Stack

The *TCP/IP protocol stack* is the collection of protocols that work together to provide communications on IP-based networks such as the Internet. To send data over a TCP/IP network requires four steps or layers:

- The Application layer encodes the data being sent.
- The Transport layer splits the data into manageable chunks and adds port number information.
- The Internet layer adds IP addresses stating where the data is from and where it is going.
- The Network Access layer adds MAC address information to specify which hardware device the message came from and which hardware device the message is going to.

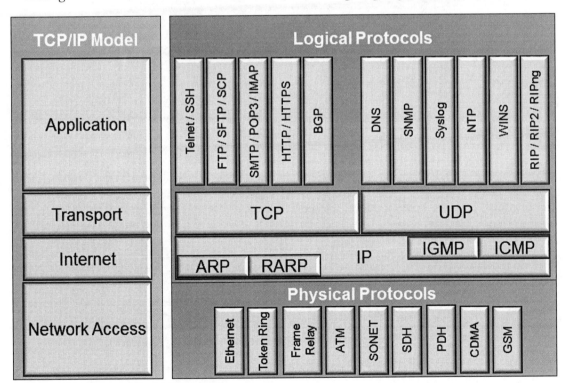

Figure 7-15: The TCP/IP protocol stack.

The terms protocol stack and protocol suite are often used interchangeably. But, you also might find that the terms can be used to convey subtle differences, such as the stack being a complete set of protocols and the suite being a subset of the stack, often supplied by a particular vendor, or the suite being the definition of the protocols and the stack being the software implementation of the suite.

Services and Daemons

A *daemon* is a background process that performs a specific operation. Daemon is a UNIX term, though daemons are supported on other operating systems. Daemons on Windows are referred to as system agents or services.

FTP

The *File Transfer Protocol (FTP)* is a TCP/IP protocol that enables the transfer of files between a user's workstation and a remote host. The FTP daemon or service must be running on the remote host, and an FTP utility may need to be installed on the client. FTP commands must be entered in lowercase and are available both as Windows command-line and UNIX commands. It works on the Application layer (Layer 7) of the OSI model and the Application layer of the TCP/IP model.

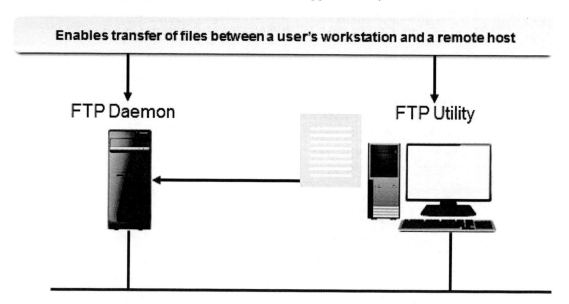

Enables transfer of files between a user's workstation and a remote host

FTP Daemon

FTP Utility

Figure 7-16: An FTP utility enables a client to access the FTP server.

FTP works on two TCP channels: TCP port 20 for data transfer and TCP port 21 for control commands. These channels work together to enable users to execute commands and transfer data simultaneously. A server-based program answers requests from FTP clients for download. A command line utility enables users to connect to an FTP server and download files. You can initiate an FTP session by entering:

```
ftp FQDN/IP address of remote host
```

You can use several options with the FTP command line utility.

Option	Used To
-v	Prevent remote server command responses being shown.
-n	Suppress auto-logon at initial connection.
-i	Disable interactive prompting when transferring multiple files.
-d	Enable debugging, displaying all commands passed between the FTP client and server.

Option	Used To
-g	Disable wildcard character support.
-s: [*filename*]	Run all the FTP commands contained in the [*filename*] file.
-a	Allow use of any local interface during data connection binding.
-w: [*windowsize*]	Override the default transfer buffer size.

Trivial File Transfer Protocol (TFTP) is a simple version of FTP that uses UDP as the transport protocol, and does not require logon to the remote host. As it uses UDP, it does not support error correction but provides for higher data integrity. It is commonly used for bootstrapping and loading applications and not for file transfer. FTP traffic is not encrypted and all transmissions are in clear text. User names, passwords, commands, and data can be read by anyone able to perform packet capture (sniffing) on the network.

Most Internet browsers can support FTP in a graphical user interface (GUI) mode. A connection to an FTP site can be made by browsing the Internet, logging on, and connecting. Once connected, you can drag files on and off the FTP site the same way you would from File Explorer. There are also a number of third-party FTP utilities that you can use for connecting to and uploading files to your FTP site.

To access most FTP servers, the client needs to connect using a valid user name and password. Some FTP servers allow limited access through an anonymous connection. If anonymous access is disabled on the remote host, users will need login credentials. To use this option, log on using the user name anonymous and enter your email address for the password.

When connecting to an FTP server, logging on poses the biggest problems. You need to provide the correct credentials to log on to the FTP server. Most users are granted only read permissions and to upload files, you need to ensure that you have the necessary permissions.

NTP

The *Network Time Protocol (NTP)* is an Internet protocol that synchronizes the clock times of devices in a network by exchanging time signals. It works on the Application layer (Layer 7) of the OSI model and the Application layer of the TCP/IP model. Synchronization is done to the millisecond against the U.S. Naval Observatory master clocks. Running continuously in the background on a device, NTP sends periodic time requests to servers to obtain the server time stamp and then adjusts the client's clock based on the server time stamp received. Implementations send and receive time stamps by using UDP on port number 123.

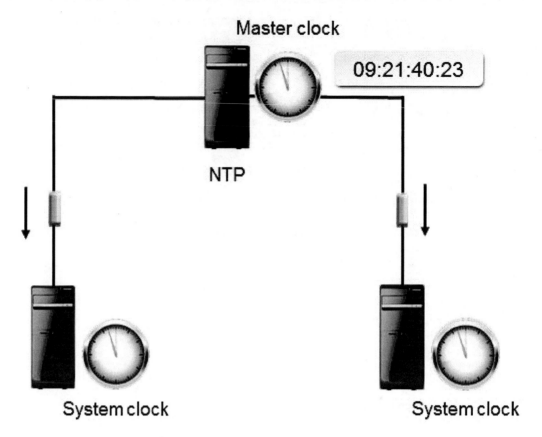

Figure 7–17: Clocks synchronized by using NTP.

 Note: The master time clocks are located in Washington, DC, and Colorado Springs, Colorado.

SNMP

The *Simple Network Management Protocol (SNMP)* is an Internet protocol that enables administrators to monitor and manage network devices and traffic. Working at the Application layer (Layer 7) of the OSI model and the Application layer of the TCP/IP model, SNMP uses ports 161 and 162 to collect information from and send configuration commands to networking devices such as routers, switches, servers, workstations, printers, and any other SNMP-enabled devices. SNMP generally runs over UDP.

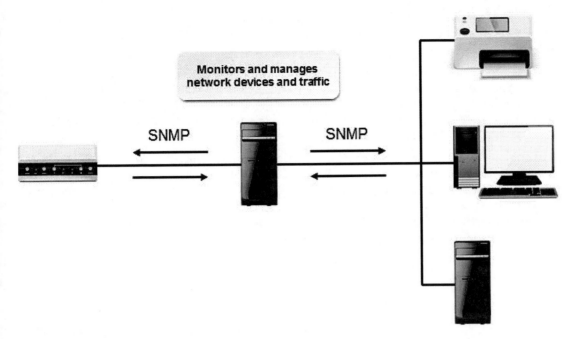

Figure 7-18: SNMP.

SMTP

The *Simple Mail Transfer Protocol (SMTP)* is a communications protocol for formatting and sending email messages from a client to a server or between servers. It works at the Application layer (Layer 7) of the OSI model and the Application layer of the TCP/IP model. Using port 25 or 587 for standard communications and port 465 for encrypted communications, SMTP runs on TCP.

SMTP uses a store-and-forward process. In SMTP, the sender starts the transfer. SMTP can store a message until the receiving device comes online. At that point, it contacts the device and hands off the message. If all devices are online, the message is sent quickly. An SMTP message consists of a header and a content section. The header, or envelope, contains the delivery information of the message and uses a colon (:) as a separator character. The content portion contains the message text, which is a sequence of ASCII characters.

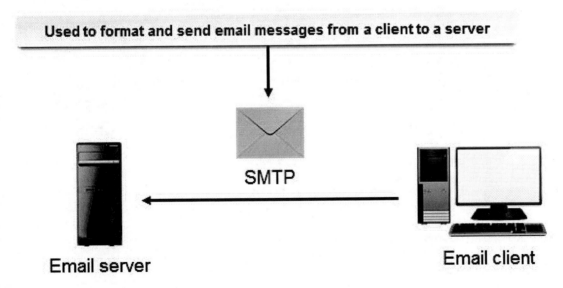

Figure 7-19: Sending email messages by using SMTP.

Because of SMTP's store-and-forward capability, it is used to send data through unreliable wide area network (WAN) links if delivery time is not critical. Data is sent to the endpoint and continues to hop from server to server until it eventually reaches its destination.

SMTP has a few limitations. The first one is related to the size of messages. Messages that are more than 64 KB cannot be handled by some older implementations. Another limitation involves timeouts. If the client and server timeouts are different, one of the systems may give up when the other is still busy, resulting in termination of the connection unexpectedly. Sometimes SMTP may also trigger infinite mail storms.

For example, consider host 1 with Mailing List A containing a few entries and host 2 with Mailing List B containing both its own entries and that of Mailing List A. In such a case, email sent to Mailing List A and copied to Mailing List B could trigger sending multiple copies of the same email message to the same set of recipients. Furthermore, if host 1 fails when mail is being forwarded, host 2 will try resending it to host 1. This generates a heavy amount of traffic on the network.

Extended SMTP (ESMTP) extends the capabilities of SMTP and helps to overcome some of these limitations.

POP3

Post Office Protocol 3 (POP3) is a protocol used to retrieve email messages from a mailbox on a mail server. POP3 works at the Application layer (Layer 7) of the OSI model and the Application layer of the TCP/IP model. POP3 uses port 110 for regular transmissions and port 195 for encrypted transmissions, and it runs on TCP.

With POP3, email messages wait in the mailbox on the server until the client retrieves them. The client can start the transfer on a set schedule, or transfer messages manually. Once the client retrieves and downloads the messages, the server deletes them unless the client configures options to leave the messages on the server. The client then works with the locally cached email messages.

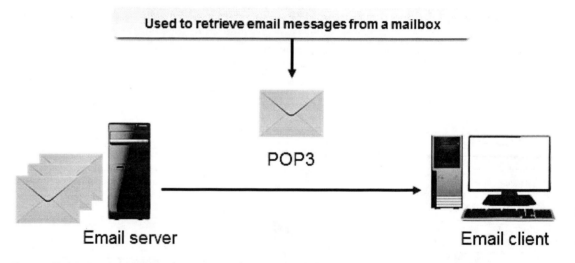

Used to retrieve email messages from a mailbox

POP3

Email server   Email client

Figure 7–20: Retrieving email messages by using POP3.

Because POP3 is designed by default to download messages to the local device and delete them from the email server, it is not the best email protocol to use when users need to access their email from multiple devices. This is because when they use POP3, they end up with their email messages downloaded and split among the devices they use instead of having all their messages in one central location. Or, if they leave their messages on the server, they will have to delete old messages manually to avoid exceeding mailbox size limits, which may also lead to messages being split across multiple devices.

IMAP4

Internet Message Access Protocol version 4 (IMAP4) is a protocol used for retrieving messages from a mail server. IMAP4 works at the Application layer (Layer 7) of the OSI model and the Application layer of the TCP/IP model. IMAP4 uses port 143 for regular transmissions and port 993 for encrypted transmissions, and it runs on TCP. Though it is similar to POP3, IMAP4 is more powerful and offers several functions. They include:

- A user can check an email header and also look for a specific string of characters in the contents of a message before downloading it.
- Messages can also remain on the server while the client works with them as if they were local.
- Users can search through messages by keywords and choose which messages to download locally.
- Messages in the user's mailbox can be marked with different status flags, such as deleted or replied to. The messages and their status flags stay in the mailbox until explicitly removed by the user.
- An email message containing multimedia files can be partially downloaded, saving bandwidth.
- A user can create, rename, or delete mailboxes on a mail server, and also arrange mailboxes in a hierarchical manner in a folder for email storage.
- Unlike POP3, IMAP4 enables users to access folders other than their mailbox.

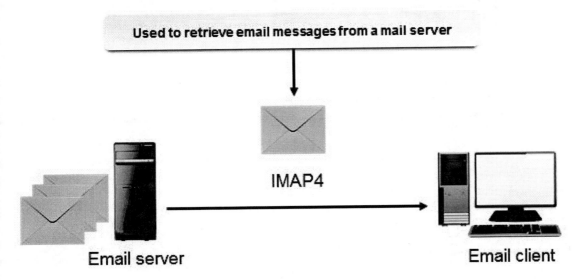

Figure 7-21: Retrieving email messages by using IMAP4.

 Note: Because IMAP4 is designed to store messages on the server, it is much easier for users to access their email messages—both new and saved—from multiple devices.

 Note: IMAP was developed at Stanford University in 1986.

HTTP

The *Hypertext Transfer Protocol (HTTP)* is a network protocol that works on the Application layer (Layer 7) of the OSI model and the Application layer of the TCP/IP model to provide web services. HTTP uses port 80 for communicating with web clients and servers and runs on TCP.

HTTP enables clients to interact with websites by allowing them to connect to and retrieve web pages from a server. It defines the format and transmission of messages, as well as what actions web servers and clients' browsers should take in response to different commands. A stateless protocol in which each command executes independently of any prior commands, HTTP supports not only persistent connections to web resources to reduce reconnection times, but also pipelining and buffering to help in the transfer process.

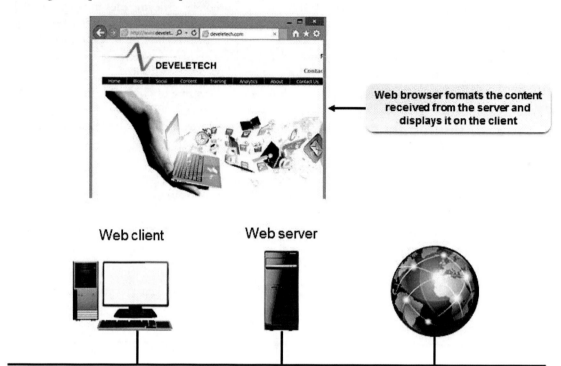

Figure 7-22: Web clients using HTTP to access a website.

Web services are application components that communicate through open protocols and can be used by other applications. Web services are based on HTTP and XML. Web services enable any operating system to access the applications you publish. The data is encoded and decoded using XML. SOAP is used to transport the data via open protocols. Programmers can create application components that are reusable and can be accessed as services. Programmers can also use web services to link existing data from various applications to make the data available across all platforms.

 Note: Because HTTP is stateless, it is difficult to implement websites that react intelligently to user input. This limitation can be overcome with a number of add-on technologies, such as ActiveX®, Java®, JavaScript®, and cookies.

HTTPS

HTTP Secure (HTTPS) is a secure version of HTTP that provides a secure connection between a web browser and a server. HTTPS runs at the Application layer (Layer 7) of the OSI model and the Application layer of the TCP/IP model. It uses port 443 and runs on TCP.

HTTPS uses the *Secure Sockets Layer (SSL)* security protocol to encrypt data. Not all web browsers and servers support HTTPS, though.

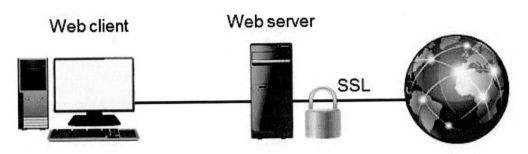

Figure 7-23: Websites that use HTTPS for secure transactions.

Note: HTTPS is also referred to as HTTP over SSL.

Telnet

Telecommunications Network (*Telnet*) is a terminal emulation protocol that enables users at one site to simulate a session on a remote host as if the terminal were directly attached. It performs this simulation by translating keystrokes from the user's terminal into instructions that the remote host recognizes, and then carrying the output back and displaying it in a format native to the user's terminal. Telnet operates at the Application layer (Layer 7) of the OSI model and the Application layer of the TCP/IP model. It uses port 23 and runs on TCP.

You can connect to any host that is running a Telnet daemon or service. Connection-oriented, Telnet handles its own session negotiations and assists network administrators in remote administration such as connecting to a remote server or to a service such as FTP. However, it is not considered a secure protocol, since it transmits in cleartext.

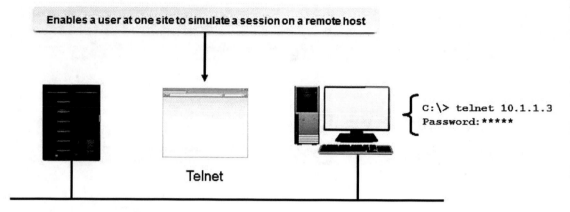

Figure 7–24: A Telnet session.

Many systems, such as a UNIX host or an IBM® mainframe running TCP/IP, include Telnet daemons. There is also a Telnet server service in older versions of Windows, such as Windows XP and Windows Server® 2003. Telnet is not installed by default in Windows Server 2012 R2. Microsoft provides directions for installing Telnet; you can view them by visiting the URL: **http://technet.microsoft.com/en-us/library/cc770501(WS.10).aspx**.

Windows includes a basic Telnet client utility. It is installed when you install TCP/IP on your Windows system. It includes Video Terminal 100 (VT100), VT52, and TeleTYpe (TTY) terminal emulation. It does not include the Telnet daemon or service, but the Telnet service can be enabled on Windows Server computers.

Telnet is defined in RFC 854, and uses the following defaults:

- Uses TCP Port 23; however, you can specify a different port if the host to which you are connecting is configured to use a different port.
- Uses 25 lines in the buffer, but you can configure it for up to 399 lines.
- Uses VT100 as the default terminal emulation, but some versions allow you to configure your system with VT220, VT52, and TTY terminal emulation support.

SSH

Secure Shell (SSH) is a program that enables a user or an application to log on to another device over a network, execute commands, and manage files. SSH operates at the Application layer (Layer 7) of the OSI model and the Application layer of the TCP/IP model. It uses port 22 and runs on TCP.

It creates a shell or session with a remote system, offers strong authentication methods, and ensures that communications are secure over insecure channels. With the SSH `slogin` command, the login session, including the password, is encrypted and protected against attacks. Secure Shell works with many different operating systems, including Windows, UNIX, and Macintosh. Windows does not provide a native SSH client. You will have to download and install an SSH client such as PuTTY, WinSCP, or Teraterm Pro with the TTSSH extension.

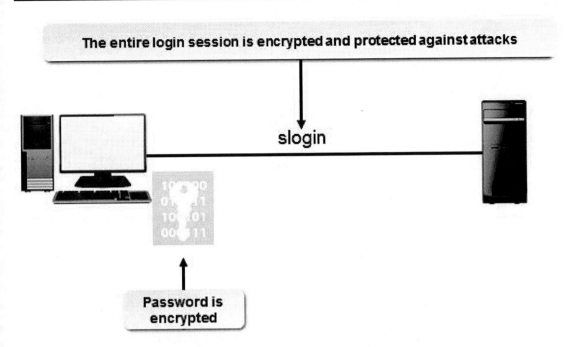

Figure 7-25: An SSH session that uses slogin.

 Note: SSH is a replacement for the UNIX-based `rlogin` command, which can also establish a connection with a remote host, but transmits passwords in cleartext.

There are two versions of Secure Shell available: SSH1 and SSH2. They are two different protocols and encrypt different parts of a data packet. To authenticate systems, SSH1 employs user keys to identify users; host keys to identify systems; session keys to encrypt communication in a single session; and server keys, which are temporary keys that protect the session key. SSH2 is more secure; it does not use server keys. SSH2 includes a secure replacement for FTP called *Secure File Transfer Protocol (SFTP)*. Because they are different protocol implementations, SSH1 and SSH2 are not compatible with each other.

 Note: Note that the acronym SFTP is used both for Secure File Transfer Protocol as well as for the now obsolete Simple File Transfer Protocol.

All traffic (including passwords) is encrypted by SSH to eliminate connection hijacking, eavesdropping, and other network-level attacks, such as IP source routing, IP spoofing, and DNS spoofing. When you implement SSH with encryption, any attacker who manages to gain access to your network can neither play back the traffic nor hijack the connection. They can only force SSH to disconnect.

SMB

The *Server Message Block (SMB)* is a protocol that works on the Application layer (Layer 7) of the OSI model and helps share resources such as files, printers, and serial ports among devices. SMB uses port 445 and runs on TCP.

In a TCP/IP network, NetBIOS clients, such as Windows systems, use NetBIOS over TCP/IP to connect to servers, and then issue SMB commands to complete tasks such as accessing shared files and printers.

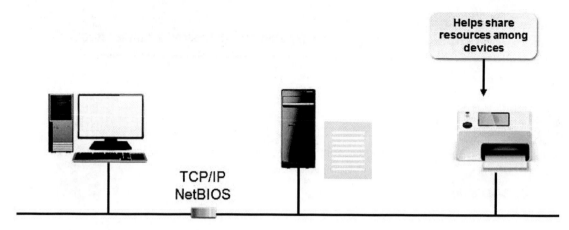

Figure 7-26: Resource sharing using SMB.

Samba is a well-known open-source product that uses SMB to enable UNIX and Windows devices for sharing directories and files. Although the SMB protocol is primarily used in Microsoft networks, there are products such as NAS appliances that use SMB to facilitate file sharing across different operating system platforms. Linux can also support SMB, as well as act as a file and print server for Windows clients, if you enable the built-in Samba service on the Linux device.

RDP

The *Remote Desktop Protocol (RDP)* is a proprietary protocol created by Microsoft for connecting to and managing devices that are not necessarily located at the same place as the administrator. It uses port 3389, runs on TCP, and works on the Application layer (Layer 7) of the OSI model. It and the remote desktop software allow a user to remotely log in to a networked device. The desktop interface, or application GUI, of the remote device looks as if it were accessed locally. RDP is a multiple-channel-capable protocol that allows for separate virtual channels for carrying device communication and presentation data from the server, as well as encrypted client mouse and keyboard data. RDP provides an extensible base and supports up to 64,000 separate channels for data transmission and provisions for multipoint transmission.

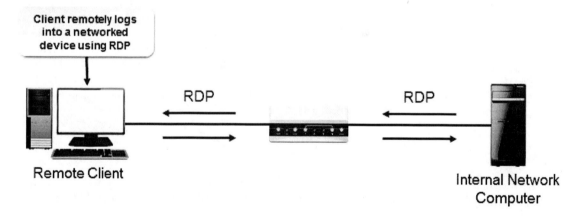

Figure 7-27: RDP.

End-to-End Communication

It can be helpful to understand how communication traverses the network. Imagine host A sends a message to host Z, which is on a different network. Host A first sends its message by using the MAC address to the local default gateway on its network, in this case a router. That router then sends the message to another router by using an IP address. This next router then sends the message over its network by using a MAC address to another router. The next hop may be another network segment or even the Internet. This process will repeat until the message finally arrives at a router on the destination network. That router will then send the message to host Z by using the MAC address.

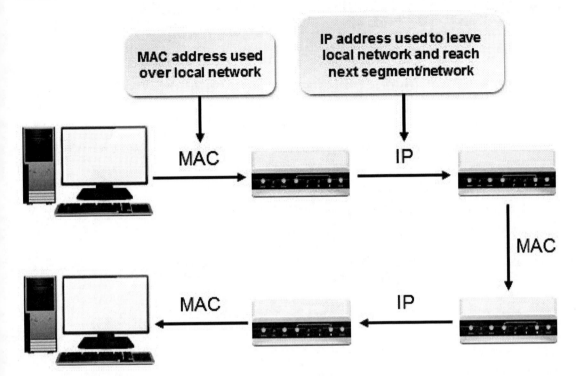

Figure 7-28: End-to-end communication.

ACTIVITY 7–5
Identifying Common TCP/IP Protocols

Scenario
The network administrator at Greene City Interiors asks you questions about TCP/IP protocols you may encounter at the branch office.

1. What are the differences between accessing email from multiple systems using IMAP4 and POP3?

   ☐ POP3 does not maintain a copy of the email once it is downloaded from a mail server.

   ☐ POP3 does not maintain a copy of the outgoing email.

   ☐ Accessing email by using POP3 is faster than IMAP4.

   ☐ IMAP4 is the messaging protocol used to access email.

2. Your sales department wants to sell supplies over the Internet and wants to make sure that the transactions are secure. Which protocol should be configured on the web server?

   ○ FTP

   ○ HTTPS

   ○ NNTP

   ○ SMTP

3. Your company has a production floor with several shared devices. The production staff needs to be able to check their email from whichever device is free. Which email protocol should you use?

   ○ POP3

   ○ NTP

   ○ IMAP4

   ○ NNTP

4. Your sales force needs to retrieve sales prospective documents and upload completed sales order forms to corporate headquarters while they are on the move. What service should you use?

   ○ HTTP

   ○ NNTP

   ○ NTP

   ○ FTP

5. What are the differences between FTP and HTTP?

6. True or False? Telnet is a terminal emulation protocol that allows users at one site to simulate a session on a remote host as if the terminal were directly attached.

   ☐ True

   ☐ False

7. Which is a program that enables a user or an application to log on to another device over a network, execute commands, and manage files over an encrypted connection?

   ○ SFTP

   ○ SSH

   ○ SMB

   ○ FTP

8. Which is a protocol that works on the Application layer and helps share resources such as files, printers, and serial ports among devices?

   ○ SSH

   ○ FTP

   ○ SMB

   ○ SFTP

Summary

In this lesson, you identified the major services used on IP networks. Understanding TCP/IP services and tools will enable you to configure, monitor, manage, and troubleshoot your TCP/IP network.

How do you assign IP addresses in your network? Why?

Which TCP/IP commands do you use in your network?

 Note: Check your LogicalCHOICE Course screen for opportunities to interact with your classmates, peers, and the larger LogicalCHOICE online community about the topics covered in this course or other topics you are interested in. From the Course screen you can also access available resources for a more continuous learning experience.

8 | WAN Infrastructure

Lesson Time: 1 hour, 30 minutes

Lesson Objectives

In this lesson, you will identify the infrastructure of a WAN implementation. You will:

- Identify basic WAN concepts and terminology.

- Identify the major WAN connectivity methods.

- Identify the major transmission technologies used in WANs.

- Identify the basic elements of unified communication technologies.

Lesson Introduction

In the previous lessons, you identified common components of a local area network (LAN) implementation. There are other technologies that can be implemented on a wide area network (WAN). In this lesson, you will identify the components of a WAN implementation.

Many local networks have a wide area connection to a distant network. Moreover, virtually every network connects in one way or another to the biggest WAN of them all, the Internet. As a networking professional, you will need to understand the infrastructure of these WAN connections so that you can ensure connectivity in the networks that you support.

TOPIC A

WAN Basics

In this lesson, you will describe various facets of WAN infrastructure. To begin, you will identify basic WAN concepts and terminology.

Both LANs and WANs allow for interconnectivity between devices. LANs are used for localized networking, whereas WANs cover larger areas, such as cities, and even allow devices in different nations to connect. Even if you don't administer a WAN, your network will most likely connect to one, and understanding some basic components will allow you to do that successfully.

Introduction to WAN Technologies

A WAN is a network that spans a large area, often across multiple geographical locations. WANs typically connect multiple LANs and other networks by using long-range transmission media. This facilitates communication among users and devices in different locations. WANs can be private, such as those built and maintained by large, multinational corporations, or they can be public, such as the Internet. When a WAN includes sites and networks around the world, it is considered a global area network (GAN).

Besides geographical coverage, the primary distinction between a LAN and a WAN is the Layer 2 protocol that each uses. With a few exceptions, most Layer 2 protocols were designed to work in either one network type or the other, but not in both. In addition, a company typically owns its own LAN infrastructure and equipment, but it will pay a service provider to connect the company's LANs through the provider's WANs.

WAN Devices

WAN connectivity devices enable you to connect LANs together. The most common WAN devices include those described in the following table.

WAN Device	Description
Modem	A *modem* enables digital data to be sent over an analog medium such as a telephone wire or cable provider's line. Digital signals are converted into an analog format suitable for transmission through analog carriers and then restored to digital format on the receiving end. The three main types of modems that you will encounter are: • *DSL modems*: hardware devices that connect subscribers to a telephone line that provides the digital subscriber line service for connectivity to the Internet. This connectivity is sometimes referred to as DSL broadband. DSL speed varies widely and depends on several factors. It is best to communicate with the service providers to determine the bandwidth available for a particular location. • *Cable modems*: hardware devices that connect subscribers to the Internet service provider's (ISP's) cable systems. Service providers use a cable modem to connect the subscriber's device to the Internet by using twisted pair cabling and a network port or USB connection. On the other end, the cable modem connects to the wall jack by using coaxial cabling. Most cable companies provide access for up to 25 or 50 Mbps. If the cable system is fiber-based, speeds might reach up to 1 Gbps. Cable modems operate at the Physical (Layer 1) and Data Link (Layer 2) layers of the OSI model. • *Dial-up modems*: communication devices that convert a computer's digital signals into analog signals before transmission over telephone lines. A dial-up modem can be either internal or external. Internal dial-up modems exist as part of the motherboard and use the device's power supply; external dial-up modems connect via the serial or USB port as separate expansion boxes. Unlike internal dial-up modems, external modems require a separate power supply. The disadvantage of a dial-up modem is that it is slow when compared to broadband modems.
Access server	An access server manages dial-in and dial-out user communications. It can have a mixture of analog and digital interfaces and support hundreds of simultaneous users. Network access servers function as control points for roaming and remote users so that they can access internal resources (or connect to an ISP) from external locations.
WAN switch	A WAN switch is a multiport internetworking device that normally switches traffic and operates at the Data Link layer (Layer 2) of the OSI model. WAN switches can share bandwidth among allocated service priorities, recover from outages, and provide network design and management systems.
CSU/DSU	A *Channel Service Unit/Data Service Unit (CSU/DSU)* is a combination of two WAN connectivity devices that work together to connect a digital WAN line with a customer's LAN. The DSU receives the signal from the LAN and passes it to the CSU. The CSU converts the signal format to make it compatible with the Digital Data Service (DDS) on the WAN line.

WAN Device	Description
ISDN terminal adapter	An *Integrated Services for Digital Network (ISDN)* terminal adapter is similar to a modem in that it joins Basic Rate Interface (BRI) connections to different physical interfaces on a router. Unlike a modem, it does not convert between analog and digital signaling.

> **Note:** You will discuss ISDN in greater depth later in this lesson.

WAN Termination Equipment

The WAN Physical layer describes the interface between the *data termination equipment (DTE)* and the *data communications equipment (DCE)*. In most cases, the DCE belongs to the service provider, and the DTE is the customer's device. The DCE will almost always be a modem or CSU/DSU that is installed on the customer's premises.

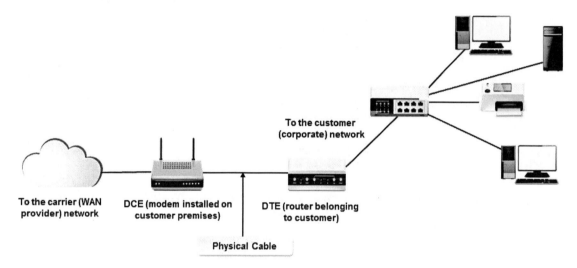

Figure 8-1: WAN termination equipment.

Circuit Switching and Packet Switching

As you know, switching is a technique used for transmitting information over a network to the destination network device. The two main types of switching are circuit switching and packet switching.

In *circuit switching,* one endpoint creates a single path connection to another, depending on the requirement. In circuit switching, the word "circuit" refers to the connection path between endpoints. Once the circuit is established, data is transmitted through that path until the circuit is active. Bandwidth is dedicated to the connection until it is not needed anymore. There is no guarantee that data will be transmitted through the same path through the network in different sessions.

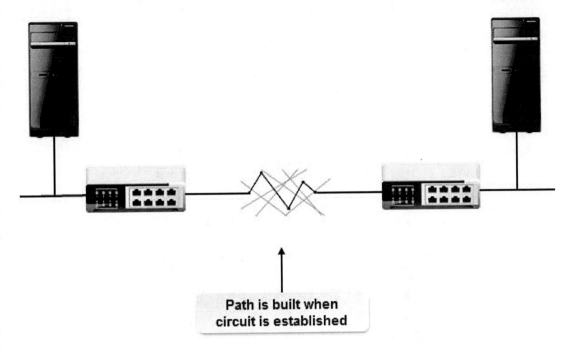

Path is built when
circuit is established

Figure 8-2: Transfer of data in a circuit switching network.

The public switched telephone network (PSTN) is an example of a circuit switching network.

In *packet switching networks,* data to be transmitted is broken into small units known as packets that move in sequence through the network. Each packet takes the best route available at any given time rather than following an established circuit path. Each data packet contains all of the routing and sequencing information required to transmit it from one endpoint to another, after which the data is reassembled. Packet switching assumes that a network is constantly changing and adjustments need to be made to compensate for network congestion or broken links.

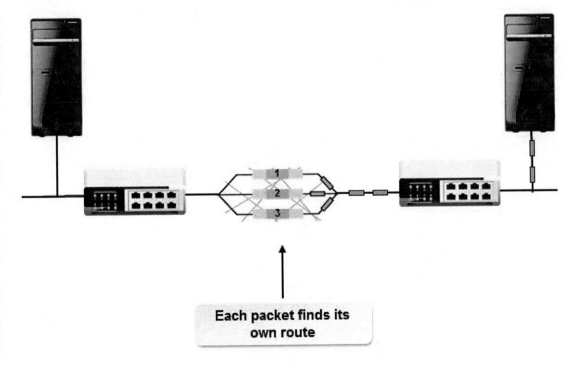

Each packet finds its
own route

Figure 8-3: Transfer of data in a packet switching network.

Packet switching is not the best choice for streaming media such as live video and audio feeds. Because all packets do not necessarily arrive at the destination in order, or soon after each other, time-sensitive applications can end up stuttering or delayed, or a streaming connection may drop entirely.

Virtual Circuit Switching

Virtual circuit switching is a switching technique to transfer packets on logical circuits that do not have physical resources, such as frequencies or time slots allocated. This technique merges both packet and circuit switching techniques to its advantage. These logical paths are assigned to identities, rather than to physical locations, and can be either permanent or switched. Each of the packets carries a virtual circuit identifier (VCI) that is local to a link and updated by each switch on the path, from the source to the destination of the packet.

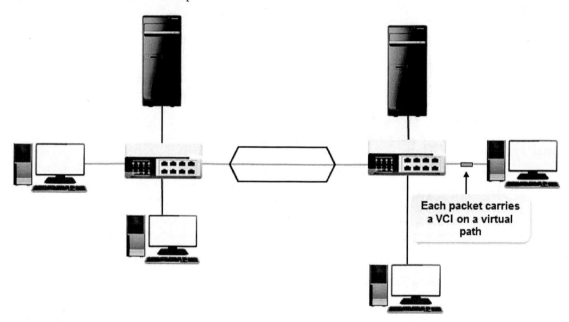

Each packet carries a VCI on a virtual path

Figure 8-4: Packets flow in a virtual circuit using VCI.

There are two types of virtual circuits: permanent virtual circuits (PVCs) and switched virtual circuits (SVCs).

Virtual Circuit Type	Description
Permanent	*PVCs* are usually associated with leased lines. They connect two endpoints and are always on, which is why they are referred to as permanent. When a PVC is established, it is manually built and maintained by a telephone company (telco). The telco identifies the endpoints with a data link connection identifier (DLCI). PVCs provide a fast, reliable connection between endpoints because the connection is always on. Customers pay a fixed monthly fee per connection.
Switched	*SVCs* are associated with dial-up connections. SVCs provide more flexibility than PVCs and allow a single connection to an endpoint to be connected to multiple endpoints as needed. When a network device attempts to connect to a WAN, an SVC is requested and the carrier establishes the connection. Customers typically pay by connection time (like a long-distance phone call) and the monthly charge is less than that of a PVC. SVCs are useful when you need a part-time connection. But keep in mind that connection time can be slow, and if usage increases, so can an SVC's cost.

Cell Switching Networks

Cell switching networks are similar to packet switching networks, except that data is transmitted as fixed-length *cells* instead of in variable-length packets. If data does not fill up an entire cell, the remainder of the space is filled with blank or filler data until the cell reaches its fixed size. The advantage of cell switching over packet switching is its predictability. Cell switching technologies make it easy to track how much data is moving on a network.

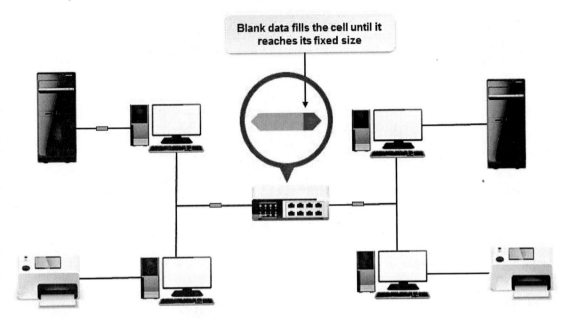

Blank data fills the cell until it reaches its fixed size

Figure 8-5: Cell switching uses fixed-length cells instead of variable-length packets.

Point-to-Point Connectivity

Like LANs, WANs use bus, star, mesh, and ring topologies. Some simple WAN implementations also use point-to-point and point-to-multipoint connections.

A *point-to-point connection* is a simple WAN topology that provides a direct connection between two nodes. A point-to-point connection is a type of bus, but with only two nodes on it. It has its own IP subnet, with a /30 subnet mask. The nodes, typically routers, are at either end of the link. This topology is used most commonly by dedicated leased lines and dial-up connections.

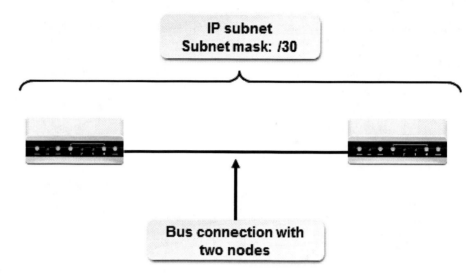

Figure 8-6: A point-to-point connection between two routers.

Point-to-Multipoint Connectivity

Another common WAN topology is *point-to-multipoint*. This is a physical star, in which a central site is the hub, and multiple branch sites are spokes. Logically, a point-to-multipoint connection behaves like a hub. All nodes belong to the same subnet, even though traffic physically passes through the central site. Point-to-multipoint is often used in frame relay networks.

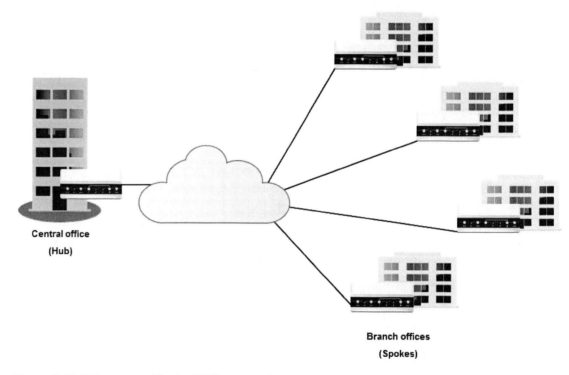

Figure 8-7: Point-to-multipoint WAN connections.

ACTIVITY 8-1
Discussing WAN Basics

Scenario

At the Greene City Interiors branch office, the network administrator quizzes you to test your knowledge of WAN basics.

1. In which switching network is there one endpoint that creates a single path connection to another?
   - ○ Circuit switching networks
   - ○ Virtual circuit switching
   - ○ Cell switching networks
   - ○ Packet switching networks

2. In which switching network is data broken into small units that move in sequence through the network?
   - ○ Packet switching networks
   - ○ Cell switching networks
   - ○ Circuit switching networks
   - ○ Virtual circuit switching

3. For what reasons might an organization want to connect to a WAN?

TOPIC B

WAN Connectivity Methods

In the previous topic, you identified basic WAN concepts and terminology. With that basic knowledge, you can now identify major WAN connectivity methods.

In order to gain access to a WAN, your LAN will have to connect to one. How do you connect your self-contained LAN to a WAN that uses completely different technologies? Understanding the various WAN connectivity devices and methods will help you implement your WAN connections appropriately.

Dial-Up and Broadband Connectivity

Three of the most common methods used to provide Internet connectivity to customers are dial-up, broadband DSL, and broadband cable.

Method	Description
Dial-up lines	*Dial-up lines* are local loop *public switched telephone network (PSTN)* connections that use modems, existing phone lines, and long-distance carrier services to provide low-cost, low-bandwidth WAN connectivity, and remote network access.
	PSTN is also known as the plain old telephone system (POTS). As a data carrier, the PSTN operates at Layers 1 and 2 of the OSI model. The Layer 2 protocol that manages the call is the Point-to-Point Protocol (PPP).
	PSTN is a telephone system that carries analog voice data. PSTN offers traditional telephone services to residences and establishments. PSTN includes telephones and fax machines that set up temporary but continuous connections. During a call, a circuit is established between two users and is kept open even during periods of silence. This provides guaranteed Quality of Service (QoS) but uses bandwidth inefficiently.
Broadband DSL	Broadband DSL offers high-speed Internet access with much higher speeds than dial-up connections. Telephone companies use DSL to offer data, video, and voice services over existing phone lines.
Broadband cable	Broadband cable offers high-speed Internet access with higher speeds than dial-up connections and broadband DSL. It also allows the simultaneous use of a telephone line.

DSL

A *digital subscriber line (DSL)* is a point-to-point, public network access broadband Internet connection method that transmits digital signals over existing phone lines. DSL accomplishes this connection by transporting voice as low-frequency signals and data as high-frequency signals. It has become a popular way to connect small businesses and households to the Internet because of its affordability and high download speeds. However, distance and the quality of lines affect the total bandwidth available to a customer.

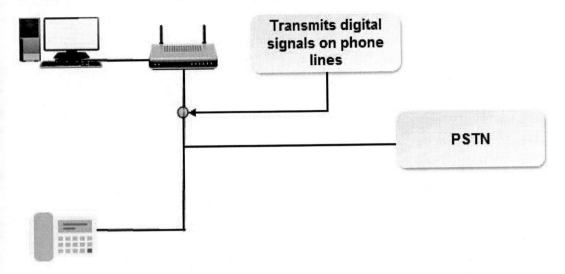

Figure 8-8: DSL transmits digital signals over phone lines.

DSL uses ATM as its underlying technology. DSL operates at Layers 1 and 2 of the OSI model. DSL then uses a tunneling protocol, the Point-to-Point Protocol over Ethernet (PPPoE) to carry data on top of the ATM infrastructure. PPPoE is used to provision DSL services for customers. It provides the ability for the DSL modem to "dial" the provider, authenticate the user, and then compress and encrypt the packets. It also allows the provider to monitor and regulate bandwidth utilization by the customer.

If you have an analog (POTS) telephone on the same line as your computer (highly likely in a consumer environment), you will have to use a DSL filter to separate the low-frequency analog voice from the high-frequency DSL data. Connecting the DSL filter improperly to your phone system causes considerable data noise on the telephone, while disrupting service to the device.

DSL is commonly referred to as xDSL, denoting the different types of DSL technologies.

DSL Technology	Description
Asymmetric DSL	ADSL is the most popular DSL technology. It allows residential customers to access the Internet and receive phone calls simultaneously. Provides high bandwidth, high-speed transmission over regular telephone lines. Called asymmetric as most of the bandwidth is used for information moving downstream. Widely used where users download more information than what they send. Offers speeds of up to 8 Mbps.
Symmetric DSL	Unlike ADSL, SDSL provides symmetric connectivity to users. Although it also uses telephone lines, it offers other services on the same line. Often used by small and medium businesses who don't need the service guarantees of frame relay or the higher performance of a leased line. Offers speeds of up to 2.3 Mbps.
High-bit-rate DSL	Unlike other types of DSL, where downloads speeds tend to be significantly faster than upload speeds, HDSL receives and sends data at the same speed. To accomplish this, it requires two lines that are separate from the normal phone line. HDSL provides transfer rates of 1.54 Mbps, which are comparable to a T1 line.
Very high-bit-rate DSL	VDSL is an asymmetric solution that provides extremely fast connections over short distances on standard copper phone wiring. VDSL offers speeds up to 52 Mbps.

Cable Internet Access

Cable Internet access uses a cable television connection and a cable modem to provide high-speed Internet access to homes and small businesses. With cable Internet access, your data is carried on two premium TV channels, one for transmit and one to receive. Cable access is contention-based, with users arranged in contention groups of nodes that split television and data signals at the cable provider's end. The speed of the network varies depending on the number of nodes in the contention group.

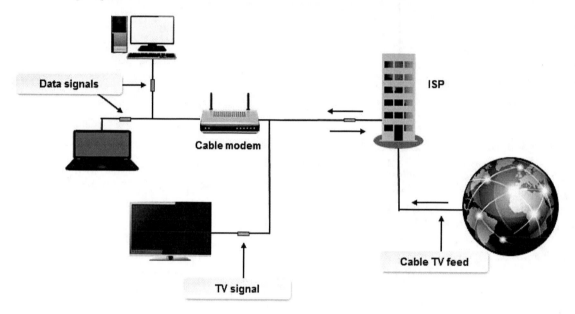

Figure 8-9: Cable providing high-speed Internet access.

Dial-Up Connections

Dial-up connections are PSTN connections that use modems, existing phone lines, and long-distance carrier services to provide low-cost, low-bandwidth WAN connectivity and remote network access. Generally limited to 56 Kbps, dial-up connections are sometimes used as backups for higher-bandwidth WAN services. Dial-up connections have two major drawbacks: They are slow and they can have a considerable connection wait time. Despite these limitations, dial-up connections are still used because they provide enough bandwidth for affordable basic Internet connectivity services over the existing telephone infrastructure, especially in geographical areas where other connectivity methods are not available.

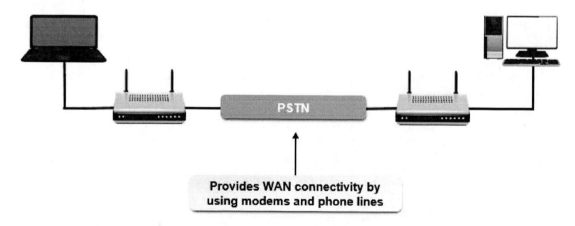

Figure 8-10: Dial-up connections provide WAN connectivity.

Leased Data Lines

A *dedicated line* is a telecommunication path that is available 24 hours a day for use by a designated user; dedicated lines and *leased lines* are essentially the same thing. With dedicated or leased lines, bandwidth availability varies with technology, but is usually between 56 Kbps and 2 Mbps. A company can lease the connection for a fixed fee, typically based on the distance between endpoints. Leasing a line can be advantageous because it guarantees a fixed bandwidth over a dedicated line.

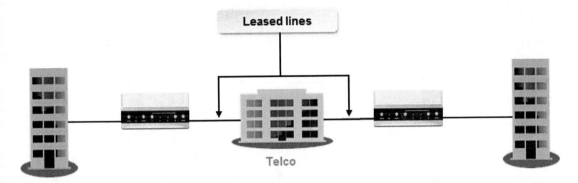

Figure 8–11: Leased lines for communication.

While still used in some situations, leased lines are used less frequently with the rise of other high-speed connectivity options. Many companies find it less expensive to deploy VPNs over higher-speed Internet connections than spending on dedicated leased lines.

Satellite Media

Satellite media provide for long-range, global WAN transmissions. A physical link transfers the signal to a satellite link at some point for transmission, and the satellite link then transmits the signal back to a physical link at the other end of the transmission for data delivery. Due to the greater distances the signal must travel, average latency is high, so satellite transmissions do not always work well for real-time applications. Weather conditions also affect the signal. Satellite services provide varying speeds depending on the service agreement.

Figure 8–12: Signal transmission using a satellite.

Satellite Internet access is an example of direct, unbounded WAN transmissions. Depending upon the provider, satellite TV customers can choose to receive Internet access through the same satellite dish that receives their TV signals.

ACTIVITY 8-2
Discussing WAN Connectivity Methods

Scenario

At the Greene City Interiors branch office, the network administrator engages you in a conversation about WAN connectivity methods.

1. When would you use satellite media?

2. Which statement is true of satellite media?
   - ○ Used for short-range transmissions
   - ○ Offers high-speed connections
   - ○ Has a low latency
   - ○ Transmits data at the same speed

3. True or False? The bandwidth availability for a dedicated line is usually between 28 Kbps and 2 Mbps.
   - ☐ True
   - ☐ False

4. When would leased data lines be used?

TOPIC C

WAN Transmission Technologies

Earlier in the course, you identified the transmission technologies and characteristics of a LAN implementation. When multiple LAN implementations need to communicate, the LANs can connect to form the larger framework of a WAN, which often uses different transmission technologies than a LAN would. In this topic, you will identify the transmission technologies used in a WAN implementation.

Present day communications span the globe. A WAN covers a very large geographical area and can connect multiple smaller networks. The transmission method used on your WAN might affect overall network performance and cost more than any other factor. From the slowest dial-up to the fastest fiber optic service, you will need to understand the capabilities of and limitations to your network's transmission method to choose the one best suited for your network.

ATM

Asynchronous transfer mode (ATM) is a cell-switching network technology that supports high-speed transfer of voice, video, and data in LANs, WANs, and telephone networks. ATM was standardized by the International Telecommunication Union (ITU) in 1988. It operates at Layers 1 and 2 of the OSI model. It was designed to be the "glue" that would connect all manner of disparate networks together, making LAN-to-WAN connectivity seamless. Due to its complexity and cost, relatively few companies have implemented it in their campus LAN backbones. However, ATM WAN implementations have become reasonably popular because of their versatility and high bandwidth availability. Information is transferred in fixed-size packets, called cells, each consisting of 53 bytes. ATM networks are made up of switches, which transport data cells among networks.

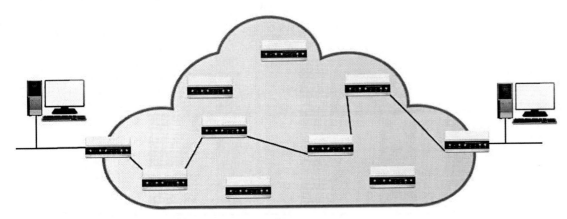

Cells travel along an agreed-upon pathway (virtual circuit) in a provider's cloud.

Figure 8–13: ATM provides high–speed data transfer.

ATM provides connection-oriented, end-to-end QoS. Unlike frame relay, it can guarantee QoS for a particular virtual channel (circuit) because all switches along a path agree upon the bandwidth before the connection is established. ATM uses a Layer 2 addressing scheme that is similar to telephone numbers. It has its own variant of the Address Resolution Protocol (ATM ARP), which maps Layer 3 network addresses such as Internet Protocol (IP) or Internet Packet Exchange (IPX) to the Layer 2 address. It can carry all manner of data, from very low-speed telemetry and low priority email and file transfers to voice, video, and high-speed real-time implementations such as high-definition video and teleradiology. Cell sequencing numbers guarantee that the data is reassembled in the proper order at the receiving end.

ATM offers reliable QoS. In the early 1990s, it was is envisioned as the underlying technology of broadband Integrated Services Digital Network (BISDN), the anticipated standard for the emerging information superhighway. In the end, it was not ATM and BISDN, but IP and packet switching that became the de facto standard for the World Wide Web. ATM is still used in the backbone of most service providers. It is also the underlying technology for digital subscriber line (DSL).

ATM handles broadband applications efficiently, and at the same time, allows users to assign priority to traffic on the network. ATM, like its predecessor frame relay, is currently being phased out, with major carriers migrating their customers' backbones to IP over multiprotocol label switching (MPLS).

The versatility of ATM can be attributed to a variety of features.

Feature	Description
Bandwidth options	Provides a wide range of high-bandwidth options. Although it has no inherent bandwidth limitations, typical ATM implementations can support from 51.84 Mbps to 2.488 Gbps, with 155 Mbps to 622 Mbps being the most common. Interfaces capable of 160 Gbps ATM throughput were introduced to the IEEE as early as 2001. In the other direction, both consumer and business DSL implementations tend to be lower speed, typically ranging from 192 Kbps to 100 Mbps.
Types of traffic	Allows the capability to carry data, voice, and video simultaneously on the same channel.
Fixed cell size	The fixed 53-byte cell size enables ATM to be implemented in hardware, reducing overhead and drain on resources required to move data on a network.
QoS	Built-in QoS features in the design aid in the flow of data between endpoints of the ATM network.
Traffic contracting and shaping	Traffic contracting assigns a set data rate to an endpoint. When an endpoint connects to an ATM network, it enters into a contract with the network for service quality. The ATM network will not contract more services than it can provide. Traffic shaping optimizes data flow on an ATM network. It includes control of bursts and optimizing bandwidth allocation.
Real-time and non-real-time data support	Real-time data support is used for time-sensitive data such as voice or video and travels at a higher priority than non-real-time data.

ATM Network Interface Types

ATM network interfaces connect ATM devices and fall into two categories: *User-to-Network Interface (UNI)* and *Network-to-Network Interface (NNI)*. The UNI, as a user device, is an ATM border device that connects one ATM network to another ATM network or a LAN. NNI is a switch that is inside an ATM network. Individual devices can connect to an ATM network, but this is rare.

ATM Connections

ATM is not a channelized service and does not waste channels by assigning them to nodes that are not talking. In a situation when the device is offline, ATM does not hold the channel. It makes that bandwidth available to other nodes, exhibiting traffic contracting to allocate the necessary bandwidth without wasting it by reservation.

An ATM switch makes virtual connections with other switches to provide a data path from endpoint to endpoint. Individual connections are called virtual channels (VCs). VCs support the connection-oriented transport between endpoints and are identified by a virtual channel identifier (VCI). VCs with a common path are tied together into virtual paths (VPs) and are identified by a virtual path identifier (VPI). You can form a transmission path (TP) by combining multiple VPs.

 Note: An ATM endpoint (or end system) contains an ATM network interface adapter.

Frame Relay

Frame relay is a WAN protocol that functions at the Physical and Data Link layers (Layers 1 and 2) of the OSI model. It is a packet-switched technology that allows transmission of data over a shared network medium and bandwidth using virtual circuits. As virtual circuits consume bandwidth only when they transport data, each device can use more bandwidth and transmit data at higher speeds. Frame relay provides reliable communication lines and efficient error-handling mechanisms that discard erroneous data frames.

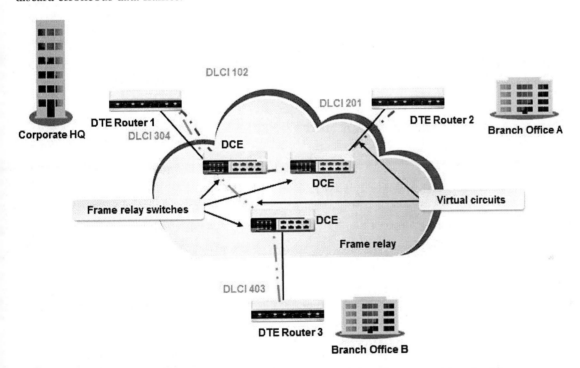

Figure 8-14: Frame relay allows stations to share the network medium and bandwidth.

Frame relay is the successor of X.25, and the predecessor of ATM. Mostly implemented at Layer 2, it eliminates the error correction features found in X.25, depending instead on a reliable digital network infrastructure. In frame relay, either a permanent or switched (on demand) virtual circuit is established in the provider's network for customer traffic. It uses traffic shaping and congestion management techniques, with upstream routers (configured as frame relay switches) matching the speed of the next hop, and even discarding lower priority traffic, if necessary. Because of its "bursty" nature, frame relay was not originally suited for real-time voice or video, although later developments sought to remedy this. Frame relay can still be found in some networks, but has largely been replaced by MPLS VPNs.

Frame Relay Characteristics

Frame relay link speeds can range from 56 Kbps to 1.544 Mbps, with the lower speeds, such as 56, 64, 128, 384, and 512 Kbps, being the most popular. Unlike a dedicated point-to-point lease line, frame relay has the concept of a committed information rate (CIR), which is the minimum bandwidth that a customer's virtual circuit is guaranteed to have. If the network is not busy, the circuit bandwidth may be allowed to exceed the CIR. If the network is congested, however, any traffic that exceeds the CIR is marked "discard eligible" and will be dropped. Some providers sell service plans with a CIR of 0, meaning that your traffic will be the lowest priority among all the customers and will always be dropped first.

Frame relay uses a Layer 2 address called a data link connection identifier (DLCI). Each customer's connection to the provider's DCE (a frame relay switch known as a point of presence, or POP) has its own DLCI number, distinguishing it from other customer connections to that particular POP. The POP then maps the customer's DLCI to a specific virtual circuit inside the cloud.

Frame Relay Network Components

Frame relay uses DCEs and DTEs to connect to the appropriate frame relay network, referred to as the Frame Relay Bearer Service (FRBS). Inside the FRBS—or frame relay network cloud—is a network of switches that makes connections between endpoints. A virtual circuit is established between two DTE devices. DTE equipment can consist of a single network device such as a router. A DCE typically is a CSU/DSU that sends signals to an *edge system (ES)*, a switch on the frame relay network.

The virtual circuits used in frame relay prevent you from seeing the complexity of communication inside the cloud. There are two types of virtual circuits: permanent and switched. Permanent virtual circuits (PVCs) are created by service providers inside their devices and the circuit is constant. Switched virtual circuits (SVCs) are established during data transmission and when the data "conversation" is over, the connection is closed.

Advantages and Disadvantages of Frame Relay

The advantages of frame relay are:

- It offers facilities like that of a leased line, but at a significantly lower cost.
- It delivers increased performance with reduced network complexity.
- It can be implemented over the existing technology.
- It can be easily configured to combine traffic from different networking protocols.
- It offers a pay-as-you-go structure.
- It can carry traffic that is not IP traffic.

The disadvantages of frame relay are:

- Data transmission may exceed network capacity as clients use a common network, and this results in the slowing down of the network.
- The "bursty" nature of traffic in a frame relay cloud, along with the use of variable-length frames, makes it difficult to provide QoS. During its most popular years in the 1990s, it was considered unsuitable for real-time traffic such as voice or video. By 1997, the Frame Relay Forum finally developed a standard for Voice over Frame Relay (VoFR).

X.25 Switched Networks

X.25 was the first widely implemented packet-switching network technology. It was developed in the 1970s before the OSI model, but its functionality corresponds to Layers 1, 2, and 3 of the OSI model. X.25 was designed to move data across the less-than-reliable analog long-distance public carrier lines of the time. Its emphasis on reliable delivery introduced a lot of overhead to the network, which reduced performance.

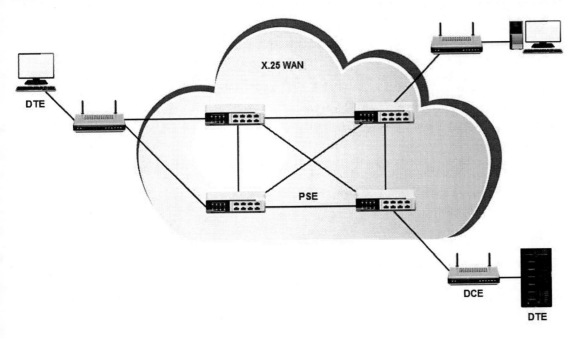

Figure 8–15: X.25 networks.

MPLS

Multiprotocol label switching (MPLS) is a high-performance, multi-service switching technology that is used in packet data networks. It is defined by a set of Internet Engineering Task Force (IETF) specifications that enable Layer 3 devices such as routers to establish and manage network traffic. It ensures faster switching of data as it follows *label switching* that helps save processing time of packets by the label-switching routers.

MPLS is a packet-forwarding technology that uses labels to make its forwarding decisions. The *labels* are special headers that are 4 bytes long, inserted between the Layer 2 and Layer 3 headers of the packet. A router that has MPLS enabled on its interface is referred to as a *label switching router (LSR)*. It uses the label, rather than the Layer 3 header, to forward the packet to its neighbor. In this way, costly routing table lookups are avoided. Each router rebuilds the label with information for the next hop.

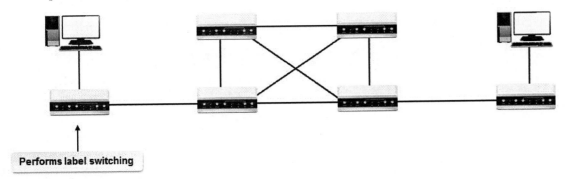

Performs label switching

Figure 8–16: MPLS performs multi–service label switching using Layer 3 routers.

MLPS provides the following benefits:

- Virtual private networking (VPN).
- Traffic engineering (TE).
- Quality of Service (QoS).
- Any Transport over MPLS (AToM).

The labels contain a special designation called the Forward Equivalence Class (FEC). The FEC is applied to a particular stream of packets. It may correspond with a prefix (destination network), or may be based on a class of service (such as IP precedence). A downstream router sends FECs to its upstream neighbor. The upstream neighbor in turn places the correct FEC in the label of a particular packet and passes the packet to the appropriate downstream neighbor. In this way, the path for a particular traffic stream in MPLS is pre-determined. Traffic always follows the same path, with the packets being quickly switched from one router to the next.

MPLS has succeeded frame relay and ATM as the dominant private WAN service. While expensive, it has very good reliability (99.9 – 99.99 percent). Companies use it mostly to connect branch offices to each other or to the corporate data center. Most providers have migrated, or are in the process of migrating, their frame relay/ATM customers to MPLS.

ISDN

ISDN is a digital circuit switching technology that carries both voice and data over digital phone lines or PSTN wires. It was the first widely used technique to bring simultaneous voice and data to a customer's home. It uses identifiers similar to a telephone number to establish a demand-dial connection to another ISDN device.

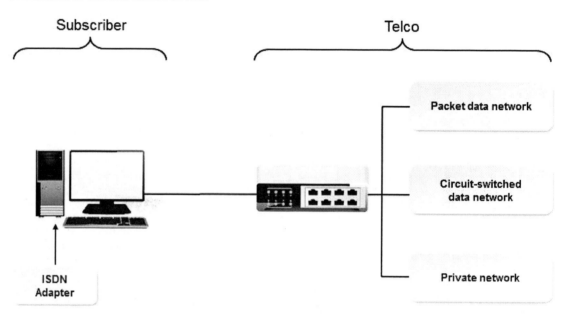

Figure 8-17: ISDN carries voice and data over digital phone lines or PSTN wires.

ISDN uses digital channels to carry the payload and manage the call. The two types of channels are the "B" (bearer) channel, and the "D" (delta) channel. B channels have a bandwidth of 64 kb. D channels have a bandwidth of either 16 kb or 64 kb, depending on the type of service.

ISDN comes in two service types:

*   Basic Rate Interface (BRI): 2 B channels + one 16 kb D channel for 128 kb throughput
*   Primary Rate Interface (PRI): 23 B channels + one 64 kb D channel for (near) T1 throughput

ISDN was the first successful attempt to digitize the "last mile" of existing copper wire between the customer and the phone company. ISDN works at Layers 1, 2, and 3 of the OSI model. At Layer 1, the frames are 48 bits long and differ in structure depending on the direction of traffic. At Layer 2, the connection is balanced, meaning there is no master/slave relationship where the master (DCE) sets the clock rate and the slave (DTE) must adhere to the DCE's speed. Both the DCE and DTE are treated equally by the protocol. At Layer 3, end-to-end connections are created for user-to-user, circuit-switched or packet-switched functionality similar to X.25.

ISDN has largely been replaced by DSL, but can still be found in areas where the distance to the customer premises exceeds DSL's capabilities. Specialized equipment is required to use it, or to adapt it to existing telephone systems.

ISDN Hardware

ISDN hardware includes *terminal equipment (TE)*, *terminal adapters (TAs)*, *network termination (NT)* devices, line termination (LT), and exchange termination (ET) equipment. TEs are communications equipment that stations use to accomplish tasks at both ends of a communications link. TAs form the hardware interface between a computer and an ISDN line. NTs are devices that connect the local telephone exchange lines to a customer's telephone or data equipment. ISDN lines terminate at a customer's premises by using an RJ-45 connector in a configuration called a U-interface, which usually connects to a *network termination unit (NTU)*. The NTU can directly connect to ISDN-aware equipment, such as phones or ISDN network interface cards (NICs) in devices. This type of equipment is called Terminal Equipment type 1 (TE1).

T–Carrier Systems

The *T-carrier system* is a digital and packet-switched system designed to carry multiplexed telephone connections. It makes communications more scalable than analog, circuit-switched systems. T-carrier systems use two twisted pairs of copper wires. The first pair is used for transmission and the second pair for reception. Therefore, T-carrier systems support full-duplex communication. T1 and T3 are the two most common T-service levels. E-1 and E-3 are European leased lines, roughly equivalent to United States T-1 and T-3 lines. T-services can be used to support a point-to-point WAN where the service provider sets up a dedicated connection between two T-service endpoints.

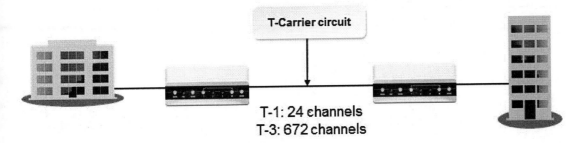

Figure 8–18: T–carrier systems allow multiplexed telephone connections.

T-services connect a customer's office with the service provider's network. The internal connection is over frame relay. The T-service can also connect an office to the telephone company for remote access. Individual remote clients dial in to a number and the service provider before being routed to the office through the T-service. This way, a server can service multiple dial-in connections without needing many modems.

T-carriers operate at Layer 1 of the OSI model, and refer to the speed of the link. They can be used by several Layer 2 WAN protocols, including frame relay, primary rate ISDN, and PPP and high-level data link control (HDLC) in dedicated leased lines.

Digital Signal Services

Digital signal (DS) services are a hierarchy of different digital signals that transfer data at different rates. The T-carrier system is the most common physical implementation of the American National Standards Institute (ANSI) *Digital Signal Hierarchy (DSH)* specifications. DSH is a channelized data transmission standard used to multiplex several single data or voice channels for a greater total bandwidth. It was established in the 1980s, primarily for use with digital voice phones. In T-carrier implementations, DSH systems have become the standard building block of most channelized systems in the United States today.

DSH defines a hierarchy of DSx specifications numbered DS0 to DS5. The basic DS0 level specifies a single voice channel of 64 Kbps. A DS1 signal bundles 24 DS0 channels and uses a T1 carrier line. The different types of DS services vary depending upon their data transmission rates.

- **DS0:** Carries data at the rate of 64 Kbps.
- **DS1:** Carries data at the rate of 1.5 Mbps.
- **DS2:** Carries data at the rate of 6.3 Mbps.
- **DS3:** Carries data at the rate of 44.4 Mbps.
- **DS4:** Carries data at the rate of 274.2 Mbps.

T-Lines

In order to implement a different DS service, telephone companies use T-lines whose carrying capacities match the data rates of DS services.

Depending on the number of DS0 links bundled together, you can get different amounts of bandwidth. Often, you will hear of links being referred to as fractional T1s, meaning that the customer has purchased less than the full 24 DS0s required to create a T1.

E-Carrier Systems

The E-carrier system is a dedicated digital line that transmits voice or data. It is used in Europe, Mexico, and South America. The different E-carriers transmit data at different rates.

T-Carrier and E-Carrier Levels

Level	T-Carrier	E-Carrier
Level zero (channel data rate)	64 Kbps (DS0)	64 Kbps
First level	1.544 Mbps (DS1, 24 Ch., T1)	2.048 Mbps (E1, 32 Ch.)
Intermediate level, T-carrier only	3.152 Mbps (DS1C, 48 Ch.)	-
Second level	6.312 Mbps (DS2, 96 Ch., T2)	8.448 Mbps (E2, 128 Ch.)
Third level	44.736 Mbps (DS3, 672 Ch., T3)	34.368 Mbps (E3, 512 Ch.)
Fourth level	274.176 Mbps (DS4, 4032 Ch.)	139.264 Mbps (E4, 2048 Ch.)
Fifth level	400.352 Mbps (DS5, 5760 Ch.)	565.148 Mbps (E5, 8192 Ch.)

Metro-Ethernet

Metro-Ethernet is a metropolitan area network (MAN) that uses Ethernet standards. Metro-Ethernets can connect LANs and individual users to a WAN or to the Internet. Organizations in large cities can use Metro-Ethernet to connect branch locations or offices to an intranet. A typical Metro-Ethernet has a star network or mesh network topology with servers or routers interconnected through cable or fiber optic media. For example, Comcast Business offers a Metro-Ethernet service for businesses with different locations within a city to communicate with using a wider bandwidth.

Metro-Ethernet operates at Layer 2 of the OSI model. The Metro Ethernet Forum does not specify exactly how Metro-Ethernet must be provided. Carriers are free to use pure Ethernet, Synchronous Optical Networking (SONET), MPLS, or a combination of IP-related protocols. Metro-Ethernet topology can be ring, star, or full or partial mesh. Popular implementations of Metro-Ethernet currently offer 1 Gbps over fiber optic cable at a distance of 100 kilometers, or 100 Gbps at a distance of 10 km. Recent developments promise to provide terabit data rates. Metro-Ethernet can be connected to using Layer 2 switches or Layer 3 routers. Companies can extend their VLANs to other locations by using 802.1q VLAN tagging over Metro-Ethernet. Although it is inexpensive and easy to implement, Metro-Ethernet does not currently scale as well as other MPLS implementations. As such, large organizations are using it as their core backbone, particularly for replicating between data centers or for aggregating call center traffic to their data centers. The following diagram shows the use of Metro-Ethernet, MPLS, and the Internet for WAN connectivity.

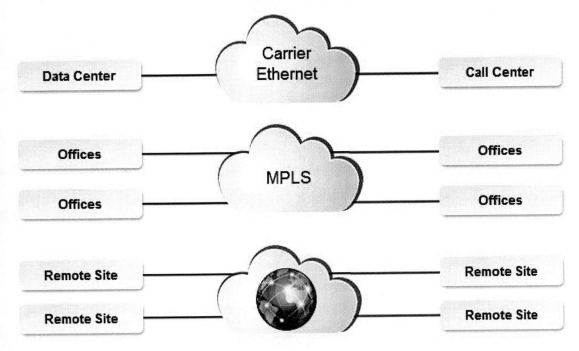

Figure 8-19: Metro-Ethernet.

Metro-Ethernet is now popularly known by its marketing term "Carrier Ethernet."

Digital Network Hierarchies

Digital networks have two hierarchical structures that define them: the *plesiochronous digital hierarchy (PDH)* and the *synchronous digital hierarchy (SDH)*. PDH networks carry data over fiber optic or microwave radio systems. In this type of network, the different parts are ready, but are not synchronized. They have largely replaced PDH for a synchronized network in which the movement of data is highly synchronized along different parts. In SDH, data moves on an optical fiber using LEDs. Basic data transmission occurs at a rate of 155.5 Mbps.

SONET/SDH

The *Synchronous Optical Network (SONET)* is a standard for synchronous data transport over a fiber optic cable. SONET is the U.S. version of the standard published by ANSI, whereas SDH is the European version of the standard published by the *International Telecommunications Union (ITU)*.

SONET has two specifications: the Optical Carrier (OC) specification for fiber optic cabling and the Secure Transfer specification (STS) for copper wire, although SONET over copper has severe limitations. SONET is deployed in a self-healing dual-fiber ring topology, similar to Fiber Distributed Data Interface (FDDI). When one ring works, the other is a standby. Whenever the working ring fails, SONET recognizes the failure and switches over to the second ring.

SONET is most widely used inside service providers to act as a high-speed backbone for other systems, such as frame relay, ATM, and Metro-Ethernet. It operates at Layer 1 of the OSI model. SONET/SDH can be used on an ATM network, and connections to the lines can be made by using single-mode or multi-mode optical fiber. In such a setup, ATM would be the switching technology, and SONET/SDH would be the transmission technology on the network.

SONET is divided into three areas. Each area is controlled by an integrated management system.

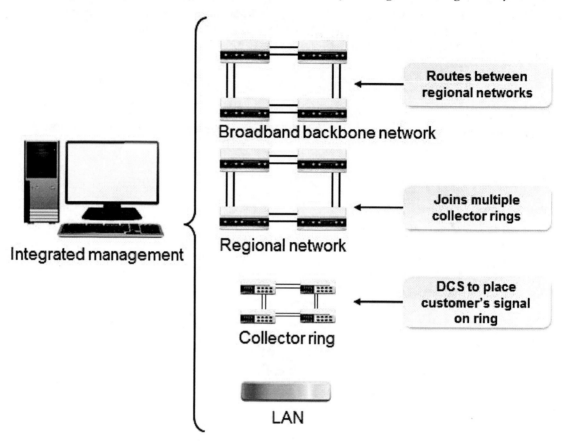

Figure 8–20: Divisions of a SONET.

Area	Description
Local collector ring	A local collector ring interfaces with users and comprises digital cross-connect switches (DCSs) at the user's location or connects to the user's location by a T-carrier. The DCS acts as a concentrator to transmit signals from a user to the SONET ring. It supports connections from different technologies and from multiple users. The technologies that can connect to the ring include ATM, T1, or T3 lines; ISDN; or DSL voice.
Regional network	A regional network combines multiple collector rings by using add/drop multiplexers (ADMs). The ADM allows data from collector rings to be added to the regional ring. The data that is not accepted by the service requester is discarded or sent back to the ADM. By managing bandwidth on the regional network, it becomes more efficient. When data moves between two networks that the same regional network supports, the connection can be through the regional network.
Broadband backbone network	The broadband backbone network routes data between regional networks. It is capable of carrying a large amount of data simultaneously in the ring, and the requester picks the data as it is transmitted.

The key advantages of SONET are its excellent bandwidth management, built-in fault recovery features, and support for data transfer speeds of up to 2.48 Gbps. A particular advantage to SONET deployments is its interoperability. The technology often is used to aggregate multiple lines (T1, T3 for example).

SONET's transmission bandwidth ranges from 51.84 Mbps to 2.48 Gbps. Its hardware actually operates at speeds in the 10 Gbps range, but the SONET standard has not been expanded to include it.

The ITU is an international organization within the United Nations that defines global technical standards for telecommunications. ITU also coordinates the widespread use of the radio spectrum, ensuring interference-free wireless communications. ITU also sponsors exhibitions and forums to exchange ideas and discuss issues affecting international telecommunications.

Dense wavelength division multiplexing (DWDM) is a multiplexing technology that uses light wavelengths to transmit data. DWDM is often used as an alternative to SONET to carry Metro-Ethernet. It operates at Layer 1 of the OSI model. Signals from multiple sources using different technologies are carried simultaneously on separate light wavelengths. DWDM can multiplex up to 80 separate data channels into a lightstream for transmission over an optical fiber. Data from different protocols and technologies such as IP, SONET, and ATM can all travel simultaneously within an optical fiber. SONET is combined with WDM functions by sending SONET data streams out on different colors of light. The sending SONET multiplexer connects light streams to the WDM card. At the receiving end, the fiber demultiplexes the light into a single color stream and sends it to SONET equipment.

Coarse wavelength division multiplexing (CWDM) is a method of combining multiple signals on laser beams at various wavelengths for transmission along fiber optic cables, such that the number of channels is fewer than in DWDM. It uses increased channel spacing to allow less sophisticated and thus cheaper transceiver designs. DWDM and CWDM are based on the same concept of using multiple wavelengths of light on a single fiber, but differ in the spacing of the wavelengths, number of channels, and the ability to amplify the multiplexed signals in the optical space.

The Optical Carrier System

The *Optical Carrier x (OCx)* standard specifies the bandwidth for fiber optic transmissions. It is a channelized technology based on the same 64 Kbps channel as DSH but with a base rate of 810 channels. The OCx standard is open-ended, enabling manufacturers to add specifications as they develop hardware that supports faster transmission speeds.

OCx specifications correspond with the data rates of SONET. As one OC channel corresponds to a data rate of 51.84 Mbps, using multiple channels increases the rate by 51.84 Mbps per channel.

OCx Specification	Description
OC1	1 OC channel with a data rate of 51.84 Mbps.
OC3	3 OC channels with a data rate of 155.52 Mbps.
OC9	9 OC channels with a data rate of 466.56 Mbps.
OC12	12 OC channels with a data rate of 622.08 Mbps.
OC18	18 OC channels with a data rate of 933.15 Mbps.
OC24	24 OC channels with a data rate of 1.24 Gbps.
OC36	36 OC channels with a data rate of 1.87 Gbps.
OC192	192 OC channels with a data rate of 9.95 Gbps.

The passive optical network (PON) is a point-to-multipoint optical network that is used for broadcast transmissions using optical systems. As the optical transmission requires no power or active electronic parts when the signal passes through the network, it is referred to as passive. A PON contains a central office node, known as optical line termination (OLT) and optical network units (ONUs) near end users. An OLT can connect to up to 32 ONUs.

Satellite Transmission Systems

A satellite-based network offers immense geographical coverage, allowing for high-speed connections anywhere in the world to transmit data between endpoints. Satellite transmission systems are used as an alternative to conventional communications, and as a cost-effective method to transmit information to different locations globally. Satellite communications systems use line-of-sight (LoS) microwave transmission.

A satellite system consists of two segments: space and ground.

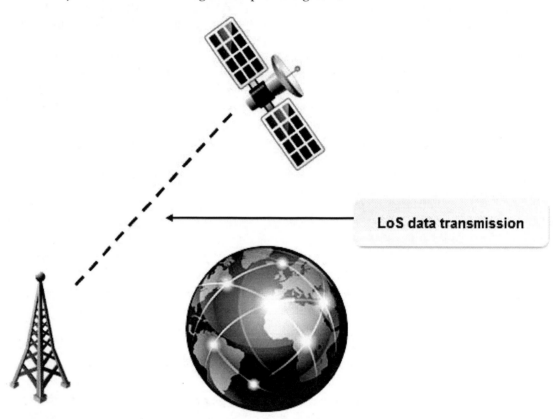

LoS data transmission

Figure 8–21: A satellite–based network.

Segment	Description
Space	A space segment contains one or more satellites organized into a constellation and a ground station that provides operational control of the satellites.
Ground	A ground segment provides access from Earth stations to the satellite to meet the communication needs of users. The ground segment contains terminals that utilize the communication capabilities of the space segment. The ground segment contains three basic types of terminals. • Fixed terminals access satellites while they are stationary. • Transportable terminals are portable, but remain stationary during transmission. • Mobile terminals can communicate with satellites even when they are in motion.

Satellites are used for a variety of purposes and each satellite service has different requirements.

Satellite Service	Description
Satellite Internet	The *satellite Internet* is a method of connecting to the Internet by using a satellite network. This method can be broadly classified as a one-way or two-way connection, based on how the request for an Internet connection reaches the satellite. In a one-way connection, the request for an Internet connection goes to the ISP via a phone line and is forwarded to the satellite.
Satellite phone network	A *satellite phone* is a telephone system that relies on the satellite network to provide services, instead of the local telephone switch infrastructure. Satellite phones can be handheld or fixed, usually connected to an antenna at the top of a building.
	When a call is made from a satellite phone to another satellite phone, the call is routed directly via the satellite. If a call is made to a regular phone, the satellite routes the call to the landline or cellular network via an Earth station known as the gateway. The gateway converts the signals so that the landline or cellular network can read them. Satellite phones work well in open spaces, but they do not have a good reception within buildings and enclosed spaces.
Satellite television	*Satellite television* is a method of relaying video and audio signals directly to a subscriber's television set by using satellites. A satellite TV network consists of a programming source that provides the original program.
	The satellite TV provider, also known as the direct broadcast (DB) center, then broadcasts these channels to the satellites, which receive the signals and rebroadcast them to Earth. The subscriber's dish antenna picks up the signals and sends them to the TV via a receiver, also known as the set-top box (STB). The satellite TV technology overcomes the disadvantage of broadcast networks, where an LoS arrangement is necessary.
VSAT	A *very small aperture terminal (VSAT)* is a telecommunication Earth station that consists of an antenna to transmit and receive signals from satellites. The size of a VSAT ranges from 1.2 to 2.4 meters in diameter.
	A network of VSATs provides a cost-effective solution to users who need to connect several sites or offices that are dispersed geographically. VSATs support transmission of voice, data, and video. A typical VSAT network consists of an antenna placed on top of a building and connected to a transceiver and modem by a cable. The modem converts the signals from the satellite into data or voice signals, and vice versa. VSAT networks can be connected in a point-to-point, star, or mesh network.
GPS	The *global positioning system (GPS)* is a navigational system that consists of a network of 27 satellites: 24 active and 3 in the standby mode. These satellites are arranged in such a pattern that at least four of them are visible from any part of the world. A GPS receiver receives the distance and time information from the four visible satellites and uses that information to calculate its current position. A GPS receiver needs an unobstructed view of the sky.

WWAN

A *wireless WAN (WWAN)* uses wireless network technology to allow users to check email, surf the web, and connect to corporate resources accessible within wireless network boundaries. Users connect to a WWAN by using a WWAN card. WWANs use a number of technologies to transfer data and connect to the Internet, such as PPP. Each of these technologies, however, falls into one of three families: GSM/UMTS, cdmaOne/CDMA2000, and WiMAX. The GSM/UMTS and cdmaOne/CDMA2000 protocols started out as mobile phone technologies but now support data transmission. WWAN technologies also use the Wireless Application Protocol (WAP), which enables you to access the Internet from your mobile device.

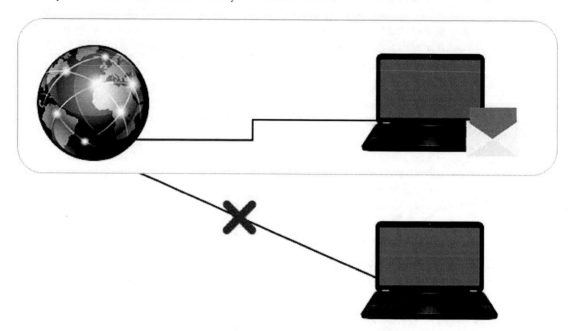

Figure 8–22: WWAN allows users access within wireless network boundaries.

 Note: Wireless Application Protocol shares its acronym with wireless access point.

The following table compares coverage, speeds, security, and costs of WLANs and WWANs.

Factor	WLAN	WWAN
Coverage	Used in a single building of an organization, a home, or a hotspot such as a coffee shop. Usually limited to 100 meters.	Used wherever a cellular network provider has coverage—can be regional, national, or even global.
Speed	Typically 1 to 4 Mbps depending on the number of users that share the connection.	Typically 30 to 50 Kbps.
Security	Susceptible to hacking and interoperability issues between WLANs. Operates on a globally allocated frequency that does not require a license.	Tightly regulated frequencies spectrum requiring licenses to operate within the frequency. WWANs incorporate military security technology with a high-level of authentication and encryption.
Cost	No cost for the wireless connection within the range but a cost to access the Internet via the WLAN access point.	The subscription fee is similar to a mobile phone contract. Can be a monthly fee, per minute or per megabyte charge.

LTE

Long-term evolution (LTE) is a radio technology for wireless broadband access. It was introduced in 3GPP Release 8. LTE will be backward compatible with the Global System for Mobile Communications (GSM) and the High Speed Packet Access (HSPA) protocol. This compatibility will enable users to make voice calls and have access to data networks even when they are in areas without LTE coverage. LTE will offer data rates about 100 times faster than 3G networks, a downlink rate that exceeds 100 Mbps, and an uplink rate of more than 50 Mbps.

HSPA

High Speed Packet Access (HSPA) refers to a family of technologies based on the 3GPP Release 5 specification, which offers high data rate services in mobile networks. HSPA offers a downlink speed of up to 14 Mbps and an uplink speed of up to 5.8 Mbps, making it possible for users to upload or download data at a high speed without having to wait for cellular service providers to upgrade their hardware. The HSPA family includes High Speed Downlink Packet Access (HSDPA), High Speed Uplink Packet Access (HSUPA), and HSPA+.

HSPA+ uses multicarrier technologies in which multiple 5 MHz carriers are aggregated and a bigger data channel is used for data transmission. This large data channel also decreases *latency* and provides an increased capacity for bursty traffic, such as web applications. Evolved HSPA also aims to use an all-IP architecture, where all base stations will be connected to the Internet via the ISP's edge routers.

PON

A *passive optical network (PON)* is a system that brings optical fiber cabling and signals all or most of the way to the end user. Depending on where the PON terminates, the system can be described as fiber-to-the-curb (FTTC), fiber-to-the-building (FTTB), or fiber-to-the-home (FTTH). A PON consists of an OLT at the service provider's central office and a number of ONUs near end users. A PON reduces the amount of fiber and central office equipment required compared with point-to-point architectures. A passive optical network is a form of fiber optic access network.

GSM and CDMA

Global System for Mobile Communications (GSM) and *Code Division Multiple Access (CDMA)* are both standards that describe protocols for 2G digital cellular networks used by mobile phones. They both use radio signals for voice and data communications. They both have derivatives for use with 3G phones. GSM uses Universal Mobile Telecommunications System (UMTS) and CDMA uses CDMA2000. The major difference between the two is how the carrier connects to the phone and how they turn voice data into radio waves. Enhanced Data rates for GSM Evolution (EDGE) is a 3G standard based on GSM. It is approximately three times as fast as GSM and provides up to 384 Kbps speeds.

Mobile phone carriers T-Mobile® and AT&T® use GSM for their cell phone networks, whereas Sprint, Virgin Mobile®, and Verizon Wireless® use the CDMA standard.

With 4G phones, GSM and CDMA can be used with the main standards, LTE, and WiMax. Since 4G technologies work using an IP network, the radio signals from both are translated into electronic data for use on the network or the phone.

WiMAX

Wireless Interoperability for Microwave Access (WiMAX) is a packet-based wireless telecommunication technology that provides wireless broadband access over long distances. Based on the IEEE 802.16 standard, it is intended for wireless MANs. WiMAX provides fixed as well as mobile broadband access. It covers a range of about 30 miles for fixed stations and 3 to 10 miles for mobile stations. WiMAX also provides LoS and non-line-of-sight (NLoS) communication, and can provide connection speeds of about 70 Mbps. WiMAX operates in the wireless frequency ranges of between 2 and 11 GHz of the wireless spectrum.

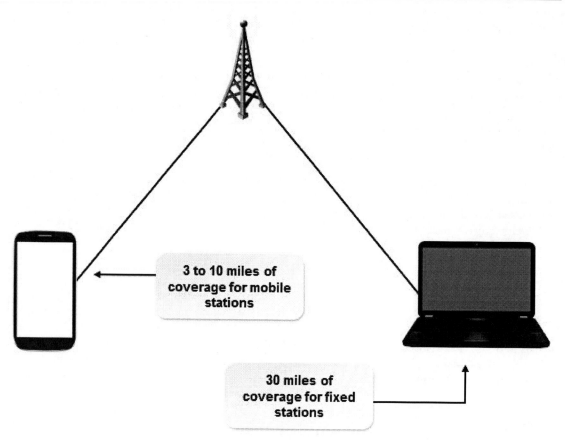

Figure 8–23: Wireless broadband access using WiMAX.

 Note: WiMAX was created by an organization known as the WiMAX Forum.

WiMAX offers two different services: LoS and NLoS.

- *Line-of-sight (LoS)*: Signals travel over a direct path from a transmitter to a receiver.
- *Non-line-of-sight (NLoS)*: Signals reach a receiver through reflections and diffractions.

WiMAX is of two types: fixed and mobile.

Type	Description
Fixed	Optimized for fixed applications in LoS and NLoS environments. The main disadvantage of fixed WiMAX is its difficulty to compete with established wired technologies such as DSL in places where the wired telecommunication infrastructure is well developed.
Mobile	Optimized for portable and mobile applications in an NLoS environment. Mobile WiMAX includes additional features such as power management, handoff, frequency reuse, channel bandwidth scalability, and better NLoS performance and indoor penetration.

ACTIVITY 8–3
Discussing WAN Transmission Technologies

Scenario

At the Greene City Interiors branch office, the network administrator continues your discussion and asks about WAN transmission technologies.

1. **On which type of network is ATM most commonly implemented?**

   ○ LAN

   ○ MAN

   ○ WAN

   ○ PAN

2. **How many bytes of data can an ATM cell transfer?**

   ○ 56

   ○ 53

   ○ 52

   ○ 58

3. **Which technologies do OCx specifications match to?**

   ☐ ATM

   ☐ SONET

   ☐ Frame relay

   ☐ SDH

   ☐ T1

4. **What are the channels used by BRI ISDN?**

   ○ Two D channels and one B channel

   ○ Two B channels and one D channel

   ○ Three B channels and one D channel

   ○ Three B channels and two D channels

5. **Which of these technologies allows for more downstream traffic than upstream?**

   ○ SDSL

   ○ SHDSL

   ○ ADSL

   ○ VDSL

6. **Which of these are features of a network with MPLS?**

   ☐ Label switching

   ☐ Used with voice traffic

   ☐ Multiprotocol adaptability

   ☐ Carries frame relay as its Layer 2 protocol

7. **On which OSI layer does frame relay operate?**

○   Transport

○   Application

○   Network

○   Physical

○   Data Link

TOPIC D

Unified Communication Technologies

In the previous topics, you identified the data transmission technologies and connectivity methods used in WAN implementations. Another aspect of WAN implementations is the implementation of unified communications (UC) technologies. In this topic, you will describe the basic elements of unified communications technologies.

The use of unified communications is prevalent in many workplaces. Users value the real-time integration of technologies such as instant messaging, presence information, IP telephony, and web and video conferencing, among others, to collaborate with other users and increase their productivity. You need to understand unified communications so that you are able to manage and support your users who use them.

UC Technologies

Unified communication (UC) technologies are a group of integrated real-time communication services and non-real-time services that provides a consistent user experience across multiple devices and media types. Real-time communication services and products can be integrated with non-real-time services and products, with the ultimate result being that a user can send a message on one medium and receive the same communication on another medium. For example, if you receive a voice-mail message, you might choose to access it through email or a mobile phone. Medianets enable video teleconferencing (VTC or VC) over ISDN or other high-speed broadband connections using IP and SIP protocols. This technology enables IP and SIP protocols to carry both video and audio data so that a conference between multiple locations can be carried out.

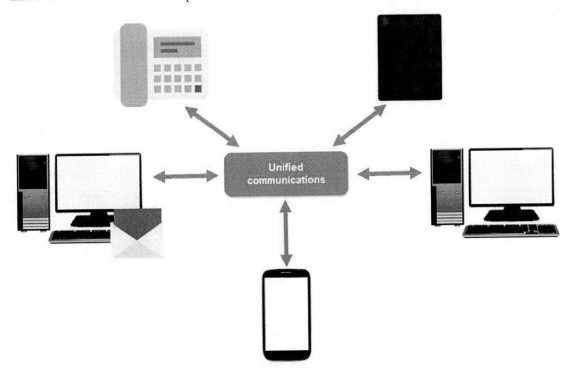

Unified communications provides a consistent user experience across many electronic devices

Figure 8–24: UC technologies.

Real-time UC technologies include:

- Voice over data systems, such as Voice over IP (VoIP).
- Video conferencing.
- Presence information.
- Instant messaging.
- Desktop sharing.
- Data sharing.
- Speech recognition.

Non-real-time UC technologies include:

- Voice mail
- Email
- SMS (text) messaging
- Fax messaging

UC Hardware

The most prevalent types of hardware devices used to provide UC services include servers, devices, and gateways.

UC Hardware	Description
UC servers	Unified communications servers provide the voice, video, fax, messaging, and more services that users will use. It can be a proprietary appliance bundled with the desired features and powered Ethernet switchports, or it could also be a generic server with the appropriate hardware specifications and the UC software product installed on it. As with many UC products, it can also be a virtual server in a provider's cloud.
UC devices	Unified communications devices are client-side devices that allow end users to use unified communications services. They can include IP or video-enabled phones, headsets, webcams and busy lights, and other meeting room devices.
UC gateways	Unified communications gateways connect your private UC network with a public network. It is the interface that allows users to connect with the outside world. It also allows mobile users to connect from the outside into the private network. The public network can be the PSTN, the Internet, or a cellular provider—any network that will extend the reach of your UC system to everyone else. The data that your UC gateway processes will be voice, video, conferencing, collaboration, messaging—any service or protocol that you have chosen to implement in your UC system. The gateway can be a dedicated appliance or a generic server with software installed. It can also be a service in a provider's cloud.

Voice-over-Data Systems

Voice-over-data systems are communication systems that replace traditional telephone links by transmitting analog voice communications over digital WAN technologies. Digital WANs provide more bandwidth than analog phone systems, and there is no long-distance service cost involved. Because voice communications are time-sensitive, the voice-over-data system must ensure that packets arrive complete and in sequence. In a voice-over-data system, voice software interfaces with an analog voice device, such as a microphone, to convert the analog voice into a data signal and to translate the dialing destination into a network address.

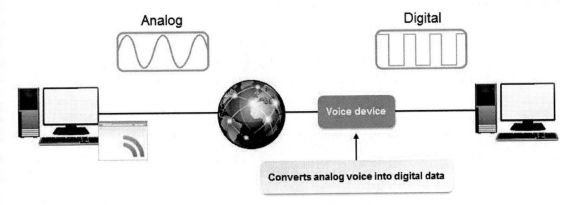

Figure 8–25: Voice software converts analog voice into digital signals.

Voice-over-data systems have included voice-over-frame-relay (VoFR), voice-over-ATM (VoATM), and voice over IP (VoIP).

VoIP

Voice over IP (VoIP) is a voice-over-data implementation in which voice signals are transmitted in real or near-real time over IP networks. In VoIP telephony, analog voice signals are converted into digital signals. As in a typical packet-switched network, digital signals are broken down into packets, to transmit voice as data. After reassembling the packets, the digital signals are reconverted into audio signals.

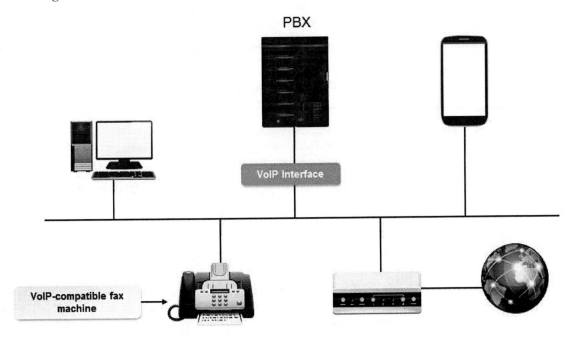

Figure 8–26: VoIP transmits voice signals over IP networks.

When you make a telephone call, the network connection transmits signals over data networks, and transfers them to the standard phone system if the called party does not have a VoIP service. Conversely, when you dial a number that maps to a VoIP device, VoIP routes the call to the IP host. VoIP relies on the existing, robust infrastructure of IP networks and the near-universal implementation of IP. It also eliminates per-call costs, especially for long-distance calls, because it uses data channels to transmit voice signals.

Unified voice services integrate a telecommunication network with an IP network. Typically, an IP-based PBX phone system is used to implement unified voice services. These services are implemented using VoIP phones. The phones can be hardware-based phones which look like traditional phones, but contain components that allow the phone to connect to the network. VoIP phones can also be software-based, where a device with a microphone and a sound card are used to make and receive calls. A VoIP provider or a SIP server are required to make and receive calls.

Compared to traditional circuit-switched telephony, VoIP telephony provides various benefits for users and is thus gaining popularity.

Benefit	Description
Cost reduction	The most attractive benefit of VoIP telephony is the cost savings it offers. You can make a call to anywhere in the world, yet pay at the rates of downloads. For a business, the savings are especially considerable.
Mobility	Depending on the setup, you can make a VoIP call from anywhere you have Internet access.
Reduced infrastructure	With no need to provide for the cabling for a separate phone system, VoIP telephony reduces infrastructure and its inherent costs.
Integrated communication	As it is based on IP, some VoIP software integrates the transmission of not just voice data, but other forms of data. Thus, in addition to speaking with someone else, you can send image files and exchange video, such as through a webcam.
Complementary features	VoIP service providers usually offer many features for free, such as the caller ID and call forwarding, which are typically charged by fixed line service providers.

Although VoIP telephony is gaining in popularity, it has many issues that need to be addressed before replacing or even competing with traditional telephony.

Issue	Description
Connectivity	Because of the variable latency and unreliability of the Internet, it is not always a dependable choice for VoIP calls. Connections to the Internet are still not completely reliable with most providers, and there are times when you are not able to go online or you get disconnected often. An option would be to switch to a more reliable provider.
Voice delivery	As voice is delivered as packets, there may be periods of silence resulting from delays in packet delivery. This can not only be annoying, but it also consumes online time, as a conversation may take longer to complete.
Power outage	During a power outage, you are not able to go online and therefore cannot make a VoIP call. This is usually not a problem with traditional telephony, as phone companies provide for reserve power. An option would be to install a backup system.
Security	With the increasing popularity of VoIP telephony, security vulnerabilities, though not a big concern presently, are bound to increase. Hackers could not only listen to and intercept sensitive data, but even break in to systems and accounts to utilize VoIP services.
Emergency 911 calls	An emergency call from a traditional phone, in the event the caller is unable to speak, can be traced. However, it is difficult to trace a VoIP call, as voice packets bear an IP address rather than a location address. The problem gets more complicated if the person is using a portable device.

VoIP Protocols

A VoIP session may use one or more protocols, depending on session parameters. Some consumer products such as Skype™ and Google Hangouts™ do not use traditional VoIP protocols such as SIP or RTP. Skype for Business, however, does implement these protocols.

Protocol	Description
Session Initiation Protocol (SIP)	Initiates, modifies, and terminates a session. It is a signaling protocol for multimedia communication sessions. SIP must work with other protocols because it is responsible only for the signaling portion of a communication session.
Session Description Protocol (SDP)	Describes the content of a multimedia communication session.
Real-Time Transport Protocol (RTP)	Transmits audio or video content and defines the packet for delivery including the type of content, sequence numbering, time stamping, and delivery monitoring. Has no specific UDP or TCP port number; rather, it has a dynamic range of port numbers, a feature that makes traversing firewalls difficult.
Real-Time Transport Control Protocol (RTCP)	Monitors QoS in RTP transmissions. Acts as a partner to RTP to package and deliver data but does not transport data.
Microsoft Notification Protocol (MSNP)	Is an instant messaging protocol used by Skype.

These real-time protocols are designed to be used in both multicast and unicast network services.

The quality of a voice service is affected by latency and *jitter* on a packet network. Therefore, there is a need to ensure QoS for protecting voice from data and to ensure that other critical data applications, which compete with voice, do not lose out on bandwidth. The QoS implementation should also take care of packet loss, delays, and efficient use of bandwidth.

Latency is the time delay for a packet to go from the source to the destination and back to the source. Jitter is the variability of latency over time across a network. Jitter should be minimum for real-time applications using voice and video.

There are two items that can aid QoS, *Class of Service (CoS)* and *Differentiated Services Code Point (DSCP)*. CoS is a parameter used in data and voice protocols to differentiate the types of payloads contained in the packet being transmitted. The focus is generally to assign priorities to the data payload or access levels to the telephone call. DSCP is a field in an IP packet that enables different levels of service to be assigned to network traffic. This is achieved by marking each packet on the network with a DSCP code and associating it with the corresponding level of service.

VoIP Software

There are various scenarios where VoIP can be used, such as phone calls, web conferences, or enabling voice mail and faxes to be delivered through email. These capabilities are achieved through different VoIP applications that are available.

VoIP Software	Description
Microsoft Lync	Microsoft Lync is a messaging application for smartphones and desktops that allows users to connect to other users and provides presence information, instant messaging, voice calls, video calls, and online meetings. Users can now also connect to Skype users.

VoIP Software	Description
Skype	Skype is a messaging application for smartphones and desktops that allows users to connect to other users and provides presence information, instant messaging, voice calls, and video calls. Users can now also connect to Microsoft Lync users.
Google Hangouts	Google Hangouts is a messaging application for smartphones and desktops that allows users to connect to other users and provides presence information, instant messaging, photos, voice calls, and video calls.
GoToMeeting	GoToMeeting is an online meeting application for smartphones and desktops that provides the ability to participate in online meetings, share desktops, and participate in video conferencing.
Viber	Viber is a messaging application for smartphones and desktops that allows users to connect to other users and provides presence information, instant messaging, photos, voice calls, and video calls.
OnSIP	OnSIP is a business-level VoIP service that provides an enterprise class phone system.
Ekiga	Ekiga is a phone and video conferencing application for desktops that allows users to connect to other users and provides instant messaging, voice calls, and video calls.
Vonage	Vonage is a telephone application and service for smartphones and desktops that allows users to make voice calls.
Tango	Tango is a messaging application for smartphones that allows users to connect to other users and provides presence information, social networking, instant messaging, photos, music, games, voice calls, and video calls.
ShoreTel Sky	ShoreTel Sky is a business-level VoIP service that provides an enterprise class phone system.

Video Conferencing

Video conferencing uses telecommunication technologies that allow two or more locations to communicate by simultaneous two-way video and audio transmissions. Video conferencing is different from videophone calls in that it's designed to serve a conference or multiple locations rather than individuals. Video conferencing uses digital compression of audio and video streams in real time. The hardware or software that performs compression is called a *codec*.

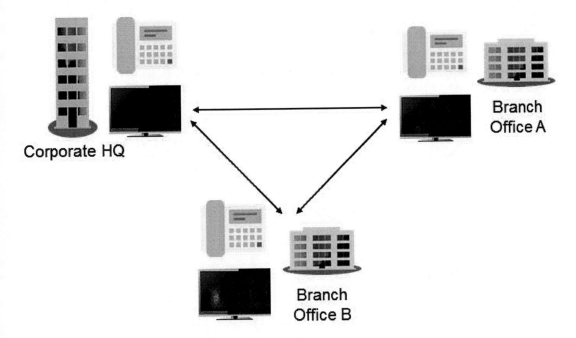

Figure 8-27: Video conferencing enables people at multiple locations to communicate.

Presence Information

Presence is knowing where a computing device is, usually linked to a person, and if it is available, in real time. A user's client provides presence information via a network connection to a presence service, and can be made available for distribution to other users to convey their availability for communication. Presence information has wide application in many communication services such as instant messaging, phones, and GPS, among others.

Figure 8-28: Presence information for instant messaging.

Instant Messaging

Instant messaging (IM) is a type of chat that has real-time text transmission over the Internet or a local connection. Short messages are typically transmitted bidirectionally between two parties when a user selects **Send**. Some IM applications can use push technology to provide real-time text, in which messages are transmitted character by character, as they are typed. Some instant messaging applications include file transfer, selectable hyperlinks, VoIP, or video chat.

Instant messaging systems tend to provide connections between specified known users. Depending on the IM protocol, the technical architecture can be peer-to-peer (direct point-to-point transmission) or client-server (a central server retransmits messages from the sender to the receiver).

Other Real-Time UC Technologies

Other real-time UC technologies include:

- Desktop sharing: Technologies and products that allow remote access and remote collaboration on a person's computer desktop through a graphical terminal emulator.
- Speech recognition: Technology that translates spoken words into text.
- Data sharing: Technologies that allow the sharing of data such as screen sharing or interactive whiteboards.
- Call control: Software that decodes addressing information and routes telephone calls from one endpoint to another. It also creates the features that can be used to adapt standard switch operation to the needs of users.

Non-Real-Time UC Technologies

Other non-real-time UC technologies include:

- Unified messaging: The integration of different electronic messaging and communications media technologies into a single interface. Traditional communications systems deliver messages into different types of stores such as voice mail systems, email servers, and stand-alone fax machines. With unified messaging, all types of messages are stored in one system.
  - Voice mail: A computer-based system that allows users and subscribers to exchange personal voice messages, and to process transactions relating to individuals, organizations, products and services, by using a telephone.
  - Email: A method of exchanging digital messages from an author to one or more recipients. Email operates across the Internet or other networks.
  - SMS: A text messaging service component of a phone, web, or mobile communication system. It uses standardized communications protocols to allow fixed line or mobile phone devices to exchange short text messages.
  - Fax: A telephonic transmission of scanned printed material, normally to a telephone number connected to a printer or other output device.

ACTIVITY 8-4
Discussing Unified Communication Technologies

Scenario

At the Greene City Interiors branch office, the network administrator asks you about the characteristics of unified communication technologies.

1. **What are the advantages of VoIP as compared to traditional telephone systems?**

   ☐ Reduced long-distance call costs

   ☐ Increased bandwidth

   ☐ Portability

   ☐ Power independent

2. **Describe a scenario in which real-time communication services and products are integrated with non-real-time services and products.**

3. **Which statements are valid regarding voice-over-data systems?**

   ☐ Transmits digital signals over WAN technologies.

   ☐ Voice communications are not time-sensitive.

   ☐ Voice software converts digital data to analog voice signals.

   ☐ Voice software translates a dialing destination to a network address.

4. **What are some of the different unified communications technologies that you have used?**

5. **Which VoIP protocol transmits audio or video content and defines the packet for delivery?**

   ○ Real-Time Transport Control Protocol

   ○ Real-Time Transport Protocol

   ○ Session Initiation Protocol

   ○ Session Description Protocol

Summary

In this lesson, you identified the infrastructure of a WAN implementation. Understanding the infrastructure of WAN connections will help you ensure connectivity in the networks that you support.

What methods have you used in your environments to connect to WANs?

Share your experiences with using and managing unified communication technologies.

 Note: Check your LogicalCHOICE Course screen for opportunities to interact with your classmates, peers, and the larger LogicalCHOICE online community about the topics covered in this course or other topics you are interested in. From the Course screen you can also access available resources for a more continuous learning experience.

9 Cloud and Virtualization Technologies

Lesson Time: 1 hour

Lesson Objectives

In this lesson, you will identify the components used in cloud computing and virtualization. You will:

- Identify virtualization technologies.

- Identify storage area network technologies.

- Identify cloud computing technologies.

Lesson Introduction

In the last lesson, you identified the major components of a WAN infrastructure. A WAN connection can enable access to services such as cloud computing and even virtualization. In this lesson, you will identify components of cloud computing and virtualization.

Virtualizing hardware enables companies to consolidate devices and maximize the use of their internal computing power. Cloud services allow companies to outsource computing power and are becoming more popular all the time. Having a solid grasp of both will enable you to better manage and implement these technologies in your environment.

TOPIC A

Virtualization

In this topic, you will define virtualization and what it encompasses. There are different types of virtualization and several devices that can be virtualized. It is important to understand them if you want to implement virtualization in your environment.

Virtualization

Virtualization is a technology through which one or more simulated computing devices run within a physical computer. The physical computer is called the host. The simulated devices are typically called virtual machines (VMs), though other terms may be used. The virtual machines communicate with each other by using virtual switches.

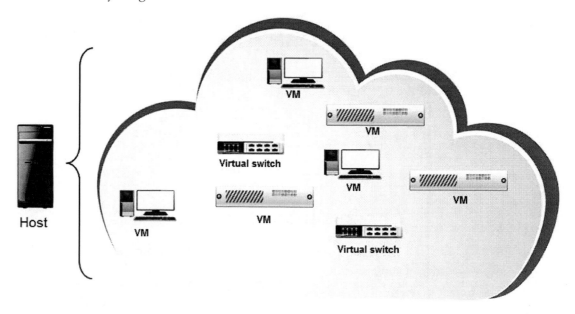

Figure 9-1: Virtualization.

Virtualization offers a range of benefits such as server consolidation, improved disaster recovery, versatile lab environments, and energy savings. Many user and system functions typically consume far less than the full power of a modern device. For example, if a user's activities on her PC use just 30 percent of the computer's capabilities, 70 percent is being wasted. Through virtualization, potentially three VMs could be run on a single system at this level of utilization, giving similar performance levels.

Rather than run on its own hardware (as computers traditionally have done), a virtual machine runs as an application on a host. In this way, virtualization provides for software-defined networking. The VM is fully functional, with its own operating system, applications, and services. It shares the hardware of the host, and from a networking perspective appears as its own node with its own media access control (MAC) address, Internet Protocol (IP) address, and Transmission Control Protocol/User Datagram Protocol (TCP/UDP) client/server sessions.

The software or firmware that creates a virtual machine on the host hardware is called a *hypervisor* or virtual machine manager. The hypervisor provides the guest operating systems with a virtual operating platform and manages the execution of the guest operating systems. Different operating systems may share the virtualized hardware resources.

There is also *software-defined networking (SDN)*, which is an approach to designing, building, and managing networks that allows network administrators to manage network services through abstraction of lower-level functionality. This is done by decoupling the system that makes decisions about where traffic is sent from the underlying systems that forward traffic to the selected destination.

Types of Server Virtualization

There are two main methods of executing server virtualization, as described in the following table.

Server Virtualization Method	Description
Hardware-based	In this method, the hypervisor runs directly on the host's hardware to control the hardware and to manage guest operating systems. They are sometimes referred to as bare metal hypervisors. A guest operating system runs as a process on the host. Examples of hardware-based virtualization include Oracle® VM Server, Citrix® XenServer®, VMware® ESX®/VMware® ESXi™, and Microsoft® Hyper-V®.
Client-based	In this method, the hypervisor runs on an operating system like other applications. These hypervisors abstract guest operating systems from the host operating system. Examples of client-based virtualization include VMware® Workstation™, VirtualBox®, and Microsoft Hyper-V. (It can be installed as either hardware- or client-based.)

Virtual Servers

Virtual servers are VMs that are running a network operating system or other server software. Often, virtual servers store their data on a central storage device, such as a storage area network (SAN) or disk array. A typical host would be a rack-mounted blade computer without optical drives. Additionally, hosts can be configured with no local disk storage, and may instead use a network storage device. For example, you can run multiple print servers as virtual machines in a single host.

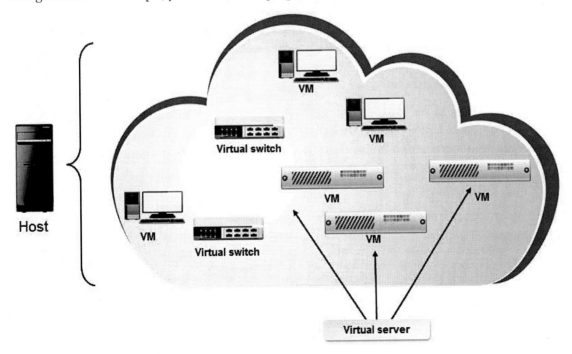

Figure 9–2: Virtual servers.

The primary benefits of virtual servers include better utilization of hardware, easier provisioning (set up new servers), easier backup, and easier disaster recovery. If your organization uses virtual local area networks (VLANs), each virtual server can be logically located within the network segments serving individual departments, yet the host can be in the central server room and not out on the floor. This system reduces opportunities for theft and hacking.

Virtual NICs

A *virtual network interface card (VNIC)* is a program that virtualizes a physical network interface card, and is used by a virtual machine as its network interface. A virtual NIC is assigned a MAC address, and each MAC address corresponds with a single virtual NIC. The virtual NIC enables the virtual machine to communicate with other virtual machines on the same host, but not on physical networks unless it is configured to bridge to the host NIC.

Virtual Switches

A *virtual switch* is a software application that enables communication between virtual machines. In addition to forwarding data packets, a virtual switch intelligently directs the communication on a network by checking data packets before moving them on.

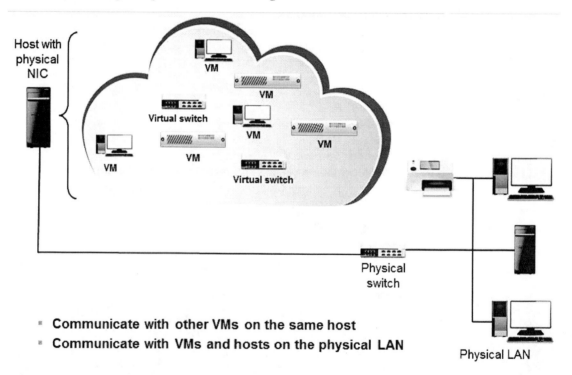

- Communicate with other VMs on the same host
- Communicate with VMs and hosts on the physical LAN

Figure 9–3: Virtual switches.

Virtual switches can be embedded into the virtualization software, but they can also be included in server hardware as part of server firmware. Virtual switches connect to NICs. A virtual NIC can connect to a virtual switch, which can be bound to a physical NIC, allowing VMs that have their virtual NICs connected to that virtual switch to access physical networks.

Virtual Routers

A *virtual router* is a software-based routing framework that enables the host to act as a hardware router over a LAN. The virtual router performs the network and packet routing functionality of a router. Using the Virtual Router Redundancy Protocol (VRRP), you can implement virtual routers to increase the reliability of your network. This is achieved by advertising a virtual router as the default gateway, which is backed by a group of physical routers that provide redundancy in case one fails.

Virtual Firewalls

A *virtual firewall* is a firewall service or appliance running entirely within a virtualized environment. This can be a software firewall on a guest VM, a virtual security appliance designed for virtual network security, a virtual switch with additional security capabilities, or a managed kernel process running within the host hypervisor that sits below all VM activity.

Virtual firewalls can operate in different modes to provide different security services.

- *Bridge mode* operates by diagnosing and monitoring all incoming and outgoing traffic bound for other virtual networks or machines. In bridge mode, the firewall does not actively participate in routing the traffic. A bridging firewall does not require any IP routing changes or subnetting to be inserted into place.
- *Hypervisor mode* resides in the core hypervisor kernel and monitors the virtual host machine's incoming and outgoing traffic.

Virtual PBX

Virtualized phone services use Voice over IP (VoIP) to provide an organization with a virtual switchboard and private branch exchange (PBX), or private telephone network. *Virtual PBX* services receive and route calls to appropriate individuals based on callers' responses to recorded questions and prompts. The virtual phone system is housed on a service provider's servers, so the organizations taking advantage of virtual PBX don't have to invest in analog phone lines or in the devices and software needed to manage PBX services locally.

 Access the Checklist tile on your LogicalCHOICE course screen for reference information and job aids on How to Implement Virtualization in Hyper-V Environments.

ACTIVITY 9-1
Managing Virtual Switches in Hyper-V

 Note: Hyper-V is not supported when running inside a virtual machine and it may not be fully functional. The steps in this activity will function on a virtual machine, but if you try to perform steps not listed here, they may not work.

Scenario

At the Greene City Interiors branch office, the software development team has notified you that they are working on an application and they want to do thorough testing on different operating systems. You have decided to use virtual machines to provide access to clean machines with different operating systems. The virtual machines don't need access to the Internet but they will need access to the host in order to copy files.

1. Observe the MAC address settings for virtual network adapters.

   a) In Server Manager, select **Tools→Hyper-V Manager**.

   b) In the Hyper-V Manager window, in the **Actions** pane, if necessary select **COMPUTER##** to expand its list, and then select **Virtual Switch Manager**.

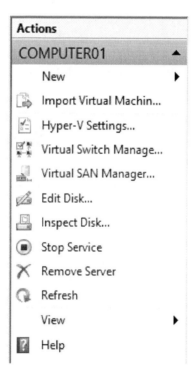

c) In the **Virtual Switch Manager for COMPUTER##** dialog box, in the left pane, select **MAC Address Range**.

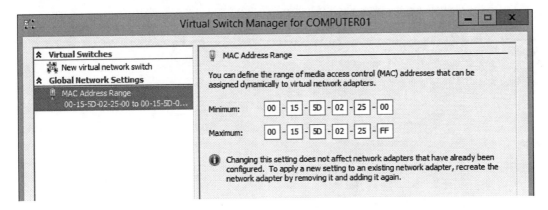

d) In the **MAC Address Range** pane, observe how you can select a range for MAC addresses assigned to virtual network adapters.

2. Create an internal virtual switch.
   a) In the **Virtual Switch Manager for COMPUTER##** dialog box, in the left pane, select **New virtual network switch**.
   b) In the **Create virtual switch** pane, under **What type of virtual switch do you want to create?**, select each option and read the description.
   c) Select **Internal**, and then select **Create Virtual Switch**.

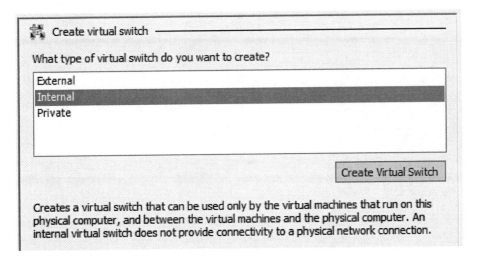

   d) In the **Virtual Switch Properties** pane, in the **Name** box, type *Internal Virtual Switch*
   e) In the **Connection Type** section, observe the options and how the virtual switch can be changed to **Internal** or **Private**.
   f) Select **OK**.

3. Create a virtual machine that uses the internal virtual switch.
   a) In the Hyper-V Manager window, in the **Actions** pane, select **New→Virtual Machine**.
   b) In the **New Virtual Machine Wizard**, select **Next**.
   c) On the **Specify Name and Location** page, in the **Name** box, type *QA Test Machine* and select **Next**.
   d) On the **Specify Generation** page, select **Next**.
   e) On the **Assign Memory** page, in the **Startup memory** box, type *4096* and select **Next**.
   f) On the **Configure Networking** page, in the **Connection** drop-down list, select **Internal Virtual Switch** and select **Next**.
   g) On the **Connect Virtual Hard Disk** page, select **Next**.

h) On the **Installation Options** page, select **Next**.

i) On the **Completing the New Virtual Machine Wizard** page, select **Finish**.

j) Close the Hyper-V Manager window.

TOPIC B

SAN Implementations

In this topic, you will describe storage area network implementations. Different technologies of varying scope can be used for implementing storage area networks. If you plan to implement one, you need to understand the strengths of each so that it fits your needs.

SANs

A *storage area network (SAN)* is a high-speed data transfer network that provides access to consolidated *block-level storage*. A SAN moves storage resources off the network and reorganizes them into an independent, high-performance network. This allows server operating systems to access the shared storage list as if it were a locally attached drive. SANs are primarily used to enhance storage devices, such as disk arrays, tape libraries, and optical jukeboxes.

- ▪ **Cabling**
- ▪ **HBAs**
- ▪ **Switches**
- ▪ **Storage devices**

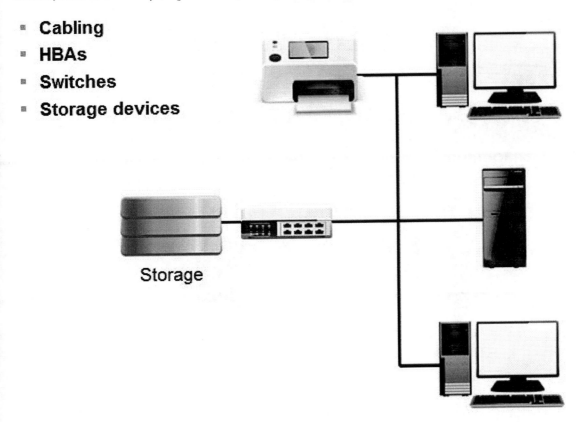

Storage

Figure 9-4: SANs.

A SAN is typically assembled by using cabling, *host bus adapters (HBAs)*, and switches. Each storage system and switch on the SAN must be interconnected, and the physical interconnections must support bandwidth levels that can handle data activities.

SANs are available in two types:

- *Fibre Channel (FC)*: Storage and servers are connected via a high-speed network of interconnected Fibre Channel switches. This is used for mission-critical applications in which uninterrupted data access is required.

- *Internet Small Computer System Interface (iSCSI)*: A protocol that describes how Small Computer System Interface (SCSI) packets should be transported on a Transmission Control Protocol/ Internet Protocol (TCP/IP) network.

Fibre Channel

Fibre Channel is a technology for transmitting data between computing devices at data rates of up to 16 Gbps. Fibre Channel is typically used for connecting servers to shared storage devices and for interconnecting storage controllers and drives. Fibre Channel has become a common connection type for SANs in enterprise storage. Optical fiber is not required for Fibre Channel, and it works by using coaxial cable and ordinary telephone twisted pair.

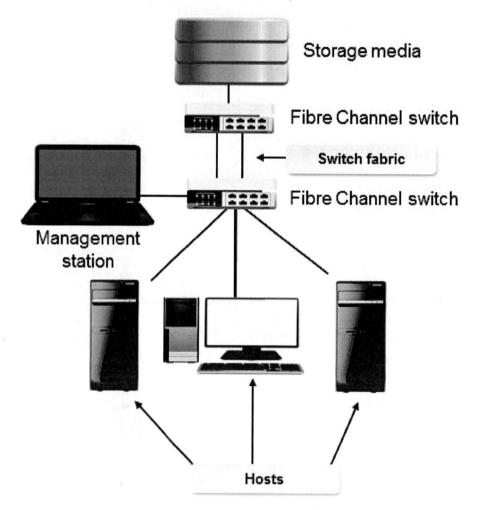

Figure 9–5: Fibre Channel.

There are three major Fibre Channel topologies that describe how several ports are connected together. In Fibre Channel terminology, a port is any entity that actively communicates over the network.

Fibre Channel Topology	Description
Point-to-point (FC-P2P)	Two devices are connected directly to each other. This is the simplest topology and has limited connectivity.
Arbitrated loop (FC-AL)	All devices are in a loop or ring, similar to token ring networking. The loop is interrupted whenever a device is removed or fails.

Fibre Channel Topology	Description
Switched fabric (FC-SW)	All devices or loops of devices are connected to Fibre Channel switches, similar to Ethernet implementations.

iSCSI

iSCSI is an IP-based storage networking standard for linking data storage facilities. iSCSI is used to facilitate data transfers over intranets and to manage storage over long distances by carrying SCSI commands over IP networks. iSCSI can be used to transmit data over LANs, WANs, or the Internet, and can enable location-independent data storage and retrieval. The iSCSI protocol allows clients, called initiators, to send SCSI commands to SCSI storage devices, called targets, on remote servers.

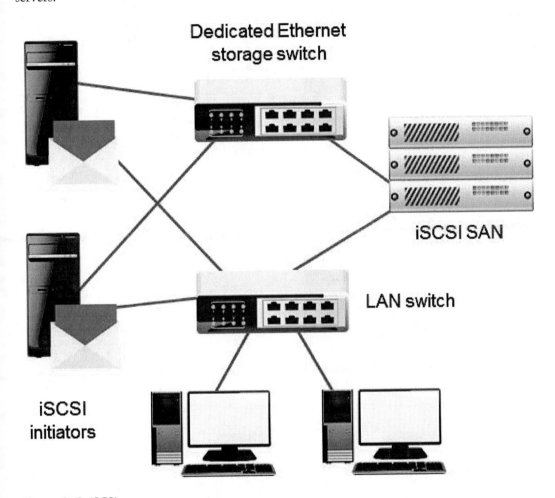

Figure 9–6: iSCSI.

In a virtualized environment, the iSCSI protocol is used to make the storage accessible to all of the hosts within the cluster, and the cluster nodes communicate with the storage pool over the network.

What makes iSCSI so popular is that you can use your existing Ethernet network to connect the servers to the SAN. You don't need to invest in expensive Fibre Channel cabling. Most organizations separate their iSCSI connectivity onto its own VLAN.

NAS

Network-attached storage (NAS) is a computing device or appliance that provides only file-based data storage services to other devices on the network. NAS devices are specialized for the file server task either by their hardware, software, or configuration of both. NAS devices typically do not have a keyboard or display, and are configured through a web-based management utility. Some NAS devices will run a standard operating system, while others may run their own proprietary operating system.

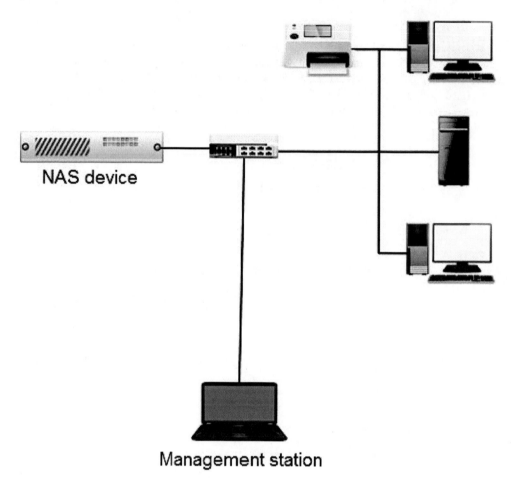

Figure 9–7: A NAS.

NAS uses file-based protocols such as Network File System (NFS), on UNIX® systems; Server Message Block/Common Internet File System (SMB/CIFS), on Microsoft® Windows® systems; or Apple Filing Protocol (AFP), on Apple® Macintosh® computers).

Jumbo Frames

A *jumbo frame* is an Ethernet frame with a payload greater than the standard maximum transmission unit (MTU) of 1,500 bytes. MTU is the size (in bytes) of the largest protocol data unit that the layer can pass onward. Jumbo frames are used on LANs that can support at least 1 Gbps and can be as large as 9,000 bytes. This includes NAS devices and the SAN technologies iSCSI and Fibre Channel.

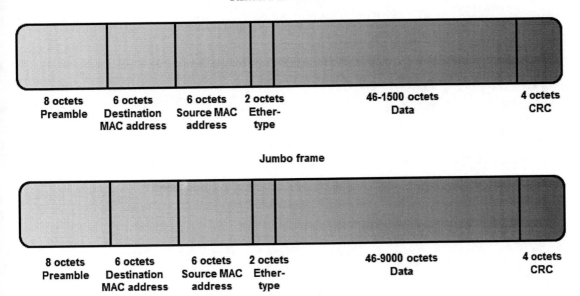

Standard Ethernet frame

| 8 octets
Preamble | 6 octets
Destination
MAC address | 6 octets
Source MAC
address | 2 octets
Ether-
type | 46-1500 octets
Data | 4 octets
CRC |

Jumbo frame

| 8 octets
Preamble | 6 octets
Destination
MAC address | 6 octets
Source MAC
address | 2 octets
Ether-
type | 46-9000 octets
Data | 4 octets
CRC |

Figure 9–8: Jumbo frames.

Jumbo frames can improve network performance by making data transmissions more efficient. Each received Ethernet frame needs the network hardware and software to process it, no matter the size. Increasing the frame size means that a larger amount of data is transferred with the same amount of processing. This reduces central processing unit (CPU) utilization and increases throughput by reducing the number of frames needing processing.

To use jumbo frames, each link in the network path, including servers and endpoints, must be configured at the same MTU. Otherwise, performance may actually decrease as incompatible devices drop frames or fragment them.

ACTIVITY 9–2
Identifying SAN Technologies

Scenario

The network administrator at Greene City Interiors questions you on various storage area network technologies.

1. Which is a specialized file-based data storage server?
   - ○ NAS
   - ○ iSCSI
   - ○ Jumbo Frame
   - ○ Fibre Channel

2. Jumbo frames are used on LANs that can support at least...?
   - ○ 9,000 bps
   - ○ 16 Gbps
   - ○ 1 Gbps
   - ○ 1,500 bps

3. Which are the three major Fibre Channel topologies?
   - ☐ Point-to-point
   - ☐ Arbitrated loop
   - ☐ Client-server
   - ☐ Switched fabric

TOPIC C

Cloud Computing

In this topic, you will define cloud computing. Cloud computing encompasses different implementations and services. If you plan to use a cloud service, you need to know what the choices are and the advantages and disadvantages.

Cloud Concepts

Cloud computing is a model for providing or purchasing off-premise computing services over the Internet. In broad terms, cloud computing is a service (that you purchase or set up on your own) by which you can dynamically expand or contract computation or storage capabilities on an as-needed basis.

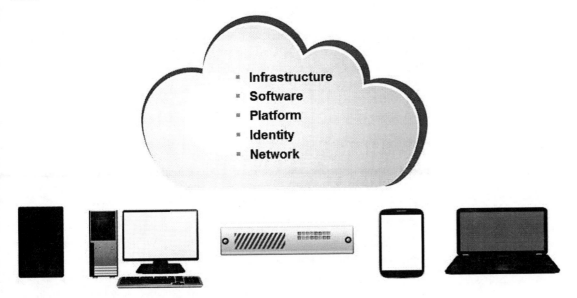

* Infrastructure
* Software
* Platform
* Identity
* Network

Figure 9-9: Cloud computing.

There are several common types of services that are normally associated with cloud computing, including:

* Infrastructure as a Service (IaaS)
* Software as a Service (SaaS)
* Platform as a Service (PaaS)
* Identity as a Service (IDaaS)
* Network as a Service (NaaS)

Cloud Computing Features

Key features of cloud computing include:

* Dynamic, or elastic, provisioning (addition or removal of resources), which can give the illusion of infinite supply.
* Cost benefits, namely a low entry price and accounting differences. Because cloud computing is typically implemented as an outsourced service, it shifts IT expenditures from a capital expense to an operational expense.

- A standardized application programming interface (API) for using or developing applications that run "within the cloud."
- Simplified installation and maintenance because you don't have to install applications on users' devices. End-user cloud-based applications are typically accessed via a web browser.
- Multi-tenancy, meaning that your data and the computing resources you consume are intermingled with others' resources in the provider's pool of resources.
- Improved reliability and redundancy because of the device independence and elastic provisioning.

Cloud Computing Implementations

Cloud computing can be deployed following a public, private, or mixed model.

Cloud Computing Method	Description
Private cloud	A private cloud is cloud infrastructure operated solely for a single organization. It can be managed internally or by a third party, and hosted either internally or externally. A private cloud project requires a significant degree of engagement to virtualize the business environment. The OpenStack project (**www.openstack.org**) is the key example of a technology you could use to implement your own cloud computing infrastructure.
Public cloud	A public cloud provides its services over a network that is open for public use. There may be little or no difference between public and private cloud architecture; however, since the services are made available for a public audience over a potentially non-trusted network, security considerations may be substantially different. Rackspace or Amazon are examples of public clouds.
Community cloud	A community cloud is where multiple organizations from a specific community with common interests share the cloud infrastructure. They can be managed internally or by a third party, and either hosted internally or externally. The costs are spread over fewer users than a public cloud, but more than a private cloud.
Hybrid cloud	A hybrid cloud is a combination of two or more clouds that remain distinct but are bound together, offering the benefits of multiple deployment models. Google's "Gov Cloud" is an example. This cloud can be used by government branches within the United States, but it is not available to consumers or businesses.

IaaS

Infrastructure as a Service (IaaS) is an arrangement in which, rather than purchasing equipment and running your own data center, you rent those resources as an outsourced service. In an IaaS arrangement, you are typically billed based on the resources you consume, much like a utility company bills you for the amount of electricity you use.

Examples of IaaS include Rackspace's CloudServers offering, in which you rent a virtual server running an operating system of your choice. You then install the applications you need onto that virtual server. Other examples include Amazon's Elastic Compute Cloud® (EC2) service and Simple Storage Service (S3).

SaaS

Software as a Service (SaaS) enables a service provider to make applications available over the Internet. This capability eliminates the need to install software on user devices, and it can be helpful for mobile or transient workforces.

Perhaps the most well-known SaaS example is the Google Apps™ suite of office applications. Other notable SaaS examples are the Zoho™ suite of applications and Microsoft's Office Web Apps.

PaaS

Platform as a Service (PaaS) enables you to rent a fully configured system that is set up for a specific purpose.

An example is Rackspace's CloudSites offering, in which you rent a virtual web server and associated systems (such as a database or email server). Amazon's Relational Database Service (RDS) enables you to rent fully configured MySQL and Oracle database servers.

IDaaS

Identity as a Service (IDaaS) is an authentication infrastructure that you can rent from a service provider. Essentially, it provides single sign-on capabilities for the cloud. It is an approach to digital identity management in which an organization or individual performs an electronic transaction that requires identity data managed by a service provider. Functionality includes authentication, registration, identity verification, federation, risk and activity monitoring, roles and entitlement management, provisioning, and reporting, among others.

NaaS

Network as a Service (NaaS) provides network-based services through the cloud, including monitoring and Quality of Service (QoS) management.

Some service models are:

- **Virtual Private Network (VPN):** Extends a private network and the resources contained in the network across networks like the public Internet.
- **Bandwidth on Demand (BoD):** Technique by which network capacity is assigned based on requirements between different nodes or users. Under this model link rates can be dynamically adapted to the traffic demands of the nodes connected to the link.
- **Mobile network virtualization:** Model in which a telecommunications manufacturer or independent network operator builds and operates a network (wireless, or transport connectivity) and sells its communication access capabilities to third parties (commonly mobile phone operators) charging by capacity utilization.

ACTIVITY 9–3
Identifying Cloud Computing Technologies

Scenario

At the Greene City Interiors branch office, the network administrator asks you to identify various cloud computing technologies.

1. Which of the following are key features of cloud computing?

   ☐ Local access to resource

   ☐ Dynamic provisioning

   ☐ Cost benefits

   ☐ Simplified installation and maintenance

2. How is a community cloud different from a public cloud?

3. True or False? Bandwidth on Demand is a service model of PaaS.

   ☐ True

   ☐ False

4. With which service do you rent computing resources as an outsourced service?

   ○ NaaS

   ○ PaaS

   ○ IaaS

   ○ SaaS

Summary

In this lesson, you identified the components of cloud and virtualization solutions. A solid understanding of cloud and virtualization solutions will enable you to better manage and implement these technologies in your environment.

Which aaS do you plan to implement? Why?

Describe common roadblocks you might encounter while trying to implement virtualization.

 Note: Check your LogicalCHOICE Course screen for opportunities to interact with your classmates, peers, and the larger LogicalCHOICE online community about the topics covered in this course or other topics you are interested in. From the Course screen you can also access available resources for a more continuous learning experience.

10 | Network Security Basics

Lesson Time: 2 hours, 30 minutes

Lesson Objectives

In this lesson, you will describe basic concepts related to network security. You will:

- Describe basic security terminology and concepts.

- List common network security vulnerabilities.

- List common network security threats and attacks.

- Identify different methods used for network authentication.

- Describe data encryption methods.

Lesson Introduction

You have identified the basic components and concepts for implementing a network. A network's security is only as strong as the security of its individual systems. In this lesson, you will describe basic concepts related to network security.

Just as the construction of a building is started with bricks and mortar, each security implementation starts with a series of fundamental building blocks. No matter what the final result is, you will always start with the same fundamentals. As a networking professional, it is part of your responsibility to understand these fundamental concepts so that you can ensure appropriate security levels in your organization.

TOPIC A

Introduction to Network Security

In this lesson, you will describe basic concepts related to network security. To begin, it's important to have a solid foundation and awareness of industry terminology that is used when discussing network security. In this topic, you will describe basic security terminology and concepts.

There are many different ways in which networks can be attacked and just as many ways for making networks more secure. You will need a basic understanding of the security risks, and security methods and tools in order to protect your network.

CIA Triad

Information security seeks to address three specific principles: confidentiality, integrity, and availability. This is called the *CIA triad*. If one of the principles is compromised, the security of the organization is threatened.

Principle	Description
Confidentiality	This is the fundamental principle of keeping information and communications private and protecting them from unauthorized access.
	Confidential information includes trade secrets, personnel records, health records, tax records, and military secrets.
Integrity	This is the property of keeping organizational information accurate, free of errors, and without unauthorized modifications.
	For example, in the 1980s movie *War Games*, actor Matthew Broderick was seen modifying his grades early in the movie. This means that the integrity of his grade information was compromised by unauthorized modification.
Availability	Availability is the fundamental principle of ensuring that systems operate continuously and that authorized persons can access the data that they need.
	Information available on a computing device is useless unless users can get to it. Consider what would happen if the Federal Aviation Administration's air traffic control system failed. Radar images would be captured but not distributed to those who need the information.

Security Factors

Most security systems rely on four major factors to achieve security goals:

- *Authorization* is the process of determining what rights and privileges a particular entity has.
- *Access control* is the process of determining and assigning privileges to various resources, objects, or data.
- *Accountability* is the process of determining who to hold responsible for a particular activity or event, such as a logon.
- *Auditing* or *accounting* is the process of tracking and recording system activities and resource access.

Authorization

Access control

Accountability

Auditing

Figure 10-1: System security factors.

Non-repudiation

Non-repudiation is the goal of ensuring that data remains associated with the party that creates it or sends a transmission with that data. It is supplemental to the CIA triad. You should be able to independently verify the identity of the sender of a message, and the sender should be responsible for the message and its data.

Least Privilege

The principle of *least privilege* dictates that users and software should have only the minimal level of access that is necessary for them to perform their duties. This level of minimal access includes facilities, computing hardware, software, and information. Where a user or system is given access, that access should conform to the least privilege level required to perform the necessary task.

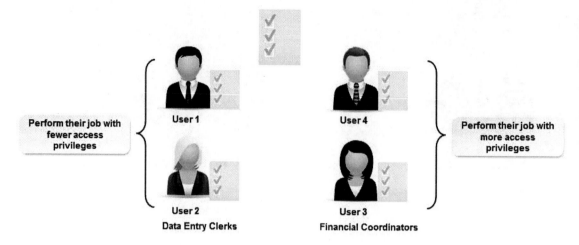

Figure 10-2: Least privilege allows appropriate levels of access to users.

The network or security administrator can use *privilege bracketing* to allow privileges only when needed, and then revoke them as soon as the user finishes the task or the need has passed.

Risks

As applied to information systems, *risk* is a concept that indicates exposure to the chance of damage or loss. It signifies the likelihood of a hazard or threat occurring. In information technology, risk is often associated with the loss of a device, power, or network, and other physical losses. Risk also affects people, practices, and processes.

For example, a disgruntled former employee is a threat. The amount of risk this threat represents depends on the likelihood that the employee will access their previous place of business and remove or damage data. It also depends on the extent of harm that could result.

Risk is the determining factor when looking at information systems security. If an organization chooses to ignore risks to operations, it could suffer a catastrophic outage that would limit its ability to survive.

Data Breaches

A *data breach* is a security incident in which sensitive, protected, or confidential data is copied, transmitted, viewed, stolen, or used by an individual unauthorized to do so. The breach can be intentional or unintentional. Incidents can range from attacks by hackers, organized crime, or national governments to the careless disposal of used computer equipment or data storage media. Data breaches may involve financial information such as credit card or bank details, personal health information (PHI), personally identifiable information (PII), trade secrets of corporations, or intellectual property.

Unauthorized Access

Unauthorized access is any type of network or data access that is not explicitly approved by an organization. It can be a deliberate attack by an outsider, a misuse of valid privileges by an authorized user, or an inadvertent action. Unauthorized access does not necessarily result in data loss or damage, but it could be the first step in mounting a number of attacks against the network.

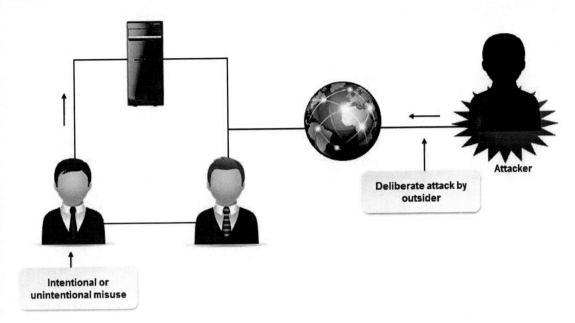

Figure 10-3: Unauthorized users can mount a number of attacks against a network.

Hackers and Attackers

Hackers and *attackers* are related terms for individuals who have the skills to gain access to computing devices through unauthorized or unapproved means. Originally, a hacker was a neutral term for a user who excelled at computer programming and computer system administration. "Hacking" into a system was a sign of technical skill and creativity that also became associated with illegal or malicious system intrusions. "Attacker" is a term that always represents a malicious system intruder.

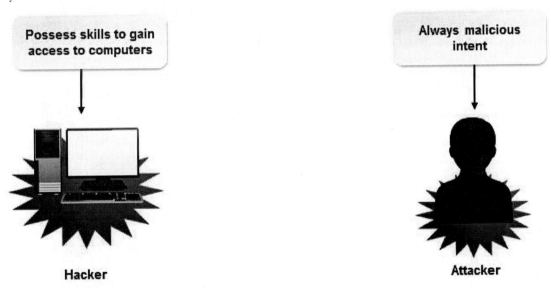

Figure 10-4: A hacker and an attacker.

 Note: The term *cracker* refers to an individual who breaks encryption codes, defeats software copy protections, or specializes in breaking into systems. The term "cracker" is sometimes used to refer to a hacker or an attacker.

Hackers are sometimes categorized as white hats and black hats.

- A *white hat* is a hacker who discovers and exposes security flaws in applications and operating systems so that manufacturers can fix them before they become widespread problems. The white hat often does this on a professional basis, working for a security organization or a system manufacturer. This is sometimes called an "ethical hack."

- A *black hat* is a hacker who discovers and exposes security vulnerabilities for financial gain or for some malicious purpose. Although the black hats might not break directly into systems the way attackers do, widely publicizing security flaws can potentially cause financial or other damage to an organization.

People who consider themselves white hats also discover and publicize security problems, but without the organization's knowledge or permission. They consider themselves to be acting for the common good. In this case, the only distinction between a white hat and a black hat is one of intent. There is some debate over whether this kind of unauthorized revelation of security issues really serves the public good or simply provides an avenue of attack.

 Note: White hats and black hats get their names from characters in old Western movies: The good guys always wore white hats, whereas the bad guys wore black hats.

Security Controls

Security controls are safeguards or countermeasures to avoid, counteract, or minimize security risks relating to personal or company property. For example, a firewall is a type of security control because it controls traffic by allowing only traffic that has specifically been permitted by a system administrator. Security controls can be classified by several criteria, such as by the time that they act relative to a security incident, according to their nature, or by people, technology, and operations/processes. In this course, we will categorize the security controls by their nature:

- Physical controls such as fences, doors, locks, and fire extinguishers
- Procedural controls such as incident response processes, management oversight, security awareness, and training
- Technical controls such as user authentication (login) and logical access controls, antivirus software, and firewalls
- Legal and regulatory or compliance controls such as privacy laws, policies, and clauses

Security Policies

A *security policy* is a formalized statement that defines how security will be implemented within a particular organization. It describes the means that the organization will take to protect the confidentiality, availability, and integrity of sensitive data and resources, including the network infrastructure, physical and electronic data, applications, and the physical environment. It often consists of multiple individual policies. All implemented security measures should conform to the stated policy.

A good security policy provides functions similar to a government's foreign policy. The policy is determined by the needs of the organization. Just as a nation needs a foreign policy in part because of real and perceived threats from other countries, organizations also need a policy to protect their data and resources.

A nation's foreign policy defines what the threats are and how the government will handle those threats. A security policy does the same for an organization; it defines threats to its resources and how those threats will be handled. A policy forms the plan that ties everything together. Without a formal policy, you can only react to threats instead of anticipating them and preparing accordingly.

A security policy may include a consent to monitoring clause. While using the organization's network or resources, any activity may be intercepted, monitored, recorded, copied, audited, inspected, and disclosed to the organization. Many sites, in particular government sites, often include a banner stating their security policy in regards to their ability to monitor your access to the site. The ability of the administrator to monitor your actions while on the site can be stated explicitly or can be assumed to be the case without actually stating it. The consent to monitor banner usually states that:

- You agree to be monitored in real time.
- You are actually authorized to access or download specific data or files.
- You and the network owner have a reasonable expectation of privacy.
- You consent to reasonable law enforcement searches.

Example: A Password Security Policy

Greene City Interiors has a password policy to which all employees must adhere. Each employee is responsible for using strong passwords and protecting those passwords accordingly. It contains guidelines for strong passwords to use and weak passwords to avoid.

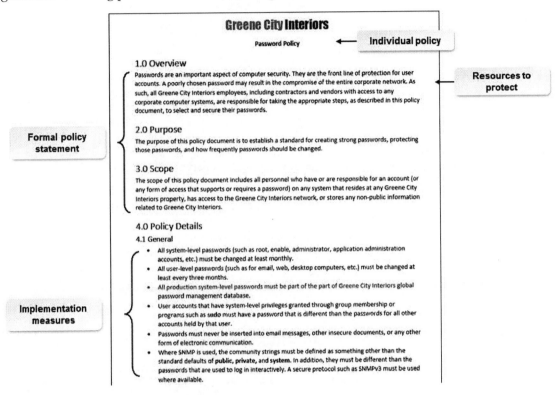

Figure 10-5: Password policy of Greene City Interiors.

Security Policy Components

Each subsection of a security policy typically consists of several standard components.

Component	Description
Policy statement	Outlines the plan for the individual security component.
Standards	Define how to measure the level of adherence to the policy.
Guidelines	Suggestions, recommendations, or best practices for how to meet the policy standard.
Procedures	Step-by-step instructions that detail how to implement components of the policy.

Common Security Policy Types

Administrators use several common security policy types as part of most corporate security policies.

Type	Description
Acceptable Use Policy	Defines the acceptable use of an organization's physical and intellectual resources.
Audit Policy	Details the requirements and parameters for risk assessment and audits of the organization's information and resources.
Extranet Policy	Sets the requirements for third-party entities that desire access to an organization's networks.
Password Policy	Defines standards for creating password complexity. It also defines what an organization considers weak passwords and the guidelines for protecting password safety.
Wireless Standards Policy	Defines what wireless devices can connect to an organization's network and how to use them in a safe manner that protects the organization's security.

Security Policy Standards Organizations

The SysAdmin, Audit, Networking and Security (SANS) Institute has identified a list of standard policy types and policy templates, ranging from the acceptable encryption policy to the wireless communication policy.

To view the complete list of policies from the SANS Institute, see **www.sans.org/resources/policies/**.

Other organizations, such as the IETF, have provided RFC 2196 for different security policies. To view RFC 2196, see **www.cse.ohio-state.edu/cgi-bin/rfc/rfc2196.html**.

ISO has published ISO/IEC 27002:2005, which is a standard for information security. To view information on ISO/IEC 27002:2005, see **www.iso.org**.

Adherence to Standards and Policies

It is not enough to just have standards and policies. Your organization and its employees and contractors need to adhere to them as well. For employees and contractors, this requires that they read the standards and policies, and understand that they need to follow them. For the organization, it also needs to follow the standards and policies, regardless of who is acting on the organization's behalf. In addition, the organization may also have regulatory compliance and additional adherence to laws, regulations, guidelines, and specifications relevant to its business. Violations of regulatory compliance regulations often result in legal punishment, including federal fines.

ACTIVITY 10-1
Identifying a Security Policy

Before You Begin

You have a Windows Server® 2012 R2 computer with the name Child##, where ## is a unique number. Log on as Administrator with the password P@ssw0rd12.

The policy document is stored on your workstation at **C:\093012Data\Network Security Basics \GreeneCityInteriorsPasswordPolicy.rtf**.

Scenario

At the Greene City Interiors branch office, you have found that not all users follow the Greene City Interiors security policies. You may need to update the policies to fit activities performed at the branch office. To do this you first need to review the existing policy documents to see if there is anything that is not covered.

1. Open and review the policy file. What type of policy document is this?

   - ○ Acceptable Use Policy
   - ○ Audit Policy
   - ○ Extranet Policy
   - ○ Password Policy
   - ○ Wireless Standards Policy

2. Which standard policy components are included in this policy?

   - ☐ Statement
   - ☐ Standards
   - ☐ Guidelines
   - ☐ Procedures

3. How often must system-level administrators change their passwords to conform to this policy?

4. To conform to this policy, how often must regular system users change their passwords?

5. According to this policy, what is the minimum character length for a password and how should it be constructed?

6. Why is "password1" not a good choice for a password?

Windows Security Policies

Windows security policies are configuration settings within Windows® operating systems that control the overall security behavior of the system. They are found in a policy object in the **Computer Configuration\Windows Settings\Security Settings** node. These are local policies that are applied to the local device only. Policies can also be set on a centralized basis, through a group policy in Windows Server® systems, which can apply to single devices or users, to groups of devices or users, or to all devices and users.

Group Policy

A *group policy* is a centralized account management feature available for Active Directory® on Windows Server systems. A group policy can be used to control certain workstation features within an enterprise, such as specifying that all workstations display the company logo as their wallpaper, or that the default browser should have pre-loaded settings. It is also used to control security features, such as limiting the desktop icons that get displayed, granting permission to access certain servers but not others, or totally locking down a desktop.

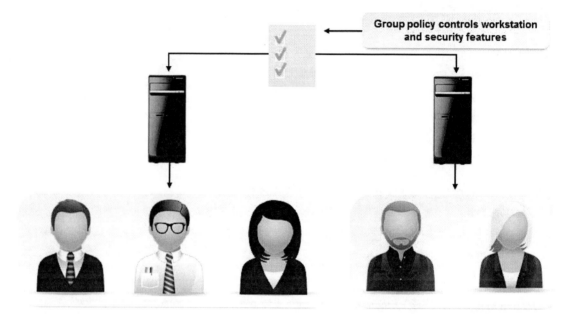

Figure 10–6: A group policy controls certain workstation features.

Permissions

A *permission* is a security setting that determines the level of access a user or group account has to a particular resource. Permissions can be associated with a variety of resources, such as files, printers, shared folders, and network directory databases. Permissions can typically be configured to allow different levels of privileges or to deny privileges to users who should not access a resource.

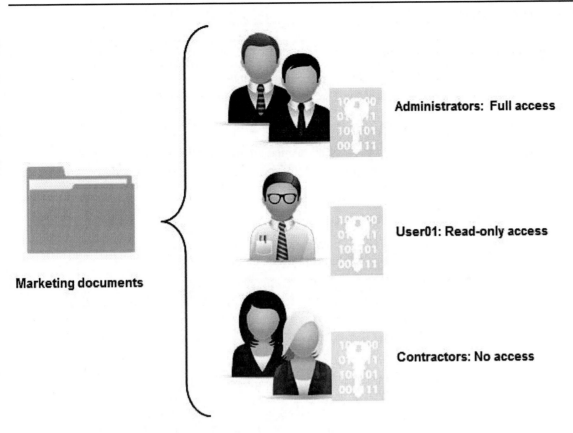

Figure 10-7: Permissions determine the user access level.

Rights and permissions can be assigned to individual user accounts. However, this is an inefficient security practice, because so many permission assignments must be duplicated for users with similar roles and because individual users' roles and needs can change frequently. It is more efficient to create groups of users with common needs, and assign the rights and permissions to the user groups. As the needs of individual users change, the users can be placed in groups with the appropriate security configuration.

NTFS Permissions

On Windows operating systems, file-level security is supported on drives that are formatted to use the Windows NT File System (NTFS). These permissions can be applied either to folders or to individual files. NTFS permissions on a folder are inherited by the files and subfolders within it. There are several levels of NTFS permissions, which can determine, for example, whether users can read files or run applications; write to existing files; and modify, create, or delete files.

Permission	Allows the User To
Read	• Permits viewing and listing of files and subfolders. • Permits viewing or accessing of the file's contents.
Write	• Permits adding of files and subfolders. • Permits writing to a file.
Read & Execute	• Permits viewing and listing of files and subfolders as well as executing of files. • Permits viewing and accessing of the file's contents as well as executing of the file.
List Folder Contents	• Permits viewing and listing of files and subfolders as well as executing of files.

Permission	Allows the User To
Modify	• Permits reading and writing or deletion of files and subfolders. • Permits reading and writing or deletion of the file.
Full Control	• Permits reading, writing, changing, and deleting of files and subfolders.
Special Permissions	• Permits specific actions that are part of other permissions to be performed on folders and files. These permissions are limited to very specific actions.

UNIX Permissions

Because UNIX® and related systems are multiuser by nature, there is a series of permissions associated with all files and directories. There are three types of permissions.

Permission	Allows the User To
r (read)	• View file content. • See what is in the directory.
w (write)	• Modify file contents. • Create and delete directory contents.
x (execute)	• Run the file (if it is an executable program and is combined with read). • Move into the directory. When combined with read, you can also see a long listing of the contents of the directory.

Segmentation

With all of the threats and attacks on networks, servers, services, and clients that are out there in the world today, it can be intimidating and difficult to make sure that your assets are secure. One way that you can help increase the security of your systems is to implement network segmentation. Network segmentation reduces the attack surface available to attackers. There may also be compliance requirements for certain services where segmentation is needed, or you can simply reduce the scope of compliance by placing those devices in their own segment. You might also create different network segments for load balancing purposes, where devices are grouped into different segments to distribute the load on the network.

With network segmentation, each subsystem is placed in its own area or zone. The zone is defined by a logical or physical boundary, separating it from the rest of the network. Each zone has a security zone that contains a group of logical or physical assets that require similar security measures. There needs to be a physical or logical border that separates the zone from other network resources.

A conduit is then established that connects the defined zone with other network resources. The conduit provides the measures to safely and securely communicate between the defined zone and other network zones. Conduits can include network security features such as firewalls and VPNs. All communication between any zones must take place through one of the implemented conduits to protect the data and systems.

Some network elements you may consider segmentation for include:

• SCADA/ICS: SCADA and ICS networks are in this segment. They may be impractical to upgrade and thus will not have the latest security.
• Legacy systems: Legacy or vulnerable systems that perform a crucial business function are in this segment. These systems may be more vulnerable than the rest of your network, so keeping them separate helps reduce the risk that the rest of your network will be compromised.

- Private networks: All of the devices used by the employees and all servers containing data not for public access are in this segment. This allows you to reduce the attack surface by limiting it to only specific groups of users.
- Public networks: Devices that are used for public access are in this segment. If one of your public servers is compromised, it is separate from the rest of the network.
- Testing lab: Devices that are used for testing applications, updates, and patches are in this segment. A test environment should be completely removed from the live environment, and segmentation enables that.
- Honeynet: Only devices that are used as honeypots are in this segment. A honeypot is a device that is set to detect, deflect, or counteract attempts at unauthorized use of the device or network. A honeynet is a special type of honeypot; a specific network segment populated with, and only with, honeypots.

ACTIVITY 10–2
Testing Permissions

Data Files

C:\093012Data\HR Files\CEOSalary.txt

C:\093012Data\HR Files\CompanyPicnicSuggestions.txt

Scenario

At the Greene City Interiors branch office, the human resources department tells you that they have sensitive information on the file server that they want to ensure other users don't have access to. The HR department uses a single folder named HR Files for works in progress that may contain sensitive materials, but because they would like additional control over file access, you have decided to use individual file permissions to limit access to certain users.

1. Locate the HR data files.
   a) Open **File Explorer**, and navigate to the **C:\093012Data\HR Files** folder.
   b) Double-click **CEOSalary**.
   c) In the CEOSalary - Notepad window, observe the sensitive information that HR does not want users to have access to.
   d) Close the CEOSalary - Notepad window.
   e) Double-click **CompanyPicnicSuggestions**.
   f) In the CompanyPicnicSuggestions - Notepad window, observe that the information is not of a sensitive nature.
   g) Close the CompanyPicnicSuggestions - Notepad window.

2. Apply permissions to the files.
   a) Right-click **CEOSalary**, and select **Properties**.
   b) In the **CEOSalary Properties** dialog box, select the **Security** tab.

c) Under **Group or user names**, select **Users** and then select **Edit**.

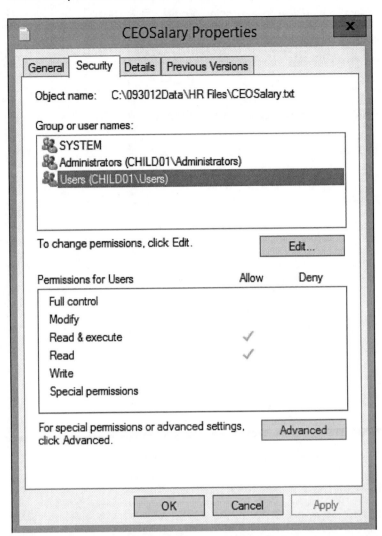

CEOSalary Properties

General | Security | Details | Previous Versions

Object name: C:\093012Data\HR Files\CEOSalary.txt

Group or user names:

- SYSTEM
- Administrators (CHILD01\Administrators)
- Users (CHILD01\Users)

To change permissions, click Edit.   [Edit...]

Permissions for Users	Allow	Deny
Full control		
Modify		
Read & execute	✓	
Read	✓	
Write		
Special permissions		

For special permissions or advanced settings, click Advanced.   [Advanced]

[OK]   [Cancel]   [Apply]

 Note: Notice that domain users can open and read the file but they can't make any changes. You don't want them to have any access to this file.

d) In the **Permissions for CEOSalary** dialog box, under **Group or user names**, select **Users**.
e) Under **Permissions for Users**, in the **Deny** column, select **Full control**.
f) Select **OK**.
g) In the **Windows Security** message box, select **Yes**.
h) Select **OK**.
i) Right-click **CompanyPicnicSuggestions**, and select **Properties**.
j) In the **CompanyPicnicSuggestions Properties** dialog box, select the **Security** tab.
k) Under **Group or user names**, select **Users**, and then select **Edit**.

 Note: Notice that domain users can open and read the file but they can't make any changes. Users should be able to edit and save changes to this file.

l) In the **Permissions for CompanyPicnicSuggestions** dialog box, under **Group or user names**, select **Users**.

m) Under **Permissions for Users**, in the **Allow** column, select **Modify**.

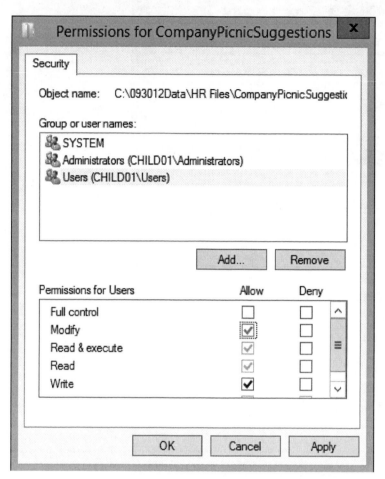

n) Select **OK**.

o) Select **OK**.

3. Test the permissions.

a) Select **Start→Administrator→Sign Out**.

b) Sign in as **CHILD##\User##** with a password of **P@ssw0rd12**.
c) Open **File Explorer**, and navigate to the **C:\093012Data\HR Files** folder.
d) Double-click **CEOSalary**.
e) In the **Notepad** message box, observe the text stating that Access is denied.
f) Select **OK**.
g) Close the Untitled - Notepad window.
h) Double-click **CompanyPicnicSuggestions**.
i) In the CompanyPicnicSuggestions - Notepad window, select the blank line under **-Skylar Stadium**.
j) Type *-Greene City BBQ*
k) Select **File→Save**.
l) Close the CompanyPicnicSuggestions - Notepad window.
m) Close **File Explorer**.
n) Log off **Child##\User##** and log on as **Child##\Administrator** with a password of **P@ssw0rd12**.

Wireless Security

Wireless security is any method of securing your WLAN to prevent unauthorized network access and network data theft. You need to ensure that authorized users can connect to the network without any hindrances. Wireless networks are more vulnerable to attacks than any other network system. For one thing, most wireless devices such as laptops, mobile phones, and tablets search and connect automatically to the access point offering the best signal, which can be coming from an attacker. Wireless transmissions can also be scanned or sniffed out of the air, with no need to access physical network media. Such attacks can be avoided by using relevant security protocols.

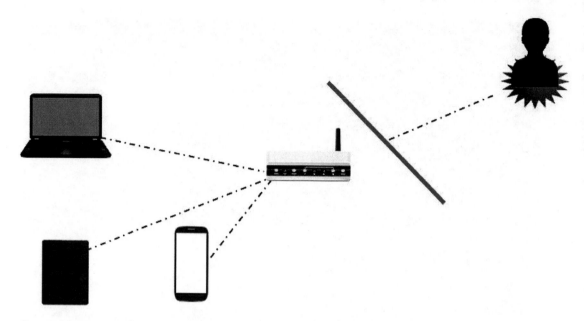

Figure 10-8: A wireless security environment.

A *site survey* is an analysis technique that determines the coverage area of a wireless network, identifies any sources of interference, and establishes other characteristics of the coverage area. Although an authorized site survey is a standard part of planning or maintaining a wireless network, unauthorized site surveys or compromise of the site survey data can be a security risk. You use a site survey to help you install and secure a WLAN.

Wireless connectivity devices such as a wireless access point (WAP) or wireless routers come with a default service set identifier (SSID). An administrator can accept a device's default SSID or specify an SSID manually to more clearly identify the device.

Another method of securing a wireless connection is by disabling the broadcast of the SSID of the wireless device. Disabling the broadcast causes the wireless device to not appear on the network. Therefore, when a client device scans the network, it will not be able to locate the disabled SSID. Though disabling the broadcast of SSID is a comparatively easy task, this method is not completely effective because hackers can still access the WLAN by using sniffing software.

Disaster Recovery

A *disaster* is a catastrophic loss of device functioning due to a cause that cannot reasonably be prevented. Disasters can affect personnel, buildings, devices, communications, resources, and data. *Disaster recovery* is the administrative function of protecting people and resources while restoring a failed network or device as quickly as possible. The first priority is to ensure the safety of personnel, and then to ensure continuity of business functions.

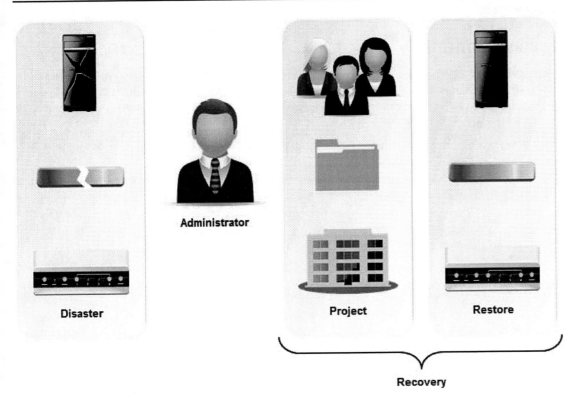

Figure 10-9: Disasters and disaster recovery.

Disasters that can affect network functioning fall into one of three main categories.

Disaster Category	Description
Natural disaster	Natural disasters include fires, storms, floods, and other destructive forces. Natural disasters involve the involuntary destruction of network hardware. Data loss is usually related to destruction of network infrastructure and hardware. The best defense against this type of disaster is excellent documentation and physical security for data backups. In the worst-case scenario, nothing remains of the office after the disaster, and the network has to be completely rebuilt from documentation alone.
Data destruction	Data loss due to causes other than natural disaster can be easier to recover from. This kind of data loss includes accidental deletion, malicious destruction, or a virus attack. Again, the key is a good quality data backup.
Hardware failure	Most day-to-day network disasters relate to failure of network hardware. Not only can hardware failure cause a loss of data, but it can also cause a loss of productivity in the office. Defense against equipment failure can be as simple as having a relationship with a vendor who can get replacement parts quickly or contracting a service provider that stocks parts. Many companies keep high-risk spares on hand in order to quickly replace failures. One major mistake that many administrators make is to standardize uncommon hardware or rely too heavily on older hardware that might be hard to replace. If a network goes down because older equipment fails, it could be down for an unacceptable length of time while a replacement is found or the network is reconfigured.

Business Continuity

Business continuity is a defined set of planning and preparatory activities that are used during a serious incident or disaster to ensure that an organization's critical business functions will continue to operate, or will be recovered to an operational state within a reasonably short period. As such, business continuity includes three key elements:

- Resilience: Critical business functions and infrastructure are designed so that they are materially unaffected by most disruptions.
- Recovery: Arrangements are made to recover or restore critical and less critical business functions that fail for some reason.
- Contingency: A generalized capability and readiness to cope effectively with major incidents and disasters. Contingency preparations are a last-resort response in the case where the resilience and recovery arrangements were inadequate.

Single Point of Failure

A *single point of failure* is a part of a system, in this case a network, that if it fails, will stop the entire network from working. Redundancy can be added to the network to avoid a single point of failure. For instance, a network has a single router that connects it to another network or the Internet. If that router fails for any reason, devices on that network will no longer be able to connect to another network or the Internet. Redundancy can be achieved at various levels. For instance, the network administrator may have a router in storage that can be put on the network in case the first one fails. To avoid any downtime, that second router could be placed on the network with the first router and provide a second option for connecting outside of the local network. The assessment of a potential single point of failure involves identifying the critical nodes or assets of a network that would cause a network failure in case of malfunction.

ACTIVITY 10-3
Discussing Network Security Basics

Scenario

The network administrator at Greene City Interiors wants to question you on some basic network security topics.

---

1. An employee in charge of social media writes a blog post that includes details on products that will be released later in the year. The intent was to make consumers excited about upcoming products, but the employee didn't realize that the company didn't want this information public. What is this an example of?

   ○ Risks

   ○ Security policy

   ○ Data breach

   ○ Unauthorized access

2. What is the main difference between Windows security policies and group policy?

3. What are the three principles of the CIA triad?

   ○ Integrity

   ○ Confidentiality

   ○ Accountability

   ○ Availability

4. When would you perform a site survey?

5. Which of these describes the concept of least privilege?

   ○ End-user jobs and software access should be restricted so that no one wields too much administrative power over the network.

   ○ End users should at least hold administrative privileges over their local workstations.

   ○ Technological and physical access should be granted only when it is needed, and then revoked as soon as the task or need has ended.

   ○ End users should be given the minimal level of technological and physical access that is required for them to perform their jobs.

6. Describe how you would alleviate or eliminate single points of failure in your network.

TOPIC B

Vulnerabilities

In the previous topic, you covered basic security terminology and concepts. Networks have different weak points that can be exploited and used as points of attack. In this topic, you will identify network vulnerabilities.

Vulnerabilities in your network can leave it open to attacks that can result in downtime, data theft, or other malicious results. Before you can harden your network and remove these vulnerabilities, you need to know what they are and how they make your network less secure.

Vulnerabilities

At the most basic level, a *vulnerability* is any condition that leaves a device open to attack. Vulnerabilities can come in a wide variety of forms, including:

- Improperly configured or installed hardware or software
- Bugs in software or operating systems
- Misuse of software or communication protocols
- Poorly designed networks
- Poor physical security
- Insecure passwords
- Design flaws in software or operating systems
- Unchecked user input

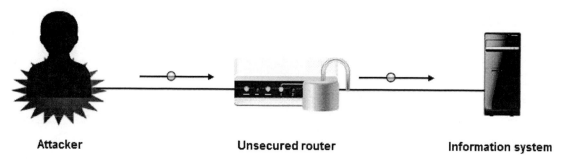

Attacker **Unsecured router** **Information system**

Figure 10-10: A system open to attack.

A device can still be vulnerable, even if there is no active threat against it.

There are vulnerability scanners that can help you automate security auditing. They scan your network and websites for thousands of different security risks. They generate a list of issues that should be patched, describe the vulnerabilities, and provide remediation steps. Some vulnerability scanners can automate the patching process.

Physical Security Threats and Vulnerabilities

Physical security threats and vulnerabilities can come from many different areas.

Threat/Vulnerability	Description
Internal	It is important to always consider what is happening inside an organization, especially when physical security is concerned. For example, disgruntled employees may be a source of physical sabotage of important network security-related resources.

Threat/Vulnerability	Description
External	It is impossible for any organization to fully control external security threats. For example, an external power failure is usually beyond a network technician's control because most organizations use a local power company as their source of electrical power. However, risks posed by external power failures may be mitigated by implementing devices such as an uninterruptible power supply (UPS) or a generator.
Natural	Although natural threats are easy to overlook, they can pose a significant risk to the physical security of a facility. Buildings and rooms that contain important computing assets should be protected against likely weather-related problems including tornadoes, hurricanes, snow storms, and floods.
Man-made	Whether intentional or accidental, people can cause a number of physical threats. Man-made threats can be internal or external. For example, a backhoe operator may accidentally dig up fiber optic cables and disable external network access. On the other hand, a disgruntled employee may choose to exact revenge by deliberately cutting fiber optic cables.

Environmental Threats and Vulnerabilities

Natural, environmental threats pose security risks and can be addressed with specific mitigation techniques.

Environmental Threat	Effects and Mitigations
Fire	Fire, whether natural or deliberately set, is a serious network environment security threat because it can destroy hardware and therefore the data contained in it. In addition, it is hazardous to people and systems. You need to ensure that key systems are installed in a fire-resistant facility, and that there are high-quality fire detection and suppression systems onsite so that the damage due to fire is reduced.
Hurricanes and tornadoes	Catastrophic weather events such as hurricanes and tornadoes are major network security threats due to the magnitude of the damage they can cause to hardware and data. You need to ensure that your information systems are well-contained and that your physical plant is built to appropriate codes and standards so that damage due to severe weather is reduced.
Flood	A flood is another major network security threat that can cause as much damage as fire can. Your organization should check the history of an area to see if you are in a flood plain before constructing your physical plant, and follow appropriate building codes as well as purchase flood insurance. When possible, construct the building so that the lowest floor is above flood level; this saves the systems when flooding does occur. Spatial planning together with protective planning in concurrence with building regulations and functional regulations are precautionary measures that should be looked into as well.
Extreme temperature	Extreme temperatures, especially heat, can cause some sensitive hardware components to melt and degrade, resulting in data loss. You can avoid this threat by implementing controls that keep the temperature in your data center within acceptable ranges.

Environmental Threat	Effects and Mitigations
Extreme humidity	Extreme humidity can cause device components, data storage media, and other devices to rust, deteriorate, and degrade, resulting in data loss. You can avoid this threat by ensuring that there is enough ventilation in your data centers and storage locations, and by using temperature and humidity controls and monitors.

Unnecessary Running Services

Services generally refer to programs that listen for and respond to network traffic, and some allow direct access to a device. So running a network service on a device provides a potential for communications with other devices. *Unnecessary running services* are services running on a device that are not necessary for its intended purpose or operation. Any service may be subject to software flaws or poor configurations that introduce security vulnerabilities. These services can be used to provide unauthorized access to a device.

Most operating system vendors have acknowledged the risk of unnecessary network services, and have configured their operating systems to have fewer unnecessary running services by default. These devices still can and do have services running that may not be needed. In addition to the operating system, some user-installed applications provide network services to communicate with other devices. Most often these are required, but some applications may enable services that are not required or may be configured improperly in regards to security.

Open Ports

An *open port* is a Transmission Control Protocol (TCP) or User Datagram Protocol (UDP) port number that is configured to accept packets. Services such as web pages or File Transfer Protocol (FTP) require their ports to be open on the server in order to be reachable. In order for a port to be considered open for security purposes, it needs to be unfiltered, which means it is reachable, and there needs to be an application actually listening on that port. If a port is unfiltered but there is no application listening on a port, incoming packets to that port will simply be rejected by the computer's operating system. Open ports can be used to gain unauthorized access to your devices.

Unpatched and Legacy Systems

An *unpatched system* is a current operating system (OS) that is supported by the manufacturer but does not have the latest security updates. A *legacy system* is a device running an older OS that is no longer supported by the manufacturer. Legacy systems are often kept in service because they support a legacy application that will not function properly on a newer OS. Both of these systems are security risks because native security features are either non-existent or have very well-known exploits that are difficult to defend against. In addition, legacy operating systems may no longer be supported by most security tools.

Unencrypted Channels

Unencrypted channels are connections in which the data being sent is not encrypted. An unencrypted channel uses one or more unsecure (unencrypted or unsigned) protocols to make a connection. Unencrypted data that is intercepted can be viewed by anyone who intercepts it. Transferring a file over FTP, basic authentication that sends authentication credentials in plaintext over Hypertext Transfer Protocol (HTTP), form-based authentication credentials sent via HTTP, or plaintext transmission of any other information over HTTP are examples of this.

Cleartext Credentials

Cleartext credentials are user passwords that are transmitted or stored unencrypted. This means that if anyone obtains the passwords they can be read as plain text. Examples of this are unencrypted passwords stored in a database, passwords sent via email, and passwords used over unencrypted channels.

Unsecure Protocols

Unsecure protocols are ones that expose data and/or credentials in cleartext. This allows the potential for the credentials or data to be viewed and captured by someone else.

- Telnet: Passes authentication and data by using cleartext.
- HTTP: Is subject to eavesdropping attacks that can let attackers gain access to website accounts and sensitive information.
- Serial Line Internet Protocol (SLIP): Passes authentication using cleartext.
- FTP: All authentication is done in cleartext, and data is sent in cleartext.
- Trivial File Transfer Protocol (TFTP): Even less secure than FTP because it does not require any authentication to the remote host by the user.
- Simple Network Management Protocol (SNMP) (v1 and v2): Authentication is done in cleartext.

Radio Frequency Emanation

Radio frequency emanation is where electronic equipment can emit unintentional radio signals, from which eavesdroppers may reconstruct processed data from a remote but nearby location. This allows someone with the proper equipment to use those radio signals to see what is being displayed on a monitor or other display.

TEMPEST is a National Security Agency (NSA) specification and North Atlantic Treaty Organization (NATO) certification referring to spying on information systems through leaking emanations, including unintentional radio or electrical signals, sounds, and vibrations. TEMPEST covers both methods to spy upon others and also how to shield equipment against such spying. The protection efforts are also known as emission security (EMSEC), which is a subset of communications security (COMSEC).

ACTIVITY 10–4
Discussing Vulnerabilities

Scenario

The network administrator at Greene City Interiors questions you on network vulnerabilities to see how well you understand the concept.

---

1. **What are applicable forms of vulnerabilities?**

   ☐   Improperly configured software

   ☐   Misuse of communication protocols

   ☐   Poor physical security

   ☐   Lengthy passwords with a mix of characters

2. **What are some examples of physical security vulnerabilities?**

3. **You suspect that one of your workstations has been compromised by an external entity. What are some vulnerabilities you should examine to see if they are allowing external connections?**

   ☐   Open ports

   ☐   Permissions

   ☐   Unpatched system

   ☐   Unnecessary running services

4. **Describe some situations in which user credentials could be viewed as cleartext.**

TOPIC C

Threats and Attacks

In the previous topic, you identified network vulnerabilities. Security is an ongoing process that includes setting up organizational security systems, hardening them, monitoring them, responding to attacks in progress, and deterring attackers. In this topic, you will identify the various types of security threats and vulnerabilities that you might encounter.

Unsecured devices can result in compromised data and, ultimately, lost revenue. But you cannot protect devices from threats you do not understand. Once you understand the types of possible threats and identify individuals who will try to use them against your network, you can take the appropriate steps to protect your network and keep your resources and revenue safe from potential attacks.

Threats

In the realm of information security, a *threat* is any event or action that could potentially result in the violation of a security requirement, policy, or procedure. Regardless of whether a violation is intentional or unintentional, malicious or not, it is considered a threat. Potential threats to device and network security include:

- Unintentional or unauthorized access or changes to data.
- Interruption of services.
- Interruption of access to assets.
- Damage to hardware.
- Unauthorized access or damage to facilities.

An email containing sensitive information that is mistakenly sent to the wrong person would be considered a potential threat, even though the misdirection of the information was not intentional.

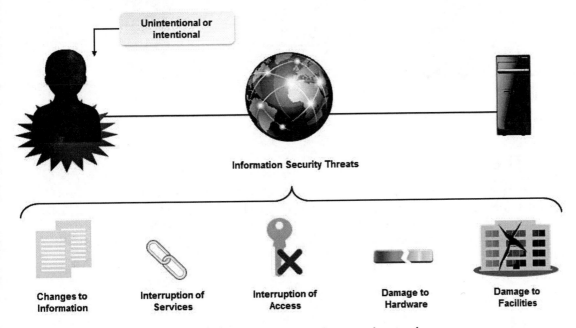

Figure 10-11: Threats cause a violation of security policies and procedures.

Attacks

In the realm of information security, an *attack* is a technique that is used to exploit a vulnerability in any application on a device without the authorization to do so. Attacks on devices and networks include:

- Physical security attacks
- Network-based attacks
- Software-based attacks
- Social engineering attacks
- Web application-based attacks

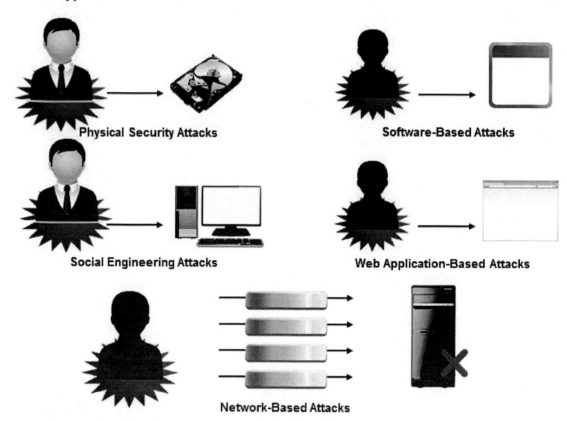

Figure 10–12: Types of attacks.

Data Theft

Data theft is a type of attack in which an attacker uses unauthorized access to obtain protected network information. The attacker can use stolen credentials to authenticate to a server and read data stored in files. Or, the attacker can steal data in transit on the network media by using a hardware- or software-based *packet sniffer*, which is a device or program that monitors network communications and captures data.

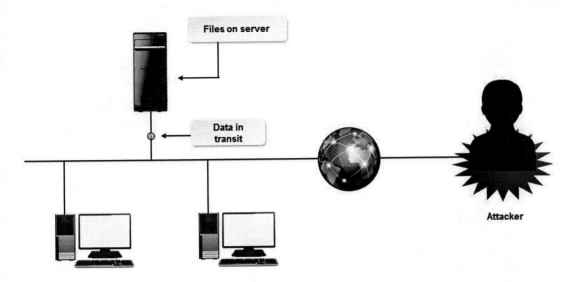

Figure 10-13: An unauthorized user obtaining protected network information.

An equivalent term that is used in the industry is *data exfiltration*.

Social Engineering Attacks

A *social engineering attack* is a type of attack that uses deception and trickery to convince unsuspecting users to provide sensitive data or to violate security guidelines. Social engineering is often a precursor to another type of attack. Because these attacks depend on human factors rather than on technology, their symptoms can be vague and hard to identify. Social engineering attacks can come in a variety of methods: in person, through email, or over the phone.

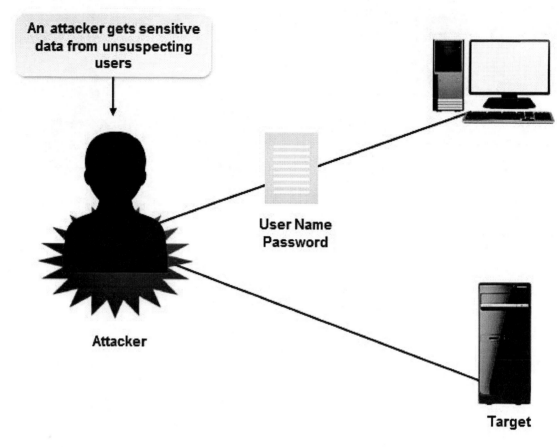

Figure 10-14: A social engineering attack using the obtained password.

These are a few typical social engineering attack scenarios:

- An attacker creates an executable program file (for example, a file that has a VBS or EXE file extension) that prompts a network user for his user name and password. The attacker then emails the executable file to the user with the story that the user must double-click the file and log on to the network again to clear up some logon problems the organization has been experiencing.
- An attacker contacts a help desk pretending to be a remote sales representative who needs assistance setting up his dial-in access. Through a series of phone calls, the attacker obtains the phone number for remote access and the phone number for accessing the organization's private phone and voice-mail system.
- An attacker sends an executable file disguised as an electronic greeting card (e-card) or as a patch for an operating system or a specific application. The unsuspecting user launches the executable, which might install email spamming software or a key-logging program, or turn the device into a remote "zombie" for the hacker.

Social engineering typically takes advantage of users who are not technically knowledgeable, but it can also be directed against technical support staff if the attacker pretends to be a user who needs help.

 Note: For additional information, check out the LearnTO **Recognize Social Engineering Attacks** presentation in the LearnTOs for this course on your LogicalCHOICE Course screen.

Types of Social Engineering Attacks

Hackers use various types of social engineering attacks.

Social Engineering Type	Description
Spoofing	This is a human- or software-based attack in which the goal is to pretend to be someone else for the purpose of concealing their identity. Spoofing can occur by using IP addresses, a network adapter's hardware media access control (MAC) addresses, and email. If used in email, various email message headers are changed to conceal the originator's identity.
Impersonation	This is a human-based attack in which an attacker pretends to be someone he is not. A common scenario is when the attacker calls an employee and pretends to be calling from the help desk. The attacker tells the employee he is reprogramming the order-entry database, and he needs the employee's user name and password to make sure it gets entered into the new system.
Phishing	This is a common type of email-based social engineering attack. In a phishing attack, the attacker sends an email message that seems to come from a respected bank or other financial institution. The message claims that the recipient needs to provide an account number, Social Security number, or other private information to the sender in order to "verify an account." Ironically, the phishing attack often claims that the "account verification" is necessary for security reasons. Individuals should never provide personal financial information to someone who requests it, whether through email or over the phone. Legitimate financial institutions never solicit this information from their clients. A similar form of phishing called *pharming* can be done by redirecting a request for a website, typically an e-commerce site, to a similar-looking, but fake, website.
Vishing	This is a human-based attack for which the goal is to extract personal, financial, or confidential information from the victim by using services such as the telephone system and IP-based voice messaging services such as VoIP as the communication medium. The term "vishing" is a shortened form of "voice phishing."
Whaling	This is a form of phishing that targets individuals who are known to be upper-level executives or other high-profile employees. It is also known as *spear phishing*. Whaling attacks are well-researched attempts to access sensitive information and often resemble a legal subpoena, customer complaint, or executive issue. The content is meant to be tailored for upper management, and usually involves an alleged company-wide concern. Like phishing messages, spear phishing and whaling attacks try to convince the target to access malicious content such as a hyperlink, file, or attachment.
Spam and *spim*	Spam is an email-based threat in which the user's inbox is flooded with email messages that act as vehicles carrying advertising material for products or promotions for get-rich-quick schemes and can sometimes deliver viruses or malware. Spam can also be used within social networking sites such as Facebook and Twitter. Spim is an IM-based attack similar to spam that is propagated through instant messaging instead of through email.

Social Engineering Type	Description
Hoax	A hoax is any type of incorrect or misleading information that is disseminated to multiple users through unofficial channels. Hoaxes can be relatively benign, such as an email message containing misinformation about historical facts. However, hoaxes often improperly alert users to the existence of unsubstantiated virus threats.
	Users then react in two ways: first, by widely disseminating the hoax email, clogging communications systems, and possibly triggering a Denial of Service (DoS) condition. Second, users react by following instructions in the hoax that direct them to defend or secure their devices in an improper or unapproved manner. The hoax email might, for example, use social engineering methods that direct users to delete legitimate files, or to go to websites and download files that might themselves contain actual viruses.

Note: A well-known website that deals with hoaxes and urban legends is **www.snopes.com**.

Insider Threats

An *insider threat* is a malicious employee who in some fashion compromises your network or uses his or her access to obtain sensitive company information. Because the employee is inside the company network, many security controls meant to keep out threats can be bypassed. Data breaches and thefts are the most common result of a malicious employee, but they can also do damage by deleting or modifying data, damaging physical equipment, or otherwise compromising the network.

Malware Attacks

Malware is malicious code, such as that contained in viruses, Trojans, or worms, that is designed to gain unauthorized access to, make unauthorized use of, or damage computing devices and networks.

A *malware attack* is a type of software attack in which an attacker inserts some type of undesired or unauthorized software into a target device. In the past, many malware attacks were intended to disrupt or disable an operating system or an application, or force the target system to disrupt or disable other devices. More recent malware attacks attempt to remain hidden on the target device, using available resources to the attacker's advantage.

Potential uses of malware include launching DoS attacks on other systems; hosting illicit or illegal data; skimming personal or business information for the purposes of identity theft, profit, or extortion; or displaying unsolicited advertisements.

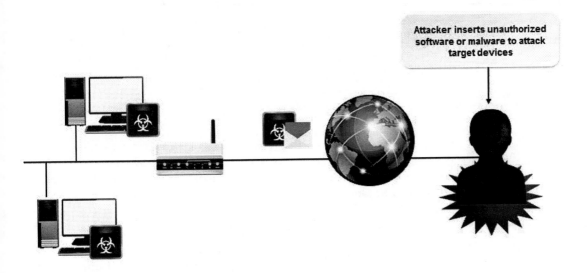

Figure 10-15: A malware attack.

Virus attacks are the most well-known type of malware attacks.

Malware is often combined with social engineering to convince a user that the malware is from a trusted or benign source. Typically, you will see the results of malware in corrupted applications, data files, and system files, unsolicited pop-up advertisements, counterfeit virus scan or software update notifications, or reduced performance or increased network traffic. Any of these could result in malfunctioning applications and operating systems.

Types of Malware Attacks

Hackers launch several major types of malware attacks to target a device. The exact method that is used to get malicious code onto a device varies by attacker and attack type.

Malware Type	Description
Virus	A sample of code that spreads from one computer to another by attaching itself to other files. The code in a virus executes when the file it is attached to is opened. Frequently, viruses are intended to enable further attacks, send data back to the attacker, or even corrupt or destroy data.
Worm	A piece of code that spreads from one device to another on its own, not by attaching itself to another file. Like a virus, a worm can enable further attacks, transmit data, or corrupt or erase files.
Trojan horse	An insidious type of malware that is itself a software attack and can pave the way for a number of other types of attacks. There is a social engineering component to a Trojan horse attack because the user has to be fooled into executing it.
Logic bomb	A piece of code that sits dormant on a target device until it is triggered by a specific event, such as a specific date. Once the code is triggered, the logic bomb "detonates," and performs whatever actions it was programed to do. Often, this includes erasing and corrupting data on the target device.

Malware Type	Description
Spyware	Surreptitiously installed malicious software that is intended to track and report on the usage of a target device, or collect other data the author wishes to obtain. Data collected can include web browsing history, personal information, banking and other financial information, and user names and passwords.
Adware	Software that automatically displays or downloads advertisements when it is used. While not all adware is malicious, many adware programs have been associated with spyware and other types of malicious software. Also, it can reduce user productivity by slowing down devices and simply by creating annoyances.
Rootkit	Code that is intended to take full or partial control of a device at the lowest levels. Rootkits often attempt to hide themselves from monitoring or detection, and modify low-level system files when integrating themselves into a device. Rootkits can be used for non-malicious purposes such as virtualization; however, most rootkit infections install backdoors, spyware, or other malicious code once they have control of the target device.
Botnet	A set of devices that have been infected by a control program called a bot that enables attackers to exploit them and mount attacks. Typically, black hats use botnets for Distributed Denial of Service, or DDoS attacks, sending spam email, and mining for personal information or passwords.

A *software attack* is any attack against software resources including operating systems, applications, protocols, and files. The goal of a software attack is to disrupt or disable the software running on the target device, or to somehow exploit the target to gain access to it, to other systems, or to a network. Many software attacks are designed to surreptitiously gain control of a device so that the attacker can use that device in the future, often for profit or for further malicious activity.

 Note: Black hats also use spam to deliver malware.

Grayware

Spyware and adware are often referred to as *grayware* because there is a possibility that these programs are not actually malicious in nature. Some security tools identify them during scans as potentially unwanted programs (PUPs). If a program is installed without user consent (along with other malware, for example), it is considered malware. If it is installed along with some other legitimate program, and is disclosed in the End User License Agreement (EULA), it is not technically malware.

Types of Viruses

Viruses can be categorized into several types.

Virus Type	Description
Boot sector	Infects any disk-based media. Writes itself into the boot sector of the disk. When a system attempts to boot from the disk, the virus is moved onto the system. Once on the system, the virus attempts to move itself to every disk placed in the system.

Virus Type	Description
Macro	A macro is a group of application-specific instructions that execute within a specific application. A macro virus uses other programs' macro engines to propagate. True macro viruses do not actually infect files or data, but attach themselves to the file's template, document, or macro code. Microsoft Office® products have been popular targets for macro viruses.
Mailer and mass mailer	A mailer virus sends itself to other users through the email system. It simply rides along with any email that is sent. A mass mailer virus searches the email system for mailing lists and sends itself to all users on the list. Often, the virus does not have a payload; its purpose is to disrupt the email system by swamping it with mail messages in the form of a DoS attack.
Polymorphic	This type of virus can change as it moves around, acting differently on different systems. It can sometimes even change the virus code, making it harder to detect.
Script	A small program that runs code by using the Windows scripting host on Windows operating systems. It is written as a script in Visual Basic® or JavaScript® and executes when the script runs. Scripts are often distributed by email and require a user to open them.
Stealth	A stealth virus moves and attempts to conceal itself until it can propagate. After that, it drops its payload.

 Note: See **http://support.microsoft.com/kb/211607/en-us** for more information on macro viruses in Microsoft products.

Viruses are an insidious threat because of their ability to replicate themselves and thus spread to multiple devices. Viruses can use different propagation methods:

- A virus on a hard disk can attach itself to removable media including flash drives, removable hard drives, and multimedia devices, which are then shared.
- A virus on the Internet can attach itself to a file. When a user downloads and runs the file, the virus is activated.
- A virus can attach to email. When a user opens or runs the attachment, the virus is activated.

Effect of Malware on the Network

Malware can have various effects on your network:

- May be used to gather data from your network.
- May cause your network connections to slow down.
- May cause your devices to slow down or crash.
- May be invisible, having no noticeable effect and running undetected if well written.
- May cause your devices to display error messages continually.
- May hijack browsers to redirect users to sites for its purposes.
- May infect your devices and use them as a server to broadcast various files or attacks.
- May cause your devices to be incapable of shutting down or restarting, as it keeps certain processes active.
- May send spam through and to user inboxes.
- May create and send email that users did not write.
- May give an attacker control of your devices and your resources.

Compromised Systems

A *compromised system* is a device that has been infected by malware or otherwise controlled by an outside entity. Due to the nature of malware, once one device is compromised, it may very well infect other devices. Compromised systems can be difficult to clean to fully remove the malware.

Buffer Overflows

Buffer overflow is an attack that targets system vulnerability to cause the device operating system to crash or reboot, and may result in loss of data or execute rogue code on devices. Buffer overflow attacks typically target desktop and server applications; however, it is also possible for applications on wireless devices to be vulnerable to buffer overflows.

A buffer overflow takes advantage of inherent weaknesses in the programming language that Linux® and Windows operating systems are created from. When programmers do not put good input controls in their code, malicious software can inject too much input, causing the service or application to run out of its allocated memory, or buffer. As the compromised system pushes out the legitimate code to make room for the malicious code, the malicious code can then inject payloads that run at system or service level privilege. Common malicious payloads include opening a network connection back to the attacker, and spawning a shell (opening a command prompt) to await the attacker's command. This gives the attacker complete control over the compromised system. Usually, the attack does not appear in system logs. Its only indicator is unusual activity from the device and instability of the service or application that has been compromised.

Any variant of the C programming language is susceptible to buffer overflows including C, C++, C#, and Objective-C. Buffer overflows are not limited to operating systems. Applications from nearly every vendor are susceptible to buffer overflows as well. Java is resistant to buffer overflows, but it can happen in unusual circumstances.

Password Attacks

A *password attack* is any type of attack in which the attacker attempts to obtain and make use of passwords illegitimately. The attacker can guess or steal passwords, or crack encrypted password files. A password attack can show up in audit logs as repeatedly failed logons and then a successful logon, or as several successful logon attempts at unusual times or locations.

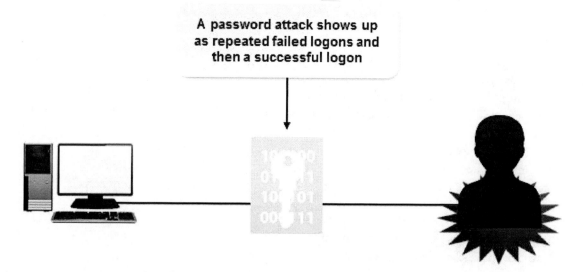

A password attack shows up as repeated failed logons and then a successful logon

Figure 10–16: Attacker guesses the password to gain network access.

Attackers know the storage locations of encrypted passwords on common systems, such as the Security Accounts Manager (SAM) database on standalone Windows systems. Password-cracking tools take advantage of known weaknesses in the security of these password databases, so security might need to be increased.

Types of Password Attacks

Hackers use several common categories of password attacks. Creating complex passwords can increase the amount of time it takes for an attack to succeed.

Password Attack Type	Description
Guessing	A *guessing attack* is the simplest type of password attack and involves an individual making repeated attempts to guess a password by entering different common password values, such as the user's name, a spouse's name, or a significant date. Most operating systems have a feature that will lock out an account after a specified number of incorrect password attempts, except for default Administrator accounts, which never lock.
Stealing	Passwords can be stolen by various means, including sniffing network communications, reading handwritten password notes, or observing a user in the act of entering the password.
Dictionary attack	A *dictionary attack* automates password guessing by comparing encrypted passwords against a predetermined list of possible password values. Dictionary attacks are successful against only fairly simple and obvious passwords, because they rely on a dictionary of common words and predictable variations, such as adding a single digit to the end of a word.
Brute-force attack	In a *brute-force attack*, the attacker uses password-cracking software to attempt every possible alphanumeric password combination. Such an attack might be used when it is not possible to take advantage of other weaknesses. When password guessing, this method is very fast when used on short passwords, but for longer passwords it takes much longer. When key guessing, the key length used in the cipher determines the practical feasibility of performing a brute-force attack, with longer keys exponentially more difficult to crack than shorter ones.
Hybrid password attack	A *hybrid password attack* uses multiple attack vectors including dictionary, brute-force, and other attack methodologies when trying to crack a password.

Network Sniffing

In network sniffing, an attacker places a sniffer on a network segment where there may be interesting traffic. The sniffer is typically a computer or wireless device with a network interface configured to capture all traffic that flows past the device. The device eavesdrops on conversations between other nodes, such as clients and servers. Depending on the sniffer software being used, the attacker can perform many types of unauthorized activities including reading emails, capturing copies of files, and collecting usernames and passwords.

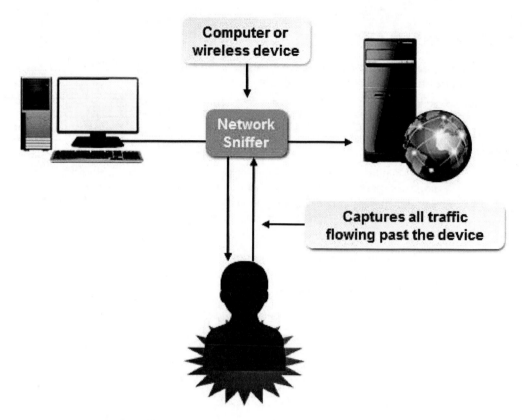

Figure 10-17: Network sniffing.

Packet sniffing is also used as a precursor to session hijacking and man-in-the-middle attacks. Like a spy planting a bug in a room to listen in on people's conversations, the attacker must place a sniffer along the traffic path for it to be effective. If it is not possible to plug a sniffer into a server's switch port, additional software can be used to spoof the switch into repeating server traffic out a second port, which the sniffer can then capture.

Packet sniffing can also be used for benign purposes such as traffic analysis and intrusion detection.

Packet and Protocol Abuse

Most of the original protocols from the TCP/IP stack, which are still used, have no built-in security, and can be abused in some way. The main abuse for a packet or protocol is when a hacking tool is used to specially craft the packet in a way that the protocol never intended. Some examples of this include:

- Spoofing the source address of an IP packet, UDP datagram, or SMTP payload to evade a firewall, intrusion detection, or a spam filter.
- Fragmenting an IP packet in a way that it cannot be reassembled, thus causing a DoS attack on the receiver.
- Monitoring the rate of TCP sequence number increases between client and server to be able to hijack the session and impersonate the client.
- Hiding a malicious payload inside of an Internet Control Message Protocol (ICMP) echo request (ping) to evade a firewall or intrusion detection.

IP Spoofing Attacks

An *IP spoofing attack* is a type of software attack in which an attacker creates IP packets with a forged source IP address and uses those packets to gain access to a remote device. One sign of an IP spoofing attack is a network packet from an external source that appears to have an internal source address.

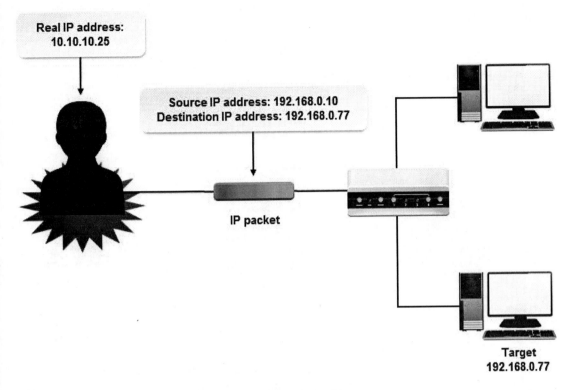

Figure 10-18: An IP spoofing attack using a forged IP address.

Consider this example: An attacker wants to access a UNIX host with an IP address of 192.168.0.77 and an application that authenticates only hosts with 192.168.0.x addresses. If the attacker's IP address is 10.10.10.25, the application will not authorize packets from this source. So the attacker creates IP packets with the forged source IP address of 192.168.0.10 and sends those packets to the UNIX host. Because the network's border router has not been configured to reject packets from outside the network with internal IP addresses, the router forwards the packets to the UNIX host, where the attacker is authenticated and given access to the system.

The term "spoofing" can also be used to describe any situation in which the source of network information is forged to appear legitimate. For example, the common social engineering technique of phishing uses forged email to try to persuade users to respond with private information.

IP spoofing attacks take advantage of:

- Applications and services that authenticate based on the IP address
- Devices that run Sun RPC (Remote Procedure Call) or X Windows, the GUI system in UNIX systems
- Services that have been secured by using TCP wrappers
- Legacy technologies such as NFS and UNIX "r" commands such as rlogin
- Routers that have not been configured to drop incoming external packets with internal IP addresses as source addresses

DoS Attacks

A Denial of Service *(DoS) attack* is a type of network attack in which an attacker attempts to disrupt or disable devices that provide network services, including:

- Flooding a network link with data to consume all available bandwidth.
- Sending data designed to exploit known flaws in an application.

- Sending multiple service requests to consume a device's resources.
- Flooding a user's email inbox with spam messages so genuine messages bounce back to the sender.

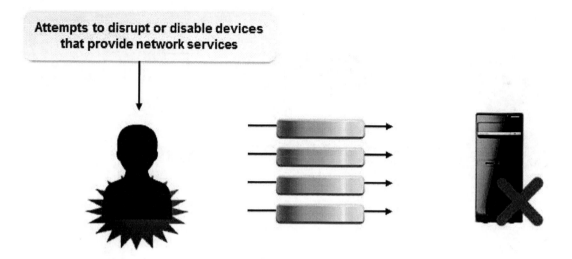

Attempts to disrupt or disable devices that provide network services

Figure 10-19: DoS attacks on a server consuming all its resources.

The attack can target any service or network device, but is usually mounted against servers or routers, preventing them from responding to legitimate network requests. A DoS attack can also be caused by something as simple as disconnecting a network cable.

Types of DoS Attacks

There are several types of DoS attacks. The main categories of these attacks are:

- DDoS, or Distributed Denial of Service.
- Reflective or amplified DoS.
- Friendly or unintentional DoS.
- Physical attack or permanent DoS.

A *Distributed Denial of Service (DDoS) attack* is a type of DoS attack that uses multiple devices on disparate networks to launch the coordinated attack from many simultaneous sources. These can sometimes be difficult to differentiate from traffic spikes when they first begin. The attacker introduces unauthorized software called a *zombie* or *drone* that directs the devices to launch the attack. A botnet is a collection of Internet-connected programs communicating with other similar programs in order to perform tasks that can be used to send spam email or participate in DDoS attacks.

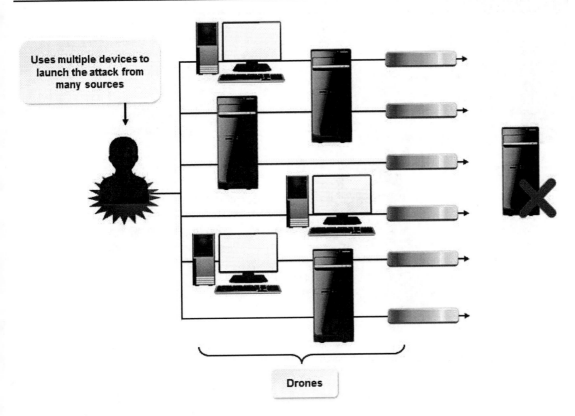

Figure 10-20: DDoS attacks using drones.

A *reflective DoS* attack involves sending forged requests of some type to a very large number of devices that will reply to the requests. Using Internet Protocol address spoofing, the source address is set to that of the targeted victim, which means all the replies will go and flood the target.

ICMP echo request attacks (smurf attacks) can be considered one form of reflected attack, as the flooding hosts send echo requests to the broadcast addresses of misconfigured networks, thereby enticing hosts to send echo reply packets to the victim.

Domain Name Service (DNS) amplification attacks involve a new mechanism that increased the amplification effect, using a much larger list of DNS servers than seen earlier. SNMP and NTP can also be exploited as a reflector in an amplification attack.

A *friendly DoS* attack is a situation in which a website ends up denied because of a sudden enormous spike in popularity. This can happen when an extremely popular website posts a prominent link to a second, less well-prepared site, for example, as part of a news story.

A *permanent DoS* is an attack that damages a system so badly that it requires replacement or reinstallation of hardware. A permanent DoS attack exploits security flaws that allow remote administration on the management interfaces of the victim's hardware, such as routers, printers, or other networking hardware. The attacker uses these vulnerabilities to replace a device's firmware with a modified, corrupt, or defective firmware image.

Man-in-the-Middle Attacks

A *man-in-the-middle attack* is a form of eavesdropping in which the attacker makes an independent connection between two victims (two clients or a client and a server) and relays information between the two victims as if they are directly talking to each other over a closed connection, when in reality the attacker is controlling the information that travels between the two victims. During the process, the attacker can view or steal information to use it fraudulently.

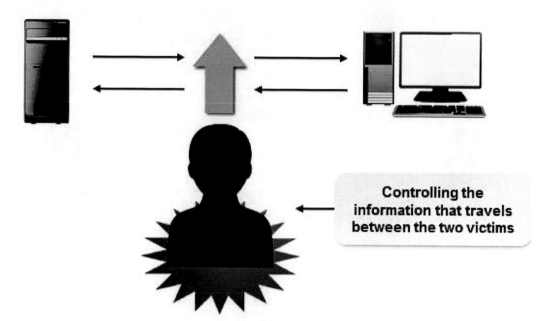

Figure 10-21: A man-in-the-middle attack.

In a typical man-in-the-middle attack, the attacker sets up a host on a network with IP forwarding enabled and a network-monitoring utility installed to capture and analyze packets. After analyzing network traffic to determine which server would make an attractive target:

1. The attacker intercepts packets from a legitimate client that are destined for the server.
2. The attacker's computer sends a fake reply to the client.
3. The attacker's computer forwards a fake packet to the server, which is modified so the attacker's computer looks like the original sender.
4. The server replies to the attacker's computer.
5. The attacker's computer replies to the server as if it were the original client.
6. The attacker stores any valuable information contained in the packets, such as sensitive data or user credentials, for use in future attacks.

Man-in-the-middle attacks are used to gain access to authentication and network infrastructure information for future attacks, or to gain direct access to packet contents. Generally, there will be no signs that a man-in-the-middle attack is in progress or has just taken place.

An *eavesdropping attack* or *sniffing attack* uses special monitoring software to intercept private network communications, either to steal the content of the communication itself or to obtain user names and passwords for future software attacks. Attackers can eavesdrop on both wired and wireless network communications. On a wired network, the attacker must have physical access to the network or tap in to the network cable. On a wireless network, an attacker needs a device capable of receiving signals from the wireless network. Eavesdropping is very hard to detect, unless you spot an unknown device leasing an IP address from a Dynamic Host Configuration Protocol (DHCP) server.

Many utilities are available that will monitor and capture network traffic. Some of these tools can sniff only the traffic that is sent to or received by the device on which they are installed. Other tools are capable of scaling up to scan very large corporate networks. Examples of these tools include: Wireshark®, the Microsoft Network Monitor Capture utility, tcpdump, and dsniff.

Session Hijacking Attacks

A *session hijacking attack* is a type of man-in-the-middle attack that involves exploiting a session to obtain unauthorized access to an organization's network or services. It involves stealing an active session cookie that is used to authenticate a user to a server and controlling the session. Session hijacking attacks also initiate denial of service to either the client's device or the server, or both.

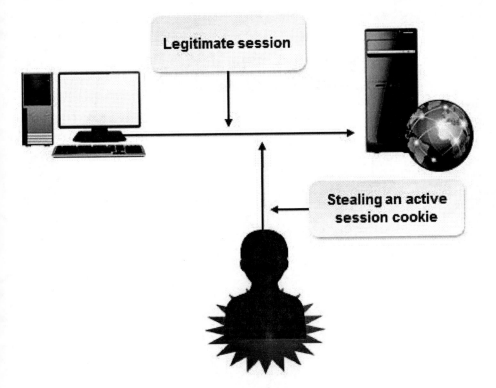

Figure 10-22: An attacker hijacking the session.

Port Scanning Attacks

A *port scanning attack* is a type of network attack in which a potential attacker scans the devices that are connected to the Internet or other networks to see which TCP and UDP ports are listening and which services are active. Port scans can be easily automated, so almost any device on the Internet will be scanned almost constantly. Some monitoring software can detect port scans, or they might happen without your knowledge.

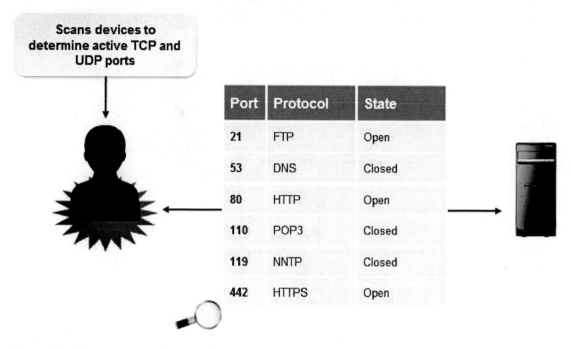

Port	Protocol	State
21	FTP	Open
53	DNS	Closed
80	HTTP	Open
110	POP3	Closed
119	NNTP	Closed
442	HTTPS	Open

Figure 10–23: A port scanning attack.

There are many utilities available that potential attackers can use to scan ports on networks, including Nmap, SuperScan, and Strobe. Many utilities can be downloaded for free from the Internet. Performing port scanning attacks is often the first step an attacker takes to identify live devices and open ports to launch further attacks with other tools.

The Xmas Scan is available on popular port scanners such as Nmap. It is used mainly to check which devices are alive or reachable, and subsequently what ports are open or responding, so that those devices or ports can be used as an avenue for a follow-up attack. The type of port scanning attack uses an Xmas packet with all flags turned on in the TCP header of the packet. The name "Xmas" refers to all flags being "on" (like lights) and so a packet is "lit up like a Christmas tree."

This scan is commonly known as a stealth scan due to its ability to hide the scan in progress, and to pass undetected through some popular firewalls, intrusion detection systems (IDSs), and other systems. However, most modern-day intrusion prevention systems (IPSs) can detect this type of scan.

Replay Attacks

A *replay attack* is a network attack in which an attacker captures network traffic and stores it for retransmitting at a later time to gain unauthorized access to a specific host or a network. This attack is particularly successful when an attacker captures packets that contain user names, passwords, or other authentication data. In most cases, replay attacks are never discovered.

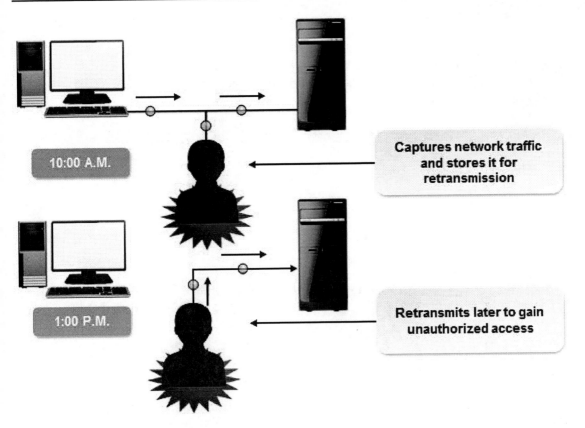

Figure 10–24: A replay attack.

Most web cracking exploits involve some form of replay attack to trick the wireless access point into revealing initialization vectors (IVs) that can lead to cracking the Wired Equivalent Privacy (WEP) key. This is possible because WEP uses a shared key and if it is ever used twice, then attackers can discover what the key is. WEP uses a 24-bit IV in each message packet to help avoid this. The RC4 key for that packet is the IV concatenated with the WEP key. The 24-bit IV only allows a little under 17 million possibilities. Therefore it is likely that for every 4,096 packets, 2 will share the same IV and hence the same RC4 key, allowing the packets to be attacked.

FTP Bounce Attacks

An *FTP bounce attack* targets the FTP vulnerability that permits connected clients to open other connections on any port on the FTP server. A user with an anonymous FTP connection can attack other systems by opening a service port on the third system and sending commands to that service.

Most FTP servers have been patched against FTP bounce attacks.

ARP Cache Poisoning Attacks

ARP cache poisoning occurs when an attacker redirects an IP address to the MAC address of a device that is not the intended recipient. Before the attack can begin, the attacker must gain access to the target network. Once the attacker has gained access to the network, he or she can poison the Address Resolution Protocol (ARP) cache on the target devices by redirecting selected IP addresses to MAC addresses that the attacker chooses. At this point, the attacker could choose to capture and/or alter network traffic before forwarding it to the correct destination, or create a denial of service condition by pointing the selected IP address at a nonexistent MAC address.

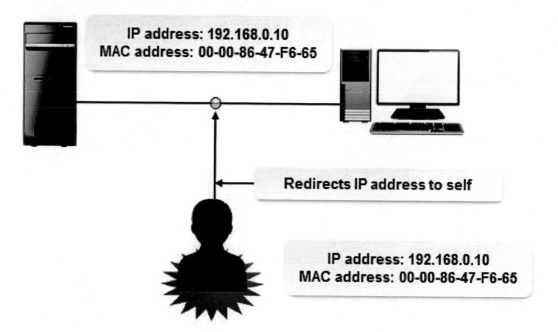

Figure 10-25: An ARP cache poisoning attack.

A common implementation of ARP cache poisoning is to poison the ARP cache of a switch. In this attack, the attacker sends frames with spoofed MAC addresses to the switch so that the switch will repeat traffic between a client and server out the port that the hacker is connected to.

VLAN Hopping

VLAN hopping is a method of attack in which an attacking host on a VLAN gains access to traffic on other VLANs that would normally not be accessible. There are two primary methods of VLAN hopping: switch spoofing and double tagging.

A switch spoofing attack is where an attacking host imitates a trunking switch by speaking the tagging and trunking protocols used in maintaining a VLAN. Traffic for multiple VLANs is then accessible to the attacking host.

A double tagging attack is where an attacking host connected on a 802.1q interface prepends two VLAN tags to packets that it transmits. The packet is forwarded without the first tag, because it is the native VLAN. The second (false) tag is then visible to the second switch that the packet encounters. This false VLAN tag indicates that the packet is destined for a target host on a second switch. The packet is then sent to the target host as though it originated on the target VLAN, bypassing the network mechanisms that logically isolate VLANs from one another.

Zero Day Attacks

A *zero day attack* is an attack that exploits a previously unknown vulnerability in an application or operating system. In such a situation, developers have not had time to address the vulnerability and patch it. It is called a "zero day" because the developer has had zero days to fix the flaw.

Wireless Threats and Attacks

Wireless networks have an increasing number of specific threats and associated attacks.

Wireless Threat/ Attack	Description
Evil twins	These are rogue access points on a network that appear to be legitimate. Although they can be installed both on corporate or private networks, typically they are found in public Wi-Fi hotspots where users do not connect transparently and automatically as they do in a corporate network, but rather select available networks from a list.
	Evil twins can be more dangerous than other rogue access points because the user thinks that the wireless signal is genuine, making it difficult to differentiate from a valid access point with the same name.
Rogue access point	This is an unauthorized wireless access point on a corporate or private network. Rogue access points can cause considerable damage to an organization's data. They are not detected easily, and can allow private network access to many unauthorized users with the proper devices. A rogue access point can allow man-in-the-middle attacks and access to private information. Organizations should protect themselves from this type of attack by implementing techniques to constantly monitor the system, such as installing an IPS.
War driving	The act of searching for instances of wireless networks by using wireless tracking devices such as tablets, mobile phones, or laptops. It locates wireless access points while traveling, which can be exploited to obtain unauthorized Internet access and potentially steal data. This process can be automated by using a GPS device and war driving software.
	Common tools that are used for war driving and war chalking include NetStumbler, Kismet, Aircrack, and Airsnort.
War chalking	The act of using symbols to mark off a sidewalk or wall to indicate that there is an open wireless network that may be offering Internet access.

> **Note:** In the terms "war driving" and "war chalking," *war* stands for wireless access receiver.

Bluejacking	This is a method used by attackers to send out unwanted Bluetooth® signals from tablets, mobile phones, and laptops to other Bluetooth-enabled devices. Because Bluetooth has a 30-foot transmission limit, this is a very close-range attack. With the advanced technology available today, attackers can send out unsolicited messages along with images and video.
	These types of signals can lead to many different types of threats. They can lead to device malfunctions, or even propagate viruses, including Trojan horses. Users should reject anonymous contacts and configure their mobile devices to the non-discoverable mode.
Bluesnarfing	This is a method in which attackers gain access to unauthorized information on a wireless device by using a Bluetooth connection within the 30-foot Bluetooth transmission limit. Unlike bluejacking, access to wireless devices such as tablets, mobile phones, and laptops by bluesnarfing can lead to the exploitation of private information including email messages, contact information, calendar entries, images, videos, and any data stored on the device.
WEP, WPA, and WPS cracking	The method used to crack the encryption keys used in WEP, WPA, and WPS installations to gain access to private wireless networks. There are many tools available that can aid attackers in cracking encryption keys, such as Aircrack.

Wireless Threat/ Attack	Description
IV attack	In this attack, the attacker is able to predict or control the *initialization vector (IV)* of an encryption process. An IV is an unpredictable random number used to make sure that when the same message is encrypted twice, the ciphertext is always different. While it is used in many cryptosystems, its implementation in wireless WEP encryption is weak. It is fairly easy, using automated tools and a replay attack, to extract enough IV data to crack the WEP key in just a few minutes. This gives the attacker the ability to connect to a WEP-encrypted wireless network along with all the other clients.
Packet sniffing	An attack on a network where an attacker captures network traffic, allowing data to be extracted from the packets. On a wireless network, a sniffer can be used not only to monitor transmitted data, but also to identify the SSID of a wireless network even if that network's SSID broadcast is disabled.

 Note: For additional information, check out the LearnTO **Recognize Threats, Risks, and Vulnerabilities** presentation in the LearnTOs for this course on your LogicalCHOICE Course screen.

ACTIVITY 10–5
Discussing Threats and Attacks

Scenario

The network administrator at Greene City Interiors describes different threats and attacks and asks you to identify them.

---

1. John is given a laptop for official use and is on a business trip. When he arrives at his hotel, he turns on his laptop and finds a wireless access point with the name of the hotel, which he connects to for sending official communications. He may become a victim of which wireless threat?

   ○ Interference

   ○ War driving

   ○ Bluesnarfing

   ○ Rogue access point

2. A new administrator in your company is in the process of installing a new wireless device. He is called away to attend an urgent meeting before he can secure the wireless network, and without realizing it, he forgot to switch the device off. A person with a mobile device who is passing the building takes advantage of the open network and hacks it. Your company may become vulnerable to which type of wireless threat?

   ○ Interference

   ○ War driving

   ○ Bluesnarfing

   ○ Rogue access point

3. A disgruntled employee copies sensitive company information to a USB drive with the intention of putting it on the Internet. This threat is which of the following?

   ☐ Insider threat

   ☐ External threat

   ☐ Data theft

   ☐ False alarm

4. What are the reasons why a hoax is dangerous?

   ☐ The hoax is an actual virus that has the potential to cause damage.

   ☐ Propagation of the hoax can create DoS conditions.

   ☐ Users are annoyed by the hoax.

   ☐ The hoax can include elements of a social engineering attack.

5. Social engineering attempt or false alarm? A supposed customer calls the help desk and states that she cannot connect to the e-commerce website to check her order status. She would also like a user name and password. The user gives a valid customer company name, but is not listed as a contact in the customer database. The user does not know the correct company code or customer ID.

   ☐ Social engineering attempt

   ☐ False alarm

6. Social engineering attempt or false alarm? A new accountant was hired and would like to know if he can have the installation source files for the accounting software package so that he can install it on his device himself and start work immediately. Last year, someone internal compromised company accounting records, so distribution of the accounting application is tightly controlled. You have received all the proper documentation for the request from his supervisor and there is an available license for the software. However, general IT policies state that the IT department must perform all software installations and upgrades.

☐ Social engineering attempt

☐ False alarm

7. While you are connected to another host on your network, the connection is suddenly dropped. When you review the logs at the other host, it appears as if the connection is still active. This could be a(n):

○ IP spoofing attack

○ DoS attack

○ Man-in-the-middle attack

○ Session hijacking attack

8. Response time on the website that hosts the online version of your product catalog is getting slower and slower. Customers are complaining that they cannot browse the catalog items or search for products. What type of attack do you suspect?

○ A Trojan horse attack

○ A spoofing attack

○ A social engineering attack

○ A DoS attack

9. The network administrator at your organization analyzes a network trace capture file and discovers that packets have been intercepted and retransmitted to both a sender and a receiver during an active session. This could be a(n):

○ IP spoofing attack

○ Session hijacking attack

○ Replay attack

○ Man-in-the-middle attack

10. Your intranet webmaster has noticed an entry in a log file from an IP address that is within the range of addresses used on your network. But the webmaster does not recognize the computer name as valid. You check the DHCP server and find out that the IP address is not similar to any in your list of IP addresses in that particular domain. This could be a(n):

○ IP spoofing attack

○ Malicious code attack

○ Man-in-the-middle attack

○ Session hijacking attack

11. A user arrives at work in the morning and finds that he cannot log on to the network. You check his account and find it was locked at 3 A.M. due to too many unsuccessful logon attempts. What type of attack do you suspect?

○ Man-in-the-middle

○ Password

○ Virus

○ Hijacking

12. **Which of these examples can be classified as social engineering attacks?**

    ☐ A customer contacts your help desk asking for her user name and password because she cannot log on to your e-commerce website.

    ☐ A user gets a call from a person who states he is a help desk technician. The caller asks the user to go to an external website and download a file so that the technician can monitor the user's system.

    ☐ The CEO of your company calls you personally on the phone to ask you to fax salary data to her personal fax number. The fax number she gives you is listed in the company directory, and you recognize her voice.

    ☐ A user receives an email that appears to be from a bank; the bank says they need the user's name, date of birth, and Social Security number to verify account information.

TOPIC D

Authentication Methods

In the previous topic, you listed common threats and attacks. In a network environment, there are security settings that control how users and devices authenticate to the network. In this topic, you will identify network authentication methods.

Strong authentication is the first line of defense to secure network resources. But authentication is not a single process; there are many methods and mechanisms involved. As a network professional, to effectively manage authentication on your network, you will need to understand these different systems and what each one can provide for your organization.

Authentication

Authentication is the method of uniquely validating a particular entity or individual's credentials. Authentication concentrates on identifying if a particular individual has the right credentials to enter a system or secure site. Authentication credentials should be kept secret to prevent unauthorized individuals from gaining access to confidential information.

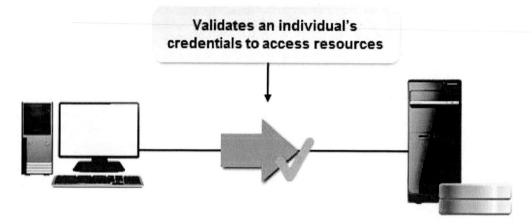

Figure 10-26: Authentication with a user name and password.

Authentication Factors

Most authentication schemes are based on the use of one or more authentication factors. The factors include:

- Something you know, such as a password
- Something you have, such as a token or access card
- Something you are, including physical characteristics, such as fingerprints or a retina pattern

Something You Do

Although not formally defined by recognized security regulatory bodies, an extension of biometrics is gaining attention as an alternative authentication factor: something you do. This factor includes the concept of keystroke authentication, where a keystroke logger measures the physical characteristics of your keystrokes. While someone might be able to forge your signature or steal your ATM card and PIN, it's highly unlikely that anyone will know how hard you press the keys while typing, or how long the keys remain pressed.

User Name and Password Authentication

The combination of a user name and a password is one of the most basic and widely used authentication schemes. In this type of authentication, a system compares the user's credentials against credentials stored in a database. It authenticates the user if the user name and password match the database. If not, the user is denied access. This method may not be very secure because the user's credentials are sometimes transmitted through the network as plaintext, making the user name and password easily accessible to an attacker.

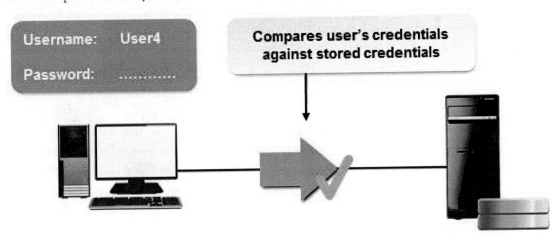

Figure 10-27: A combination of a user name and password for authentication.

Authentication based entirely on a user name/password combination is sometimes called *authentication by assertion,* because once the client has a valid set of credentials, it can use them to assert its identity to obtain access to a resource.

Two-Factor Authentication

Two-factor authentication is an authentication scheme that requires validation of two authentication factors. Requiring a physical ID card along with a secret password is an example of two-factor authentication. A bank ATM card is a common example of this.

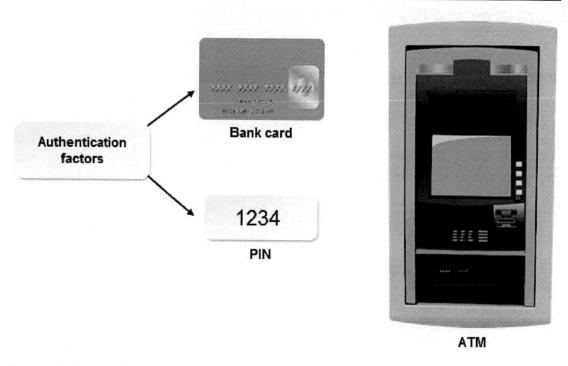

Figure 10-28: Two-factor authentication.

A user name and password is not two-factor authentication, because the user name helps in identification and the password alone acts as the authentication factor.

Multifactor Authentication

Multifactor authentication is any authentication scheme that requires validation of at least two of the possible authentication factors. It can be any combination of who you are, what you have, and what you know.

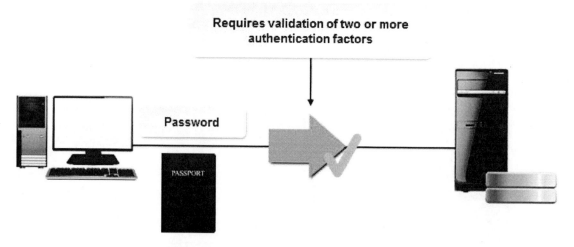

Figure 10-29: Multifactor authentication requires validation of at least two of the authentication factors.

Strong Passwords

A *strong password* is a password that meets the complexity requirements that are set by a system administrator and documented in a security policy or password policy. Strong passwords increase the security of systems that use password-based authentication by protecting against password guessing and password attacks.

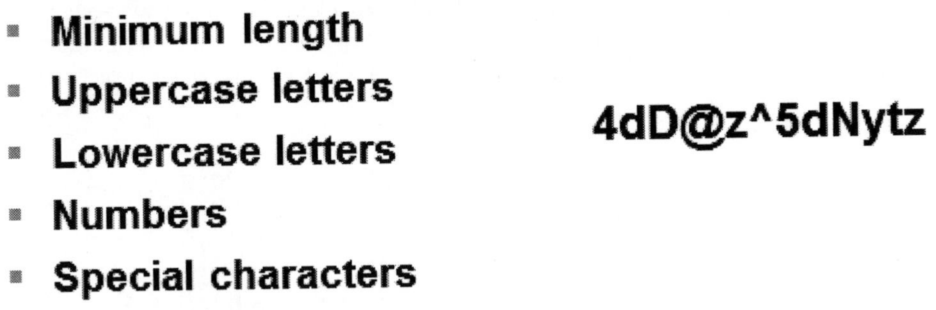

- **Minimum length**
- **Uppercase letters**
- **Lowercase letters**   **4dD@z^5dNytz**
- **Numbers**
- **Special characters**

Figure 10-30: Strong passwords increase system security.

Password complexity requirements should meet the security needs of an individual organization, and can specify:

- The minimum length of the password
- Required characters, such as a combination of letters, numbers, and symbols
- Forbidden character strings, such as the user account name or dictionary words

The types of password policies and the complexity settings they can include vary between different organizations and systems. Human resources or the IT department maintains an official password policy document that is often publicized to employees, or it can be a system configuration setting within an application or operating system.

Tokens

Tokens are physical or virtual objects, such as smart cards, ID badges, or data packets, that store authentication information. Tokens can store Personal Identification Numbers (PINs), information about users, or passwords. Unique token values can be generated by special devices or software in response to a challenge from an authenticating server or by using independent algorithms.

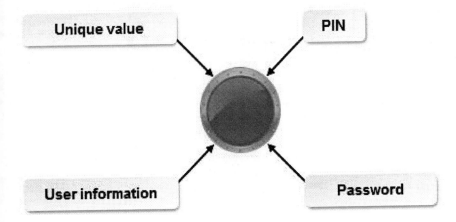

Figure 10-31: Tokens store authentication information.

Smart cards are a common example of token-based authentication. A smart card is a plastic card containing an embedded computer chip that can store different types of electronic information. The contents of a smart card can be read with a smart card reader.

Biometrics

Biometrics are authentication schemes based on an individual's physical characteristics. This system can involve a fingerprint scanner, a retina scanner, a hand geometry scanner, or voice-recognition and facial-recognition software. As biometric authentication becomes less expensive to implement, it is adopted more widely.

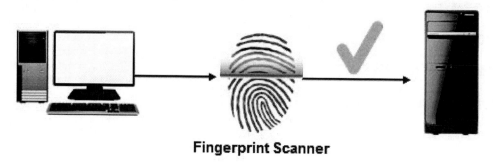

Fingerprint Scanner

Figure 10–32: Biometric authentication using a fingerprint scanner.

Mutual Authentication

Mutual authentication is a security mechanism that requires that each party in a communication verify each other's identity. A service or resource verifies the client's credentials, and the client verifies the resource's credentials. Mutual authentication prevents a client from inadvertently submitting confidential information to a non-secure server. Any type or combination of authentication mechanisms can be used.

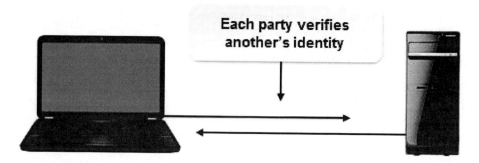

Each party verifies another's identity

Figure 10–33: Mutual authentication to verify credentials.

Mutual authentication helps in avoiding man-in-the-middle and session hijacking attacks.

Mutual authentication is most commonly used in virtual private networks (VPNs) where both the client and the server are expected to prove their identity to each other before the VPN is established between them. The authentication can be password-based, but is more likely to be a certificate.

SSO

Single sign-on (SSO) is a mechanism where a single user authentication provides access to all the devices or applications where the user has permission. The user need not enter multiple passwords each time he wants to access a device.

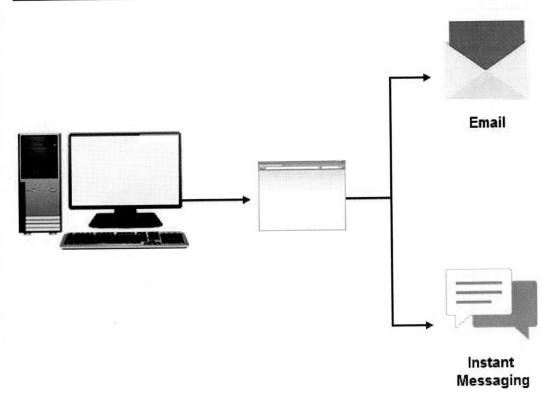

Figure 10-34: A user authenticated using SSO.

SSO is a convenience mechanism used in enterprise networks where multiple unrelated authentication systems exist. A single user might have a different user name and password (or some other authentication mechanism) in a variety of systems. Rather than require the user to remember all of the various logins (and when it is appropriate to use each one), the different systems are organized into a federation. In the federation, the user's various login accounts are all mapped to a single account that the user uses across the enterprise.

SSO is designed to make security easier for users, but this ease of use comes at a potential cost. SSO passwords must be ultra-secure.

EAP

Extensible Authentication Protocol (EAP) is a protocol that enables systems to use hardware-based identifiers, such as fingerprint scanners or smart card readers, for authentication. EAP categorizes the devices into different EAP types depending on each device's authentication scheme. The EAP method associated with each type enables the device to interact with a system's account database.

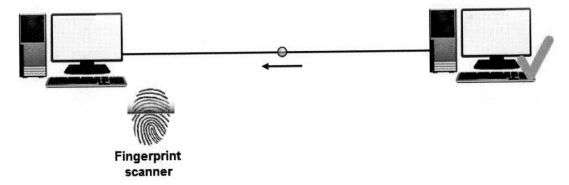

Figure 10-35: EAP allows systems to use hardware-based identifiers for authentication.

Users might need to provide a password in addition to the physical authentication. EAP allows for logon using different methods such as public-key authentication, Kerberos, and certificates. Remote Authentication Dial-In User Service (RADIUS), a centralized authentication protocol, is often used with EAP.

Other authentication protocols can be used in EAP implementations.

Protocol	Description
Extensible Authentication Protocol over LAN (EAPOL)	EAP over LAN as used in *802.1x* implementations. **Note:** The 802.1x protocol is discussed in depth later in the course.
EAP-Transport Layer Security (EAP-TLS)	This widely supported feature in wireless routers and cards provides robust security. Native support is included in: • Mac OS X 10.3 and above • Windows 7 and Windows 8 • Windows Server 2012 • Windows Mobile 7 and above
EAP-MD5	Provides minimal security and is easily bypassed or hacked.
Protected Extensible Authentication Protocol (PEAP)	PEAP, similar to EAP-TLS, was proposed as an open standard by a coalition made up of Cisco Systems®, Microsoft, and RSA Security. PEAPv0/EAP-MSCHAPv2 is a widely supported authentication method in EAP implementations.

EAP as an authentication protocol has broad functionality that can include nearly any authentication method beyond user name and password. Although it is most commonly associated with smart cards, certificates, and tokens, some vendors have also implemented EAP biometrics.

Kerberos

Kerberos is an authentication service that is based on a time-sensitive ticket-granting system. It was developed by the Massachusetts Institute of Technology (MIT) to use an SSO method in which the user enters access credentials that are then passed to the authentication server, which contains an access list and permitted access credentials. Kerberos can be used to manage access control to several services by using one centralized authentication server.

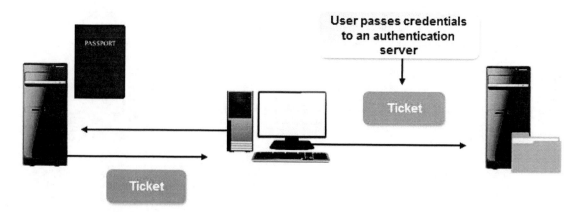

Figure 10-36: Kerberos is used to manage access control to services.

In the Kerberos authentication process:

1. A user logs on to the domain.

2. The user requests a Ticket Granting Ticket (TGT) from the authenticating server.
3. The authenticating server responds with a time-stamped TGT.
4. The user presents the TGT back to the authenticating server and requests a service ticket to access a specific resource.
5. The authenticating server responds with a service ticket.
6. The user presents the service ticket to the resource.
7. The resource authenticates the user and allows access.

Kerberos is a popular open-source authentication protocol. Microsoft adopted Kerberos version 5 (v5) as the authentication protocol for its Active Directory domains.

Wireless Authentication Methods

There are three main methods used for wireless authentication.

Authentication Method	Description
Open system	Open system authentication uses null authentication, which means that user names and passwords are not used to authenticate a user. This is the default for many access points (APs) and stations. Open system authentication enables a station to connect to any wireless AP that has open system authentication enabled, even if the service set identifier (SSID) is different from the station.
	When an AP and a station have an open system configured:
	1. The station will find an AP by sending out a probe.
	2. When it locates an AP, it sends a request for authentication to that AP.
	3. The AP responds with an authentication success.
	4. The station then associates itself with an AP by sending an association request.
	5. The AP, upon receipt of an association request, responds with a success association response.

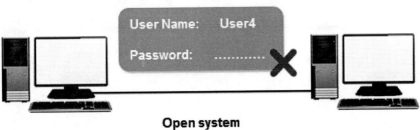

Open system

Open system is often used in conjunction with 802.1x. The wireless client is allowed to make an unauthenticated association with the AP, but until the user logs on, the client cannot connect to the network.

Authentication Method	Description
Shared-key	The shared-key authentication method verifies the identity of a station by using a WEP key. Both the station and the AP must be configured to use data encryption and the same WEP key. The station also needs to be configured to use a shared-key authentication instead of the default setting, which is open system authentication.

Once configured correctly, the communication process begins.

1. The station probes for an AP and initiates an authentication request.
2. Upon receipt of the request, the AP issues a challenge to the station.
3. The station accepts the challenge and encrypts it by using the WEP key with which it has been configured.
4. The station then sends the challenge back to the AP that decrypts the encrypted challenge using its key.
5. If both the station and the AP have the same key, the AP decrypts the challenge with the matching WEP key.
6. The AP then authenticates the station.
7. The station initiates an association request.
8. The AP accepts the association request. |

Shared WEP key

Shared-key

Shared-key is sometimes referred to as pre-shared key, or PSK.

Authentication Method	Description
802.1x and EAP	The EAP authentication method authenticates a user and not the station. This is done with a RADIUS server. An AP forwards the authentication request to the RADIUS server, and the server calls the user credential database (for example, Active Directory in Windows domains) to verify the user. The RADIUS server then passes the identity verification to the AP.

The authentication process consists of the following steps:

1. A station initiates an authentication request to the AP.
2. The AP issues an EAP identity request.
3. Once the station receives the request, it sends an EAP identity response to the AP.
4. The AP forwards the EAP identity response to the RADIUS server.
5. The RADIUS server issues a RADIUS access challenge, which passes through the AP to the station.
6. The station sends a RADIUS challenge response that the AP forwards to the RADIUS server.
7. If the RADIUS server can decrypt the challenge and verify the user, it forwards a success response to the AP.
8. The AP forwards an EAP success to the station and the station can then establish an association with the AP.

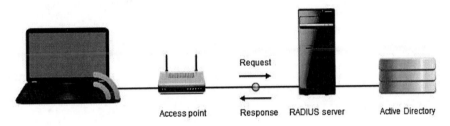

802.1x and EAP

ACTIVITY 10–6
Discussing Authentication Methods

Scenario

The network administrator at Greene City Interiors quizzes you on various authentication methods.

1. If a user needs to insert her employee ID card into a special card reader to access her laptop, this is an example of:
   ○ User name/password authentication
   ○ Biometrics
   ○ Token-based authentication
   ○ Mutual authentication

2. If a user needs to place his index finger on a fingerprint reader to access the server room, this is an example of which authentication method:
   ○ Password
   ○ Token-based
   ○ Biometric
   ○ Multifactor

3. To withdraw money from an ATM, a person needs to insert a card and type a four-digit PIN. This incorporates what types of authentication?
   ☐ Token-based
   ☐ Password
   ☐ Biometrics
   ☐ Multifactor
   ☐ Mutual

4. Which is an example of a strong password?
   ○ Password
   ○ !Passw0rd1
   ○ PaSsWoRd
   ○ drowssaP

TOPIC E

Encryption Methods

In the previous topic, you identified secure client authentication methods to prevent unauthorized access. Apart from restricting access, it is also important to ensure the integrity of data by securing it. Data encryption can be used to secure information. In this topic, you will identify major data encryption methods and standards.

However fast you secure your digital communications, hackers will test the security method and attempt to breach the systems. To stay one step ahead of the hackers and protect data, you need to understand the fundamentals of data encryption and the choices you have for implementing data encryption in your organization.

Encryption

Encryption is a cryptographic technique that converts data from plain, or *cleartext* form, into coded, or ciphertext form. Only authorized parties with the necessary decryption information can decode and read the data. Encryption can be one-way, which means the encryption is designed to hide only the cleartext and is never decrypted. Encryption can also be two-way, in which ciphertext can be decrypted back to cleartext and read.

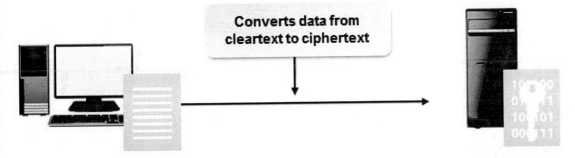

Converts data from cleartext to ciphertext

Figure 10-37: Encryption converts plain data into ciphertext.

Cryptography is the science of hiding information. The practice of cryptography is thought to be nearly as old as the written word. Current cryptographic science has its roots in mathematics and computer science and relies heavily upon technology. Modern communications and computing use cryptography extensively to protect sensitive information and communications from unauthorized access.

 Note: The word cryptography has roots in the Greek words "kryptós," meaning "hidden" and "gráphein," meaning "to write."

A *cipher* is a specific set of actions used to encrypt data. *Plaintext* is the original, unencoded data. Once the cipher is applied via *enciphering*, the obscured data is known as *ciphertext*. The reverse process of translating ciphertext to cleartext is known as *deciphering*.

Encryption and Security Goals

Encryption is used to promote many security goals and techniques. Encryption enables confidentiality by protecting data from unauthorized access. It supports integrity because it is difficult to decipher encrypted data without the secret decrypting cipher. It supports non-repudiation, because only parties that know about the confidential encryption scheme can encrypt or decrypt data. In addition, some form of encryption is employed in most authentication mechanisms to protect passwords. Encryption is used in many access control mechanisms as well.

It is becoming common to encrypt many forms of communications and data streams, as well as entire hard disks. Some operating systems support whole-disk encryption, whereas some other commercially available open-source tools are capable of encrypting all or part of the data on a disk or drive.

An encryption *algorithm* is the rule, system, or mechanism used to encrypt data. Algorithms can be simple mechanical substitutions, but in electronic cryptography, they are generally complex mathematical functions. The stronger the mathematical function, the more difficult it is to break the encryption. A letter-substitution cipher, in which each letter of the alphabet is systematically replaced by another letter, is an example of a simple encryption algorithm.

Hashing Encryption

Hashing encryption is one-way encryption that transforms cleartext into ciphertext that is not intended to be decrypted. The result of the hashing process is called a *hash, hash value,* or *message digest.* The input data can vary in length, whereas the hash length is fixed.

Two types of hashes you will encounter are MD5 and SHA. Each of these hashes is used for data verification. Typically, you will see them used to verify that the data you are downloading has not been tampered with.

MD5 (Message Digest version 5) is an algorithm that creates a 128-bit message digest from the input data. The data input can be a message of any size. The resulting hash digest is unique to the data from which it was created. The MD5 standard, created by Professor Ronald Rivest at MIT, is defined by IETF RFC 1321.

Secure Hash Algorithm (SHA) was created by the National Institute of Standards and Technology (NIST) and the NSA. It is used for US government documents and other documents to create a digital signature. SHA-2 and SHA-3 have four variations: SHA-224, SHA-256, SHA-384, and SHA-512.

Key–Based Encryption

Data encryption depends on the use of a key to control how information is encoded and decoded. There are two main categories of key-based encryption.

- In *shared-key,* or *symmetric,* encryption systems, the same key is used both to encode and to decode the message. The secret key must be communicated securely between the two parties involved in the communication.

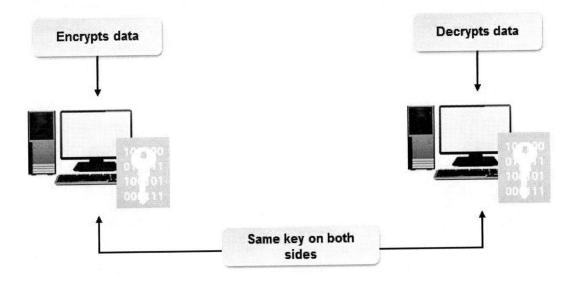

Shared-key (symmetric) encryption

Figure 10-38: Shared-key encryption uses the same key for encoding and decoding.

- In *key-pair,* or *asymmetric,* encryption systems, each party has two keys: a *public key,* which anyone can obtain, and a *private key,* known only to the individual. Anyone can use the public key to encrypt data; only the holder of the associated private key can decrypt it.

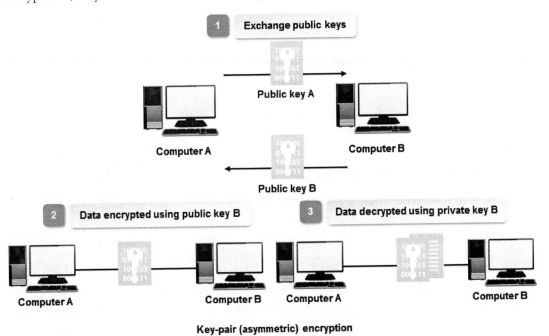

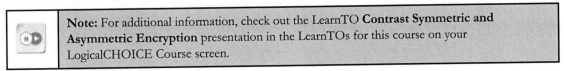

Key-pair (asymmetric) encryption

Figure 10-39: Key-pair encryption uses two separate keys for encoding and decoding.

> **Note:** For additional information, check out the LearnTO **Contrast Symmetric and Asymmetric Encryption** presentation in the LearnTOs for this course on your LogicalCHOICE Course screen.

Digital Certificates

A *digital certificate* is an electronic document that associates credentials with a public key. Both users and devices can hold certificates. The certificate validates the certificate holder's identity and is also a way to distribute the holder's public key. A server called a *Certificate Authority (CA)* issues certificates and the associated public/private key pairs. A root CA is typically the first or only CA installed. A root certificate is an unsigned public key certificate or a self-signed certificate that identifies the root CA.

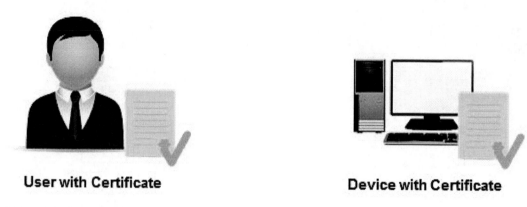

User with Certificate   **Device with Certificate**

Figure 10–40: Digital certificates associate credentials with a public key.

A CA can issue multiple certificates in the form of a tree structure. A root certificate is at the top of the tree, and is the private key that is used to sign other certificates. All certificates immediately below the root certificate inherit the trustworthiness of the root certificate. Certificates further down the tree also depend on the trustworthiness of the intermediate CAs.

An *encryption key* is a specific piece of information that is used in conjunction with an algorithm to perform encryption and decryption. A different key can be used with the same algorithm to produce different ciphertext. Without the correct key, the receiver cannot decrypt the ciphertext even if the algorithm is known. The longer the key, the stronger the encryption.

In a simple letter-substitution algorithm, the key might be "replace each letter with the letter that is two letters following it in the alphabet." If the same algorithm were used on the same cleartext but with a different key—for example, "replace each letter with the one three letters before it"—the resulting ciphertext would be different.

Certificates and Encryption

Certificates can be used for data encryption. The certificate encryption process consists of four steps:

1. A security principal obtains a certificate and a public/private key pair from a CA.
2. The party that encrypts data obtains the user's public key from the user or from the CA's certificate repository.
3. The encrypting party then uses the public key to encrypt the data and sends it to the other user.
4. The other user uses the private key to decrypt the data.

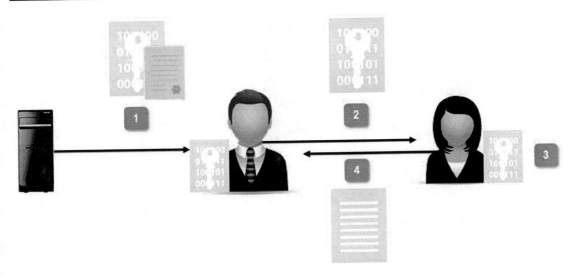

Figure 10-41: Users share keys and certificates to encrypt and decrypt data.

The *Encrypting File System (EFS)* is a file-encryption tool available on Windows devices that have partitions formatted with NT File System (NTFS). EFS encrypts file data by using digital certificates. If a CA is not available to issue a file-encryption certificate, the local device can issue a self-signed encryption certificate to users who want to encrypt files. Unlike NTFS permissions, which control access to the file, EFS protects the contents of the file. With EFS, you can keep data secure even if NTFS security is breached—for example, if an attacker steals a laptop and moves the laptop's hard drive to another system to bypass the NTFS security implementations.

PKI

A *Public Key Infrastructure (PKI)* is an encryption system that is composed of a CA, certificates, software, services, and other cryptographic components. It is used to verify data authenticity and validate data and entities. PKI can be implemented in various hierarchical structures, and may be publicly available or maintained privately by an organization. It can also be used to secure transactions over the Internet.

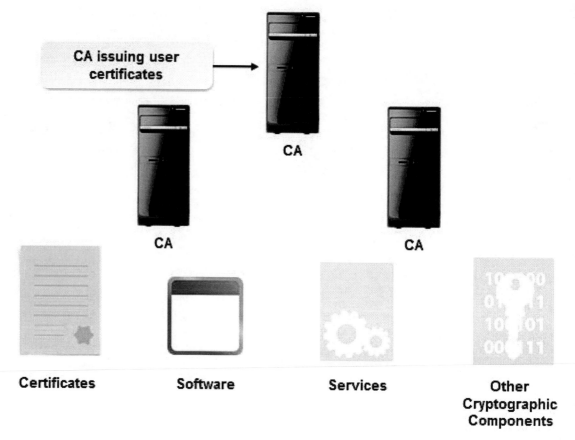

Figure 10–42: PKI consists of a CA, certificates, software, and services.

PKI contains several components:

- Digital certificates, to verify the identity of entities
- One or more CAs, to issue digital certificates to computers, users, or applications
- A *Registration Authority (RA),* responsible for verifying users' identities and approving or denying requests for digital certificates
- A *certificate repository database,* to store the digital certificates
- A *certificate management system,* to provide software tools to perform the day-to-day functions of the PKI

Certificates and Authentication

Certificate authentication is the process of identifying users in a transaction by carrying out a series of steps before confirming the identity of the user. These can include:

1. Initiating a secure transaction such as a client requesting access to a secure site.
2. The secure site presents its digital certificate to the client with its public key and verified digital signature enclosed.
3. The client browser compares it to a library of certificate authorities and validates the signature against its cache of trusted and acknowledged certificates. This comparison includes checking to see if the certificate has been issued and signed by a trusted CA, if it is expired, and if it has been revoked.
4. Once the client accepts the digital signature, then the certificate authentication is successful.

   If the issuing CA does not match the library of certificate authorities in the client, then certificate authentication is unsuccessful and the user obtains a notification that the digital certificate supplied is invalid.

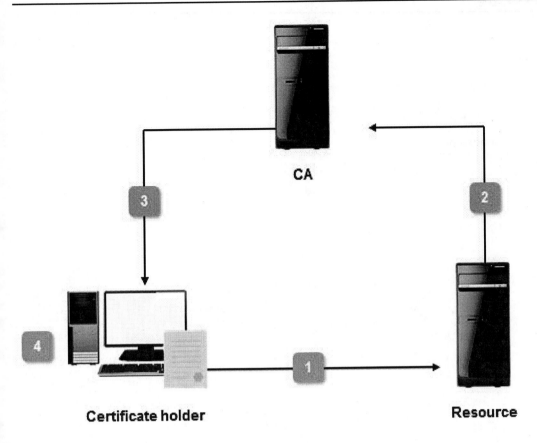

CA

3

2

4

Certificate holder

1

Resource

Figure 10-43: Certificate authentication identifies end users in a transaction.

Digital Signatures

A *digital signature* is a message digest that has been encrypted with a user's private key. Asymmetric encryption algorithms can be used with hashing algorithms to create digital signatures. The sender creates a hashed version of the message text, and then encrypts the hash itself with the sender's private key. The encrypted hash is attached to the message as the digital signature.

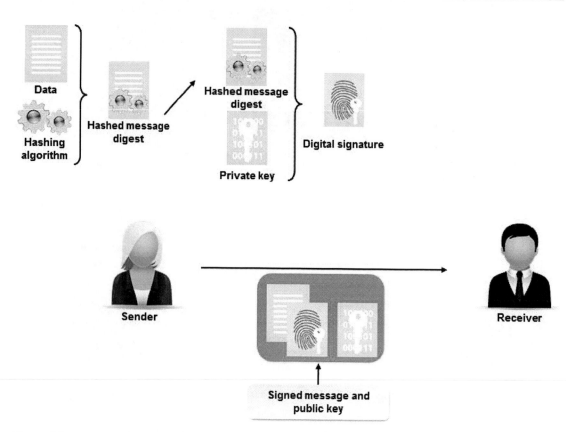

Figure 10–44: Digital signature creation and transmission.

The sender provides the receiver with the signed message and the corresponding public key. The receiver uses the public key to decrypt the signature to reveal the sender's version of the hash. This proves the sender's identity, because, if the public and private keys did not match, the receiver would not be able to decrypt the signature. The receiver then uses the same hashing algorithm to create a new hash version of the document. If the two hash versions match, this proves that the data has not been altered.

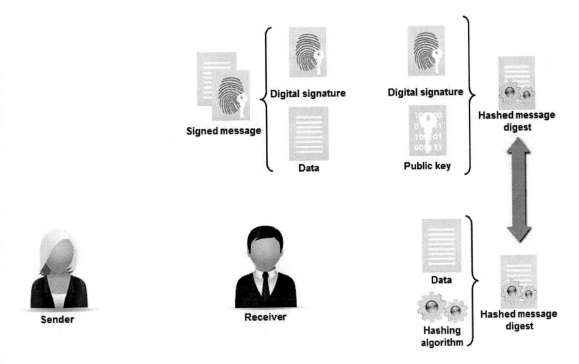

Figure 10-45: Digital signature used to verify sender identity and message integrity.

Digital signatures support message integrity because if the signature is altered in transit, the receiver's version of the hash will not match the original hash value. They support non-repudiation because the specific encrypted hash value is unique to a sender.

It is important to remember that a digital signature is a hash that is then encrypted. Without the second round of encryption, another party could easily:

1. Intercept the file and the hash.
2. Modify the file.
3. Re-create the hash.
4. Send the modified file to the recipient.

Encryption Devices

In *encryption devices*, encryption, decryption, and access control are enforced by a cryptographic module called a *Hardware Security Module (HSM)*. Encryption devices do not allow the execution of external programs, which attempt either to reset any counters or access their memory. The lockdown in the event of unauthenticated use can also destroy data and encryption keys that are present on a USB drive or a hard drive, based on the level of security enforced in the HSMs.

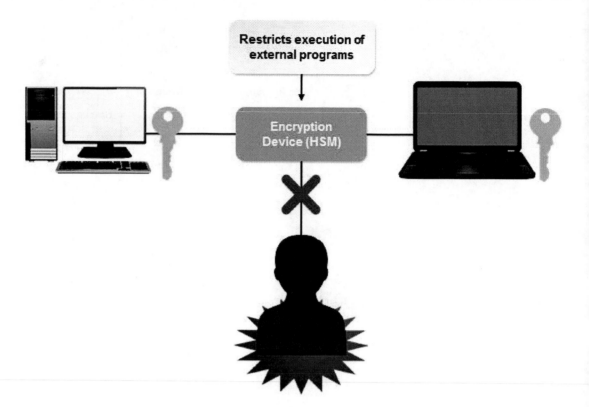

Figure 10–46: HSM enforces encryption and decryption.

Benefits of Encryption Devices

Encryption devices provide benefits such as:

- Preventing storage mapping from the drive to the file system until a user inserts a plug-in smart card into a slot connected to the hard drive.
- Preventing attackers from copying the drive contents without the assigned HSM.
- Providing security controls that are self-governed and not dependent on the operating system; therefore, the hard drive is not affected by malicious code.
- Providing an organization with the proof that each machine is encrypted.

If a machine is lost due to a security attack, this will act as an assurance to customers that none of the data has been lost or compromised.

SSL

Secure Sockets Layer (SSL) is a security protocol that combines digital certificates for authentication with public key data encryption. SSL is a server-driven process; any web client that supports SSL, including all current web browsers, can connect securely to an SSL-enabled server.

Figure 10-47: SSL combines digital certificates for authentication.

SSL is used specifically to protect network traffic. It works at Layer 6 of the OSI model. Its most common use is to work in conjunction with HTTPS to encrypt web connections.

SSL and Encryption

The encryption process in SSL consists of the following steps:

1. A client requests a session from a server.
2. The server responds by sending its digital certificate and public key to the client.
3. The server and client then negotiate an encryption level.
4. The client generates and encrypts a session key using the server's public key, and returns it to the server.
5. The client and server then use the session key for data encryption.

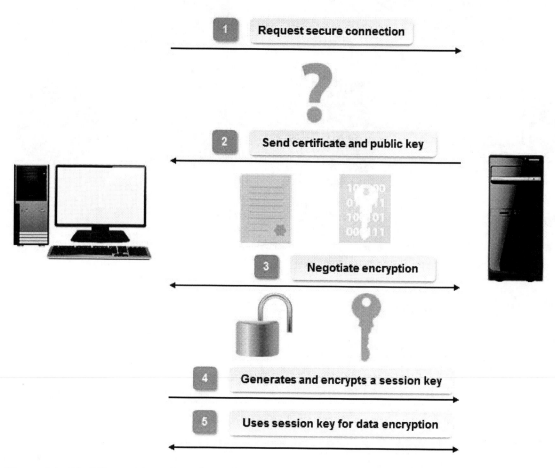

Figure 10–48: SSL combines digital certificates with public–key data encryption.

TLS

Transport Layer Security (TLS) is a security protocol that protects sensitive communication from being eavesdropped and tampered with. It does this by using a secure, encrypted, and authenticated channel over a TCP/IP connection. TLS uses certificates and public key cryptography for mutual authentication and data encryption using negotiated secret keys. TLS take place in Layer 6 of the OSI model.

Figure 10–49: TLS uses a secure channel over a TCP/IP connection.

TLS is the successor to SSL. Most modern browsers support both.

TLS is very similar to SSL, but the two protocols are incompatible with each other.

TLS1.2 is the current version of the TLS protocol and 1.3 is in process. TLS1.2 has a variety of security measures:

- It prevents downgrade of the protocol to a previous (less secure) version or a weaker cipher suite.
- It uses sequence numbering based on application records in authentication code for messages.
- It uses a message digest upgraded with a key to ensure that a MAC can be checked only by a key holder.

Wireless Encryption Protocols

There are three main encryption protocols used in wireless networking:

- WEP
- WPA
- WPA2

Wired Equivalent Privacy (WEP) is a protocol that provides 64-bit, 128-bit, and 256-bit encryption using the Rivest Cipher 4 (RC4) algorithm for wireless communication that uses the 802.11a and 802.11b protocols. Although WEP might sound like a good solution at first, it is ironically not as secure as it should be. The problem stems from the way WEP produces the keys that are used to encrypt data. Because of a flaw in the method, attackers could easily generate their own keys by using a wireless network capture tool, such as Airsnort or WEPCrack, to capture and analyze data transferred through the air.

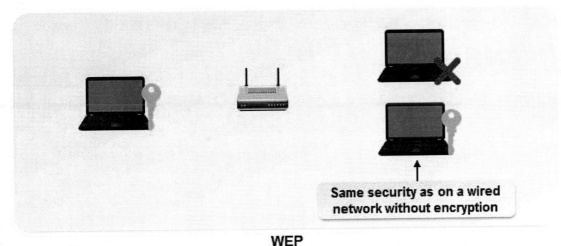

Same security as on a wired network without encryption

WEP

Figure 10–50: WEP provides encryption using the RC4 algorithm.

Wi-Fi Protected Access (WPA) is a security protocol introduced to address some of the shortcomings in WEP. It provides for dynamic reassignment of keys to prevent the key-attack vulnerabilities of WEP. WPA provides improved data encryption through the *Temporal Key Integrity Protocol (TKIP)*, which is a security protocol created by the IEEE 802.11i task group to replace WEP. It is combined with the existing WEP encryption to provide a 128-bit encryption key that fixes the key length issues of WEP.

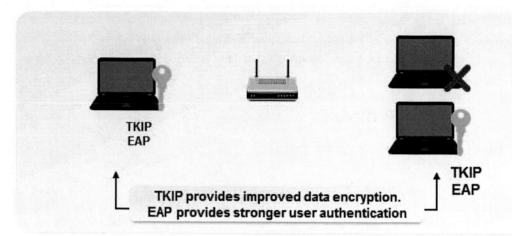

WPA/WPA2

Figure 10-51: WPA/WPA2 protects against WEP key-attack vulnerabilities.

In addition to TKIP, *WPA2* adds Advanced Encryption Standard (AES) cipher-based *Counter Mode with Cipher Block Chaining Message Authentication Code Protocol (CCMP)* encryption for even greater security and to replace TKIP.

In order to use WPA, you may need to use devices that support WPA. Older WAPs may support WEP. WPA can operate in two modes: WPA-Personal and WPA-Enterprise.

Mode	Description
WPA-Personal	In this mode, the WAP is configured with a value known as the preshared key, which is used to encrypt data. It is used for personal use and by small businesses. Also known as WPA-PSK.
WPA-Enterprise	This mode is designed for enterprise networks. It assigns a unique encryption key for every client when they log on to the network. This encryption key is regularly updated, making it impossible for a Wi-Fi snooper to decode the key. WPA-Enterprise uses a RADIUS server for authentication, which provides logging and accounting information. It also uses EAP to provide authentication.

ACTIVITY 10-7
Identifying Network Encryption Methods

Scenario
The network administrator at Greene City Interiors asks you questions to see if you are ready to handle the encryption methods used at the branch office.

1. True or False? Encryption is only a two-way format in which data can be decrypted and read.
   - ☐ True
   - ☐ False

2. Which is the least secure wireless security protocol?
   - ○ WPA
   - ○ WEP
   - ○ TKIP
   - ○ WPA2

3. With key pair encryption, what type of key is used to decrypt the data?
   - ○ Shared key
   - ○ Public key
   - ○ Decrypt key
   - ○ Private key

4. Which are security protocols that combine digital certificates for authentication with public key data encryption?
   - ☐ SSL
   - ☐ TLS
   - ☐ PKI
   - ☐ DES

5. Which is not a step in the certificate encryption process?
   - ○ Encrypting party uses public key to encrypt data and sends it to the other user.
   - ○ The party that decrypts data obtains the public key from the CA's certificate repository.
   - ○ A security principal obtains a certificate and a public/private key pair from a CA.
   - ○ Other user uses the private key to decrypt the data.

ACTIVITY 10-8
Installing a CA

Scenario

At the Greene City Interiors branch office, you want to prevent users from receiving unapproved certificates and accessing information that they are not supposed to and also to prevent attackers from getting data. You have decided to implement a secure CA using Windows Server 2012 R2 CAs.

 Note: Although Certificate Services is running on a domain controller for classroom and testing purposes, this is a security risk and should not be replicated on a real-time network.

1. Install **Active Directory Certificate Services** on the CA.
   a) Select **Start→Server Manager**.
   b) In the Server Manager Dashboard window, select the **Add roles and features** link.
   c) In the **Add Roles and Features Wizard**, on the **Before You Begin** page, select **Next**.
   d) On the **Select installation type** page, verify that **Role-based or feature-based installation** is selected and select **Next**.
   e) On the **Select destination server** page, verify that **Computer##.Child##.GCInteriors.com** is selected and select **Next**.
   f) On the **Select server roles** page, check the **Active Directory Certificate Services** check box.
   g) In the **Add Roles and Features Wizard** dialog box, select **Add Features** to add all the suggested features.
   h) Select **Next**.
   i) On the **Select features** page, select **Next**.
   j) On the **Active Directory Certificate Services** page, select **Next**.
   k) On the **Select Role Services** page, check the **Certification Authority Web Enrollment** check box.
   l) In the **Add Roles and Features Wizard** dialog box, select **Add Features** to add all the suggested features.
   m) Select **Next**.
   n) On the **Confirm Installation Selections** page, select **Install**.
   o) On the **Installation Progress** page, when the installation is complete, under Active Directory Certificate Services, select the **Configure Active Directory Certificate Services on the destination server** link.
   p) In the **AD CS Configuration** wizard, on the **Credentials** page, select **Next**.
   q) On the **Role Services** page, check **Certification Authority** and **Certification Authority Web Enrollment** and select **Next**.

r) On the **Specify Type** page, verify that the **Standalone CA** option is selected. Select **Next**.

Enterprise certification authorities (CAs) can use Active Directory Domain Services (AD DS) to simplify the management of certificates. Standalone CAs do not use AD DS to issue or manage certificates.

○ Enterprise CA

Enterprise CAs must be domain members and are typically online to issue certificates or certificate policies.

◉ Standalone CA

Standalone CAs can be members or a workgroup or domain. Standalone CAs do not require AD DS and can be used without a network connection (offline).

s) On the **CA Type** page, with the **Root CA** option selected, select **Next**.
t) On the **Private Key** page, with the **Create a new private key** option selected, select **Next**.
u) On the **Cryptography for CA** page, select **Next** to accept the default values.
v) On the **CA Name** page, in the **Common name for this CA** text box, type *GCInteriorsCA##* as the common name for the CA. Select **Next**.
w) On the **Validity Period** page, select **Next** to accept the default validity period for the certificate.
x) On the **CA Database** page, select **Next** to accept the default storage location for the CA database and log.
y) On the **Confirmation** page, select **Configure**.
z) On the **Results** page, select **Close** and then select **Close** again.

2. Verify that **Active Directory Certificate Services** was installed properly.
   a) In **Server Manager**, select **Tools→Certification Authority**.
   b) In the certsrv window, in the console tree, select **GCInteriorsCA##**.
   c) Select **Action→Properties**.

d) In the **GCInteriors## Properties** dialog box, the name should appear as you configured it during installation. Select **View Certificate**.

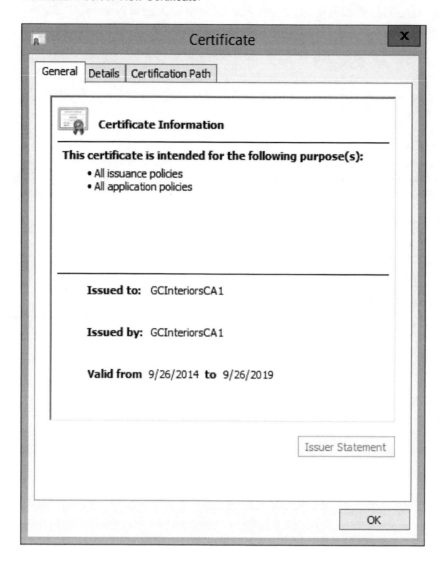

e) The certificate should expire in 5 years. Select **OK** to close the **Certificate** dialog box.

f) Select **OK** to close the **GCInteriorsCA## Properties** dialog box, and close the Certification Authority window.

Summary

In this lesson, you described basic concepts related to network security. Understanding the fundamental security concepts enables you to ensure the appropriate security levels in your organization.

Can you describe any exploited network vulnerabilities and/or threats and attacks that you have encountered?

Can you describe some situations in which you have used basic network security techniques such as authentication or encryption?

 Note: Check your LogicalCHOICE Course screen for opportunities to interact with your classmates, peers, and the larger LogicalCHOICE online community about the topics covered in this course or other topics you are interested in. From the Course screen you can also access available resources for a more continuous learning experience.

11 | Preventing Security Breaches

Lesson Time: 3 hours

Lesson Objectives

In this lesson, you will prevent security breaches. You will:

- Describe physical security controls.

- Describe network access controls.

- Install and configure firewalls.

- Implement network hardening techniques.

- Describe methods for detecting and preventing data breaches.

- Facilitate user awareness of security issues and countermeasures.

Lesson Introduction

In the last lesson, you described basic concepts related to network security. With that foundation in place, you are now ready to investigate ways to prevent security issues. In this lesson, you will prevent security breaches.

Each day, the number and complexity of threats against network security increases. In response to these threats, there are more and more security tools and techniques available to increase network security. Because you are a networking professional, your organization and users will be looking to you to ensure that your network environment provides the appropriate level of security, without compromising network performance.

TOPIC A

Physical Security Controls

In this lesson, you will prevent security breaches. To begin, you will examine ways to enhance the physical security of your facilities and network. In this topic, you will describe physical security controls.

Part of securing a network is to ensure that it is physically secure from threats and disasters, which includes access to the building and certain areas. The three principles of the CIA triad also apply to physical security. An understanding of procedures and hardware that increase the physical security of your network will help reduce the potential for security issues.

General Physical Security Considerations

Physical security is as important as network security in protecting an organization and employees from crime. An organization's physical components have vulnerabilities that should be mitigated by employing appropriate physical security measures.

Physical Resource	Vulnerabilities and Countermeasures
Building and grounds	Location: • Is the building located in a high-crime area or in a relatively remote location that would be hard to access in the event of a natural disaster? • If so, what protections do you have in place to deter theft or vandalism, and to recover from disaster? • Is it in a flood area? Fire risks: • Is the building adequately covered by a fire-suppression system? Not just the server room, but other general areas as well. • Are critical devices and server rooms equipped with special fire-protection methods? Will a fire accidentally destroy the storage systems? Will data be compromised? • Is network cabling in the plenum areas of the building fire-resistant? Electrical shielding: Are the building and the network equipment protected from electrical surges and other interference from the outside? Physical access control: • Are there physical barriers in place, such as fences, locks, mantraps, and monitored reception areas, to protect the building from unauthorized access? • Are strict physical access controls, such as biometric authorization, deployed to restrict access to sensitive areas? • Is there video or still-image surveillance in place to deter or help prosecute any unwanted access?

Physical Resource	Vulnerabilities and Countermeasures
Devices	Servers: • Are all the servers in one physical location? • If someone gains access to a server room, does she have access to every server in the company? Laptops/Tablets: These items are easily misplaced or stolen and often contain highly sensitive information. Mobile phones: Confidential conversations about proprietary company information should be held on land lines and not over wireless channels that do not use encryption. You may also want to disallow the use of unencrypted wireless devices for business purposes. Other wireless devices: Cameras, iPods, and similar digital devices can carry enormous amounts of data. Do you want those being carried around the building?
Communications	Telecommunications: Phone company cables, transformers, and switches can be intentionally or unintentionally damaged or tapped. Service providers: Third-party ISPs and other service providers may have security holes that your organization has no control over. Can your provider maintain your service if they have a loss or failure and, if not, do you have a backup plan? Wireless cells: Are your wireless access points placed and secured properly so that outside parties cannot connect to your network?

Door Access Controls

Door access controls provide an electronic and programmable device that people have to interact with in order to gain access to a door. Some of these controls can also limit access based on the time and date. This includes devices such as electronic keypads, card readers, and intercoms.

• Electronic keypads require that the user enter a code before the door will unlock. You can program different codes for different users and remove codes for users who no longer require access.

Figure 11-1: Electronic keypad.

- Card readers require that a user insert their card before the door will unlock. The card identifies the user and the user's profile determines which doors they have access to. User profiles can be edited or removed as necessary.

Figure 11-2: Card reader.

- Intercoms require that a user press a button to speak to a user inside the building and request access. The user inside the building can then press a button to unlock the door.

Figure 11-3: Intercom.

Proximity Readers and Key Fobs

There are also *proximity readers* that require the user to place a key fob near the reader to gain access. A proximity reader is a card reader that can read a smart card when it is held near it. The proximity card is held near an electronic reader for a moment. The reader usually produces a beep or other sound to indicate the card has been read. Proximity cards typically have a range of around 5 cm (2 inches) for reading.

Figure 11–4: Proximity reader.

Electronic *key fobs* are small devices which can be used for activating things such as remote keyless entry systems on motor vehicles, and in buildings for access to certain areas. Electronic key fobs now use a challenge-response authentication over radio frequency, and do not need line-of-sight to operate. The fob operates in much the same manner as a proximity card to communicate with a central server for the building, which can be programmed to allow access only to certain areas, or only within certain time frames.

Figure 11–5: Electronic key fob.

Biometric Locks

A *biometric lock* is a lock that is activated by biometric features, such as a fingerprint, voice, retina, or signature. Biometric locks make it more difficult for someone to counterfeit the "key" used to open the lock. An example of a biometric lock is an optical or thermal scanner that reads and stores the fingerprints of authorized users. The user then places his or her hand on the scanner to gain access to a door.

Figure 11-6: Thermal fingerprint scanner.

Keypads and Cipher Locks

Cipher locks require that a user press buttons in the correct sequence in order to open a door. The buttons may be mechanical and built into the door handle, or they may be in the form of a keypad. A cipher lock may have four or five push buttons, depending on the manufacturer, and the code may be one to five digits. The codes can be changed at any time. Some organizations use keyed locks to maintain physical security, and use cipher locks to control access, limiting unannounced intrusions or unescorted entry to particular areas of a building.

Figure 11-7: A keypad cipher lock.

Mantraps

A *mantrap* is two sets of interlocking doors inside a small space, where the first set of doors must close before the second set opens. If the mantrap is manual, a guard locks and unlocks each door in sequence. In this case, an intercom or video camera is typically used to allow the guard to control the trap from a remote location. If the mantrap is automatic, identification or a key of some kind may be required for each door, and sometimes different measures may be required for each door. Metal detectors are often built in, in order to prevent entrance of people carrying weapons. Such use is particularly frequent in banks and jewelry shops.

Figure 11–8: A mantrap.

Video Monitoring

Video monitoring allows you to increase the visual awareness of your organization. On your video monitoring system, you can use traditional closed circuit (CC) analog cameras with a CCTV network. You can also use Internet Protocol (IP) cameras, which are digital video cameras that connect to an IP network. IP cameras can be accessed across the network or the Internet. Some IP cameras also include local storage in case the network connection is lost. When the camera is connected to the network again, the data stored locally is downloaded to the video monitoring network. Video monitoring can take two forms:

- A video intercom that has a camera and a monitor so that users can see who is requesting access. This adds an added level of security when you are visually able to identify the person requesting entry.

Figure 11-9: Video intercom.

- Video surveillance cameras don't restrict access by themselves but they do provide security. They allow you to monitor and document who has gained access to the building or sensitive areas. They can also act as a deterrent to those who want to violate your security.

Figure 11-10: Video surveillance camera.

Security Guards

Security guards protect the property, people, and assets of an organization. They can be employed by the organization or through an agency. They act to protect property by maintaining a high-visibility presence to deter illegal and inappropriate actions. They watch for signs of crime, fire, or disorder and then take action and report any incidents to the client and emergency services as appropriate.

Figure 11-11: Security guard.

Network Closets and Server Rooms

Network closets and server rooms provide a place to store your network hardware and your servers. At a minimum, they allow you to organize and remove equipment from open areas where it can be exposed to accidental damage or interference. They also provide an opportunity to secure and limit access to equipment. Physical access controls can be used to limit the users who can enter these rooms.

A network closet contains the hubs, switches, and other network components for that floor or building. A server room contains some or all of the servers for an organization. Both rooms should be dry and have adequate electricity available. A server room may also require air-conditioning. Depending on the layout of the building and the requirements of the organization, these two areas can be in the same room or in separate rooms.

Rack Security

Rack security involves physically securing the racks so that they cannot be tampered with. Lockable doors and covers will prevent access to the rack, and some allow an unobstructed view of knob settings. Server boots can be added to a rack system to fully enclose servers within the rack. Patch panel protectors and cable tracks with covers can be used to restrict unauthorized access to patch panels and cables.

Air Flow

Proper air flow management is the effort to maximize cooling by either supplying cooling air to equipment, or by eliminating the mixing and recirculation of hot equipment exhaust air. Most network equipment has an optimal temperature and humidity that it needs to be kept at to ensure proper performance. If it gets too hot or cold it may not run effectively or even fail. An ambient temperature range of 68° to 75°F (20° to 24°C) and humidity levels between 45 and 55 percent is generally recommended for performance and reliability. Your heating, ventilation, and air conditioning (HVAC) system is an important part of keeping your network devices running. Providing proper air flow in server rooms helps keep servers and network devices from overheating. Rows of servers should be placed with fronts facing fronts, creating a cold aisle, and the rear of units creating a hot aisle where ventilation systems can gather up the hot air, cool it, and recirculate the cooled air. There are several techniques and equipment that can help you control temperature and humidity levels. Some of these are:

- Position diffusers so that they deliver cool air directly to the equipment.
- Use blanking panels on unused rack spaces so that air passes through the equipment rather than around it.
- Use structured cabling systems to eliminate disorganized and excess cables that might restrict exhaust air flow from rack mounted equipment. Also consider cutting cables and power cords to the correct length to allow more room for air to flow away from the back of the rack.
- Remove unnecessary sub–floor obstructions to increase air flow. For example, cabling in the sub-floor plenum can impede proper air circulation.
- Use floor grommets to improve cooling by sealing areas where cables enter and exit plenums.
- Consider getting a professional air flow assessment to help identify ways to improve cooling efficiency.

Emergency Procedures

In the event of an emergency, your organization needs to have established emergency procedures and the proper equipment. In the case of a fire, earthquake, or similar disaster, employees need to know where the emergency exits are and where to gather once outside the building. There also need to be procedures in place to inform employees how to act if hostile intruders gain access to the premises. Emergency equipment such as smoke detectors, fire extinguishers, and fire and security alarms need to be in place and maintained. Document these procedures and ensure that each employee is familiar with them.

If there is ever an emergency in your building, you need to get everyone out safely and protect your network assets at the same time. The building layout can be an important key to keeping people and assets safe. Server rooms that are in the center of the building are better positioned not only for running cables to all areas, but also this location provides some protection from people on the street easily gaining access to it. Someone posing as an emergency responder who is actually there to attack or steal network assets would have to pass many employees and other emergency personnel to reach a server room located in the center of the building.

Your building should have clearly marked safety and emergency exits, and the fire escape plan should be drilled at least twice a year. In the event of a fire, hostage situation, or natural disaster, employees should be alerted to any potential problems through an emergency alert system. This might include sirens and lights within the building, being included on lists of business and school closings, and phone or text messages to alert network users to the problem.

When developing applications or allowing network access, developers need to determine what will happen if an error or exception is encountered. Fail open and fail closed relate to the behavior of applications and networks when an error or exception is encountered. After the error, a fail open system continues to allow access; a fail closed system denies access.

A Material Safety Data Sheet (MSDS) is a technical bulletin that is designed to give users and emergency personnel information about the proper procedures for the storage and handling of a hazardous substance. This applies to any situation in which an employee is exposed to a chemical under normal use conditions or in the event of an emergency. The manufacturers supply MSDSs with the first shipment to a new customer and with any shipment after the MSDS is updated with significant and new information about safety hazards. You can get MSDSs online; the Internet has a wide range of free resources. The Occupational Health and Safety Administration (OSHA) regulations govern the use of MSDSs and the information an MSDS must contain in the U.S.

Battery Backups and UPSs

A backup battery is a device that provides power to a computing device when the primary source of power is unavailable. Backup batteries can range from small single cells used to retain clock time and date inside computers and devices, to large battery room facilities that power uninterruptible power supply (UPS) systems for large data centers.

A UPS is different from battery backup because it will provide near-instantaneous protection from power interruptions, power conditioning by removing power quality problems, and real-time monitoring and controlled shutdown of protected equipment. A UPS is typically used to protect hardware such as computers, data centers, telecommunication equipment, or other electrical equipment in which an unexpected power disruption could cause serious business disruption or data loss.

ACTIVITY 11-1
Identifying Physical Security Controls

Scenario

The network administrator at Greene City Interiors quizzes you on some of physical security controls used at the branch office.

---

1. True or False? An emergency procedure can inform employees on what to do in the event of an armed intruder.

   ☐ True

   ☐ False

2. What are some of the techniques to implement good air flow in a network closet or data center?

3. Which is the most efficient physical security control to limit access to multiple rooms for multiple users?

   ○ Card/proximity reader

   ○ Intercom

   ○ Cipher lock

   ○ Security guard

4. What is the main difference between battery backups and UPSs?

5. In which ways can security cameras improve the security of a building?

   ☐ Act as a deterrent.

   ☐ Prevent access.

   ☐ Monitor and document access to the building.

TOPIC B

Network Access Controls

In the last topic, you identified physical security controls. Once the physical premises and its contents are secure, you can begin to determine ways to protect your network from unauthorized access. In this topic, you will describe network access controls.

NAC

Network access control (NAC) is a general term for the collected protocols, policies, and hardware that govern access on network interconnections. NAC provides an additional security layer that scans devices for conformance and allows or quarantines updates to meet policy standards. Security professionals will deploy a NAC policy according to an organization's needs based on three main elements: the authentication method, endpoint vulnerability assessment, and network security enforcement. Once the NAC policy is determined, professionals must determine where NAC will be deployed within their network structure.

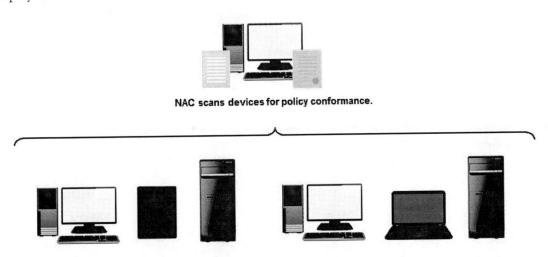

NAC scans devices for policy conformance.

Figure 11–12: NAC governs access on device network interconnections.

Posture Assessment

Sometimes authorization in NAC can be done by using a compliance check. This process is called *posture assessment*. In this process, a network's security is assessed based on the security applications that are running on the network. These might include things such as Windows® registry settings or the presence of security agents such as antivirus or personal firewall.

NAC and Protocols

IEEE 802.1x is a standard for securing networks by implementing Extensible Authentication Protocol (EAP) as the authentication protocol over either a wired or wireless Ethernet LAN, rather than the more traditional implementation of EAP over Point-to-Point Protocol (PPP). IEEE 802.1x, often referred to as port authentication, employs an authentication service, such as Remote Authentication Dial-In User Service (RADIUS), to secure clients, removing the need to implement security features in access points (APs), which typically do not have the memory or processing resources to support complex authentication functions.

In 802.1x, the switch or wireless access point puts the client session on hold and does not allow it to enter the network until either the device or user is authenticated and authorized by a RADIUS server. If you have ever been to a wireless hotspot where you had to enter a user name and password in a browser before you could access the Internet, you have experienced 802.1x.

An IEEE standard is used to provide a Port-based Network Access Control (PNAC), using the 802.11a and 802.11b protocols. 802.1x uses EAP to provide user authentication against a directory service.

ACLs

An *access control list (ACL)* is a set of data (user names, passwords, time and date, IP addresses, media access control [MAC] addresses, and so on) that is used to control access to a resource such as a device, file, or network. ACLs are commonly implemented as MAC address filtering on wireless routers and access points. When a wireless client attempts to access the network, that client's MAC address is compared to the list of authorized MACs and access is granted or restricted based on the result.

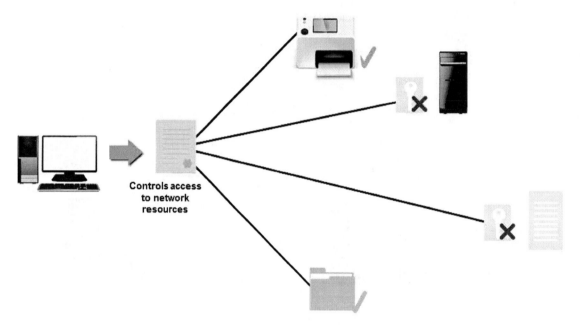

Controls access to network resources

Figure 11-13: ACLs control access to network resources.

Guest Networks

A *guest network* is a subset of an organization's network that is designed for temporary use by visitors. Typically, guest networks provide full Internet connectivity while severely restricting access to the internal intranet. This helps keep an organization's internal information private, and helps avoid spreading any malware that visitors may have on their devices.

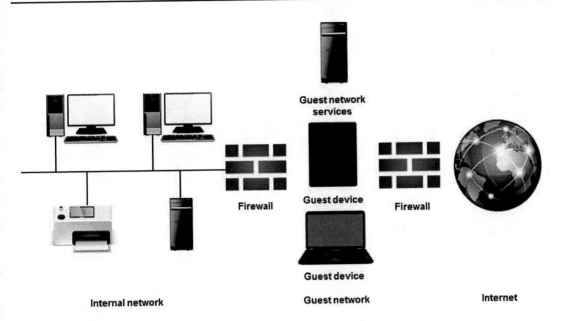

Figure 11-14: A guest network.

Persistent and Non-persistent Agents

The code that authenticates users and devices on behalf of an application for network access control can be a persistent or non-persistent agent. The agent can verify that the user or device meets specific requirements before being allowed access. This might include verifying that the device has or does not have certain applications installed and that the antivirus software is up-to-date.

A *persistent agent* is a piece of software that installs on the client device, and can respond continuously to queries from the NAC about the device's health. It stays on the device until uninstalled.

A *non-persistent agent*, also known as a dissolvable agent, is one that is installed on demand and then removed after it is used. The agent installs, responds to NAC queries to check the health of the device, authenticates the device, and then disappears when the session is over.

There is also an "agentless" approach. This uses a device's Active Directory domain membership to verify health. Services that already exist on any Microsoft® operating system are used to perform the task. You have to enable the services before you can use them.

Quarantine Networks

A *quarantine network* is a restricted network that provides users with routed access only to certain hosts and applications. Users are denied access to the network and are assigned to a quarantine network when a NAC product determines that an end user's device is out-of-date. They are assigned to a network that is routed only to patch and update servers, and not to the rest of the network. They can then update their devices to bring them up to NAC standards and gain access to the network.

Another commonly used term for quarantine network is *remediation network*.

These are often implemented using VLAN configurations.

Edge Networks

An *edge network* is a network located on the periphery of a centralized network. It is where an organization's network actually connects to the Internet, or to a provider's carrier network. It is the least secure of all the organization's networks. Physically located on the customer's premises, it is a link between the provider's demarc and the organization's router. Providers too can have an edge network, where they connect to other providers. Most edge devices are routers or firewalls.

Edge Networks and Access Control

Access control starts at the edge network. A virtual private network (VPN) server, or even a firewall itself, can accept client VPN connections at the edge. These clients and their users have to pass some sort of access control to authenticate, and the client may also have to prove its health before the connection is accepted. If there is no VPN connection, the firewall will still have many access control rules to filter out undesirable or uninvited traffic.

Proxy and Reverse Proxy Servers

A *proxy server* is a system that isolates internal clients from the servers by downloading and storing files on behalf of the clients. It intercepts requests for web-based or other resources that come from the clients, and, if it does not have the data in its cache, it can generate a completely new request packet by using itself as the source, or simply relay the request. In addition to providing security, the data cache can also improve client response time and reduce network traffic by providing frequently used resources to clients from a local source.

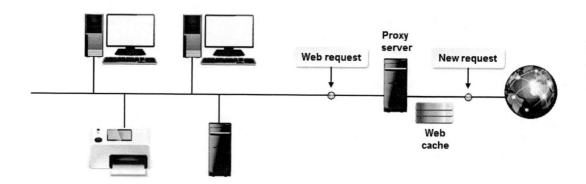

Figure 11-15: A proxy server isolates internal clients from the server.

A proxy puts the client session on hold while it fetches the content for the client. It will then cache the fetched data for the next client that wants the same content. One potential issue with a proxy is that the cached content can quickly become stale. This is especially a nuisance for businesses that depend on quick updates such as stock availability on a website, continually updated news or stock market quotes, or website developers that are constantly uploading web pages to remote servers and then displaying the results. An administrator will have to accurately judge how long cached content should be kept, and configure the proxy accordingly.

Depending on your traffic level and network needs, different proxy servers can be configured for different external services. For example, one proxy server can handle HTTP requests, while another server can handle FTP content.

A *reverse proxy* is a type of proxy server that retrieves resources on behalf of a client from one or more servers. These resources are returned to the client as if they originated from the reverse proxy server itself. A reverse proxy acts as an intermediary for its associated servers and returns resources provided by those associated servers only.

Web Proxy Features

A *web proxy* is a proxy server that provides anonymous access to web-based content. Web proxies can incorporate several enhanced features.

Feature	Description
User security	Enables an administrator to grant or deny Internet access based on user names or group membership.
Gateway services	Enables proxies to translate traffic between protocols.
Auditing	Enables administrators to generate reports on users' Internet activity.
Remote access services	Provides access to the internal network for remote clients.
Content filtering	Evaluates the content of websites based on words or word combinations, and blocks content that an administrator has deemed undesirable.

Website Caching

The website caching process enables web proxies to cache web data for clients.

Step	Description
Step 1: Client request	The client requests data from a website.
Step 2: Packet intercepted	The proxy server intercepts the packet, generates a new request, and transmits it to the website.
Step 3: Download content	The proxy server downloads all requested content, caches it, and sends it to the client.
Step 4: Verify cache	If the client requests the same data, the proxy server intercepts the request, verifies that the files are current based on the time-to-live (TTL) values in its cache index, and sends the cached data to the client.
Step 5: Update cache	If the files are not current, the proxy server updates both cache contents from the external website and the TTL on the cache.
Step 6: Purge cache	The proxy server purges its cache once the TTL value on an indexed item expires.

One important danger of using a proxy server is that, if an external website updates its contents before the TTL of the cache on the web proxy expires, a client might get outdated information from the web proxy's cache. Proxy servers can use either passive or active caching to ensure that cache data is current.

- In passive caching, the proxy server does not cache any data marked as time sensitive, but sends repeated requests to external sites to ensure that data is current.
- In active caching, the proxy server profiles cache indexes of websites based on the volume of use.

The proxy server actively refreshes the cache contents for sites that have had multiple hits from internal clients. Another technique the proxy server can use is to request time stamps from the external website, compare them to the stamp in its cache, and download only new data. The time stamp requests generate only a small amount of traffic and eliminate unnecessary content downloads.

 Access the Checklist tile on your LogicalCHOICE course screen for reference information and job aids on How to Install and Configure Proxy and Reverse Proxy Servers.

NAT

Network address translation (NAT) conceals internal addressing schemes from external networks such as the Internet. A router is configured with a single public IP address on its external interface and a nonroutable address on its internal interface. A NAT service running on the router or on another device translates between the two addressing schemes. Packets sent to the Internet from internal hosts all appear as if they came from a single IP address, thus preventing external hosts from identifying and connecting directly to internal devices.

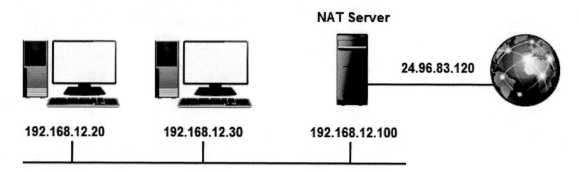

Figure 11-16: NAT conceals internal addressing schemes from the public Internet.

 Note: An internal network can be configured with a private IP address, which makes NAT both secure and cost-efficient.

Both proxy servers and NAT devices readdress outgoing packets. However, NAT simply replaces the original source address on the packet. Proxy servers actually examine the packet contents and then generate a new request packet, thus providing an additional level of protection between the original requesting client and the external network.

NAT can be implemented as software on a variety of systems, or as hardware in a dedicated device such as a router. Internet Connection Sharing (ICS) in Windows systems includes a simple software-based NAT implementation, but requires a separate device, such as a modem, to provide Internet connectivity. Hardware-based NAT devices, such as cable modems and digital subscriber line (DSL) routers, often have extended functionality and can double as Internet access devices.

In static NAT, an unregistered address is mapped to a single specific registered address. In dynamic NAT, a single unregistered address is mapped to the first registered address in an address pool.

In Windows, you can configure NAT in Routing and Remote Access. In Linux®, you can configure it by entering the following commands as root:

```
modprobe iptable_nat
echo 1 > /proc/sys/net/ipv4/ip_forward
iptables -t nat -A POSTROUTING -o eth0 -j MASQUERADE
iptables -A FORWARD -i eth1 -j ACCEPT
```

Port address translation (PAT) is a subset of dynamic NAT functionality that maps either one or more unregistered addresses to a single registered address using multiple ports. PAT is also known as overloading.

SNAT is an intensely debated acronym that can stand for Secure NAT, Stateful NAT, Source NAT, or Static NAT, depending on the source of information. Per Cisco, the originators of NAT, SNAT stands for Stateful NAT. SNAT includes two or more routers working together to perform NAT. Dynamic NAT (DNAT) uses a group of public IP addresses, rather than mapping to a specific public IP address.

The NAT Process

The NAT process translates external and internal addresses based on port numbers.

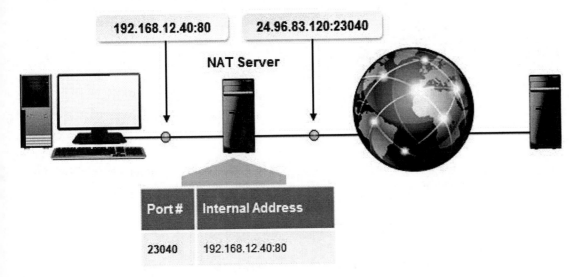

Figure 11-17: Steps in the NAT process.

Step	Description
Step 1: Client request	An internal client sends a request to an external service, such as a website, using the external destination IP address and port number.
Step 2: Source address conversion	The NAT device converts the source address in the request packet to its own external address, and adds a reference port number to identify the originating client.
Step 3: Data return	The service returns data to the NAT device's external address using the reference port number.
Step 4: Internal source identification	NAT uses the reference port number to identify the correct internal source address.
Step 5: Data delivery	NAT readdresses the packet to the internal system and delivers the data.

 Note: For additional information, check out the LearnTO **Understand the NAT Process** presentation in the LearnTOs for this course on your LogicalCHOICE Course screen.

ACTIVITY 11-2
Configuring NAT

Scenario

At the Greene City Interiors branch office, you want to limit the number of public IP addresses used by the branch office when users connect to the Internet. You decide to configure the NAT service on your network to help with this.

1. Enable NAT for routing.

   a) In **Server Manager**, select **Tools→Routing and Remote Access**.

   b) In the Routing and Remote Access window, in the console tree, expand **Computer##, IPv4**.

   c) Select **General**.

   d) Right-click **General** and select **New Routing Protocol**.

   e) In the **New Routing Protocol** dialog box, verify that **NAT** is selected and select **OK**.

   f) Observe that in the console tree, a new entry called **NAT** appears under **IPv4**.

2. Exclude reserved IP addresses and configure NAT.

   a) Right-click **NAT** and select **Properties**.

   b) In the **NAT Properties** dialog box, select the **Address Assignment** tab.

   c) Check the **Automatically assign IP addresses by using the DHCP allocator** check box.

   d) Select **Exclude.**

   e) In the **Exclude Reserved Addresses** dialog box, select **Add**.

   f) Enter the IP address of a partner computer, and select **OK**.

   g) In the **Exclude Reserved Addresses** dialog box, select **OK**.

   h) In the **NAT Properties** dialog box, select **Apply** and then select **OK**.

   i) Right-click **NAT** and select **New Interface** to create an interface for NAT.

   j) In the **New Interface for Network Address Translation** dialog box, select **Loopback Adapter** and select **OK**.

   k) In the **Network Address Translation Properties** dialog box, select **Public interface connected to the Internet**.

   l) Check the **Enable NAT on this interface** check box, select **Apply** and then select **OK**.

   m) Close the Routing and Remote Access window.

Port Forwarding

Port forwarding, also called port mapping, enables a permanent translation entry that maps a protocol port on a gateway to an IP address and protocol port on a private LAN. Network clients cannot see that port forwarding is being done. This allows communications from an external source to a destination within a private LAN. For example, a remote device could connect to a specific device or service within a private LAN by using port forwarding.

DMZs

A *demilitarized zone (DMZ)* is a small section of a private network that is located between two firewalls and made available for public access. A DMZ enables external clients to access data on private devices, such as web servers, without compromising the security of the internal network as a whole. The external firewall enables public clients to access the service, whereas the internal firewall prevents them from connecting to protected internal hosts.

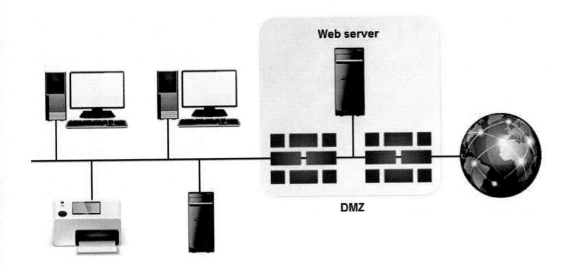

Figure 11-18: A section of a private network available for public access.

 Note: You will examine firewalls in depth in the next topic.

ACTIVITY 11-3
Discussing Network Access Controls

Scenario

The network administrator at Greene City Interiors wants to see what you know of network access controls.

---

1. In the NAT process, in which step does the NAT readdress the packet to the internal system?
   - ○ Source address conversion
   - ○ Client request
   - ○ Data delivery
   - ○ Data return

2. Why might you want to implement NAC on your network?

3. What is a system that isolates internal clients from the servers by downloading and storing files on behalf of the clients?
   - ○ Reverse proxy server
   - ○ Proxy server
   - ○ Quarantine network
   - ○ Website caching

4. Describe a common use for ACLs.

5. You are visiting a client's office and connected to a wireless network with your laptop. You have full Internet connectivity but no access to the internal intranet. What sort of network are you on?
   - ○ Guest network
   - ○ DMZ
   - ○ Edge network
   - ○ Quarantine network

6. How does a NAT differ from a DMZ?

TOPIC C

Install and Configure Firewalls

In the last topic, you described network access controls. One of the most popular means of controlling access to network resources from outside the network is to use firewalls. In this topic, you will install and configure firewalls.

Although firewalls are a popular means of controlling external access to network resources, they need to be configured correctly in order to block unwanted traffic while still allowing approved traffic. Having a solid understanding of how firewalls work and how to configure them will enable you to increase your network security without blocking traffic that users need.

Firewalls

Firewalls permit traffic that has specifically been permitted by a system administrator, based on a defined set of rules. Information about the incoming or outgoing connections can be saved to a log and used for network monitoring or hardening purposes. Firewalls use complex filtering algorithms that analyze incoming packets based on destination and source addresses, port numbers, and the data type.

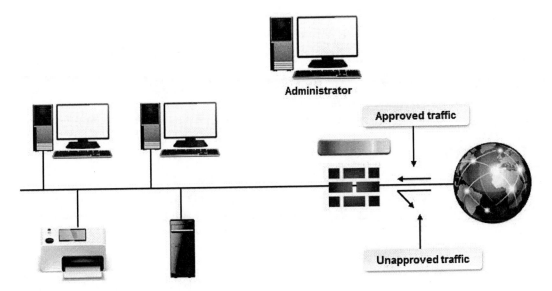

Figure 11-19: A firewall blocks unwanted network traffic.

Firewalls are universally deployed between private networks and the Internet. They can also be used between two separate private networks, or on individual systems, to control data flow between any two sources.

Firewalls can be of different types based upon the requirements of the network. There are four common types of firewalls.

Firewall Type	Description
Packet filters	Packet filters are the simplest implementation of a firewall and work at the Network layer (Layer 3) of the OSI model. Each packet being passed along the network is compared to a set of default criteria or a set of rules configured by a network administrator. Once a packet is compared to the criteria, it is passed or dropped, or a message is sent back to the originator. Packet filters are usually a part of a router.
Stateful inspection firewall	Stateful inspection firewalls work at the Session layer (Layer 5) of the OSI model by monitoring the condition, or state, of the connection. It monitors the TCP connection-establishment to determine if a request is legitimate. Stateful inspection firewalls are also known as circuit-level gateways. **Note:** Stateful inspection is covered in greater detail later in this topic.
Proxy firewall	Proxy firewalls work at the Application layer (Layer 7) of the OSI model and require incoming and outgoing packets to have a proxy to access services. This functionality allows proxy firewalls to filter application-specific commands. Proxy firewalls can be used to log user activity and logons, which offers administrators a high level of security but significantly affects network performance. Also known as Application-level gateways.
Hybrid firewall	Hybrid firewalls combine the functions of a packet filter, a stateful inspection firewall, and a proxy firewall. They operate on all three OSI layers, Network, Session, and Application, simultaneously.

Note: For additional information, check out the LearnTO **Understand the Firewall Process** presentation in the LearnTOs for this course on your LogicalCHOICE Course screen.

Port Filtering

Port filtering is a technique of selectively enabling or disabling TCP and UDP ports on computers or network devices. It ensures that no traffic, except for the protocol that the administrator has chosen to allow, can pass through an open port. Port filtering works by examining the packet's header, source address, destination address, and port number. However, a packet's header can be spoofed; a sender can fake his IP address or any other data stored in the header.

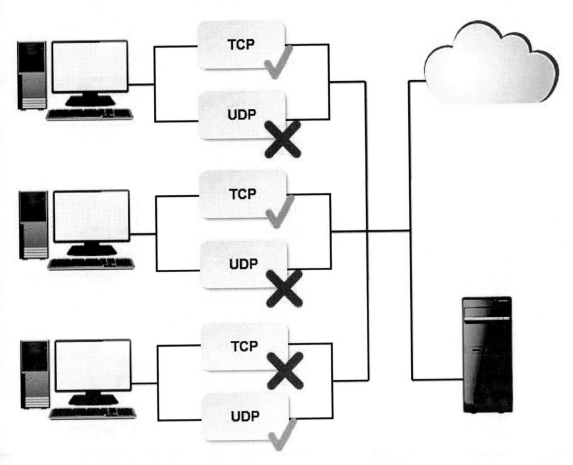

Figure 11-20: TCP and UDP ports disabled in computers on a network.

Port filtering is most often used in firewalls and for device hardening. Normally, in organizations, administrators disable/block ports above 1024 as a security measure. They selectively enable ports above 1024 during the installation of the associated services that use the port number.

Traffic Filtering

Traffic filtering is a method that allows only legitimate traffic through to the network. It blocks unwanted traffic, thereby minimizing valuable resource consumption. Traffic is filtered based on rules that accept or deny traffic based on the source or destination IP address. Whenever a filtering device receives traffic, it attempts to match the traffic with a rule. Firewalls and servers are the most commonly used traffic filtering devices. Some devices filter traffic that originates only from the internal network, whereas other, more sophisticated, devices filter traffic from external networks also.

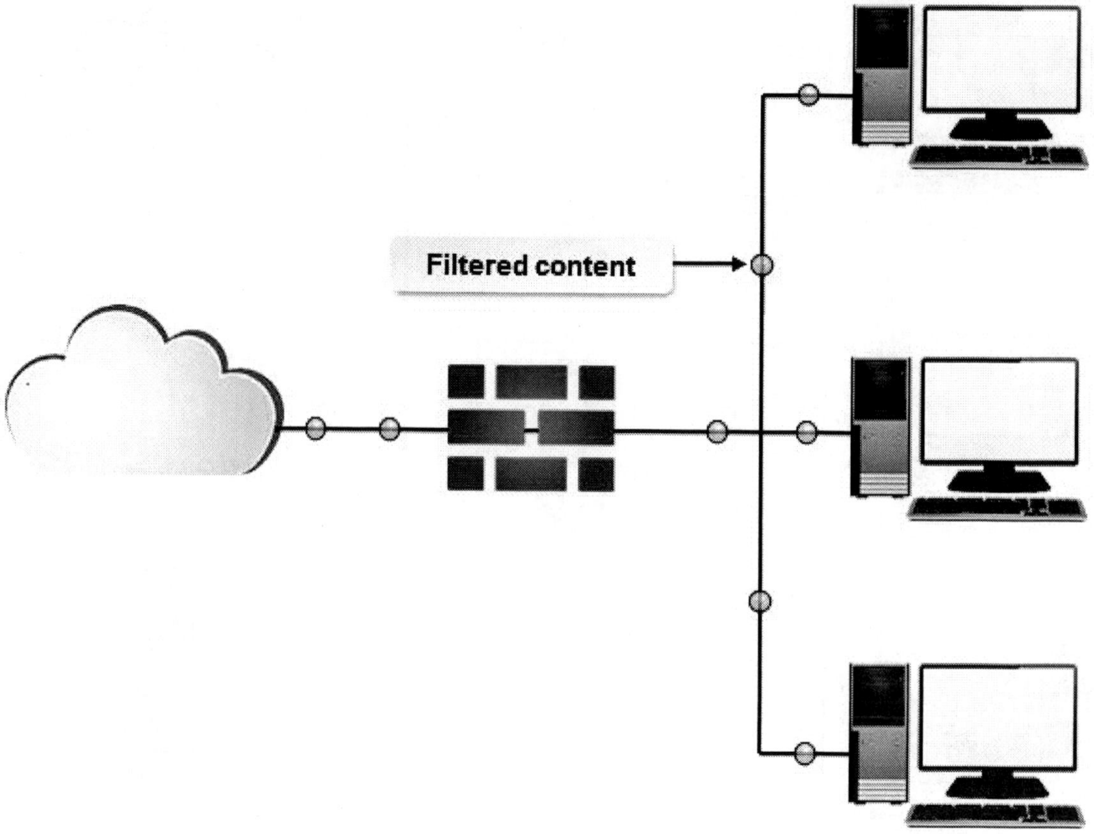

Figure 11-21: Data packets filtered by a firewall.

Firewalls will sometimes block network discovery from other devices. In the case of Windows, the option for network discovery is disabled. Network discovery is a method for devices to find each other on the network. In order to use this feature, it will need to be enabled.

Common Firewall Features

Modern firewall software and hardware can offer many features and a great deal of functionality.

Firewall Feature	Description
Scanning services	Provides the ability to scan incoming and outgoing packets and perform some action based on the content of those packets.
Content filtering	Blocks restricted websites or content. This can be accomplished by URL filtering, or inspection of each file or packet. Some firewalls have this functionality built in; in other cases, each request is passed to a filtering server that can approve or deny the request.
Signature identification	Many modern firewalls can scan for and detect indicators and patterns that may indicate that a network-based attack is under way. These indicators could also signify that data in question is not legitimate or could be infected with a virus, Trojan, or other malicious code. These indicators are compared against a list of known features, or signatures, of common threats including network-based attacks and viruses. The data is then handled according to the rules established by the firewall administrator.

Firewall Feature	Description
Zones	Firewall zones are used to create a virtual or physical network topology or architecture that creates separate areas (zones) with differing security levels. For example, web servers may be placed inside firewalls with increased security due to frequent attacks, while a departmental file server might be placed in a medium security zone because it is less likely to be directly attacked.
Port security	*Port security* is the process of properly securing ports on a network. The process includes: • Disabling unnecessary services. • Closing ports that are by default open or have limited functionality. • Regularly applying the appropriate security patches. • Hiding responses from ports that indicate their status and allow access to pre-configured connections only.

In higher-security environments, you also can configure firewalls to block unapproved outbound traffic from leaving the private network.

Host-Based and Network-Based Firewalls

A *network-based firewall* is a dedicated hardware/software combination that protects all the devices on a network behind the firewall. A *host-based firewall* (also known as a personal firewall) is software that is installed directly on a host and filters incoming and outgoing packets to and from that host.

 Note: Some popular personal firewalls are ZoneAlarm® and Norton™ Personal Firewall.

Software Firewalls and Hardware Firewalls

Software firewalls can be useful for small home offices and businesses, as well as providing extra protection to clients and servers on the internal network. The firewall provides many features that can be configured to suit various computing needs. Some features include:

• Enabling or disabling port security on certain ports.
• Filtering inbound and outbound communication. A user can set up rules or exceptions in the firewall settings to limit access to the web.
• Reporting and logging activity.
• Protecting systems from malware and spyware.
• Blocking pop-up messages.
• Assigning, forwarding, and triggering ports.

A hardware firewall is a hardware device, either stand-alone or built into a router. A router configured with an ACL (a packet filtering router) can also be used as a simple stateless firewall. By today's standards, however, this is considered insufficient to provide any real network security, and would ordinarily be used by an upstream router to help "weed out" undesirable traffic before it reaches the firewall. Software and hardware firewalls can be used together, where the hardware firewall provides protection for the entire network and the software firewall provides additional protection for individual systems.

 Note: ACLs and stateless firewalls are discussed in greater depth later in this topic.

Application–Aware and Context–Aware Firewalls

Application-aware firewalls provide the same capabilities as traditional firewalls, and they can also enforce security rules on applications, regardless of port or protocol. This allows them to protect against threats that can run over any port, use encryption, or tunnel to evade security.

Context-aware firewalls include application-aware capabilities and include the ability to extract the user identity, origin of the access, and the type of device used for the access. It can then permit or deny the access based on these attributes, thus giving you even more ways to protect against threats.

SOHO Firewalls

Small office/home office (SOHO) firewalls are typically derived from enterprise-level firewalls. They have more features than just using the broadband router's firewall provided through NAT. SOHO firewalls retain many of the features of enterprise firewalls with features such as NAT, stateful packet inspection, and port forwarding. Typically, SOHO firewalls have two interfaces, with one connection to the external or public Internet connection and one for the internal private network.

A SOHO will have very simple firewall needs and therefore could use any traditional firewall. Typically, the rules for a SOHO will be to block all unsolicited inbound traffic, and permit all outbound traffic and its responses. A few ports or protocols might be permitted and mapped to an internal computer, such as a gaming server. There would be no need for a DMZ, and typically no host-to-site VPN, though you might have a site-to-site VPN if the SOHO had two locations. There would also be little or no need for monitoring or alerts. SOHOs would typically not host any public servers such as web, email, or Domain Name System (DNS) servers. They would use a provider to host these services instead. A SOHO may not have a separate firewall. In this case, it would use the firewall capabilities of its router.

Stateful and Stateless Inspection

Stateful inspection examines the data within a packet as well as the state of the connection between the internal and external devices. Stateless inspection examines the data within a packet but ignores the state of the connection between the internal and external devices.

An Application-layer gateway builds on the process of stateful inspection by analyzing each packet to ensure that the content matches the expected service it is communicating with. For example, an Application-layer gateway would check web traffic data to ensure that it is HTML data. If the data type did not match the acceptable use for the service, the Application-layer gateway would block the packet from passing through. Application-layer gateways can perform deep packet inspection, even when files are compressed with products such as winzip and winrar. It is possible to do antivirus checks and even quarantine suspicious data if it matches certain criteria.

An Application-layer gateway is a very powerful feature, but it comes at a cost. The processing overhead incurred in analyzing every individual packet passing through the filter is extremely resource intensive. Many products have a separate service for each protocol that will be inspected. Significant processor and memory resources are required in order to provide the stateful inspection capability and to minimize network latency. In addition, Application-layer gateways are typically expensive.

A *stateless firewall* performs a *stateless inspection* by comparing each individual packet to a rule set to see if there is a match, and then if there is a match, acts on that packet (permits or denies) based on the rule. It does not track the lifetime of a connection. It has no memory of whether there was a starting handshake, and cannot detect if an address, port, or protocol has changed in the middle of the conversation. Stateless firewalls can be easily deceived by specially crafted packets. For example, when the TCP ACK flag is raised, that normally indicates that the packet is part of an already existing conversation. A stateless firewall, having no memory of whether the conversation actually started, will permit such a packet to enter the internal network on the assumption that it is part of a legitimate response from an external server to an internal host.

In contrast, a *stateful firewall* performs stateful inspections and monitors entire conversations from start to finish. It can detect if the communication has suddenly changed ports (often an indication of hacking activity), if an appropriate TCP three-way handshake occurred, or if packets have TCP flags raised illegally in an effort to spoof the firewall into letting them pass.

UTM

Unified Threat Management (UTM) is a network security solution that is used to monitor and manage a wide variety of security-related applications and infrastructure components through a single management console. UTMs provide multiple security functions such as network firewalling, network intrusion prevention, anti-malware, VPN, spam and content filtering, load balancing, data leak prevention, and on-appliance reporting. UTMs can be network appliances or a cloud service.

 Note: Security functions like network intrusion prevention are covered later in the course.

Firewalls and ACLs

Firewall functionality was initially performed by ACLs, usually on routers. ACLs have good scalability and high performance, but cannot read past packet headers in the way some firewalls can. For that reason, ACL packet filtering alone does not have the capacity to keep threats out of the network.

Routed Mode and Virtual Wire Mode

In Routed mode, the firewall is considered to be a router hop in the network. It can perform NAT between connected networks, and can use Open Shortest Path First (OSPF) or Routing Information Protocol (RIP) (in single context mode). Routed mode supports many interfaces in which each is on a different subnet.

In Virtual Wire mode, the firewall logically binds two ports together and passes all traffic to the other port without any switching or routing. It is not seen as a router hop to connected devices. Full inspection and control for all traffic is enabled, and no networking protocol configuration is required.

Implicit Deny and Firewalls

The principle of *implicit deny* dictates that when using a firewall, anything that is not explicitly allowed is denied. Users and software should only be allowed to access data and perform actions when permissions are specifically granted to them. No other action is allowed.

Most hardware firewalls are configured out of the box with implicit deny in both directions, inbound and outbound. It is then up to the administrator to permit traffic as desired. Most administrators will allow some level of outbound traffic, but will continue to deny inbound traffic that is not already part of an established connection. Most software firewalls on a host are configured to permit all outbound traffic originating from the host, but with an implicit deny disallowing inbound traffic from entering the host. Usually, when an application or service is configured on a host, the host firewall is also automatically configured to permit the traffic by that service.

Traffic Control

Firewalls control traffic by blocking or allowing communications. Inbound and outbound traffic can be blocked or allowed by firewall rules. These rules are specific to inbound or outbound traffic and thus one kind of traffic may be allowed when outbound but blocked when it is inbound, depending on the rules. Typically, rules can be configured to specify the device, user, program, service, or port and protocol that they apply to. A firewall may be configured to allow or block all traffic for either inbound or outbound. If all traffic is blocked by default, then you can create rules to allow specific traffic. If all traffic is allowed by default, then you can create rules to block specific traffic. Blocking all traffic and adding exceptions to allow specific traffic is more secure.

Firewall Placement

It is important to consider where firewalls should be placed in your network. Typically, firewalls are placed on the network perimeter where the private LAN connects to the Internet or other public WAN. This is a critical placement because the private-public network edge is still considered particularly vulnerable to intrusions from external sources. Firewalls should also be placed throughout the internal network in key locations. This will help protect against internal threats. To increase protection from internal threats, firewalls can also be placed at internal network perimeters. Examples of these perimeters, or trust boundaries, are between switches and back-end servers, between different departments, and where a wireless LAN connects the wired network. Placing firewalls in multiple network segments also helps organizations comply with the latest corporate and industry governance mandates. Sarbanes-Oxley, Gramm-Leach-Bliley (GLB), Health Insurance Portability and Accountability Act (HIPAA), and Payment Card Industry Data Security Standard (PCI-DSS), for example, contain requirements about information security auditing and tracking.

 Access the Checklist tile on your LogicalCHOICE course screen for reference information and job aids on How to Install and Configure a Firewall.

ACTIVITY 11-4
Configuring Windows Firewall

Scenario

At the Greene City Interiors branch office, you want to improve network security by allowing only the types of connections needed for the branch to conduct business. To accomplish this, you will verify that Windows Firewall is on and configured correctly.

---

1. Turn on Windows Firewall.

   a) In the Server Manager window, in the **Welcome to Server Manager** section, select the **Configure this local server** link.

   b) In the **Properties** section, for **Windows Firewall**, select the **Domain: Off** link.

   c) In the Windows Firewall window, in the left pane, select the **Turn Windows Firewall on or off** link.

   d) In the Customize Settings window, in each of the three sections **Domain network settings**, **Private network settings**, and **Public network settings**, select the **Turn off Windows Firewall (not recommended)** option and select **OK**.

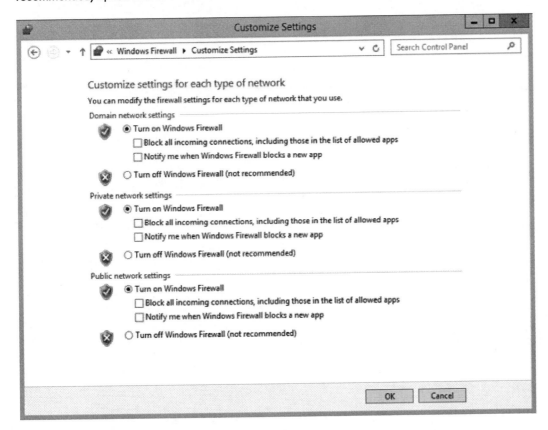

2. Configure Windows Firewall.

   a) In the **Domain networks** section, observe the settings summary.

   b) In the left pane, select the **Advanced Settings** link.

   c) In the Windows Firewall with Advanced Security window, in the center pane, select **Windows Firewall Properties**.

d) In the **Windows Firewall with Advanced Security on Local Computer** dialog box, verify that the **Domain Profile** tab is selected.

e) In the **Firewall state** section, select **Customize.**

f) In the **Protected Network Connections for the Domain Profile** dialog box, verify that all network connections are selected and select **OK.**

g) In the **Settings** section, select **Customize.**

h) In the **Customize Settings for the Domain Profile** dialog box, in the **Display a notification** drop-down list, select **Yes** and select **OK.**

i) In the **Windows Firewall with Advanced Security on Local Computer** dialog box, select **OK.**

j) Close the Windows Firewall with Advanced Security window.

k) Close the Windows Firewall window.

TOPIC D

Harden Networks

In the last topic, you installed and configured a firewall. That's a good start, but protecting your network will involve additional tasks. In this topic, you will implement network hardening techniques.

Because networks have so many different points of vulnerability, protecting them requires multiple layers of security. Understanding the techniques used to harden a network is crucial to increasing the level of security on your network.

Software Updates

Software manufacturers regularly issue different types of system updates that can include security-related changes to software.

System Update Type	Description
Patch	A small unit of supplemental code meant to address either a security problem or a functionality flaw in a software package or operating system.
Hotfix	A patch that is often issued on an emergency basis to address a specific security flaw.
Rollup	A collection of previously issued patches and hotfixes, usually meant to be applied to one component of a device, such as the web browser or a particular service.
Service pack	A larger compilation of operating system updates that can include functionality enhancements, new features, and typically all patches, updates, and hotfixes issued up to the point of the release of the service pack.

Patch Management

Patch management is the practice of monitoring for, obtaining, evaluating, testing, and deploying software patches and updates. As the number of computing devices in use has grown over recent years, so has the volume of vulnerabilities and corresponding patches and updates intended to address those vulnerabilities. So, the task of managing and applying them can be very time-consuming and inefficient without an organized patch management system. In typical patch management, software updates are evaluated for their applicability to an environment and then tested in a safe way on non-production devices. Finally, an organized plan for rolling out a valid patch across the organization is executed.

When vulnerabilities are found in the operating system, updates are made available to users. You will want to test the functionality of the updates before allowing your users to install the updates. Some updates might interfere with the functionality of how some of your applications work. However, you might need to weigh the balance between known vulnerabilities and the functioning of the applications on your network.

In order for some updates to function properly, you might need to also update system firmware and drivers. Firmware updates and driver updates should also be thoroughly tested before deploying them in a large rollout.

Additional features might be available with some updates. Be sure you know how the feature changes and updates will affect your users before installing updates. Updates will usually be a minor version number update. For example, if the current version of an application is version 5.4, a minor version might be 5.4.1 or 5.4a. A major version update will usually go from 5.4 to 5.5.

If vulnerabilities in the firmware or operating system software on a server, workstation, or other network device are detected, and an update is issued, you should immediately begin testing the updates. Leaving a vulnerability unprotected can open up your network to attack or failure. Be sure to back up your systems before applying updates. This way, if something goes wrong with updates or additional problems are found after deploying the updates, you can downgrade again to the previous version. If possible, keep a configuration backup of all devices stored so that the devices can easily be restored to the previous configuration if necessary.

Patch Management Policies

Many organizations have taken to creating official patch management policies that define the who, what, where, when, why, and how of patch management for that organization.

Example: Patch Management

A patch management program might include:

- An individual responsible for subscribing to and reviewing vendor and security patches and updating newsletters
- A review and triage of the updates into urgent, important, and non-critical categories
- An offline patch-test environment where urgent and important patches can be installed and tested for functionality and impact
- Immediate administrative "push" delivery of approved urgent patches
- Weekly administrative "push" delivery of approved important patches
- A periodic evaluation phase and "pull" rollout for non-critical patches

Anti-malware Software

Anti-malware software is a category of protective software that scans devices and sometimes networks for known viruses, Trojans, worms, and other malicious programs. Some anti-malware programs attempt to scan for unknown harmful software. It is advisable to install anti-malware software on all devices and keep it updated according to your organization's patch management policy. In addition to detection, most anti-malware software is capable of logging scan and detection information. These logs should be monitored to make sure that scans are taking place and ensure that infections are reported properly.

Anti-malware can be host-based, where the application runs on the host and protects only that device. That system also needs to download its own updates. Server-based and cloud-based anti-malware can manage anti-malware applications installed on other hosts and provide the updates to them. In some cases, they can also run scans on the other hosts. Network-based anti-malware scans traffic entering and leaving the network for malware.

Anti-malware software vendors maintain and update the libraries of virus definitions and malware signatures; the customer must periodically update the definitions on all systems where the software is installed. Most vendors provide an automatic update service that enables customers to obtain and distribute current virus definitions on a schedule. Periodically, administrators should manually check to verify that the updates are current. When there is a known active threat, administrators should also manually update definitions.

Some vendors offer enterprise malware suites that include malware protection for all devices in a company, automatic updating, and the ability to download and distribute updates from a central server. Distributing the updates from a local server instead of obtaining them directly from the vendor enables the administrator to review and verify virus definitions before they are deployed.

Because almost all devices today are connected to the Internet, email is a source of serious virus threats. Companies can implement Internet email virus protection by:

- Screening the Internet gateway devices for viruses

- Employing reliable desktop antivirus software
- Scanning incoming email between the Internet and the email server
- Scanning email again at the device level
- If a virus attack is detected, disabling all Internet connections and isolating affected devices

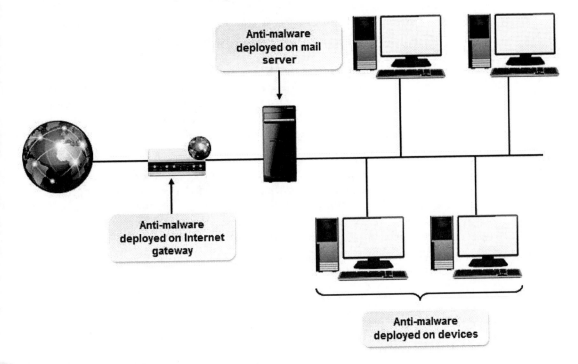

Figure 11-22: Anti-malware software deployed on different network locations.

Switch Port Security

There are different methods for implementing security for switch ports.

Switch Port Security Method	Description
DHCP snooping	Can harden the security on the network to allow only clients with specific IP or MAC addresses to have access to the network. It uses information from the Dynamic Host Configuration Protocol (DHCP) server to track the physical location of hosts, ensure that hosts use only the IP addresses assigned to them, and ensure that only authorized DHCP servers are accessible.
ARP inspection	Validates Address Resolution Protocol (ARP) packets in a network. ARP inspection determines the validity of packets by performing an IP-to-MAC address binding inspection before forwarding the packet to the appropriate destination. ARP packets with invalid IP-to-MAC address bindings that fail the inspection are dropped.

Switch Port Security Method	Description
MAC address filtering	Provides a simple method of securing a wireless network. By configuring a wireless access point (WAP) to filter MAC addresses, you can control which wireless clients can access your network. Typically, an administrator configures a list of client MAC addresses that are allowed to join the network. Those pre-approved clients are granted access if the MAC address is "known" by the access point. A note of caution, though: It is not difficult for someone with a little skill and know-how to change a MAC address, falsely gain authorization by using another computer, and gain access to your network. Although MAC filtering is usually implemented on wireless networks, it can also be used on wired networks.
IP filtering	Determines which packets will be allowed to pass and which packets will be dropped by screening the packet based on certain criteria. An administrator can set criteria to determine which packets to filter, such as the protocol type, source IP address, and destination IP address. When a packet is dropped, it is deleted and treated as if it was never received. IP filtering operates mainly at Layer 2 of the TCP/IP protocol stack and is generally performed by a screening router, although other network devices can also perform IP filtering.
VLAN assignments	Can segment a network so that traffic from one VLAN does not interfere with the traffic on other VLANs.

Secure Protocols

Secure protocols are ones that do not expose data and/or credentials in cleartext, so they are less likely to allow for the credentials or data to be viewed and captured by someone else.

- Secure Shell (SSH): Is used for secure data communication, remote command-line login, remote command execution, and other secure network services between two networked devices. It was designed as a replacement for Telnet and other insecure remote shell protocols.
- Hypertext Transfer Protocol Secure (HTTPS): Is used for secure communication over a network, with especially wide deployment on the Internet. The main purpose for HTTPS is to prevent wiretapping and man-in-the-middle attacks.
- Transport Layer Security/Secure Sockets Layer (TLS/SSL): Are used to provide communication security over the Internet. Several versions of the protocols are in widespread use in applications such as web browsing, electronic mail, Internet faxing, instant messaging, and Voice over IP (VoIP).
- Secure File Transfer Protocol (SFTP): Is used for secure file access, file transfer, and file management functionalities.
- Simple Network Management Protocol (SNMP) (v3): Is used for managing devices on IP networks. Version 3 added cryptographic security to secure data and user credentials.
- Internet Protocol Security *(IPSec)*: Is used for securing IP communications by authenticating and encrypting each IP packet of a communication session.

Wireless Security Controls

There are different controls that can be used to harden wireless networks.

Wireless Security Control	Description
WEP	Wired Equivalent Privacy (WEP) encrypts wireless communications, making them less vulnerable. It was designed to provide the same level of security as wired networks, but WEP has many well-known security flaws.
WPA/WPA2	Wi-Fi Protected Access (WPA) and WPA2 both encrypt wireless communications, making them less vulnerable to unauthorized access. Both offer better security that WEP, with WPA2 being more secure. Both protocols have a Personal and Enterprise mode. Personal mode uses a preshared key that all clients use for encryption. Enterprise mode uses 802.1x authentication and a unique encryption key for every client who logs on to the network.
TKIP/AES	Temporal Key Integrity Protocol (TKIP) is what provides the encryption for the WPA protocol, and Advanced Encryption Standard (AES) is what provides the encryption for the WPA2 protocol.
TLS/TTLS	Transport Layer Security (TLS) is a security protocol that protects sensitive communication from being eavesdropped and tampered. Tunneled Transport Layer Security (TTLS) is an Extensible Authentication Protocol (EAP) protocol that extends TLS by providing authentication that is as strong as TLS, but it does not require that each user be issued a certificate. Instead, only the authentication servers are issued certificates.
MAC filtering	MAC filtering restricts access to a wireless network by allowing access only to devices with specified MAC addresses.

Guidelines for Hardening Networks

 Note: All of the Guidelines for this lesson are available as checklists from the **Checklist** tile on the LogicalCHOICE Home screen.

Follow these guidelines to harden networks:

- Keep devices up-to-date with the latest security patches.
- Use an organized patch management system to optimize the task of managing and applying patches.
- Use an anti-malware application to protect devices from malicious programs.
- Keep anti-malware applications up-to-date.
- Consider using switch port security methods to make switches more secure.
- Use secure protocols whenever transmitting secure data or user credentials.
- Employ wireless security controls to make your wireless networks more secure.
- Consider disabling unneeded network services to reduce the possible avenues for attacks.
- Disable unneeded user accounts.
- Change default passwords.
- Implement security settings based on the concept of least privilege.
- Implement access lists such as web content/filtering, port filtering, IP filtering, and implicit deny to improve network security.
- Be sure to use some form(s) of user authentication, such as Challenge Handshake Authentication Protocol (CHAP)/Microsoft Challenge Handshake Authentication Protocol (MSCHAP), Password Authentication Protocol (PAP), EAP, Kerberos, multifactor authentication, two-factor authentication, and single sign-on (SSO).
- Consider using vulnerability testing tools to scan the system for any remaining vulnerabilities.

ACTIVITY 11-5
Hardening Networks

Scenario

The network administrator at Greene City Interiors asks you questions related to hardening the branch office network.

1. When should an anti-malware administrator manually check for malware updates?

   ○ When a known threat is active

   ○ After each automatic update

   ○ Never

   ○ Daily

2. Describe the process you would use to install OS patches in your environment.

3. You manage a small office network with a single gateway to an Internet service provider. The ISP maintains your corporate email on its own email server. There is an internal server for file and print services. As the administrator for this network, where should you deploy anti-malware software?

   ☐ Desktops

   ☐ Gateways

   ☐ Email server

   ☐ File and print server

TOPIC E

Intrusion Detection and Prevention

In the previous topic, you implemented network hardening techniques. No matter how many steps you take to secure your network, there is always a chance that it can be breached. In this topic, you will describe methods of threat detection and prevention.

At one time, computers were connected to an internal organization's network and most people did not access the Internet daily. Since the mid-1980s, there has been a tremendous surge in Internet usage. With millions of connections comes the very real potential for malicious attacks on an organization's network. As a network administrator, you must be aware of potential threats to your network and methods you can employ to protect data and resource availability.

Intrusion Detection

Intrusion detection is the process of monitoring the events occurring on a device or a network, and analyzing them to detect possible incidents. An *incident* is a violation or an imminent threat of violation of both information security policies and standard security practices. Though this process cannot prevent intrusions from occurring, it is predominantly used to monitor events, gather information, create a log of events, and alert you to the incident. The incidents may be unintentional or deliberate, but many of them are malicious. Intrusion detection can be performed manually or automatically.

The most popular way to detect intrusions is by using the audit data generated by the operating system. It is a record of activities logged chronologically. As almost all activities are logged, it is possible that a manual inspection of the logs would allow intrusions to be detected. Audit trails are particularly useful because they can be used to establish the attacker's guilt. In any case, they are often the only way to detect unauthorized and subversive user activity.

IDSs

An *intrusion detection system (IDS)* is software or hardware, or a combination of both, that scans, audits, and monitors the security infrastructure for signs of attacks in progress and automates the intrusion detection process. It is used to quickly detect malicious behavior that compromises the integrity of a device so that appropriate action can be taken. IDS software can also analyze data and alert security administrators to potential infrastructure problems. A variety of hardware sensors, intrusion detection software, and IDS management software can comprise an IDS. Each implementation is unique, depending on the security needs and the components chosen.

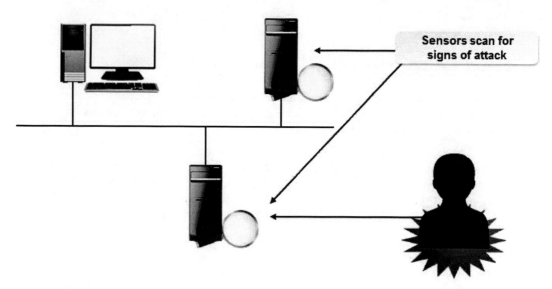

Figure 11-23: IDS detects an attack.

Both a firewall and an IDS enforce network policies, but the way they accomplish that task is significantly different. An IDS collects information and will either notify you of a possible intrusion or block packets based on configuration settings determined by a defined signature. A firewall filters traffic based on configuration settings alone. It can be helpful to keep in mind that many firewall and IDS systems have functionality that overlaps, or is integrated into the same device or appliance.

Snort is an open-source, free IDS software available for detecting and preventing intrusions. It is available at **www.snort.org**. This software has the capability to log data, such as alerts and other log messages, to a database.

Types of IDSs

There are several general categories of IDSs that you can use, alone or in combination with each other.

Category	Description
Network-based	An IDS that monitors network traffic and restricts or alerts when unacceptable traffic is seen in the system. It can be connected to a switch and is most often referred to as a *network intrusion detection system (NIDS)*. An example of an NIDS is Snort.
	A network-based IDS primarily uses passive hardware sensors to monitor traffic on a specific segment of the network. A network-based IDS cannot analyze encrypted packets because it has no method for decrypting the data. It can sniff traffic and send alerts about anomalies or concerns. Many network-based IDSs allow administrators to customize detection rules so that they may be tailored to a specific environment.

Category	Description
Host-based	An IDS capability installed on a workstation or server to protect that device. It monitors the device internally, and detects which program accesses the particular resource(s). It checks the host completely, and gathers information from the file system, log files, and similar places and detects any deviations from the security policy. This types of IDS is most often referred to as a *host intrusion detection system (HIDS)*.
	A host-based system primarily uses software installed on a specific host, such as a web server. Host-based IDSs can analyze encrypted data if it is decrypted before reaching the target host. However, host-based IDSs use the resources of the host they are installed on, and this can add to the processing time from other applications or services. Many host-based IDSs allow administrators to customize detection rules so that they can be tailored to a specific environment.
Pattern- or signature-based	An IDS that uses a predefined set of rules to identify traffic that is unacceptable. These rules can contain patterns and signatures provided by software vendors to identify known security issues.
Anomaly- or behavior-based	An IDS that uses a database of unacceptable traffic patterns identified by analyzing traffic flows. Anomaly-based systems are dynamic and create a baseline of acceptable traffic flows during their implementation process.
Protocol-based	An IDS installed on a web server and used to monitor the protocol(s) used by the device. It contains a system or agent at the front end of a server that is used for the monitoring and analysis of the communication protocol between a connected device and the system.
Application protocol-based	An IDS that monitors the application protocol(s) in use by the system. Contains an agent that interfaces between a process, or between multiple servers, and analyzes the application protocol between two devices.
	Application-based IDSs monitor traffic within or related to a specific application. They may be used in conjunction with a network- or host-based IDS to add another layer of protection to a critical application, such as a customer database.

Passive and Active IDSs

An IDS can be either passive or active. A *passive IDS* detects potential security breaches, logs the activity, and alerts security personnel. An *active IDS* does the same, and then takes the appropriate action to block the user from the suspicious activity. Some people consider the active IDS a type of *intrusion prevention system (IPS)*, and not a separate system.

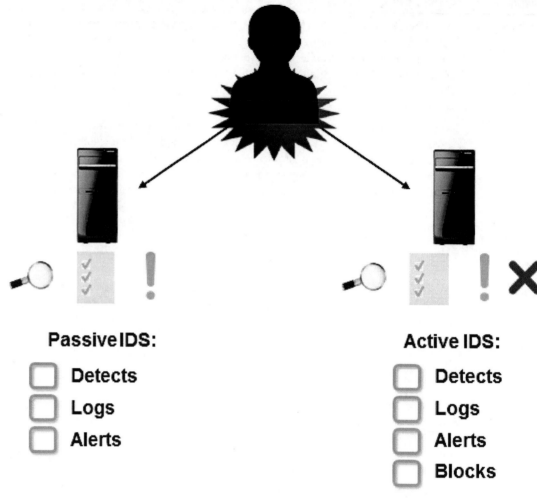

Passive IDS:

- Detects
- Logs
- Alerts

Active IDS:

- Detects
- Logs
- Alerts
- Blocks

Figure 11–24: Passive and active IDSs.

HIDS and NIDS

This table will help you compare the two most popular types of IDS implementations.

Characteristic	NIDS	HIDS
Components	Primarily hardware sensors	Primarily software applications
Monitoring method	Monitors traffic on a specific network segment	Monitors traffic on the host it is installed on
Monitoring target	Packets for protocol anomalies and known virus signatures	Log files, inadvisable settings or passwords, and other policy violations
Encrypted data	Cannot analyze encrypted data	Can analyze encrypted data if it is decrypted before it reaches the target host
Passive vs. active	Passive	Passive or active
Resource utilization	Uses resources from the network	Uses computing resources from the host it is monitoring
Capabilities	Broad scope; very general	Narrow scope; very specific

Characteristic	NIDS	HIDS
Alerts	Management console or email messages	Management console or email messages
Best use	To secure a large area with non-critical data, provide broad-based overall security; most cost effective	To secure a specific resource, such as a web server, that has critical data; cost prohibitive
Management issues	Can be installed on a network	Service agreements or other policy restrictions prevent the installation on a host
Legal issues	Hard to use as evidence in a lawsuit	May be admissible as evidence in a lawsuit

IPSs

An IPS is an inline security device that monitors suspicious network and/or device traffic and reacts in real time to block it. An IPS may drop packets, reset connections, sound alerts, and, at times, even quarantine intruders. It can regulate traffic according to specific content, because it examines packets as they travel through the IPS. This is in contrast to the way a firewall behaves, which blocks IP addresses or entire ports.

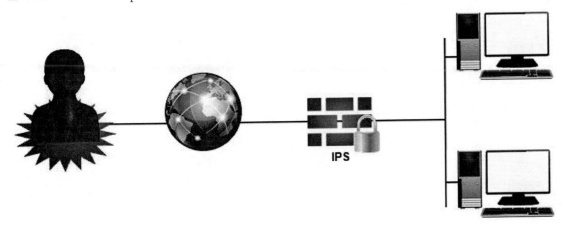

Figure 11-25: An IPS blocks suspicious network traffic.

 Note: Network behavior analysis is a behavior-based IPS that constantly monitors network traffic and identifies potential threats such as Distributed Denial of Service (DDoS), malware, and policy violations.

Types of IPSs

There are two major types of IPS: host-based and network-based.

IPS	Description
HIPS	A *host-based IPS (HIPS)* is an application that monitors the traffic from a specific host or a list of host addresses. This method is efficient because it blocks traffic from a specific host or an attack targeted against a specific host. The host-based IPS is also effective against internal attacks and threats from viruses, worms, Trojan horses, and keyloggers, among others.

IPS	Description
NIPS	A *network-based IPS (NIPS)* monitors the entire network and analyzes its activity. It detects malicious code and unsolicited traffic, and takes the necessary action. The NIPS is built to identify distorted network traffic; analyze protocols; and secure servers, clients, and network devices from various threats and attacks. NIPS is deployed in an organization and is considered a checkpoint to all incoming traffic.

Port Scanners

A *port scanner* is a type of software that searches a network host or a range of IP addresses for open TCP and UDP ports. A port scanner looks for open ports on the target device and gathers information including whether the port is open or closed, what services are running on that port, and any available information about the operating system. Administrators can use a port scanner to determine what services are running on the network and potential areas that are vulnerable. A port scanning attack occurs when an attacker scans your devices to see which ports are listening in an attempt to find a way to gain unauthorized access.

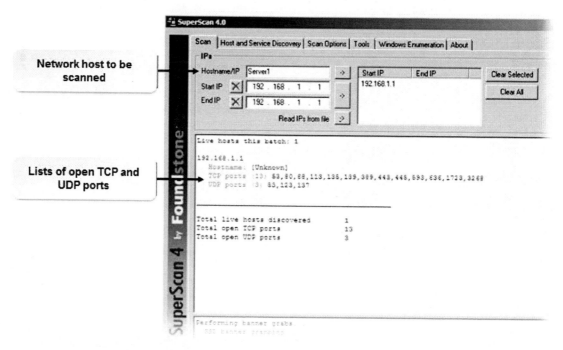

Figure 11–26: A port scanner on a network.

Note: When multiple hosts are scanned simultaneously or consecutively, it is called portsweeping.

Nmap is a widely available open source port scanner. It can rapidly scan a single host or an entire network. It can determine what hosts are available on a network, what services are offered, what types of operating systems are being used, what types of firewalls are being used, and numerous other characteristics of the target.

There are many utilities available that potential attackers can use to scan ports on networks, including Nmap, SuperScan, and Strobe. Many utilities can be downloaded for free from the Internet. Performing port scanning attacks is often the first step an attacker takes to identify live devices and open ports to launch further attacks with other tools.

Honeypots and Honeynets

A *honeypot* is a security tool that lures attackers away from legitimate network resources while tracking their activities. Honeypots appear and act as a legitimate component of the network but are actually secure lockboxes in which security professionals can block the intrusion and begin logging activities for use in court or even launch a counterattack. The act of luring individuals in could potentially be perceived as entrapment or violate the code of ethics of your organization. These legal and ethical issues should be discussed with your organization's legal counsel and human resources department.

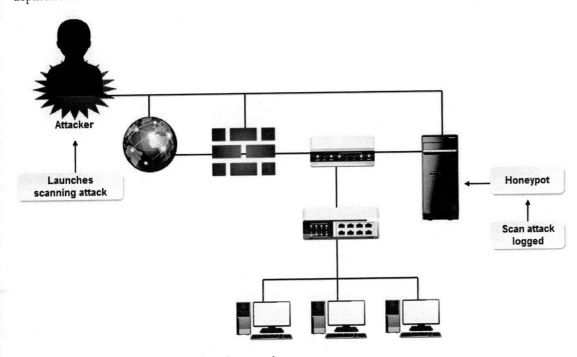

Figure 11-27: A honeypot scanning for attacks.

Honeypots can be software emulation programs, hardware decoys, or an entire dummy network, known as a *honeynet*. A honeypot implementation often includes some kind of IDS to facilitate monitoring and tracking of intruders. Some dedicated honeypot software packages can be specialized types of IDSs.

Network Scanners

Network scanners are computer programs used for scanning networks to obtain user names, host names, groups, shares, and services. Some network scanners provide information about vulnerabilities or weak spots on the network. Network scanners are sometimes used by attackers to detect and exploit the vulnerabilities on a network. Network scanners are also known as network enumerators.

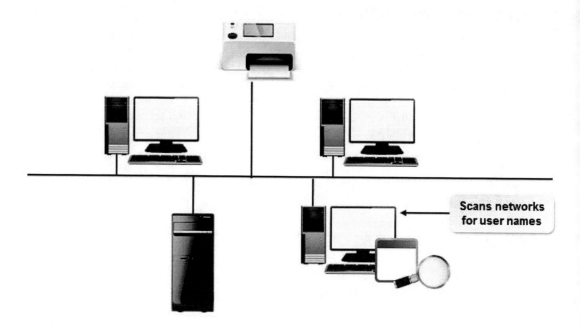

Figure 11-28: A network scanner scanning for user names on the network.

There are several network scanners available. Nmap and QualysGuard are popular among them. Another popular and effective network scanner you can use on both Windows and Linux is Nessus. The home version is free for personal use. You can download it from **www.tenable.com**.

Penetration Testing

Penetration testing is an attack authorized by the owner of a computing device or a network, with the purpose of finding security weaknesses that could be exploited by a real attacker. The goal is to determine if the device or network has any weaknesses. A penetration test may be a white box or black box. A white box is where all background and device information is provided to the attacker, and a black box is where only basic or even no information is provided except the company name. Penetration testing can help discover if a device's defenses prevented a successful attack, if it is vulnerable to attack, and which defenses, if any, were defeated. The results of the penetration test should then be reported to the owners so that they are aware of any issues they need to address. Penetration test reports may also assess the potential impact to the organization and suggest countermeasures to reduce risks.

ACTIVITY 11-6
Scanning for Port Vulnerabilities

Before You Begin

Ensure that the services running on the Child## computer include Active Directory, DNS, and Certificate Services. SuperScan is available in the **C:\093012Data\Tools** folder.

Scenario

At the Greene City Interiors branch office, you want to remove a potential security vulnerability of your servers by scanning them for open ports. The branch has had problems in the past with attackers getting access to applications on servers by getting through the firewall and accessing open ports on the servers. You have already hardened your servers and now want to check your work.

---

1. Install SuperScan.
   a) Open **File Explorer** and navigate to the **C:\093012Data\Tools** folder.
   b) Double-click the **superscan-4.1** compressed folder and, in the folder, double-click the **SuperScan4.1** application.
   c) In the **Compressed (zipped) Folders** dialog box, select **Run**.
   d) In the **Open File - Security Warning** dialog box, select **Run**.

2. Use SuperScan to scan the default ports on your server.
   a) In the SuperScan 4.1 window, on the **Scan** tab, in the **IPs** section, in the **Hostname/IP** box, type *Computer##*
   b) Select the **Host and Service Discovery** tab.
   c) Verify that the **UDP port scan** and **TCP port scan** check boxes are checked, and that a default list of ports appears in each scan area. The default ports are loaded from a configuration file.
   d) Select the **Scan** tab, and select the **Start** ▶ button to start the scan.

3. Examine the scan results.
   a) When the scan is complete, select **View HTML Results**.
   b) The report opens in the browser window. Scroll down to view a list of open ports. The right column shows how the server responds to a scan of each port.
   c) Close all open dialog boxes and windows.

TOPIC F

Educate Users

In the last topic, you described intrusion detection and prevention methods. But all of the steps you take to secure the network infrastructure can be negated at one stroke if a user provides the right information to the wrong person. In this topic, you will facilitate user awareness of security issues and countermeasures.

An attacker calls Maria, poses as a network administrator, and hangs up after asking for and receiving her user ID and password. John leaves his laptop on his desk, unlocked, over the weekend, and it is stolen by a member of the cleaning crew. Tina always logs in to her computer as Administrator with a blank password because it is easier. It is clear that none of these users are following good security practices and, if nobody told them how to do things any better, it is not necessarily their fault. How can you prevent these scenarios? It is your responsibility to educate or coach your users about their individual security responsibilities. An educated user is the IT professional's best partner in preventing security breaches.

Employee Education

Information security is not the exclusive responsibility of information professionals. A comprehensive security plan can succeed only when all members of an organization understand and comply with the necessary security practices. IT professionals are often the ones responsible for educating employees and encouraging their compliance with security policies. You will need a process for implementing end-user awareness and training.

The process of employee security education consists of three components.

Step	Description
Awareness	Education begins with awareness. Employees must be aware of the importance of information security and be alert to its potential threats. Employees also need to be aware of the role they play in protecting an organization's assets and resources. A network security professional can create awareness through seminars, email, or information on a company intranet.
Education	Employees should be trained and educated in security procedures, practices, and expectations from the moment they walk through the door. Employees' responsibility for organizational security starts the second they join the organization and have access to the physical building and resources, as well as the intellectual property inside. Education should continue as the technology changes and new information becomes available. Education takes many forms, from training sessions to online courses employees can take at work. Educated users are one of your best defenses against social engineering attacks.
Communication	Once employees are aware of security issues and the role they play in protecting the organization's assets, the lines of communication between employees and the security team must remain open. Network security professionals can accomplish this by encouraging employees to ask questions and provide feedback on security issues. Also, the security team must take responsibility for keeping the workforce informed of ongoing security concerns and updated practices and standards.

Online Resources for Employee Education

A common way to promote all phases of the employee education process is to provide employees with access to security-related resources and information online. You can provide proprietary, private security information, such as your corporate security policy document, through an organization's intranet. You can also point employees to a number of reputable and valuable security resources on the Internet.

However, both you and employees should be cautious whenever researching information on the Internet, as not all sources are trustworthy. Just because information is posted on a website does not mean it is factual or reliable. Monitor the websites you recommend to your employees periodically to make sure that they are providing worthwhile information, and encourage employees to verify any technical or security-related information with a reliable third party before acting on the information or passing it along to others.

Here are just a few of the valuable information security resources from technology vendors and other organizations that you can find on the Internet:

- **www.microsoft.com/security/default.mspx**
- **tools.cisco.com/security/center/home.x**
- **www.symantec.com/business/index.jsp**
- **www.sans.org**

User Security Responsibilities

Because security is most often breached at the end-user level, users need to be aware of their specific security responsibilities.

Security Area	Employee Responsibilities
Physical security	Employees should not allow anyone in the building without a proper ID. Employees should not allow other individuals to "piggyback" on a single ID badge. Employees should be comfortable approaching and challenging unknown or unidentified persons in a work area. Access within the building should be restricted to only those areas an employee needs to access for job purposes. Hard copies of confidential files must be stored securely where they are not visible to others.
System security	Employees must use their user IDs and passwords properly. This information should never be shared or written down where it is accessible to others. All confidential files should be saved to an appropriate location on the network where they can be secured and backed up, not just on a hard drive.
Device security	Employees must use correct procedures to log off all devices and shut them down when not in use. Wireless communication devices must be approved by the IT department and installed and secured properly. Portable devices, such as laptops, tablets, and cell phones, must be properly stored and secured when not in use.

Guidelines for Educating Users

Consider the following guidelines when educating users.

Educating Users

When you educate your users, you give them the ability to participate in the process of ensuring the security of the organization. Because many attacks involve the unwitting participation of unsuspecting users, educating them to raise their level of awareness of proper security procedures can greatly increase the overall security of your organization. To educate your users on security practices, follow these guidelines:

- Train new users on how to use their devices and applications, and follow organizational security policies. Focus on potential security problems throughout the training. For example, don't trust messages with attachments or links, even if you know the sender.
- Consider implementing humor or other means to help users remember the messages you are trying to convey. For instance, you might create posters or other communications with messages like "Is it legit? If not, quit!" and "Passwords are like toothbrushes. Change them often, and never share them with others!"
- Post all relevant security policies so that they are easily available to all users.
- Notify users when changes are made to the policies. Educate them on the changes.
- Test user skills periodically after training to ensure that they are implementing proper security. For example, you can use planned social engineering attacks.
- Post information such as a link to **http://hoaxbusters.org/** on the company website to assist users in determining whether or not email messages they receive are hoaxes.
- In a high-security or highly regulated environment, consider requiring all users to take a pass/fail quiz or some other validation method immediately after training to verify the training's effectiveness and gather metrics on training results.
- Periodically refresh the users' training, including any relevant updates that they should be aware of.

Example: Educating Users at Greene City Interiors

At Greene City Interiors, during new-hire orientation, all new employees are briefed on the security standards of the company. A representative from the security team shows them how to connect to the company's intranet and locate links to all the company's security policy documents from the security page. The security representative also demonstrates basic device security procedures, such as how to create a strong password.

After training, you email the address of the intranet security page to all new employees, along with the addresses of other Internet resources they can consult to identify email threats, such as spam and hoaxes. Any time there is a change to any policy, you update the policy and notify users of the change. Significant policy changes are rolled out in conjunction with security training refresher sessions, which all employees are required to attend.

ACTIVITY 11-7
Educating Users

Scenario

As the network administrator for the Greene City Interiors branch office, one of your responsibilities is coordinating the employee security education program. The branch office has recently experienced several security incidents involving improper user behavior. Other IT staff and management personnel have come to you for recommendations on how to implement proper employee training procedures to prevent similar problems in the future.

1. A virus has spread throughout your organization, causing expensive downtime and corruption of data. You find that the virus sent to many users was an email attachment that was forwarded by an employee. The employee that received the original message was fooled into believing the link it contained was a legitimate marketing survey. You quickly determine that this is a well-known email hoax that has already been posted on several hoax-related websites. When questioned, this employee says that he thought it sounded as if it could be legitimate, and he could not see any harm in "just trying it." How could better user education have helped this situation?

2. What education steps do you recommend taking in response to this incident?

3. You come in on a Monday morning to find laptops have been stolen from several employees' desks over the weekend. After reviewing videotapes from the security cameras, you find that as an employee exited the building through the secure rear door on Friday night, she held the door open to admit another individual. You suspect this individual was the thief. When you question the employee, she states that the individual told her that he was a new employee who had not yet received his employee badge, that he only needed to be in the building for a few minutes, and that it would save him some time if she could let him in the back door rather than having to walk around to the receptionist entrance. Your security policy states that no one without identification should be admitted through the security doors at any time, but the employee says she was unaware of this policy. You ask her to locate the security policy documents on the network, and she is unable to do so. How could better user education have helped this situation?

4. What education steps do you recommend taking in response to this incident?

5. One of your competitors has somehow obtained confidential data about your organization. There have been no obvious security breaches or physical break-ins, and you are puzzled as to the source of the leak. You begin to ask questions about any suspicious or unusual employee activity, and you start to hear stories about a sales representative from out of town who did not have a desk in the office and was sitting down in open cubes and plugging her laptop into the corporate network. You suspect that the sales representative was really an industrial spy for your competitor. When you ask other employees why they did not ask the sales representative for identification or report the incident to security, the other employees said that, given their understanding of company policies, they did not see anything unusual or problematic in the situation. You review your security policy documents and, in fact, none of them refer to a situation like this one. How could better user education have helped this situation?

6. What education steps do you recommend taking in response to this incident?

Summary

In this lesson, you gained a better understanding of how to prevent security breaches. Ensuring that your network environment provides the appropriate level of security, without compromising on network performance is very important when maintaining a network.

What physical security controls have been employed at organizations you have worked at?

What types of firewalls have you worked with? Where in the network were they placed?

Note: Check your LogicalCHOICE Course screen for opportunities to interact with your classmates, peers, and the larger LogicalCHOICE online community about the topics covered in this course or other topics you are interested in. From the Course screen you can also access available resources for a more continuous learning experience.

12 | Responding to Security Incidents

Lesson Time: 1 hour

Lesson Objectives

In this lesson, you will respond to security incidents. You will:

- Describe practices related to managing and responding to security incidents.

- Identify basic forensic concepts.

Lesson Introduction

In the last lesson, you prevented network security breaches. Even with all the preparation you take to guard your network and its data, there will undoubtedly come a time when you encounter a security incident. In this lesson, you will respond to security incidents.

Many organizations learn how to respond to security incidents only after an attack has occurred. Because of this, incidents are often more costly than they could have been because it takes longer and more effort to respond. A proper incident response should be an integral part of your overall security policy and risk mitigation strategy.

TOPIC A

Incident Management and Response

In this lesson, you will respond to security incidents. To start, there are some general concepts and practices that can help in almost any security situation. In this topic, you will describe practices related to managing and responding to security incidents.

Responding to an incident without a plan will require more time and effort and increases the chance that you may miss something. Establishing a plan will allow responders to have a clear idea of what to do and will guide them through the process.

Security Incident Management

A *security incident* is a specific instance of a risk event occurring, whether or not it causes damage. Security *incident management* is the set of practices and procedures that govern how an organization will respond to an incident in progress. The goals of incident management are to contain the incident appropriately, and ultimately minimize any damage that may occur as a result of the incident. Incident management typically includes procedures to log, and report on, all identified incidents and the actions taken in response.

IRPs

An *incident response policy (IRP)* is the security policy that determines the actions that an organization will take following a confirmed or potential security breach. The IRP usually specifies:

- Who determines and declares if an actual security incident has occurred.
- What individuals or departments will be notified.
- How and when they are notified.
- Who will respond to the incident.
- Guidelines for the appropriate response.

Incident response will usually involve several departments and, depending on the severity of the incident, may involve the media. The human resources and public relations departments of an organization generally work together in these situations to determine the extent of the information that will be made available to the public. Information is released to employees, stockholders, and the general public on a need-to-know basis.

First Responders

A *first responder* is the first experienced person or a team of trained professionals that arrive on the scene of an incident. In a non-IT environment, this term can be used to define the first trained person, such as a police officer or firefighter, to respond to an accident, a damage site, or a natural disaster. In the IT world, first responders can include security professionals, human resource personnel, or IT support professionals.

Change Management

Change management is a systematic way of approving and executing change in order to ensure maximum security, stability, and availability of information technology services. When an organization changes its hardware, software, infrastructure, or documentation, it risks the introduction of unanticipated consequences. Changes may also be necessary in response to a security incident where modifications are required to resolve the issue. Therefore, it is important that an organization be able to properly assess risk; to quantify cost of training, support, maintenance, or implementation; and to properly weigh benefits against the complexity of a proposed change. By maintaining a documented change management procedure, an organization can protect itself from potential adverse effects of hasty change.

 Note: Change management is covered in more detail later in the course.

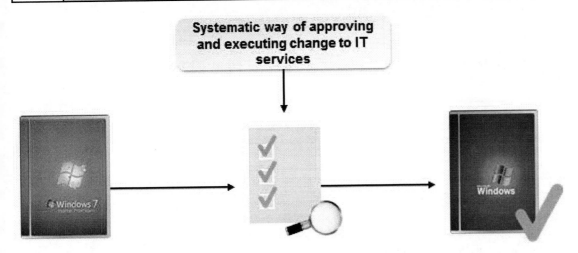

Figure 12-1: Change management of service packs.

ACTIVITY 12–1
Discussing Incident Management and Response

Scenario

The network administrator at Greene City Interiors poses some incident scenarios and asks you how you would respond.

1. An employee reports that he thinks his laptop was hacked and that sensitive information may have been stolen. What determines the actions that you will take for this potential security breach?

   ○ Security incident management

   ○ IRP

   ○ Change management

   ○ Security policy

2. When responding to the potential stolen information from the laptop, what types of actions would be specified?

3. It is determined that there was a security breach on the laptop but no sensitive information was stolen. What step(s) should be taken next?

TOPIC B

Basic Forensic Concepts

In the last topic, you described methods for managing and responding to incidents. To protect yourself and your organization from legal ramifications, you might need to provide evidence of a security incident. In this topic, you will describe basic forensic concepts.

Investigating an incident without a process in place will be inefficient and can lead to improper evidence collection and possible legal ramifications. Establish a clear forensic process that informs responders how to properly investigate an incident so that you avoid any legal issues.

A Basic Forensic Process

Any time you have an incident that needs to be investigated, you need to have a forensic process established to help you perform it properly. Although each organization might develop its own forensic process, it is recommended that the following steps be included:

1. The first responder(s) arrive on the scene of an incident.
2. Secure the area to preserve the scene of the incident.
3. Documentation of the scene can begin.
4. Electronic discovery (eDiscovery) is performed to identify and collect any electronically stored information.
5. Collect any other evidence and data related to the incident.
6. Preserve the chain of custody when evidence is collected and until the end of the investigation.
7. If data needs to be transported to another entity, then follow proper data transport procedures.
8. Report your forensic findings.
9. If there is litigation, then follow legal hold procedures.

Area Security

In a situation that requires investigation, try to secure the area as best you can. If it is a physical location such as a room, then close off the area using doors. You can put up signs and send out a notice that the area is off limits until further notice. If it is a digital location, then you can try to take it offline if it won't have a negative impact on operations. If it is a single device, then you can put that in a secure location.

The main idea is that you want to preserve the area as it is so that you can investigate without other people adding, removing, or altering any evidence that may exist. If you have trouble getting the area secured because other people insist they need to be there, escalate the issue to a manager or other senior employee who can help you.

Documentation

Documentation of the scene begins with the first responder. It is important to start taking notes from the time of arrival at the scene. Include any details on the condition of the scene, and talk to witnesses, if any, and get their statements. Stick to the facts at this stage, and do not include your opinions or thoughts and guesses. You can also take photos and videos to help document the scene.

eDiscovery

Electronic discovery, also known as eDiscovery, is the electronic aspect of identifying, collecting, and producing electronically stored information (ESI) in response to a request in a lawsuit or investigation. ESI includes, but is not limited to, email, documents, presentations, databases, voice mail, audio and video files, social media, and websites. The nature of the incident and the investigation will determine what information will be ESI.

Evidence and Data Collection

As you document a scene or perform eDiscovery, you can collect evidence or data. If you are investigating an issue of some kind, then you can collect any evidence or data as you see fit. However, if you are investigating a legal issue that may involve other parties, then you should consult your manager and possibly a lawyer, as there may be legal restrictions you need to follow.

If you are trying to retrieve data that has been erased or damaged, then you may need to consult with a data collection and recovery specialist. They are trained and possess tools that enable them to recover data that is not normally recoverable through standard tools.

Chain of Custody

The idea of *chain of custody* is borrowed from law enforcement. The premise is to track the evidence from the time it is collected until it is released back to the owner. It will track the chronological handling of the evidence and is a paper trail, showing the seizure, custody, control, transfer, analysis, and disposition of physical or electronic evidence.

A chain of custody document might also contain basic information about the organization, any affected clients, details about the seized media such as brand, type, and serial number, as well as other information. The form can also track each person who has touched the media for purposes of collection, imaging, and return of property.

Data Transport

In certain situations, you may need to transport data from your organization to another entity. Digital evidence can be altered, damaged, or destroyed due to improper handling. If this occurs, the data may be unreadable or inadmissible, or lead to an inaccurate conclusion. You will need to transport the data securely by using some sort of encrypted portable drive. You can also obtain devices built specifically for this purpose.

Forensic Reports

A forensic report simply and succinctly summarizes the substantive evidence. It typically contains several sections to help the reader understand not only what was found (or not found) by the investigator, but also to detail the steps performed to acquire and analyze the data.

Legal Holds

A *legal hold* is a process that an organization uses to preserve all forms of relevant information when litigation is reasonably anticipated. The legal hold is initiated by a notice or communication from legal counsel to an organization that suspends the normal disposition or processing of records, such as backup tape recycling, archived media, and other storage and management of documents and information. A legal hold will be issued as a result of current or anticipated litigation, audit, government investigation, or other such matter to avoid evidence spoliation. Legal holds can encompass business procedures affecting active data, including, but not limited to, backup tape recycling.

ACTIVITY 12-2
Discussing Basic Forensic Concepts

Scenario

The network administrator at Greene City Interiors engages you in a conversation about the various techniques used in the forensic process.

1. **What is the purpose of a chain of custody document?**

   ○ Includes facts about the scene of the incident.

   ○ Tracks evidence from the time it is collected until it is released back to the owner.

   ○ Summary of the substantive evidence.

   ○ Document items affected by a legal hold.

2. **Which methods can be used to document the scene?**

   ☐ Take a video.

   ☐ Take notes.

   ☐ Take evidence.

   ☐ Take pictures.

3. **What is the first step you perform when you become aware of a situation?**

   ○ Document the scene.

   ○ Perform eDiscovery.

   ○ Secure the area.

   ○ Collect evidence.

4. **True or False? Data that has been erased can never be retrieved.**

   ☐ True

   ☐ False

Summary

In this lesson, you responded to security incidents. Implementing a proper incident response strategy will enable you to properly and efficiently respond to incidents.

Have organizations you have worked for had incident response policies? What did they specify?

Have you ever had to use a forensic process to investigate an incident? What tasks did you have to perform?

 Note: Check your LogicalCHOICE Course screen for opportunities to interact with your classmates, peers, and the larger LogicalCHOICE online community about the topics covered in this course or other topics you are interested in. From the Course screen you can also access available resources for a more continuous learning experience.

13 | Remote Networking

Lesson Time: 1 hour

Lesson Objectives

In this lesson, you will identify the components of a remote network implementation. You will:

- Identify the architectures used for remote access networking.

- Identify remote access networking implementations.

- Identify the major components of a VPN implementation.

- Identify VPN protocols.

Lesson Introduction

So far in this course, you have described technologies for implementing networks where users have a device with a direct connection to the network. Many WANs also include remote users who connect to the network by using indirect, remote-networking technologies. In this lesson, you will identify the components of a remote network implementation.

Almost every organization needs to support remote users. Whether it is the employee who is always on the move, works from a home office, or connects to the organization's network from an occasional offsite conference, all your remote users need reliable, secure access to your network from their offsite locations. As a network professional, you will need to understand all components required for remote network implementations so that you can support your remote users effectively.

TOPIC A

Remote Network Architectures

You are familiar with common network implementations. Many remote network implementations have similar configurations, or architectures. In this topic, you will identify remote network architectures.

The needs of remote users are often different from those of other network users. Several common implementation schemes have evolved to meet the most sophisticated remote user requirements. As a network professional, you may need to provide network connectivity to remote users. To provide remote users with the functionality they need, you need to understand the basics of remote networking.

Remote Networking Overview

Remote networking is a type of networking that enables users who are not at the same physical location to access network resources. The remote device uses specific protocols for connectivity and an established connection mechanism to connect to the network. Remote networking can be used to enable a user to connect to a device for basic access, or it can be a full-service connection with the same functionality that the user would expect to have at the office.

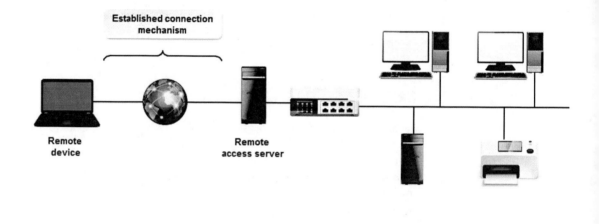

Figure 13-1: Infrastructure in a remote networking environment.

The biggest limitations of remote networks are the available bandwidth, link latency, and security.

Remote Access Networking

In remote access networking, a node uses a remote connection to connect to a network. Once connected, the node can access resources and function as if it is on the same physical network. There is a possibility of the connection being slower due to bandwidth constraints. The server that provides remote access also provides security and authenticates users to access the network. All network traffic to and from the remote node passes through the server.

Remote Desktop Connectivity

A *remote desktop* is a connection mode that enables users to access any network node from their workstation and perform tasks on the remote device as if they were working locally. *Remote desktop control* uses a special software package that enables a remote client to control a host on the network, or run applications from a server. Once connected, the remote client can send keyboard and mouse inputs and receive the resultant information on-screen.

Remote desktop networking solutions include Windows® Remote Desktop Connection and Remote Assistance, Symantec™ pcAnywhere™ (it is being discontinued but is still in use), LogMeIn, WebEx® PCNow®, Bomgar™, various virtual network computing (VNC) clients and servers, Citrix® GoToMyPC® and XenApp®, and Apple® Remote Desktop.

Remote desktop control can be used on a WAN or on a local network. Remote desktop control can be used for remote server administration and to enable help-desk personnel to provide remote assistance. Unless there are sufficient servers to balance the load, remote desktop control requires expensive centralized hardware and software to manage use and maintenance.

Remote desktop control can also be used by the host as an access point to a remote network. When a host is used to access a network, the host should be a dedicated system.

Traditional models of centralized computing are based on a central server that has attached terminals. Modern interpretations of centralized computing include remote desktop, hosted and web-based applications, and "thin client" computing, in which most of the hardware resources reside on the server side.

There is also *remote desktop assistance,* which is similar except that both the user making the remote connection, and the local user on the target device see the same screen. Both users can also have control of the device. The intent is for the remote user to connect to the device and help the local user with an issue.

Benefits of Remote Desktop Connectivity

Remote desktop connectivity provides several benefits for both administrators and end users.

Benefit	Description
Centralized application deployment and access	Applications are installed on the terminal servers and clients access the applications from their desktops. Applications are not installed on each client, and have centralized upgradability and maintenance.
Multiple device support	Servers and clients can run on a wide variety of hardware configurations. These can be different hardware or multiple devices such as low configuration PCs or thin clients.
Server administration and maintenance	Allows an administrator to connect to a server remotely and perform administrative tasks using the graphical user interface (GUI) of the server.
Enhanced security	Implements basic and advanced encryption schemes.

RAS Servers

Remote Access is a feature that allows a remote user to dial in to or use a virtual private network (VPN) to connect to the network. The user can be working from home, a hotel, an airport, a client site, or any other remote location. If Internet access is not available for that remote user, that person can use a dial-up modem to make a connection over the public switched telephone network (PSTN). Remote access can also be used by an administrator to access client devices from any location on the network. A *Remote Access Services (RAS)* server is a combination dial-up and VPN server. It can accept multiple client connections, terminate their VPN tunnels, and route their traffic into the private network.

Note: In modern implementations of remote access, dial-up may not be required. Many administrators have chosen to disable or not implement the dial-up capabilities of their RAS servers.

Microsoft®, Apple, IBM®, and many other UNIX® and Linux® vendors offer remote access server implementation either included with their server operating systems or as separate software. In addition, there are several third-party software vendors that provide remote access solutions, including Cisco®, EMC®, Perle®, Citrix, and Patton™.

Microsoft's remote server implementation is called Routing and Remote Access Services (RRAS). On Microsoft networks, using RRAS instead of a third-party remote access server means that the user can dial in and authenticate with the same account as he or she uses at the office. With third-party remote access servers, there must be some mechanism in place to synchronize user names and passwords.

RADIUS

Remote Authentication Dial-In User Service (RADIUS) is a protocol that enables a server to provide standardized, centralized authentication for remote users. When a network contains several remote access servers, you can configure one of them to be a RADIUS server and all of the others as RADIUS clients. The RADIUS clients will pass all authentication requests to the RADIUS server for verification. User configuration, remote access policies, and usage logging can be centralized on the RADIUS server. RADIUS is supported by VPN servers, Ethernet switches requiring authentication, wireless access points (WAPs), as well as other types of network devices.

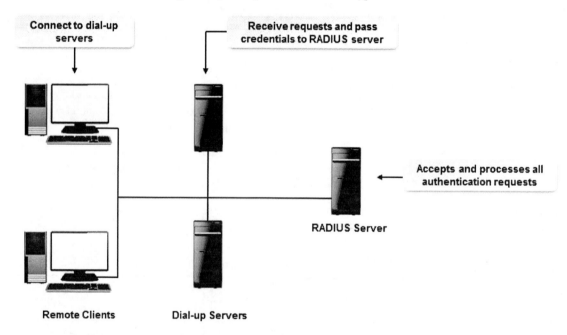

Figure 13-2: The architecture of a RADIUS network.

RADIUS was originally developed by AT&T as an accounting protocol to charge customers for network usage. Its role, however, eventually expanded to include authentication and authorization. RADIUS uses User Datagram Protocol (UDP) ports 1812 and 1813. Some RADIUS implementations use UDP ports 1645 and 1646.

In Windows Server® 2012 R2, a network policy server (NPS) can be used as a RADIUS server to perform authentication, authorization, and accounting for RADIUS clients. FreeRADIUS is a popular open-source software that you can use to turn your Linux computer into a RADIUS server.

Diameter

Diameter is an authentication protocol that is an updated version of RADIUS and improves on some of its features. Diameter is not backward-compatible with RADIUS, but it does provide an upgrade path. Diameter is a stronger protocol that provides more advanced features, but is not as widespread in its implementation due to the lack of compatible products.

 Note: The name Diameter is a reference to the mathematical term that indicates that the diameter is two times the RADIUS.

Diameter works well as a base protocol to provide authentication, authorization, and accounting (AAA) for mobile IP applications, remote access, and VoIP. It is widely used by IP Multimedia Subsystem (IMS) telecommunication providers to exchange AAA-related information across their services. Cisco, Juniper®, and other vendors have added Diameter, along with RADIUS and Terminal Access Controller Access Control System/Terminal Access Controller Access Control System Plus (TACACS/TACACS+), to their AAA solutions.

AAA

AAA is a framework for controlling access to computing resources. It is a generic term that refers to how remote access systems permit, control, and audit remote client connections. RADIUS, TACACS, TACACS+, and Diameter all have their own implementations of AAA.

ACTIVITY 13–1
Implementing RADIUS for Remote Access

Before You Begin
Open the Server Manager window.

Scenario
At the Greene City Interiors branch office, several users have complained that they are not able to connect to the network remotely. You plan to implement RADIUS for remote authentication, and you want to use it in tandem with wireless authentication for an added layer of security on a wireless network that is mainly accessed by traveling employees. You want to test RADIUS in a lab environment before deploying it in production. On a test RRAS system, you will install a RADIUS server and reconfigure an RRAS server to use RADIUS authentication.

1. View the current remote access authentication methods.
   a) In Server Manager, select **Tools→Routing and Remote Access**.
   b) In the Routing and Remote Access window, in the console tree, right-click **Computer##** and select **Properties**.
   c) In the **Computer## (local) Properties** dialog box, select the **Security** tab.
   d) In the **Authentication provider** section, select **Authentication Methods**.
   e) In the **Authentication Methods** dialog box, observe the options selected by default.

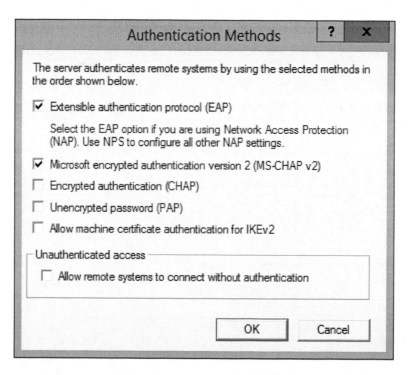

This dialog box allows you to select which authentication methods you want to use. For this activity, you will use the default settings.
   f) Select **Cancel** to close the **Authentication Methods** dialog box.
   g) Select **Cancel** to close the **Routing and Remote Access Properties** dialog box.
   h) Close the Routing and Remote Access window.

2. Install the Network Policy and Access Services.
   a) If necessary, in Server Manager, select **Dashboard**.
   b) In the Server Manager window, select the **Add roles and features** link.
   c) In the **Add Roles and Features Wizard**, on the **Before You Begin** page, select **Next**.
   d) On the **Select installation type** page, verify that **Role-based or feature-based installation** is selected, and select **Next**.
   e) On the **Select destination server** page, verify that **Computer##.Child##.GCInteriors.com** is selected, and select **Next**.
   f) On the **Select role services** page, check the **Network Policy and Access Services** check box.
   g) In the **Add Roles and Features Wizard** dialog box, select **Add Features** to add all the suggested features.
   h) Select **Next**.
   i) On the **Select features** page, select **Next**.
   j) On the **Network Policy and Access Services** page, select **Next**.
   k) On the **Select role services** page, verify that **Network Policy Server** is selected, and select **Next**.
   l) Confirm what you are about to install and then select **Install**.

To install the following roles, role services, or features on selected server, click Install.

☐ Restart the destination server automatically if required

Optional features (such as administration tools) might be displayed on this page because they have been selected automatically. If you do not want to install these optional features, click Previous to clear their check boxes.

Network Policy and Access Services
    Network Policy Server

Remote Server Administration Tools
    Role Administration Tools
        Network Policy and Access Services Tools

Export configuration settings
Specify an alternate source path

[< Previous] [Next >]   [Install] [Cancel]

   m) Once the installation is complete, select **Close** to close the **Add Roles and Features Wizard** and complete the installation.

3. Configure a RADIUS client.
   a) In Server Manager, select **Tools→Network Policy Server**.
   b) In the Network Policy Server window, select the **RADIUS Clients and Servers** folder.
   c) In the details pane, select **Configure RADIUS Clients**.
   d) Select **Action→New**.
   e) In the **New RADIUS Client** dialog box, in the **Name and Address** section, in the **Friendly name** box, select and type *My RADIUS Client*
   f) In the **Address (IP or DNS)** section, select **Verify**.

g) In the **Verify Address** dialog box, select **Resolve**.

h) In the IP address list, select **192.168.2.XX**, where **XX** is the IP address of the system, and select **OK**.

i) In the **Shared Secret** section, select the **Generate** option and then select **Generate**.

j) Observe that in the **Shared secret** text box, the key is generated. Select the warning message icon next to the text box.

k) Observe the text displayed as a tool tip and select **OK**.

4. Reconfigure the RRAS server to use RADIUS authentication.

a) In the Network Policy Server window, in the console tree, select the **NPS (Local)** object.

b) In the **Standard Configuration** section, from the drop-down list, select the **RADIUS server for 802.1X Wireless or Wired Connections** option.

c) Read the description and then select the **Configure 802.1X** link.

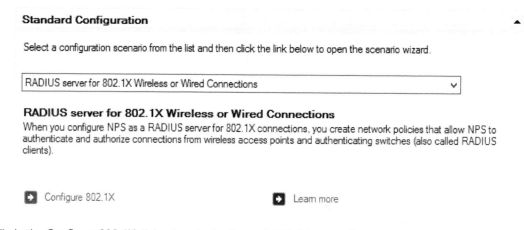

d) In the **Configure 802.1X** dialog box, in the **Type of 802.1X connections** section, select the **Secure Wireless Connections** option and select **Next**.

e) On the **Specify 802.1X Switches** page, verify that **My RADIUS Client** appears in the RADIUS clients list, and select **Next**.

f) On the **Configure an Authentication Method** page, from the **Type (based on method of access and network configuration)** drop-down list, select the **Microsoft: Secured password (EAP-MSCHAP v2)** option and select **Next**.

g) On the **Specify User Groups** page, select **Next**.

h) On the **Configure Traffic Controls** page, select **Next** and select **Finish**.

5. Verify the RADIUS port settings.

a) In the Network Policy Server window, in the console tree, right-click the **NPS (Local)** object and select **Properties**.

b) In the **Network Policy Server (Local) Properties** dialog box, select the **Ports** tab.

c) Verify that **1812**, the default port for RADIUS, is listed in the **Authentication** text field. After examining the other port settings, select **Cancel**.

d) Close the **Network Policy Server** window.

Remote Control Protocols

There are several remote control protocols that you can use, depending on the remote networking needs.

Remote Control Protocol	Description
Remote Desktop Protocol (RDP)	*RDP* is the backbone of Microsoft's Remote Desktop system. Its capabilities include data encryption, remote audio and printing, access to local files, and redirection of the host's disk drives and peripheral ports. In client versions 6.1 and later, any application that can be accessed via the normal remote desktop can serve as a standalone remote application. The server component, the terminal server, is available on most Windows operating systems, except for Windows Vista® Home Edition, and a desktop client is available for most operating systems. The server listens on port 3389.
Virtual Network Computing (VNC)	*VNC* is a platform-independent desktop sharing system. VNC client and server software is available for almost any operating system (and for Java®), so a VNC viewer on a Linux system can connect to a VNC server on a Microsoft system and vice versa. VNC uses the *Remote Frame Buffer (RFB)* protocol, which allows the client and server to determine the best version of RFB they can support during a session. VNC is not an inherently secure system, but does offer varying levels of password and content encryption, depending on the implementation.
Independent Computing Architecture (ICA)	The Citrix ICA protocol is a remote terminal protocol used by Citrix WinFrame and Citrix Presentation Server software as an add-on to Microsoft Terminal Services. ICA enhances and expands on the core thin-client functionality found in Terminal Services, and provides client support for additional protocols and services.
X Window system	The *X Window system* is a protocol that uses a client-server relationship to provide a GUI and input device management functionality to applications. Current X Windows systems are based on the X11 protocol and are normally used on UNIX- and Linux-based systems to display local applications. Because X is an open cross-platform protocol and relies on client-server relationships, remote connections are often easy to implement.

Nested Remote Connections

Nested remote connections are when a user connects remotely to a device and then, from that remote device, they establish a remote connection to another device. Support for nested connections typically extends only to one level of nesting, and they may not be supported in older remote connection applications. You may be able to nest more connections, but any issues you experience will not be supported by the manufacturer. Using nested remote connections can also create additional latency with the remote connections.

ACTIVITY 13-2
Enabling Remote Desktop Connections

Before You Begin

RAIDIUS for Remote Access is installed and configured. You will need a partner to complete this activity.

Scenario

At the Greene City Interiors branch office, you discover that the former IT person originally used Telnet to manage and troubleshoot servers remotely. As the branch has grown since those early days, there are more dedicated servers, and you decide to manage and troubleshoot remotely by using Remote Desktop, which is more secure than Telnet.

Additionally, because Remote Desktop allows for creating and accessing files on the remote computer, accessing files on the server is more efficient. You now do not need to keep FTP ports open to transfer individual files. In this activity, you will enable Remote Desktop Connections on your workstation to connect to a partner's computer, which is simulating a dedicated file server running Windows Server 2012 R2.

1. Enable remote desktop connections.
    a) Select a fellow student to be your partner for this activity. You will take turns connecting to each other's computers.
    b) Select **Start→Control Panel**.
    c) In the Control Panel window, select **System and Security**.
    d) In the System and Security window, under **System**, select **Allow remote access**.
    e) In the **System Properties** dialog box, under **Remote Desktop**, select **Allow remote connections to this computer**.
    f) Select **Select Users**.
    g) In the **Remote Desktop Users** dialog box, select **Add**.
    h) In the **Select Users or Groups** dialog box, select **Locations**.

i)   In the **Locations** dialog box, select **GCInteriors.com**.

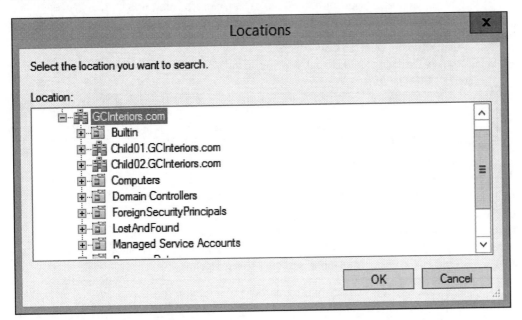

j)   Select **OK**.
k)   In the **Select Users or Groups** dialog box, in the **Enter the object names to select** box, type your partner's *Student##* and select **OK**.
l)   In the **Remote Desktop Users** dialog box, select **OK**.
m) In the **System Properties** dialog box, select **OK**.

2. Allow remote connections to the server.

a)   In **Server Manager**, select **Tools→Group Policy Management**.
b)   In the Group Policy Management window, in the console tree, expand **Forest: GCInteriors.com→Domains→Child##.GCInteriors.com→Domain Controllers** and select **Default Domain Controllers Policy**.
c)   If necessary, in the **Group Policy Management Console** message box, select **OK**.
d)   Select **Action→Edit**.
e)   In the Group Policy Management Editor window, expand **Computer Configuration→Policies→Windows Settings→Security Settings→Local Policies**.
f)   Select **User Rights Assignment**.
g)   In the details pane, double-click **Allow log on through Remote Desktop Services**.
h)   In the **Allow log on through Remote Desktop Services Properties** dialog box, check **Define these policy settings**.
i)   Select **Add User or Group**.
j)   In the **Add User or Group** dialog box, select **Browse**.
k)   In the **Select Users, Computers, Service Accounts, or Groups** dialog box, select **Advanced**.
l)   In the **Select Users, Computers, Service Accounts, or Groups** dialog box, select **Find Now**.
m) In the **Search results** section, select **Authenticated Users** and select **OK**.
n)   In the **Select Users, Computers, Service Accounts, or Groups** dialog box, select **OK**.
o)   In the **Add User or Group** dialog box, select **OK**.
p)   In the **Allow log on locally Properties** dialog box, select **OK** to close it.
q)   Close the Group Policy Management Editor and Group Policy Management windows.
r)   Open **Windows PowerShell**.
s)   In the Windows PowerShell window, type *gpupdate /force* and press **Enter**.
t)   When the policy has updated, close the Windows PowerShell window.

3. Connect to a partner computer by using remote desktop connection.

Note: You and your partner will take turns performing this last step. Decide who will go first.

a) Select **Start→Remote Desktop Connection**.

b) In the **Remote Desktop Connection** dialog box, in the **Computer** box, type the computer name of your partner's computer.

Note: The computer name will follow the naming standard of **Computer##**.

c) Select **Connect**.

d) In the **Windows Security** dialog box, select **Use another account**.

e) In the **User name** field, type *GCInteriors\Student##*, where **##** is your student ID number.

f) In the **Password** box, type *P@ssw0rd12*

g) Select **OK**.

h) In the **Remote Desktop Connection** dialog box, select **Yes**.

i) On the desktop of the remote computer, observe the **Computer##** bar at the top of the screen.

j) On the Start menu, select **Student##**, and then select **Sign out**.

Note: Once you complete this activity, it is your partner's turn.

TOPIC B

Remote Access Networking Implementations

In the last topic, you identified remote network architectures. These architectures can be used for different implementations of remote networks. In this topic, you will identify remote access networking implementations.

For many, connecting to a remote network while on the move is a way of life. From telecommuters to traveling sales representatives to a manager attending an annual conference, these remote users need a reliable way to access network services when they are not in an office environment. As a network professional, you need to recognize the components commonly used in remote access networking so that you can support your remote users.

Remote Access Protocols

A *remote access protocol* enables a user to access a remote access server and transfer data. Remote access protocols can provide direct dial-in connections via modems, or they can provide connections via ISPs and the Internet. There are various remote access protocols such as Point-to-Point Protocol (PPP), Point-to-Point Protocol over Ethernet (PPPoE), and Extensible Authentication Protocol (EAP) that provide remote access.

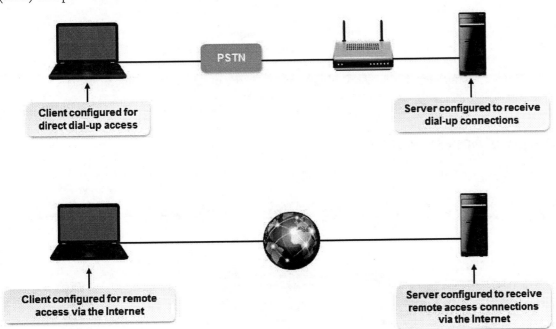

Figure 13–3: A remote access protocol environment.

PPP

The *Point-to-Point Protocol (PPP)* is a remote networking protocol that works on the Data Link layer (Layer 2) of the TCP/IP protocol suite. It is used to send IP datagrams over serial point-to-point links. It can be used in synchronous and asynchronous connections. PPP can dynamically configure and test remote network connections, and is often used by clients to connect to networks and the Internet. It also provides encryption for passwords, paving the way for secure authentication of remote users. To log on to a remote session via PPP, you need to enable a remote authentication protocol.

Note: Serial Line Internet Protocol (SLIP) is a legacy remote access protocol used for sending IP data streams over serial lines such as modem or phone connections. In Windows Server 2012 R2, SLIP is automatically upgraded by the network operating system (NOS) to PPP.

PPP Variants

There are four commonly used variants of PPP: PPPoE, EAP, Protected EAP (PEAP), and multilink PPP.

Variant	Description
PPPoE	A standard that provides the features and functionality of PPP to DSL connections that use Ethernet to transfer signals from a carrier to a client. In addition, it contains a discovery process that determines a client's Ethernet media access control (MAC) address prior to establishing a connection. PPPoE and Point-to-Point Protocol over ATM (PPPoA) are used by many DSL broadband Internet connections.
EAP	A protocol that is an extension of PPP and provides support for additional authentication methods, such as tokens, smart cards, and certificates.
PEAP	A protocol that secures EAP by creating an encrypted channel between a remote client and a server. PEAP can also be used with *Microsoft Challenge Handshake Authentication Protocol v2 (MS-CHAPv2)* to strengthen the protocol's password authentication.
Multilink PPP	A protocol that provides a method for spreading traffic across multiple distinct PPP connections. Multilink PPP enables a computer to use two PPP ports together as a single port with greater bandwidth. Examples of multilink PPP include a home computing device connecting to an ISP using two traditional 56k modems, or connecting a company through two leased lines.

Remote Access Authentication

To authenticate a remote session connection, you need to perform several steps.

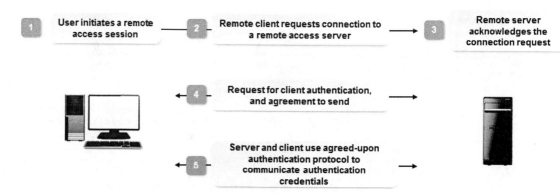

Figure 13-4: Remote access authentication.

Step	Description
Step 1: Session initiation	A user initiates a session by using a remote device.
Step 2: Connection request	The remote device requests a connection to a remote access server so that it can connect to another device.
Step 3: Link establishment	The remote access server acknowledges the connection request, and establishes the physical link between the two devices.

Step	Description
Step 4: Client authentication	The remote access server requires the client to authenticate itself by using a remote authentication protocol. If the client does not agree to provide the requested authentication data, the server refuses to create a connection and the physical link is dropped. If the client agrees to send the authentication data, the server establishes a connection and authenticates the client.
Step 5: Authentication credentials communications	The server and client use the agreed-upon authentication protocol to communicate authentication credentials. If the server does not accept the authentication credentials provided by the client, the server closes the connection and drops the physical link. If the server accepts the authentication credentials provided by the client, the server allows the client to access resources.

Web-Based Remote Access

Web-based remote access implementations provide access to services and data via web browsers. A well-deployed web-based service enables clients to access web-based applications and data without any additional software installed on their system. However, proper security mechanisms should be in place when you use these implementations. Web-based remote access also enables administrators to manage application servers from remote locations. Web-based remote access applications require a higher configuration of web servers when clients access the server.

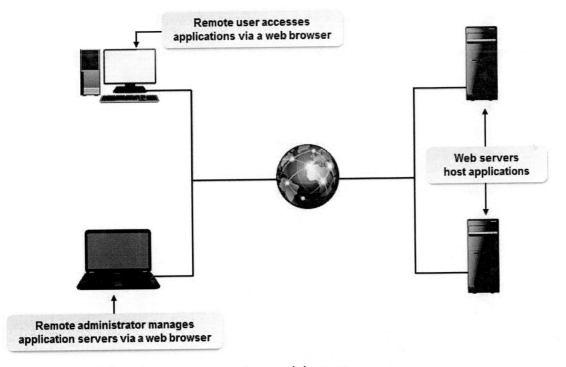

Figure 13-5: Web-based remote access using a web browser.

In Windows Server 2012 R2, Windows 7, and Windows 8, web-based remote access is available through the Remote Desktop Web Connection (RDWC). The remote device connects through a web browser, and the web server requires RDWC to be installed and running. RDWC is a component of Remote Desktop Services and is included with Windows Server, but must be downloaded separately for Windows 7.

Another web-based access feature in Windows Server 2012 R2 is called Web Interface For Remote Administration. Designed for remote management of application servers, it enables administrators to access a server from any browser (though Internet Explorer® is still the only browser that supports web single sign-on [SSO]. This is because web SSO still requires ActiveX.) On the application server, which cannot be a domain controller, Web Interface For Remote Administration must be installed. Windows Server 2012 R2 can make use of the Remote Server Administration tools available for Windows 7 and 8.

ACTIVITY 13-3
Identifying Remote Access Networking Implementations

Scenario

The network administrator at Greene City Interiors questions you on remote access networking implementations.

1. EAP is an extension of:
   - ○ PEAP
   - ○ CHAP
   - ○ PAP
   - ○ PPP

2. Which of these statements about PPP are true?
   - ☐ It sends IP datagrams over serial point-to-point links.
   - ☐ It works on the Physical layer of the TCP/IP protocol suite.
   - ☐ It is used for both asynchronous and synchronous connections.
   - ☐ It provides secure authentication for remote users.

3. Describe remote access authentication.

TOPIC C

Virtual Private Networking

In the last topic, you identified remote access networking protocols and implementations. In some organizations, the sheer number of remote users makes the implementation of traditional remote access networking cost-prohibitive. This is where a virtual private network (VPN) comes into the picture. In this topic, you will identify the major components of VPN implementations.

Although standard dial-up implementations can still be found in some network environments, other considerations, such as security and the number of remote users to be supported, require additional measures to provide remote connections. When organizations opt to take advantage of public networks such as the Internet, the issue of securing data transmissions becomes critical. To counter the security risks associated with public networks, organizations implement a VPN within the public network to ensure secure communications. As a network professional, you need to recognize the components of VPN implementations to support remote users.

Tunneling

A *tunnel* is a logical path through the network that appears like a point-to-point connection. *Tunneling* is a data transport technique in which a data packet from one protocol, called the passenger protocol, is transferred inside the frame or packet of another protocol, called the carrier protocol. Tunneling enables data from one network to pass from one endpoint of a tunnel to the other through the infrastructure of another network. The carrier protocol can encapsulate and route nonroutable passenger protocols, or it can provide additional security by hiding passenger data from the carrier network.

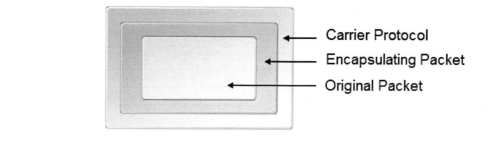

Carrier Protocol
Encapsulating Packet
Original Packet

Figure 13-6: Tunneling through a network.

Essentially, there are two tunnel types: voluntary and compulsory.

- *Voluntary tunnels* are created between endpoints at the request of a client. When a user runs a software application that supports encrypted data communications, the client establishes an encrypted tunnel to the other end of the communication session, whether it is on a local network or the Internet.
- *Compulsory tunnels* are VPNs between routers. They are established by routers across the Internet with no involvement on the part of their clients. From the client's perspective, it is simply sending unencrypted data to its default gateway for delivery to the remote network. The router then establishes a VPN tunnel with its peer at the remote location, and all data is sent through

the tunnel without affecting the client. Compulsory tunnels can be in place permanently (static), or they can be put in place based on the data or client type (dynamic).

VPNs

A *virtual private network (VPN)* is a private network that is configured by tunneling through a public network such as the Internet. Because tunneling is used to encapsulate and encrypt data, VPNs ensure that connections between endpoints, such as routers, clients, and servers, are secure. To provide VPN tunneling, security, and data encryption services, special VPN protocols are required.

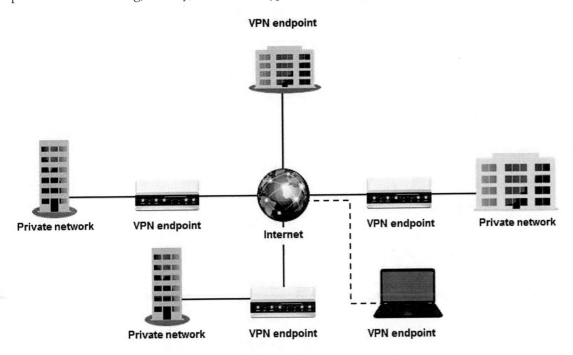

Figure 13-7: VPN infrastructure makes a private network secure.

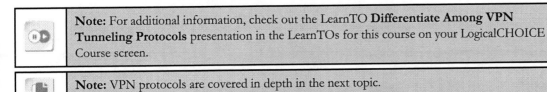

Note: For additional information, check out the LearnTO **Differentiate Among VPN Tunneling Protocols** presentation in the LearnTOs for this course on your LogicalCHOICE Course screen.

Note: VPN protocols are covered in depth in the next topic.

A *Secure Socket Layer VPN (SSL VPN)* is a VPN format that works with a web browser—without needing the installation of a separate client. SSL ensures that the connection can be made only by using HTTPS instead of HTTP. This format works well in schools and libraries where easy access is required but security is still a concern.

VPN Types

There are several types of VPNs that you might encounter.

VPN Type	Description
Intranet VPNs	Connects sections of a network, such as remote offices tying into a corporate headquarters.

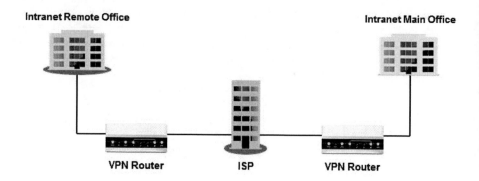

| Extranet VPNs | Connects networks belonging to different companies for the purposes of sharing resources. |

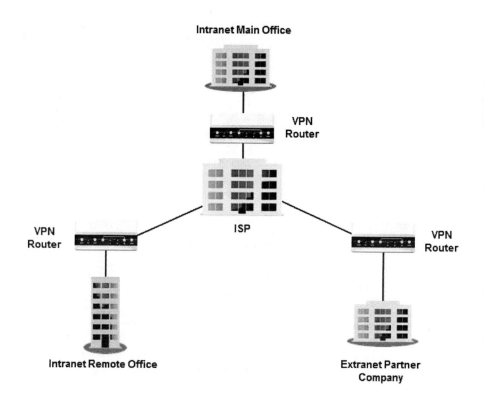

VPNs can also be classified by their implementations.

Implementation	Description
Hardware-based	Uses hardware such as encrypting routers.
Firewall-based	Uses a firewall's security mechanisms.
Software-based	Uses software when VPN endpoints are not controlled by the same organization.

Advantages of VPNs

The two biggest reasons that most organizations implement VPNs are cost savings and data confidentiality. The cost of maintaining a VPN is generally lower than other remote access technologies. For instance, if a remote access technology depends on long-distance or toll-free calls, an organization's communication expenditure can become very high. Another reason for implementing VPNs is versatility. One VPN endpoint connected to a T1 or T3 line through the service provider can accommodate hundreds of simultaneous connections from any type of client using any type of connection.

VPN Data Encryption

In most VPNs, data encryption is accomplished by either MPPE or IPSec.

Encryption Method	Description
MPPE	*Microsoft Point-to-Point Encryption (MPPE)* is often used with Point-to-Point Tunneling Protocol (PPTP). It provides both strong (128-bit key) and standard (40- or 56-bit key) data encryptions. MPPE requires the use of MS-CHAP, MS-CHAPv2, or EAP remote authentication, because the keys used for MPPE encryption are derived from the authentication method.
IPSec	IPSec in Tunnel mode is often used with Layer Two Tunneling Protocol (L2TP). Data encryption is accomplished by IPSec, which uses Data Encryption Standard (DES) or Triple DES (3DES) encryption to provide data confidentiality. IPSec can also be used on its own to provide both tunneling and encryption of data.

VPN Concentrators

A *VPN concentrator* is a device that incorporates advanced encryption and authentication methods to handle a large number of VPN tunnels. It is geared specifically toward secure, remote access or site-to-site VPNs. VPN concentrators provide high performance, high availability, and impressive scalability.

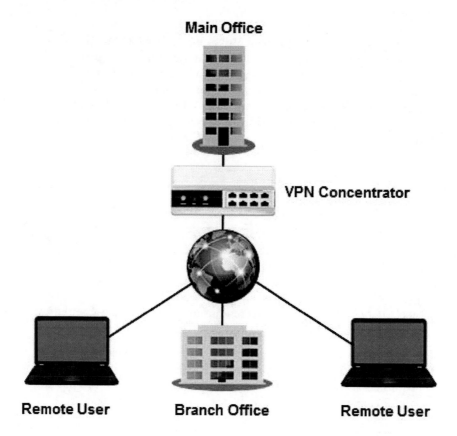

Main Office

VPN Concentrator

Remote User   **Branch Office**   **Remote User**

Figure 13-8: A VPN concentrator used in a corporate environment.

Although most connections to a VPN concentrator are incoming remote access client connections, the VPN concentrator can also create site-to-site VPNs.

VPN Connection Models

There are several popular connection models for VPNs.

Connection Model	Description
Site-to-site	In the site-to-site VPN connection model, each node on the network is connected to a remote network that may be separated by public or other unsecured networks. Site-to-site VPNs may be either open or closed. In case of an open site-to-site VPN connection, the exchange of data among nodes can be unsecured. In case of a closed site-to-site VPN connection, data can be communicated only by using the VPN in a secure mode. In both types of VPNs, IPSec is implemented to ensure secure data transactions.
Host-to-site	In the host-to-site VPN connection model also, there are two types of networks—open and closed. In the case of an open VPN, the path between the end node and the IPSec gateway is not secured. In the case of a closed VPN, the path between the end node and the IPSec gateway is secured. A host-to-site VPN connection establishes the connection to the network over an intermediary network such as the Internet. VPN software and protocols must be configured on both the client (host) and the server or router (site) to which the user is connecting.

Connection Model	Description
Host-to-host	In the host-to-host VPN connection model, rather than connecting to another network, a single device makes a secure connection to another single device. This can be used either internally or on the Internet. Where this is most common is when one server needs a secure connection to another server. A host-to-host VPN connection is usually established by using IPSec. This creates a secure, encrypted connection between the two hosts. All network traffic between the two hosts uses the tunnel to send and receive the encrypted information.

VPNs can also connect offsite to the virtual network components of VLANs or to other virtual networks that are onsite. The offsite components can also include proxy or reverse proxy servers.

ACTIVITY 13–4
Verifying VPN Configuration on RRAS

Scenario

At the Greene City Interiors branch office, some remote users need VPN access to the network. Before you configure VPN, you want to verify that VPN support is configured in RRAS.

---

1. Verify that VPN support is enabled on the WAN miniport that uses PPTP.
   a) In the Server Manager window, select **Tools→Routing and Remote Access**.
   b) In the Routing and Remote Access window, in the console tree, select the **Ports** object.
   c) Select **Actions→Properties**.
   d) In the **Ports Properties** dialog box, select the WAN miniport that uses PPTP and select **Configure**.

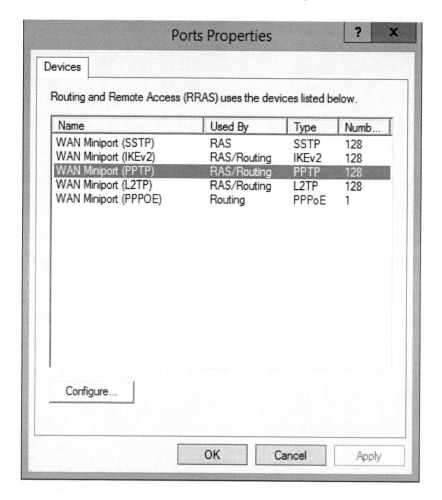

   e) In the **Configure Device - WAN Miniport (PPTP)** dialog box, verify that the **Remote access connections (inbound only)** and **Demand-dial routing connections (inbound and outbound)** check boxes are checked and select **OK**.

2. Verify that VPN support is enabled on the WAN miniport that uses L2TP.

a) Select the WAN miniport that uses L2TP and select **Configure**.

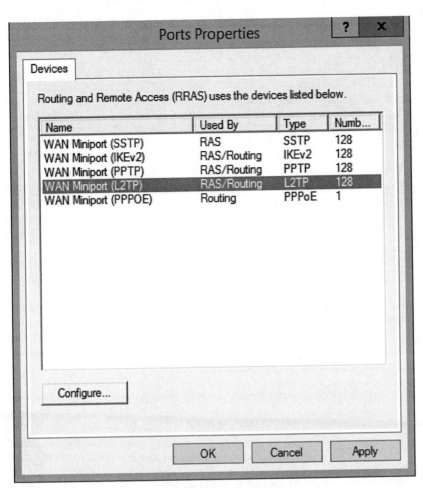

b) In the **Configure Device - WAN Miniport (L2TP)** dialog box, verify that the **Remote Access Connections (inbound only)** and **Demand-dial routing connections (inbound and outbound)** check boxes are checked and select **OK**.

c) Verify that the **Used By** column for the two ports displays **RAS/Routing**.

d) In the **Ports Properties** dialog box, select **OK**.

e) Close the Routing and Remote Access window.

TOPIC D

VPN Protocols

In the last topic, you identified the basic characteristics of VPNs. VPNs have additional data packet formatting and security requirements for which they use specific protocols. In this topic, you will identify the protocols that are used on VPNs.

When organizations are using a public network as a channel for communication, they need to deploy additional layers of security to mitigate threats and attacks. VPNs have built-in protocols to address this security risk because one of the key benefits to implementing a VPN is the security provided by the protocols that it uses. As a network professional, you should be aware of VPN protocols and their characteristics. This background information will ensure that you will be able to implement VPNs successfully.

PAP

The *Password Authentication Protocol (PAP)* is a remote-access authentication method that sends client IDs and passwords as cleartext. It is generally used when a remote client is connecting to a non-Windows PPP server that does not support password encryption. When the server receives a client ID and password, it compares them to its local list of credentials. If a match is found, the server accepts the credentials and allows the remote client to access resources. If no match is found, the connection is terminated.

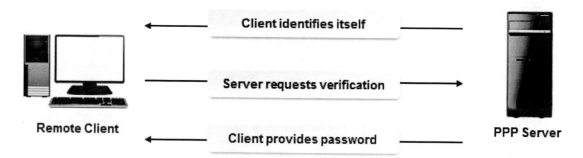

Figure 13-9: PAP authentication of a client by a server.

CHAP

The *Challenge Handshake Authentication Protocol (CHAP)* is a RAS protocol that uses an encryption method to transmit authentication information. Generally used to connect to non-Microsoft servers, CHAP was developed so that passwords would not have to be sent in plaintext. CHAP uses a combination of Message Digest 5 (MD5) hashing and a challenge-response mechanism, and authenticates without sending passwords as plaintext over the network.

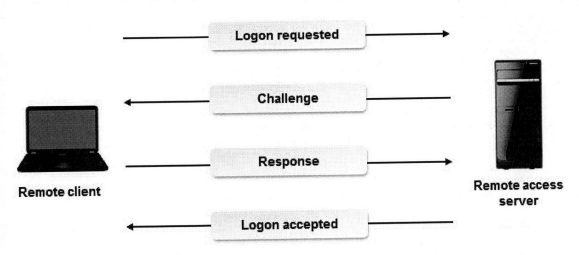

Figure 13-10: CHAP between a remote client and server.

Note: CHAP does not support PAP or Secure PAP unencrypted authentication.

MS-CHAP is a Microsoft extension of CHAP that is specifically designed for authenticating remote Windows workstations. MS-CHAPv2 provides all the functionality of MS-CHAP, and in addition provides security features such as two-way authentication and stronger encryption keys.

The Challenge-Response Authentication Process

In the challenge-response authentication process used in CHAP, the password is never sent across the network. The challenges that are tokens are encrypted.

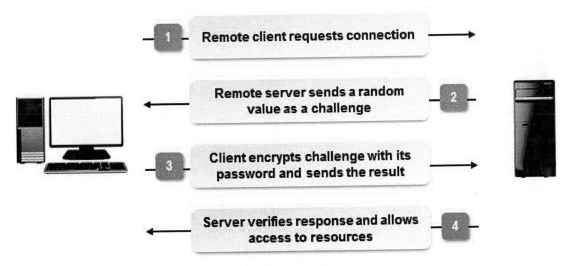

Figure 13-11: The challenge-response authentication process.

Step	Description
Step 1: Client requests a connection	A remote client requests a connection to a RAS.
Step 2: Server sends the challenge sequence	The remote server sends a challenge sequence, which is usually a random value. This is to receive an acknowledgment from the client.

Step	Description
Step 3: Client encrypts the challenge sequence	The remote client uses its password as an encryption key to encrypt the challenge sequence and sends the modified sequence to the server.
Step 4: Server encrypts the challenge sequence and compares the results	The server encrypts the original challenge sequence with the password stored in its local credentials list and compares the results with the modified sequence received from the client. • If the two sequences do not match, the server closes the connection. • If the two sequences match, the server allows the client to access resources.

TACACS+

Terminal Access Controller Access Control System (TACACS) and *TACACS Plus (TACACS+)* are authentication protocols that provide centralized authentication and authorization services for remote users. TACACS includes process-wide encryption for authentication, whereas RADIUS encrypts only passwords. TACACS uses TCP instead of UDP and supports multiple protocols. Extensions to the TACACS protocols exist, such as Cisco's TACACS+ and XTACACS.

TACACS+, which is open standard, uses TCP port 49 and also supports multifactor authentication. TACACS+ is considered more secure and more scalable than RADIUS because it accepts login requests and authenticates the access credentials of the user. TACACS+ is not compatible with TACACS because it uses an advanced version of the TACACS algorithm.

PPTP

The *Point-to-Point Tunneling Protocol (PPTP)* is a Layer 2 VPN protocol that increases the security of PPP by providing tunneling and data encryption for PPP packets. It uses the same authentication methods as PPP, and is the most widely supported VPN protocol among older Windows clients. Deployed over public, unsecured networks such as the Internet, PPTP encapsulates and transports multiprotocol data traffic over IP networks on port 1723.

Generic Routing Protocol (GRE) is used with PPTP and IPSec for VPN connections between clients and servers, or between clients. GRE encapsulates packets at the Network layer (Layer 3) of the OSI model. When you have established a PPTP connection between the client and the server, and you use the `ifconfig` or `ipconfig` command, one of the items listed is **P-t-P** with an IP address. The address listed after **P-t-P** is the IP address of the server.

L2TP

The *Layer Two Tunneling Protocol (L2TP)* is a protocol that works on the Internet and combines the capabilities of PPTP and Layer 2 Forwarding (L2F) to enable the tunneling of PPP sessions across network protocols such as IP, frame relay, or asynchronous transfer mode (ATM). L2TP uses UDP port 1701. L2TP was specifically designed to provide tunneling and security interoperability for client-to-gateway and gateway-to-gateway connections. L2TP packets look like IP packets because they also have a header, footer, and cyclic redundancy check (CRC).

L2TP does not provide any encryption on its own, so it uses IPSec as the transport mode for authentication, integrity, and confidentiality. This is referred to as L2TP/IPSec. If there is a device configured with network address translation (NAT) between the client and the server, then NAT Traversal must be used. NAT Traversal maintains IP connections traversing NAT gateways, which break end-to-end connectivity.

Note: L2TP has wide vendor support because it addresses the IPSec shortcomings of client-to-gateway and gateway-to-gateway connections.

 Note: If you are using the DirectAccess VPN protocol, which uses IPSec tunnels from the client to the DirectAccess server, it is always on. It will connect automatically when the computer establishes an Internet connection.

Windows Server 2008, Windows Server 2012 R2, Windows 7, and Windows 8 support a new tunneling protocol, *Secure Socket Tunneling Protocol (SSTP)*. SSTP uses the HTTP over SSL protocol. It encapsulates a data packet from IP with an SSTP header. The IP packet and SSTP header are encrypted by SSL. An IP header containing the destination addresses is then added to the packet.

ACTIVITY 13-5
Identifying VPN Protocols

Scenario

The network administrator at Greene City Interiors asks you to identify the characteristics of VPN protocols.

1. Name the benefits of using TACACS+ authentication compared to RADIUS.

2. Which statements are true of PAP?

   ☐ Encrypts user credentials.

   ☐ Connects a remote client to a non-Windows PPP server.

   ☐ Updates its local list of credentials when it receives a new set of credentials on the server.

   ☐ Compares credentials from a remote client with local credentials to allow access to resources.

3. What could you use a VPN for?

4. Do you have to use IPSec to enable a VPN?

5. Which statements are true of CHAP?

   ☐ Sends passwords as plaintext.

   ☐ Used to connect to non-Microsoft servers.

   ☐ Does not send passwords as plaintext.

   ☐ Uses MD5 hashing.

Summary

In this lesson, you identified the components required for remote networking. You need an understanding of all components required for remote network implementations so that you can support your remote users effectively.

What remote administration tools are used in your workplace? Would you suggest others based on what you just learned?

Share your experiences with using VPNs. What protocols did you use? Can you think of any reasons why you would not update the protocols?

 Note: Check your LogicalCHOICE Course screen for opportunities to interact with your classmates, peers, and the larger LogicalCHOICE online community about the topics covered in this course or other topics you are interested in. From the Course screen you can also access available resources for a more continuous learning experience.

14 | Network Management

Lesson Time: 1 hour

Lesson Objectives

In this lesson, you will identify the tools, methods, and techniques used in managing a network. You will:

- Describe major system and network monitoring tools.

- Identify the major types of configuration management documentation.

- Identify network performance optimization techniques.

Lesson Introduction

You have designed your network, chosen the hardware and software it will require, and secured it. Your next step is to manage your network for optimal performance. In this lesson, you will investigate some monitoring tools and network management methods that will help you determine your network's baseline and optimize your network's performance.

Managing your network for optimal performance is an essential task for network technicians to understand and be able to perform. By monitoring your network, determining your network's baseline, and optimizing your network to perform at its peak performance, your network can provide reliable service to your users. An effectively managed network has low downtime and improved availability of services no matter what the network size is. This aligns with the Information Technology Infrastructure Library (ITIL) set of practices for IT service management (ITSM) that focuses on aligning IT services with the needs of business. ITIL describes processes, procedures, tasks, and checklists that are not organization-specific, but can be applied by an organization for establishing integration with the organization's strategy, delivering value, and maintaining a minimum level of competency. There are various network monitoring and troubleshooting tools that can help you to achieve this outcome.

TOPIC A

Network Monitoring

Monitoring the activities on your network is the first step in efficiently managing it. With monitoring tools, you can compile information about your network that will help you manage it. In this topic, you will use monitoring tools to analyze your network's performance.

There are several major types of monitoring tools that you can use to assess the overall functioning of your network and to diagnose the cause of general complaints such as "The network is too slow" or "I'm having problems getting on and off this server." You can use these tools to keep tabs on your network's performance, in order to recognize and correct problems as well as to anticipate and eliminate problems before they disrupt services on the network.

Network Management Overview

Network management is the management of functions such as operation, administration, maintenance, and provisioning of systems on a network by using various activities, methods, procedures, and tools.

- Operation deals with procedures that allow for the smooth running of the network, and includes monitoring of the network to spot problems as they arise.
- Administration involves keeping track of the assignment and utilization of devices on the network.
- Maintenance involves repairing and upgrading network components, and taking necessary measures to ensure that devices are running optimally.
- Provisioning assigns resources to support a service.

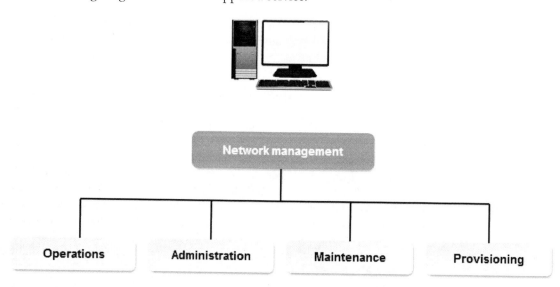

Figure 14-1: Functions of network management.

The goal of network management is to make operations more efficient. The cost of ownership of the network should come down, including the cost of the equipment and of operating the network.

The quality of the network and its services includes reliability and availability. Increased revenue can be obtained through network management when a service provider attracts more customers with management-related capabilities such as tracking accounting charges online and configuring service features over the web.

Network management has its share of challenges. For one, the number of services to be delivered over a network is usually large, and each of these services has specific requirements relating to bandwidth, connections, and other similar requirements that need to be fulfilled. These services along with other existing services on the network impact the overall performance. Moreover, networks expand constantly and require reconfiguration and upgrades. Any new management tools must adapt to the network in the shortest possible time, or they may impact network performance.

SNMP

Simple Network Management Protocol (SNMP) is an Application-layer (Layer 7) protocol used to collect information from network devices for diagnostic and maintenance purposes. SNMP includes two components: management systems and agent software, which are installed on network devices such as servers, routers, and printers. The agents send information to an SNMP manager. The SNMP manager can then notify an administrator of problems, run a corrective program or script, store the information for later review, or query the agent about a specific network device.

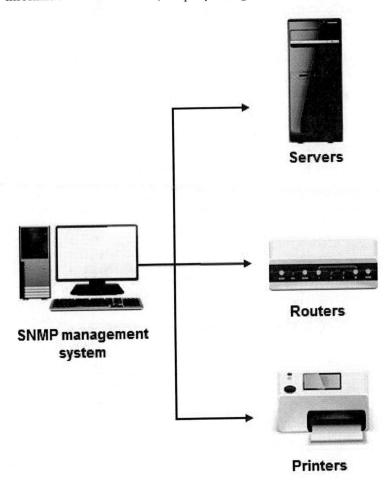

Figure 14-2: SNMP collects information from network devices for diagnostic purposes.

SNMP does not define which information a managed system will offer. Instead the available information is defined by management information bases (MIBs). MIBs describe the structure of the management data of a device subsystem. MIBs use a hierarchical namespace containing object identifiers (OIDs). Each OID identifies a variable that can be read or set via SNMP. MIBs will typically allow you to do SNMP operations such as GET, TRAP, and WALK. The GET operation is a request to retrieve the value of a variable or list of variables. The TRAP operation enables an agent to notify the management station of significant events by way of an unsolicited SNMP message. The WALK operation is essentially a GET operation performed on an MIB node that has child nodes or column nodes, and performs the OID walk through the child nodes or column nodes.

There are currently three versions of SNMP.

Version	Description
SNMPv1	Original specification defined in 1988.
SNMPv2	Introduced in 1993. Added several protocol operations and initial security measures.
SNMPv3	Introduced in 2002. Added security features and remote configuration capabilities. Three important services added: authentication, privacy, and access control.

SNMP uses User Datagram Protocol (UDP) ports 161 and 162. Not all monitoring solutions are SNMP-based. Microsoft® System Center Operations Manager uses Microsoft's proprietary Remote Procedure Call at Transmission Control Protocol (TCP) port 135 instead.

Network Monitoring Tools

Network monitoring tools can capture and analyze traffic; create logs; alert you to events you define; monitor different interfaces such as routers, switches, and servers; indicate areas of traffic congestion; help you construct baselines; determine upgrade and forecast needs; and generate reports for management.

There are many different network monitoring tools, each of which has a specific purpose.

Purpose	Tools
LAN monitoring	• Remote Monitoring (RMON) • pathping • OpManager • Distinct Network Monitor • Solarwinds® ipMonitor®
QoS monitoring	• QoS parameters • Router parameters • Load balancing • XenMon • RT Audio and RT Video • Avaya® Converged Network Analyzer
Bandwidth monitoring	• Netflow analyzer • Rokario • DU Meter
WAN monitoring	• Exinda® • Router monitoring • CastleRock SNMPc • Visual UpTime® • Observer

Purpose	Tools
Security information and event management (SIEM)	• McAfee® Enterprise Security Manager • CNAM Threat Defense Platform NETMONASTERY • EiQ Networks SecureVue® • HP® ArcSight • IBM® Security QRadar® SIEM • NetIQ® Sentinel™

Throughput Testers

Throughput testers are software tools that you can use to measure network throughput and capacity. These software tools send large data packets from one destination to another and measure the time taken to transfer the packets. The throughput is then calculated by dividing the packet size by the time taken.

Connectivity Tools and Utilities

There are several built-in connectivity tools and utilities in Windows® or UNIX® operating systems that you can use to troubleshoot network connectivity issues. Connectivity software utilities are used to troubleshoot connectivity issues. Some of these utilities also support network monitoring. Ping, pathping, tracert, and netstat are examples of connectivity utilities. Popular third-party connectivity tools include Wireshark® and Nagios®.

Network Monitoring Tool Categories

There are thousands of software tools for managing or monitoring a network. These tools are generally part of an operating system such as Windows or UNIX. However, they are also available as add-on applications. They are broadly classified into three functional categories: status, traffic, and route monitoring tools.

Functional Category	Description
Status monitoring	Used to gather data related to the status of a network. Examples of these tools include the `ping` and `nslookup` commands.
Traffic monitoring	Used to gather data related to the traffic generated in a network. The `ping` command can be used as a traffic monitoring tool. The command used repeatedly enables a user to calculate the percentage of packet loss. Another example of a traffic monitoring tool is the `iptrace` command used in UNIX systems. The command is used to measure the performance of gateways.
Route monitoring	Used to trace the route taken by packets and detect routing delays, if any. Some examples of the route monitoring tools include the `tracert` and `arp` commands.

Network Traffic Analysis

Network traffic analysis is the study of various network activities. It includes:

- Identification of the inbound and outbound protocols.
- Checking whether the protocols acknowledge each other. This step helps identify if the protocols communicate unidirectionally or bidirectionally.
- Identifying if ports are open and closed.
- Checking the traffic that passes through a firewall.
- Packet flow monitoring.

- Checking *goodput* (throughput), threshold limits, and overall network performance.
- Identifying *top talkers*, which are the hosts sending the most data, and *top listeners*, which are the hosts receiving the most data, on the network.
- Tracing packets on the network.
- Studying network utilization.

When doing network analysis, you need to have an appropriate sampling size. This sample size should reflect the load your network will need to support. It is not realistic to expect your entire network population to carry out testing of your updated or optimized network, so by using a sample you can extrapolate how the changes will affect your total network population.

Network Diagnostics

There are various tools available to perform network diagnostic tests to determine areas of concern and issues. The tools provide real-time issues and methods to troubleshoot most common issues. Some of the activities performed by network diagnostics tools are:

- Monitor end-to-end application response time.
- Analyze network traffic.
- Manage device performance.
- Monitor and alert for availability, bandwidth utilization, and health of devices.
- Provide network diagnostics for troubleshooting and resolving issues.
- Offer network discovery tools that facilitate IP address management, port mapping, and ping sweeps.

    - Port mapping translates addresses of packets to a new address. The translated packets are then routed based on the routing table.
    - Ping sweeps establish a range of IP addresses to locate active hosts within a given range. Ping sweep can be performed by using tools such as fping and map.

- Provide tools for real-time *NetFlow* analysis, configuration, and device management.

System Performance Monitors

A *performance monitor* is a software tool that monitors the state of services or daemons, processes, and resources on a computing device. Performance monitors track one or more *counters*, which are individual statistics about the operation of different objects on the device, such as software processes or hardware components. Some objects can have more than one instance; for example, a device can have multiple CPUs.

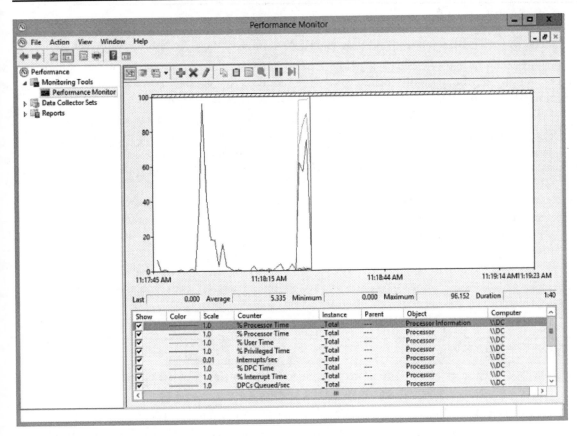

Figure 14-3: A performance monitor.

When a counter value reaches a given *threshold*, it indicates that the object of the counter may be functioning outside acceptable limits. System administrators generally take action when counter values they are monitoring reach a threshold value. These values can be set in different ways that vary depending on the monitoring tool and system. Some counters have thresholds that depend upon the device or its criticality. You will need to consult the documentation from your equipment's manufacturer, and establish a baseline for performance before setting these thresholds.

There are many counters that cover a wide range of components in a network. Counters that deal with the utilization of resources are commonly used because they provide you with an insight of how much of the resources are being used. Individual counters will be different from monitor to monitor, but here are some of the groups of counters that will be available.

Type of Counter	Description
Bandwidth	Counters measure different aspects of network bandwidth. Types of counters include: Bytes received/sent, Interface counts and rates, Transfers per Second.
Storage	Counters measure disk space and storage-related performance. Types of counters include: Free Space, Transfers per Second, Reads/Writes per Second.
Network device CPU	Counters measure CPU utilization data. Types of counters include: % user time, % processor time, Interrupts.
Network device memory	Counters measure memory utilization. Types of counters include: Available bytes, Page Ins/Page Outs, Active/Inactive Pages, Free/Shared/Buffered/Cached Pages, Swap Ins/Swap Outs.

Some monitoring tools can also provide the link status of a device's network interface card (NIC). The link status indicates whether the NIC has a valid link or not. Some tools can also provide data on the wireless channel utilization of a wireless network. This can help you determine how well your wireless network is being utilized and then you can determine if it can be optimized further.

Many operating systems include basic network performance monitoring tools, or you can obtain more complex third-party tools, including network monitors that are based on the SNMP and Remote Monitoring (RMON) systems designed to handle large clusters or server farms.

- Most Linux/UNIX systems provide a CPU usage monitoring tool called *top* as part of their default installation. top can provide either a static snapshot, or a real-time display of the processes currently running on a given CPU. top's various data displays include columns for memory use, virtual memory, and the process ID. The -u flag is useful for ordering the list by CPU usage. The process with the highest use is displayed at the beginning of the list.
- Windows Performance Monitor is included in Windows Server® 2008 and later and allows network administrators to observe, monitor, and record a wide variety of system-related information including CPU usage, network usage, process and thread behavior, and memory usage.

Syslog is a term used to define the process of logging program messages or data logs. The term collectively includes the software or operating system that generates, reads, and analyzes log files. A *log file* is a record of actions and events performed on an operating system. There are three common types of log files: system, general, and history files.

Type	Description
System	System logs are often predetermined by the operating system itself and are a record of events logged by the operating system.
General	General logs are a type of system log that contains information about device changes, installation/uninstallation of device drivers, and any other system changes.
History	History logs record information, such as the type of log, the time of event occurrence, the name of the user who was logged on at the time of the event (or who caused the event), keywords, any identification numbers, and what category (or categories) the event belongs to. The format may differ based on the operating system used.

Protocol Analysis

A *network analyzer,* also known as a packet or protocol analyzer, or a packet sniffer, is a software or hardware management tool that integrates diagnostic and reporting capabilities to provide a comprehensive view of an organization's network. As data flows across a network, the analyzer can monitor the packet flow by intercepting it, logging it, and analyzing the information according to baseline specifications.

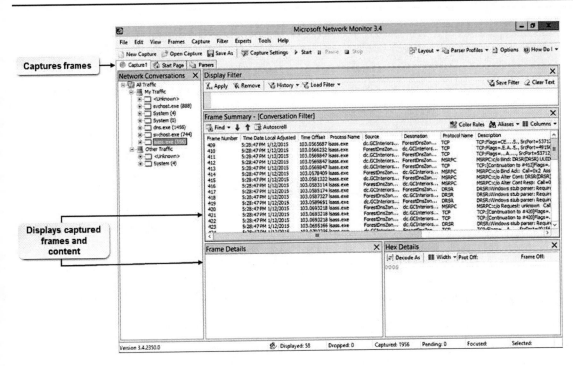

Captures frames

Displays captured frames and content

Figure 14-4: The Network Monitor utility provides network statistics.

Basic network analyzers enable a technician to analyze network traffic on a LAN or DSL connection. Network analyzers also have the ability to provide an administrator with an overview of systems and reports from one location on the network. Full-featured network analyzers offer a variety of monitoring, analyzing, and reporting functions. A network analyzer can be used during troubleshooting to locate problems, but it can also be used as a long-term network monitoring solution or for packet flow monitoring.

Wireshark® and Microsoft Network Monitor are software that can analyze networks.

Similar to a packet sniffer, a network sniffer can identify and capture data packets on a network, record and analyze traffic, and identify open ports on the network. They can possibly analyze data packets from different protocols and identify data vulnerabilities on the network.

You can measure the throughput, or goodput, of a network by using various tools available on different operating systems. One of the methods will be to measure maximum data throughput in bits per second of network access or a communication link. Another method of measuring the network performance is to transfer a "large" file from one system to another and calculate the time required to complete the transfer of the file or to copy it. The throughput can be determined by dividing the file size by the total time and expressed as megabits, kilobits, or bits per second.

Log Management

Log management is the approach to dealing with computer-generated log messages for the network. Devices and applications generate log data on a variety of processes. These can range from simple status events to errors. They can be very brief or contain detailed information on events and processes running. Log management can be used to monitor the health of systems or to troubleshoot issues. The built-in log system can be used, or there are log management tools available that give you more control and options for filtering and managing logs.

Network Fault Tolerance

Fault tolerance is the ability of a network or device to withstand a foreseeable component failure and continue to provide an acceptable level of service. Fault tolerance measures include protecting power sources, disks and data storage, and network components. The critical components of a network need to be fault tolerant so as to ensure base-level functioning of the network.

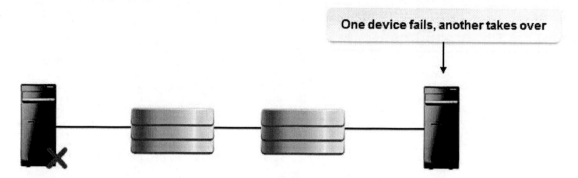

One device fails, another takes over

Figure 14–5: A backup server takes over when the main server fails.

 Note: For more information about fault tolerance, see Appendix B, Network Fault Tolerance and Disaster Recovery.

Alerts

Many network monitoring tools have the ability to send alerts. An alert can be a notification that appears within the tool, or even an email or SMS message that is sent to a preconfigured user. The alert informs the user of an event that occurred. The conditions that triggered the alert are usually configurable so that you can control what you want to be alerted about. After receiving an alert, the user can then investigate the event and take the appropriate action, if any.

Power Monitoring Tools

Power monitoring tools increase your awareness of power quality issues and the ability to address them. Poor quality of power can cause physical damage to equipment and can also result in downtime. Power monitoring tools can provide reliable information about power quality, demand, and flow. Most power monitoring tools allow you to perform remote monitoring, optimize energy consuming equipment, and perform regular remote maintenance routines and emergency service.

There is also data center infrastructure management (DCIM), which is a category of solutions that were created to extend the traditional data center management function to include all of the physical assets and resources found in the facilities and IT domains. It is a combination of hardware and software tools that can be used to constantly monitor power consumption of the data center, including networking equipment, which allow you to proactively strike a continual balance between efficiency and availability. You can look for areas where the power load is too great or too light, and re-route power availability as needed.

Rack Monitoring

Rack monitoring involves using sensors to monitor the ambient conditions where rack systems are in place. Fluctuations in temperature or air humidity outside of recommended parameters can cause hardware defects. Monitoring of these parameters is required to ensure properly functioning operability. Rack monitoring systems can send alerts, record information, and forward it to a higher-level management system. Some monitoring systems can connect to environmental systems, respond to changing conditions, and automatically perform actions to adjust those conditions, such as activating additional fans.

Interface Monitoring

Interface monitoring is typically a feature built into a switch, router, or server. The device can provide statistics about its own interfaces. Usually these are transmit (TX) and receive (RX) traffic loads, packet errors, and link status. In most cases, you can get a point-in-time snapshot, as well as some history. You can use classic SNMP-based third-party monitoring tools to continuously query many devices and report their status to a central console in a graphical format. You can typically also set alerts and track trends on interfaces/devices of interest.

Wireless Survey Tools

A wireless survey is the process of planning and designing a wireless network that provides a wireless solution that will deliver the required wireless coverage, data rates, network capacity, roaming capability, and QoS. The survey will require a site visit to identify installation locations for access points and to test for *radio frequency (RF)* interference. Wireless survey tools will be required to perform parts of the site survey.

Most surveys can be performed by using software, a wireless access point (WAP), and either a client with a Wi-Fi adapter or a field-strength measuring device. You place the WAP and then move the client/field-strength measuring device to test the signal strength of connections within the range that WAP will service, preferably testing from actual client desk locations. You can perform site surveys by using tools such as NetStumbler or AirSnort. These will also allow you to see if any rogue access points have been installed on the network.

An RF spectrum survey requires specialized RF equipment. There are various types of spectrum analyzers ranging from large and expensive bench-top units to portable and PC-based analyzers.

The signal-to-noise ratio (SNR) is a comparison of a wireless network signal with noise generated from other devices such as florescent lights, microwave ovens, and other wireless devices. Determining the SNR is often part of performing a site survey of your wireless network, and the tool you use for your site survey might include a function to calculate the SNR. A higher SNR value indicates a better signal strength in relation to the surrounding noise levels. The value is expressed in decibels. For example, a SNR of 40 dB or more is an excellent connection, and when shown with bars in the system tray, will show 5 bars. A value of 15 to 25 dB SNR is usually a low signal, showing 3 bars. A value of 5 to 10 dB SNR results in no signal and no bars.

Wireless Analyzers

A wireless analyzer is piece of software or hardware that is used to analyze the physical aspects of wireless networks. This includes items such as: spectrum analysis, finding WAPs, reporting service set identifiers (SSIDs), channel usage, signal strength, and identifying noise sources.

Wireless Heat Maps

A wireless heat map, also known as a wireless coverage map, is a map with an overlay of colors representing different values related to wireless coverage. Typically, red represents the best signal levels and blue represents the worst. By looking at the heat map, you can identify areas of low and high signal strength. The results from a site survey can be displayed as a heat map.

ACTIVITY 14–1
Monitoring Data on the Network

Scenario

At the Greene City Interiors branch office, you want to capture data about network traffic on the network to analyze if there is anything suspicious or out of place. You decide to use Network Monitor to accomplish this.

1. Use Network Monitor to capture data.
   a) On the desktop, double-click **Microsoft Network Monitor 3.4.**
   b) Maximize the Microsoft Network Monitor 3.4 window.
   c) In the **Select Networks** pane, in the **Friendly Name** list, check any unchecked networks.
   d) On the toolbar, select **New Capture**.
   e) Select **Start**.

2. Perform tasks that generate network traffic.
   a) Open **Windows PowerShell**, type `ping -6 computer##` and press **Enter**, where XX corresponds to another student's ID number.
   b) Select **Start→Remote Desktop Connection**.
   c) In the **Remote Desktop Connection** dialog box, in the **Computer** box, type the computer name of your partner's computer.

    Note: The computer name will follow the naming standard of Computer##. Use the same partner you had from the Remote Networking lesson.

   d) Select **Connect**.
   e) In the **Windows Security** dialog box, select **Use another account**.

    Note: If you already connected to this student's computer previously, then you will not have to select **Use another account** and can instead enter the password.

   f) In the **User name** field, type *GCInteriors\Student##* where ## is your student ID number.
   g) In the **Password** box, type *P@ssw0rd12*
   h) Select **OK**.
   i) In the **Remote Desktop Connection** dialog box, select **Yes**.
   j) On the desktop of the remote computer, observe the **Computer##** bar at the top of the screen.

k) On the Start menu, select **Student##**, and then select **Sign out**.

3. Analyze the traffic in the capture log.
   a) In the Network Monitor window, on the toolbar, select **Stop**.
   b) In the **Display Filter** pane, in the text field, select and type *RDP* and then select **Apply**.
   c) In the **Frame Summary** pane, select a frame.
   d) In the **Frame Details** pane, review the frame information.

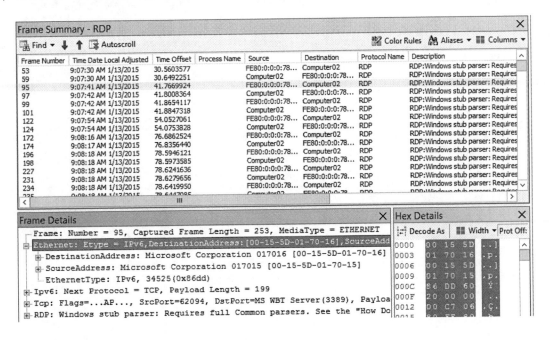

   e) In the **Display Filter** pane, on the toolbar, select **Remove**.
   f) In the **Display Filter** pane, on the toolbar, select **Clear Text**.
   g) In the **Display Filter** pane, in the text field, select and type *RIP* and then select **Apply**.
   h) In the **Frame Summary** pane, select a frame.
   i) In the **Frame Details** pane, review the frame information, and identify the port used for RIP traffic.
   j) In the **Display Filter** pane, on the toolbar, select **Remove**.
   k) In the **Display Filter** pane, on the toolbar, select **Clear Text**.

l) In the menu, select **Filter→Display Filter→Load Filter→Standard Filter→Authentication Traffic**.

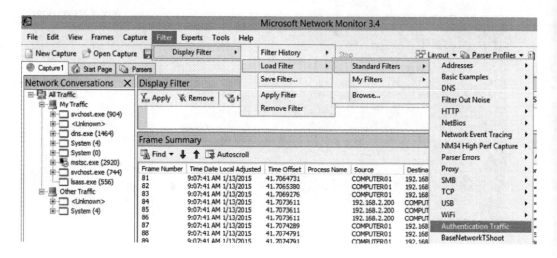

m) In the **Display Filter** pane, review the code for the filter.

n) Select **Apply**.

o) Review the authentication traffic data in the **Frame Summary** and **Frame Details** panes.

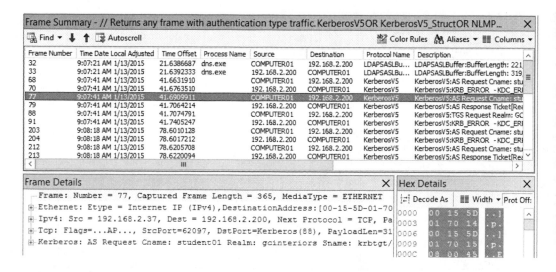

p) In the **Display Filter** pane, on the toolbar, select **Remove**.

q) In the **Display Filter** pane, on the toolbar, select **Clear Text**.

r) In the **Network Conversations** pane, review the types of traffic listed.

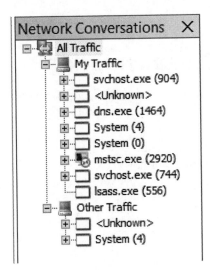

s) Under **Other Traffic**, expand **<Unknown>**.

t) Select each group of **IPv6** traffic and then review the traffic information in the **Frame Summary** and **Frame Details** panes.

4. **What types of IPv6 traffic were captured?**

TOPIC B

Configuration Management Documentation

In the last topic, you identified network monitoring tools. However, there may be times when you need to refer to the actual network configuration documentation. In this topic, you will identify configuration management documentation.

In case of a disaster, it is imperative that you already have critical documentation in place that will help you rebuild as quickly as possible. Without detailed documentation, you would have to rely on memory to determine your network layout, which would likely be very time consuming, costly, and ultimately inaccurate. A complete set of configuration documentation will give you a solid base from which you can begin rebuilding your network.

Configuration Management

Configuration management is a process of setting up and changing the configuration of the network and its components. The information on configuration management is present on managed objects such as switches and routers. Configuration management therefore involves the setting up of parameters for these devices. There are three main configuration types:

- The static configuration, which is the permanent configuration of the network.
- The current running configuration.
- The planned configuration, when the configuration data changes as the network changes.

Configuration management documentation focuses on maintaining a database of the hardware and software components on a network. The database stores a detailed inventory of network elements such as the part number, version number, description, wire schemes, and a record of the network topology being implemented. The database is updated as the network grows or shrinks. The `arp` command facilitates in updating this database because it can discover any new network component having an IP address.

Network Documentation

Although each network is unique, there are common documents that each network administrator should have at hand.

Document	Used To
Network diagrams	Provide the location and routing information for network devices. They are also known as network maps.
Device information	List the hardware, software, and configuration information for each device on the network. This includes serial numbers and software license keys, unique identifications, and date. Changes to device information should be noted and dated as they occur. Special cases should be called out so that a new network administrator can come up to speed quickly. This list must be updated for the onboarding and offboarding of mobile devices as they are added and removed from the network.
Utilization statistics	Provide usage logs and reports to measure network utilization and performance.
Policies and procedures	Provide guidelines and the appropriate method for performing network management tasks. Documented procedures can include: hardware selection, new user creation, security policies and procedures, and troubleshooting tips.

Document	Used To
Graphing	Provide visual representation of network-related data, such as the graph from a network performance monitor.
Vendor documentation	List the vendors used to service any aspects of your network, including ISPs, computer/device retailers, equipment/computer technicians, and so on. This list should include their contact information, services they provide, rate, and any additional comments about their service or performance.

Physical Network Diagrams

A *physical network diagram* is a graphical representation of the locations of all network devices and endpoints, and depicts their connections with one another. A network diagram illustrates the physical relationship between nodes, but not necessarily their exact location in a building or a floor.

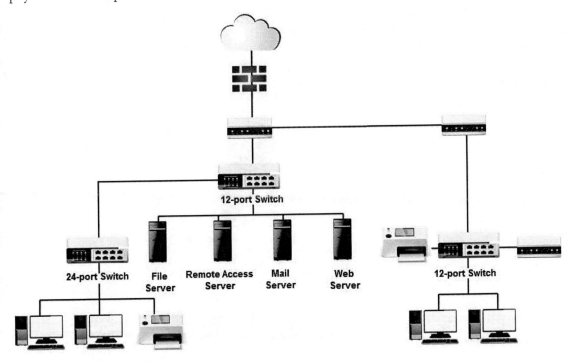

Figure 14-6: A physical network diagram.

A physical network diagram typically depicts:

- Routers and switches
- Servers
- Workstations, printers, and fax machines
- Remote access equipment
- Firewalls
- Wireless access points
- Cable management information
- Channel Service Unit/Data Service Unit (CSU/DSU)

You may also want to include a floor plan in your physical network diagram. A floor plan or physical layout should also include the locations of the demarc, wiring closets, and cable runs.

A network *wiring schematic* or *wiring diagram* is a combination of a floor plan and a physical network topology diagram. As with physical network diagrams, you can see the nodes on the network and how they are physically connected. Schematics show the nodes and network wiring superimposed on a floor plan of the facility with the actual equipment and cables depicted on the schematic in their real-world locations.

Just as it is possible to follow a map from one place to another, it should be possible to use a wiring schematic to locate nodes and follow wires within a facility. The schematic is usually drawn to scale so that it is easy to estimate distances and locate drops, wiring closets, and cable runs. Cable management techniques and tools can be used to group and organize cables together to keep them out of the way and hidden from the general working space.

Logical Network Diagrams

A *logical network diagram* documents the protocols and applications that control the flow of network traffic. Logical network diagrams do not attempt to depict the physical relationship of the nodes; rather, they show how the data should move, regardless of the physical implementation. A logical network diagram depicts:

- IP addresses of each network device.
- Fully Qualified Domain Name (FQDN) of a device.
- Application type of each server.
- Trust relationships that exist between nodes.
- The routing topology.

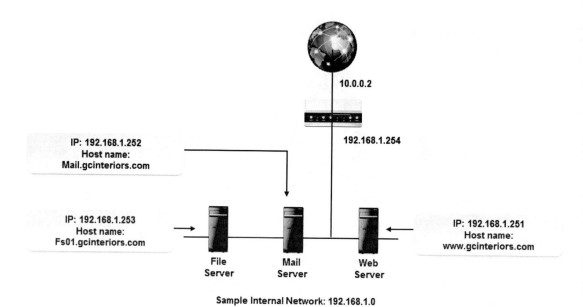

Figure 14-7: A logical network diagram.

Typical logical network diagrams also include the direction of traffic flow as well as the protocols and services provided by different parts of the network.

IT Asset Management

IT asset management is the set of management policies that include information about the financial and contractual specifications of all the hardware and software components present in an organization's inventory. Some organizations have exclusive asset management for hardware and software components.

Critical Hardware Inventory

A hardware inventory provides insurance documentation and helps determine what you need to rebuild the network.

Hardware Inventory Entry	Information to Include
Standard workstation	A basic description of a standard client workstation. Include minimum requirements and the installed operating system as well as how many workstations of this type are deployed. For workstations that deviate from the norm, be sure to document the deviations.
Specialty workstation	A description of any specialty workstations deployed. Include a brief description of their roles and special configurations implemented on them.
Basic server	A list of the basic server hardware configuration and the role of these servers. List their internal hardware and any special configuration settings and software. Include a configuration list for the operating system.
Connectivity hardware	A list of all connectivity hardware in as much detail as possible. This includes the device brand and model numbers, but a description of each feature ensures that replacements can be made without research.
Backup hardware	Document critical information about backup hardware, such as the vendor and model number of a tape drive, backup hard drives, DVD drives, and network attached storage, if applicable.

> **Note:** For more information about backups, see Appendix B, Network Fault Tolerance and Disaster Recovery.

Critical Software Inventory

A software inventory provides insurance documentation and helps determine what you need to rebuild the network.

Software Inventory Entry	Information to Include
Operating system software	All operating system software, including desktop and server operating systems. Include documentation on licensing and copies of the bulk licenses, if possible. Many vendors retain records of software licenses sold to their customers. If this is the case, include this fact in your documentation.
Productivity and application software	Off-the-shelf productivity software, including any applications installed on client devices and servers.
Maintenance utilities	The utilities used to maintain a network, especially backup software and software configuration.
Backup documentation	Records of when backups were made, how frequently to make them, what backups contain, where backups are stored, and credentials needed to restore backups. Document the backup software and version. Special setup and configuration considerations need to be documented too.

Software Inventory Entry	Information to Include
Overall asset inventory	If your company maintains an overall asset inventory, attach a copy. Many companies use the inventory as a base to track hardware and maintenance. This usually includes most of the information needed.

Network Policies

A *network policy* is a formalized statement or set of statements that defines network functions and establishes expectations for users, management, and IT personnel. It describes, in detail, the acceptable use policies of network equipment for a particular organization, including the appropriate methods to maintain, upgrade, and troubleshoot the network. Policies may also include specific information about security and network functioning such as the use of removable drives and other detachable media, instant messaging, wireless devices, the Internet, backup storage, network monitoring procedures, and vendor agreements. Network policies may include other areas of network functioning depending on the size and needs of an organization.

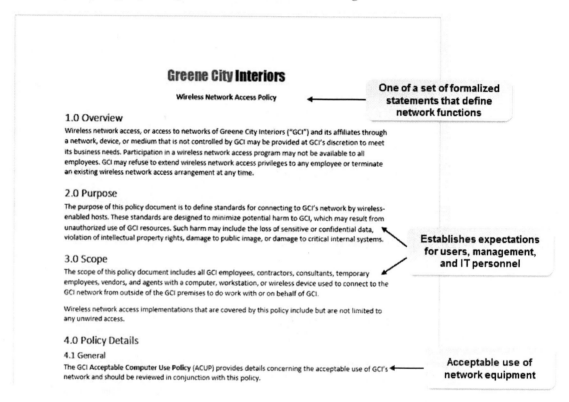

Figure 14–8: Network policy defines network functioning.

Each subsection of a network policy typically consists of several standard components.

Policy Component	Description
Policy statement	The *policy statement* outlines the plan for individual components.
Standards	*Standards* define how to measure the level of adherence to the policy.
Guidelines	Policy *guidelines* are suggestions, recommendations, or best practices for how to meet the policy standard.
Procedures	*Procedures* are step-by-step instructions that detail how to implement components of the policy.

Legal Compliance Requirements and Regulations

All organizations must consider their legal obligations, rights, liabilities, and limitations when creating policies. Because incidents can potentially be prosecuted as technology crimes, organizations must be prepared to work with civil authorities when investigating, reporting, and resolving each incident. Information security practices must comply with legal requirements that are documented in other departmental policies, such as human resources. A company's response to any incident must conform to the company's legal limitations as well as the civil rights of individuals involved.

Legal issues can affect different parties within each organization.

Affected Party	Legal Considerations
Employees	There may be a policy that governs what is allowed in social media. Employees are expected to know the policy and if they violate it, the organization can state that there was a policy in place and that the employee violated it.
	Who is liable for misuse of email and Internet resources—the organization, the employee, or both?
	What is the extent of liability for an organization for criminal acts committed by its employees?
	What rights to privacy do employees have regarding electronic communications?
Customers	An organization will have a privacy policy in regard to customers who do business with them. The policy will govern how private customer data, such as credit card information or contact information, is handled and what, if any of it, is made available to any other entities.
	What customer data is considered private and what is considered public?
	How will a company protect the privacy and confidentiality of customer information?
Business partners	Business partners working together on a project may have a mutual non-disclosure agreement (NDA) in place where both parties are not allowed to share any project details, patents, designs, and so on with external entities.
	Who is liable if the data resides in one location and processing takes place in another location?
	Who is responsible for the security and privacy of the information transmitted between an organization and a business partner—the sender or the receiver?

Standard Business Documents

There are various business documents that you may come into contact with. Here are some common documents you should be familiar with.

Document	Description
Service Level Agreement (SLA)	This document is a part of a service contract in which a service is formally defined between two or more parties. This can be a legally binding formal or an informal "contract" (for example, internal department relationships). Particular aspects of the service, such as scope, quality, and responsibilities are agreed upon between the service provider(s) and the customer. A common feature of an SLA is a contracted delivery time of the service or performance. In this case, the SLA will typically have a technical definition in terms of mean time between failures (MTBF); mean time to repair or mean time to recovery (MTTR); identifying which party is responsible for reporting faults or paying fees; responsibility for various data rates; throughput; jitter; or similar measurable details.
Memorandum of Understanding (MOU)	This document describes a bilateral or multilateral agreement between two or more parties, including each party's requirements and responsibilities. It is often used in cases where parties either do not imply a legal commitment, or in situations where the parties cannot create a legally enforceable agreement. It is far more formal than a handshake and is given weight in a court of law should one party fail to meet the obligations of the memorandum.
Master License Agreement (MLA)	This document describes an agreement between two or more parties, where one party is providing a service or product and the other party agrees to certain terms and conditions in order to use it.
Statement of Work (SOW)	This is a formal document that defines the work activities, deliverables, and timeline a vendor must execute in performance of specified work for a client. The SOW usually includes detailed requirements and pricing, with standard regulatory and governance terms and conditions. The main purpose of a SOW is to define the liabilities, responsibilities, and work agreements between clients and vendors.

Network Baselines

A *baseline* is a record of a device's performance statistics under normal operating conditions. A *network baseline* documents the network's current performance level and provides a quantitative basis for identifying abnormal or unacceptable performance. It can also reveal where *bottlenecks* are impeding performance, and provide evidence for upgrading devices to improve performance.

For example, if a company is expanding a remote office that is connected to the corporate office with a fractional T1, the baseline can help determine if there is enough reserve bandwidth to handle the extra user load, or if the fractional T1 needs to be upgraded to a full T1.

The Network Baselining Process

Creating and applying a baseline is a cyclical process.

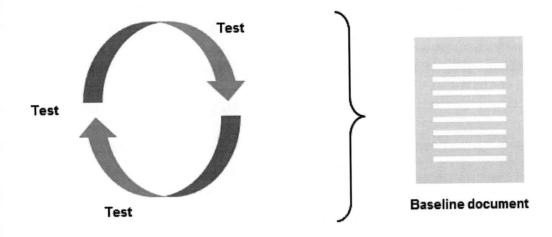

Figure 14-9: The baselining process involves repeated testing.

The number, type, and frequency of tests performed and recorded in the baseline will vary depending upon the systems and the needs of the organization. The organization must also decide how often to establish a new baseline to reflect current performance.

Typically, you will record baseline measurements to a log file that you can review later, rather than examining the measurements in real time. Most performance or network monitoring systems enable you to save log data. For example, in Windows Server 2012 R2, Performance Monitor gives you the option to record data directly to log format. When you log data in Performance Monitor, you can select all counters for a selected object, or specific counters. You can examine the counter values by selecting the counters to add when you open the log file in Chart view.

Change Management Procedures

Each individual organization will have its own customized process for change management, but most processes will include at least the following stages:

1. Identify potential change.
2. Document rationale for the change.
3. Create a change request, which should include:
   - Configuration procedures
   - Rollback processes
   - Potential impact
   - Notification processes
4. Initiate and work through an established approval process.
   - Analyze the change request to determine the feasibility of the request.
   - Determine the costs and benefits of the proposed change.
   - Evaluate the change based on the feasibility, costs, benefits, and need.
5. Plan the change.
   - Identify what is required in order to make the change.
   - Determine the time required to implement the change.
   - Identify the maintenance window, including authorized downtime, when the change can be implemented.
6. Implement the change.
   - Notify affected parties of downtime, if any.
   - Execute the change.

- Test the change.
- Provide notification of the change to affected parties.

7. Ensure adequate documentation exists and is updated, including:

- Network configuration diagrams
- Network additions
- Physical location changes

ACTIVITY 14-2
Using Performance Monitor to Establish a Baseline

Scenario

At the Greene City Interiors branch office, a part of your regular duties as the network administrator is to take and record baseline performance measurements for key systems on your network. The next system you are scheduled to baseline is a corporate file server running on Windows Server 2012 R2. This system is a dedicated file server, and does not run any special services.

1. Create and set up the performance log.
   a) In Server Manager, select **Tools→Performance Monitor**.
   b) In the Performance Monitor window, in the console tree, expand **Data Collector Sets**.
   c) Select the **User Defined** object, and select **Action→New→Data Collector Set**.
   d) In the **Create new Data Collector Set** dialog box, in the **Name** field, type *Baseline* and select **Next**.
   e) In the **Template Data Collector Set** list, select **Basic** and select **Next**.
   f) Accept the default settings for saving data by selecting **Next** and then select **Finish**.
   g) In the right pane, double-click the **Baseline** object.
   h) Right-click **Performance Counter** and select **Properties**.
   i) In the **Performance Counter Properties** dialog box, with the **\Processor(*)*** item selected, select **Remove**.
   j) Select **Add** to add a new performance counter.

k) In the **Available counters** section, scroll up and expand the **Memory** object.

![Performance Counter dialog box showing Available counters with Memory object expanded, listing % Committed Bytes In Use, Available Bytes, Available KBytes, Available MBytes, Cache Bytes, Cache Bytes Peak, Cache Faults/sec, and Added counters panel](performance-dialog)

l) Select **Add**.

m) Select **OK**.

2. Create the log file and set its parameters.

a) In the **Performance Counter Properties** dialog box, in the **Log format** drop-down list, verify that **Binary** is selected.

b) In the **Sample interval** text box, type *15*

c) Verify that the **Units** drop-down list displays **Seconds** and select the **File** tab.

d) For **File name format**, select the right arrow button .

e) Select **yyyy Full year including century**.

f) For **File name format**, select the right arrow button .

g) Select **MM Numeric month with leading zero**.

h) For **File name format**, select the right arrow button .

i) Select **dd Day of the month with leading zeros**.

j) Check the **Prefix file with computer name** check box.

k) Observe that in the **Example file name** text box, a log file name appears that displays the criteria just selected.

l) In the **Log mode** section, check **Overwrite**.

m) Select **Apply** and then select **OK**.

3. Track server activity with the log.

a) In the console tree, right-click **Baseline** and select **Start**.

 Note: Verify that a green arrow appears over the icon, indicating that the monitor is running.

b) In the console tree, select **Performance Monitor**.

c) Observe the graph that is plotted.

d) Run the log for two minutes, while you generate system activity by opening and closing programs, documents, and connecting to other systems on the network.

 Note: Open different applications from the **Start** menu and ping or navigate to other student computers on the network. After two minutes, close the windows you opened.

e) Return to Performance Monitor and observe the graph that is plotted.

4. Examine the log data.

a) In the console tree, expand **Reports→User Defined** and then select **Baseline**.

b) In the right pane, double-click the object that displays today's date.

c) Select **Application Counters** to expand that section of the report.

d) Observe that this report provides baseline information for the counters you specified, as each counter gets a Mean, Minimum, and Maximum score.

e) Close the Performance Monitor window.

TOPIC C

Network Performance Optimization

Now that you have determined your configuration and baseline measurements, you may want to change the network configuration or utilization to increase performance. In this topic, you will review techniques for network performance optimization.

If all you did was to monitor the network and take baseline measurements, the data you gathered would be relatively useless. You need to use the data to tweak the performance of existing devices and make the necessary changes to ensure that the network performs to its peak efficiency. This, in turn, provides higher availability of data and resources to your users and optimizes the performance.

QoS

Quality of Service (QoS) is a set of parameters that controls the quality provided to different types of network traffic. QoS parameters include the maximum amount of delay, signal loss, and noise that can be accommodated for a particular type of network traffic, bandwidth priority, and CPU usage for a specific stream of data. These parameters are agreed upon by the transmitter and the receiver, the transmitter being the ISP and the receiver being the subscriber. Both the transmitter and receiver enter into an agreement known as the *service level agreement (SLA)*. In addition to defining QoS parameters, the SLA describes remedial measures or penalties to be incurred by an ISP in the event that the ISP fails to provide the QoS promised in the SLA.

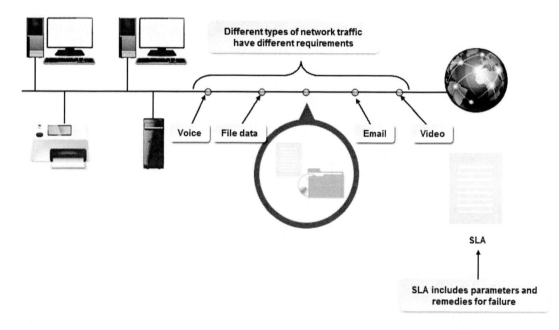

Figure 14-10: QoS controls the quality provided to different types of network traffic.

The Need for QoS

The amount of data being transmitted over networks is rising every day. Also, the type of data being transferred is changing. Traditional applications such as FTP and Telnet are now outnumbered by real-time multimedia applications such as IP telephony, multimedia applications, and videoconferencing. FTP and Telnet are very sensitive to packet loss but are tolerant to delays in data delivery. The reverse is applicable to multimedia applications; they can compensate for some amount of packet loss, but are very sensitive toward delays in data delivery.

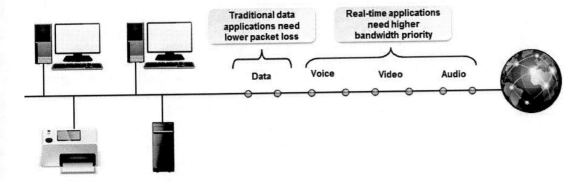

Figure 14-11: Bandwidth is prioritized to provide better QoS.

Therefore, an optimum usage of bandwidth becomes very critical while dealing with multimedia applications. Low bandwidth may result in a bad quality transmission of real-time applications, leading to dropouts or data loss. To avoid this, certain parameters were developed to prioritize bandwidth allocation for real-time applications on networks, such as the Internet, and guarantee a specific QoS.

QoS Parameters

Several parameters affect QoS on a network.

Parameter	Description
Bandwidth	Network *bandwidth* is the average number of bits of data that can be transmitted from a source to a destination over the network in one second.
Latency	*Latency,* also called lag or delay, is the time difference between transmission of a signal and when it was received.
	Some delay is inevitable; packets are held up in queues, or take less congested routes that take longer, but excessive delay can render applications insensitive to delay.
	To account for latency on a network, technicians need to consider the applications that will predominantly use the network, and design the network with devices that allow for lower processing delays or provision for bandwidth expansion when needed. Latency can be minimized by increasing the network bandwidth, fragmenting data packets, or prioritizing data on a network.

Parameter	Description
Jitter	*Jitter* is the variability over time in latency between sequentially transmitted data packets.
	Packets are delayed when processed in queues and routers along the transmission route and often reach the destination at variable times. Although packets are sent continuously with even spacing, the spacing becomes uneven because the delay between each packet is variable due to network congestion, improper queuing, or errors in configuration. The variation in the arrival of packets pauses the conversation and garbles the speech.
	A very low amount of jitter is important for real-time applications using voice and video. Jitter is resolved by using the dejitter or play-out delay buffer. This buffer stores packets and plays them into a steady stream so that they are converted into a proper analog stream. However, dejitter buffers increase latency on a network.
Packet loss	*Packet loss* is the number of packets that are lost or damaged during transmission.
	Packets can be dropped when they arrive at a destination that has buffers that are already full. To minimize packet loss, the receiving application asks for a retransmission of packets. Unfortunately, this can add to latency.
Echo	Echo is a reflected sound, a distinct repetition of the original sound—a familiar phenomenon in phone calls when you hear your own voice after a few milliseconds (ms).
	Echoes can occur during many locations along the route. Splices and improper terminations in the network can cause a transmission packet to reflect back to the source, which causes the sound of an echo. To correct for echo, network technicians can introduce an echo canceller to the network design. This will cancel out the energy being reflected.

Latency Sensitivity

Some applications, protocols, and processes are sensitive to the time it takes for their requests and results to be transmitted over the network. This is known as *latency sensitivity*. Examples of latency-sensitive applications include VoIP, video conferencing, and other real-time applications. In VoIP, high latency can result in an annoying and counterproductive delay between a speaker's words and the listener's reception of those words.

Network management techniques such as QoS, load balancing, traffic shaping, and caching can be used to optimize the network and reduce latency for sensitive applications. By regularly testing for latency and monitoring those devices that are susceptible to latency issues, you can provide a higher level of service to users.

Traffic Shaping

Traffic shaping, also known as *bandwidth shaping* is a mechanism in QoS for introducing some amount of delay in traffic that exceeds an administratively defined rate. Traffic shaping smooths down traffic bursts that occur when the transmitter sends packets at a rate higher than the capacity of the receiver. During such times, packets are stored in a buffer and released after a specific time interval. Traffic shaping is implemented on edge devices, before packets enter the core network. Traffic shaping does not drop packets and is implemented only on the outbound interface of a device, whereas traffic policing can be implemented on both outbound and inbound interfaces.

Traffic policing is the method of governing and regulating a flow of packets in conformity with the standards and limits specified in the SLA. Packets not conforming to the SLA are either dropped or marked to a lower precedence value.

Dividing a network into segments can improve network performance. With segments, traffic is confined to a portion of the network containing nodes that communicate with each other most often. However, performance can suffer if nodes must regularly communicate with nodes on other segments. Devices such as switches and routers that link segments can lead to slower transmission between segments.

Packet Shapers

A *packet shaper*, also known as a traffic shaper, is the mechanism that enables traffic shaping. It works by delaying metered traffic so that each packet complies with the relevant traffic contract. Metering may be implemented with algorithms such as the leaky bucket or token bucket. All traffic shaper implementations have a finite buffer, and must be able to deal with a full buffer. A simple and common approach is to drop traffic arriving while the buffer is full (tail drop), thus resulting in traffic policing as well as shaping.

Load Balancing

Another network performance optimization method is *load balancing*. Load balancing is a method of dividing work among the devices on a network. By sharing the work, more resources are available and data is processed faster. Because the workload is balanced between devices, all devices in the network perform at their optimum efficiency. Often, a dedicated program or hardware device is used to balance the load on different devices. Clustering servers is also another way to create load balancing. In a cluster, a main server is used to determine which server in the cluster will provide the data processing capability. *Load balancers* are stand-alone network devices that perform load balancing as their primary function.

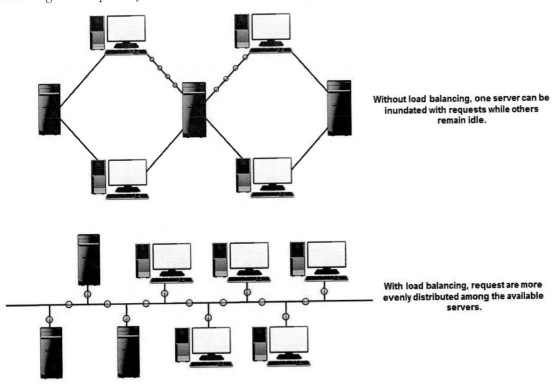

Without load balancing, one server can be inundated with requests while others remain idle.

With load balancing, request are more evenly distributed among the available servers.

Figure 14-12: Load balancing.

Common Address Redundancy Protocol (CARP) allows a number of devices to be grouped together to use a single virtual network interface between them. One of the devices acts as the master and it responds to all packets sent to that virtual interface address. All of the other devices just act as hot spares. If the master device fails, one of the spares would immediately take over with virtually no downtime. It is also possible to have two different CARP groups using the same IP address. This allows for the load balancing of any traffic destined for that IP. The spreading of the load improves network performance.

High Availability

High availability is a rating that expresses how closely devices approach the goal of providing data availability 100 percent of the time while maintaining a high level of performance. High availability devices are usually rated as a percentage that shows the proportion of uptime to total time.

"Five nines" and other availability rating figures are determined through a series of industry-standard calculations that take into account a variety of factors, such as the amount of time between failures and the time required to restore the device.

Caching Engines

A *caching engine* is an application or a service that stores, or indexes, data in order to provide faster responses to requests for that data. Rather than having to run a database query or send a request to a web server every time data is needed, caching engines retrieve the data and store it until it is requested. The engine uses various parameters to determine when it should update the cached data, and is usually configured to deliver the most up-to-date information available. Caching engines are useful for responding to requests for frequently used data. The presence of a caching engine is usually hidden to both the requester and originator of data.

High-Bandwidth Applications

A *high-bandwidth application* is a software application or program that requires large amounts of network bandwidth for data transmission. With these high-intensity, high-bandwidth applications, bandwidth issues will become more frequent, resulting in degradation of QoS on a network. High-bandwidth applications can be managed by ensuring a certain amount of bandwidth availability for them. High-bandwidth applications can include:

- VoIP
- HDTV
- Real-time video
- Multimedia

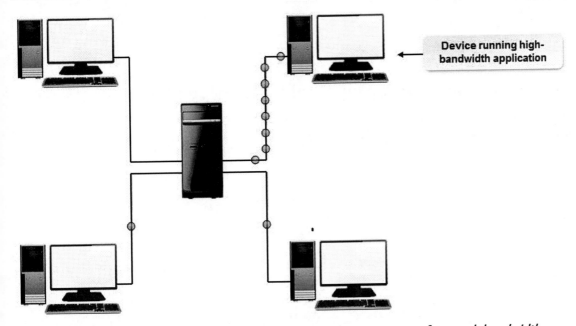

Figure 14–13: A high-bandwidth application consumes large amounts of network bandwidth.

Factors Affecting a QoS Implementation

Proper QoS mechanisms ensure that a network performs at the desired level and delivers predictable results to its users. There are various factors that affect the QoS implementation on a network.

Factor	Description
Packet classification	Each packet coming to a router is classified based on its QoS requirements. This classification enables the router to process the packet based on its resource requirement. For example, a packet classified as FTP will need less bandwidth than a packet classified as IP telephony.
Policing	An application requests the required amount of network resources, and it must always adhere to this request. An application must not send packets at a rate of more than what was requested. In order to make sure the application is adhering to the parameters, policing of packets is implemented at the router end.
Resource allocation	A network may receive both data and voice packets simultaneously. It is the network device's responsibility to appropriately allocate resources to both these types of data.

ACTIVITY 14-3
Identifying Network Performance Optimization Techniques

Scenario

The network administrator at the Greene City Interiors branch office questions you on various network performance optimization techniques.

1. What network setting could you configure to ensure that VoIP traffic is smooth and free of jitters?

2. Which are examples of latency-sensitive applications?
   - ☐ VoIP
   - ☐ Video conferencing
   - ☐ Online gaming
   - ☐ Email

3. How does CARP help provide fault tolerance?

4. Which statements are true of QoS?
   - ☐ A set of parameters that controls the quality provided to different types of wireless network traffic.
   - ☐ QoS parameters are agreed upon by the transmitter and the receiver, the receiver being the ISP and the transmitter being the subscriber.
   - ☐ QoS parameters include the maximum delay, signal loss, and noise that can be accommodated for a type of network traffic, bandwidth priority, and CPU usage for a specific stream of data.
   - ☐ The transmitter and receiver enter into an SLA to ensure QoS.

5. True or False? Traffic shaping smooths down traffic bursts that occur when the transmitter sends packets at a rate higher than the capacity of the receiver.
   - ☐ True
   - ☐ False

6. Which is a method of dividing work among the devices on a network?
   - ○ High availability
   - ○ Caching engine
   - ○ Traffic shaping
   - ○ Load balancing

Summary

In this lesson, you investigated a number of monitoring tools and network management methods that will help you determine your network's baseline and optimize your network's performance. Managing your network for optimal performance is an essential task for network technicians to perform so that your network can provide reliable service to your users.

What network monitoring tasks have you used in your organization?

What configuration management documentation have you used in your organization?

Note: Check your LogicalCHOICE Course screen for opportunities to interact with your classmates, peers, and the larger LogicalCHOICE online community about the topics covered in this course or other topics you are interested in. From the Course screen you can also access available resources for a more continuous learning experience.

15 Troubleshooting Network Issues

Lesson Time: 2 hours, 30 minutes

Lesson Objectives

In this lesson, you will describe troubleshooting of issues on a network. You will:

- List the components of a troubleshooting model.

- Describe various utilities for troubleshooting networks.

- Describe commonly used hardware troubleshooting tools.

- Identify the causes and solutions of common network connectivity issues.

- Troubleshoot security configuration issues.

- Troubleshoot security issues.

Lesson Introduction

So far in this course, you have learned about all the different components, theories, technologies, and tasks that network administrators will draw upon to perform their job functions. One of the most important of those functions, which requires knowledge about all aspects of the network, is network troubleshooting. In this lesson, you will identify major issues, models, tools, and techniques in network troubleshooting.

Network problems can arise from a variety of sources outside your control. As a network professional, your users, your managers, and your colleagues will all look to you to identify and resolve those problems efficiently. To do that, you will need a strong fundamental understanding of the tools and processes involved in troubleshooting a network.

TOPIC A

Network Troubleshooting Models

You have learned about securing, monitoring, and managing a network. Despite these measures, unforeseen issues do arise on a network that require you, as a network professional, to identify and troubleshoot issues. The first step in troubleshooting your network is to select a troubleshooting model. In this topic, you will list the components of a network troubleshooting model.

Because troubleshooting network problems is such a big part of a network administrator's or network professional's job, you should always use a systematic approach to problem solving. Troubleshooting models provide you with processes on which to base your troubleshooting techniques. Learning and using a troubleshooting model can help you resolve problems speedily and effectively.

Troubleshooting

Troubleshooting is the recognition, diagnosis, and resolution of problems. Troubleshooting begins with the identification of a problem, and does not end until services have been restored and the problem no longer adversely affects users. Troubleshooting can take many forms, but all approaches have the same goal: to solve a problem efficiently with a minimal interruption of service.

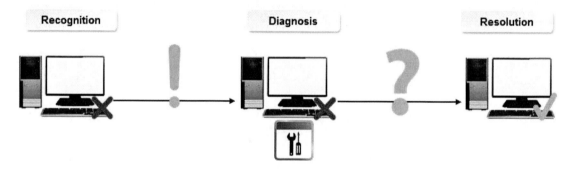

Figure 15–1: Troubleshooting.

Troubleshooting Models

A *troubleshooting model* is a standardized step-by-step approach to the troubleshooting process. The model serves as a framework for correcting a problem on a network without introducing further problems or making unnecessary modifications to the network. Models can vary in the sequence, number, and name of the steps involved, but all models have the same goal: to move in a methodical and repeatable manner through the troubleshooting process.

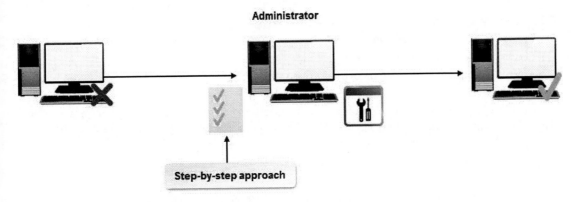

Administrator

Step-by-step approach

Figure 15-2: Resolving user issues by using a troubleshooting model.

 Note: For additional information, check out the LearnTO **Follow the Troubleshooting Process** presentation in the LearnTOs for this course on your LogicalCHOICE Course screen.

The Network+ Troubleshooting Model

There are seven stages in the CompTIA® Network+® troubleshooting model.

1. Identify the problem. This stage includes:

   - Gathering information
   - Duplicating the problem, if possible
   - Questioning users to gain experiential information
   - Identifying the symptoms
   - Determining if anything has changed
   - Approaching multiple problems individually

2. Establish a theory of probable cause. This stage includes:

   - Questioning the obvious
   - Considering multiple approaches, such as examining the OSI model from top to bottom and bottom to top and dividing and conquering

3. Test the theory to determine the cause.

   a. When the theory is confirmed, determine the next steps to resolve the problem.

   b. If the theory is not confirmed, establish a new theory or escalate the issue.

4. Establish a plan of action to resolve the problem, while identifying the potential effects of your plan.

5. Implement the solution, or escalate the issue.

6. Verify full system functionality and, if applicable, implement preventative measures.

7. Document your findings, actions, and the outcomes.

Troubleshooting Documentation Template

Some of the things you might want to include in a troubleshooting documentation template are:

- A description of the initial trouble call, including date, time, who is experiencing the problem, and who is reporting the problem.
- A description of the conditions surrounding the problem, including the type of device, the type of network interface card (NIC), any peripherals, the desktop operating system and version, the network operating system and version, the version of any applications mentioned in the problem report, and whether or not the user was logged on when the problem occurred.
- Whether or not you could reproduce the problem consistently.

- The exact issue you identified.
- The possible cause or causes you isolated.
- The correction or corrections you formulated.
- The results of implementing each correction you tried.
- The results of testing the solution.
- Any external resources you used, such as vendor documentation, addresses for vendor and other support websites, names and phone numbers for support personnel, and names and phone numbers for third-party service providers.

ACTIVITY 15-1
Discussing Troubleshooting Models

Scenario

The network administrator at Greene City Interiors quizzes you on the elements of the Network+ troubleshooting model.

1. **Users on the third floor cannot connect to the Internet, but they can log on to the local network. What should you check first?**

   ○ Router configuration tables

   ○ If viruses exist

   ○ If users on other floors are having similar problems

   ○ If the power cable to the switch is connected

2. **You reinstall the operating system for a user who is having problems. Later, the user complains that she cannot find her familiar desktop shortcuts. What step of the troubleshooting model did you omit?**

   ○ Documenting findings, actions, and outcomes

   ○ Verifying full system functionality and implementing preventative measures

   ○ Testing the theory to determine cause

   ○ Establishing a plan of action to resolve the problem

3. **Which techniques will help you establish a theory of probable cause of the problem?**

   ☐ Ask the user open-ended questions about the problem.

   ☐ Try to replicate the problem on a nearby workstation.

   ☐ Make a list of problems that can all cause the same symptoms.

   ☐ Find out if users in other parts of the building are facing the same problem.

4. **A user calls to say that his computer will not boot. He mentions that everything was fine until a brief power outage on his floor. What stage of the troubleshooting model can this information help you with most directly?**

   ○ Establishing a theory of probable cause

   ○ Establishing a plan of action to resolve the problem

   ○ Documenting findings, actions, and outcomes

   ○ Identifying the problem

5. **A user calls the help desk and says he is unable to open a file. You are not able to visit the user's workstation because he is in a different location. What are the first steps you need to take to diagnose the problem?**

6. What are some of the questions you should ask?

7. Through your diagnostic questions, you establish that the file is a word-processing document stored on a network file server. The user last accessed the file three months ago. By reviewing the activity logs on the file server, you find that there is a bi-monthly cleanup routine that automatically backs up and removes user data files that have not been accessed since the last cleanup date. The backups are stored in an offsite facility for one year. Given this information, what is your action plan, how will you implement it, and what potential side effects of the plan do you need to consider?

8. What steps should you take to test, verify, and document the solution?

TOPIC B

Network Troubleshooting Utilities

In the previous topic, you identified the steps in a troubleshooting model. To implement the model, you will use various troubleshooting utilities. In this topic, you will identify the functions of network troubleshooting utilities.

It does not pay to try to drive in a nail with a screwdriver or loosen a bolt with a hammer. Knowing the right tool for the job is an important part of correcting any problem. As a networking professional, you will need to be familiar with the uses of several tools. With TCP/IP being the most commonly implemented network protocol today, the TCP/IP utility suite will often be the first place you will turn to start figuring out a network communication problem and fixing it.

Troubleshooting with IP Configuration Utilities

With TCP/IP networking problems, a common first step is to verify that the host's IP addressing information is correct. Use `ipconfig` or `ifconfig`, as appropriate, to determine if the host is configured for static or dynamic IP addressing and if it has a valid IP address. If the host is getting an incorrect dynamic IP address and you believe there is a valid Dynamic Host Configuration Protocol (DHCP) server, you can use the utility to release and renew the address.

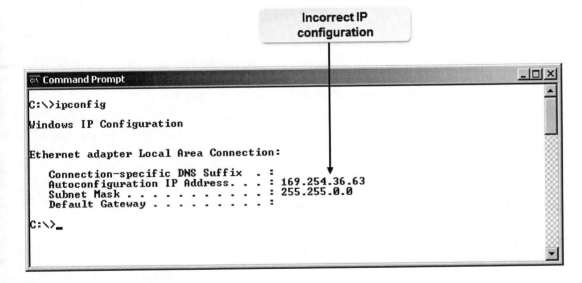

Figure 15-3: The ipconfig utility.

The ping Utility

Use the `ping` utility as an initial step in diagnosing general connectivity problems. To use `ping` with IPv6 addresses, use `ping -6` for Windows® or `ping6` for Linux®. The steps can include:

1. Ping the loopback address (127.0.0.1 or ::1 for IPv6) to test whether TCP/IP has initialized on an individual device.
2. Ping a specific device to verify that it is running and is connected to the network.
3. Ping by IP address instead of host name to determine if it is a problem related to name resolution.
4. Localize the problem:
   - Ping the local loopback address.

- Ping the device's own IP address.
- Ping the address of the default gateway.
- Ping the address of a remote host.

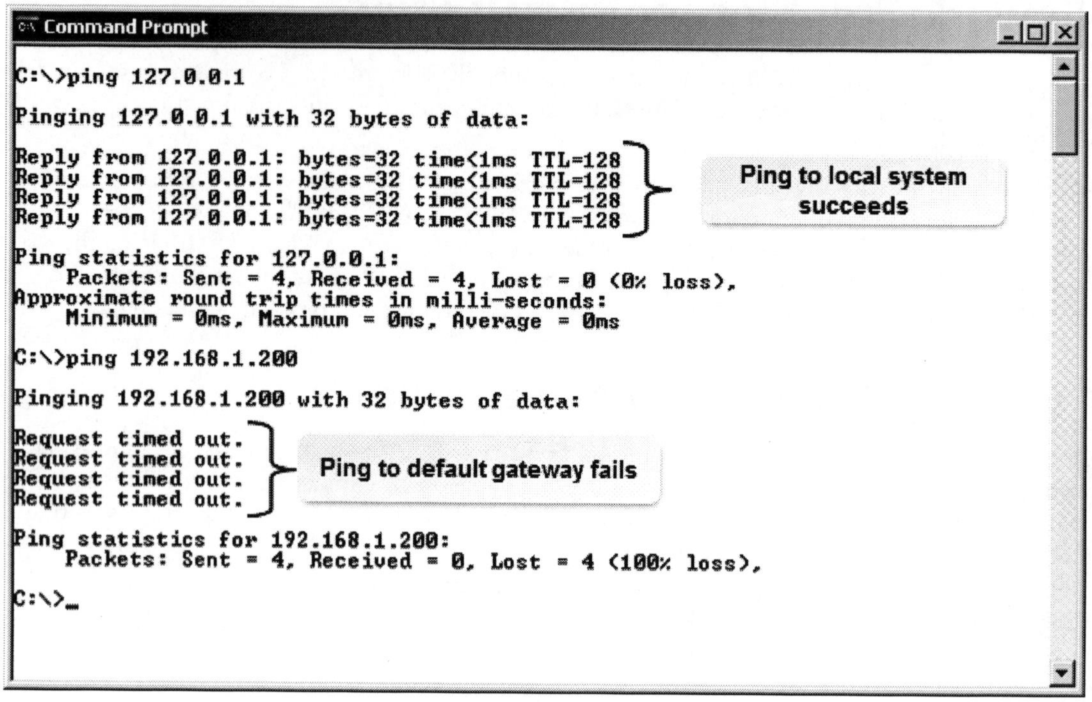

```
Command Prompt                                                    _ |□| x|

C:\>ping 127.0.0.1

Pinging 127.0.0.1 with 32 bytes of data:

Reply from 127.0.0.1: bytes=32 time<1ms TTL=128  ⎫
Reply from 127.0.0.1: bytes=32 time<1ms TTL=128  ⎬  Ping to local system
Reply from 127.0.0.1: bytes=32 time<1ms TTL=128  ⎪      succeeds
Reply from 127.0.0.1: bytes=32 time<1ms TTL=128  ⎭

Ping statistics for 127.0.0.1:
    Packets: Sent = 4, Received = 4, Lost = 0 (0% loss),
Approximate round trip times in milli-seconds:
    Minimum = 0ms, Maximum = 0ms, Average = 0ms

C:\>ping 192.168.1.200

Pinging 192.168.1.200 with 32 bytes of data:

Request timed out.  ⎫
Request timed out.  ⎬  Ping to default gateway fails
Request timed out.  ⎪
Request timed out.  ⎭

Ping statistics for 192.168.1.200:
    Packets: Sent = 4, Received = 0, Lost = 4 (100% loss),

C:\>_
```

Figure 15-4: Successful and unsuccessful responses using the ping utility.

When you ping a device, it will respond with one of the following responses:

- **Reply from...:** The device responds normally with requested data for different parameters.
- **Destination Network / Host Unreachable:** The target device was identified but was not reachable by the default gateway.
- **Unknown Host:** The target device is unknown and is not reachable.
- **Request timed out:** The ping command timed out because there was no response.
- **Hardware Error:** Your network adapter is disabled or unplugged.

The traceroute and tracert Utilities

On a UNIX® or Linux device, if you cannot connect to a particular remote host, you can use `traceroute`, or `traceroute6` for IPv6, to determine where the communication fails. Issue a `traceroute` command from the local device to see how far the trace gets before you receive an error message. By using the IP address of the last successful connection, you will know where to begin troubleshooting the problem and potentially even pinpoint a specific failed device. On Windows devices, the `tracert`, or `tracert -6` for IPv6, utility provides similar functionality.

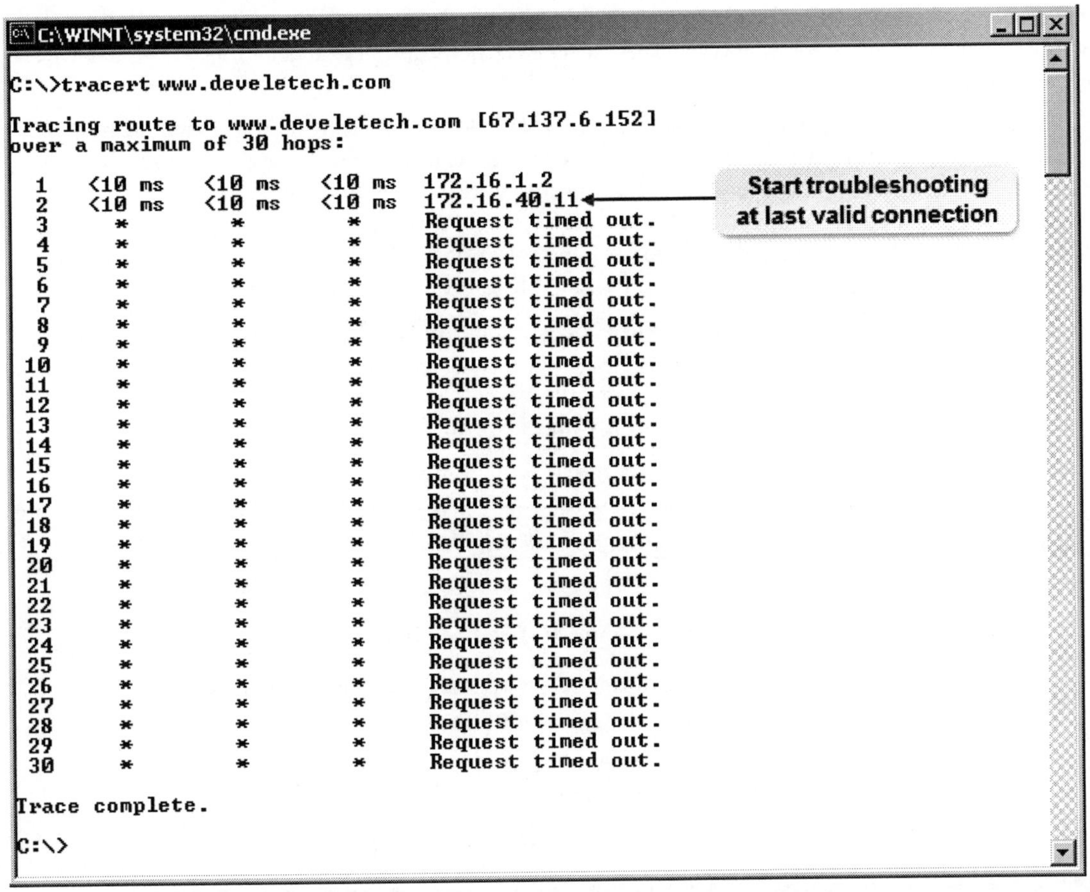

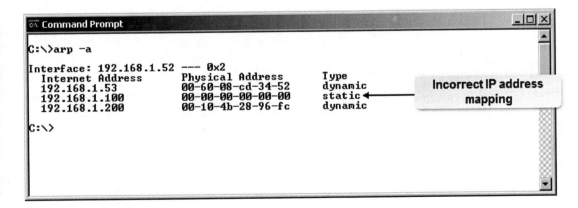

Figure 15-5: Sample tracert output.

The arp Utility

The *arp* utility supports the Address Resolution Protocol (ARP) service of the TCP/IP protocol suite. It enables an administrator to view the ARP cache and add or delete cache entries. It is also used to locate a node's hardware address. Any added entry becomes permanent until it is deleted or the device is shut down.

```
C:\>arp -a

Interface: 192.168.1.52  ---  0x2
  Internet Address     Physical Address     Type
  192.168.1.53         00-60-08-cd-34-52    dynamic
  192.168.1.100        00-00-00-00-00-00    static
  192.168.1.200        00-10-4b-28-96-fc    dynamic

C:\>
```

Incorrect IP address mapping

Figure 15-6: The ARP cache entries.

The *ARP cache* is a table used for maintaining the correlation between each media access control (MAC) address and its corresponding IP address. To reduce the number of address resolution requests, a client normally has all addresses resolved in the cache for a short period of time. The

ARP cache is of a finite size; if no limit is specified, all incomplete and obsolete entries of unused devices will accumulate in the cache. The ARP cache is, therefore, periodically flushed of all entries to free up memory.

arp can be used both to help troubleshoot duplicate IP address problems and to diagnose why a workstation cannot connect to a specific host. If a host is reachable from one workstation but not from another, you can use the arp command on both workstations to display the current entries in the ARP table. If the MAC address on the problem workstation does not match the correct MAC address, you can use arp to delete the incorrect entry. On both UNIX and Windows systems, the arp -a command will return a tabular listing of all ARP entries in the node's ARP cache.

You can refer to online MAC address lookup tables to identify an address on a switch, in network command results, or in the ARP cache that you don't think belongs on your network. Identifying the MAC address helps you identify the manufacturer of the device to help you narrow down the device you are looking for and remove it from your network.

There are several options available for use with arp. They follow the syntax: arp [option]

Option	Description
inet_addr	Used with other options to specify an Internet address.
eth_addr	Used with other options to specify a physical address.
if_addr	Used with other options to specify the Internet address of the interface whose ARP table should be modified.
-a	Displays the current ARP entries in the cache. Can add inet_addr to specify a particular IP address.
-g	Displays the same information as the -a option.
-N if_addr	Displays the ARP entries for the network interface specified by if_addr.
-d	Deletes a single host entry if followed by if_addr. Deletes all host entries if followed by *.
-s inet_addr eth_addr	Adds a host. The Internet address is set by adding an inet_addr value and the physical address is set by adding an eth_addr value.

arp can be used in conjunction with ping to troubleshoot more complex network problems. If you ping a host on the network and there is no reply, the host may not necessarily be unavailable. The increased use of firewalls today can prevent a ping from returning accurate information. Instead, you can use the arp command to find the host by the MAC address and bypass the IP address resolution.

The NBTSTAT Utility

NBTSTAT is a Windows utility that is used to view and manage NetBIOS over TCP/IP (NetBT) status information. It can display NetBIOS name tables for both the local device and remote devices, and also the NetBIOS name cache. The table names enable you to verify the connection establishment. With NBTSTAT, you can refresh the NetBIOS name cache as well as the names registered with the Windows Internet Name Server (WINS) server.

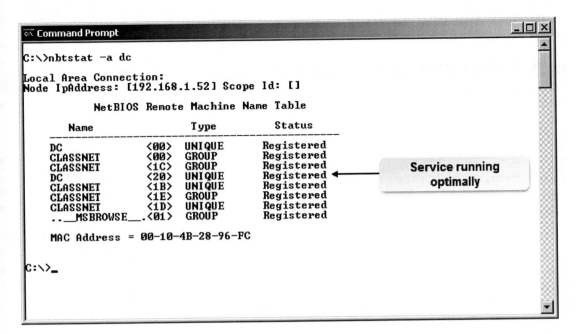

Figure 15-7: Output of the NBTSTAT utility.

NBTSTAT can be very helpful in identifying problems that are specific to Windows devices using NetBIOS naming. NBTSTAT was developed specifically as a NetBIOS diagnostic tool, and it displays NetBIOS information that is not available with other TCP/IP utilities.

There are several case-sensitive options you can use with the NBTSTAT command. They follow the syntax:

NBTSTAT [option]

Option	Description
-a [RemoteName]	Displays the NetBIOS name table of the remote device specified by the name.
-A [IPAddress]	Displays the NetBIOS name table of the remote device specified by the IP address.
-c	Displays the NetBIOS name cache of the local device.
-n	Lists the local NetBIOS name table along with the service code, type, and status.
-r	Lists NetBIOS names resolved by broadcast and via WINS.
-R	Purges the cache and reloads static entries from the LMHOSTS file.
-S	Lists NetBIOS connections and their state with destination IP addresses.
-s	Lists NetBIOS connections and their state, converting destination IP addresses to computer NetBIOS names.
-RR	Sends name release packets to the WINS server and then starts refresh.

The NETSTAT Utility

The *NETSTAT* utility shows the status of each active network connection. NETSTAT (network statistics) will display statistics for both TCP and UDP, including protocol, local address, foreign address, and the TCP connection state. Because UDP is connectionless, no connection information will be shown for UDP packets.

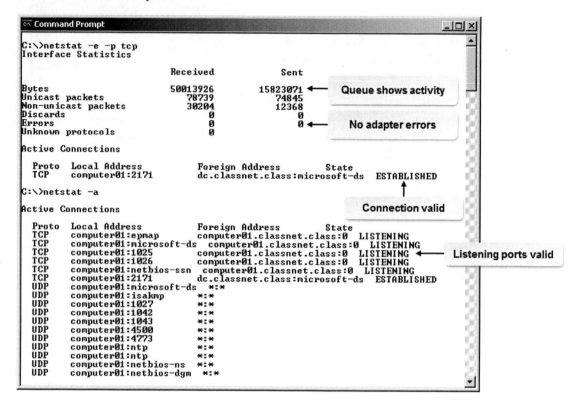

Figure 15–8: Output of the NETSTAT utility.

NETSTAT is a versatile troubleshooting tool that can serve several functions. You can:

- Use NETSTAT to find out if a TCP/IP-based program, such as SMTP or FTP, is listening on the expected port. If not, the system might need to be restarted.
- Check statistics to see if the connection is good. If there is a bad connection, this usually means there are no bytes in the send or receive queues.
- Use statistics to check network adapter error counts. If the error count is high, it could be a problem with the card, or could indicate generally high network traffic.
- Use NETSTAT to display routing tables and check for network routing problems.

There are several options available to use with the NETSTAT command.

Option	Displays
-a	All connections and listening ports.
-e	Ethernet statistics.
-n	Addresses and port numbers in numerical form.
-o	The process ID associated with each connection.
-p [protocol]	Connections for the protocol specified in place of [protocol] in the command syntax. The value of the [protocol] variable may be TCP, UDP, TCPv6, or UDPv6.
-r	The routing table.
-s	Statistics grouped by protocol—IP, IPv6, ICMP, ICMPv6, TCP, TCPv6, UDP, and UDPv6.

Option	Displays
[interval]	Refreshes and redisplays the statistics specified in the command at the stated number of seconds specified in place of [interval] in the code syntax. Ctrl+C stops the command from refreshing.

Socket States

NETSTAT will display one of several states for each socket.

Socket State	Description
SYN_SEND	Connection is active and open.
SYN_RECEIVED	The server just received the synchronize flag set (SYN) from the client.
ESTABLISHED	The client received the server's SYN and the session is established.
LISTEN	The server is ready to accept a connection.
FIN_WAIT_1	The connection is active, but closed.
TIMED_WAIT	The client enters this state after FIN_WAIT_1.
CLOSE_WAIT	Passive close. The server just received FIN_WAIT_1 from a client.
FIN_WAIT_2	The client just received an acknowledgement of its FIN_WAIT_1 from the server.
LAST_ACK	The server is in this state when it sends its own FIN.
CLOSED	The server received an acknowledgement (ACK) from the client and the connection is closed.

 Note: A SYN packet contains information regarding the return path for the data.

The nslookup Utility

The *nslookup* utility is used to test and troubleshoot domain name servers. nslookup has two modes: the *interactive mode* enables you to query name servers for information about hosts and domains, or to print a list of hosts in a domain. The *non-interactive mode* prints only the name and requested details for one host or domain. The non-interactive mode is useful for a single query.

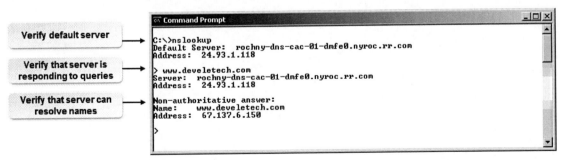

Figure 15-9: Output of the nslookup utility.

You can use nslookup to display information about DNS servers. You can verify that:

- The device is configured with the correct DNS server.
- The server is responding to requests.

- The entries on the server are correct.
- The DNS server can communicate with other servers in the DNS hierarchy to resolve names.

nslookup is available on UNIX and Windows systems. The syntax for the nslookup command is nslookup [-option ...] [computer-to-find | - [server]]

- To enter the interactive mode of nslookup, type nslookup without any arguments at a command prompt, or use only a hyphen as the first argument and specify a domain name server in the second. The default DNS name server will be used if you do not enter anything for the second argument.
- To use the non-interactive mode, in the first argument, enter the name or IP address of the device you want to look up. In the second argument, enter the name or IP address of a domain name server. The default DNS name server will be used if you do not enter anything for the second argument.

Domain Internet Groper (DIG) is a UNIX/Linux command-line tool that can be used to display name server information. Some experts consider it to be generally easier to use than nslookup, and that it supports more flexible queries and is easier to include in command scripts. It is included with the BIND version of DNS, and can be downloaded from many UNIX and Linux resource sites on the Internet.

ACTIVITY 15-2
Using the Network Troubleshooting Utilities

Scenario

At the Greene City Interiors branch office, the tasks you have to perform are starting to pile up. You decide to train a member of the staff in some basic troubleshooting techniques that he can perform in certain situations and report his findings to you. You will demonstrate the use of various network troubleshooting utilities.

1. Use the NETSTAT command to identify the connections that are active on your system.

   a) Select **Start→Command Prompt** to display the Command Prompt window.

   b) In the Command Prompt window, type *NETSTAT -a* and press **Enter** to identify the active connections.

   c) Observe the UDP connections that are listed in the output.

2. Use the NBTSTAT command to see the names in your NetBIOS name cache.

   a) Type *NBTSTAT -c -n* and press **Enter** to view your NetBIOS name cache.

   b) Observe the name cache entries that are displayed in the output.

3. Use the nslookup command to obtain the host name of the DNS server.

   a) Type *nslookup* and press **Enter** to open the nslookup interactive mode.

   b) Type *set querytype=ptr* and press **Enter** to change the query type to pointer.

   c) Type *Computer##* and press **Enter**, where ## will be the IP address of your local system.

   d) Observe the results of the output.

   e) Type *exit* and press **Enter** to quit nslookup.

4. Use the arp command to view the entries in your system's ARP cache.

   a) Type *arp /?* and press **Enter** to view the syntax of the arp command.

   b) Type *arp -a | more* and press **Enter** to view the first page of the entries in your system's ARP cache.

   c) Press the **Spacebar** to view the next page of the entries in your system's ARP cache.

   d) Observe the entries displayed in the output.

   e) Close the Command Prompt window.

WLAN Survey Software

WLAN survey software is used to plan, simulate, and implement WLANs. WLAN survey software can simulate WLAN performance during the planning phase even before any installation takes place. Technicians can use the software to analyze WLAN performance before and after implementation to determine the health of the network based on defined, measurable criteria. WLAN survey software can also be used to define network coverage areas before implementation.

SNIPS

System and Network Integrated Polling Software (SNIPS) is a system and network monitoring software tool that runs on UNIX devices. It offers both command-line and web interfaces to monitor network and system devices. The monitoring functions of SNIPS determine and report the status of services running on the network. Reports can be viewed in real time by the systems administrator through a terminal or web interface. Alarms created by SNIPS can be set to set off an alarm or to simply log the event based on monitoring levels the administrator can configure. The four monitoring levels supported by SNIPS are: info, warning, error, and critical.

 Note: Network Operations Center Online, or nocol, was Netplex's network monitoring tool that supports both a command-line interface and web interface and was the predecessor of SNIPS.

Loopback Interface

A *loopback interface* is a virtual network interface that network applications can communicate with when executing on the local device. The loopback interface has no hardware associated with it, and it is not physically connected to a network. Any traffic that a computer program sends to a loopback IP address is passed back up the network software stack as if it had been received from another device. The loopback interface allows IT professionals to test IP software without any potential issues from broken or corrupted drivers or hardware. The IPv4 loopback address is 127.0.0.1 and the IPv6 loopback address is ::1.

Speed Test Sites

Speed test sites are a web service that measure the bandwidth (speed) and latency of a visitor's Internet connection. Tests typically measure the data rate for the downloads and the upload data rate. A server located in the visitor's geographic location is typically used for the test. The tests are performed within the user's web browser and the sites will provide statistics based on test results. These sites allow you to test your connection speeds and latency in a real world setting to see what the actual performance is.

Looking Glass Sites

A *looking glass site* is a web server that allows external users to get a look at routing and network behavior as it originates from the remote network. A looking glass site accesses a remote router and performs commands, allowing a view of the IP and Border Gateway Protocol (BGP) route tables. The information is then presented to the user. Looking glass sites are used for verifying routing between providers, and for verifying that routes are propagating correctly across the Internet.

ACTIVITY 15-3
Troubleshooting Network Problems

Scenario

At the Greene City Interiors branch office, an employee has contacted you, reporting that she is unable to connect to the Internet. After checking the physical cables and verifying that everything is working correctly, you run `ipconfig` and discover that the computer has been leased an IP address of 192.168.0.200. Your company uses private IP addresses that begin with 172.16.0.2, and so you need to start troubleshooting the problem.

1. Which of the these would be the best first step?
    - ○ Reboot the computer.
    - ○ Load a new browser.
    - ○ Drop the IP address and lease a new address.
    - ○ Drop the IP address and assign a static address.

2. If you lease a new IP address and it is also in the 192.168 scope, then, based on the evidence, what seems to be the problem so far?
    - ○ The employee's computer is functioning as a DHCP server.
    - ○ There is another DHCP server on the network leasing addresses.
    - ○ The computer is looking at the incorrect network interface.
    - ○ The loopback adapter is not working.

3. After the user in the next cubicle reports the same problem, based on the diagnostic methodology, you discover that an administrator in a nearby conference room has set up a wireless router so that visiting clients can access the Internet during a meeting. Based on this information, what is the most likely reason for the IP addressing problem?

4. In order to correct the problem, you have to physically connect a computer to the wireless router and log in as an administrator. What kind of cable would be best to connect the wireless router to a laptop in order to access the admin features?
    - ○ Crossover
    - ○ Coaxial
    - ○ Category 5
    - ○ Category 3

ACTIVITY 15-4
Discussing Network Troubleshooting Utilities

Scenario

The network administrator at Greene City Interiors poses different network scenarios to you and asks you what troubleshooting steps you would take.

1. You have installed a Linux device in your test lab so that application developers can test new software. Because the lab is isolated from the main network, there is no DHCP service running. A software engineer has loaded a network application on the device, but cannot connect to it from a client. She has already tried to ping the Linux device by name and IP address. What should you check next and why?

2. A user is having trouble connecting to your company's intranet site (internal.gcinteriors.com), which is on your company's private network inside your firewall. She is not having general Internet connectivity problems. What is the best first step to take to try to narrow down the possible problem?

3. You can connect to the intranet site with no difficulty. You check your IP configuration against the user's and find that you are configured with different DNS server addresses. You do not have DNS administrative utilities installed on your workstation. What can you do to diagnose the DNS problem?

4. You had to stop and start the DHCP server service earlier in the day. A Windows user calls to say that she has no network connectivity at all. What can you do to correct the problem?

5. Your test environment includes a number of different clients, including Windows devices, Linux devices, and Mac OS® X clients. You would like to be able to examine the network performance of each device while you run a batch file to generate network load. What utility can you use?

6. You are experiencing a number of dropped packets and slow response time on your routed private network. You suspect there may be a routing loop and you would like to look more closely at packet transmissions through the network. How can you examine the path of the transmissions?

7. Servers on your internal network are manually configured with IP addresses in the range 192.168.2.200 through 192.168.2.225. You are trying to open an FTP session with the FTP server that is located on your internal network at 192.168.2.218. Although you can ping the device by IP address, sometimes you can connect over FTP and sometimes you cannot. You suspect there may be two hosts configured with duplicate addresses. How can you verify which physical host system is using the FTP server's address?

TOPIC C

Hardware Troubleshooting Tools

In the last topic, you identified the functions of TCP/IP troubleshooting utilities. Another common category of troubleshooting utilities is hardware troubleshooting tools. In this topic, you will identify the functions of various hardware troubleshooting tools.

As a network technician, you might not pick up a screwdriver or a pair of pliers as often as a cable installer or an electrician does, but there are still cases in which hardware and hand tools come in handy. You should know which hardware tools you will need to use in your job, and when and how to use them.

Network Hardware Tools

As a network technician, you might find that you occasionally need basic hand tools, such as:

- A variety of screwdrivers and spare screws
- Long-nose pliers
- Small diagonal cutting pliers
- A small adjustable wrench
- A variety of wrenches or nut drivers
- A small flashlight
- An anti-static wrist strap with clip

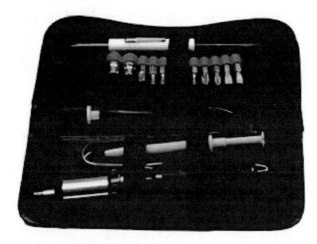

Figure 15-10: Basic hand tools.

Because of the variety of tasks you will encounter as a network technician, you'll also require more specialized tools, such as those used to install and terminate network cables and connectors, including:

- Cable crimpers.
- Punch down tool.
- Wire strippers.
- Snips.
- Optical time-domain reflectometers (OTDRs).
- Cable certifier.

Figure 15-11: A typical network installation toolkit.

There are also certain tools that you'll use while troubleshooting network issues:

- Line testers.
- Certifiers.
- Multimeter.
- Cable tester.
- Light meter.
- Toner probe.

Other general tools and supplies that you might find useful include cable ties/zip strips, electrical tape, a lightweight laptop or notebook computer capable of both wired and wireless connectivity. The laptop should have Wi-Fi spectrum analyzer software installed on it such as NetStumbler, InSSIDer, or WiSpy. (It is also common for network technicians to carry desktop support software such as operating system boot disks and recovery disks, as well as a removable drive.)

Safety Rules

Only a professional electrician should install, test, and maintain electric power equipment. Network technicians can safely install and test low-power communication circuits in network cabling. When you work with electrical power, you need to follow certain basic safety rules:

- Always disconnect or unplug electrical equipment before opening or servicing it.
- Work with a partner.
- Never bypass fuses or circuit breakers.
- Use anti-static mats and wristbands to protect yourself and equipment from static discharge.

- Prevent an electrostatic discharge (ESD) from damaging components by standing on a totally insulated rubber mat to increase the resistance of the path to ground. In some cases, workstations are located in areas with grounded floors and workbenches, so static electricity has a low-resistance, non-destructive path to ground.
  - Use grounding conductive materials and self-grounding methods before touching electronic equipment. You can prevent ESD injuries by using ESD straps that can be attached to your ankle or wrist.
  - Eliminate unnecessary activities that create static charges. By removing unnecessary materials that are known charge generators, you can protect against ESD-related damage and injuries.
- Perform only the work for which you have sufficient training.
- Check the area for potential causes of secondary injuries.
- Do not attempt repair work when you are tired; you may make careless mistakes, and your primary diagnostic tool, deductive reasoning, will not be operating at full capacity.
- Do not assume anything without checking it out for yourself.
- Do not wear jewelry or other articles that could accidentally contact circuitry and conduct current.
- Wear rubber-soled shoes to insulate yourself from ground.
- Suspend work during an electrical storm.
- Do not handle electrical equipment when your hands or feet are wet or when you are standing on a wet surface. Perform tests with the power supply turned off.
- Power supplies have a high voltage in them any time the device is plugged in, even if the device's power is turned off. Before you start working inside the device case, disconnect the power cord and press the power button to dissipate any remaining power in the circuitry. Leave the power off until you are done servicing the unit.

Similarly, when you are installing, maintaining, and troubleshooting equipment, you should follow these safety rules:

- Check tools before you begin to ensure they are in good condition and functioning properly. Do not misuse tools.
- When lifting equipment, always assess the situation first to determine if you can lift or move items safely.
- When you lift, bend at your knees and not at your waist. This will prevent strain on your back muscles and pressure on your spine.
- Use lifting equipment for heavy and/or bulky items.
- When installing a rack system, follow safety guidelines to ensure your safety and the safety of any equipment.
- Make sure you use proper placement of equipment and devices as prescribed by the manufacturer.

Wire Crimpers

A *wire crimper*, also called a cable crimper, is a tool that attaches media connectors to the ends of cables. You can use it if you need to make your own network cables or trim the end of a cable. There are different crimpers for different types of connectors, so select the one that is appropriate for the type of network media you are working with.

Cable Strippers

A *cable stripper*, also called a wire stripper, is often part of a wire crimper, allowing the user to strip wires of their protective coating, and then use the crimping tool to attach a media connector.

Figure 15-12: A cable stripper.

Punch Down Tools

A *punch down tool* is used in a wiring closet to connect cable wires directly to a patch panel or punch down block. The tool strips the insulation from the end of the wire and embeds the wire into the connection at the back of the panel.

Figure 15-13: A punch down tool.

 Note: The technical name for a punch down tool is an insulation displacement connector (IDC).

The punch down tool makes connecting wires to a patch panel easier than it would be to connect them by hand. Without the punch down tool, you would have to strip the wire manually and connect it by twisting it or tightening it around a connection pole or screw.

Circuit Testers

A *circuit tester* is an electrical instrument that is used for testing whether or not current is passing through the circuit. This is normally used when there is a problem in testing electricity flows through two points. Plug the circuit tester into the socket and it will display a pattern of lights depicting the status of wiring of a circuit, which will help identify whether or not power is passing through the points.

Plugs into socket

Displays circuit status

Figure 15-14: A circuit tester.

Multimeters

A *multimeter*, also known as a volt/ohm meter, is an electronic measuring instrument that takes electrical measurements such as voltage, current, and resistance. A multimeter can be a handheld device for field service work or a bench-top model for in-house troubleshooting. Multimeters can be either analog or digital. The digital multimeter (DMM) and digital volt-ohm meter (DVOM) are examples of digital models, whereas the analog multimeter (AMM) is an example of the analog model.

Digital   **Analog**

Figure 15-15: Digital and analog multimeters.

Not all circuits are the same. Some circuits carry much higher electrical loads than others. Be sure that you know the approximate current and impedance that the circuit you are testing should be running at, and use the appropriately rated multimeter for the job. Connecting an underrated multimeter to a main electrical line could result in damage to the multimeter, and possible injury to the operator.

There are several items to be aware of when reading a multimeter. You must select all of these correctly, otherwise you will get a confusing or misleading reading, or possibly damage your meter. A multimeter has a positive probe and a negative probe. This is significant when measuring DC volts or DC current. You must get the polarity correct; in other words, touch the positive probe to the positive side of the power supply or battery, and the negative probe to the negative side of the power supply or battery. If your power supply is bi-polar, meaning that it has a positive, a ground, and a negative, you must touch the positive probe to ground and the negative probe to negative.

You must select the type of measurement you want. This could be the following.

Measurement	Description
AC volts	This is typically used to test an AC outlet, a power strip, or a UPS. • You must put the probes in parallel to the voltage source, with one probe on each side of the outlet.
DC volts	This is typically used to test a computer power supply. • You put the probes in parallel to the voltage source, such as an unused molex plug coming out of the power supply. • Touch the positive probe to a positive source, such as a red or yellow wire. • Touch the negative probe to a negative or ground source such as a black wire.
Ohms	Typically used to check for breaks in the wires. Should be close to zero ohms resistance. • You must MAKE SURE the circuit has NO power on it, or you will damage the meter. • Touch the two probes to the two ends of the cable. • If the cable is good, the resistance (the reading) will show zero or very close to zero. • If the cable is broken, the resistance will show infinity. • When using probes, make sure they make very firm, unmoving contact with what they're measuring.

There are various categories of multimeters that are used in different situations.

Multimeter Category	For Use In
I	Conditions where current levels are low.
II	Interior residential branch circuits.
III	Distribution panels, motors, and appliance outlets.
IV	High-current applications, such as service connections, breaker panels for wiring mains, and household meters.

Voltmeters

A *voltmeter* measures voltage and resistance between two points in a circuit. Like multimeters, voltmeters come in both digital and analog forms. A *digital volt meter (DVM)* provides scales for reading voltage in both AC and DC and different resistances. It can be used to test resistances between cable endpoints or voltages inside a low-power system. It should not be used to service high-power or high-frequency equipment.

A *voltage event recorder (VER)* is another tool to use in conjunction with or in addition to a voltmeter to test and verify that the electrical signals transmitting through the network cables are within the required specifications. VERs are attached to electrical lines or outlets and remain there undisturbed to monitor the flow of electricity across the lines or within an outlet. VERs can help diagnose electrical faults or intermittent problems regarding low or high voltage.

Cable Testers and Line Testers

A *cable tester,* also called a *line tester,* is an electrical instrument that verifies if a signal is transmitted by a cable. A simple cable tester will determine whether a cable has an end-to-end connection and can detect shorts or opens, but cannot certify the cable for transmission quality, which is the cable installer's responsibility. Cable testers can differ based on their intended purpose.

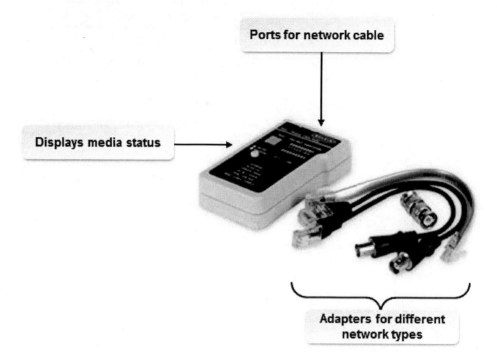

Ports for network cable

Displays media status

Adapters for different network types

Figure 15-16: Network cable testers with adapters for testing.

Unshielded twisted pair (UTP) cable links are limited to a distance of 295 feet. The speed will be either 10 Mbps or 100 Mbps depending on the type of switch used.

Cable Certifiers

A *cable certifier* allows you to perform tests, such as cable testing and validity testing. It can detect shorts and crosstalk on a cable, test for the cable type and whether a cable is straight-through or crossover, and check if the NIC is functioning and at what speed: half or full duplex. Cable certifiers can also be attached to devices. The collected data can be used to print certification reports.

Types of Cable Testers and Certifiers

The types of cable testers and certifiers that are available vary based on the task they are used for.

Tool	Used To
Certification tester	Determine whether a cable meets specific ISO or TIA standards (CAT5e, CAT6, or CAT7). Should be used if a network is wired with both copper and fiber.
Qualification tester	Measure the speeds at which a network can transmit data. Also used to troubleshoot a network. It is not used to test networks. A qualification tester tests the continuity of UTP/STP cables and verifies the adherence to 10BASE-T, 100BASE-T, TIA-568A, TIA-568B, and token ring wiring standards. It also verifies ring wiring standards and shield integrity.
LAN tester	Test transmission speed, cable skew, cable propagation delay, cable typing (CAT3, 5, 5E, 6), attenuation, and cable verification. A LAN tester carries out a cable conduction test and a mis-wiring detection test.
Network cable certifier	Test transmission speed and performance.

Crossover Cables

In Ethernet UTP installations, crossover cables enable you to connect devices without using a hub or a switch. In a crossover cable, the transmit and receive lines are crossed to make them work like a loopback—a function that the switch does. In troubleshooting, crossover cables let you connect two stations' network adapters directly without a switch so that you can test communications between them.

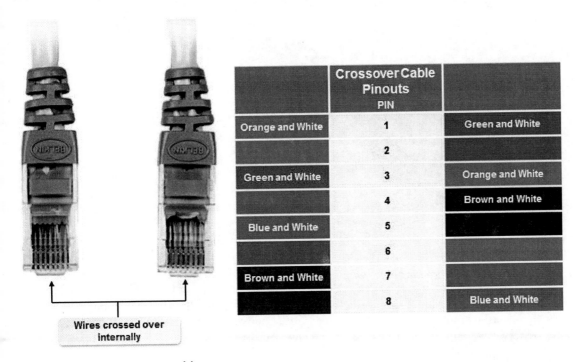

	Crossover Cable Pinouts PIN	
Orange and White	1	Green and White
	2	
Green and White	3	Orange and White
	4	Brown and White
Blue and White	5	
	6	
Brown and White	7	
	8	Blue and White

Wires crossed over internally

Figure 15-17: A crossover cable.

T1 crossover cable is used to connect two T1 CSU/DSU devices by using T568B pairs. Crossover cables are very much like straight-through cables with the exception that TX and RX lines are crossed.

Connector A	Connector B
Pin 1	Pin 3
Pin 2	Pin 6
Pin 3	Pin 1
Pin 4	Pin 7
Pin 5	Pin 8
Pin 6	Pin 2
Pin 7	Pin 4
Pin 8	Pin 5

If you suspect that a server's NIC might be corrupt, you can use a crossover cable to attach a laptop's NIC directly to the server's NIC. Provided that both NICs are configured correctly, you should be able to log on to the server if the server's NIC is good.

Hardware Loopback Plugs

A *hardware loopback plug* is a special connector used for diagnosing transmission problems such as redirecting electrical signals back to the transmitting device. It plugs into a port and crosses over the transmit and receive lines. Some loopback plugs are small and plug into a port with no visible wires, whereas others have wires that loop visibly into the connector. Hardware loopback plugs are commonly used to test Ethernet NICs. The plug directly connects Pin 1 to Pin 3 and Pin 2 to Pin 6.

Crosses over transmit/receive lines

Figure 15-18: A hardware loopback plug.

If a NIC comes with hardware diagnostic capabilities, the loopback plug will be included with the NIC. Connect the loopback plug to the installed NIC's network port, and run the diagnostic software to verify that the NIC can send and receive data.

There are standards for loopback wiring.

Wiring Standard	Connects
Ethernet	• Pin 1 to Pin 3 • Pin 2 to Pin 6
T1	• Pin 1 to Pin 4 • Pin 2 to Pin 5

Time-Domain Reflectometers

A *time-domain reflectometer (TDR)* is a measuring tool that transmits an electrical pulse on a cable and measures the reflected signal. In a cable without any problems, the signal does not reflect and is absorbed by a terminator, if present. Bends, short circuits, and connector problems on the cable modify a signal's amplitude before it returns to a TDR. These modifications change how the signal reflects back. A TDR analyzes the returned signal, and based on the signal's condition and its rate of return, it checks the time span and determines cable problems. In addition, if a TDR is attached on a coaxial cable network, the TDR will indicate whether terminators are installed properly and are functioning correctly.

Optical time-domain reflectometers (OTDRs) are a variation of TDRs used specifically for fiber optic cabling to determine cabling issues. An OTDR transmits light signals of different wavelengths over fiber. Depending on the quality of the signal returned, an OTDR can accurately measure the length of the fiber; determine locations of faulty splices, breaks, connectors, and bends; and measure signal attenuation over the length of the fiber cable.

Tone Generators and Locators

A *tone generator* is a device that sends an electrical signal through one pair of UTP wires. A *tone locator* or a tone probe is a device that emits an audible tone when it detects a signal in a pair of wires. Tone generators and tone locators are most commonly used on telephone systems to trace wire pairs. A digital toner and toner probe trace and locate voice, audio, and video cabling on a network. In addition to confirming the cable location, a toner and probe can verify continuity and detect faults.

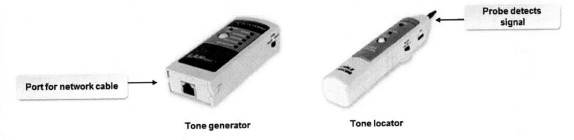

Figure 15-19: A tone generator and a tone locator.

 Note: The combination of a tone generator and tone locator is frequently referred to as "fox and hound."

Do not confuse tone generators and tone locators with cable testers. Tone generators and tone locators can only help you differentiate between different UTP cables.

To locate a cable in a group of cables, connect the tone generator to the copper ends of the wires; then move the tone locator over the group of cables. A soft beeping tone indicates that you are close to the correct wire set; when the beeping is loudest, you have found the cable.

 Caution: Do not connect a tone generator to a cable that is connected to a NIC. The signal sent by the tone generator can destroy network equipment.

Environment Monitors

Environment monitors are hardware tools that ensure that environmental conditions do not spike or plummet to place temperatures above or below equipment specifications. In addition to temperature, environment monitors allow you to monitor the humidity in the environment in which the network devices are placed. By monitoring humidity, you can ensure that condensation does not build in devices, and that there is enough humidity to decrease static electricity buildup.

You can monitor a computer room with a humidity monitor or you can use sensors to monitor the temperature inside servers, workstations, and components such as hard drives.

Butt Sets

A *butt set*, also known as a lineman's test set, is a special type of telephone handset used by telecom technicians when installing and testing local lines. It is called a butt set because the technician "butts" into telephone lines to detect issues. The butt set allows a technician to bridge onto wire pairs with clips in order to monitor the line and use dialing features as if it was a physical phone on the system. This feature allows a technician to determine any problems that exist. Some butt sets can detect polarity reversals and other line faults to troubleshoot performance issues.

Figure 15–20: A butt set.

LED Indicators

Light-emitting diode (LED) indicators on network adapters, switches, routers, and cable and DSL modems can give you information about the status of the network connection.

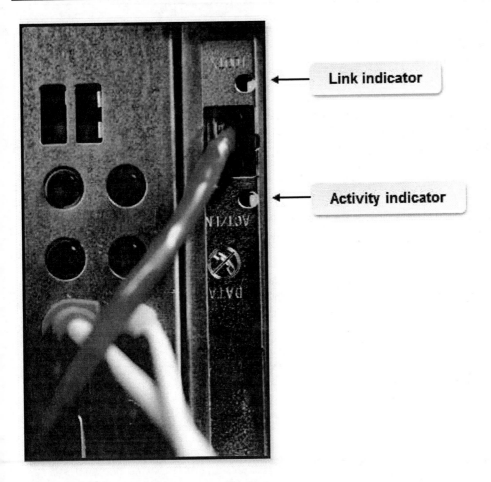

Figure 15-21: Indicators on a network adapter.

There are different types of LED indicators.

Indicator	Description
Link indicators	Most adapters have a link indicator to visually indicate signal reception from the network. If the link indicator is not lit, it could indicate a problem with the cable or the physical connection.
Activity indicators	Most adapters also have an activity indicator that flickers when data packets are received or sent. If the indicator flickers constantly, the network might be overused or there is a system generating noise.
Speed indicators	Dual-mode adapters have a speed indicator to display whether the adapter is operating at 10 Mbps, 100 Mbps, or at 1 Gbps.
Dual-color indicators	Uses dual-color indicators to indicate different network states. For example, a green flickering indicator might indicate normal activity, whereas an amber flickering indicator indicates collisions on the network.

Network Analyzers

Earlier in the course, you saw that a network analyzer, also known as a packet or protocol analyzer, or a packet sniffer, is a software or hardware tool that integrates diagnostic and reporting capabilities to provide a comprehensive view of an organization's network. Network analyzers can be used to troubleshoot network problems and detect network intrusions. They can identify anomalous network issues or diagnose and troubleshoot complex network and application performance issues.

They can look inside the header of the packets, which helps to determine if the packets, route, and destination are all what you expect.

Demarc

Earlier in the course, you saw that a demarc, or demarcation point, is where a building's wiring ends and the provider company's wiring begins. Any premises connected to the telephone company wiring include a demarc, including residential buildings as well as commercial and industrial buildings. A demarc can be installed on the outside of the building, as is common with residential demarcs, or it can be installed inside the building, as is the case with most commercial and industrial demarcs.

A *smart jack* is a device that serves as the demarcation point between the end user's inside wiring and local access carriers' facilities. The smart jack is capable of looping a diagnostic signal back to the provider. The provider can thus remotely test the line up to the smart jack, without having to send a technician to the premises. Sometimes the provider also installs a physical jack on the backboard next to the demarc that you can plug a device into ad hoc. The customer would typically either perform a visual inspection of the wiring from the demarc to the punch down block, or might possibly put a telephone toner on the demarc posts if they are accessible. The customer would then use a wand to trace the tone signal.

The demarc is the point at which the telephone company's responsibility for the line ends, and your responsibility begins. Usually, the telephone company will not troubleshoot issues past the demarc unless you pay for that service.

Wireless Testers

A *wireless tester*, or a Wi-Fi analyzer, is a Wi-Fi spectrum analyzer used to detect devices and points of interference, as well as analyze and troubleshoot network issues on a WLAN or other wireless networks. Like network analyzers, wireless testers give an overview of the health of a WLAN in one central location, enabling technicians to troubleshoot problems efficiently.

A spectrum analyzer is an instrument that displays the variation of signal strength against the frequency.

Light Meters

Light meters, also known as optical power meters, are devices used to measure the power in an optical signal. A typical light meter consists of a calibrated sensor, measuring amplifier, and display. The sensor primarily consists of a photodiode selected for the appropriate range of wavelengths and power levels. The display will show the measured optical power and set wavelength. A traditional light meter responds to a broad spectrum of light, and the user sets the wavelength to test. If there are other spurious wavelengths present, then wrong readings can result.

ACTIVITY 15-5
Identifying Hardware Troubleshooting Tools

Scenario

The network administrator at Greene City Interiors asks you questions about the various hardware troubleshooting tools you may need to use at the branch office.

1. You have a cable with a frayed end. You want to trim the cable and reattach the connector. You need a:
   - ○ Punch down tool
   - ○ Wire crimper
   - ○ Cable tester
   - ○ Cable stripper

2. You need to trace a UTP cable in a bundle of cables. You need a:
   - ○ Butt set
   - ○ Circuit tester
   - ○ Cable tester
   - ○ Tone generator and locator

3. A workstation and server on your small office network cannot communicate. To see if one of the network adapters is bad, you can connect them directly by using a:
   - ○ Crossover cable
   - ○ Hardware loopback plug
   - ○ Tone generator and locator
   - ○ Punch down tool

4. A user tells you he cannot log on to the network. You direct him to check his network adapter and he notices that there is one steady indicator and one flashing indicator. What does this indicate to you about the status of the connection?
   - ○ There is a network connection but there is no data transfer.
   - ○ There is no network connection.
   - ○ There is a network connection that is transferring data.
   - ○ The network adapter is faulty.

5. What does an amber indicator on a NIC indicate?
   - ○ A frame error
   - ○ A dysfunctional transceiver
   - ○ Bad network connectivity
   - ○ Data collisions
   - ○ A cable break

6. You recently replaced the NIC in a user's device. You receive a call from the user, who complains that there is no network connectivity. Which LED indicator on the NIC should you check first? Why?

   ○ Activity

   ○ Collision

   ○   Link

   ○ Cable

7. Your instructor will show examples of various types of hardware tools. Identify each tool and its function, and give an example of how you would use it in network troubleshooting.

ACTIVITY 15-6
Assembling a Patch Cable

Before You Begin

To perform this activity, you will need a cable, connectors, a wire crimper, and a cable tester. An eye loupe is optional.

Scenario

The network administrator at Greene City Interiors needs you to attach a new computer to the network. They have given you an extra length of patch cable to attach a computer to the network. Although you do not have a cable assembled, you do have some cable wire and loose connectors.

1. Strip the cable jacket back about 3/4 of an inch. Do not cut or nick the inner wires.

2. Place the pairs in the order of their color so that they lie flat and slip into the connector.

3. Slip the wires into the connector and ensure that they are properly seated and in the correct order. Ensure that the outer jacket is far enough into the connector that it will be captured by the strain relief tab.

 Note: A 5x magnification eye loupe will help you examine the wires.

4. Insert the cable/connector assembly into the crimping tool and crimp it.

5. Use the cable tester to test your cable.

TOPIC D

Common Connectivity Issues

Now that you are familiar with the common software and hardware tools used in network troubleshooting, you should also familiarize yourself with the types of connectivity issues you may encounter as a network administrator. In this topic, you will describe common network connectivity issues.

A network can be simple or complex—but even at the simplest level, numerous connectivity issues occur regularly. Each time a problem with network connectivity surfaces, you will be faced with a large number of very unhappy users. To restore connectivity as quickly as possible, you will need to be aware of the possible connectivity issues you may face and the appropriate fixes.

Physical Issues

When troubleshooting network problems, it is helpful to understand the issues that can arise. Having this understanding will enable you to solve problems more efficiently. There are several categories of physical connectivity issues.

Source of Problem	Description
Crosstalk	**Symptoms:** Slow network performance and an excess of dropped or unintelligible packets. In telephony applications, users hear garbled voice or conversations from another line.
	Causes: Generally, crosstalk occurs when two cables run in parallel and the signal of one cable interferes with the other. Crosstalk can also be caused by crossed or crushed wire pairs in twisted pair cabling.
	Resolution: The use of twisted pair cabling or digital signals can reduce the effects of crosstalk. Maintaining proper distance between cables can also help.
Near-end crosstalk	**Symptoms:** Signal loss or interference.
	Causes: Near-end crosstalk occurs more closely along the transmitting end of the cable. Often occurs in or near the terminating connector.
	Resolution: Test with cable testers from both ends of the cable and correct any crossed or crushed wires. Verify that the cable is terminated properly and that the twists in the pairs of wires are maintained.
Far-end crosstalk	**Symptoms:** Signal loss or interference.
	Causes: Similar to near-end crosstalk, far-end crosstalk occurs at the other end of the cable from the transmitter that is causing the interference.
	Resolution: Test with cable testers from both ends of the cable and correct any crossed or crushed wires. Verify that the cable is terminated properly and that the twists in the pairs of wires are maintained.

Source of Problem	Description
Attenuation	**Symptoms:** Slow responses from the network. **Causes:** Degradation of signal strength. **Resolution:** In case of wired networks, use shorter cable runs. In case of wireless networks, add more access points and signal boosters along the transmission path. A longer cable length, poor connections, bad insulation, a high level of crosstalk, or EMI can all increase attenuation. Evaluate the environment for interference. The type of signal interference would depend on the wireless spectrum used.
Collisions	**Symptoms:** High latency, reduced network performance, and intermittent connectivity issues. **Causes:** Collisions tend to occur on networks as nodes attempt to access shared resources. **Resolution:** Depends on the network. For example, on a network still using hubs, replacing a hub with a switch will often alleviate the problem.
Shorts	**Symptoms:** Electrical shorts—complete loss of signal. **Causes:** Two nodes of an electrical circuit that are meant to be at different voltages create a low-resistance connection, causing a short circuit. **Resolution:** Use a TDR to detect and locate shorts. Replace cables and connectors.
Open impedance mismatch	**Symptoms:** There is an echo on either the talker or listener end of the connection. **Causes:** The mismatching of electrical resistance. **Resolution:** Use a TDR to detect impedance. Collect and review data, interpret the symptoms, and determine the root cause in order to correct the cause.
Interference (EMI/RFI)	**Symptoms:** Crackling, humming, and static are all signs of interference. Additionally, low throughput, network degradation, and poor voice quality are also symptoms of interference. **Causes:** Electromagnetic and radio-frequency interference can be caused by a number of devices including cordless phones, Bluetooth® devices, cameras, paging systems, unauthorized access points, and clients in the ad-hoc mode. For a WAN connection, the distance of a WAN link, including all the networks and connections it may have to traverse, could make it more susceptible to interference, especially for DSL links that have practical distance limits, or radio transmissions that can be easily interfered with. **Resolution:** Remove or avoid environmental interferences as much as possible. This may simply entail turning off competing devices or relocating them. Ensure that there is adequate LAN coverage. To resolve problems proactively, test areas prior to deployment by using tools such as spectrum analyzers.
SFP/GBIC issues	**Symptoms:** There is no communication through the device. The system console may display error lights or message. **Causes:** Modules in SFPs/GBICs get corrupted, there is a cable mismatch, or a cable is bad. **Resolution:** Check cables, replace the faulty SFPs/GBICs.

Source of Problem	Description
Cable problems	**Symptoms:** The nodes on the network cannot communicate. The router, switches, and the individual nodes on the network are fully functional, but the problem still persists. **Causes:** There is a problem with the network cables. **Resolution:** There could be issues with the network cables. Identify the issue and determine a suitable solution. Bad connectors: Check and replace the faulty connectors. Verify that the cables are properly secured to the connectors and are properly crimped. Bad wiring: Check and replace the wires that are in bad condition. Open, short cables: Use cable testers and locate open or short cables. Repair the cables and recheck that the issues are resolved. If not, replace the cables. Split cables: Identify the split cables and replace them with compatible cables. DB loss: Check the cable for defects or damage, crimping, and connection with the connectors. Identify and remove sources of interference. Tx/Rx reversed: Check the network port indicators on the system; if the link light is off, there is an issue with the network adapter. Replace the network adapter. Cable placement: Verify that the cable is placed away from sources of EMI. Identify and remove the sources of interference. Distance limitations: Verify that the cables are run only for the maximum distance they are supported. For example, multimode fiber optic cables for Gigabit Ethernet range from 300 meters to 1,040 meters at 850 nm, or 600 meters at 1,310 nm. Dirty fiber connectors: Inspect and clean the connector. Fiber bend radius limitations: Excessively bent fiber cable needs to be replaced.
Bad cables/ improper cable types	**Symptoms:** The nodes on the network cannot communicate. The router, switches, and the individual nodes on the network are fully functional, but the problem still persists. **Causes:** Cables are cut or shorted. A short can happen when the wire conductor comes in contact with another conductive surface, changing the path of the signal. **Resolution:** Cable testers can be used to detect many types of cable problems such as: cut cable, incorrect cable connections, cable shorts, interference, and faulty connectors. After identifying the source of the issue, move the cable to prevent it from coming in contact with other conductive surfaces.
Mismatched fiber optic cables/ connectors	**Symptoms:** Signal loss or slow responses from the network. **Causes:** There is a fiber type mismatch, connector mismatch, or wavelength mismatch. These cause a mismatch of the chosen light wavelength and the cable that conducts it. Because both the core and cladding of fiber optic cable are designed to be optimal for specific wavelengths, you do not want to mix and match the various cable types or connectors. **Resolution:** Replace mismatched fiber cables and terminations to use the same type.

Source of Problem	Description
Incorrect termination	**Symptoms:** Intermittent problems with a network connection. **Causes:** Copper cables may not be properly terminated. **Resolution:** Ensure that straight-through cables are used unless you specifically need to use a crossover cable.
Hardware failure	**Symptoms:** Intermittent problems with a network connection or no connection. **Causes:** A device had a hardware failure which causes it to function intermittently or not all. The entire device may have failed, or in case of a computer, it may be just one component that has failed. **Resolution:** Investigate the issue and trace it to the source hardware that has failed. Test the device to determine if it is just a component that has failed or if the entire device has failed. Have the device repaired or replaced.

Logical Issues

In addition to physical connectivity issues, your network can suffer from logical connectivity issues, which range from no connectivity to lost connectivity and can vary in severity.

Source of Problem	Description
Port speed	**Symptoms:** No or low-speed connectivity between devices. **Cause:** Ports are configured to operate at different speeds and are therefore incompatible with each other. **Resolution:** Verify that equipment is compatible and is operating at compatible speeds. For example, if you're running a switch at 100 Mbps, but a device's NIC runs at 10 Mbps, the device will be slow. Replace the NIC with one that runs at 100 Mbps and you will increase the throughput to a higher level (or at least a theoretical higher level since there are other variables such as network congestion).
Port duplex mismatch	**Symptoms:** Late collisions, port alignment errors, and FCS errors are present during testing. **Causes:** Mismatches are generally caused by configuration errors. They occur when the switch port and a device are configured to use a different set of duplex settings, or when both ends are set to auto negotiate the settings. **Resolution:** Verify that the switch port and device are configured to use the same duplex setting. This may entail having to upgrade one of the devices.
Wrong VLAN/ Incorrect VLAN assignment	**Symptoms:** No connectivity between devices. **Causes:** Devices are configured to use different VLANs. **Resolution:** Reconfigure devices to use the same VLAN.

Source of Problem	Description
Incorrect interface/ Interface misconfiguration	**Symptoms:** No connectivity between devices. **Causes:** Either the source or destination device has an incorrect IP address or subnet mask. **Resolution:** Use the `ping` command to determine if there is connectivity between devices. Resolution will depend on the problem. If a network is running a rogue DHCP server, for example, two devices could have been leased the same IP address. Check TCP/IP configuration info by using `ipconfig /all` on Windows devices, and `ifconfig` on Linux/UNIX/Mac devices. After confirming the issue, troubleshoot DHCP. It could also be the case that a static IP address was entered incorrectly. Check IP addresses, and empty the ARP cache on both devices. Check the subnet mask on both devices. Change the incorrect subnet mask to a correct one and test connectivity.
Interface errors	**Symptoms:** No connectivity between devices, device is generating error messages, or WAN connection is down. **Causes:** The device is misconfigured or it, or another device, is failing. For WAN connections, there may be issues such as a protocol mismatch between the two routers, an improperly configured DCE/DTE relationship, or there might be PPP authentication mismatch between the two sides. **Resolution:** Review system messages for the device, if any, to see if there is information that indicates what the issue is. You can use utilities to look for errors such as CRC errors, collisions, and frame errors.
Wrong default gateway address	**Symptoms:** No connectivity between devices. **Causes:** The IP address of the default gateway is incorrect for the specified route. **Resolution:** Change the IP address of the default gateway to the correct address.
Misconfigured DHCP	**Symptoms:** No connectivity for some or all devices. **Causes:** DHCP is misconfigured and not assigning the correct IP addresses for the network, or did not assign enough IP addresses to cover all devices. **Resolution:** Check the DHCP server configuration and verify that it is using the correct IP address range. Determine the number of addresses in the IP address range and compare that against the number of connecting devices to see if there are enough.
Misconfigured DNS	**Symptoms:** No connectivity between devices when using device names, or unable to resolve names on Internet connection. **Causes:** A device is configured to use the wrong DNS server which prevents using device names or resolving names on the Internet. **Resolution:** Open TCP/IP properties and check the IP address of the DNS server listed for the client. Replace with the correct IP address and test connectivity.

Source of Problem	Description
Duplicate IP address	**Symptoms:** System displays notification that the same IP address is in use on the network. No connectivity between devices. **Causes:** The same IP address is assigned to more than one device. **Resolution:** In case the network is DHCP-enabled, try to identify the devices that are assigned IP addresses manually and change the IP address of such devices to be outside the DHCP scope. If the network is not DHCP-enabled, locate the devices that have the same IP address, and change the IP address in one of the devices.
Power failure	**Symptoms:** There is a power failure that affects switches and routers. **Causes:** Switch and router adapters connect to cable modems which depend on the availability of power. **Resolution:** Use cable modems and other network devices with battery-backed power supplies to ensure that there is uninterrupted service of several hours in case of local power failures.
Bad/missing IP routes	**Symptoms:** The router is sending packets using an invalid path. **Causes:** The router setting is incorrect. Missing IP routes are either the result of missing or misconfigured routing protocols, or an unconfigured or misconfigured default gateway address. **Resolution:** Check and change the router setting and reboot the router for the changes to be effected.
NIC teaming misconfiguration	**Symptoms:** There is a switching loop on the network related to NIC team. **Causes:** Administrator misconfigures a NIC team so that it ends up being not one aggregate link, but several parallel links. Something happens to the hardware that causes the aggregate to break apart. Any broadcast or multicast would then cause an instant storm. **Resolution:** Configure "active" and "passive" features of the Link Aggregation Control Protocol (LACP) to prevent the NIC team from losing aggregation. You can have both sides of the links be in active mode, thus guaranteeing link aggregation. You can also have one side be active and the other passive to create link aggregation.
Unpatched firmware/OS	**Symptoms:** Network devices or computers are targets of exploit attacks. **Causes:** Attackers are taking advantage of a security flaw in the firmware of a device or OS of a computer. **Resolution:** Apply patches that address the security flaw in the firmware or OS.
Loss of Internet connectivity	**Symptoms:** One or more devices cannot connect to the Internet. **Cause:** Loss of Internet connectivity could be related to many different issues such as hardware failure, misconfigured settings, Internet service provider (ISP) issue, and more. **Resolution:** Try to determine if the entire network has lost Internet or if it is localized to certain segments or computers. If it is not the entire network, then troubleshoot the affected segments and computers that have lost connectivity. If it is the entire network, then check the WAN devices to ensure they are functioning properly. Call your ISP and have them validate that there are no issues on their end.

Source of Problem	Description
Split horizon	**Symptoms:** One branch office sends a route update to the main office; the hub office will NOT repeat the route to the other branch office.
	Causes: Split horizon becomes a problem on a multipoint link in a hub and spoke topology where you have two or more branch offices connected to the same interface of a main (hub) office.
	Resolution: To fix this unintended consequence of split horizon, break the multipoint connection into two separate links. If you cannot use two separate physical interfaces on the hub, then you turn the one physical interface into two logical subinterfaces on the hub site's router. Each subinterface creates its own point-to-point link with its corresponding branch office. The routing protocol now treats the subinterfaces as separate interfaces, allowing an incoming routing update on one subinterface from one branch office to be repeated out the other subinterface to the other branch office.
Router configurations	**Symptoms:** No WAN connectivity or limited connectivity.
	Causes: Since it is the router that has the WAN interface, any number of things can be misconfigured, including the Layer 2 protocol, the clock rate, route tables, possible router-to-router authentication, or IPSec VPN settings, and inappropriate access control lists (ACLs) set on the router.
	Resolution: Troubleshoot the issue by checking the different configuration settings on the router. Check each group of settings and verify that they are correct and then check the connection again to see if it is now working.
Customer premise equipment	**Symptoms:** No WAN connectivity or limited connectivity.
	Cause: There can be an issue with the customer premise equipment. The demarc, smart jack, or Channel Service Unit/Data Service Unit (CSU/DSU) could have failed or been misconfigured. If copper line drivers/repeaters are in use, they may have been placed too far away from the transmitting source.
	Resolution: Check the components inside the building such as the demarc, smart jack, and CSU/DSU to verify that they have power and are functioning. Most CSU/DSUs are built into the WAN interface card, but older routers may require a separate CSU/DSU between the router's serial port and the provider's demarc. Ensure that the repeaters are placed no farther than 80% of the recommended distance. In some cases, it should be closer if there is more EMI/RFI in the environment.
Company security policy	**Symptoms:** WAN connection is not performing as well as it should.
	Causes: Your company policy may limit and/or block certain traffic or protocols. It may limit how much bandwidth a connection can utilize. It may block many types of traffic/protocols for security reasons, especially going out on the Internet. Common protocols that are blocked for security reasons include ICMP, RDP, SMB, RPC, telnet, and SSH. It may disallow users from using more than their fair share of WAN bandwidth, and thus impose limits on utilization.
	Resolution: If the company security policy is interfering with legitimate work-related traffic, then it can be re-evaluated to see if it needs to be changed, or perhaps an exception can be created for certain traffic. If the policy is not interfering with legitimate work-related traffic, then remind the users of the company policy.

Source of Problem	Description
Satellite issues	**Symptoms:** Satellite connectivity is slow or intermittent.
	Causes: Due to the greater distances the signal must travel, average latency is high, and weather conditions also affect the signal.
	Resolution: Check to see if there is a closer connection that can be used that has lower latency. Much of the slowdown associated with satellite connections is that for each request, many roundtrips must be completed before any useful data can be received by the requester. Special IP stacks and proxies can reduce latency through lessening the number of roundtrips, or simplifying and reducing the length of protocol headers. These types of technologies are generally referred to as TCP acceleration, HTTP pre-fetching, and DNS caching.

Routing and Switching Issues

There are several common router and switch issues that can occur on a network.

Source of Problem	Description
Switching loop	**Symptoms:** There is a switching loop on the network.
	Causes: Packets are switched in a loop.
	Resolution: A switching loop needs STP to ensure loop-free switching of data. Rework on the network arrangement and cabling to prevent the switching loop.
Routing loop	**Symptoms:** There is a routing loop on the network.
	Causes: Packets are routed in a loop.
	Resolution: Recheck the router configuration and adjust it to prevent a routing loop.
Route problems	**Symptoms:** Packets do not reach their intended destination.
	Causes: This could be caused by configuration problems, route convergence, broken segments, or router malfunctioning.
	Resolution: Verify that the router is functional. If necessary, replace the router.
Proxy arp	**Symptoms:** The proxy server is not functional.
	Causes: The proxy settings are misconfigured. This may lead to DoS attacks.
	Resolution: Correct the proxy settings to resolve the issue.
Broadcast storms	**Symptoms:** The network becomes overwhelmed by constant broadcast traffic generated by a device on the network.
	Causes: There are too many broadcast messages being sent in parallel, causing high network traffic.
	Resolution: Identify the device and reconfigure it to increase the interval of broadcast messages. On the network, apply restrictive settings to prevent network nodes from sending broadcast messages.

Source of Problem	Description
Port configuration	**Symptoms:** Port configuration is incorrect.
	Causes: The recent changes made to the port configuration were incorrect.
	Resolution: On the system console of the switch, verify the port properties of the individual nodes and check their status. If required, restore the port configuration to its default setting from the last backup.
VLAN assignment	**Symptoms:** Nodes on the network cannot communicate with one other.
	Causes: By default, computers on different segments are added to different VLANs, and they cannot communicate with one another, unless the switch is configured to allow communication between computers on different VLANs.
	Resolution: Check the VLAN assignment on the switch console and reassign the computers to the VLAN to enable communication among them. Ensure that the IOS of the switch is updated to reflect the latest settings.
Mismatched MTU/MTU black hole	**Symptoms:** MTU is inaccessible or there are intermittent errors.
	Causes: In case of a mismatch of the MTU, the TCP/IP connection handshake does not occur between the devices (routers) and the connection cannot be established. For black holes, the router receives a packet that is larger than the size of the MTU and it sends an ICMP message saying to change the size but the message is never received.
	Resolution: Reconfigure the MTU to check whether the problem gets resolved. If not, replace the device. For black holes, configure the router to send ICMP Type 3 Code 4 messages.

At times, you will encounter issues that need to be escalated in order to be solved. This is an important aspect of network troubleshooting, because solutions may require input from people who are more experienced in switching or routing configurations and operations.

Wireless Issues

In addition to the physical and logical connectivity issues you can encounter while troubleshooting a wired network, wireless networks present their own issues.

Source of Problem	Description
Interference	**Symptoms:** Low throughput, network degradation, dropped packets, intermittent connectivity, and poor voice quality are all symptoms caused by interference.
	Causes: RF interference can be caused by a number of sources, including cordless phones, Bluetooth devices, cameras, paging systems, unauthorized access points, metal building framing, and clients in ad-hoc mode.
	Resolution: Determine the signal-to-noise ratio and try to locate the sources of interference. Remove or avoid environmental interference as much as possible.

Source of Problem	Description
Incorrect encryption/Wrong encryption type	**Symptoms:** If the encryption types between two devices (access point and client) do not match, no connection is established. Similarly, if different encryption keys are used between two devices, they cannot negotiate key information for verification and decryption in order to initiate communication. **Causes:** Improper configuration and different encryption types. **Resolution:** Ensure that security settings match between and among devices.
Congested/ overlapping channels	**Symptoms:** Very slow speeds or no connectivity. **Causes:** Interference from neighboring wireless networks that are on the same channel; mismatched channels will prevent connectivity; congested network channels. **Resolution:** Many wireless routers are set to autoconfigure the same wireless channel. Try logging in to the router and manually change the channel the wireless router is operating on.
Incorrect frequency	**Symptoms:** No connectivity. **Causes:** Devices must operate on the same frequency. For example, a device designed to communicate at 5 GHz frequency cannot communicate with one designed to communicate at 2.4 GHz. **Resolution:** Deploy devices that operate on the same frequency.
SSID mismatch/ Wrong SSID	**Symptoms:** No connectivity between devices. **Causes:** Devices are configured to use different ESSIDs. **Resolution:** Set the devices to use the same SSID. Ensure that the wireless client and the access point are the same. **Note:** SSIDs are case-sensitive.
Standard mismatch	**Symptoms:** No connectivity between devices. **Causes:** Devices are configured to use different standards such as 802.11a/b/g/n. **Resolution:** Devices chosen to work together should use the same standard to operate. 802.11a, for example, is incompatible with 802.11b/g because the first operates at 5 GHz and the second at 2.4 GHz. Or, an 802.11g router could be set only for "g" mode and you are trying to connect with an 802.11b wireless card. Both 802.11b and 802.11g transmit at 2.4 GHz. Their throughput is different with 802.11b at 11 Mbps and 802.11g at 54 Mbps. Change the mode on the router.

Source of Problem	Description
Signal strength/loss	**Symptoms:** Low or no signal strength and throughput.
	Causes: The distance between two points causes this connectivity issue. The longer the distance between two devices, the lower the signal strength. Issues that can occur because of low signal strength include latency, packet loss, retransmission, or transient traffic. Physical environmental factors can also have an impact on signal strength. Signal strength can be lost when the signal encounters objects such as concrete walls, window film, or metal studs. If it is a multiple input, multiple output wireless access point (MIMO WAP) that does not have the superior signal strength, then it could be that one or both antennas is loose, unscrewed, or broken off. A MIMO WAP needs both antennas in order to deliver the superior signal strength.
	Resolution: Add another access point to increase coverage. Use a spectrum analyzer to determine coverage and signal strength. You might need to use directional antennas or additional APs to improve signals when such environmental factors are encountered. Make sure that antennas are not loose and are screwed on properly.
Bounce	**Symptoms:** No or low connectivity between devices.
	Causes: Signals from a device bounce off obstructions and are not received by the receiving device.
	Resolution: If possible, move one of the devices to avoid obstructions. Monitor performance and check for interference.
Antenna placement	**Symptoms:** No or low signal and connectivity.
	Causes: The position of your antenna can negatively affect overall performance, if placed incorrectly.
	Resolution: Alter the position of your antenna and monitor device performance.

Source of Problem	Description
AP configuration	**Symptoms:** The wireless modem is active, but clients cannot access the Internet.

Causes: Configuration of the wireless modem is incorrect.

Resolution:

- Check the configuration of the wireless modem by accessing the web admin interface.
- Check the encryption type, SSID, and passphrase text that is specified and confirm that the wireless modem was rebooted after the configuration change.
- Ensure that the clients can also support the same encryption type.
- Verify that the same SSID and key phrase are defined in the network connection.
- Verify that the wireless receiver on the client is configured properly with the correct compatible drivers installed.
- Similarly, for a laptop, check that the wireless network adapter is functional and is turned on. If needed, update the device driver on the client systems.
- Check to see if any untested updates were applied to your wireless routers or devices. As with updates on any other part of your network, you should test any updates to your wireless routers and devices before deploying the updates on a wide scale. Troubleshooting a single update on a single device is much easier than troubleshooting it on an organization-wide basis.
- Determine whether the access point is stand-alone (thick) or controller based (thin). A thick AP is a stand-alone device so you will only have to check configuration settings for it. For a thin AP, it will also connect to a wireless LAN controller and will use the LWAPP protocol. The controller will need to be accessed to check configuration settings.

 Note: Typically, **http://192.168.1.1** will be the address for accessing the admin interface. This may vary for some routers. Refer the user manual or the manufacturer's site for the actual address.

Incompatibilities	**Symptoms:** The wireless device is not accessible from the client.

Causes: The settings on the wireless device are not compatible with the clients.

Resolution: Check the configuration of the wireless modem by accessing the web admin interface. Verify that the clients can support the same configuration. If not, identify the configuration, such as the encryption type, supported on both the clients and the server and apply the same on the wireless device and the client systems.

Source of Problem	Description
Incorrect channel	**Symptoms:** The wireless signal is not accessible even within the expected range.
	Causes: A number of factors can cause the signal of the WAP to deteriorate and the performance of your network will dip lower than normal. The most common cause could be another wireless device or application that operates at the same frequency level creating a conflict.
	Resolution: Identify the conflicting device and move it to another location that is outside the reach of the WAP. If it is not possible to relocate devices, change the channel of one of the devices such that they operate at a different frequency. Ensure that the cordless phones, microwaves, and other electrical equipment are kept a safe distance away from the access point.
Latency	**Symptoms:** Delay in data transmission on the network is very high.
	Causes: The signal strength is weak or the position of the wireless antenna is modified.
	Resolution: Verify that the wireless modem is functional. Change the antenna position to the position that gives the best performance. Ensure that your antenna is maintained in the same position.
AP placement	**Symptoms:** AP performance is considerably reduced.
	Causes: There is a conflicting device in the range which is causing the interference that results in the WAP performance being degraded.
	Resolution: Locate the conflicting device and, if possible, move it to another location. If that is not possible, work on your network layout and determine a better position for the WAP such that there is no conflict with the other devices. Monitor the WAP performance periodically to prevent further occurrence of the issue.
Device/bandwidth saturation	**Symptoms:** Very slow speeds or no connectivity.
	Causes: On a wireless network, you can only have a certain number of devices connected before performance begins deteriorating. When you reach the device saturation limit, transmissions will be lost and need to be re-sent, thus decreasing the throughput to the device. Bandwidth saturation on wireless networks can also be reached if you have a lot of devices connected, or a device is transferring a large volume of data.
	Resolution: Replace the WAP with one that provides better bandwidth, or add another WAP to support the needed traffic demands. Investigate to see if some devices could use a wired connection instead.
Open network	**Symptoms:** Unauthorized devices are connected to your wireless network; you suspect your wireless traffic is being intercepted by an external entity.
	Causes: An open network is a wireless network that is unsecured. It doesn't use any type of security or encryption. This makes any information you send or receive available for grabbing by anyone. It also gives anyone on that wireless network access to your device.
	Resolution: Configure security and encryption settings for all WAPs and devices that connect to the wireless network.

Source of Problem	Description
Power levels	**Symptoms:** Wireless devices connect to a WAP that is not the closest; the coverage area of the WAP is smaller than it should be.
	Causes: The power level on the WAP may be set too high or too low. This will cause it to extend its range too far or make it too small.
	Resolution: Set the power to 50% and make small increments up and down to find a good balance of power and coverage.
Rogue access point	**Symptoms:** Unauthorized access through the wireless network.
	Causes: A wireless access point that is added to a network without the administrator's consent or knowledge is considered a rogue access point. These are usually installed by employees who want wireless access to the network when no wireless access is available. Rogue access points can also be used as an evil twin. An evil twin operates outside of the organization's network and receives beacons transmitted by the legitimate network with the intent of gaining access to the organization's network by unauthorized users.
	Resolution: Remove the rogue access point from the network. Administrators can routinely monitor their managed wireless access points. If any additional access points are detected, they should immediately be removed from the network to protect the network.
Wrong antenna type	**Symptoms:** The range of the wireless signal is either too short or too far.
	Causes: Installing the wrong antenna type can make your Wi-Fi signal not reach far enough or it can make it so that the signal can be picked up outside the area you intend your network to reach. The range covered depends on the access point type (802.11b, g, or n) and the type of antenna connected to it. The standard antenna that comes with an 802.11g AP can usually reach about 100 meters. However, if a semi-parabolic antenna is installed, the same AP can often reach as far as 20 miles. You would not want your AP to broadcast so far. An 802.11n AP can often reach twice as far.
	Resolution: Replace the wrong antenna type with the correct one. You can also use directional antennas to improve the distance the AP can reach without going outside of the desired area you want covered. Some APs allow you to install upgraded antennas to improve coverage in this way.

Simultaneous Wired/Wireless Connections

Simultaneous wired and wireless connections are not an issue in and of themselves. Sometimes issues can be created when a device has both connections. For example, if you are connected to both, you may want to use the wired connection for its higher transfer rate but the wireless connection may be the one used. If a device is connected using the wired connection and then the user disconnects it to move to another location where they will rely on the wireless connection, they will lose their network connection while the device switches from the disconnected NIC to the wireless adapter. Normally this only results in a brief interruption of network connectivity. If the user was connected to an application, it may need to be closed and reopened for it to use the new connection. Users should be educated on how the two connections work when both are available and what happens when one is added or removed.

If both the wired and wireless connections are on the same subnet then either one connection will have a lower route cost than the other, or routes will be ambiguous and unpredictable. For example, if your wired LAN connection has a lower cost, the wireless connection will always be used whenever it is active. However, if both connections have the same cost, some packets may be routed to the wired LAN and others to the wireless network. In this case change the subnet of one of the networks.

Discovery of Neighboring Devices and Nodes

Network discovery is a method for devices to find each other on the network. This is usually a configuration option as it can lead to some security issues, mostly on public networks. When not working, devices typically can be pinged but cannot be connected to. If network discovery is used but not functioning, then the first step to take is to make sure that the option has been enabled. Check network connectivity in general to make sure there isn't another issue causing the problem.

Typically there are certain services that need to be running in order for the network discovery to work properly. For example, for Windows these typically include: DNS Client, SSDP Discovery, UPnP Device Host, and Function Discovery Resource Publication services. For your system, verify that the required services are running. Some security applications such as firewalls may interfere with network discovery. Research what traffic needs to be allowed and determine if your firewall or other security application is causing the issue.

ACTIVITY 15–7
Troubleshooting Network Connectivity

Scenario

In this activity, you will identify the cause of network connectivity problems.

1. You receive a call from a network user who has lost all network connectivity. You examine the network components on the user's workstation and segment and discover the situation shown in the graphic.

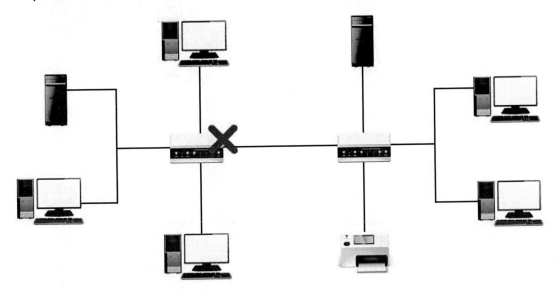

   Which network component has failed?

2. Which network device(s) will be affected? Why?

3. Another network user calls complaining that he cannot connect to a server. You try to connect to various network devices and examine the network components and discover the situation shown in the graphic.

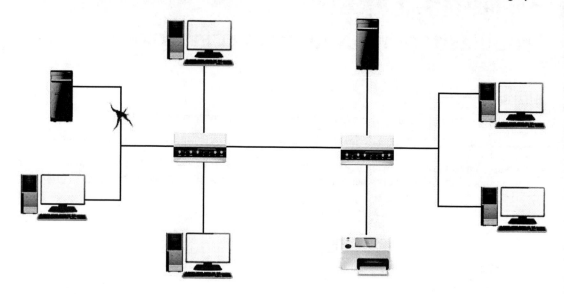

What is the cause of the connectivity failure?

4. Which network device(s) will be affected? Why?

5. Your company's network is spread across several locations within the city. One of your network operations centers has experienced a power surge and you are concerned about the effect on network connectivity. You try to connect to various network devices and discover the situation shown in the graphic.

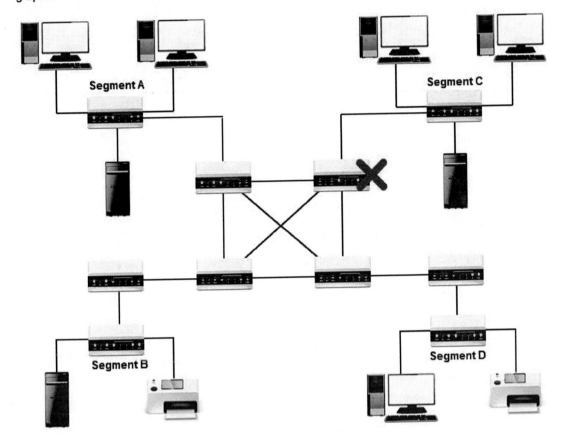

Which network device has failed?

6. What area of the network will be affected?

7. Your network uses UTP CAT5 cable throughout the building. There are a few users who complain of intermittent network connectivity problems. You cannot determine a pattern for these problems that relates to network usage. You visit the users' workstations and find that they are all located close to an elevator shaft. What is a likely cause of the intermittent connectivity problems?

8. How might you correct the problem?

9. A client visiting your company found that his 802.11b wireless card cannot connect to your company's 802.11g wireless network. Of the following choices, which is most likely?

   ○ 802.11b broadcasts at 5 GHz, while 802.11g is 2.4 GHz

   ○ Incompatibility between 802.11b and g

   ○ A rogue DHCP server

   ○ Too many wireless devices sharing the access point

10. An employee has complained that conference calls in Conference Room 1 routinely get interrupted by periods of white noise, and that the speaker often has every other word cut off. You have discovered that the room's network cable has been run over by a chair's wheel, and that the wires have been crushed. What is this an example of?

○ Packet loss

○ Near-end crosstalk

○ Far-end crosstalk

○ Network drain

TOPIC E

Troubleshoot Security Configuration Issues

In the last topic, you described common network connectivity issues. Sometimes you will need to troubleshoot issues related to security configuration. In this topic, you will discover some troubleshooting steps for common security configuration issues.

Improperly configured or conflicting security settings can cause issues that affect the network just as much as other issues. Understanding how to troubleshoot and resolve security configuration issues is a very important part of maintaining a network.

Common Security Configuration Issues

Some of the more common security configuration issues that you are likely to encounter include:

- Misconfigured firewalls
- Misconfigured access control lists (ACLs) and applications
- Open or closed ports
- Authentication issues
- Domain or local group configurations

Misconfigured Firewalls

The first step you typically take in troubleshooting a Windows Firewall problem is to view which rules are currently being applied to the device. Many firewalls have a monitoring node that enables you to see the rules currently being applied to a device. Many firewalls also allow for the logging of processed rules. This will also allow you to research which rules are being applied.

Only one firewall rule is used to determine if a network packet is allowed or dropped. If the network packet matches multiple rules, then you need to determine how your system handles multiple rules. Some firewalls process the first rule that applies, and others allow certain types of rules to take precedence.

Misconfigured ACLs and Applications

ACL misconfigurations, whether on a router or from operating systems or applications that have their own ACLs, can cause issues that need to be tracked down. Some common ACL misconfigurations with routers are:

- A "deny" ACL has been applied for specific conditions, but there is no "permit" ACL for all other conditions (which has the net result of denying all traffic).
- The rules in the ACL are out of order.
- ACL is applied to wrong interface.
- ACL is applied in the wrong direction (inbound or outbound).
- ACL is applied to the wrong protocol or port.
- Source and destination IP are reversed.
- Wrong mask or IP range is applied to the ACL (the intended target is not in the range).

The best way to approach troubleshooting router ACLs is to draw a network diagram showing the router, its connected networks, and how traffic flows through the router. Use the diagram to determine where to place the ACL (the interface and direction). Make sure if you deny specific traffic, that the ACL includes a "permit any" at the bottom of the list of rules to allow other traffic to flow through it. Test the ACL by attempting to send both permitted and denied traffic through.

Operating systems and applications have their own ACLs. Windows has five ACLs: NTFS, Share, Printer, Registry, and Active Directory. Linux has comparable ACLs, though there is no registry and the directory service will not be Active Directory, but instead something like RedHat Directory Services or OpenLDAP. In addition, for any operating system, applications like database management systems, email servers, web servers, and so on have their own ACLs.

What makes operating system or application ACLs difficult is that users can belong to many roles or groups that can potentially have conflicting permissions. You will have to compare all the groups/ roles that the user belongs to with the permissions assigned to that group/role in the ACL. Generally, if a user belongs to multiple groups, the user gets the permissions of ALL the groups together, meaning the least restrictive. The exception is Deny. If any of the groups the user belongs to is denied, the user is denied that particular action, even if the user is an administrator. Windows has an "Effective Permissions" tab to help sort out a user's ultimate permission level on an object, but that is only for the NTFS ACL. In Windows, any folder that is shared will be subject to both the Share and NTFS ACLs. A user will have to get past both ACLs to perform an action. This is true of not only the shared folder, but also of the contents inside the share.

Troubleshooting operating system/application ACLs might take some investigation, especially if the administrator did not follow best practice regarding assigning permissions to users and groups. Test to see if some other person can perform the action. The best practice is you always assign permissions to a group, and then put users in or out of the group. You create groups based on roles or common security need. You make exceptions such as Deny sparingly.

Open or Closed Ports

Open and closed ports are generally used in hacking, rather than regular troubleshooting. A port scanner can determine if a port is open or closed. If it is open, then the host has a service that is responding on that port. If it is a TCP port, the usual response is SYN ACK. That port can then have a vulnerability scan performed against it to see if the service is vulnerable. A closed port means that there is a device at that IP address, but that there is no service listening on that port. If it is a TCP port, the target device will send back a TCP RST (reset) meaning that it is not accepting connections on that port.

Open and closed ports can be used for troubleshooting to see if a firewall permits traffic to a protected host on a particular port. If you use a port scanner to connect to port 80 and get no response where there should be a response, then perhaps the firewall is misconfigured. If you get an RST, then the firewall may be permitting the traffic, but the target host is not listening on that port. This may be particularly useful if the target host is using a non-standard port. In addition, if the port is open but the service does not respond properly, then there is something wrong with the service. For example, if you scan TCP port 80 and get a SYN ACK response, you know you are getting port 80 traffic to the target. If you then open a browser and do not get the response you expect, you know that the web server is misconfigured or has a problem, but that there is no problem with the network itself. The only exception to that would be if the firewall was acting as a reverse proxy and perhaps has some additional rules that filter or block the content.

Authentication Issues

Because there are often multiple authentication mechanisms to the same host, troubleshooting authentication issues can involve a few steps. The first thing to determine is if the problem is truly authentication and not some other problem with the network, the device, or the application. See if someone else can authenticate. If no one can authenticate by using one method, then see if users can authenticate by using some other method, such as sitting directly at the console, or across the network via remote access, RDP, SSH, telnet, remote PowerShell, and so on. Also try, if available, a different authentication protocol, such as Kerberos, NTLM, smart card/token, MS-CHAP v2 (for remote access), and more. Check the Event Viewer logs or error messages to see if there is any indication of the problem. Common problems include expired certificates, wrong user name or password, locked or disabled account, and client not configured to use correct authentication protocol or encryption level.

Another source of possible authentication issues is TACACS/RADIUS misconfigurations. There are many possible causes of TACACS/RADIUS misconfigurations. The policy that controls how clients can connect has many possible components, any one of which could be mismatched between the remote access client (computer, laptop, or wireless device) and the remote access server/device, which is also known as the RADIUS/TACACS client (router, switch, wireless access point, or VPN server). These components include:

- Authentication protocol.
- Encryption level.
- Certificates.
- Permitted connection type such as VPN, wireless, and wired.
- Permitted connection conditions such as user group, time of day, and type of protocol.

In addition, you could have a mismatch between the RADIUS/TACACS client (router, switch, WAP, or VPN server) and the RADIUS/TACACS server, especially the following items:

- Encryption key
- Default port

Domain or Local Group Configuration

Troubleshooting groups can be challenging if you don't know what group the user is supposed to be in. Groups are meant to funnel users down to the object's ACL:

- Universal groups are forest wide. They go into global groups.
- Global groups are domain wide. They go into domain local groups.
  - Domain local groups get permissions in an object's ACL.

Groups tend to quickly get out of hand if not carefully designed, well-documented, and tightly controlled. They change, with groups being added or deleted, and members coming and going. The two things you need to check for in group configurations are:

1. Who is a member of the group, including users and other groups?
2. Which groups, if any, is this group a member of?

You also must evaluate the group type and scope, to see if they are appropriate for your usage scenario.

ACTIVITY 15-8
Troubleshooting Windows Firewall

Scenario

At the Greene City Interiors branch office, you have some users who need to use a remote desktop connection from their homes. They say they have not been able to accomplish this so you decide to review the firewall rules on the device they are attempting to connect to and see if they are configured properly.

1. Monitor active Windows Firewall rules.

   a) In the Server Manager window, select **Tools→Windows Firewall with Advanced Security**.

   b) In the console tree, expand **Monitoring**, and select **Firewall**.

   c) In the center pane, observe the currently active inbound and outbound rules applied to this computer.

   This list of currently active inbound and outbound rules applied to this computer can be used to discover a rule that might be blocking traffic, or to discover if a rule that should be blocking or allowing traffic is not present. The firewall on this computer is currently configured to block all traffic except the traffic allowed by rules.

   d) Double-click the **Remote Desktop - User Mode (TCP-In)** rule.

Remote Access Management (WMI-In)	All	Allow
Remote Access Quarantine (TCP-In)	All	Allow
Remote Desktop - Shadow (TCP-In)	Domai...	Allow
Remote Desktop - User Mode (TCP-In)	Domai...	Allow
Remote Desktop - User Mode (UDP-In)	Domai...	Allow
Routing Information Protocol (RIP-In)	All	Allow
RPC (TCP, Incoming)	All	Allow

   e) In the **Remote Desktop - User Mode (TCP-In) Properties** dialog box, observe the Profile information.

   This field lists which firewall connection profile the rule applies to. In this case, it is the Domain and Private profiles only.

   f) Select the **Programs and Ports** tab, and observe the **Protocol** and **Local port** settings.

   These two fields list the protocol and the port affected by this rule. In this case, it is the TCP protocol on port 3389.

   g) Select **Cancel**.

   h) In the console tree, select **Connection Security Rules**.

   There are currently no active connection security rules that would implement IPSec requirements on network traffic.

2. Enable an inbound rule.

   a) In the console tree, select **Inbound Rules**.

b) In the center pane, double-click the **Remote Desktop - User Mode (TCP-In)** rule for the **Public** profile, and verify that this rule is not enabled.

Remote Access Quarantine (TCP-In)	Remote Access Quarantine	All	Yes	Allow
Remote Desktop - Shadow (TCP-In)	Remote Desktop	Public	No	Allow
Remote Desktop - Shadow (TCP-In)	Remote Desktop	Domai...	Yes	Allow
Remote Desktop - User Mode (TCP-In)	Remote Desktop	Public	No	Allow
Remote Desktop - User Mode (TCP-In)	Remote Desktop	Domai...	Yes	Allow
Remote Desktop - User Mode (UDP-In)	Remote Desktop	Domai...	Yes	Allow
Remote Desktop - User Mode (UDP-In)	Remote Desktop	Public	No	Allow

c) In the **Remote Desktop - User Mode (TCP-In) Properties** dialog box, in the **Action** section, verify that **Allow this connection** is selected.

d) Select the **Protocols and Ports** tab and verify that the **Protocol type** is **TCP** and the **Local port** is **3389**.

e) Select the **General** tab, and then check **Enabled**.

f) Select **OK**.

ACTIVITY 15-9
Troubleshooting Security Configuration Issues

Scenario

The network administrator at Greene City Interiors poses different scenarios to you and asks what troubleshooting steps you would take for security configuration problems.

1. A user complains of no longer being able to access the Internet from her workstation. After some initial investigation, you decide the issue is because of a firewall. In your environment, you have hardware firewalls protecting the entire network. What troubleshooting steps would you take?

2. A user comes to you and says that he is no longer able to log in to the network. He says that yesterday he was able to log in just fine. What troubleshooting steps would you take?

3. In the previous scenario, you verified that there were no issues with the user account. What steps would you take next?

4. A user who recently moved from one department to a new department is unable to find the printer on the network for the new department. What troubleshooting steps would you take?

5. You are attempting to use the `tracert` or `traceroute` command to investigate a routing issue on your network. The command fails even though you are able to use the `ping` command. What troubleshooting steps would you take?

TOPIC F

Troubleshoot Security Issues

In the last topic, you discovered some troubleshooting steps for common security configuration issues. Issues can arise when the security of the network has been compromised. In this topic, you will identify troubleshooting steps for security issues.

When the security of your network has been breached, you want to be able to track down and identify the source of the incident as quickly as possible. Having a good understanding of how to locate and resolve issues related to a security breach will allow you to reduce the exposure time to the security incident.

Malware

Malware is often difficult to troubleshoot because the symptoms can be vague or not obvious. Some malware, such as browser hijacking, has obvious telltale signs. Other malware, such as zero-day infections or root kits, are very difficult to trace. A lot of malware is difficult to remove. The best way to search for infections is to use a good up-to-date virus scanner. However, some malware such as spyware, adware, root kits, and hijacked browsers do not show up in a virus scan.

Use antivirus products that scan for all of these, or that specialize in one thing, such as spyware. However, do not install two antivirus products on the same device, as they tend to conflict and will usually cause severe performance degradation. Sometimes, the easiest way to remove a serious infection from a Windows device is to apply a restore point, which takes the device back to a previously saved state. In a really serious case, you can refresh the device by wiping the hard drive and reinstalling the operating system. Both of these methods come with the inconvenience that you may have to reinstall applications that were added after the restore point was created. You will also spend time re-applying updates that came after the restore point was created. In addition, this will not fix the user behavior, such as visiting certain websites or trading flash drives with other people, that caused the computer infection to begin with. Without careful education, the user will most likely reinfect his or her device again very quickly. In an enterprise environment, carefully locking down devices through policy or even desktop virtualization can go a long way toward limiting or preventing malware infections.

DoS Attacks

A Denial of Service (DoS) attack has an obvious symptom but usually no quick solution. Most DoS attacks are network-based, where the network is being flooded with traffic. This can be quickly determined by querying routers or switches for congestion on their interfaces. Any network monitoring tool will be able to identify a network-based DoS. The only fix for a network-based DoS is to wait for it to stop. You can disconnect yourself from the network until it is done. You might also be able to filter the offending traffic on upstream routers. That may not be so useful, unless you have redundant links that will allow normal traffic to come to you through some other path. The best defense against network-based DoS is to have redundancy and load balancing.

If the DoS is based on malicious code that consumes all of a server's CPU, memory, or disk space, that is not so obvious to detect, because it usually only takes a few packets to deliver that malicious payload. In that case, you will want your network intrusion detection system (NIDS) to watch for those types of signatures. If there is no signature for it, the NIDS will allow the attack to happen. The quickest way to deal with a malicious code DoS is to disconnect the power on the target and force it to reboot from a cold start. If you perform a proper shutdown, the infection might simply pop up again on restart. This does have the risk that it will corrupt unsaved data. Even with a sudden restart, if the malicious code was somehow saved on the machine, it will run again. You can run an antivirus scan to see if you can find and remove the code. The best defense is network load balancing in which you have multiple servers perform the same service.

ICMP–Related Issues

ICMP can be misused by hackers and cause problems. ICMP smurf attacks can cause a DoS. ICMP redirect messages can cause clients to use a fake gateway so that a hacker can capture user names, passwords, and data. ICMP echo and echo reply packets can carry malicious payloads as a covert channel. ICMP is used in `ping` and `tracert` commands, and if you block ICMP on a firewall or in a router ACL, then you won't be able to ping to test network connectivity. A NIDS can be used to actively monitor the network for malicious ICMP traffic. The challenge with this is that there needs to be accurate signatures to detect malicious ICMP traffic. Host-based IDS is another option, but it will also require accurate inputs to monitor the traffic accurately. You can filter ICMP traffic to minimize potential threats. To do this, you need to know what type of ICMP messages should only be allowed in and out of the network.

You may receive an ICMP "unreachable" message from the gateway. The gateway router has no specific route or default route to send the packet to. It then drops the packet and sends an ICMP "unreachable" message to the sender. Verify that the router has a route defined to send the packets to. Perform a traceroute for the destination that was unreachable to see where the traffic stops.

A ping of death is a type of attack on a computer that involves sending a malformed or otherwise malicious ping to a computer. Historically, many computer systems could not properly handle a ping packet larger than the maximum IPv4 packet size of 65,535 bytes. Larger packets could crash the target computer. Operating systems were patched to avoid this type of attack. A new form of the ping of death, called ping flooding, will flood the victim with so much ping traffic that normal traffic fails to reach the system, a basic DoS attack.

Malicious Users

Malicious users are an interesting problem. If they are very careful, it can be quite hard to detect their activity if they are inside the organization. They can be untrusted users who actively cause damage or violate security on purpose, or they can be trusted users who inadvertently cause damage to the network or violate security. The list of issues that malicious users can create ranges from using packet sniffing to examine traffic on the trusted network, to damaging equipment, to simply copying data and releasing it outside of the network. You will need good auditing and monitoring with someone actually looking at the logs and alerts to try to detect malicious users. Lock down machines very tightly with host-based IDS and lots of auditing. Automate the monitoring system as much as possible so that there is less chance of activity getting past you.

Improper Access

Improper access is usually an authorized person going into an unauthorized area or doing something they shouldn't be doing. It is not always malicious. It can be accidental by a user or by a developer who is trying to create software for the company to use internally. It can also be a hacker using a backdoor to gain access to your network. A backdoor not only allows the hacker to access the network, potentially undetected, it also provides them with the means to return and enter the system. Troubleshooting improper access is the same as for malicious users. It goes back to tightening all access controls, implementing IDS, granting least privilege, and auditing/monitoring for unauthorized or improper access. You should also always have backups and redundancy to get your system back to normal quickly in case there was damage due to improper access.

ARP Issues

Because ARP is both dynamic and broadcast-based, it is quite easy to spoof ARP packets, poisoning host ARP caches and misdirecting LAN traffic to an undesirable MAC address. Some network monitoring tools can be used to detect ARP flooding and ARP spoofing attack events. In some attacks, a rogue host is sending ARP requests sourced from a different host MAC address. In this case, you need to identify the port on which the MAC address is learned. You then backtrack until you reach the rogue host. The only way to defeat this is to hard-code ARP to IP mappings, or to use software that regularly checks the accuracy of the ARP table.

Banner Grabbing

Banner grabbing is one of the easiest ways to fingerprint an operating system or an application or service. In many cases, you can configure the service (web server, email server, and so on) to not respond to clients with any banner. Firewalls can also be configured to block banners.

Jamming

Jamming is a very crude but effective form of radio-based DoS. It is effective if the jamming device emits a relatively stronger signal than the legitimate transmitter. The jammer itself can produce a fairly weak signal, but if it is close to the receiver and the legitimate transmitter is farther away, the jammer's signal will be relatively strong. You can identify jamming by using a spectrum analyzer. You will then need to use several mobile devices/laptops with directional antennas to triangulate the location of the jammer. Jammers can be very small, and well hidden, even on a person, so you have to look carefully and use a good directional antenna to find them.

ACTIVITY 15-10
Troubleshooting Security Issues

Scenario

The network administrator at Greene City Interiors poses different scenarios to you and asks what troubleshooting steps you would take for security issues.

1. Users and customers are complaining that your company website is not responding. You check and the web server is up and running. What troubleshooting steps would you take?

2. It has been discovered that a user in the sales department is able to access resources in the finance department. It is suspected that the user is disgruntled and may be trying to find sensitive information. What troubleshooting steps would you take?

3. It is suspected that a workstation has malware running on it. What troubleshooting steps would you take?

4. Mobile users in your office inform you that they are no longer able to access the wireless network. What troubleshooting steps would you take?

Summary

In this lesson, you identified major issues, models, tools, and techniques in network troubleshooting. Having a strong fundamental understanding of the tools and processes involved in troubleshooting a network will allow you to identify and resolve problems efficiently.

Can you describe some issues that you had to troubleshoot and how you identified them?

Have you used a troubleshooting model at your organization? If so, which one and why?

Note: Check your LogicalCHOICE Course screen for opportunities to interact with your classmates, peers, and the larger LogicalCHOICE online community about the topics covered in this course or other topics you are interested in. From the Course screen you can also access available resources for a more continuous learning experience.

Course Follow-Up

Congratulations! You have completed the *CompTIA® Network+® (Exam N10-006)* course. You have gained the skills and information you will need to create a secure and efficiently operating network, including selecting the appropriate bounded and unbounded network media for your network; to set up and configure a TCP/IP Ethernet network; configure LAN and WAN services with appropriate network devices; establish connections to cloud and virtualized services; configure the network to prevent security breaches; and to respond to security incidents and troubleshoot network issues.

You also covered the objectives that you will need to prepare for the CompTIA Network+ (Exam N10-006) certification examination. If you combine this class experience with review, private study, and hands-on experience, you will be well prepared to demonstrate your expertise both through professional certification and with solid technical competence on the job.

What's Next?

Your next step after completing this course will probably be to prepare for and obtain your CompTIA Network+ certification. In addition, there are a number of other CompTIA courses and certifications that you might want to pursue following the *CompTIA® Network+® (Exam N10-006)* course, including *CompTIA® Server+® (Exam SK0-004)*, and *CompTIA® Security+® (Exam SY0-401)*. You might also wish to pursue further technology-specific training in operating system or network design, implementation and support, or in application development and implementation.

You are encouraged to explore networking setup, support, and configuration further by actively participating in any of the social media forums set up by your instructor or training administrator through the **Social Media** tile on the LogicalCHOICE Course screen.

A | Mapping Course Content to the CompTIA Network + Exam

Obtaining CompTIA® Network+® certification requires candidates to pass exam N10-006. This table describes where the objectives for exam N10-006 are covered in this course.

Domain and Objective	Covered In
Domain 1.0 Network Architecture	
1.1 Explain the functions and applications of various network devices	Lesson 4, Topic D
• Router	
• Switch	Lesson 4, Topic D
• Multilayer switch	Lesson 4, Topic D
• Firewall	Lesson 4, Topic D
• HIDS	Lesson 11, Topic E
• IDS/IPS	Lesson 11, Topic E
• Access point (wireless/wired)	Lesson 3, Topic B
• Content filter	Lesson 11, Topics B and C
• Load balancer	Lesson 14, Topic C
• Hub	Lesson 4, Topic D
• Analog modem	Lesson 4, Topic D
• Packet shaper	Lesson 14, Topic C
• VPN concentrator	Lesson 13, Topic C
1.2 Compare and contrast the use of networking services and applications	Lesson 13, Topics C and D
• VPN	
• Site to site/host to site/host to host	
• Protocols: IPSec, GRE, SSL VPN, PTP/PPTP	

Domain and Objective	Covered In
• TACACS/RADIUS	Lesson 13, Topics A and D
• RAS	Lesson 13, Topic A
• Web services	Lesson 7, Topic D
• Unified voice services	Lesson 8, Topic D
• Network controllers	Lesson 4, Topic D
1.3 Install and configure the following networking services/applications	Lesson 7, Topic A
• DHCP	
• Static vs. dynamic IP addressing	
• Reservations	
• Scopes	
• Leases	
• Options (DNS servers, suffixes)	
• IP helper/DHCP relay	
• DNS	Lesson 7, Topic B
• DNS servers	
• DNS records (A, MX, AAAA, CNAME, PTR)	
• Dynamic DNS	
• Proxy/reverse proxy	Lesson 11, Topic B
• NAT	Lesson 11, Topic B
• PAT	
• SNAT	
• DNAT	
• Port forwarding	Lesson 11, Topic B
1.4 Explain the characteristics and benefits of various WAN technologies	Lesson 8, Topic C
• Fiber	
• SONET	
• DWDM	
• CWDM	
• Frame relay	Lesson 8, Topic C
• Satellite	Lesson 8, Topics B and C
• Broadband cable	Lesson 8, Topic B
• DSL/ADSL	Lesson 8, Topic C
• ISDN	Lesson 8, Topic C
• ATM	Lesson 8, Topic C
• PPP/Multilink PPP	Lesson 8, Topic B; Lesson 13, Topic B

Domain and Objective	Covered In
• MPLS	Lesson 8, Topic C
• GSM/CDMA	Lesson 8, Topic C
• LTE/4G	
• HSPA+	
• 3G	
• Edge	
• Dial up	Lesson 8, Topic B
• WiMAX	Lesson 8, Topic C
• Metro-Ethernet	Lesson 8, Topic C
• Leased lines	Lesson 8, Topics B and C
• T-1	
• T-3	
• E-1	
• E-3	
• OC3	
• OC12	
• Circuit switch vs. packet switch	Lesson 8, Topic A
1.5 Install and properly terminate various cable types and connectors using appropriate tools	Lesson 2, Topics A and C
• Copper connectors	
• RJ-11	
• RJ-45	
• RJ-48C	
• DB-9/RS-232	
• DB-25	
• UTP coupler	
• BNC coupler	
• BNC	
• F-connector	
• 110 block	
• 66 block	
• Copper cables	Lesson 2, Topics A and C
• Shielded vs. unshielded	
• CAT3, CAT5, CAT5e, CAT6, CAT6a	
• PVC vs. plenum	
• RG-59	
• RG-6	
• Straight-through vs. crossover vs. rollover	

Domain and Objective	Covered In
• Fiber connectors	Lesson 2, Topic B
• ST	
• SC	
• LC	
• MTRJ	
• FC	
• Fiber coupler	
• Fiber cables	Lesson 2, Topic B
• Single mode	
• Multimode	
• APC vs. UPC	
• Media converters	Lesson 2, Topic C
• Single mode fiber to Ethernet	
• Multimode fiber to Ethernet	
• Fiber to coaxial	
• Single mode to multimode fiber	
• Tools	Lesson 15, Topic C
• Cable crimpers	
• Punch down tool	
• Wire strippers	
• Snips	
• OTDR	
• Cable certifier	
1.6 Differentiate between common network topologies	Lesson 4, Topic A
• Mesh	
• Partial	
• Full	
• Bus	Lesson 4, Topics A and B
• Ring	Lesson 4, Topics A and B
• Star	Lesson 4, Topics A and B
• Hybrid	Lesson 4, Topic A
• Point-to-point	Lesson 8, Topic A
• Point-to-multipoint	Lesson 8, Topic A
• Client-server	Lesson 1, Topic C
• Peer-to-peer	Lesson 1, Topic C
1.7 Differentiate between network infrastructure implementations	Lesson 1, Topic C
• WAN	

Domain and Objective	Covered In
• MAN	Lesson 1, Topic C
• LAN	Lesson 1, Topic C
• WLAN	Lesson 3, Topic C
• Hotspot	
• PAN	Lesson 1, Topic C; Lesson 3, Topic A
• Bluetooth	
• IR	
• NFC	
• SCADA/ICS	Lesson 1, Topic C
• ICS server	
• DCS/closed network	
• Remote terminal unit	
• Programmable logic controller	
• Medianets	Lesson 8, Topic D
• VTC (ISDN, IP/SIP)	
1.8 Given a scenario, implement and configure the appropriate addressing schema	Lesson 5, Topic E; Lesson 7, Topic A
• IPv6	
• Auto-configuration (EUI 64)	
• DHCP6	
• Link local	
• Address structure	
• Address compression	
• Tunneling 6to4, 4to6 (Teredo, miredo)	
• IPv4	Lesson 5, Topics B and D; Lesson 7, Topic A
• Address structure	
• Subnetting	
• APIPA	
• Classful A, B, C, D	
• Classless	
• Private vs. public	Lesson 5, Topic C
• NAT/PAT	Lesson 11, Topic B
• MAC addressing	Lesson 4, Topic C
• Multicast	Lesson 5, Topic E; Lesson 6, Topic B
• Unicast	Lesson 5, Topic E
• Broadcast	Lesson 5, Topic C; Lesson 6, Topic A
• Broadcast domains vs. collision domains	Lesson 4, Topic D

Domain and Objective	Covered In
1.9 Explain the basics of routing concepts and protocols	Lesson 15, Topic B
• Loopback interface	
• Routing loops	Lesson 6, Topic B
• Routing tables	Lesson 6, Topic A
• Static vs. dynamic routes	Lesson 6, Topic B
• Default route	Lesson 6, Topic A
• Distance vector routing protocols (RIP v2)	Lesson 6, Topic B
• Hybrid routing protocols (BGP)	Lesson 6, Topic B
• Link state routing protocols (OSPF, IS-IS)	Lesson 6, Topic B
• Interior vs. exterior gateway routing protocols	Lesson 6, Topic B
• Autonomous system numbers	Lesson 6, Topic A
• Route redistribution	Lesson 6, Topic B

• High availability
  • VRRP
  • Virtual IP
  • HSRP
	Lesson 6, Topic A; Lesson 9, Topic A

• Route aggregation	Lesson 6, Topic A

• Routing metrics
  • Hop counts
  • MTU, bandwidth
  • Costs
  • Latency
  • Administrative distance
  • SPB
	Lesson 4, Topic D; Lesson 6, Topic A; Lesson 9, Topic B

1.10 Identify the basic elements of unified communication technologies	Lesson 8, Topic D
• VoIP	
• Video	Lesson 8, Topic D

• Real time services
  • Presence
  • Multicast vs. unicast
	Lesson 8, Topic D

• QoS
  • DSCP
  • COS
	Lesson 8, Topic D

Domain and Objective	Covered In

• Devices
  • UC servers
  • UC devices
  • UC gateways
	Lesson 8, Topic D

1.11 Compare and contrast technologies that support cloud and virtualization	Lesson 9, Topic A

• Virtualization
  • Virtual switches
  • Virtual routers
  • Virtual firewall
  • Virtual vs. physical NICs
  • Software defined networking	

• Storage area network
  • iSCSI
  • Jumbo frame
  • Fibre Channel
  • Network attached storage
	Lesson 9, Topic B

• Cloud concepts
  • Public IaaS, SaaS, PaaS
  • Private IaaS, SaaS, PaaS
  • Hybrid IaaS, SaaS, PaaS
  • Community IaaS, SaaS, PaaS
	Lesson 9, Topic C

1.12 Given a set of requirements, implement a basic network	Lesson 2, Topic C; Lesson 3, Topic C
• List of requirements	
• Device types/requirements	Lesson 2, Topic C; Lesson 3, Topic C; Lesson 4, Topic D
• Environment limitations	Lesson 2, Topic C; Lesson 3, Topic C
• Equipment limitations	Lesson 2, Topic C; Lesson 3, Topic C; Lesson 4, Topic D
• Compatibility requirements	Lesson 2, Topic C; Lesson 3, Topic C; Lesson 4, Topic D
• Wired/wireless considerations	Lesson 2, Topic C; Lesson 3, Topic C
• Security considerations	Lesson 2, Topic C; Lesson 3, Topic C; Lesson 10, Topics A, B, C, D, E

Domain and Objective	Covered In
2.0 Network Operations	
2.1 Given a scenario, use appropriate monitoring tools	Lesson 5, Topic A; Lesson 14, Topic A; Lesson 15, Topic C
• Packet/network analyzer	
• Interface monitoring tools	Lesson 14, Topic A

Domain and Objective	Covered In
• Port scanner	Lesson 11, Topic E
• Top talkers/listeners	Lesson 14, Topic A
• SNMP management software	Lesson 14, Topic A
• Trap	
• Get	
• Walk	
• MIBS	
• Alerts	Lesson 1, Topic E; Lesson 14, Topic A
• Email	
• SMS	
• Packet flow monitoring	Lesson 14, Topic A
• SYSLOG	Lesson 14, Topic A
• SIEM	Lesson 14, Topic A
• Environmental monitoring tools	Lesson 15, Topic C
• Temperature	
• Humidity	
• Power monitoring tools	Lesson 14, Topic A
• Wireless survey tools	Lesson 14, Topic A
• Wireless analyzers	Lesson 14, Topic A
2.2 Given a scenario, analyze metrics and reports from monitoring and tracking performance tools	Lesson 14, Topic B
• Baseline	
• Bottleneck	Lesson 14, Topic B
• Log management	Lesson 14, Topic A
• Graphing	Lesson 14, Topic B
• Utilization	Lesson 14, Topic A
• Bandwidth	
• Storage	
• Network device CPU	
• Network device memory	
• Wireless channel utilization	
• Link status	Lesson 14, Topic A

Domain and Objective	Covered In
• Interface monitoring	Lesson 14, Topic A
• Errors	
• Utilization	
• Discards	
• Packet drops	
• Interface resets	
• Speed and duplex	
2.3 Given a scenario, use appropriate resources to support configuration management	Lesson 14, Topics A and B; Appendix B, Topic B
• Archives/backups	
• Baselines	Lesson 14, Topic B
• On-boarding and off-boarding of mobile devices	Lesson 14, Topic B
• NAC	Lesson 11, Topic A
• Documentation	Lesson 14, Topic B
• Network diagrams (logical/physical)	
• Asset management	
• IP address utilization	
• Vendor documentation	
• Internal operating procedures/policies/ standards	
2.4 Explain the importance of implementing network segmentation	Lesson 10, Topic A
• SCADA systems/Industrial control systems	
• Legacy systems	Lesson 10, Topic A
• Separate private/public networks	Lesson 10, Topic A
• Honeypot/honeynet	Lesson 10, Topic A
• Testing lab	Lesson 10, Topic A
• Load balancing	Lesson 10, Topic A
• Performance optimization	Lesson 10, Topic A; Lesson 14, Topic C
• Security	Lesson 10, Topic A
• Compliance	Lesson 10, Topic A
2.5 Given a scenario, install and apply patches and updates	Lesson 11, Topic D
• OS updates	
• Firmware updates	Lesson 11, Topic D
• Driver updates	Lesson 11, Topic D
• Feature changes/updates	Lesson 11, Topic D

Domain and Objective	Covered In
• Major vs. minor updates	Lesson 11, Topic D
• Vulnerability patches	Lesson 11, Topic D
• Upgrading vs. downgrading	Lesson 11, Topic D
• Configuration backup	
2.6 Given a scenario, configure a switch using proper features	Lesson 4, Topic E
• VLAN	
• Native VLAN/Default VLAN	
• VTP	
• Spanning tree (802.1d)/rapid spanning tree (802.1w)	Lesson 4, Topic D
• Flooding	
• Forwarding/blocking	
• Filtering	
• Interface configuration	Lesson 4, Topics D and E
• Trunking/802.1q	
• Tag vs. untag VLANs	
• Port bonding (LACP)	
• Port mirroring (local vs. remote)	
• Speed and duplexing	
• IP address assignment	
• VLAN assignment	
• Default gateway	Lesson 4, Topic D; Lesson 5, Topic C
• PoE and PoE+ (802.3af, 802.3at)	Lesson 4, Topic C
• Switch management	Lesson 4, Topic D
• User/passwords	
• AAA configuration	
• Console	
• Virtual terminals	
• In-band/Out-of-band management	
• Managed vs. unmanaged	Lesson 4, Topic D
2.7 Install and configure wireless LAN infrastructure and implement the appropriate technologies in support of wireless capable devices	Lesson 3, Topic B
• Small office/home office wireless router	
• Wireless access points	Lesson 3, Topics A and B; Lesson 4, Topic E
• Device density	
• Roaming	
• Wireless controllers (VLAN pooling, LWAPP)	

Domain and Objective	Covered In
• Wireless bridge	Lesson 3, Topic B
• Site surveys	Lesson 3, Topic C; Lesson 14, Topic A
• Heat maps	
• Frequencies	Lesson 3, Topic A
• 2.4 GHz	
• 5.0 GHz	
• Channels	Lesson 3, Topic A
• Goodput	Lesson 3, Topic C
• Connection types	Lesson 3, Topic A
• 802.11a-ht	
• 802.11g-ht	
• Antenna placement	Lesson 3, Topic B
• Antenna types	Lesson 3, Topic B
• Omnidirectional	
• Unidirectional	
• MIMO/MUMIMO	Lesson 3, Topic A
• Signal strength	Lesson 3, Topic B
• Coverage	
• Differences between device antennas	
• SSID broadcast	Lesson 3, Topic C
• Topologies	Lesson 3, Topic C
• Ad hoc	
• Mesh	
• Infrastructure	
• Mobile devices	Lesson 3, Topic C
• Cell phones	
• Laptops	
• Tablets	
• Gaming devices	
• Media devices	

Domain and Objective	Covered In
3.0 Network Security	
3.1 Compare and contrast risk related concepts	Lesson 10, Topic A
• Disaster recovery	
• Business continuity	Lesson 10, Topic A
• Battery backups/UPS	Lesson 11, Topic A

Domain and Objective	Covered In
• First responders	Lesson 12, Topic A
• Data breach	Lesson 10, Topic A
• End user awareness and training	Lesson 11, Topic F
• Single point of failure	Lesson 10, Topic A
• Critical nodes	
• Critical assets	
• Redundancy	
• Adherence to standards and policies	Lesson 10, Topic A
• Vulnerability scanning	Lesson 10, Topic B
• Penetration testing	Lesson 11, Topic E
3.2 Compare and contrast common network vulnerabilities and threats	Lesson 10, Topic C
• Attacks/threats: Denial of service	
• Distributed DoS (Botnet, Traffic spike, Coordinated attack)	
• Reflective/amplified (DNS, NTP, Smurfing)	
• Friendly/unintentional DoS	
• Physical attack (Permanent DoS)	
• Attacks/threats: ARP cache poisoning	Lesson 10, Topic C
• Attacks/threats: Packet/protocol abuse	Lesson 10, Topic C
• Attacks/threats: Spoofing	Lesson 10, Topic C
• Attacks/threats: Wireless	Lesson 10, Topic C
• Evil twin	
• Rogue AP	
• War driving	
• War chalking	
• Bluejacking	
• Bluesnarfing	
• WPA/WEP/WPS attacks	
• Attacks/threats: Brute force	Lesson 10, Topic C
• Attacks/threats: Session hijacking	Lesson 10, Topic C
• Attacks/threats: Social engineering	Lesson 10, Topic C
• Attacks/threats: Man-in-the-middle	Lesson 10, Topic C
• Attacks/threats: VLAN hopping	Lesson 10, Topic C
• Attacks/threats: Compromised system	Lesson 10, Topic C
• Attacks/threats: Effect of malware on the network	Lesson 10, Topic C

Domain and Objective	Covered In
• Attacks/threats: Insider threat/malicious employee	Lesson 10, Topic C
• Attacks/threats: Zero day attacks	Lesson 10, Topic C
• Vulnerabilities: Unnecessary running services	Lesson 10, Topic B
• Vulnerabilities: Open ports	Lesson 10, Topic B
• Vulnerabilities: Unpatched/legacy systems	Lesson 10, Topic B
• Vulnerabilities: Unencrypted channels	Lesson 10, Topic B
• Vulnerabilities: Clear text credentials	Lesson 10, Topic B
• Vulnerabilities: Unsecure protocols	Lesson 10, Topic B

- TELNET
- HTTP
- SLIP
- FTP
- TFTP
- SNMPv1 and SNMPv2

• Vulnerabilities: TEMPEST/RF emanation	Lesson 10, Topic B
3.3 Given a scenario, implement network hardening techniques	Lesson 11, Topic D
• Anti-malware software	

- Host-based
- Cloud/server-based
- Network-based

• Switch port security	Lesson 11, Topic D

- DHCP snooping
- ARP inspection
- MAC address filtering
- VLAN assignments (Network segmentation)

• Security policies	Lesson 10, Topic A
• Disable unneeded network services	Lesson 10, Topic B
• Use secure protocols	Lesson 11, Topic D

- SSH
- SNMPv3
- TLS/SSL
- SFTP
- HTTPS
- IPSec

Domain and Objective	Covered In
• Access lists	Lesson 11, Topics C and D

• Web/content filtering
   • Port filtering
   • IP filtering
   • Implicit deny	

• Wireless security	Lesson 10, Topics D and E; Lesson 11, Topic D

• WEP
   • WPA/WPA2 (Enterprise, Personal)
   • TKIP/AES
   • 802.1x
   • TLS/TTLS
   • MAC filtering	

• User authentication	Lesson 10, Topic D; Lesson 13, Topics B and D

• CHAP/MSCHAP
   • PAP
   • EAP
   • Kerberos
   • Multifactor authentication
   • Two-factor authentication
   • Single sign-on	

• Hashes	Lesson 10, Topic E; Lesson 13, Topic D
• MD5 • SHA	
3.4 Compare and contrast physical security controls	Lesson 11, Topic A
• Mantraps	
• Network closets	Lesson 11, Topic A
• Video monitoring	Lesson 11, Topic A
• IP cameras/CCTVs	
• Door access controls	Lesson 11, Topic A
• Proximity readers/key fob	Lesson 11, Topic A
• Biometrics	Lesson 11, Topic A
• Keypad/cipher locks	Lesson 11, Topic A
• Security guard	Lesson 11, Topic A

Domain and Objective	Covered In
3.5 Given a scenario, install and configure a basic firewall	Lesson 11, Topic C
• Types of firewalls	
• Host-based	
• Network-based	
• Software vs. hardware	
• Application aware/context aware	
• Small office/home office firewall	
• Stateful vs. stateless inspection	
• UTM	
• Settings/techniques	Lesson 11, Topics B and C
• ACL	
• Virtual wire vs. routed	
• DMZ	
• Implicit deny	
• Block/allow (Outbound traffic, Inbound traffic)	
• Firewall placement (Internal/external)	
3.6 Explain the purpose of various network access control models	Lesson 11, Topic B
• 802.1x	
• Posture assessment	Lesson 11, Topic B
• Guest network	Lesson 11, Topic B
• Persistent vs. non-persistent agents	Lesson 11, Topic B
• Quarantine network	Lesson 11, Topic B
• Edge vs. access control	Lesson 11, Topic B
3.7 Summarize basic forensic concepts	Lesson 12, Topic B
• First responder	
• Secure the area (Escalate when necessary)	Lesson 12, Topic B
• Document the scene	Lesson 12, Topic B
• eDiscovery	Lesson 12, Topic B
• Evidence/data collection	Lesson 12, Topic B
• Chain of custody	Lesson 12, Topic B
• Data transport	Lesson 12, Topic B
• Forensics report	Lesson 12, Topic B
• Legal hold	Lesson 12, Topic B

Domain and Objective	Covered In
4.0 Troubleshooting	
4.1 Given a scenario, implement the following network troubleshooting methodology	Lesson 15, Topic A

- Identify the problem
  - Gather information
  - Duplicate the problem, if possible
  - Question users
  - Identify symptoms
  - Determine if anything has changed
  - Approach multiple problems individually

• Establish a theory of probable cause	Lesson 15, Topic A

- Question the obvious
- Consider multiple approaches (Top-to-bottom/bottom-to-top OSI model, Divide and conquer)

• Test the theory to determine cause	Lesson 15, Topic A

- Once theory is confirmed, determine next steps to resolve problem
- If theory is not confirmed, re-establish new theory or escalate

• Establish a plan of action to resolve the problem and identify potential effects	Lesson 15, Topic A
• Implement the solution or escalate as necessary	Lesson 15, Topic A
• Verify full system functionality and if applicable implement preventative measures	Lesson 15, Topic A
• Document findings, actions, and outcomes	Lesson 15, Topic A
4.2 Given a scenario, analyze and interpret the output of troubleshooting tools	Lesson 7, Topic C; Lesson 15, Topic B

- Command line tools
  - ipconfig
  - netstat
  - ifconfig
  - ping/ping6/ping -6
  - tracert/tracert -6/traceroute6/traceroute -6
  - nbtstat
  - nslookup
  - arp
  - mac address lookup table
  - pathping

• Line testers	Lesson 15, Topic C
• Certifiers	Lesson 15, Topic C

Domain and Objective	Covered In
• Multimeter	Lesson 15, Topic C
• Cable tester	Lesson 15, Topic C
• Light meter	Lesson 15, Topic C
• Toner probe	Lesson 15, Topic C
• Speed test sites	Lesson 15, Topic B
• Looking glass sites	Lesson 15, Topic B
• Wi-Fi analyzer	Lesson 15, Topic C
• Protocol analyzer	Lesson 14, Topic A; Lesson 15, Topic C
4.3 Given a scenario, troubleshoot and resolve common wireless issues	Lesson 15, Topic D
• Signal loss	
• Interference	Lesson 15, Topic D
• Overlapping channels	Lesson 15, Topic D
• Mismatched channels	
• Signal-to-noise ratio	Lesson 14, Topic A; Lesson 15, Topic D
• Device saturation	Lesson 15, Topic D
• Bandwidth saturation	Lesson 15, Topic D
• Untested updates	Lesson 15, Topic D
• Wrong SSID	Lesson 15, Topic D
• Power levels	Lesson 15, Topic D
• Open networks	Lesson 15, Topic D
• Rogue access point	Lesson 10, Topic C; Lesson 15, Topic D
• Wrong antenna type	Lesson 15, Topic D
• Incompatibilities	Lesson 15, Topic D
• Wrong encryption	Lesson 15, Topic D
• Bounce	Lesson 15, Topic D
• MIMO	Lesson 15, Topic D
• AP placement	Lesson 15, Topic D
• AP configurations	Lesson 15, Topic D
• LWAPP	
• Thin vs. thick	

Domain and Objective	Covered In

• Environmental factors
   • Concrete walls
   • Window film
   • Metal studs
	Lesson 15, Topic D

• Wireless standard related issues
   • Throughput
   • Frequency
   • Distance
   • Channels
	Lesson 15, Topic D

4.4 Given a scenario, troubleshoot and resolve common copper cable issues	Lesson 15, Topic D
• Shorts	
• Opens	Lesson 15, Topic D

• Incorrect termination (mismatched standards)
   • Straight-through
   • Crossover
	Lesson 15, Topic D

• Cross-talk
   • Near end
   • Far end
	Lesson 15, Topic D

• EMI/RFI	Lesson 15, Topic D
• Distance limitations	Lesson 15, Topic D
• Attenuation/Db loss	Lesson 15, Topic D
• Bad connector	Lesson 15, Topic D
• Bad wiring	Lesson 15, Topic D
• Split pairs	Lesson 15, Topic D
• Tx/Rx reverse	Lesson 15, Topic D
• Cable placement	Lesson 15, Topic D
• Bad SFP/GBIC - cable or transceiver	Lesson 15, Topic D
4.5 Given a scenario, troubleshoot and resolve common fiber cable issues	Lesson 15, Topic D
• Attenuation/Db loss	
• SFP/GBIC - cable mismatch	Lesson 15, Topic D
• Bad SFP/GBIC - cable or transceiver	Lesson 15, Topic D
• Wavelength mismatch	Lesson 15, Topic D
• Fiber type mismatch	Lesson 15, Topic D
• Dirty connectors	Lesson 15, Topic D

Domain and Objective	Covered In
• Connector mismatch	Lesson 15, Topic D
• Bend radius limitations	Lesson 15, Topic D
• Distance limitations	Lesson 15, Topic D
4.6 Given a scenario, troubleshoot and resolve common network issues	Lesson 15, Topic D
• Incorrect IP configuration/default gateway	
• Broadcast storms/switching loop	Lesson 15, Topic D
• Duplicate IP	Lesson 15, Topic D
• Speed and duplex mismatch	Lesson 15, Topic D
• End-to-end connectivity	Lesson 15, Topic C
• Incorrect VLAN assignment	Lesson 15, Topic D
• Hardware failure	Lesson 15, Topic D
• Misconfigured DHCP	Lesson 15, Topic D
• Misconfigured DNS	Lesson 15, Topic D
• Incorrect interface/interface misconfiguration	Lesson 15, Topic D
• Cable placement	Lesson 15, Topic D
• Interface errors	Lesson 15, Topic D
• Simultaneous wired/wireless connections	Lesson 15, Topic D
• Discovering neighboring devices/nodes	Lesson 15, Topic D
• Power failure/power anomalies	Lesson 15, Topic D
• MTU/MTU black hole	Lesson 15, Topic D
• Missing IP routes	Lesson 15, Topic D
• NIC teaming misconfiguration	Lesson 15, Topic D
• Active-active vs. active-passive	
• Multicast vs. broadcast	
4.7 Given a scenario, troubleshoot and resolve common security issues	Lesson 15, Topic E
• Misconfigured firewall	
• Misconfigured ACLs/applications	Lesson 15, Topic E
• Malware	Lesson 15, Topic F
• Denial of service	Lesson 15, Topic F
• Open/closed ports	Lesson 15, Topic E

Domain and Objective	Covered In
• ICMP related issues	Lesson 15, Topic F
• Ping of death	
• Unreachable default gateway	
• Unpatched firmware/OSs	Lesson 15, Topic D
• Malicious users	Lesson 15, Topic F
• Trusted	
• Untrusted users	
• Packet sniffing	
• Authentication issues	Lesson 15, Topic F
• TACACS/RADIUS misconfigurations	
• Default passwords/settings	
• Improper access/backdoor access	Lesson 15, Topic F
• ARP issues	Lesson 15, Topic F
• Banner grabbing/OUI	Lesson 15, Topic F
• Domain/local group configurations	Lesson 15, Topic E
• Jamming	Lesson 15, Topic F
4.8 Given a scenario, troubleshoot and resolve common WAN issues	Lesson 15, Topic D
• Loss of Internet connectivity	
• Interface errors	Lesson 15, Topic D
• Split horizon	Lesson 15, Topic D
• DNS issues	Lesson 15, Topic D
• Interference	Lesson 15, Topic D
• Router configurations	Lesson 15, Topic D
• Customer premise equipment	Lesson 15, Topics B, C, D
• Smart jack/NIU	
• Demarc	
• Loopback	
• CSU/DSU	
• Copper line drivers/repeaters	
• Company security policy	Lesson 15, Topic D
• Throttling	
• Blocking	
• Fair access policy/utilization limits	
• Satellite issues	Lesson 15, Topic D
• Latency	

Domain and Objective	Covered In
5.0 Industry Standards, Practices, and Network Theory	
5.1 Analyze a scenario and determine the corresponding OSI layer	Lesson 1, Topic B
• Layer 1 – Physical	
• Layer 2 – Data link	Lesson 1, Topic B
• Layer 3 – Network	Lesson 1, Topic B
• Layer 4 – Transport	Lesson 1, Topic B
• Layer 5 – Session	Lesson 1, Topic B
• Layer 6 – Presentation	Lesson 1, Topic B
• Layer 7 – Application	Lesson 1, Topic B
5.2 Explain the basics of network theory and concepts	Lesson 1, Topic B
• Encapsulation/de-encapsulation	
• Modulation techniques	Lesson 1, Topic E
• Multiplexing	
• De-multiplexing	
• Analog and digital techniques	
• TDM	
• Numbering systems	Lesson 1, Topic A; Lesson 5, Topic B
• Binary	
• Hexadecimal	
• Octal	
• Broadband/base band	Lesson 1, Topic E
• Bit rates vs. baud rate	Lesson 1, Topic E
• Sampling size	Lesson 14, Topic A
• CDMA/CD and CSMA/CA	Lesson 1, Topic E
• Carrier detect/sense	Lesson 4, Topic C
• Wavelength	Lesson 1, Topic E
• TCP/IP suite	Lesson 5, Topic A
• ICMP	
• UDP	
• TCP	
• Collision	Lesson 4, Topics A and D; Lesson 15, Topic D
5.3 Given a scenario, deploy the appropriate wireless standard	Lesson 3, Topic A
• 802.11a	

Domain and Objective	Covered In
• 802.11b	Lesson 3, Topic A
• 802.11g	Lesson 3, Topic A
• 802.11n	Lesson 3, Topic A
• 802.11ac	Lesson 3, Topic A
5.4 Given a scenario, deploy the appropriate wired connectivity standard	Lesson 2, Topic A; Lesson 4, Topic C
• Ethernet standards	
• 10BaseT	
• 100BaseT	
• 1000BaseT	
• 1000BaseTX	
• 10GBaseT	
• 100BaseFX	
• 10Base2	
• 10GBaseSR	
• 10GBaseER	
• 10GBaseSW	
• IEEE 1905-2013 (Ethernet over HDMI, Ethernet over power line)	
• Wiring standards	Lesson 2, Topic A
• EIA/TIA 568A/568B	
• Broadband standards	Lesson 1, Topic B
• DOCSIS	
5.5 Given a scenario, implement the appropriate policies or procedures	Lesson 10, Topic A
• Security policies	
• Consent to monitoring	
• Network policies	Lesson 14, Topic B
• Acceptable use policy	Lesson 10, Topic A
• Standard business documents	Lesson 14, Topic B
• SLA	
• MOU	
• MLA	
• SOW	
5.6 Summarize safety practices	Lesson 2, Topic D; Lesson 15, Topic C
• Electrical safety	
• Grounding	
• ESD	Lesson 15, Topic C
• Static	

Domain and Objective	Covered In
• Installation safety	Lesson 15, Topic C
• Lifting equipment	
• Rack installation	
• Placement	
• Tool safety	
• MSDS	Lesson 11, Topic A
• Emergency procedures	Lesson 11, Topic A
• Building layout	
• Fire escape plan	
• Safety/emergency exits	
• Fail open/fail close	
• Emergency alert system	
• Fire suppression systems	Lesson 11, Topic A
• HVAC	Lesson 11, Topic A
5.7 Given a scenario, install and configure equipment in the appropriate location using best practices	Lesson 2, Topic C
• Intermediate distribution frame	
• Main distribution frame	Lesson 2, Topic C
• Cable management	Lesson 2, Topic C
• Patch panels	
• Power management	Lesson 2, Topic C
• Power converters	
• Circuits	
• UPS	
• Inverters	
• Power redundancy	
• Device placement	Lesson 2, Topic C
• Air flow	Lesson 11, Topic A
• Cable trays	Lesson 2, Topic C
• Rack systems	Lesson 2, Topic C
• Server rail racks	
• Two-post racks	
• Four-post racks	
• Free-standing racks	

Domain and Objective	Covered In
• Labeling	Lesson 2, Topic C
• Port labeling	
• System labeling	
• Circuit labeling	
• Naming conventions	
• Patch panel labeling	
• Rack monitoring	Lesson 14, Topic A
• Rack security	Lesson 11, Topic A
5.8 Explain the basics of change management procedures	Lesson 14, Topic B
• Document reason for a change	
• Change request	Lesson 14, Topic B
• Configuration procedures	
• Rollback process	
• Potential impact	
• Notification	
• Approval process	Lesson 14, Topic B
• Maintenance window	Lesson 14, Topic B
• Authorized downtime	
• Notification of change	Lesson 14, Topic B
• Documentation	Lesson 14, Topic B
• Network configurations	
• Additions to network	
• Physical location changes	
5.9 Compare and contrast the following ports and protocols	Lesson 7, Topic A
• 80 HTTP	
• 443 HTTPS	Lesson 7, Topic A
• 137-139 NetBIOS	Lesson 7, Topic A
• 110 POP	Lesson 7, Topic A
• 143 IMAP	Lesson 7, Topic A
• 25 SMTP	Lesson 7, Topic A
• 5060/5061 SIP	Lesson 7, Topic A
• 2427/2727 MGCP	Lesson 7, Topic A
• 5004/5005 RTP	Lesson 7, Topic A
• 1720 H.323	Lesson 7, Topic A

Domain and Objective	Covered In
• TCP	Lesson 5, Topic A
• Connection-oriented	
• UDP	Lesson 5, Topic A
• Connectionless	
5.10 Given a scenario, configure and apply the appropriate ports and protocols	Lesson 7, Topic A
• 20, 21 FTP	
• 161 SNMP	Lesson 7, Topic A
• 22 SSH	Lesson 7, Topic A
• 23 Telnet	Lesson 7, Topic A
• 53 DNS	Lesson 7, Topic A
• 67, 68 DHCP	Lesson 7, Topic A
• 69 TFTP	Lesson 7, Topic A
• 445 SMB	Lesson 7, Topic A
• 3389 RDP	Lesson 7, Topic A

B | Network Fault Tolerance and Disaster Recovery

Appendix Introduction

Ensuring that data and other network resources are available to users is part of a network professional's responsibilities. This can be challenging when hardware fails or a natural disaster strikes. In this appendix, you will describe concepts related to network fault tolerance.

TOPIC A

Plan for Fault Tolerance

The first step in ensuring the availability of network data and resources is to create a plan of action to follow. In this topic, you will plan for fault tolerance.

RAID

The *Redundant Array of Independent Disks (RAID)* standards are a set of vendor-independent specifications for fault-tolerant configurations on multiple-disk devices. If one or more of the disks fails, data can be recovered from the remaining disks. In RAID, the central control unit provides additional functionality so that the individual disks can be utilized to achieve higher fault tolerance and performance. The disks appear as a single storage unit to the devices to which they are connected.

 Note: The original RAID specifications were titled Redundant Array of Inexpensive Disks. As the disk cost of RAID implementations has become less of a factor, the term "Independent" disks has been widely adopted instead.

A disk system consists of physical storage disks kept side-by-side. It has a central unit that manages all the input and output and simplifies the integration with other devices such as other disk systems and servers. Disk systems are usually used for online storage due to their superior performance.

Non-RAID Disk Fault-Tolerance Features

RAID systems are the primary means of providing disk fault tolerance. There are other fault-tolerance methods that you might encounter on your network.

Fault-Tolerance Method	Description
Sector sparing	After a block of data is written to a hard disk or database, it is read back from the destination and compared to the original data in memory. If, after several attempts, data read from the destination does not match the data in memory, the software stores the data in a block in a temporary area, marks the bad area so that it will not be used again, and attempts to write the data to a new location.
Read-after-write verification	Media that connects devices to a network and transmits data between the devices.
TTSs	Transaction Tracking Systems (TTSs) monitor write and change processes that occur in a system to ensure successful completion, providing the ability to back out of transactions, such as changes in a database file, that have been interrupted by the failure of a component.
	For example, in a banking system, if power is interrupted after funds are deducted from a customer's savings account but before they are credited to the customer's checking account, the system will roll back the transaction to the original savings account balance.

Link Redundancy

Link redundancy is a network fault-tolerance method that provides alternative connections that can function even if a critical primary connection is interrupted. The duplicate link can be fully redundant and provide the same level of performance, service, and bandwidth as the primary link. Alternatively, the redundant link can be a broadband connection to provide basic connectivity until the main link is restored.

For a small office, a fully fault-tolerant network might be too expensive, but a backup dial-in connection might be a reasonable and cost-effective precaution. Some broadband routers include a serial port where you can attach an external modem so that you can create a dial-up connection when a DSL or cable connection fails.

Not all network links must be made redundant. Each company must evaluate how critical each of its LAN and WAN links is to ongoing operations, and weigh the impact of losing connectivity for a given period of time against the cost of maintaining a redundant link.

 Access the Checklist tile on your LogicalCHOICE course screen for reference information and job aids on How to Create an Enterprise Fault Tolerance Plan.

TOPIC B

Prepare for Disaster Recovery

In the last topic, you planned for fault tolerance. With this plan in place, you are prepared to deal with hardware issues as they arise. Next, you'll need to plan for handling catastrophes. In this topic, you will prepare for disaster recovery.

Disaster Recovery Plans

A *disaster recovery plan* is a policy and set of procedures that document how people and resources will be protected in case of disaster, and how the organization will recover from the disaster and restore normal functioning. The plan should be developed and implemented cooperatively among and between different functional groups.

The disaster recovery plan incorporates many components, including:

- A complete list of responsible individuals
- A critical hardware and software inventory
- Detailed instructions on how to reconstruct the network

 Note: A complete disaster recovery plan will be highly detailed and completely customized to suit the needs and circumstances of a particular organization. This section provides only a broad overview of the components and considerations involved in constructing a recovery plan.

The network administrator has the biggest responsibility for drafting, testing, and documenting the plan. Corporate managers and administrators should contribute to the plan and should fully understand their role in implementing the plan, if needed. Vendors and regular contractors should understand their responsibilities and what service levels they will guarantee.

Network Reconstruction Plans

A network reconstruction plan provides the steps to rebuild the network.

Plan Component	Description
Network documentation	Physical and logical network diagrams will enable networking staff to begin to reconstruct the network with minimal downtime. An administrator's access credentials need to be documented so that the network is accessible after the restore. Decryption or recovery agents and digital certificates need to be documented as well. In addition, critical hardware and software inventory documentation will aid in ensuring that you have all the documentation and information needed to rebuild the network.
Fall-back plan	A *fall-back plan* is an alternate design that can be implemented temporarily to enable critical network elements to function. It should include a list of minimum required hardware and software as well as implementation instructions.
Data restoration plan	A data restoration plan details exactly how to retrieve and restore data backups in the correct sequence.

Many administrators have the valid concern that writing down security information, such as administrative and service account passwords, provides opportunities for security breaches. However, a network is useless when restored if there is no administrative access. The security information must be in the recovery documentation, but it can be stored securely and accessed separately by the appropriate individuals; it certainly should not be distributed to everyone working on or reviewing the plan.

Network Reconstruction Plan Maintenance

A network is a living entity—most organizations do not maintain the status quo. A disaster recovery plan needs to reflect changes to the organization. You should formally review the disaster recovery plan at least twice a year, and informally review it quarterly. A formal review should include business managers, the CIO, corporate staff, and IT managers. A formal review makes many employees, including corporate personnel, aware of the review. An informal review can be done by the appropriate administrator and his or her staff. During a review, check administrative passwords, recovery agents, and changes to the backup scheme. Review time is also a good time to train new IT personnel on the recovery plan.

Once the plan has been reviewed and accepted, it needs to be distributed to the appropriate people. To ensure that you can access the plan in the event of an actual disaster, at least one copy must be stored offsite in a secure but known location, such as a remote corporate office. If your company uses an offsite data storage location, keep copies there. If your company uses an offsite storage/ management company, keep copies on file with them. Key managers might also want to keep copies of the plan at their homes.

Hot, Warm, and Cold Sites

Backup site locations and replacement equipment can be classified as hot, warm, or cold, depending on how much configuration would be necessary to bring the location or spare equipment online.

- A *hot site* is a fully configured alternate network that can be online quickly after a disaster.
- A *warm site* is a business site that performs noncritical functions under normal conditions, but which can be rapidly converted to a key operations site if needed.
- A *cold site* is a predetermined alternate location where a network can be rebuilt in case of a disaster.

A *hot spare* is a fully configured and operational piece of backup equipment that can be swapped into a system with little to no interruption in functionality. A *cold spare* is a duplicate piece of backup equipment that can be configured to use as an alternate if needed.

UPS

An *Uninterruptible Power Supply (UPS)* is a device that provides backup power when the electrical power fails or drops to an unacceptable voltage level. This helps reduce or eliminate data loss and limit or prevent hardware damage during power surges or brownouts. UPSs can be online or offline models.

With an online UPS, power always flows through the UPS to the devices connected to it. Because it is always actively monitoring power, it provides an added benefit by functioning as a line conditioner, reducing or eliminating surges and brownouts to the attached equipment. Online UPS systems tend to be more expensive than offline systems.

With an offline UPS, the UPS monitors power and activates only when there is a drop, so there is a very slight delay before the UPS becomes active. However, system power is not usually lost because the delay is so short. Some operating systems provide UPS monitoring so that users can be alerted to log off and the operating system can be shut down properly if there is a power outage.

Specialized Data Backups

Certain data types may require specialized procedures or additional software components to perform a successful backup.

Specialized Backup Type	Description
Databases	Databases are essentially big, open files. Some backup software handles simple databases with nothing more than an open files agent. However, larger databases have special considerations. In a database, the actual data on the drive might not be current because of write-behind caching, a technique that temporarily stores database changes in server memory while the server is busy. Sometimes, database logs need to be reset when a database is backed up. Log files are often stored on a different drive than the database itself. These databases may require either a manual backup procedure to close open files and clear logs, or the use of a database agent, which can back up the database and reset the logs while the database is online.
Email	Email servers are essentially modified database servers that store users' mailboxes. Data is still in a database data store, which means that the email server can be backed up just like a database server. In fact, a standard backup and restore of a mail server contains all the same elements that backing up a database does. When a mail server is backed up, like a database, one restore option is to restore all the data and then extract the damaged mailbox.
	There is another type of mail server backup called the brick-level backup, which uses a special agent that is aware of the database's data structure. Brick-level backups enable a database to be backed up mailbox by mailbox, which takes longer, and then restored one mailbox at a time. Some agents even enable the mail to be restored message by message.
Power user workstations	Some power users on your network might have sensitive data on their personal workstations that you would choose to include in a backup plan. Workstations are easy to back up when they have an agent installed that enables backup software to access them. However, they have to be powered on to be backed up. This used to be a problem, but today most network cards and PCs support a technology called Wake on LAN (WOL), in which backup software sends a signal to the workstation (awakens it), waits for it to boot up, backs it up, and then turns it off again.
Remote network backups	When remote users are on the network, they are backed up the same way that workstations are. However, when they are primarily offline, backups require a different solution. Many backup software manufacturers use a remote agent to back up remote users when the users connect to the network. The agent copies changed data from the laptop to a network drive.
	This is always a partial backup, so it is faster than copying all the data off the laptop. But how do you back up remote users if they are not connected to the network? Some backup software uses over-the-web backups. The process is the same as already described except that the user attaches to a secure website and uploads data.
Enterprise backups	Many companies have moved to an enterprise-wide solution for data backups. A high-performance backup solution is deployed from a central location and all backup data is stored in the central location. Many of these solutions cross manufacturers' boundaries, enabling one setup to get backups from PC servers, UNIX® mainframes, mid-range servers, and workstations, regardless of manufacturer and operating system.

Specialized Backup Type	Description
Snapshot backups	Snapshots can be used to take complete backups of drives and databases, as well as to copy open files. There are a number of different snapshot technologies that are implemented in software, in hardware, or in combinations of the two. Depending on the technology in use, snapshots might clone an entire copy of a volume to another physical drive, or they might record only file changes or only pointers to file locations. See your storage or backup vendors for specifics on the snapshot backup implementation they offer.

Offline Files

Windows® 8, Windows Server® 2012, and various other operating systems support offline files, which can serve as a backup method for remote users. The offline files process synchronizes a copy of a file on the network with a copy of the same file on a remote computer or a website. This enables other users to access and use the network copy of the file at the same time that the remote user edits the remote copy. Any changes to the file are synchronized with the remote user's copy whenever the remote user connects to the network.

Types of Distributed Storage Systems

Many systems include built-in support for distributed storage, and there are also third-party implementations for both software and hardware that you can purchase if you need improved performance.

For example, Microsoft's Distributed File System (DFS) is a software-based distributed hierarchical storage implementation that was built into Windows Server 2008 R2 and into other Windows server software. It provides users with a simple and convenient way to access shared folders that are distributed throughout the network. With DFS, administration can make files that are distributed across multiple servers appear to users as if they all reside in a single location on the network. DFS comprises three main components. The first is the DFS root, which is a visible network share that contains folders and files. The DFS link resides below the root and it redirects the user to a share that exists somewhere on the network. The DFS target (or replica) allows you to group two identical shares, usually stored on different servers, as DFS targets under the same link.

Backup Policies

Each organization will need to maintain a backup policy that documents its own backup requirements, procedures, and systems. The policy should include specifications for all the components of the backup plan, including the backup software, hardware, media, schedule, and testing plans, as well as designating administrative responsibility for the system.

When you devise a backup policy and implement a backup system, you should consider these factors:

- Hardware and media: What is appropriate for your environment? How do you balance cost against performance?
- Software: Can you use the utilities built into your operating system, or will you need a dedicated third-party backup application?
- Backup administration: Who is responsible for performing backup functions?
- Backup frequency: How much data you can afford to lose determines how often you will back up.
- Backup methods: Which of several backup media-rotation schemes is appropriate for your organization?
- Backup types: Which of several schemes will you use for backing up new and existing data efficiently? What is the balance between partial and complete backups?

- Backup set: How many tapes or other media will you need for each backup?
- Backup scheduling: What time of day and when during the week will you run the backups? Will users be logged on? Will files be open?
- Media identification: What are the standards for labeling backup media?
- Media storage: Where will backup media be kept? Onsite or offsite, or in multiple locations?
- Recovery testing: When and how will you perform test restorations of data? Who is responsible?
- Maintenance: What scheduled maintenance or replacement is required for the hardware, software, and media? When will this be performed? How will you budget for it?
- Restoration timeline: Do you have a complete plan for recovering all lost data? How long is recovery expected to take?

C | Planning and Implementing a SOHO Network

Appendix Introduction

Just as you design a large network, you need to be able to design smaller SOHO networks that suit the physical boundaries of a smaller location. By being aware of the best practices for setting up a small network, you will be able to accurately identify the requirements and resources that match the location.

TOPIC A

Introduce a SOHO Network

In this topic, you'll learn how to plan and implement a SOHO network.

SOHO Networks

A *small office/home office (SOHO)* network is a small network that can be composed of up to 10 nodes. SOHO networks can either be wired or wireless. It is necessary that all the computers in a SOHO network be present at the same physical location. A SOHO can include devices such as switches or routers.

 Note: The upper limit of 10 nodes is the generally accepted limit, but you might encounter SOHO networks that include more than 10 nodes.

 Note: Small office/home office is sometimes referred to as single office/home office.

SOHO Network Hardware

The list of device types and other requirements to implement a SOHO network is:

- Computers and laptops: About 1 to 10 computing devices that are to be connected on the network.
- Specialized connectivity devices: SOHO hubs, switches, and routers.
- Peripheral devices: Printers, fax machines, access points, and biometric devices can also be added to the network.
- Multipurpose network devices such as WAPs, firewalls, routers, and the like.
- Modem: An ADSL modem to connect to the Internet.

Routing in a SOHO network does not require the same type of routing hardware as large networks and the Internet. There are several popular, relatively inexpensive, and easy to implement router products that are designed to support both wired and wireless SOHO networks, available from D-Link, Linksys, and NETGEAR.

Wired and Wireless Considerations

SOHO networks can be built using wired or wireless technology, or a combination of the two. Wired and wireless have their advantages and both represent viable options for a SOHO network.

Wired	Wireless

Installation

Ethernet cables need to be run to each computer and to the central device. The cables will need to be tucked away from foot traffic areas, or run under the floor or through walls, which can be difficult and time consuming. Some homes and offices are pre-wired with CAT5 cable, greatly simplifying the cabling process.

The cabling configuration will vary depending on the type of Internet connection, the different devices on the network, and if internal or external modems are used. Regardless of these options, the setup should not be very difficult.

After hardware installation, the steps to configure either a wired or wireless LAN will not differ much.

Installation

WLANs require an access point that must be installed in a central location where wireless radio signals can reach it with minimal interference. Each device that will connect wirelessly requires a wireless network adapter.

Performance

Wired LANs offer superior performance over wireless LANs. Ethernet connections have a higher maximum bandwidth than wireless and are sufficient for file sharing, gaming, and high-speed Internet access. Wired LANs using hubs can suffer performance slowdown if devices heavily use the network simultaneously. Using Ethernet switches instead of hubs can help avoid this problem.

Performance

Wireless LANs have a lower maximum bandwidth than wired LANs. Wi-Fi performance will also degrade on devices that are farther away from the access point. As more wireless devices use the WLAN more heavily, performance degrades even further.

Reliability

Ethernet cables, hubs, and switches are extremely reliable. Loose cables can be a source of failure in a wired network. When installing a wired LAN or moving any devices later, be sure to check the cable connections and ensure they are not loose.

Reliability

Some wireless signals are subject to interference from other appliances such as cordless telephones and garage door openers. This interference can be minimized with proper planning.

Security

Firewalls are the primary security consideration for any wired LAN connected to the Internet. A hardware or software firewall can be used to help secure the connection to the Internet. Some routers have built-in firewalls or you can purchase a separate hardware firewall device. Otherwise, software firewalls can be installed and/or configured on the computers themselves.

Security

In addition to the security concerns shared with a wired LAN, WLANs also have communication signals that travel through the air that can be intercepted. WLANs should be configured to protect their signals by enabling encryption.

Limitations of a SOHO Network

There are some environment limitations in setting up a SOHO network. All the computing devices and peripheral devices should be spread over a short range, as long-distance networking is not supported.

A SOHO setup has some equipment limitations and is recommended for a maximum of 10 devices that include workstations and other computing devices, printers, and fax machines with one hub, switch, or router. SOHO networks cannot support more devices. Segmentation of the network is also not possible.

As SOHO is intended for smaller networks or domestic purposes, multiple devices and technologies such as switches, routers, VLANs, and VPNs are not recommended. Switches and routers designed for medium-sized or larger networks are expensive to be used in SOHO environments.

Guidelines for Planning a SOHO Network

SOHO networks require meticulous planning to set up. Planning a SOHO network is not the same as planning a regular enterprise network. There are specific requirements that need to be met to successfully set up a SOHO network. To plan a SOHO network:

- Identify up to 10 devices to be included in the SOHO network.
- Connect up to 10 devices in the SOHO network.
- Ensure that the access points are distributed strategically to maintain seamless connectivity, if your SOHO network is implemented using wireless technology.
- Use routers and switches that can scale up, to handle the data transmission requirements of the devices on the network. Personal-use routers and switches may not support a SOHO.
- Plan the connectivity and placement of other devices such as printers and fax machines if needed on your network.
- Conceal the cabling to avoid disruption or outages on wired SOHOs.

 Access the Checklist tile on your LogicalCHOICE course screen for reference information and job aids on How to Implement a SOHO Network.

D | Legend for Icons Used in Network+ Figures

The following table describes some of the icons used in the figures throughout this course.

Device	Icon
Cell phone	

Device	Icon
Mainframe computer	
Modem	
Multiplexer	
Rack server	

Device	Icon
Router	
Switch	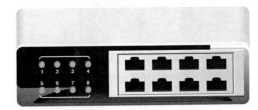
Tablet	
VPN concentrator	

Device	Icon
WAP	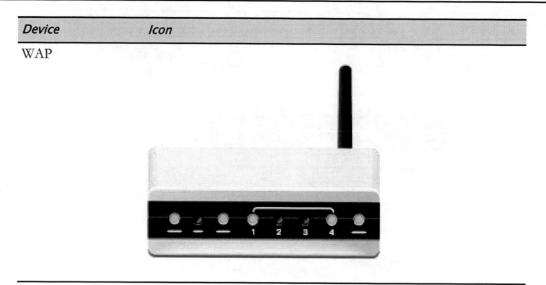

Solutions

ACTIVITY 1–1: Defining Networking Terminology

1. What is a network device that shares resources with and responds to requests from other devices called?
   - ○ Client
   - ◉ Server
   - ○ Terminal
   - ○ Mainframe

2. What is a network device that transmits data a user enters to a mainframe for processing and displays the results?
   - ○ Server
   - ○ Mainframe
   - ◉ Terminal
   - ○ Client

3. What is a device that acts as both a server and a client?
   - ○ Mainframe
   - ○ Client
   - ○ Server
   - ◉ Peer

4. True or False? A mainframe computer transmits data to another device for processing and displays the result to a user.
   - ☐ True
   - ☑ False

5. In which type of network are multiple switches connected by a single backbone cable?
   - ○ Distributed
   - ◉ Serial
   - ○ Collapsed
   - ○ Parallel

ACTIVITY 1-2: Identifying the Layers in the OSI Model

1. What layer transmits bits from one device to another and regulates the transmission stream over a medium?
   - ⊙ Physical
   - ○ Network
   - ○ Transport
   - ○ Data Link

2. In which layer do programs on a network node access network services?
   - ○ Data Link
   - ○ Physical
   - ⊙ Application
   - ○ Presentation
   - ○ Session

3. Which OSI layer is responsible for establishing connections between two devices?
   - ⊙ Transport
   - ○ Presentation
   - ○ Application
   - ○ Physical
   - ○ Data Link

4. Which layer packages bits of data from the Physical layer into frames, transfers them from one device to another, and receives acknowledgment from the addressed device?
   - ○ Presentation
   - ○ Session
   - ○ Transport
   - ⊙ Data Link
   - ○ Application

ACTIVITY 1-3: Identifying Network Types

1. Greene City Interiors has a remote office that accesses its corporate office with relatively high bandwidth. Which network category does it use?
   - ○ LAN
   - ⊙ WAN
   - ○ CAN
   - ○ MAN

2. The Greene City Interiors headquarters occupies four floors in their building. What category does this network fit into?

   - ◉ LAN
   - ○ WAN
   - ○ CAN
   - ○ MAN

3. This figure represents the Greene City Interiors company with a central office, an attached warehouse, and a remote supplier. Which portions of the network are LANs?

   - ☑ Section A—Greene City Headquarters and Greene City Warehouse
   - ☐ Section B—Greene City Warehouse and Wethersfield Supplier
   - ☑ Section C—Greene City Headquarters

4. This figure represents the Greene City Interiors company with a central office, an attached warehouse, and a remote sales office. Which portion of the network is a WAN?

   - ○ Section A—Greene City Headquarters
   - ○ Section B—Greene City Headquarters and Greene City Warehouse
   - ◉ Section C—Greene City Warehouse and Plainstown Sales Office

5. Which network type employs elements of both LANs and WANs?

   - ○ MAN
   - ○ WAN
   - ○ CAN
   - ◉ Enterprise network

ACTIVITY 1–4: Identifying Network Models

1. On a company's network, users access a single computer via a terminal for all of their data processing and storage. Which network model does this network use?

   - ○ Peer-to-peer
   - ○ Mixed mode
   - ○ Client/server
   - ◉ Centralized

2. On a company's network, users directly share files stored on their devices with other users. Additionally, they access shared storage, printing, and fax resources, which are connected to a department-wide server. Which network model does this network use?

   - ○ Peer-to-peer
   - ○ Client/server
   - ○ Centralized
   - ◉ Mixed mode

3. A company has four employees who need to share information and hardware, such as a scanner and printer. They also need Internet access. None of the users have advanced computing skills. Which type of network would best suit their needs?

- ○ Client/server
- ◉ Peer-to-peer
- ○ Centralized
- ○ Mixed mode

ACTIVITY 1-5: Identifying Data Transmission Methods

---

1. Identify the transmission method depicted in the graphic.

- ◉ Unicast
- ○ Broadcast
- ○ Multicast

2. True or False? Multicasting is more efficient in the use of network media than unicast transmission when many clients need to receive the same information from a server.

- ☑ True
- ☐ False

3. Which transmission method allows digital signals to be sent as DC pulses over a single, unmultiplexed signal channel?

- ○ Broadband
- ○ Parallel
- ◉ Baseband
- ○ Serial

4. Which of these devices use serial data transmission?

- ☑ Keyboard
- ☑ Mouse
- ☑ USB hard drive
- ☐ Internal bus

5. True or False? With the deterministic media access method, the nodes themselves negotiate for media access time.

- ☐ True
- ☑ False

6. Which transmission method allows data to be sent to a node, and then that node transmits the data to the next nearest node?

- ○ Broadcast
- ◉ Anycast
- ○ Baseband
- ○ Parallel

ACTIVITY 2-1: Identifying Bounded Copper Network Media

1. Identify the type of network cabling shown in the graphic.
    - ◉ Twisted pair
    - ○ Coax
    - ○ Fiber optic
    - ○ Video

2. Identify the type of network cabling shown in the graphic.
    - ○ Unshielded twisted pair
    - ○ Shielded twisted pair
    - ◉ Coax
    - ○ Fiber optic

3. True or False? The connector shown in the graphic is a BNC connector.
    - ☑ True
    - ☐ False

ACTIVITY 2-2: Identifying Bounded Fiber Network Media

1. In an industrial setting, which fiber connector would provide greater strength and durability?
    - ○ Straight tip
    - ○ Biconic
    - ◉ Ferrule connector
    - ○ Local connector

2. True or False? Multimode fiber can be used in longer distances than singlemode.
    - ☐ True
    - ☑ False

3. The network administrator says you will need to work with network patch panels. Which fiber connector would you use?
    - ○ Ferrule connector
    - ◉ Straight tip
    - ○ Standard connector
    - ○ FDDI

4. The network administrator says that the branch office could be experiencing a high amount of back reflection with their fiber media. Which ferrule polish would you select to reduce the back reflection the most?
    - ○ Ultra physical contact
    - ○ Physical contact
    - ◉ Angled physical contact
    - ○ Ferrule connector

ACTIVITY 2-3: Identifying Bounded Network Installation Media

1. Which of the following are reasons why a plenum cable is commonly used in air handling spaces and run through firebreaks?

   ☑ It does not give off poisonous gases when burning.

   ☐ Fire cannot travel through the cable because of the insulated metal shield that surrounds the conductors.

   ☑ Fire cannot travel through the cable because the jacket is closely bound to the conductors.

   ☐ It is more durable than using a PVC cable.

2. Which is not a factor that can affect the performance of network media?

   ⊙ Refraction

   ○ Attenuation

   ○ Impedance

   ○ Noise

3. Which structured cabling subsystem provides connections between equipment rooms and telecommunication closets?

   ○ Horizontal wiring

   ○ Attenuation

   ○ Cross-connects

   ⊙ Backbone wiring

   For remote participants, encourage them to explore their local environments and try to determine the network hardware that is used.

4. Identify the cable types that connect the devices in the classroom.

   A: The cable types used will vary, but may include the most common type of bounded media—twisted pair cable. Other possible cable types are coax and fiber optic.

5. Identify the types of connectors used in the classroom network.

   A: The connector types used will vary, as it depends on the cables used on the network. For example, if the cable type is twisted pair, the connectors will be RJ-45.
   For remote participants, be sure to use your webcam to display the media and connectors.

6. Your instructor will provide samples of a variety of media and connector types. Identify each of the media and connectors.

   A: Answers will vary depending upon the media samples provided.

ACTIVITY 2-4: Identifying Electrical Noise Control Measures

1. What is electrical noise?
   - ○ Solar radiation or man-made sources of data signals
   - ◉ Extraneous signals introduced onto network media
   - ○ The reception of transmitted signals from a source
   - ○ Extraneous signals that enhance the quality of received transmission

2. The network administrator says that the branch office is experiencing electrical noise. What are some of the possible sources?
   - ☑ Fluorescent lights
   - ☑ Solar storms
   - ☐ Wind storms
   - ☑ HVAC equipment

3. True or False? Differential signaling reduces electrical noise by distinguishing between the signals on two different inputs.
   - ☑ True
   - ☐ False

4. What is the process of installing a resistor on the end of a cable to prevent signal reflections?
   - ○ Draining
   - ○ Grounding
   - ◉ Terminating
   - ○ Shielding

5. True or False? The unwinding of a twisted pair cable's conductors does not affect its performance characteristics.
   - ☐ True
   - ☑ False

ACTIVITY 3-1: Identifying Wireless Transmission Technologies

1. Select the characteristics of unbounded media.
   - ☐ Use a physical medium.
   - ☑ Transmit both voice and data signals.
   - ☑ Use electromagnetic energy.
   - ☐ Operate only within a 10-mile radius.

2. At what radio frequency does Bluetooth operate?
   - ○ 5 GHz
   - ◉ 2.4 GHz
   - ○ 300 GHz
   - ○ 100 GHz

3. Which form of wireless transmission transmits signals in the 10 KHz to 1 GHz frequency range?

   ⦿ Radio

   ○ Infrared

   ○ Spread spectrum

   ○ Microwave

4. Which forms of wireless media operate only when there are no obstacles in the transmission path?

   ☑ Infrared

   ☐ Radio

   ☑ Microwave

   ☐ Broadcast

5. Which unbounded media transmission method uses multiple frequencies to reduce interference and the likelihood of eavesdropping?

   ○ Infrared

   ○ Microwave

   ⦿ Spread spectrum

   ○ Broadcast radio

ACTIVITY 3-2: Identifying Wireless Devices and Components

1. Select the characteristics of directional antennas.

   ☑ Used in point-to-point networks

   ☐ Have low gain

   ☑ Transmit narrow and focused beams

   ☐ Are prone to interference

2. Which device can be used to connect two wired networks using a wireless connection?

   ⦿ Wireless bridge

   ○ Wireless controller

   ○ Wireless access point

   ○ Wireless antenna

3. What is the purpose of an SSID?

   ○ Control multiple Wi-Fi wireless access points.

   ○ Identify each device on a wireless network.

   ⦿ Identify a WAP and all devices attached to it.

   ○ Identify the protocol of a wireless network.

ACTIVITY 3-3: Installing a Wireless Router

5. Greene City Interiors has installed a wireless network. There are ceiling dome transmitters at various locations in your building, and you have upgraded the users' laptops with wireless NICs. There is one wireless antenna to serve the warehouse area. The coverage area is adequate; however, users in the warehouse report intermittent connectivity problems as they move in and out of the tall metal storage shelving. What problem do you suspect?

   A: The metal in the shelves is interfering with the omni-directional radio signals from the transmitter. If you need complete coverage in the warehouse area, you might need to install additional antenna stations in the areas between the shelving units.

6. A user on your network uses a tablet computer to keep track of her calendar and contact list. She synchronizes the tablet data frequently with her laptop computer via the systems' infrared ports. She complains that she intermittently loses the infrared connection between the two devices. You visit her workstation and find that she is seated in close proximity to a large window. What problem do you suspect?

   A: Bright sunlight from the window can occasionally interfere with the infrared transmission. There could also be a line-of-sight problem where the transmitter and receiver are not directly aligned.

ACTIVITY 4-1: Identifying Physical Network Topologies

1. Identify the physical network topology depicted in the graphic.
   - ○ Star
   - ○ Bus
   - ◉ Mesh
   - ○ Ring

2. Identify the physical network topology depicted in the graphic.
   - ○ Mesh
   - ◉ Bus
   - ○ Star
   - ○ Hybrid

3. Identify the physical network topology depicted in the graphic.
   - ○ Mesh
   - ○ Bus
   - ○ Star
   - ◉ Hybrid

ACTIVITY 4-2: Identifying Logical Network Topologies

1. One of your servers is suffering from intermittent poor performance. As the CPU, RAM, and disk utilization are normal, you suspect it is the target of a network-based hacking attack. You would like to place a sniffer with a protocol analyzer next to the server's network interface to monitor traffic. The server is connected to an Ethernet switch, but the switch does not have port mirroring capability. You also do not want to add to the server's load by running the sniffer on the server itself. What logical network topology do you need to place a sniffer next to the server, and how would you implement it?

   ⦿ You need to configure the server and the sniffer in a logical bus. Unplug the server from its switch port, plug a hub in its place, and then plug both the switch and the sniffer into the hub.

   ○ You need to configure the server and the sniffer in a logical star. Plug the sniffer into the switch port that is next to the server's switch port.

   ○ You need to configure the server and the sniffer in a logical ring. Unplug the server from the switch port, plug a hub into the switch, and then plug the server and the sniffer into the token ring hub.

2. Briefly explain the thought process you used to arrive at the answer in the preceding question.

   A: Using a logical bus will work. Because the hub is a logical bus, it will repeat all traffic out all ports. The sniffer will receive all traffic sent to and from the server. The only disadvantage is that a hub is a half-duplex device. The server will have to take turns transmitting and receiving, so this may have a negative impact on performance. Using a logical star will not work because the switch will not pass any of the server's traffic to the sniffer. Using a logical ring will not work because Ethernet does not use a ring topology.

3. You are part of a team helping to troubleshoot and upgrade the network at an older facility. Until the new equipment arrives, you need to restore connectivity to some old mini mainframe computers and other workstations. None of the computers can communicate with any other computer. All of the computers connect to a central hub device. You inspected the hub and noticed that the chassis has no place for status lights, no power switch, and does not appear to have any way to plug into power. All of the connectors, which are unusually large, seem to be firmly plugged into the hub. Meanwhile, your colleague discovered a frayed-looking connector at the back of one of the computers. You are able to bring the network back up by holding the connector in place, though as soon as you let go the network goes down again. You are wondering how the failure of a single node could impact the entire network. What do you think is the problem?

   ○ Although the network is hub and spoke (physical star), it is a logical bus. The break at the end of one of the spokes is causing reflections in the signal, thus bringing the network down.

   ○ Although the network is a hub and spoke (physical star), it is also a logical star. The break at the end of one of the spokes is disrupting network continuity for all nodes.

   ⦿ Although the network is a hub and spoke (physical star), it is a logical ring. The broken connector at one computer is breaking the ring, thus taking the network down. When you manually hold the connector in place, the wiring reconnects and the ring resumes conducting traffic.

4. Briefly explain the thought process you used to arrive at the answer in the preceding question.

A: The first option is incorrect. While it is true that a break in a bus will cause reflections, holding the connector so that the broken wires will reconnect is not likely to heal the reflection problem. Even a nick in a cable, frayed strands, a mismatched connector, or a bad kink in the cable can cause reflections. The second option is also incorrect. The convenience of a logical star is that if one node loses connectivity, it will not impact the other nodes. The third option is correct. The description of the cabling and hub, as well as the environment of an older network of mini mainframes, suggests that the network is token ring based, meaning that the direction of traffic is in a logical ring. Token ring hubs are passive in nature, and do not plug into a power outlet. Although the physical topology is that of a star, the logical topology is that of a ring. The traffic is passed from node to node, with each node repeating the packets for the next node.

5. You are troubleshooting intermittent connectivity in a departmental network. In the entire department, two devices continue to have connectivity problems. All of the other devices seem to be fine. Each device is plugged into a wall jack by using a CAT5 cable with RJ-45 connectors. Because the wiring is in the wall, you are unable to determine where the wiring leads to. You suspect that a locked door in the hallway leads to a wiring closet. While you are waiting for maintenance to arrive and unlock the door, your assistant theorizes that the problem is that the network is in a ring topology, that there is a break somewhere in the cable, and the reason why the two nodes cannot connect is that they exist on either side of the break. Do you agree with this theory?

◉ No, you disagree. Because only two nodes are affected, your idea is that this is a logical star, keeping the problem limited to those nodes only.

○ Yes, you agree. Since only two nodes are affected, you agree that this must be a logical ring, and that the two affected nodes must be on either side of the break.

○ No, you disagree. Because only two nodes are affected, you think that they must be at the far end of a logical bus, and that the break in the cabling is between them and the rest of the network.

6. Briefly explain the thought process you used to arrive at the answer in the preceding question.

A: The first option is correct. The hallmark of a logical star is that if one node has a broken cable, it will not affect the rest of the network. The fact that two nodes are affected does not contradict this idea, as the rest of the network is operating normally. The second option is incorrect. If the network was a logical ring, any break in the ring would bring the entire network down. The third option is incorrect. Although it is true that in some cases even an unterminated bus can still function (a bus with a break in it would end up being two networks), the fact that you have Category 5 cable with RJ-45 connectors means you are not using a bus. Bus connectors are either BNC (coax) or AUI (15-pin D connector) style.

ACTIVITY 4-4: Describing Ethernet Networks

1. Which of the following is an example of a proper MAC address?

○ 192.168.1.1

○ FG:12:1A:N0:22:42

◉ 00:25:1D:12:3E:48

○ 01:15:2E:10:2B:48:5A

2. True or False? The 802.2 standard specifies the frame size and transmission rate of the Ethernet technology.

☑ True

☐ False

3. Which field of the Ethernet frame provides error detection information?
   - ○ PRE
   - ◉ FCS
   - ○ SFD
   - ○ SA

4. Which is a Gigabit Ethernet standard?
   - ○ 100Base-T
   - ◉ 1000Base-LX
   - ○ 10Base-F
   - ○ 10000Base-P

ACTIVITY 4–5: Identifying Network Connectivity Devices

1. True or False? The main purpose of a switch is to optimize performance by providing users with higher bandwidth for transmission.
   - ☑ True
   - ☐ False

2. You need to connect multiple networks that use the same protocol. Which networking device would best meet your needs?
   - ◉ Router
   - ○ Firewall
   - ○ Gateway
   - ○ Switch

3. Which of these network devices is a common connecting point for various nodes or segments?
   - ○ Hub
   - ○ Router
   - ○ Gateway
   - ◉ Switch

4. True or False? A gateway subdivides a LAN into segments.
   - ☐ True
   - ☑ False

5. Which statements are valid for a gateway?
   - ☑ It can connect networks with dissimilar protocols.
   - ☑ It can be implemented in a router.
   - ☐ It can be implemented only as a computer program.
   - ☑ It can be implemented as hardware or software.

6. You have a logical bus network formed by connecting devices with twisted-pair cables. As you expect considerable traffic on the network, you need maximum transmission speeds between the nodes on the network. Which network device would you use to handle this requirement?

   ○ Router

   ○ Modem

   ◉ Switch

   ○ Gateway

7. True or False? A collision domain associates itself only with a single broadcast domain.

   ☐ True

   ☑ False

8. What is used to prevent switching loops?

   ○ Gateway

   ◉ Spanning Tree Protocol

   ○ Collision Domain

   ○ Switch

ACTIVITY 4–6: Describing VLANs

1. What are some of the common uses for employing VLANs?

   ☑ Security

   ☑ Separate traffic types for Quality of Service

   ☐ Increase bandwidth and reliability

   ☑ Traffic management

2. Why should VLANs be carefully planned before implementing them?

   A: Because the switch will not forward frames between VLANs. If a node in one VLAN needs to communicate with a node in another VLAN, some other mechanism must be used to allow that communication.

3. True or False? VLANs can be extended beyond a single switch.

   ☑ True

   ☐ False

4. When would you use port mirroring?

   A: It is often used to analyze and debug data, or diagnose errors on a network. It is also used for network appliances that require monitoring of network traffic such as an intrusion detection system.

ACTIVITY 5–3: Converting Binary and Decimal Numbers

1. Convert the binary number of 10110010 to its decimal equivalent.

   A: 178.

2. Convert the binary number of 10111011 to its decimal equivalent.

   A: 187.

3. Convert the binary number of 1010001 to its decimal equivalent.

   A: 81.

4. Use the calculator app on your computer and select the Programmer view (or an equivalent display mode that includes binary and decimal number options) and verify each of your conversions from steps 1, 2, and 3.

   A: 178, 187, 81

ACTIVITY 5-4: Identifying Default IP Addressing Schemes

2. For the Ethernet adapter named Ethernet, what are the IPv4 Address, Subnet Mask, and Default Gateway?

   A: Answers will vary based on the device setup but should resemble this: IPv4 Address - 192.168.2.36, Subnet Mask - 255.255.255.0, Default Gateway - 192.168.2.200.

3. How will you determine the class of this IPv4 address?

   A: You can determine the class of an IP address from the first octet of the IP address. This is a Class C address.

4. How many valid IP addresses are available for internal hosts?

   A: There are 253 valid IP addresses available.

ACTIVITY 5-5: Creating Custom IP Addressing Schemes

1. How many bits do you need to move the mask?

   A: 1

2. What is the new mask?

   A: 255.255.255.128 (/25)

3. What is the delta?

   A: 128

4. What are the subnet IDs for each network?

   A: 192.168.1.0 /25, 192.168.1.128 /25

5. What are the first and last assignable IP addresses for each subnet?

   A: 192.168.1.1 – 126, 192.168.1.129 – 254

6. What is the broadcast for each subnet?

   A: 192.168.1.127, 192.168.1.255

7. What are the recommended IP addresses for each router interface?

   A: The first legitimate host ID of each subnet

ACTIVITY 5-6: Implementing IPv6 Addressing

2. **For the Ethernet adapter named Ethernet, what is the IPv6 address?**

    A: Answers will vary based on computer setup, but should resemble this: fe80::78a7:da22:4ef6:de19.

3. **What type of IPv6 address do you have?**

    A: The fe80 prefix is a link-local address.

ACTIVITY 5-7: Identifying Data Delivery Techniques

1. **Which techniques would you use for error detection?**

    ☐ Sliding windows

    ☑ Parity checking

    ☑ CRC

    ☑ EDAC

2. **True or False? Parity checking adds overhead to network transmissions.**

    ☑ True

    ☐ False

3. **Which statement is true of sliding and fixed-length windows?**

    ○ Sliding windows are groups of packets selected at random from transmitted data, whereas fixed-length windows always include the same sequence of packets.

    ○ Fixed-length windows always contain the same number of packets, while sliding windows contain 8, 16, or 32 packets.

    ◉ Sliding windows contain a variable number of packets in a block, whereas fixed-length windows always contain the same number.

    ○ Fixed-length windows contain a variable number of packets in a block; sliding windows always contain the same number.

4. **Buffer flooding is the process of:**

    ○ Sending data at a speed the receiver can handle.

    ○ Corrupting the buffers in the receiver.

    ○ Filling the buffer of the receiver with padding (empty) packets.

    ◉ Overfilling the buffers in the receiver.

ACTIVITY 6-2: Identifying Routing Entries

1. **Which route determines the destination for packets to the 172.16.0.0 network? What adapter will they be delivered to?**

    A: The fifth route in the table with a network destination of 172.16.0.0. These packets will be delivered to the 172.16.0.1 network adapter.

2. Which interfaces will receive internetwork broadcasts?

   A: Both interfaces as well as the loopback adapter will receive internetwork broadcasts. This is because the last three routes in the table have a destination address of 255.255.255.255.

3. You connect a second router in parallel to the default gateway for testing purposes. Its IP address is 192.168.1.254. Both routers lead to the 10.10.10.0/24 network. You want to ping 10.10.10.22. How can you configure your host to use the second router to reach the 10.10.10.0 network without changing the default gateway on your host?

   A: Configure a static route, pointing to 192.168.1.254: *Route add 10.10.10.0 MASK 255.255.255.0 192.168.1.254*

ACTIVITY 7-5: Identifying Common TCP/IP Protocols

---

1. What are the differences between accessing email from multiple systems using IMAP4 and POP3?

   ☑ POP3 does not maintain a copy of the email once it is downloaded from a mail server.

   ☑ POP3 does not maintain a copy of the outgoing email.

   ☑ Accessing email by using POP3 is faster than IMAP4.

   ☐ IMAP4 is the messaging protocol used to access email.

2. Your sales department wants to sell supplies over the Internet and wants to make sure that the transactions are secure. Which protocol should be configured on the web server?

   ○ FTP

   ◉ HTTPS

   ○ NNTP

   ○ SMTP

3. Your company has a production floor with several shared devices. The production staff needs to be able to check their email from whichever device is free. Which email protocol should you use?

   ○ POP3

   ○ NTP

   ◉ IMAP4

   ○ NNTP

4. Your sales force needs to retrieve sales prospective documents and upload completed sales order forms to corporate headquarters while they are on the move. What service should you use?

   ○ HTTP

   ○ NNTP

   ○ NTP

   ◉ FTP

5. What are the differences between FTP and HTTP?

   A: Answers will vary, but may include: although both FTP and HTTP enable file transfer across the Internet, there are important differences between the two protocols. Both have a GET command for downloading files. Both have a PUT command for uploading files. But FTP is optimized for large file transfers, and is more efficient at it than HTTP. In addition, FTP uses two separate channels, one for control (sending commands) and one for sending the data. HTTP uses only one channel, for both commands and data transfer.

6. True or False? Telnet is a terminal emulation protocol that allows users at one site to simulate a session on a remote host as if the terminal were directly attached.

   ☑ True

   ☐ False

7. Which is a program that enables a user or an application to log on to another device over a network, execute commands, and manage files over an encrypted connection?

   ○ SFTP

   ◉ SSH

   ○ SMB

   ○ FTP

8. Which is a protocol that works on the Application layer and helps share resources such as files, printers, and serial ports among devices?

   ○ SSH

   ○ FTP

   ◉ SMB

   ○ SFTP

ACTIVITY 8-1: Discussing WAN Basics

1. In which switching network is there one endpoint that creates a single path connection to another?

   ◉ Circuit switching networks

   ○ Virtual circuit switching

   ○ Cell switching networks

   ○ Packet switching networks

2. In which switching network is data broken into small units that move in sequence through the network?

   ◉ Packet switching networks

   ○ Cell switching networks

   ○ Circuit switching networks

   ○ Virtual circuit switching

3. For what reasons might an organization want to connect to a WAN?

   A: Answers will vary, but may include: They need to connect to offices in different geographic locations, enable access to local resources from external users, or access to the Internet.

ACTIVITY 8-2: Discussing WAN Connectivity Methods

1. **When would you use satellite media?**

    A: Answers will vary, but may include: For satellite Internet and TV consumers, to provide backbone links to geographically dispersed LANs, or to provide connectivity in remote areas that have no other available Internet infrastructure.

2. **Which statement is true of satellite media?**
    - ○ Used for short-range transmissions
    - ◉ Offers high-speed connections
    - ○ Has a low latency
    - ○ Transmits data at the same speed

3. **True or False? The bandwidth availability for a dedicated line is usually between 28 Kbps and 2 Mbps.**
    - ☐ True
    - ☑ False

4. **When would leased data lines be used?**

    A: Answers will vary, but may include: to connect geographically distant offices, for a data center that's connected to the Internet or other WAN.

ACTIVITY 8-3: Discussing WAN Transmission Technologies

1. **On which type of network is ATM most commonly implemented?**
    - ○ LAN
    - ○ MAN
    - ◉ WAN
    - ○ PAN

2. **How many bytes of data can an ATM cell transfer?**
    - ○ 56
    - ◉ 53
    - ○ 52
    - ○ 58

3. **Which technologies do OCx specifications match to?**
    - ☐ ATM
    - ☑ SONET
    - ☐ Frame relay
    - ☑ SDH
    - ☐ T1

4. What are the channels used by BRI ISDN?
   - ○ Two D channels and one B channel
   - ◉ Two B channels and one D channel
   - ○ Three B channels and one D channel
   - ○ Three B channels and two D channels

5. Which of these technologies allows for more downstream traffic than upstream?
   - ○ SDSL
   - ○ SHDSL
   - ◉ ADSL
   - ○ VDSL

6. Which of these are features of a network with MPLS?
   - ☑ Label switching
   - ☑ Used with voice traffic
   - ☑ Multiprotocol adaptability
   - ☐ Carries frame relay as its Layer 2 protocol

7. On which OSI layer does frame relay operate?
   - ○ Transport
   - ○ Application
   - ○ Network
   - ○ Physical
   - ◉ Data Link

ACTIVITY 8–4: Discussing Unified Communication Technologies

1. What are the advantages of VoIP as compared to traditional telephone systems?
   - ☑ Reduced long-distance call costs
   - ☑ Increased bandwidth
   - ☑ Portability
   - ☐ Power independent

2. Describe a scenario in which real-time communication services and products are integrated with non-real-time services and products.

   A: Answers will vary, but may include: Receiving a voice-mail message through email or a mobile phone, viewing presence information from an instant messaging service in your email client.

3. Which statements are valid regarding voice-over-data systems?
   - ☑ Transmits digital signals over WAN technologies.
   - ☐ Voice communications are not time-sensitive.
   - ☐ Voice software converts digital data to analog voice signals.
   - ☑ Voice software translates a dialing destination to a network address.

4. **What are some of the different unified communications technologies that you have used?**

   A: Answers will vary, but may include: VoIP, video conferencing, voice mail, SMS messaging, presence information, instant messaging, email, data sharing, fax messaging, or speech recognition.

5. **Which VoIP protocol transmits audio or video content and defines the packet for delivery?**

   ○ Real-Time Transport Control Protocol

   ◉ Real-Time Transport Protocol

   ○ Session Initiation Protocol

   ○ Session Description Protocol

ACTIVITY 9–2: Identifying SAN Technologies

1. **Which is a specialized file-based data storage server?**

   ◉ NAS

   ○ iSCSI

   ○ Jumbo Frame

   ○ Fibre Channel

2. **Jumbo frames are used on LANs that can support at least...?**

   ○ 9,000 bps

   ○ 16 Gbps

   ◉ 1 Gbps

   ○ 1,500 bps

3. **Which are the three major Fibre Channel topologies?**

   ☑ Point-to-point

   ☑ Arbitrated loop

   ☐ Client-server

   ☑ Switched fabric

ACTIVITY 9–3: Identifying Cloud Computing Technologies

1. **Which of the following are key features of cloud computing?**

   ☐ Local access to resource

   ☑ Dynamic provisioning

   ☑ Cost benefits

   ☑ Simplified installation and maintenance

2. **How is a community cloud different from a public cloud?**

   A: A public cloud offers its services to the public in general, whereas a community cloud is restricted to a group of organizations or users who have a common focus.

3. True or False? Bandwidth on Demand is a service model of PaaS.

☐ True

☑ False

4. With which service do you rent computing resources as an outsourced service?

○ NaaS

○ PaaS

◉ IaaS

○ SaaS

ACTIVITY 10-1: Identifying a Security Policy

---

1. Open and review the policy file. What type of policy document is this?

○ Acceptable Use Policy

○ Audit Policy

○ Extranet Policy

◉ Password Policy

○ Wireless Standards Policy

2. Which standard policy components are included in this policy?

☑ Statement

☑ Standards

☑ Guidelines

☐ Procedures

3. How often must system-level administrators change their passwords to conform to this policy?

A: The password policy states that administrator passwords should be changed every month to remain secure.

4. To conform to this policy, how often must regular system users change their passwords?

A: The password policy states that regular system users should change their passwords every three months to stay secure.

5. According to this policy, what is the minimum character length for a password and how should it be constructed?

A: Eight characters is the minimum length for security purposes, and you should try and include numbers and special characters to make it more secure.

6. Why is "password1" not a good choice for a password?

A: It is easy to guess and therefore not very secure.

ACTIVITY 10-3: Discussing Network Security Basics

1. An employee in charge of social media writes a blog post that includes details on products that will be released later in the year. The intent was to make consumers excited about upcoming products, but the employee didn't realize that the company didn't want this information public. What is this an example of?

   ○ Risks

   ○ Security policy

   ◉ Data breach

   ○ Unauthorized access

2. What is the main difference between Windows security policies and group policy?

   A: Windows security policies reside on each local Windows device and apply to that device only. Group policy resides in Active Directory on a Windows server and can apply to any Windows device in the domain.

3. What are the three principles of the CIA triad?

   ◉ Integrity

   ◉ Confidentiality

   ○ Accountability

   ◉ Availability

4. When would you perform a site survey?

   A: You would use a site survey to help you install and secure a WLAN. A site survey is an analysis technique that determines the coverage area of a wireless network, identifies any sources of interference, and establishes other characteristics of the coverage area.

5. Which of these describes the concept of least privilege?

   ○ End-user jobs and software access should be restricted so that no one wields too much administrative power over the network.

   ○ End users should at least hold administrative privileges over their local workstations.

   ○ Technological and physical access should be granted only when it is needed, and then revoked as soon as the task or need has ended.

   ◉ End users should be given the minimal level of technological and physical access that is required for them to perform their jobs.

6. Describe how you would alleviate or eliminate single points of failure in your network.

   A: Answers will vary but may include: having replacements for any network devices that are single points of failure, and adding redundant devices to the network.

ACTIVITY 10-4: Discussing Vulnerabilities

1. What are applicable forms of vulnerabilities?

   ☑ Improperly configured software

   ☑ Misuse of communication protocols

   ☑ Poor physical security

   ☐ Lengthy passwords with a mix of characters

2. What are some examples of physical security vulnerabilities?

    A: Answers will vary but may include: disgruntled employees performing some sort of physical sabotage, weather-related problems such as floods, an external power failure, and workers accidentally digging up fiber optic cables.

3. You suspect that one of your workstations has been compromised by an external entity. What are some vulnerabilities you should examine to see if they are allowing external connections?

    ☑ Open ports

    ☐ Permissions

    ☑ Unpatched system

    ☑ Unnecessary running services

4. Describe some situations in which user credentials could be viewed as cleartext.

    A: Answers will vary but may include: form-based authentication credentials sent via HTTP, unencrypted passwords stored in a database, downloading/uploading files by using FTP, and passwords sent via email.

ACTIVITY 10–5: Discussing Threats and Attacks

1. John is given a laptop for official use and is on a business trip. When he arrives at his hotel, he turns on his laptop and finds a wireless access point with the name of the hotel, which he connects to for sending official communications. He may become a victim of which wireless threat?

    ○ Interference

    ○ War driving

    ○ Bluesnarfing

    ◉ Rogue access point

2. A new administrator in your company is in the process of installing a new wireless device. He is called away to attend an urgent meeting before he can secure the wireless network, and without realizing it, he forgot to switch the device off. A person with a mobile device who is passing the building takes advantage of the open network and hacks it. Your company may become vulnerable to which type of wireless threat?

    ○ Interference

    ◉ War driving

    ○ Bluesnarfing

    ○ Rogue access point

3. A disgruntled employee copies sensitive company information to a USB drive with the intention of putting it on the Internet. This threat is which of the following?

    ☑ Insider threat

    ☐ External threat

    ☑ Data theft

    ☐ False alarm

    Students may disagree with the answer for this question. Use this as an opportunity to solicit feedback from other students and discuss why they disagree or what social engineering attacks they have come across. You can also discuss what category each attacker might fall into and the attacker's possible motivation in each case.

4. What are the reasons why a hoax is dangerous?

☐ The hoax is an actual virus that has the potential to cause damage.

☑ Propagation of the hoax can create DoS conditions.

☐ Users are annoyed by the hoax.

☑ The hoax can include elements of a social engineering attack.

5. Social engineering attempt or false alarm? A supposed customer calls the help desk and states that she cannot connect to the e-commerce website to check her order status. She would also like a user name and password. The user gives a valid customer company name, but is not listed as a contact in the customer database. The user does not know the correct company code or customer ID.

☑ Social engineering attempt

☐ False alarm

6. Social engineering attempt or false alarm? A new accountant was hired and would like to know if he can have the installation source files for the accounting software package so that he can install it on his device himself and start work immediately. Last year, someone internal compromised company accounting records, so distribution of the accounting application is tightly controlled. You have received all the proper documentation for the request from his supervisor and there is an available license for the software. However, general IT policies state that the IT department must perform all software installations and upgrades.

☐ Social engineering attempt

☑ False alarm

7. While you are connected to another host on your network, the connection is suddenly dropped. When you review the logs at the other host, it appears as if the connection is still active. This could be a(n):

○ IP spoofing attack

○ DoS attack

○ Man-in-the-middle attack

◉ Session hijacking attack

8. Response time on the website that hosts the online version of your product catalog is getting slower and slower. Customers are complaining that they cannot browse the catalog items or search for products. What type of attack do you suspect?

○ A Trojan horse attack

○ A spoofing attack

○ A social engineering attack

◉ A DoS attack

9. The network administrator at your organization analyzes a network trace capture file and discovers that packets have been intercepted and retransmitted to both a sender and a receiver during an active session. This could be a(n):

○ IP spoofing attack

○ Session hijacking attack

○ Replay attack

◉ Man-in-the-middle attack

10. Your intranet webmaster has noticed an entry in a log file from an IP address that is within the range of addresses used on your network. But the webmaster does not recognize the computer name as valid. You check the DHCP server and find out that the IP address is not similar to any in your list of IP addresses in that particular domain. This could be a(n):

- ◉ IP spoofing attack
- ○ Malicious code attack
- ○ Man-in-the-middle attack
- ○ Session hijacking attack

11. A user arrives at work in the morning and finds that he cannot log on to the network. You check his account and find it was locked at 3 A.M. due to too many unsuccessful logon attempts. What type of attack do you suspect?

- ○ Man-in-the-middle
- ◉ Password
- ○ Virus
- ○ Hijacking

12. Which of these examples can be classified as social engineering attacks?

- ☑ A customer contacts your help desk asking for her user name and password because she cannot log on to your e-commerce website.
- ☑ A user gets a call from a person who states he is a help desk technician. The caller asks the user to go to an external website and download a file so that the technician can monitor the user's system.
- ☐ The CEO of your company calls you personally on the phone to ask you to fax salary data to her personal fax number. The fax number she gives you is listed in the company directory, and you recognize her voice.
- ☑ A user receives an email that appears to be from a bank; the bank says they need the user's name, date of birth, and Social Security number to verify account information.

ACTIVITY 10–6: Discussing Authentication Methods

1. If a user needs to insert her employee ID card into a special card reader to access her laptop, this is an example of:

- ○ User name/password authentication
- ○ Biometrics
- ◉ Token-based authentication
- ○ Mutual authentication

2. If a user needs to place his index finger on a fingerprint reader to access the server room, this is an example of which authentication method:

- ○ Password
- ○ Token-based
- ◉ Biometric
- ○ Multifactor

3. To withdraw money from an ATM, a person needs to insert a card and type a four-digit PIN. This incorporates what types of authentication?
   - ☑ Token-based
   - ☑ Password
   - ☐ Biometrics
   - ☑ Multifactor
   - ☐ Mutual

4. Which is an example of a strong password?
   - ○ Password
   - ◉ !Passw0rd1
   - ○ PaSsWoRd
   - ○ drowssaP

ACTIVITY 10–7: Identifying Network Encryption Methods

1. True or False? Encryption is only a two-way format in which data can be decrypted and read.
   - ☐ True
   - ☑ False

2. Which is the least secure wireless security protocol?
   - ○ WPA
   - ◉ WEP
   - ○ TKIP
   - ○ WPA2

3. With key pair encryption, what type of key is used to decrypt the data?
   - ○ Shared key
   - ○ Public key
   - ○ Decrypt key
   - ◉ Private key

4. Which are security protocols that combine digital certificates for authentication with public key data encryption?
   - ☑ SSL
   - ☑ TLS
   - ☐ PKI
   - ☐ DES

5. Which is not a step in the certificate encryption process?

    ○ Encrypting party uses public key to encrypt data and sends it to the other user.

    ◉ The party that decrypts data obtains the public key from the CA's certificate repository.

    ○ A security principal obtains a certificate and a public/private key pair from a CA.

    ○ Other user uses the private key to decrypt the data.

ACTIVITY 11–1: Identifying Physical Security Controls

1. True or False? An emergency procedure can inform employees on what to do in the event of an armed intruder.

    ☑ True

    ☐ False

2. What are some of the techniques to implement good air flow in a network closet or data center?

    A: Answers will vary but may include: diffusers in proper position to deliver cool air directly to equipment, structured cabling systems to eliminate disorganized and excess cables, floor grommets to improve cooling by sealing areas where cables enter and exit plenums, blanking panels on unused rack spaces so that air passes through the equipment, or removal of unnecessary sub-floor obstructions to increase air flow.

3. Which is the most efficient physical security control to limit access to multiple rooms for multiple users?

    ◉ Card/proximity reader

    ○ Intercom

    ○ Cipher lock

    ○ Security guard

4. What is the main difference between battery backups and UPSs?

    A: Battery backups provide power only in case of a power outage, whereas UPSs will also provide power conditioning by removing power quality problems and real-time monitoring and controlled shutdown of protected equipment.

5. In which ways can security cameras improve the security of a building?

    ☑ Act as a deterrent.

    ☐ Prevent access.

    ☑ Monitor and document access to the building.

ACTIVITY 11–3: Discussing Network Access Controls

1. In the NAT process, in which step does the NAT readdress the packet to the internal system?

    ○ Source address conversion

    ○ Client request

    ◉ Data delivery

    ○ Data return

2. **Why might you want to implement NAC on your network?**

   A: You can make sure all systems comply with your security policies, thereby eliminating many of the threats posed by the end-user stations connected to your network.

3. **What is a system that isolates internal clients from the servers by downloading and storing files on behalf of the clients?**

   ○ Reverse proxy server

   ◉ Proxy server

   ○ Quarantine network

   ○ Website caching

4. **Describe a common use for ACLs.**

   A: Answers may vary but can include: MAC address filtering on wireless routers and access points, and packet filtering on a router.

5. **You are visiting a client's office and connected to a wireless network with your laptop. You have full Internet connectivity but no access to the internal intranet. What sort of network are you on?**

   ◉ Guest network

   ○ DMZ

   ○ Edge network

   ○ Quarantine network

6. **How does a NAT differ from a DMZ?**

   A: NAT is an isolation technique in which the device translates private IP addresses to a public address, whereas a DMZ is a design or topology architecture in which two firewalls create a protected, semi-public network for public-facing servers such as web servers, email servers and DNS servers. A DMZ might use NAT to provide the necessary network isolation. Other techniques such as packet filtering and payload inspection could be used as well.

ACTIVITY 11–5: Hardening Networks

1. **When should an anti-malware administrator manually check for malware updates?**

   ◉ When a known threat is active

   ○ After each automatic update

   ○ Never

   ○ Daily

2. **Describe the process you would use to install OS patches in your environment.**

   A: Answers will vary but may include: Evaluate the patches to determine how applicable they are to the system, test the patches in an offline patch-test environment, or implement the patches in the live environment if there is no negative effect.

3. You manage a small office network with a single gateway to an Internet service provider. The ISP maintains your corporate email on its own email server. There is an internal server for file and print services. As the administrator for this network, where should you deploy anti-malware software?

- ☑ Desktops
- ☑ Gateways
- ☐ Email server
- ☑ File and print server

ACTIVITY 11-7: Educating Users

---

1. A virus has spread throughout your organization, causing expensive downtime and corruption of data. You find that the virus sent to many users was an email attachment that was forwarded by an employee. The employee that received the original message was fooled into believing the link it contained was a legitimate marketing survey. You quickly determine that this is a well-known email hoax that has already been posted on several hoax-related websites. When questioned, this employee says that he thought it sounded as if it could be legitimate, and he could not see any harm in "just trying it." How could better user education have helped this situation?

   A: If the employees had been aware of the dangers of opening email attachments, and had been more knowledgeable about how to identify email hoaxes, it is unlikely that the virus would have spread as far. If the initial employee, in particular, had been better informed, you might have been able to keep the virus out of your organization altogether.

2. What education steps do you recommend taking in response to this incident?

   A: Because this was a widespread incident, your response must include better security information for all users. You could distribute or prominently post a notice regarding the incident, reviewing proper guidelines for opening email attachments and for identifying email hoaxes. You could distribute links to common hoax-debunking websites to make it easy for employees to research possible hoaxes. You could also review your new-hire training procedures to be sure they include information on email security.

3. You come in on a Monday morning to find laptops have been stolen from several employees' desks over the weekend. After reviewing videotapes from the security cameras, you find that as an employee exited the building through the secure rear door on Friday night, she held the door open to admit another individual. You suspect this individual was the thief. When you question the employee, she states that the individual told her that he was a new employee who had not yet received his employee badge, that he only needed to be in the building for a few minutes, and that it would save him some time if she could let him in the back door rather than having to walk around to the receptionist entrance. Your security policy states that no one without identification should be admitted through the security doors at any time, but the employee says she was unaware of this policy. You ask her to locate the security policy documents on the network, and she is unable to do so. How could better user education have helped this situation?

   A: Regardless of the specific policy, if the employee had been informed of some common-sense security guidelines, she might have not admitted the stranger without question.

4. What education steps do you recommend taking in response to this incident?

   A: This seems to be an isolated incident, so you should be sure to address it with the employee in question by reviewing all security policies with her and emphasizing the possible consequences of her actions. You should probably also post all security policies in an easily accessible location on the network and send out a company-wide reminder about them. However, because this employee never even attempted to refer to the policy, the inaccessibility of the policy documents was not a contributing factor in this incident. Finally, you should review your new-hire security training procedures to be sure they include common-sense tips on building security.

5. One of your competitors has somehow obtained confidential data about your organization. There have been no obvious security breaches or physical break-ins, and you are puzzled as to the source of the leak. You begin to ask questions about any suspicious or unusual employee activity, and you start to hear stories about a sales representative from out of town who did not have a desk in the office and was sitting down in open cubes and plugging her laptop into the corporate network. You suspect that the sales representative was really an industrial spy for your competitor. When you ask other employees why they did not ask the sales representative for identification or report the incident to security, the other employees said that, given their understanding of company policies, they did not see anything unusual or problematic in the situation. You review your security policy documents and, in fact, none of them refer to a situation like this one. How could better user education have helped this situation?

A: In this case, it is not apparent that there were any problems in the education process. Users were aware of the presence of policy documents, but the documents themselves were inadequate because they did not deal with the dangers of this type of situation.

6. What education steps do you recommend taking in response to this incident?

A: You need to update your acceptable network use policy to make it clear what kind of authorization an individual needs in order to access the corporate network from within the building. You also need to disseminate this new information to all employees. You might want to follow this up in a few weeks or months with a "staged" attack of a similar nature, to see how employees respond.

ACTIVITY 12-1: Discussing Incident Management and Response

1. An employee reports that he thinks his laptop was hacked and that sensitive information may have been stolen. What determines the actions that you will take for this potential security breach?

   ○ Security incident management

   ◉ IRP

   ○ Change management

   ○ Security policy

2. When responding to the potential stolen information from the laptop, what types of actions would be specified?

   A: Answers will vary but may include: who determines and declares if an actual security incident has occurred, what individuals or departments will be notified, how and when they are notified, who will respond to the incident, and guidelines for the appropriate response.

3. It is determined that there was a security breach on the laptop but no sensitive information was stolen. What step(s) should be taken next?

   A: The security issue should be resolved and change management procedures should be followed before making the change and to document it after it is made.

ACTIVITY 12-2: Discussing Basic Forensic Concepts

1. What is the purpose of a chain of custody document?
   - ○ Includes facts about the scene of the incident.
   - ◉ Tracks evidence from the time it is collected until it is released back to the owner.
   - ○ Summary of the substantive evidence.
   - ○ Document items affected by a legal hold.

2. Which methods can be used to document the scene?
   - ☑ Take a video.
   - ☑ Take notes.
   - ☐ Take evidence.
   - ☑ Take pictures.

3. What is the first step you perform when you become aware of a situation?
   - ○ Document the scene.
   - ○ Perform eDiscovery.
   - ◉ Secure the area.
   - ○ Collect evidence.

4. True or False? Data that has been erased can never be retrieved.
   - ☐ True
   - ☑ False

ACTIVITY 13-3: Identifying Remote Access Networking Implementations

1. EAP is an extension of:
   - ○ PEAP
   - ○ CHAP
   - ○ PAP
   - ◉ PPP

2. Which of these statements about PPP are true?
   - ☑ It sends IP datagrams over serial point-to-point links.
   - ☐ It works on the Physical layer of the TCP/IP protocol suite.
   - ☑ It is used for both asynchronous and synchronous connections.
   - ☑ It provides secure authentication for remote users.

3. Describe remote access authentication.

   A: A user first initiates a connection, the remote device requests a connection, the remote access server acknowledges the connection request, the remote access server requests the client to authenticate itself by using a remote authentication protocol, and then the server and client use the agreed-upon authentication protocol to communicate authentication credentials.

ACTIVITY 13–5: Identifying VPN Protocols

1. **Name the benefits of using TACACS+ authentication compared to RADIUS.**

   A: It uses TCP rather than UDP for more reliable transport. It includes process-wide encryption for authentication, whereas RADIUS encrypts only passwords.

2. **Which statements are true of PAP?**

   ☐ Encrypts user credentials.

   ☑ Connects a remote client to a non-Windows PPP server.

   ☐ Updates its local list of credentials when it receives a new set of credentials on the server.

   ☑ Compares credentials from a remote client with local credentials to allow access to resources.

3. **What could you use a VPN for?**

   A: Typically, VPNs are used to give home-office users or traveling users access to file servers, email servers, and custom applications that are normally accessible only while users' devices are connected to the physical internal corporate LAN.

4. **Do you have to use IPSec to enable a VPN?**

   A: No. IPSec is one technique for providing encrypted transmission across a public IP network. There are other techniques, though they are less commonly used.

5. **Which statements are true of CHAP?**

   ☐ Sends passwords as plaintext.

   ☑ Used to connect to non-Microsoft servers.

   ☑ Does not send passwords as plaintext.

   ☑ Uses MD5 hashing.

ACTIVITY 14–1: Monitoring Data on the Network

4. **What types of IPv6 traffic were captured?**

   A: Answers will vary, but may include ICMPv6, LLMNR, or DHCPv6.

ACTIVITY 14–3: Identifying Network Performance Optimization Techniques

1. **What network setting could you configure to ensure that VoIP traffic is smooth and free of jitters?**

   A: QoS settings help prioritize certain types of traffic to help ensure smooth transmission.

2. Which are examples of latency-sensitive applications?

☑ VoIP

☑ Video conferencing

☑ Online gaming

☐ Email

3. How does CARP help provide fault tolerance?

A: CARP allows multiple devices to use the same IP address, helping to ensure that if one device fails, the other configured devices can take over.

4. Which statements are true of QoS?

☐ A set of parameters that controls the quality provided to different types of wireless network traffic.

☐ QoS parameters are agreed upon by the transmitter and the receiver, the receiver being the ISP and the transmitter being the subscriber.

☑ QoS parameters include the maximum delay, signal loss, and noise that can be accommodated for a type of network traffic, bandwidth priority, and CPU usage for a specific stream of data.

☑ The transmitter and receiver enter into an SLA to ensure QoS.

5. True or False? Traffic shaping smooths down traffic bursts that occur when the transmitter sends packets at a rate higher than the capacity of the receiver.

☑ True

☐ False

6. Which is a method of dividing work among the devices on a network?

○ High availability

○ Caching engine

○ Traffic shaping

◉ Load balancing

ACTIVITY 15-1: Discussing Troubleshooting Models

1. Users on the third floor cannot connect to the Internet, but they can log on to the local network. What should you check first?

○ Router configuration tables

○ If viruses exist

○ If users on other floors are having similar problems

◉ If the power cable to the switch is connected

2. You reinstall the operating system for a user who is having problems. Later, the user complains that she cannot find her familiar desktop shortcuts. What step of the troubleshooting model did you omit?

○ Documenting findings, actions, and outcomes

◉ Verifying full system functionality and implementing preventative measures

○ Testing the theory to determine cause

○ Establishing a plan of action to resolve the problem

3. Which techniques will help you establish a theory of probable cause of the problem?

- ☐ Ask the user open-ended questions about the problem.
- ☑ Try to replicate the problem on a nearby workstation.
- ☑ Make a list of problems that can all cause the same symptoms.
- ☑ Find out if users in other parts of the building are facing the same problem.

4. A user calls to say that his computer will not boot. He mentions that everything was fine until a brief power outage on his floor. What stage of the troubleshooting model can this information help you with most directly?

- ○ Establishing a theory of probable cause
- ○ Establishing a plan of action to resolve the problem
- ○ Documenting findings, actions, and outcomes
- ⦿ Identifying the problem

5. A user calls the help desk and says he is unable to open a file. You are not able to visit the user's workstation because he is in a different location. What are the first steps you need to take to diagnose the problem?

A: You need to detail the problem. You then need to define the specific symptoms of the problem so that you can begin to consider potential causes; find out if other users are affected and, if so, who that is; and find out if anything has changed on the user's system or the network since he last accessed the file.

6. What are some of the questions you should ask?

A: Ask the user to describe his system and his physical location. What application is he using to open the file? Can he open other files with that application? If so, the problem is with the file and not the software. Ask him to describe the specific problem he is having. Can he find the file but receives an error when he opens it? Or does the file open but look corrupted? To localize the problem, ask where the file is saved; is it on a local disk or on a network drive? Can he open other files from that location? If not, it may be a problem with the storage media itself. Or is it in an email attachment? Find out when he could last open the file, if ever. If he could open the file previously, find out anything that might have occurred since that time to change the situation. If the file is in a network location, review network activity logs to see if there have been any issues or changes to that server.

7. Through your diagnostic questions, you establish that the file is a word-processing document stored on a network file server. The user last accessed the file three months ago. By reviewing the activity logs on the file server, you find that there is a bi-monthly cleanup routine that automatically backs up and removes user data files that have not been accessed since the last cleanup date. The backups are stored in an offsite facility for one year. Given this information, what is your action plan, how will you implement it, and what potential side effects of the plan do you need to consider?

A: You need to locate the tape backup containing the archived copy of the document and restore it to the network location. You might need to work with your company's network storage administrator to identify the tape and retrieve it from the offsite storage location. You need to ensure that you identify the correct file and restore only that file so that you do not overwrite other data. Also, you need to consider the version compatibility of the backup that you are trying to restore.

8. What steps should you take to test, verify, and document the solution?

A: Ensure that the user can open the restored file and that its contents are correct. Check the modification dates of other files in the restore location to ensure that you have not inadvertently overwritten an existing file with an archived copy. Enter the information from the service call in your service form and file it as prescribed by your company's help desk policies.

ACTIVITY 15-3: Troubleshooting Network Problems

1. Which of the these would be the best first step?
   - ○ Reboot the computer.
   - ○ Load a new browser.
   - ◉ Drop the IP address and lease a new address.
   - ○ Drop the IP address and assign a static address.

2. If you lease a new IP address and it is also in the 192.168 scope, then, based on the evidence, what seems to be the problem so far?
   - ○ The employee's computer is functioning as a DHCP server.
   - ◉ There is another DHCP server on the network leasing addresses.
   - ○ The computer is looking at the incorrect network interface.
   - ○ The loopback adapter is not working.

3. After the user in the next cubicle reports the same problem, based on the diagnostic methodology, you discover that an administrator in a nearby conference room has set up a wireless router so that visiting clients can access the Internet during a meeting. Based on this information, what is the most likely reason for the IP addressing problem?

   A: Answers will vary, but should include specific reference to the wireless router's DHCP capabilities. The employee running the conference has probably forgotten or neglected to disable the router's DHCP service, and so the wireless router is functioning as a rogue DHCP server, leasing addresses to any wireless device within range.

4. In order to correct the problem, you have to physically connect a computer to the wireless router and log in as an administrator. What kind of cable would be best to connect the wireless router to a laptop in order to access the admin features?
   - ○ Crossover
   - ○ Coaxial
   - ◉ Category 5
   - ○ Category 3

ACTIVITY 15-4: Discussing Network Troubleshooting Utilities

1. You have installed a Linux device in your test lab so that application developers can test new software. Because the lab is isolated from the main network, there is no DHCP service running. A software engineer has loaded a network application on the device, but cannot connect to it from a client. She has already tried to ping the Linux device by name and IP address. What should you check next and why?

   A: Use the `ifconfig` utility to verify that you have configured the test system with an appropriate static IP address.

2. A user is having trouble connecting to your company's intranet site (internal.gcinteriors.com), which is on your company's private network inside your firewall. She is not having general Internet connectivity problems. What is the best first step to take to try to narrow down the possible problem?

   A: Because the user does not seem to be having general TCP/IP problems, the problem may be with the web server that hosts the intranet site. You can ping internal.gcinteriors.com by name from different systems to verify that the name is being resolved. If there is no response, ping the system by IP address to see if you can connect to it at all.

3. You can connect to the intranet site with no difficulty. You check your IP configuration against the user's and find that you are configured with different DNS server addresses. You do not have DNS administrative utilities installed on your workstation. What can you do to diagnose the DNS problem?

A: Use the `nslookup` command to see if the user's server can resolve the internal.gcinteriors.com address and to examine the entries on both DNS servers.

4. You had to stop and start the DHCP server service earlier in the day. A Windows user calls to say that she has no network connectivity at all. What can you do to correct the problem?

A: Use `ipconfig /all` to see if the user is receiving a dynamic address. If not, use the utility to renew the DHCP address configuration.

5. Your test environment includes a number of different clients, including Windows devices, Linux devices, and Mac OS® X clients. You would like to be able to examine the network performance of each device while you run a batch file to generate network load. What utility can you use?

A: The `NETSTAT` utility is a versatile tool for examining general network status and performance on a variety of devices.

6. You are experiencing a number of dropped packets and slow response time on your routed private network. You suspect there may be a routing loop and you would like to look more closely at packet transmissions through the network. How can you examine the path of the transmissions?

A: Use the `tracert` command to trace the routes of packets between various source and destination hosts. This can help you locate a packet looping between routers, or the point at which a route fails.

7. Servers on your internal network are manually configured with IP addresses in the range 192.168.2.200 through 192.168.2.225. You are trying to open an FTP session with the FTP server that is located on your internal network at 192.168.2.218. Although you can ping the device by IP address, sometimes you can connect over FTP and sometimes you cannot. You suspect there may be two hosts configured with duplicate addresses. How can you verify which physical host system is using the FTP server's address?

A: First ping the device, and then use the `arp` command to view your ARP cache. The cache will display the MAC address of the device that first responded to the ping request. You can then try to open an FTP session and use the `arp` command again; if the session succeeded, you know which physical device is the FTP server; if it failed, you know which physical device is incorrectly configured.

ACTIVITY 15–5: Identifying Hardware Troubleshooting Tools

1. You have a cable with a frayed end. You want to trim the cable and reattach the connector. You need a:
   - ○ Punch down tool
   - ◉ Wire crimper
   - ○ Cable tester
   - ○ Cable stripper

2. You need to trace a UTP cable in a bundle of cables. You need a:
   - ○ Butt set
   - ○ Circuit tester
   - ○ Cable tester
   - ◉ Tone generator and locator

3. A workstation and server on your small office network cannot communicate. To see if one of the network adapters is bad, you can connect them directly by using a:
   - ◉ Crossover cable
   - ○ Hardware loopback plug
   - ○ Tone generator and locator
   - ○ Punch down tool

4. A user tells you he cannot log on to the network. You direct him to check his network adapter and he notices that there is one steady indicator and one flashing indicator. What does this indicate to you about the status of the connection?
   - ○ There is a network connection but there is no data transfer.
   - ○ There is no network connection.
   - ◉ There is a network connection that is transferring data.
   - ○ The network adapter is faulty.

5. What does an amber indicator on a NIC indicate?
   - ○ A frame error
   - ○ A dysfunctional transceiver
   - ○ Bad network connectivity
   - ◉ Data collisions
   - ○ A cable break

6. You recently replaced the NIC in a user's device. You receive a call from the user, who complains that there is no network connectivity. Which LED indicator on the NIC should you check first? Why?
   - ○ Activity
   - ○ Collision
   - ◉ Link
   - ○ Cable

7. Your instructor will show examples of various types of hardware tools. Identify each tool and its function, and give an example of how you would use it in network troubleshooting.

   A: Answers will vary depending on the tools available.

ACTIVITY 15-7: Troubleshooting Network Connectivity

1. You receive a call from a network user who has lost all network connectivity. You examine the network components on the user's workstation and segment and discover the situation shown in the graphic. Which network component has failed?

   A: One of the network switches has failed.

2. **Which network device(s) will be affected? Why?**

   A: All devices on that segment because they all rely on the switch for connectivity with each other and with the rest of the network. In addition, any communications between the segments would fail.

3. **Another network user calls complaining that he cannot connect to a server. You try to connect to various network devices and examine the network components and discover the situation shown in the graphic. What is the cause of the connectivity failure?**

   A: A cable drop has failed or broken.

4. **Which network device(s) will be affected? Why?**

   A: Only connectivity to and from the server will be affected because it is the only system to use that cable drop.

5. **Your company's network is spread across several locations within the city. One of your network operations centers has experienced a power surge and you are concerned about the effect on network connectivity. You try to connect to various network devices and discover the situation shown in the graphic. Which network device has failed?**

   A: It is a hybrid network, as there is a mesh topology between the four routers, and a star topology on each individual LAN segment—one of the routers has failed.

6. **What area of the network will be affected?**

   A: Only the nodes on Segment C will be affected. The mesh topology between the routers will enable the network to bypass the fault.

7. **Your network uses UTP CAT5 cable throughout the building. There are a few users who complain of intermittent network connectivity problems. You cannot determine a pattern for these problems that relates to network usage. You visit the users' workstations and find that they are all located close to an elevator shaft. What is a likely cause of the intermittent connectivity problems?**

   A: As the cabling is being run too close to the elevator equipment, when the elevator motor activates, it produces interference on the network wire.

8. **How might you correct the problem?**

   A: Replace the UTP cable with STP.

9. **A client visiting your company found that his 802.11b wireless card cannot connect to your company's 802.11g wireless network. Of the following choices, which is most likely?**

   ○ 802.11b broadcasts at 5 GHz, while 802.11g is 2.4 GHz

   ◉ Incompatibility between 802.11b and g

   ○ A rogue DHCP server

   ○ Too many wireless devices sharing the access point

10. **An employee has complained that conference calls in Conference Room 1 routinely get interrupted by periods of white noise, and that the speaker often has every other word cut off. You have discovered that the room's network cable has been run over by a chair's wheel, and that the wires have been crushed. What is this an example of?**

    ○ Packet loss

    ◉ Near-end crosstalk

    ○ Far-end crosstalk

    ○ Network drain

ACTIVITY 15-9: Troubleshooting Security Configuration Issues

1. A user complains of no longer being able to access the Internet from her workstation. After some initial investigation, you decide the issue is because of a firewall. In your environment, you have hardware firewalls protecting the entire network. What troubleshooting steps would you take?

   A: Answers will vary, but may include: First have other users try to reach the Internet and establish if the problem resides with one or more devices. If multiple users have the same issue, then check that the rules for the hardware firewalls are not blocking the traffic the users are trying to use. If only a single user has an issue, then check her device for connectivity in general and also check if she has a local firewall running that may be blocking traffic.

2. A user comes to you and says that he is no longer able to log in to the network. He says that yesterday he was able to log in just fine. What troubleshooting steps would you take?

   A: Answers will vary, but may include: Check the user account to verify that is hasn't been locked out; check if the user password has expired.

3. In the previous scenario, you verified that there were no issues with the user account. What steps would you take next?

   A: Answers will vary, but may include: Verify that the user has correct permissions/group membership to log in to the network, and verify that his computer has network connectivity.

4. A user who recently moved from one department to a new department is unable to find the printer on the network for the new department. What troubleshooting steps would you take?

   A: Answers will vary, but may include: Check to see if other users in that department have the same issue, verify that the user was moved from the domain group of her former department and added to the domain group for the new department, and verify that local security settings aren't interfering with access to the printer.

5. You are attempting to use the tracert or traceroute command to investigate a routing issue on your network. The command fails even though you are able to use the ping command. What troubleshooting steps would you take?

   A: Answers will vary, but may include: Check ACLs on routers to see if they are blocking ICMP traffic, and check firewalls to see if they are blocking ICMP traffic.

ACTIVITY 15-10: Troubleshooting Security Issues

1. Users and customers are complaining that your company website is not responding. You check and the web server is up and running. What troubleshooting steps would you take?

   A: Answers will vary, but may include: Query the routers for congestion on their interfaces to see if they are being flooded; use a network monitoring tool to check traffic to the web server; try to filter the offending traffic on upstream routers; wait for the DoS attack to stop.

2. It has been discovered that a user in the sales department is able to access resources in the finance department. It is suspected that the user is disgruntled and may be trying to find sensitive information. What troubleshooting steps would you take?

   A: Answers will vary, but may include: Check the user's group membership to verify that they don't have this kind of access; implement tighter group security to limit the user's access; monitor and audit the user's network activity, and if the user is using another account, then lock down that account or simply change the password. If this user is found to be malicious, then HR or a manager will need to be notified so that they can determine what steps to take.

3. **It is suspected that a workstation has malware running on it. What troubleshooting steps would you take?**

    A: Answers will vary, but may include: Run anti-malware scans with the latest definitions on the workstation to see if it will detect malware; run scans with different tools to see if they can detect malware; remove malware by using anti-malware tool or recommended steps; apply a previous restore point; and wipe the workstation and reinstall the operating system.

4. **Mobile users in your office inform you that they are no longer able to access the wireless network. What troubleshooting steps would you take?**

    A: Answers will vary, but may include: Verify that WAPs are running and configured properly; if possible, test the wireless device by connecting it to a wired connection; use a spectrum analyzer to detect jamming attacks.

Glossary

10Base standards
A set of standards that describes the media type and the speeds at which each type of media operates.

802.11 standard
An IEEE standard that specifies an over-the-air interface between a wireless client and a base station or between two wireless clients.

802.1x
A standard for securing networks by implementing EAP as the authentication protocol over either a wired or wireless Ethernet LAN, rather than the more traditional implementation of EAP over PPP.

802.2 standard
An IEEE standard used to address the need for MAC-sub-layer addressing in bridges.

802.3 standard
An IEEE standard used to standardize Ethernet and expand it to include a wide range of cable media.

802.3af standard
An IEEE standard used to describe PoE technology.

802.3at standard
An IEEE standard used to describe PoE+ technology.

802.x standards
A family of networking standards developed by IEEE to address networking technologies.

A
(Address record) A DNS record that maps the host name to its IP address using a 32-bit IPv4 address.

AAAA
(IPv6 address record) A DNS record that maps the host name to its IP address using a 128-bit IPv6 address.

AC
(Alternating Current) An electrical current that switches its flow back and forth in a circuit.

access control
In security terms, the process of determining and assigning privileges to various resources, objects, and data.

accountability
In security terms, the process of determining who to hold responsible for a particular activity or event.

accounting
See auditing.

ACL
(Access Control List) A set of data (user names, passwords, time and date, IP address, MAC address, etc.) that is used to

control access to a resource, such as a device, file, or network.

active hub
A hub that regenerates the signal similar to a repeater.

active IDS
(active intrusion detection system) A system that detects a security breach according to the parameters it has been configured with, logs the activity, and then takes the appropriate action to block the user from the suspicious activity.

ad-hoc mode
A peer-to-peer wireless configuration where each wireless workstation talks directly to other workstations.

administrative distance
A numerical value assigned to a routing protocol, static route, or a direct-connected route to signify more desirable routes.

adware
Software that automatically displays or downloads advertisements when it is used.

algorithm
In encryption, the rule, system, or mechanism used to encrypt data.

amplitude
The crest or trough of a wave from the midpoint of the waveform to its top or bottom.

analog modem
A device that modulates signals to encode digital information and demodulates signals to decode transmitted information.

analog signal
A signal that carries information as continuous waves of electromagnetic or optical energy.

ANS
(Authoritative Name Server) A name server that responds to name-related queries in one or more zones.

anti-malware software
A software program that scans a device or network for known viruses, Trojans, worms, and other malicious software.

anycast transmission
A transmission method in which data is sent from a server to the nearest node within a group, which then initiates another anycast and transmits the data to next nearest node within the group, and so forth, until all nodes in the group have received the data.

AP
(Access Point) See WAP.

APC connector
(angled physical contact connector) A fiber optic connector where the end faces are curved but are angled at an industry-standard eight degrees to maintain a tight connection.

APIPA
(Automatic Private IP Addressing) A service that enables a DHCP client device to configure itself automatically with an IP address on the 169.254.0.0 network in case no DHCP servers respond to the client's DHCP discover broadcast.

ARP
(Address Resolution Protocol) A communications protocol that resolves IP addresses to MAC addresses.

ARP cache
A table used to maintain a correlation between each MAC address and its corresponding IP address.

ARP cache poisoning
(Address Resolution Protocol cache poisoning) An attack that occurs when an attacker redirects an IP address to the MAC address of a device that is not the intended recipient.

ARP inspection
(Address Resolution Protocol inspection) A security control for switch ports that can validates ARP packets on the network.

arp utility

A command that enables an administrator to view and manipulate the ARP cache, including deleting it or adding an entry to it.

AS

(Autonomous System) A self-contained network on the Internet that deploys a single protocol and has a single administration. Also called a routing domain.

asymmetric encryption

See key-pair encryption.

asynchronous communications

A communication method in which special start and stop bit patterns are inserted between each byte of data, enabling the receiver to distinguish between the bytes in the data stream.

ATM

(Asynchronous Transfer Mode) A cell-switching network technology designed for the high-speed transfer of voice, video, and data in LANs, WANs, and telephone networks.

attack

Any technique that is used to exploit a vulnerability in any application on a computing device without authorization.

attacker

A term for a user who gains unauthorized access to devices and networks for malicious purposes.

attenuation

The fading or degradation of a signal as it travels across a network medium.

auditing

In security terms, the process of tracking and recording system activities and resource access. Also called accounting.

AUI connector

(Attachment Unit Interface connector) A 15-pin D-shaped connector. Also called a DIX connector, it is named for the three companies that invented it: Digital Equipment Corporation (DEC), Intel, and Xerox.

AUI-to-Ethernet transceiver

See MAC transceiver.

authentication

A network security measure in which a user or some other network component proves its identity to gain access to network resources.

authentication by assertion

Authentication based entirely on a user name/password combination.

authorization

In security terms, the process of determining what rights and privileges a particular entity has.

availability

The fundamental security goal of ensuring that systems operate continuously and that authorized individuals can access data that they need.

backhaul

The connection between a provider's core network and its regional subnetworks.

backoff

The random amount of time a node in a CSMA/CD network waits after a collision has occurred; a typical backoff period is a few milliseconds long.

bandwidth

The average number of bits of data that can be transmitted from a source to a destination over the network in one second.

bandwidth shaping

See traffic shaping.

base 16 numbering system

See hexadecimal numbering system.

base 2 numbering system

See binary numbering system.

base 8 numbering system

See octal numbering system.

baseband transmission
A transmission technique in which digital signals are sent via direct current pulses over a single, unmultiplexed signal channel.

baseline
A record of a device's performance statistics under normal operating conditions.

BGP
(Border Gateway Protocol) A path vector routing protocol used by ISPs to establish routing between one another.

biconic
A screw-on type connector with a tapered sleeve that is fixed against guided rings and screws onto the threaded sleeve to secure the connection.

binary numbering system
The numbering system used by electronic machines to perform calculations. Each position, starting from the rightmost, signifies a higher power of 2. Also called base 2 numbering system.

biometric lock
A physical security control that grants access to facilities according to biometric features, such as fingerprints, voice prints, retina scans, or signatures.

biometrics
Authentication schemes based on an individual's physical characteristics.

black hat
A hacker who exposes vulnerabilities for financial gain or for some malicious purpose.

bleed
A condition where wireless signals travel where they are not intended to go.

block-level storage
A data storage mechanism where raw volumes are created and every block within every volume can be controlled as if it were an individual hard drive.

bluejacking
A method used by attackers to send out unwanted Bluetooth signals from smartphones, tablets, and laptops to other Bluetooth-enabled devices.

bluesnarfing
A process in which attackers gain access to unauthorized information on a wireless device using a Bluetooth connection.

Bluetooth
A wireless technology that facilitates short-range wireless communication between devices, such as personal computers, laptops, mobile phones, and gaming consoles, thus creating a WPAN.

BNC coupler
(Bayonet-Neill-Concelman coupler) A device that enables you to connect two BNC cables together.

BOOTP
(Bootstrap Protocol) A legacy UDP network protocol that helps diskless workstation devices get an IP address before loading an operating system.

border router
A router situated on the edge of an AS that connects the AS to one or more remote networks. Also called an edge router.

botnet
A collection of software robots run by a command and control program that is controlled by a person.

bottleneck
A component of a device that performs poorly when compared to other components and reduces the overall performance of a device.

bounded media
A network medium that uses a physical conductor typically made of metal or glass.

BPL
(Broadband over power lines) A technology that allows broadband transmissions over domestic power lines.

bridge

A network device that divides a logical bus network into subnets.

bridge mode

A virtual firewall mode that diagnoses and monitors all incoming and outgoing traffic but does not actively participate in routing the traffic.

broadband transmission

A transmission technique in which a single medium carries multiple channels of data, usually through modulation.

broadcast domain

A logical area in a network where any node connected to the network can directly transmit to any other node in the domain without a central routing device.

broadcast radio

A form of RF networking that is non-directional, uses a single frequency for transmission, and comes in low- and high-power versions.

broadcast transmission

A transmission method in which data is sent from a source node to all other nodes on a network.

brute force attack

A type of password attack where an attacker uses an application to exhaustively try every possible alphanumeric combination to attempt to crack encrypted passwords.

buffer overflow

An attack that targets a device's vulnerability by causing the device's operating system to crash or reboot, which may result in the loss of data or the execution rogue code on the device.

buffering

A flow control technique in which received data is stored on a temporary high-speed memory location.

business continuity

A collection of planning and preparatory activities that are used during a serious incident or disaster to ensure that an organization's critical business functions will continue to operate or will be recovered to an operational state within a reasonably short period.

butt set

A special type of telephone used by telecom technicians when installing and testing local lines. Also called a lineman's test set.

CA

(Certificate Authority) A server that can issue digital certificates and the associated public/private key pairs.

cable basket

A type of cable tray made of wire mesh that is primarily used for lightweight cables, such as telephone and network cables.

cable certifier

A type of networking tool that enables you to perform tests, such as cable testing and validity testing.

cable Internet access

A WAN connectivity technology that uses a cable television connection and a cable modem to provide high-speed Internet access to homes and small businesses.

cable ladder

A vertical channel that network cables and electrical wires run through that provides mechanical support and protection.

cable management

The practice of neatly securing electrical, data, and other cables.

cable modem

A hardware device that connects a subscriber's device to a service provider's cable systems.

cable stripper

A device that enables you to remove the protective coating from wiring to facilitate installing a media connector.

cable tester

An electrical instrument that verifies if a signal is transmitted by a cable. Also called a media tester or line tester.

cable tray
A horizontal channel that network cables and electrical wires run through that provides mechanical support and protection.

cache
A buffer that is used when reading information from a disk or RAM.

caching engine
An application or service that stores requested data to provide faster responses to future requests for the data.

CAN
(campus area network) A network that covers an area equivalent to an academic campus or business park.

CARP
(Common Address Redundancy Protocol) A redundancy protocol that allows a number of devices to be grouped together to use a single virtual network interface among them.

CCMP
(Counter Mode with Cipher Block Chaining Message Authentication Code Protocol) An Advanced Encryption Standard (AES) cipher-based encryption protocol used in WPA2.

CDMA
(Code Division Multiple Access) A standard that describes protocols for 2G digital cellular networks.

cell
The area covered by a wireless access point. Alternatively, a cell is a type of network, similar to a packet switching network, in which data is transmitted as fixed-length packets called cells.

cell switching network
A type of network, similar to a packet switching network, in which data is transmitted as fixed-length packets called cells.

centralized network
A network in which a central mainframe computer controls all network communication and performs data processing and storage on behalf of clients.

certificate management system
A system that provides the software tools to perform the day-to-day functions of a PKI.

certificate repository
A database containing digital certificates.

chain of custody
Documentation that tracks evidence from the time it is collected until it is released back to the owner.

change management
A systematic way of approving and executing change to ensure maximum security, stability, and availability of information technology services.

CHAP
(Challenge Handshake Authentication Protocol) An encrypted remote-access authentication method that enables connections from any authentication method requested by the server, except for PAP and SPAP unencrypted authentication.

chips
Multiple data signals generated in the DSSS technique.

CIA triad
The three principles of security control and management: confidentiality, integrity, and availability. Also called the information security triad or information security triple.

CIDR
(Classless Inter Domain Routing) A subnetting method that selects a subnet mask that meets an individual network's networking and node requirements and then treats the mask like a 32-bit binary word.

cipher
A method for concealing the meaning of text.

cipher lock
A physical security control that requires users to press keypad buttons in the correct sequence to gain entry to a room or building.

ciphertext
Data that has been encoded with a cipher and is unreadable.

circuit switching
A switching technique in which one endpoint creates a single path connection to another, depending on the requirement.

circuit tester
An electrical instrument that test whether or not current is passing through a circuit.

Class A addresses
A block of IP addresses from 1.0.0.0 to 127.255.255.255 that provides the largest number of nodes (16,777,214) for the smallest number of networks (126), thus increasing the number of nodes per network.

Class B addresses
A block of IP addresses from 128.0.0.0 to 191.255.255.255 that provides a good balance between the number of networks and the number of nodes per network—16,382 networks of 65,534 nodes each.

Class C addresses
A block of IP addresses from 192.0.0.0 to 223.255.255.255 that provides the largest number of networks (2,097,150) and the smallest number of nodes per network (254).

Class D addresses
A block of IP addresses from 224.0.0.0 to 239.255.255.255 used to support multicast sessions.

Class E addresses
A block of IP addresses from 240.0.0.0 to 255.255.255.255 used for research and experimentation purposes.

cleartext
The unencrypted form of data. Also called plaintext.

cleartext credentials
User information, such as passwords that are not encrypted before being stored or transmitted.

client
A network device or process that initiates a connection to a server.

client/server network
A network in which servers provide resources to clients.

cloud computing
A model for providing or consuming off-premises computing services over the Internet.

CNAME
(Canonical name record) A DNS record that maps multiple canonical names (aliases) to one A record.

coax
(coaxial cable) A type of copper cable that features a central conductor surrounded by an insulator and braided or foil shielding.

codec
Software or hardware that performs digital compression of audio and video streams for video conferencing.

cold site
A predetermined alternate location where a network can be rebuilt after a disaster.

cold spare
A duplicate piece of backup equipment that can be configured to use as an alternate, if needed.

collision domain
A contention-based network on which a group of nodes compete with each other for access to the media.

competitive media access
See contention-based media access.

compromised system
A device that has been infected by malware or otherwise controlled by an outside entity.

compulsory tunnels
VPN tunnels that are established by the WAN carrier without involvement from client endpoints.

confidentiality

The fundamental security goal of keeping information and communications private and protecting them from unauthorized access.

configuration management

The process of setting up and changing the configuration of a network and its components.

connection

A virtual link between two nodes established for the duration of a communication session.

connection-oriented protocol

A data transmission method where a connection is established before any data can be sent, and where a stream of data is delivered in the same order as it was sent.

connectionless protocol

A data transmission method that does not establish a connection between devices and where data may be delivered out of order and may be delivered over different paths.

connector

A metal device at the end of a wire to connect video equipment and network nodes in a LAN.

contention-based media access

A media access method in which nodes compete or cooperate among themselves for media access time. Also called competitive media access.

controlled media access

A media access method in which a central device controls when and for how long each node can transmit. Also called deterministic media access.

copper media

A type of bounded media that uses one or more copper conductors surrounded by an insulated coating.

COS

(class of service) A parameter used in data and voice protocols to differentiate among the payload types contained in a transmitted packet.

cost

The number of hops along a route between two networks.

count-to-infinity loop

A routing loop that occurs when a router or network goes down and one of the other routers does not realize that it can no longer reach the router.

counter

An individual statistic about the operation of system objects, such as software processes or hardware components, monitored by a performance monitor.

cracker

A user who breaks encryption codes, defeats software copy protections, or specializes in breaking into systems.

CRC

(Cyclic Redundancy Check) An error detection method that can be applied to blocks of data, rather than individual words. Both the sender and receiver calculate EDC; if they match, the data is assumed to be valid.

crossover cable

A network cable that connects like devices.

cryptography

The science of hiding information to protect sensitive information and communications from unauthorized access.

CSMA/CA

(Carrier Sense Multiple Access/Collision Avoidance) A contention-based media access method where nodes try to avoid data collisions by transmitting when they deem the channel to be idle.

CSMA/CD

(Carrier Sense Multiple Access/Collision Detection) A contention-based media access method where nodes send data when they deem the channel to be idle, but take steps to retransmit when collisions occur.

CSU/DSU

(Channel Service Unit/Data Service Unit) A combination of two WAN connectivity devices on a frame relay network that work together to connect a digital WAN line with a customer's LAN.

custom subnet

A collection of leased IP addresses that are divided into smaller groups to serve a network's needs.

custom subnet mask

A number that is applied to an IP address to divide a single block of addresses into multiple subnets.

CWDM

(Coarse Wavelength Division Multiplexing) A multiplexing technology that combines multiple signals on laser beams at various wavelengths for transmission along fiber optic cables, resulting in fewer channels than DWDM

cycle

One complete oscillation of an analog signal.

daemon

A background process that performs a specific operation.

data breach

A security incident where sensitive, protected, or confidential data is copied, transmitted, viewed, stolen, or used by an individual who is not authorized to do so.

data exfiltration

Another industry term for data theft.

data packet

A unit of data transfer between devices that communicate on a network.

data theft

A type of attack in which unauthorized access is used to obtain protected network information.

data transmission

The exchange of data among different computers or other electronic devices through a network.

data window

A flow control technique in which multiple packets are sent as a unit. The recipient acknowledges each window rather than each packet, resulting in higher throughput.

DC

(Direct Current) A type of electric current that flows unidirectionally.

DCE

(Data Communications Equipment) An interface device, such as a modem on a frame relay network.

DCF

(distributed coordination function) A collision avoidance method that controls access to the physical medium.

DCS

(Distributed Control System) An ICS that is used in process-based industries where each main process is broken down into a series of sub-processes, each of which is assigned an acceptable tolerance level.

DDoS attack

(Distributed Denial of Service attack) A software attack in which an attacker hijacks or manipulates multiple devices (through the use of zombies or drones) on disparate networks to carry out a DoS attack.

de-encapsulation

The process of removing delivery information at each layer of the OSI model as data passes to the next-higher layer at the receiver end.

deciphering

The process of reversing a cipher.

decoy

See honeypot.

dedicated line

A telecommunication path that is always available for use by a designated user. Also called a leased line.

default gateway

An IP address of the router that routes remote traffic from the device's local subnet to remote subnets.

demand priority

A polling technique in which nodes signal their state—either ready to transmit or idle—to an intelligent hub, which grants nodes permission to transmit.

demarc

(demarcation point) The physical location where a building's wiring ends and the telephone company's wiring begins.

demarcation point

See demarc.

demultiplexer

See demux.

demultiplexing

A process that converts the multiplexed signals to independent signals.

demux

(demultiplexer) A device that performs demultiplexing at the receiving end.

deterministic media access

See controlled media access.

DHCP

(Dynamic Host Configuration Protocol) A network service that provides automatic assignment of IP addresses and other TCP/IP configuration information.

DHCP discover

A broadcast sent by a node when it is ready to communicate with a DHCP server.

DHCP relay agent

A service that captures a BOOTP broadcast and forwards it through the router as a unicast transmission to a DHCP server on a remote subnet.

DHCP request

A message returned to a DHCP server by a client that asks to lease an IP address from the DHCP server.

DHCP reservation

DHCP lease assignments that enable you to configure a permanent IP address for a client.

DHCP snooping

A security control for switch ports that can harden the security on the network to allow only clients with specific IP or MAC addresses to have access to the network.

dial-up connection

A PSTN connection that uses modems, existing phone lines, and long-distance carrier services to provide WAN connectivity and remote network access.

dial-up lines

PSTN connections that use modems, existing phone lines, and long-distance carrier services to provide low-cost, low-bandwidth WAN connectivity and remote network access.

dial-up modem

A communication device that converts a device's digital signals into analog signals before transmission over telephone lines.

dialectric

An insulator—a material that does not conduct electricity by separating the conductor and shield.—where the entire package is wrapped in an insulating layer called a sheath or jacket.

Diameter

An authentication protocol that is an updated version of RADIUS and improves on some of its features.

dictionary attack

A type of password attack that automates password guessing by comparing encrypted passwords against a predetermined list of possible password values.

digital certificate

An electronic document that associates credentials with a public key.

digital signal

An electrical signal that can have combinations of only two values: one and zero.

digital signature

An encrypted hash value that is appended to a message to identify the sender and the message.

directional antenna

A type of antenna that concentrates the signal beam in a single direction.

disaster

A catastrophic loss of device functioning due to a cause that cannot reasonably be foreseen or avoided.

disaster recovery

The administrative function of protecting people and resources while restoring a failed network or failed systems as quickly as possible.

disaster recovery plan

A policy and set of procedures that documents how people and resources will be protected in a disaster, and how the organization will recover from the disaster and restore normal functioning.

distance–vector routing

A dynamic routing method used on packet-switched networks to calculate route costs and routing table entries.

distribution frame

A device that terminates cables and enables connections with other devices.

DMZ

(demilitarized zone) A small section of a private network that is located between two firewalls and made available for public access.

DNS

(Domain Name System) The naming service used on the Internet and many TCP/IP-based networks.

domain

A grouping of devices on the Internet based on the nature of their operations.

domain name

A unique name that identifies a website on the Internet. A period is used to separate the labels of domain names.

DoS attack

(Denial of Service attack) A network attack in which an attacker disables systems that provide network services by consuming a network link's available bandwidth, consuming a single device's available resources, or exploiting programming flaws in an application or operating system.

drain

The connection point between a shield and the ground.

drone

See zombie.

DSCP

(Differentiated Services Code Point) A field in an IP packet that enables different levels of service to be assigned to network traffic.

DSH

(Digital Signal Hierarchy) A channelized data transmission standard used to multiplex several single data or voice channels for a greater total bandwidth.

DSL

(Digital Subscriber Line) A broadband Internet connection method that transmits digital signals over existing phone lines.

DSL modem

A hardware device that connects a subscriber's device to a telephone line that provides the DSL service for connectivity to the Internet.

DSSS

(Direct Sequence Spread Spectrum) A type of radio transmission in which a single data signal is converted into multiple digital data signals called chips that are sent across a wide band of adjacent frequencies.

DTE

(Data Termination Equipment) An interface device, such as a NIC or router on a frame relay network.

dual ring topology

A variation of the physical ring topology where two counter-rotating rings carry data in opposite directions.

DVM

(Digital Volt Meter) An electrical instrument that uses an analog-to-digital converter to display numeric voltage readings.

DWDM

(Dense Wavelength Division Multiplexing) A multiplexing technology that uses light wavelengths to transmit data.

dynamic routing

A type of routing that automatically builds and updates routing tables by using route discovery operations.

EAP

(Extensible Authentication Protocol) A protocol that enables systems to use hardware-based identifiers, such as fingerprint scanners or smart card readers, for authentication.

eavesdropping attack

A network attack that uses special monitoring software to gain access to private communications on the network wire or across a wireless network. Also called a sniffing attack.

EDAC

(Error Detection and Correction) The process of determining if transmitted data has been received correctly and completely, and if not, rebuilding the data to its correct form.

EDC

(Error Detection Code) The bits that are attached to transmitted data to indicate its original contents.

edge network

A network located on the periphery of a centralized network.

edge router

See border router.

EFS

(Encrypting File System) A file encryption tool available on Windows systems that have partitions formatted with NTFS.

EGP

(Exterior Gateway Protocol) The protocol responsible for exchanging routing information between two neighboring gateways.

EIA

(Electronic Industries Alliance) A trade association accredited by ANSI to develop and jointly issue standards for telecommunications and electronics.

EIGRP

(Enhanced Interior Gateway Routing Protocol) An improvement over IGRP that includes features that support VLSM and classful and classless subnet masks.

electrical noise

Unwanted signals that are introduced into network media and that interfere with the proper reception of transmitted signals.

EMI

(electromagnetic interference) A type of noise that is caused by electrical radiation or induction and that disrupts an electrical signal.

encapsulation

The process of adding delivery information to the actual data in each layer of the OSI model.

enciphering

The process of applying a cipher.

encryption

A security technique that converts data from plain, or cleartext form, into coded, or ciphertext form, so that only authorized parties with the necessary decryption information can decode and read the data.

encryption devices

A device that provides encryption, decryption, and access control using an HSM.

encryption key

A specific piece of information that is used with an algorithm to perform encryption and decryption in cryptography.

endpoint

A network node that is the source or destination for data transfer.

enterprise network

A network that includes elements of both LANs and WANs and is owned and operated by a single organization to interlink its devices and resources.

environment monitor

A hardware tool that ensures that environmental conditions do not spike or plummet temperature above or below equipment specifications.

error detection

The process of determining if transmitted data has been received correctly and completely.

ES

(Edge System) A system on a frame relay network that efficiently manages traffic between a user and the backbone network.

Ethernet

A set of networking technologies and media access methods specified for LANs.

Ethernet frame

A data packet that has been encoded on the Data Link layer for transmission from one node to another on an Ethernet network.

Ethernet transceiver

See MAC transceiver.

evil twin

A rogue access point on a network that appears to be legitimate.

exterior router

Any router entirely outside an AS.

extranet

A private network that grants controlled access to users outside of the network.

fall-back plan

An alternate network design that can be implemented temporarily to enable critical network elements to function.

Fast Ethernet

An Ethernet technology that can transmit data at speeds of 100 Mbps.

fault tolerance

The ability of a network or device to withstand a foreseeable component failure and still continue to provide an acceptable level of service.

FC

(ferrule connector) A connector used in industrial settings that has a heavy-duty ferrule in the center for more mechanical stability than SMA or ST connectors.

FC

(Fibre Channel) A high-speed network technology that is primarily used to connect device data storage at rates of up to 16 Gbps.

FCS

(Frame Check Sequence) The extra characters added to a frame for detecting and correcting errors.

FDDI

(Fiber Distributed Data Interface) A dual-ring, token-passing fiber network that operates at 100 Mbps.

FDM

(Frequency-Division Multiplexing) A multiplexing method in which data from multiple nodes is sent over multiple frequencies or channels over a network medium.

ferrule

A tubular structure made of ceramic or metal that supports optical fiber.

fiber coupler

A device that enables you to connect fiber optic cables together when a device has one or more input fibers and one or more output fibers that need to be connected.

fiber optic cable
A network cable that has a core surrounded by one or more glass or plastic strands, along with extra fiber strands or wraps, which are surrounded by a protective outer jacket.

firewall
A software program or a hardware device or a combination of both that protects a device or network from unauthorized data by blocking unsolicited traffic.

first responder
The first person or team to respond to an accident, damage site, or natural disaster in an IT company.

fixed length window
A type of data window in which each block of packets is of the same size. Typically, fixed length windows are small to avoid flooding the buffers of less-powerful receivers.

flooding
A network transmission state in which data arrives at a receiving node too quickly to be processed.

flow control
A class of technique for optimizing the exchange of data between systems.

FQDN
(Fully Qualified Domain Name) The host name combined with the host's domain name.

frame relay
A WAN protocol that operates at the Physical and Data Link layers of the OSI model.

frequency
The number of complete cycles per second in a wave. Also called the period of the wave.

friendly DoS
(friendly denial of service) An attack where a website ends up denied because of a sudden enormous spike in popularity.

FTP
(File Transfer Protocol) A TCP/IP protocol that allows the transfer of files between a user's device and a remote host.

FTP bounce attack
An attack that targets an FTP's vulnerability to permit connected clients to open other connections on any port on the FTP server.

full duplex
A communication mode that permits simultaneous two-way communication.

gain
An increase in the amplitude of a radio wave.

GAN
(global area network) A WAN that includes sites and networks around the world.

gateway
A device or software that converts data between incompatible devices.

GBIC
(Gigabit Interface Converter) A transceiver used to convert electrical signals into optical signals and vice versa.

Gigabit Ethernet
An Ethernet technology that can transmit data at speeds of 1,000 Mbps and primarily uses optical fibers for transmission.

goodput
A subset of network throughput that is calculated by excluding bits related to protocol overhead, as well as any packets that need to be retransmitted for any reason.

GPS
(Global Positioning System) A navigational system that consists of a network of satellites with 24 active satellites and three in standby mode.

grayware
A type of software that can be either malicious or non-malicious in nature. Spyware and adware are two notable examples of grayware.

grounding
The connection of a shield or conductor to an electrical ground point, such as a pipe or wire, that is in contact with the ground.

group policy
A centralized configuration management feature available for Active Directory on Windows Server systems.

GSM
(Global System for Mobile Communications) A standard that describes protocols for 2G digital cellular networks.

guessing attack
A human-based attack where the goal is to guess a password or PIN through brute force means or by using deduction.

guest network
A subset of an organization's network that is designed for temporary use by visitors.

guideline
A suggestion for meeting the policy standard or best practices on a network policy.

hacker
A user who excels at programming or managing and configuring computing devices, and has the skills to gain access to devices through unauthorized or unapproved means.

half duplex
A communication mode that permits a two-way transmission, but in only one direction at a time.

hardware loopback plug
A special connector used for diagnosing transmission problems.

hash
The value that results from hashing encryption. Also called a hash value or message digest.

hash value
See hash.

hashing encryption
One-way encryption that transforms cleartext into a coded form that is never decrypted.

HBA
(host bus adapter) An adapter that provides input/output (I/O) processing and physical connectivity between a server and a storage device.

HCC
(horizontal cross-connect) A wiring closet where the horizontal cabling connects to a patch panel that is attached to the main facility by a backbone cable.

hertz
A measure of the number of cycles per second in an analog signal. One cycle per second equals one hertz.

hexadecimal numbering system
A numbering system where each digit is the equivalent of four binary digits. Each position, starting from the rightmost, signifies a higher power of 16. Also called base 16 numbering system.

HIDS
(host intrusion detection system) Software that monitors the device on which it is installed to identify deviations from an established security policy.

high availability
A rating that expresses how closely systems approach the goal of providing data availability 100 percent of the time.

high bandwidth application
A software application or program that requires large amounts of network bandwidth for data transmission.

HIPS
(host-based intrusion prevention system) An application that monitors the traffic from a specific host or a list of host addresses, blocking traffic from a specific host or an attack targeted against a specific device.

hoax
Any type of incorrect or misleading information that is disseminated to multiple users through unofficial channels.

honeynet
An entire dummy network used to lure attackers away from actual network components.

honeypot

A security tool used to lure attackers away from the actual network components. Also called a decoy.

hop

The action of forwarding a packet from one router to the next.

host

Any device that is connected to a network.

host name

The unique name given to a network node on a TCP/IP network.

host-based firewall

A software application that is installed directly on a host and filters incoming and outgoing packets to and from that host. Also called a personal firewall.

HOSTS file

A plaintext file configured on a client machine containing a list of IP addresses and their associated host names, which can be used for host name resolution as an alternative to DNS.

hot site

A fully configured alternate network that can be online quickly after a disaster.

hot spare

A fully configured and operational piece of backup equipment that can be swapped into a device with little to no interruption to functionality.

hotfix

A patch that is often issued on an emergency basis to address a specific security flaw.

HPSA

(high speed packet access) A family of technologies based on the 3GPP Release 5 specification, offering high data-rate services in mobile networks.

HSM

(Hardware Security Module) A cryptographic module that can generate cryptographic keys.

HTTP

(Hypertext Transfer Protocol) A network protocol that works on the Application layer of the OSI and TCP/IP models and enables clients to connect to and retrieve web pages from a server to interact with websites.

HTTPS

(HTTP Secure) A secure version of HTTP that provides a secure connection between a web browser and a server.

hub

A networking device used to connect the drops in a physical star topology network into a logical bus topology. Also called a multiport repeater.

HVAC

(heating, ventilating, and air conditioning) A type of climate control system often found in large commercial or industrial buildings.

hybrid password attack

An attack that utilizes multiple attack vectors including dictionary, rainbow table, and brute force attack methodologies when trying to crack a password.

hybrid routing

A dynamic routing method that uses both distance-vector and link state routing methods.

hybrid topology

Any topology that exhibits the characteristics of more than one standard network topology.

hypervisor mode

A virtual firewall mode that runs in the core hypervisor kernel and monitors all incoming and outgoing traffic.

IaaS

(Infrastructure as a Service) A cloud computing service that enables a consumer to outsource computing equipment purchases and running their own data center.

IANA

(Internet Assigned Number Authority) An international organization established in 1993 to govern the use of IP addresses. The Internet Corporation for Assigned Names and

Numbers (ICANN) is now responsible for leasing IP addresses worldwide.

ICC
(intermediate cross-connect) An optional connection between the main cross-connect and the horizontal cross-connect.

ICMP
(Internet Control Message Protocol) A protocol used with IP that attempts to report on the condition of a connection between two nodes.

ICS
(Industrial Control System) A network or system used to support municipal services, industrial processes, and transportation systems.

IDaaS
(Identification as a Service) A cloud computing service that enables consumers to rent an authentication infrastructure from a service provider.

IDF
(Intermediate Distribution Frame) A cable rack that interconnects the telecommunications wiring between an MDF and any end-user devices.

IDS
(intrusion detection system) A software and/or hardware system that scans, audits, and monitors a security infrastructure for signs of attacks in progress.

IEEE 1394
(Institute of Electrical and Electronics Engineers 1394) This standard is used to connect up to 63 devices to form a small local network. Also called FireWire

IGMP
(Internet Group Management Protocol) A protocol in the TCP/IP suite that supports multicasting in a routed environment.

IGP
(Interior Gateway Protocol) The protocol responsible for exchanging routing information between gateways within an AS.

IGRP
(Interior Gateway Routing Protocol) A distance-vector routing protocol developed by Cisco as an improvement over RIP and RIP v2.

IMAP4
(Internet Message Access Protocol) A protocol used for retrieving email messages and folders from a mail server.

impedance
A force that opposes the flow of electricity in an AC circuit. Impedance is measured in ohms (Ω).

impersonation
A type of spoofing in which an attacker pretends to be someone they are not; typically an average user in distress or a help desk representative.

implicit deny
The principle that establishes that everything that is not explicitly allowed is denied.

in phase
When two waves of the same frequency begin at the same time.

incident management
Practices and procedures that govern how an organization will respond to an incident in progress.

information security triad
See CIA triad.

infrared radiation
An electromagnetic wave with wavelengths longer than visible light.

infrared transmission
A form of wireless transmission where signals are sent as pulses of infrared light.

infrastructure mode
A wireless configuration that uses one or more WAPs to connect wireless workstations to the cable backbone.

insider threat

A malicious employee who in some fashion compromises a network or uses their access to obtain sensitive company information.

integrity

The fundamental security goal of ensuring that electronic data is not altered or tampered with.

intelligent switch

See managed switch.

inter–domain routing

Routing a packet among different ASes.

interactive mode

This mode of the nslookup utility enables you to query name servers for information about hosts and domains, or to print a list of hosts in a domain.

interior router

A router arranged inside an AS and completely controlled by the AS administrator.

Internet

The single largest global WAN that virtually links every country in the world.

intra–domain routing

Routing a packet within an AS.

intranet

A private network that uses Internet protocols and services to share a company's information with its employees.

intrusion detection

A process of monitoring the events occurring on a device or a network and analyzing them to detect possible incidents that are violations or imminent threats of security policy violations and standard security practices.

IP

(Internet Protocol) A connectionless Network-layer protocol that is responsible for sending data packets across a network.

IP address

A unique identifier assigned to every node connected to a TCP/IP network, such as the Internet.

IP filtering

A security control for switch ports that determines the packets that will be allowed to pass and those that will be dropped by screening the packet based on certain criteria.

IP spoofing attack

A type of software attack where an attacker creates IP packets with a forged source IP address and uses those packets to gain access to a remote device.

IPS

(Intrusion Prevention System) An active, inline security device that monitors suspicious network and/or device traffic and reacts in real time to block it. Also called NIPS.

IPSec

(Internet Protocol Security) A set of open, non-proprietary standards that you can use to secure data as it travels across the network or the Internet through data authentication and encryption.

IPv4 address

See IP address.

IPv6

An addressing scheme that uses a 128-bit binary address space.

IPv6 address

A 128-bit hexadecimal number assigned to a device on a TCP/IP network.

IRP

(Incident Response Policy) The security policy that determines the actions that an organization will take following a confirmed or potential security breach.

IS–IS

(Intermediate System to Intermediate System) A link state routing protocol used within a network.

iSCSI

(Internet Small Computer System Interface) An IP-based storage networking standard for linking data storage facilities.

ISDN
(Integrated Services Digital Network) A digital circuit switching technology that carries both voice and data.

IT asset management
(information technology asset management) The set of management policies that include information about the financial and contractual specifications of all the hardware and software components present in an organization's inventory.

iterative query
A query used by a DNS server for name resolution when a client requests only the information the server already has in its cache for a particular domain name.

ITU
(International Telecommunication Union) An international organization within the United Nations that defines global technical standards for telecommunications.

IV
(initialization vector) An unpredictable random number used to make sure that, when the same message is encrypted twice, the ciphertext is always different.

IV attack
(initialization vector attack) An attack where the attacker is able to predict or control the IV of an encryption process, thus giving the attacker access to view the encrypted data that is supposed to be hidden from everyone else except for the user or network.

jitter
The variability of latency over time across a network.

jumbo frame
An Ethernet frame with a payload greater than the standard MTU of 1,500 bytes.

Kerberos
A secure method for authenticating requests for services on a network.

key fob
A small device that can be used for activating such things as remote keyless entry systems on motor vehicles and in buildings for access to certain areas.

key–pair encryption
An encryption system in which an individual has two encryption keys: the public key that anyone can use to encode the message, and the user's private key, which is used to decode messages. Also called asymmetric encryption.

L2TP
(Layer Two Tunneling Protocol) The de facto standard VPN protocol for tunneling PPP sessions across a variety of network protocols, such as IP, frame relay, or ATM.

label
A special 4-byte header used by MLPS routers to make forwarding decisions.

label switching
A switching technology that saves on the processing time of packets by routers by adding a label to each incoming data packet.

LAN
(local area network) A self-contained network that spans a small area, such as a single building, floor, or room.

latency
The time delay for a packet to go from a source to a destination and back to the source.

latency sensitivity
The susceptibility of a device to experience issues that affect delay within a network.

LC
(Local Connector) A small form factor ceramic ferrule connector for both single mode and multimode fiber.

leased line
See dedicated line.

least privilege
The security principle that establishes that users and software should only have the

minimal level of access that is necessary for them to perform the duties required of them.

legacy system

A device running an older OS that is no longer supported by the manufacturer.

legal hold

A process that an organization uses to preserve all forms of relevant information when litigation is reasonably anticipated.

line tester

See cable tester.

lineman's test set

See butt set.

link redundancy

A network fault-tolerance method that provides alternative network connections that can function if a critical primary connection is interrupted.

link state routing

A dynamic routing method that floods routing information to all routers within a network to build and maintain a more complex network route database.

load balancer

Stand-alone network devices that perform load balancing as their primary function.

load balancing

A method of dividing work among the devices on a network.

log file

A record of actions and events performed on an operating system.

logic bomb

Code that sits dormant on a target device until it is triggered by the occurrence of specific conditions, such as a specific date and time. Once the code is triggered, the logic bomb "detonates," performing whatever action it was programmed to do.

logical bus topology

A network topology in which all nodes receive a data transmission at the same time, regardless of the physical wiring layout of the network.

logical network diagram

A network diagram that documents the protocols and applications that control the flow of network traffic.

logical ring topology

A network topology in which each node receives data only from its upstream neighbor and retransmits it only to its downstream neighbor, regardless of the physical layout of the network.

logical star topology

A network topology in which a central device controls network access for nodes that are wired as a physical bus.

logical topology

A topology that describes the data-flow patterns in a network.

looking glass site

A web server that enables external users to view routing and network behavior as it originates from a remote network.

loopback interface

A virtual network interface that network applications can communicate with when executing on the local device.

LOS

(line-of-sight) A WiMAX service where signals travel over a direct path from transmitter to receiver.

LSR

(label switching router) A router that has the MPLS technology enabled on its interfaces.

LTE

(Long Term Evolution) A radio technology for wireless broadband access.

MAC address

(Media Access Control address) A unique, hardware-level address assigned to every networking device by its manufacturer. MAC addresses are six bytes long. Also called a physical address.

MAC address filtering

(Media Access Control address filtering) A security control for switch ports that provides a simple method for securing a wireless network.

MAC transceiver

A device that connects a 15-pin AUI Ethernet connector to an RJ45 Ethernet connector. Also called an Ethernet transceiver or AUI-to-Ethernet transceiver.

mainframe computer

A powerful, centralized computer that performs data storage and processing tasks on behalf of clients and other network devices.

malware

Malicious code, such as viruses, Trojans, or worms,designed to gain unauthorized access to, make unauthorized use of, or damage devices and networks.

malware attack

A type of software attack where an attacker inserts some type of undesired or unauthorized software into a target device.

MAN

(metropolitan area network) A network that covers an area equivalent to a city or a municipality.

man-in-the-middle attack

A form of eavesdropping where the attacker makes an independent connection between two victims and steals information to use fraudulently.

managed switch

A switch that enables you to monitor and configure its operation. Also called an intelligent switch.

Manchester encoding

A digital transmission encoding scheme using binary that represents the transition from positive to ground with a 0, and the transition from negative to positive in the middle of the bit period with a 1.

mantrap

A physical security control that consists of two sets of interlocking doors inside a small space, where the first set of doors must close before the second set opens.

MCC

(main cross-connect) A structured cabling connection point that connects equipment cables, backbone cables, and entrance cables.

MDF

(Main Distribution Frame) A cable rack that interconnects external communication cables and the cables that comprise the internal network.

media access method

A network communications mechanism that determines whether or not a particular node can transmit data on a network at a given time.

media converter

A network device that enables networks running on different media to interconnect and exchange signals.

media tester

See cable tester.

medianet

A network optimized for rich media, such as voice and video, which is designed to transport a mixture of rich media and other content, such as text.

message digest

See hash.

microsegmentation

A forwarding process where all nodes are logically separated until there is a need for them to be connected.

microwave transmission

A form of point-to-point wireless transmission where signals are sent via pulses of electromagnetic energy in the microwave region of the spectrum.

microwaves

An electromagnetic wave with wavelengths shorter than radio waves.

mixed mode network

A network that incorporates elements from more than one of the three standard network configurations.

modem

A device that enables digital data to be sent over an analog medium, such as a telephone wire or cable provider's line.

MPLS

(Multiprotocol Label Switching) A network technology defined by a set of IETF specifications that enable Layer 3 devices, such as routers, to establish and manage network traffic.

MPPE

(Microsoft Point-to-Point Encryption) A method of data encryption between PPP dial-up connections or PPTP VPN connections.

MS–CHAPv2

(Microsoft Challenge Handshake Authentication Protocol v2) A protocol that strengthens the password authentication provided by Protected Extensible Authentication Protocol (PEAP).

MT–RJ

(Mechanical Transfer Registered Jack) A compact snap-to-lock connector used with multimode fiber. Also called a Fiber Jack connector.

MTR

(My traceroute) A utility that is a combination of ping and traceroute used in a UNIX-based device.

MTU

(maximum transmission unit) The size, in bytes, of the largest protocol data unit that an OSI layer can pass onwards.

multicast transmission

A transmission method in which data is sent from a server to specific nodes that are predefined as members of a multicast group.

multifactor authentication

Any authentication scheme that requires validation of at least two of the possible authentication factors.

multimeter

An electronic measuring instrument that takes electronic measurements, such as voltage, current, and resistance.

multimode fiber

A type of fiber optic cable that carries multiple light signals on a single strand.

multiplexer

See mux.

multiplexing

A controlled media access method in which a central device called a multiplexer combines signals from multiple nodes and transmits the combined signal across a medium.

multiport repeater

See hub.

mutual authentication

A security mechanism that requires that each party in a communication verify their identity.

mux

(multiplexer) A device that manages multiplexing from the sending end.

MX

(Mail Exchanger) A DNS record that maps a domain name to a mail exchange server list.

NaaS

(Network as a Service) A cloud computing service that provides network-based services through the cloud, including monitoring and QoS management.

NAC

(Network Access Control) A collection of protocols, policies, and hardware that govern access on devices to and from a network.

name resolution

The process of identifying a network node by translating its host or domain name to the corresponding IP address.

NAS

(network attached storage) A device or appliance that provides only file-based data storage services to other network devices.

NAT

(Network Address Translation) A form of Internet security that conceals internal addressing schemes from external networks, such as the Internet.

NBTSTAT

A Windows utility that is used to view and manage NetBIOS name cache information.

NetFlow

A feature of Cisco routers that enables administrators to collect IP network traffic as it enters or exits an interface.

NETSTAT

A TCP/IP utility that shows the status of each active connection.

network

A group of devices that are connected together to communicate and share network resources.

network analyzer

A software or hardware tool that integrates diagnostic and reporting capabilities to provide a comprehensive view of an organization's network.

network backbone

The highest-speed transmission path that carries the majority of network data.

network baseline

A baseline that documents the network's current performance level and provides a quantitative basis for identifying abnormal or unacceptable performance.

network configuration

A design specification for how the nodes on a network are constructed to interact and communicate.

network enumerator

See network scanner.

network management

Management of systems on the network using various activities, methods, procedures, and tools that relate to the operation, administration, maintenance, and provisioning of these systems.

network media

The bounded or unbounded conduit through which signals flow.

network policy

A formalized statement that defines network functions and establishes expectations for users, management, and IT personnel.

network scanner

A program used for scanning networks to obtain user names, host names, groups, shares, and services. Also called a network enumerator.

network-based firewall

A dedicated hardware/software combination that protects all the devices on a network by blocking unsolicited traffic.

networking standard

A set of specifications, guidelines, or characteristics applied to network components to ensure interoperability and consistency among them.

NFC

(near field communications) Technology that enables wireless devices to establish radio communications by touching them together or by bringing them into close proximity with each other, typically within 10 cm or less.

NIC

(network interface card) A device that serves as an interface between the device and the network. Also called a network adapter or network card.

NIDS

(network intrusion detection system) A system that monitors network traffic and restricts or alerts when unacceptable traffic is seen in a system.

NIPS

(network-based intrusion prevention system) An application that monitors the entire network and analyzes its activity, detects malicious code and unsolicited traffic, and takes the necessary action to protect the network. Also called an IPS.

NLOS

(non-line-of-sight) A WiMAX service where signals reach receivers by means of reflections and diffractions.

NNI

(Network-to-Network Interface) A switch that is inside an ATM network.

node

Any device that can connect to the network and generate, process, or transfer data.

noise

In electronics, random changes and disturbances in an electrical signal, such as EMI or RFI.

non-interactive mode

This mode of the nslookup utility prints only the name and requested details for one host or domain and is useful for a single query.

non-persistent agent

Software that is installed on demand, responds to NAC queries about the device's health, authenticates the device, and is removed after the session ends.

non-repudiation

The security goal of ensuring that data remains associated with the party that creates it or sends a transmission.

NS

(Name Server) A DNS record that delegates a DNS zone to use the given authoritative name servers.

nslookup

A utility that is used to test and troubleshoot domain name servers.

NT

(Network Termination) In ISDN, a device that connects the local telephone exchange lines to the customer's telephone or data equipment.

NTP

(Network Time Protocol) An Internet protocol that enables synchronization of device clock times in a network of devices by exchanging time signals.

NTU

(Network Termination Unit) In ISDN, a device that can directly connect to ISDN-aware equipment, such as phones or ISDN NICs in devices.

octal numbering system

A numbering system where each digit is the equivalent of three binary digits. Each position, starting from the rightmost, signifies a higher power of 8. Also called base 8 numbering system.

OCx

(Optical Carrier x) A standard that specifies the bandwidth for fiber optic transmissions.

OFDM

(orthogonal frequency division multiplexing) A data-encoding method used on multiple carrier frequencies.

ohm

The value of electrical resistance through which one volt will maintain a current of one ampere.

omni-directional antenna

A type of antenna that radiates the signal beam out in all directions and has lower gain but a wider coverage area. Also called a unidirectional antenna.

on-off keying

A digital data transmission encoding scheme in which a change in voltage from one state to another within a predetermined interval is symbolized by a 1.

open port

A TCP or UDP port number that is configured to accept packets.

OSI model

(Open Systems Interconnection model) A standard means of describing network communication by defining it as a series of layers, each with a specific input and output.

OSPF

(Open Shortest Path First) A link-state routing protocol used on IP networks.

OTDR

(Optical Time-Domain Reflectometer) A variation of TDR that transmits light-based signals of different wavelengths over fiber optic cabling to determine cabling issues.

OUI

(Organizationally Unique Identifier) The first three bytes of a MAC address that uniquely identify a network device manufacturer.

out of phase

When two waves either start at an offset from each other or have different frequencies.

overloading

See PAT.

PaaS

(Platform as a Service) A cloud computing service that enables consumers to rent fully configured systems that are set up for specific purposes.

packet

See data packet.

packet loss

The number of packets that are lost or damaged during transmission.

packet shaper

The mechanism that enables traffic shaping by delaying metered traffic so that each packet complies with the relevant traffic contract.

packet sniffer

A device or program that monitors network communications and captures data.

packet sniffing

An attack on a network where an attacker captures network traffic, allowing data to be extracted from the packets.

packet switching network

A network in which data is broken up into separate packets and each packet is separately routed without a dedicated connection between the endpoints.

PAN

(personal area network) A network that connects two to three devices with cables and is most often seen in small or home offices.

PAP

(Password Authentication Protocol) A remote-access authentication method that sends client IDs and passwords as cleartext.

parallel data transmission

A transmission technique in which multiple bits are transmitted across multiple transmission lines.

parity check

A process used to detect errors in memory or data communication.

partial mesh

A variation of the physical mesh topology in which only a few nodes have direct links with all other nodes.

passive hub

A hub that receives data transmitted from a device on one port and broadcasts it out to the devices connected on all other ports.

passive IDS

(passive intrusion detection system) A system that detects potential security breaches, logs the activity, and alerts security personnel.

password attack

Any type of attack in which the attacker attempts to obtain and make use of passwords illegitimately.

PAT

(Port Address Translation) A subset of dynamic NAT functionality that maps either one or multiple unregistered addresses to a single registered address using multiple ports. Also called overloading.

patch

A small unit of supplemental code meant to address either a security problem or a functionality flaw in a software package or operating system.

patch management

The practice of monitoring for, evaluating, testing, and installing software patches and updates.

path–vector routing

A routing method where the router keeps track of the route from itself to the destination; however, rather than recording every individual node, path-vector routing can treat entire autonomous systems as nodes.

pathping

A TCP/IP command that provides information about latency and packet loss on a network.

PC connector

(physical contact connector) A fiber optic connector that has end faces that are polished to be slightly curved or spherical to eliminate any air gap and force the fibers into contact.

PDH

(Plesiochronous Digital Hierarchy) A communications standard that can carry data over fiber optic or microwave radio systems.

PDU

(protocol data unit) An umbrella term that refers to the data packets, frames, packets, segments, and datagrams that carry information across a network.

peer

A self-sufficient device that acts as both a server and a client.

peer–to–peer network

A network in which resource sharing, processing, and communications control are completely decentralized. Also called a workgroup.

penetration testing

An attack authorized by the owner of a computing device or network with the purpose of finding security weaknesses that could be exploited by a real attacker.

performance monitor

A software tool that monitors the state of services or daemons, processes, and resources on a device.

permanent DoS

(permanent denial of service) An attack that damages a device so badly that it must be replaced or hardware must be reinstalled.

permission

A security setting that determines the level of access a user or group account has to a particular resource.

persistent agent

Software that installs on a client device and responds continuously to NAC queries about the device's health.

personal firewall

See host-based firewall.

pharming

An attack in which a request for a website, typically an e-commerce site, is redirected to a similar-looking, but fake, website.

phase

The fixed point where a wave's cycle begins in relationship to a fixed point.

phishing

A type of email-based social engineering attack in which the attacker sends email from a spoofed source, such as a bank, to try to elicit private information from the victim.

physical bus topology

A physical topology in which network nodes are arranged in a linear format.

physical mesh topology

A network topology in which each node has a direct, point-to-point connection to every other node.

physical network diagram

A pictorial representation of the location of all network devices and endpoints, and their connections to one another.

physical ring topology

A network topology in which all network nodes are connected in a circle.

physical star topology

A network topology that uses a central connectivity device with separate point-to-point connections to each node.

physical topology

A topology that describes a network's physical layout and shape.

ping

A TCP/IP command used to verify the network connectivity of a device, and also to check if the target device is active.

PKI

(Public Key Infrastructure) An encryption system that is composed of a CA, certificates, software, services, and other cryptographic components for the purpose of verifying authenticity and enabling the validation of data and entities.

plaintext

Unencoded data. Also called cleartext.

plenum

An air handling space, including ducts and other parts of the HVAC system in a building.

plenum cable

A grade of cable that does not give off noxious or poisonous gases when burned.

PoE

(Power over Ethernet) A standard that specifies a method for supplying electrical power over Ethernet connections.

PoE+

(Power over Ethernet Plus) An updated standard that specifies a method for supplying electrical power over Ethernet connections.

point-to-multipoint connection

A WAN topology that uses a physical star/logical hub configuration to connect a central site (hub) and several branch sites (spokes)s.

point-to-point connection

A WAN topology that provides a direct connection between two routers.

poison reverse

An algorithm that prevents count-to-infinity loops by ensuring that a router broadcasts a route cost of 16 for all transmissions on its network.

policy statement

An outline of the plan for the individual component on a network policy.

polling

A controlled media access method in which a central device contacts each node to check whether it has data to transmit.

PON

(Passive Optical Network) A point-to-multipoint optical network that is used for broadcast transmissions using optical systems.

POP3

(Post Office Protocol version 3) A protocol used for retrieving email from a mailbox on the mail server.

port

The endpoint of a logical connection that client devices use to connect to specific server programs.

port filtering

A technique of selectively enabling or disabling TCP and UDP ports on devices or network devices.

port mirroring

The practice of duplicating all traffic on one port in a switch to a second port.

port scanner

A type of software that searches a network host or a range of IP addresses for open TCP and UDP ports.

port scanning attack
An attack where an attacker scans your systems to see which ports are listening in an attempt to find a way to gain unauthorized access.

port security
The process of protecting ports on a network from unauthorized access.

posture assessment
The process of performing a compliance check to provide authorization in NAC.

power management
The practice of ensuring sufficient electrical power to electronic and other devices.

PPP
(Point-to-Point Protocol) A remote networking protocol that works on the Data Link layer (Layer 2) of the TCP/IP protocol suite and is used to send IP datagrams over serial point-to-point links.

PPTP
(Point-to-Point Tunneling Protocol) A Microsoft VPN layer 2 protocol that increases the security of PPP by providing tunneling and data encryption for PPP packets and uses the same authentication methods as PPP.

premise wiring
The collection of drop cables, patch panels, and patch cables that together make a functional network.

private IP address
An address used for a node that needs IP connectivity only within the enterprise network, but not external connections to the Internet.

private key
In key-pair encryption, the key that is known only to an individual and is used to decode data.

privilege bracketing
The security method of allowing privileges to a user only when needed and revoking them as soon as the task is complete.

procedure
Instructions that detail specifically how to implement a network policy.

promiscuous mode
A mode of operation for network adapters that enables them to capture all packets sent across the network, regardless of the source or destination of the packets.

protocol analyzer
A type of diagnostic software that can examine and display data packets that are being transmitted over a network. Also called a network analyzer.

protocol binding
The assignment of a protocol to a NIC.

protocols
Rules that govern the transfer of information among computing devices.

proximity reader
A card reader that can read a smart card when the card is held near it.

proxy server
A device that isolates internal networks from the servers by downloading and storing files on behalf of clients.

PSTN
(Public Switched Telephone Network) An international telephone system that carries analog voice data.

PTR
(Pointer) A DNS record that maps the IP address to a host name for reverse lookup functionality.

public key
In key-pair encryption, the key that is available to all and is used to encode data.

punch down block
A device that connects groups of telephone or network wires within a wiring closet.

punch down tool

A tool used in a wiring closet to connect cable wires directly to a patch panel or punch down block.

PVC

(polyvinyl chloride) A flexible rubber-like plastic used to surround some twisted pair cabling.

PVC

(Permanent Virtual Circuit) A virtual circuit associated with leased lines and that connects two always-on endpoints.

QoS

(Quality of Service) A set of parameters that controls the level of quality provided to different types of network traffic.

quarantine network

A restricted network that provides users with routed access only to certain hosts and applications.

RA

(Registration Authority) An authority in a PKI that processes requests for digital certificates from users.

rack system

A standardized frame or enclosure for mounting multiple electronic equipment and devices.

radio frequency emanation

A condition where electronic equipment emits unintentional radio signals from which eavesdroppers can reconstruct processed data from a remote, but nearby, location.

radio networking

A form of wireless communications in which signals are sent via RF waves. Also called RF networking.

radio waves

An electromagnetic wave with wavelengths longer than infrared light.

RADIUS

(Remote Authentication Dial-In User Service) A protocol that enables a server to provide standardized, centralized authentication for remote users.

RAID

(Redundant Array of Independent/ Inexpensive Disks) A set of vendor-independent specifications for fault-tolerant configurations on multiple-disk systems.

RAS server

(Remote Access Services server) A server that enables a user to dial in and authenticate with the same account he or she uses at the office.

RDP

(Remote Desktop Protocol) The proprietary protocol created by Microsoft for connecting to and managing devices that are not necessarily located at the same place as the administrator.

recursive query

A query used by a DNS server for name resolution when a client requests that its preferred DNS server find data on other DNS servers.

redistribution point

A network node that is used to transfer data.

reflective DoS

(reflective denial of service) An attack that involves sending forged requests of some type to a very large number of devices that will reply to the requests.

refraction

The phenomenon of light rays bending due to a change in speed when passing from one transparent medium to another.

remediation network

An equivalent term for quarantine network.

Remote Access

A feature that allows an administrator to access client systems from any location on the network.

remote access protocol

A type of protocol that enables users to access a remote access server and transfer data.

remote desktop

A connection mode that enables a user to access any network device from their workstation and perform tasks on the remote device.

remote desktop assistance

Software that enables a remote client to control a host device on the network or run applications from a server, while both the local and remote user see the same screen and can have control of the device.

remote desktop control

Software that enables a remote client to control a host device on the network or run applications from a server.

remote networking

A type of network communication that enables users who are not at the same physical locations to access network resources.

repeater

A device that regenerates a signal to improve transmission distances.

replay attack

A type of network attack where an attacker captures network traffic and stores it for retransmission at a later time to gain unauthorized access to a network.

reservation

See DHCP reservation.

reverse proxy

A type of proxy server that retrieves resources on behalf of a client from one or more servers.

RF

(radio frequency) A frequency in which network or other communications take place using radio waves in the 10 KHz to 1 GHz range.

RFB

(Remote Frame Buffer) A protocol used in VNC for remote access and GUIs.

RFI

(radio frequency interference) A type of noise that is caused by electrical radiation or induction and that disrupts an electrical signal in wireless communication.

RIP

(Routing Information Protocol) A routing protocol that configures routers to periodically broadcast their entire routing tables. RIP routers broadcast their tables regardless of whether or not any changes have occurred on the network.

risk

An information security concept that indicates exposure to the chance of damage or loss, and signifies the likelihood of a hazard or threat.

rogue access point

An unauthorized wireless access point on a corporate or private network, which allows unauthorized individuals to connect to the network.

rollover cable

A network cable that connects a device to a router's console port.

rollup

A collection of previously issued patches and hotfixes, usually meant to be applied to one component of a device, such as a web browser or a particular service.

rootkit

Software that is intended to take full or partial control of a device at the lowest levels.

routable protocol

A network protocol which provides separate network and node addresses to work with routers.

route

The path used by data packets to reach a specified destination.

route aggregation

A method of combining routes in a routing table to save space and simplify routing decisions.

route convergence

The period of time between a network change and the router updates to reach a steady state once again.

router

A networking device that connects multiple networks that use the same protocol.

router discovery protocols

Protocols that are used to identify routers on the network.

routing

The process of selecting the best route for moving a packet from its source to destination on a network.

routing domain

See AS.

routing loop

A routing process in which two routers discover different routes to the same location that include each other but never reach the endpoint.

routing table

A database created manually or by a route-discovery protocol that contains network addresses as perceived by a specific router. A router uses its route table to forward packets to another network or router.

SaaS

(Software as a Service) A cloud computing service that enables a service provider to make applications available over the Internet.

SAN

(storage area network) A high-speed data transfer network that provides access to consolidated block-level storage.

satellite Internet

An Internet connection method that uses a satellite network.

satellite phone

A telephone system that relies on the satellite network to provide services instead of the infrastructure of the local telephone switch.

satellite television

A method of relaying video and audio signals directly to the subscriber's television sets using geosynchronous satellites.

SC

(Subscriber Connector or Standard Connector) A connector used in a duplex configuration where two fibers are terminated into two SC connectors that are molded together.

SCADA system

(Supervisory Control and Data Acquisition system) An ICS that is used in situations where sites are at great geographical distances from one another, and where centralized data collection and management is critical to industrial operations.

scope

In DHCP, the IP addresses that a DHCP server is configured with and can assign to clients.

SCSI

(Small Computer System Interface) An older personal computer connection standard that provides high-performance data transfer between the SCSI device and the other components of the computer. SCSI is pronounced "scuzzy."

SDH

(Synchronous Digital Hierarchy) Another optical communications standard that is based upon SONET and implemented widely outside the U.S.

secure protocol

A protocol that does not expose data and/or credentials in cleartext, so it is less likely to allow for the credentials or data to be viewed and captured by someone else.

security control

A safeguard or countermeasure to avoid, counteract, or minimize security risks relating to personal or company property.

security incident

A specific instance of a risk event occurring, whether or not it causes damage.

security policy

A formalized statement that defines how security will be implemented within a particular organization.

segment

A physical subdivision of a network that links multiple devices or serves as a connection between two nodes.

serial cable

A type of bounded network media that transfers information between two devices using serial transmission.

serial data transmission

The transmission of bits at one per clock cycle across a single transmission medium.

server

A network device or process that shares resources with and responds to requests from computers, devices, and other servers on the network.

service pack

A collection of operating system updates that can include functionality enhancements, new features, and typically, all patches, updates, and hotfixes issued up to the point of the service pack release.

session hijacking attack

An attack where the attacker exploits a legitimate session to obtain unauthorized access to an organization's network or services.

SFP

(Small Form Factor Pluggable) A transceiver used to convert electrical signals to optical signals.

SFTP

(Secure File Transfer Protocol) A protocol based on SSH2 that provides for secure file transfers on an IP network.

shared-key encryption

An encryption system in which a single key is shared between parties in a communication and is used to both encode and decode the message. Also called symmetric encryption.

shielding

A method of placing grounded conductive material around bounded media to prevent the introduction of noise into the media.

SIEM

(security information and event management) An umbrella approach to security management that attempts to provide a holistic view of an organization's IT security.

signal

The electromagnetic pulses that are transmitted across a network medium.

signal bounce

A condition in which the signals endlessly move from one end of a cable to the other end.

simplex

A communication mode that provides the one-way transfer of information.

single mode fiber

A type of fiber optic cable that carries a single optical signal.

single point of failure

A portion of a network, which can be a cable, a network device, a server, or any other device, that will cause the entire network to stop functioning if it fails.

site survey

An analysis technique that determines the coverage area of a wireless network, identifies any sources of interference, and establishes other characteristics of the coverage area.

SLA

(Service Level Agreement) An agreement entered into by the transmitter/ISP and the receiver/subscriber.

sliding window

A type of data window in which block sizes are variable. Window size is continually reevaluated during transmission, with the sender always attempting to send the largest window it can to speed throughput.

SMA
(Sub Multi Assembly or Sub Miniature type A) A connector with a threaded ferrule on the outside used when water or other environmental factors necessitate a waterproof connection.

smart card
A plastic card containing an embedded computer chip that can store different types of electronic information.

smart jack
A device that serves as the demarcation point between the end user's inside wiring and the local access carriers' facilities.

SMB
(Server Message Block) A protocol that works on the Application layer and is used to share files, serial ports, printers, and communications devices—including mail slots and named pipes —between devices.

SMTP
(Simple Mail Transfer Protocol) A communications protocol that enables sending email from a client to a server or between servers.

sniffing attack
See eavesdropping attack.

SNIPS
(System and Network Integrated Polling Software) System and network monitoring software that runs on UNIX systems and offers both a command-line and a web interface to monitor network and system devices.

SNMP
(Simple Network Management Protocol) An Application-layer protocol used to exchange information between network devices.

SOA
(Start of Authority) A DNS record that specifies authoritative information about a DNS zone.

social engineering attack
A type of attack that uses deception and trickery to convince unsuspecting users to provide sensitive data or to violate security guidelines.

socket
An identifier for an application process on a TCP/IP network.

software attack
Any attack that targets software resources including operating systems, applications, protocols, and files.

SOHO
(small office home office) A description used for a small network that contains up to 10 nodes.

SONET
(Synchronous Optical Network) A standard for synchronous data transmission on optical media.

spam
An email-based threat that floods the user's inbox with emails that typically carry unsolicited advertising material for products or other spurious content, and which sometimes delivers viruses.

SPB
(Shortest Path Bridging) A replacement for the Spanning Tree Protocol (STP) that simplifies network creation and configuration and enables multipath routing.

spear phishing
See whaling.

speed test site
A web service that measure the bandwidth and latency of a visitor's Internet connection.

spim
An IM-based attack similar to spam, but is propagated through instant messaging instead of through email.

split horizon
An algorithm that prevents count-to-infinity loops by prohibiting a router from broadcasting internal network information.

spoofing
A human- or software-based attack where the goal is to pretend to be someone else for the purpose of identity concealment.

spread spectrum
A form of radio transmission in which the signal is sent over more than one frequency to discourage eavesdropping.

spyware
Surreptitiously installed malicious software that is intended to track and report on the usage of a target device or collect other data the author wishes to obtain.

SRV
(Service Locator) A DNS record that specifies a generic service location record for newer protocols.

SSH
(Secure Shell) A program that enables a user or an application to log on to another device over a network, run commands in a remote machine, and transfer files from one machine to the other.

SSID
(Service Set Identifier) A 32-bit alphanumeric string that identifies a WAP and all devices attached to it.

SSID broadcast
(service set identifier) A continuous announcement by a WAP that transmits its name so that wireless devices can discover it.

SSL
(Secure Sockets Layer) A security protocol that uses certificates for authentication and encryption to protect web communication.

SSL VPN
(Secure Socket Layer virtual private network) A VPN format that works with a web browser—installing a separate client is not necessary.

SSO
(Single Sign-On) A session/user authentication process that permits a user to enter one name and password to access multiple applications.

SSTP
(Secure Socket Tunneling Protocol) Uses the HTTP over SSL protocol and encapsulates an IP packet with an SSTP header.

ST
(Straight Tip) A connector used to connect multimode fiber.

standard
A measure of adherence to the network policy.

stateful firewall
A firewall that performs stateful inspections and monitors entire conversations.

stateful inspection
The process of examining data within a packet as well as the state of the connection between the internal and external devices.

stateless firewall
A firewall that manages and maintains the connection state of a session using the filter, and ensures that only authorized packets are permitted in sequence.

stateless inspection
The process of comparing each individual packet to a rule set to see if there is a match, and then if there is a match, acting on that packet (permits or denies) based on the rule.

static routing
A type of routing used by a network administrator to manually specify the mappings in the routing table.

STP
(shielded twisted pair) A type of twisted pair cabling that includes shielding around its conductors.

STP
(Spanning Tree Protocol) A Layer 2 protocol that is used for routing and prevents network loops by adopting a dynamic routing method. Replaced by the Rapid Spanning Tree Protocol

(RSTP), IEEE 802.1w, and Shortest Path Bridging (SPB).

straight-through cable
A network cable that connects unlike devices. Also called a patch cable.

strong password
A password that meets the complexity requirements that are set by a system administrator and documented in a password policy.

stub autonomous system
An autonomous system in which the source or the destination node must exist within the system.

subnet
A logical subset of a larger network created by an administrator to improve network performance or to provide security.

subnet mask
A number assigned to each host for dividing the IP address into network and node portions.

subnetting
The process of logically dividing a network into smaller subnetworks or subnets.

SVC
(Switched Virtual Circuit) A virtual circuit associated with dial-up and demand-dial connections and provide more flexibility than PVCs, allowing a single connection to an endpoint to connect to multiple endpoints, as needed.

switch
A network device that acts as a common connecting point for various nodes or segments.

switched Ethernet
A LAN technology that connects devices using switches, enabling the devices on each switched connection to utilize the full bandwidth of the medium.

symmetric encryption
See shared-key encryption.

synchronous communications
A communication method in which a byte is sent in a standardized time interval, enabling the receiver to use the time interval as the means to distinguish between bytes in the data stream.

T-carrier system
A digital and packet switched system that makes communication more scalable than analog, circuit-switched systems.

TA
(Terminal Adapter) In ISDN, the hardware interface between a device and an ISDN line.

TACACS
(Terminal Access Controller Access Control System) An authentication protocol that provides centralized authentication and authorization services for remote users.

TACACS+
(Terminal Access Controller Access Control System Plus) An authentication protocol that uses TCP port 49, supports multifactor authentication, and is considered more secure and scalable than RADIUS.

TCP
(Transmission Control Protocol) A connection-oriented, guaranteed-delivery protocol used to send data packets between devices over a network, like the Internet.

TCP/IP
(Transmission Control Protocol/Internet Protocol) A network protocol suite that is routable and allows devices to communicate across all types of networks.

TCP/IP model
A four-layer data communication model developed by the United States Department of Defense. To some extent, it is similar to the OSI model.

TCP/IP protocol stack
The collection of protocols that work together to provide communications on IP networks.

TDM

(Time-Division Multiplexing) A multiplexing method in which the communication channel is divided into discrete time slots that are assigned to each node on a network.

TDR

(Time-Domain Reflectometer) A measuring tool that transmits an electrical pulse on a cable and measures the way the signal reflects back on the TDR to determine network issues.

TE

(Terminal Equipment) ISDN communications equipment that stations use to accomplish tasks at both ends of a communications link.

Telnet

A terminal emulation protocol that allows users at one site to simulate a session on a remote host.

terminal

An end user's device on a host-based network, dedicated to transmitting data to a host for processing and displaying the results to the user.

terminal emulator

Software that enables a standard client device to appear as a dedicated terminal to a mainframe computer .

termination

Adding a resistor to the ends of a coax network segment to prevent reflections that would interfere with the proper reception of signals.

terminator

A network component attached to the ends of a network cable that can impede or absorb signals so they cannot reflect onto the cable.

TFTP

(Trivial File Transfer Protocol) A simple version of FTP that uses UDP as the transport protocol and does not require a logon to the remote host.

ThickNet

Ethernet networking over RG8 cabling.

thin client

A device or process that depends on a server to fulfill its computational needs.

ThinNet

Ethernet networking over RG58/U or RG58A/U cabling.

threat

Any potential violation of security policies or procedures.

threshold

When monitoring network performance, the value that signals that an object or component is functioning outside acceptable performance limits.

throughput tester

A software tool that is used to measure network throughput and capacity.

TIA

(Telecommunications Industry Association) Developed the 568 Commercial Building Telecommunication Cabling standard in association with EIA.

TKIP

(Temporal Key Integrity Protocol) A security protocol created by the IEEE 802.11i task group to replace WEP.

TLS

(Transport Layer Security) A security protocol that uses certificates and public key cryptography for mutual authentication and data encryption over a TCP/IP connection.

token

A physical or virtual object that stores authentication information.

token ring

A type of technology used on ring networks in which devices pass a special sequence of bits called a token between them.

tone generator

An electronic device that sends an electrical signal through one set of UTP cables.

tone locator

An electronic device that emits an audible tone when it detects a signal in a set of wires.

top

A CPU usage monitoring tool offered in UNIX and Linux systems that provides a static snapshot or a real-time display of the processes currently running on a CPU.

top listener

A network host that receives a significant amount of network data.

top talker

A network host that generates a significant amount of network traffic by sending data.

topology

A network specification that determines the network's overall layout, signaling, and data-flow patterns.

tracert

A command that determines the route data takes to get to a particular destination.

traffic filtering

A method that allows only legitimate traffic through to the network.

traffic policing

The method of governing and regulating a flow of packets by conforming with the standards and limits specified in the SLA.

traffic shaping

A QoS mechanism that introduces some amount of delay in traffic that exceeds an administratively defined rate. Also called bandwidth shaping.

transceiver

A device that has a transmitter and a receiver integrated into it to send and receive data.

transit autonomous system

An autonomous system in which the source or the destination node does not reside within the system.

Trojan horse

An insidious type of malware that is itself a software attack and can pave the way for a number of other types of attacks.

troubleshooting

The recognition, diagnosis, and resolution of problems on a network.

troubleshooting model

A standardized step-by-step approach to the troubleshooting process.

trunking

Combining multiple network connections to increase bandwidth and reliability.

TTL

(Time To Live) A value for the ping command that determines how many hops an IP packet can travel before being discarded.

tunnel

A logical path through the network that appears as a point-to-point connection.

tunneling

A data transport technique in which a data packet is transferred inside the frame or packet of another protocol, enabling the infrastructure of one network to be used to travel to another network.

twisted pair

A type of cable in which two conductors or pairs of copper wires are twisted around each other and clad in a color-coded, protective insulating plastic sheath or jacket.

two–factor authentication

An authentication scheme that requires validation of two authentication factors.

UC technologies

(unified communication technologies) A group of integrated real-time communications services and non-real-time services that provides a consistent user experience across multiple devices and media types.

UDP

(User Datagram Protocol) A connectionless Transport-layer protocol that is one of the protocols in the Internet protocol suite and is used with IP. It is also called the Universal Datagram Protocol.

unauthorized access

Any type of network or data access that is not explicitly approved by an organization.

unbounded media

A network medium that does not use a physical connection between devices and can transmit electromagnetic signals through the air using radio waves, microwaves, or infrared radiation.

unencrypted channel

A connection that uses unsecure protocols to transfer data.

UNI

(User-to-Network Interface) A user device that is an ATM border device used to connect one ATM network to another or a LAN.

unicast transmission

A method for data transfer from a source address to a destination address.

unidirectional antenna

See omni-directional antenna.

unnecessary running service

Any service that is running on a device that is not required for its intended purpose or operation.

unpatched system

A current OS that is supported by the manufacturer but does not have the latest security updates.

unsecure protocol

A protocol that expose data or credentials in cleartext, enabling the information to be viewed or captured by unauthorized entities.

UPC connector

(ultra physical contact connector) A fiber optic connector where the end faces are given an extended polishing for a better surface finish.

UPS

(uninterruptible power supply) A device that provides backup power when the electrical power fails or drops to an unacceptable voltage level.

USB

(Universal Serial Bus) A hardware interface standard designed to provide connections for numerous peripherals.

USB connection

(Universal Serial Bus connection) A personal computer connection that enables you to connect multiple peripherals to a single port with high performance and minimal device configuration.

UTM

(unified threat management) A network security solution that is used to monitor and manage a wide variety of security-related applications and infrastructure components through a single management console.

UTP

(unshielded twisted pair) A type of twisted pair cabling that does not include shielding around its conductors.

UTP coupler

A device that enables you to connect two UTP cables together to form a longer cable.

vampire tap

A clamshell-like device that clamps over an RG8 cable, making contact with its conductors and permitting a networking device to connect to the ThickNet segment.

VCC

(vertical cross-connect) A cable that runs vertically between floors in a building, or vertically between equipment in an equipment rack.

VER

(Voltage Event Recorder) A tool to use in conjunction with or in addition to using a voltmeter to test and verify that the electrical signals transmitting through the network cables are within the required specifications.

video conferencing

A UC technology that enables users at two or more geographic locations to communicate by simultaneous two-way audio and video transmission.

virtual circuit switching

A switching technique that connects endpoints logically through a provider's network.

virtual firewall

A firewall service or appliance that runs entirely within a virtualized environment.

virtual PBX

A private communications service provider that provides a low-cost PBX service.

virtual router

A software-based routing framework that enables the host device to act as a hardware router over a LAN.

virtual server

A VM that runs a network operating system or other server software.

virtual switch

A software application that enables communication between VMs.

virtualization

Technology that enables one or more simulated devices to run within one physical device.

virus

A sample of code that spreads from one device to another by attaching itself to other files.

vishing

(voice phishing) A human-based attack where the attacker extracts information while speaking over the phone or leveraging IP-based voice messaging services, such as VoIP.

VLAN

(Virtual LAN) A logical grouping of ports on a switch.

VLAN assignment

(virtual local area network assignment) A security control for switch ports that can segment a network so that traffic from one VLAN does not interfere with traffic on other VLANs.

VLAN hopping

(virtual local area network hopping) An attack where an attacking host on a VLAN gains access to traffic on other VLANs that would normally not be accessible.

VLAN pooling

A mechanism that enables WAPs to choose from among available VLANs when they are accepting incoming client connection requests.

VLSM

(Variable Length Subnet Mask) See custom subnet mask.

VNC

(Virtual Network Computing) A platform-independent desktop sharing system.

VNIC

(virtual network interface card) A software program that enables a VM to communicate with other VMs on the shared host.

voice over data system

A communications system that replaces traditional telephone links by transmitting analog voice communications over digital WAN networking technologies.

VoIP

(Voice over IP) A voice over data implementation in which voice signals are transmitted over IP networks.

voltmeter

An electrical instrument that measures voltage and resistance between two points in a circuit.

voluntary tunnels

VPN tunnels that are created between client endpoints at the request of the client.

VPN

(Virtual Private Network) A private network that is configured within a public network, such as the Internet.

VPN concentrator
A single device that incorporates advanced encryption and authentication methods to handle a large number of VPN tunnels.

VSAT
(Very Small Aperture Terminal) A small telecommunications Earth station that consists of a small antenna that transmits and receives signals from satellites.

VTP
(VLAN Trunking Protocol) A VLAN management protocol developed by Cisco that enables switches to update each other's VLAN databases.

vulnerability
Any condition that leaves a device open to attack.

WAN
(wide area network) A network that spans multiple geographic locations connecting multiple LANs using long-range transmission media.

WAP
(Wireless Access Point) A device that provides a connection between wireless devices and can connect to wired networks.

war chalking
Using symbols to mark off a sidewalk or wall to indicate that there is an open wireless network which may be offering Internet access.

war driving
The act of searching for instances of wireless LAN networks while in motion, using wireless tracking devices like smartphones, tablets, or laptops.

warm site
A business site that performs noncritical functions under normal conditions, but which can be rapidly converted to a key operations site, if needed.

waveform
The graphical representation of a signal.

web proxy
A type of proxy server that provides for anonymous access to web content.

WEP
(Wired Equivalent Privacy) A protocol that provides 64-bit, 128-bit, and 256-bit encryption using the Rivest Cipher 4 (RC4) algorithm for wireless communication that uses the 802.11a and 802.11b protocols.

WEP cracking
(Wired Equivalent Privacy cracking) An attack that attempts to gain access to private wireless networks by cracking WEP encryption keys.

whaling
An email- or web-based form of phishing that targets individuals who are known to be upper-level executives or other high-profile employees, with the goal of obtaining sensitive information. Also called spear phishing.

white hat
A hacker who exposes security flaws in applications and operating systems so manufacturers can fix them before they become widespread problems.

WiMAX
(Worldwide Interoperability for Microwave Access) A packet-based wireless technology that provides wireless broadband access over long distances.

Windows security policy
A group of configuration settings within Windows operating systems that control the overall security behavior of a device.

wire crimper
A tool that attaches media connectors to the ends of cables.

wireless antenna
A device that converts high-frequency signals on a cable into wireless electromagnetic waves and vice versa.

wireless communication
A type of communication in which signals are transmitted over a distance without the use of a physical medium.

wireless security

Any method of securing a WLAN network to prevent unauthorized network access and network data theft while ensuring that authorized users can connect to the network.

wireless tester

A Wi-Fi spectrum analyzer used to detect devices and points of interference, as well as analyze and troubleshoot network issues on a WLAN.

wiring closet

A small room that contains patch panels. Also called a network closet or telecommunication closet.

wiring diagram

See wiring schematic.

wiring schematic

A combination of a floor plan and a physical network topology. Similar to physical network diagrams, you can see the nodes on the network and how they are physically connected. Also called a wiring diagram.

WLAN

(wireless local area network) A self-contained network of two or more devices connected using a wireless connection.

workgroup

See peer-to-peer network.

worm

Code that spreads from one device to another on its own, not by attaching itself to another file.

WPA

(Wi-Fi Protected Access) A security protocol introduced to address some of the shortcomings in WEP, WEP, WPA2, and Wi-Fi.

WPA cracking

(Wi-Fi Protected Access cracking) An attack that attempts to gain access to private wireless networks by cracking WPA encryption keys.

WPA2

(Wi-Fi Protected Access version 2) A security protocol that provides WPA with AES cipher-based CCMP encryption for even greater security and to replace TKIP.

WPAN

(wireless personal area network) A network that connects devices in very close proximity but not through a WAP.

WPS cracking

(Wi-Fi Protected Setup cracking) An attack that attempts to gain access to private wireless networks by cracking WPS encryption keys.

WWAN

(wireless wide area network) Uses wireless network technology to allow users to check email, surf the web, and connect to corporate resources accessible within the cellular network boundaries.

X Window system

A remote control protocol that uses a client-server relationship to provide GUI and input device management functionality to applications.

X.25

A legacy packet switching network technology developed in the 1970s to move data across less than reliable public carriers.

zero day attack

An attack that exploits a previously unknown vulnerability in an application or operating system.

zombie

Unauthorized software introduced on multiple devices to manipulate the devices into mounting a DDoS attack. Also called a drone.

zone

A file that physically divides the DNS database and contains the actual IP-to-host name mappings for one or more domains.

Index

I

093012S rev 1.1
ISBN-13 978-1-4246-2489-8
ISBN-10 1-4246-2489-4